lonely planet

Alaska

The Bush
p351

**Denali &
the Interior**
p262

**Anchorage &
Around** p156

**Kodiak, Katmai &
Southwest Alaska**
p326

**Kenai
Peninsula**
p217

**Prince
William
Sound**
p194

**Juneau &
the Southeast**
p76

THIS EDITION WRITTEN AND RESEARCHED BY

Brendan Sainsbury,
Greg Benchwick, Catherine Bodry

PLAN YOUR TRIP

ON THE ROAD

TUFTED PUFFIN P406

DANITA DELIMONT/A / GETTY IMAGES ©

AIR-DRYING SALMON

YVETTE CARDOZO / GET...

MENDENHALL GLACIER P11...

KIM HEACOX / GETTY IMAGES ©

Contents

JAY BERKOW PHOTOGRAPHY / GETTY IMAGES ©

HALIBUT COVE P255

Contents

ON THE ROAD

AUTUMN FOREST

TALKEETNA P281

ICE CLIMBERS OUTSIDE ANCHORAGE

Contents

Welcome to Alaska

Bears larger than bison, national parks the size of nations, and glaciers bigger than other US states. The word 'epic' barely does Alaska justice.

The Call of the Wild

Pure, raw, unforgiving, and humongous in scale, Alaska is a place that arouses basic instincts and ignites what Jack London termed the 'call of the wild'. Yet, unlike London and his gutsy, gold-rush companions, visitors today will have a far easier time penetrating the region's vast, feral wilderness. Indeed, one of the beauties of the 49th state is its accessibility. Nowhere else in North America is it so easy to climb an unclimbed mountain, walk where – quite possibly – no human foot has trodden before, or sally forth into a national park that gets fewer annual visitors than the International Space Station.

Into the Outdoors

Alaska is, without a doubt, America's grittiest outdoor playground where skilled bush pilots land with pinpoint accuracy on crevasse-riddled glaciers, and backcountry guiding companies take bravehearts on bracing paddles down almost virgin rivers. With scant phone coverage and a dearth of hipster-friendly coffee bars to plug in your iPad, this is a region for 'doing' rather than observing. Whether you go it alone with bear-spray and a backpack, or place yourself in the hands of an experienced 'sourdough' (Alaskan old-timer), the rewards are immeasurable.

Animal Magic

People-watching takes second place to wildlife-spotting in a state where brown bears snatch leaping salmon out of angry waterfalls and curious moose pose majestically on national park roadsides. But the real thrill for wilderness purists is to go off in search of fauna in its natural habitat. The landscapes of the far north might be the domain of musk oxen, gray wolves and bears, but, keep your wits about you, and they'll quietly accept you as a guest.

Meet the People

Isolation fosters peculiarities. A trip into the Alaskan wilderness can be as much about the off-beat people as the off-the-beaten-track location. Take tiny Chitina with its handful of subsistence-hunting locals, or the crusty boom-and-bust town of Nome, or the jokey gold-mining punch line that is Chicken. Ever since the US bought Alaska for 2 cents an acre in 1867, the land that styles itself as America's last frontier has attracted contrarians, rat-race escapees, wanderers, dreamers, back-to-the-landers and people imbued with the spirit of the Wild West. In a land of immense natural beauty, the Alaskan people are an oft-forgotten part of the brew.

Why I Love Alaska

By Brendan Sainsbury, Author

Like many travelers, I am drawn to roads less traveled, isolated frontier regions where spontaneity and excitement rule over certainty and home comforts. Alaska, for me, fits all of these requirements. Challenging, unpolished and, on occasions, a hard nut to crack, it is, in many ways, the antithesis of the country where I grew up (the UK). Like a stranger in a strange land, I never fail to be astonished by the state's extremes and gaping lack of people. And though travel here isn't always easy, it's a constant education.

For more about our authors, see p440

Above: Northern lights, Fairbanks (p297)

Alaska

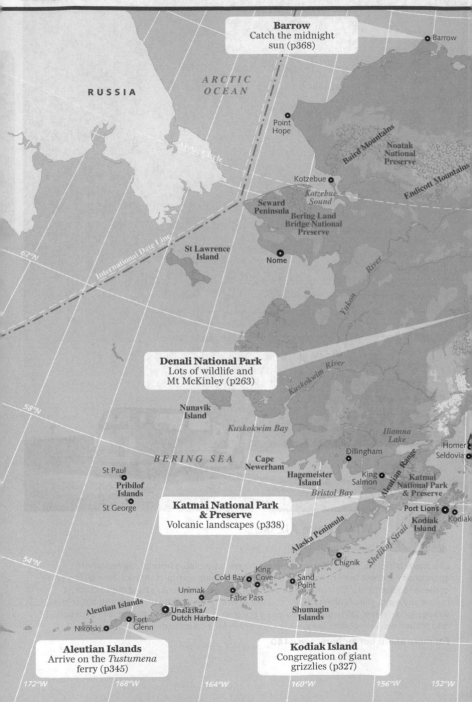

Barrow
Catch the midnight sun (p368)

ARCTIC
OCEAN

RUSSIA

Point
Hope

Baird Mountains

Noatak
National
Preserve

Endicott Mountains

Arctic Circle

Kotzebue

Kotzebue
Sound

Seward
Peninsula

Bering Land
Bridge National
Preserve

62°N

International Date Line

St Lawrence
Island

Nome

Yukon River

Denali National Park
Lots of wildlife and
Mt McKinley (p263)

Kuskokwim River

Nunavik
Island

58°N

Kuskokwim Bay

Iliamna
Lake

BERING SEA

Cape
Newerham

Dillingham

Aleutian Range

Homer
Seldovia

St Paul

Pribilof
Islands

St George

Hagemeister
Island

Bristol Bay

King
Salmon

Katmai
National Park
& Preserve

**Katmai National Park
& Preserve**
Volcanic landscapes (p338)

Port Lions

Kodiak
Island

Kodiak

54°N

Chignik

Shelikof Strait

Alaska Peninsula

King
Cove

Sand
Point

Cold Bay

Aleutian Islands

Nikolski

Fort
Glenn

Unimak

Unalaska/
Dutch Harbor

False Pass

Shumagin
Islands

Aleutian Islands
Arrive on the *Tustumena*
ferry (p345)

Kodiak Island
Congregation of giant
grizzlies (p327)

172°W   168°W   164°W   160°W   156°W   152°W

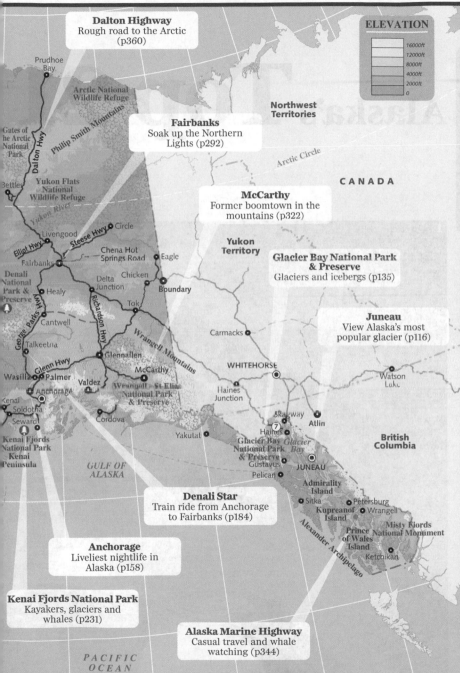

ELEVATION

16000ft
12000ft
8000ft
4000ft
2000ft
0

Dalton Highway
Rough road to the Arctic
(p360)

Fairbanks
Soak up the Northern
Lights (p292)

McCarthy
Former boomtown in the
mountains (p322)

**Glacier Bay National Park
& Preserve**
Glaciers and icebergs (p135)

Juneau
View Alaska's most
popular glacier (p116)

Denali Star
Train ride from Anchorage
to Fairbanks (p184)

Anchorage
Liveliest nightlife in
Alaska (p158)

Kenai Fjords National Park
Kayakers, glaciers and
whales (p231)

Alaska Marine Highway
Casual travel and whale
watching (p344)

Prudhoe
Bay

Arctic National
Wildlife Refuge

Gates of
the Arctic
National
Park

Dalton Hwy

Bettles

Philip Smith Mountains

Yukon Flats
National
Wildlife Refuge

Yukon River

Livengood

Circle

Elliot Hwy

Steese Hwy

Fairbanks

Chena Hot
Springs Road

Eagle

Denali
National
Park &
Preserve

Healy

Delta
Junction

Chicken

Boundary

Richardson Hwy

Tok

George Parks Hwy

Cantwell

Talkeetna

Glennallen

Wrangell Mountains

McCarthy

Wasilla
Palmer

Glenn Hwy

Anchorage

Valdez

Wrangell-St Elias
National Park
& Preserve

Kenai
Soldotna

Seward

Cordova

Kenai Fjords
National Park
Kenai
Peninsula

GULF OF
ALASKA

Yakutat

**Northwest
Territories**

Arctic Circle

CANADA

**Yukon
Territory**

Carmacks

WHITEHORSE

Watson
Lake

Haines
Junction

Skagway

Haines

7

Atlin

**British
Columbia**

Glacier Bay
National Park
& Preserve

Glacier
Bay

Gustavus

JUNEAU

Pelican

Admiralty
Island

Sitka

Petersburg

Kupreanof
Island

Wrangell

Prince
of Wales
Island

Misty Fiords
National Monument

Alexander Archipelago

Ketchikan

PACIFIC
OCEAN

148°W   144°W   140°W   136°W   132°W

0   400 km
0   200 miles

Alaska's **Top 21**

Mt McKinley

1 The Athabascans call it the Great One, and few who have seen this 20,237ft bulk of ice and granite would disagree. Seen from the Park Rd of Denali National Park, McKinley (p265) chews up the skyline, dominating an already stunning landscape of tundra fields and polychromatic ridgelines. The mountain inspires a take-no-prisoners kind of awe, and climbers know that feeling well. As the highest peak in North America, McKinley attracts over a thousand alpinists every summer, but less than 50% make it to the summit.

Riding the Alaska Ferry to the Aleutian Islands

2 There's no experience like it: three nights on a ferry (p344) that services remote Alaskan communities far along the tendril of the Aleutian chain. Commercial fishers with plastic bins full of gear, tourists lugging giant camera lenses with the hope of scoping a few birds, and even a family or two returning from a visit to the doctor in Homer are all likely to be your new friends by the time you disembark in Unalaska. In port, folks pile on these ships just to take off stacks of hamburgers – often the ship cafeterias are the only restaurants in town. Below: Harbor at King Cove (p345)

2

GLEB TARRO A / GETTY IMAGES ©

Bear-Viewing at Brooks Camp

3 Nowhere in the world are the bears more abundant, well-fed and blissfully happy as they are in Katmai National Park & Preserve (p338) where, under the watchful eye of the National Park Service, a pristine, well-protected eco-system flourishes, providing a rich supply of salmon – the bears' favorite food source. To see these brilliant ursine beasts pluck spawning salmon straight out of turbulent Brooks Falls, hire a floatplane in July and proceed to Brooks Camp. Granted, it isn't cheap, but, as 99% of previous Katmai visitors will testify, it's worth every penny.

Spotting Whales in Southeast Alaska

4 An announcement followed by a rush of passengers in the forward observation lounge of an Alaska Marine Highway ferry (p344) is a sure sign that humpback whales have been spotted. Join the crowd outside to gawk in awe at a pair of black humps and spouts less than a quarter mile away. When one of the whales breaches, heaving its near-ly 50ft-long body almost completely out of the wa-ter, it's such an incredible sight that it has everybody buzzing until the ferry ar-rives in Wrangell.

McCarthy Road & McCarthy

5 When all you need is an open road, a funky town, and 13.2 million acres of wilderness to make you happy, the McCarthy Rd is waiting. Running atop a historic rail line, the road shakes and rattles driv-ers through the heart of America's largest national park: Wrangell-St Elias. Sixty miles in, the road dead-ends at a footbridge. On the other side is Mc-Carthy (p322), a former red-light district that's now a handsome old boomtown and the perfect base for exploring this transcendent landscape of glaciers and reach-for-the-sky alpine ranges.

Anchorage Nightlife

6 You've already taken in the Anchorage Museum and climbed Flattop Mountain but who can go to bed? It's still light at 11pm and there is a bolt of energy surging through downtown Anchorage (p158). There are pushcart vendors hawking sausages on 4th Ave, horse-drawn carriages picking up passengers at Hotel Captain Cook, frisbees in the air at Delaney Park and a line out the door at Chilkoot Charlie's, where a band is certain to be rocking tonight.

Kodiak Island

7 Land of huge brown bears and lucrative crab fishing, where verdant mountains shelter quiet, crescent-shaped bays, and the people of the eponymous main town grin contentedly in their daily lives. Rarely visited by big cruise ships, the US' second-largest island (p327) is Alaska at its most authentic. You'd be mad to miss the bear-viewing and the fishing, but reserve extra time to investigate Kodiak's less heralded attractions including WWII military batteries, onion-domed Russian churches and roughshod day-hikes on the cusp of an ethereal wilderness.

Flying in a Bush Plane

8 Faster than the state bird (the mosquito), and almost as ubiquitous, the Alaskan bush plane (p418) provides an important network of passenger and freight transport. But dropping off adventurers into the remotest corners of the state is only half of what these remarkable craft can do. They can land you on a glacier 7200ft above sea level, circle an area that's a mere ball toss away from the highest peak on the continent and give a live satellite view of the top of the world.

An Alaskan Salmon Bake

9 The floatplane takes off from a bustling waterfront, crosses three glaciers and 30 minutes later lands at Taku Glacier Lodge (p128). The lodge is classic Alaska: a low-slung log building adorned with moose antlers and bear skins. Staff are grilling king salmon caught just up the Taku River and you can smell the brown-sugar sauce they're basting the fillets with. So can the bears. Two black bears pop out of the woods and are chased off before you sit down to a meal of a lifetime. Bottom: Salmon bake, Fairbanks

Mt Roberts Tramway

10 The Mt Roberts Trail is not overly difficult, but it's a steady climb. Within an hour most people break out of the trees to find stunning views of Juneau and Douglas. Even better is the nearby Mt Roberts Tramway station (p118), a great place to stop after an afternoon of alpine scrambling. For the price of a cold beer – and who couldn't use one after climbing a mountain? – you can ride the tramway back to Juneau.

Icebergs in Glacier Bay

11 Passengers have already seen sea lions, horned puffins and even a pod of orcas when icebergs of all shapes, sizes and shades of blue begin to appear in Glacier Bay National Park & Preserve (p135). By lunchtime the tour boat reaches Margerie Glacier and for the next half hour passengers see and hear the ice fall off the face of the glacier in a performance that is nothing short of dramatic.

Watching the Midnight Sun

12 'There are strange things done under the Midnight Sun,' wrote Robert Service during the gold-rush days, and it seems as true today as then. With near endless daylight in an all too short summer, Alaskans and visitors alike go into overdrive and push as much sport, travel, partying and adventure into the time they have. To catch the true midnight sun (that is, the sun above the horizon at midnight) head north to the Arctic Circle. In Barrow (p368) there are no sunsets at all for 84 days in a row. Above: Chugach State Park

Riding the Denali Star

13 The northernmost railway line in the US was one of the triumphs of gilded-age engineering when President Warren Harding ceremoniously banged in the last spike in 1923. Nearly a century later, the railway continues to work its steely magic on the *Denali Star* (p184), a luxury train that plies a route between Anchorage and Fairbanks. Replete with grazing wildlife, tiny towns and plunging gorges, there's a lot for passengers to take in, but all else is forgotten when Mt McKinley takes its cloudy hat off and shimmers above the forest.

The Magic of Mendenhall

14 Glaciers are often described with a linguistic flourish – noble ice, majestic mountains or sublime grandeur. There's a reason onlookers reach to describe this brand of beauty, and the Mendenhall Glacier (p119) demands weak-kneed prose. Take a hike around this river of ice that tumbles out of the mountains, stand in the gaping mouth of an ice cave or watch the parade of icebergs that the glacier discharges into the Mendenhall River. Come quick: scientists say most of it will be gone in 25 years.

Native Culture

15 Though Anchorage is now the biggest 'Native village' by population, and Western influences are seen everywhere, the essence of traditional culture lives on in settlements across the state. Most are just a bush-plane flight away, but the best way to begin your understanding is to visit an urban cultural center, run by Alaska Natives and largely for Alaska Natives. Afterwards, consider a visit to the Iñupiat hub of Barrow (p368) for the whaling festival.

Northern Lights

16 Natural spectacles don't get much better than this surreal, solar-powered jig. And while a good glossy photo can do the colors of the aurora justice, it simply can't capture the magic of a live performance. Starting in late August, Fairbanks (p292) is the undisputed capital with 200 shows a year. Whistle when the aurora is out, some locals say, and you can influence its movements.

A View of Juneau

17 The quintessential Juneau (p116) walk begins on S Franklin St with its gift shops and saloons. Follow the steep street uphill leaving the throngs of cruise-ship passengers behind. The state capitol and the distinctive dome of a Russian Orthodox church will quickly come into view. A pair of long stairways offer access to even higher ground where views of wild mountains dominate the backdrop. This is an ideal place to pause for breath while gazing at the prettiest state capital in the country. Above: St Nicholas Russian Orthodox Church (p119)

Chicken

18 'Space: the Final Frontier' said Captain Kirk at the beginning of *Star Trek*. He obviously hadn't been to Alaska. When feisty gold rush prospectors ran out of Californian coastline to colonize in the 1890s they pitched north and founded isolated off-the-grid communities like Chicken (population 7-ish; p310) on the Taylor Highway. It's a 'town' that epitomizes the ruggedness and eccentricities of the Alaskan Bush. Come here for gold-panning, wilderness kayaking and surprisingly good cinnamon buns. Just don't expect flushing toilets or access to your Facebook page.

The Dalton Highway

19 Belt up, stick some Springsteen on the sound system and get prepared for the ride of your life. The 500-mile trawl up the Dalton Highway (p360) from Fairbanks to the Arctic Ocean won't be the smoothest ride you'll ever take, but it could well be one of the most legendary. What the infamous 'haul road' lacks in asphalt, it makes up for with a succession of surreal ecosystems from the boreal forests of the interior to the bleak tundra of the North Slope, or even to the frigid Arctic Ocean.

Denali National Park

20 The centerpiece of this 6-million-acre park may be Mt McKinley, the highest peak in North America, but for many the bigger attraction is the chance to experience nature on its own terms. Only one route, 92-mile Park Rd, runs through Denali (p263), and if there's any place you're going to see caribou, moose and grizzlies roaming free and wild it's here. You don't even need to step off the bus, though that's recommended. Most of Denali is trackless wilderness and discovering it yourself is the way to go.

Kayaking Kenai Fjords National Park

21 As you paddle you might be treated to the thunder of calving tidewater glaciers, the honking and splashing of sea lions at a haul-out or the cacophony of a kittiwake rookery. Near Peterson Glacier you might find plump harbor seals bobbing on glacier ice or breaching whales at the mouth of Resurrection Bay. Getting an orca's-eye view of this rich marine ecosystem is just one of the many rewards of propelling yourself through the rocking waters of Kenai Fjords (p231).

Need To Know

For more information, see Survival Guide (p407)

Currency
US dollars ($)

Language
English

Visas
Most international visitors need a visa, and should have a multiple-entry one if coming from the lower 48 through Canada.

Money
Twenty-four-hour ATMs widely available, especially in cities and larger towns.

Cell Phones
Coverage is surprisingly good, even in remote areas. Pre-paid SIM cards can be used in some international mobile phones for local calls and voice mail.

Time
Alaska Time (GMT/UTC minus nine hours)

When to Go

Warm to hot summers, mild winters
Warm to hot summers, cold winters
Mild summers, cold winters
Cold climate

Fairbanks
GO Jun–Sep

Denali National Park
GO Jun–Aug

Anchorage
GO Jun–Oct

Homer
GO May–Oct

Juneau
GO May–Aug

High Season
(Jun–Aug)

➡ Solstice festivals and 20-hour days are enjoyed in June.

➡ Salmon runs peak in July and August.

➡ Mountain trails and passes are snow-free in August.

➡ Room demand and prices peak in July.

Shoulder
(May & Sep)

➡ Car rental rates are 30% lower than in June.

➡ Southeast Alaska is sunny during May, but rainy in September and October.

➡ The northern lights begin to appear in late September.

Low Season
(Oct–Apr)

➡ Brrrrr! Bundle up, it's cold.

➡ Longer days and warmer temps make late February the best time for winter sports.

➡ Avoid March, when ice break-up suspends most ice- and water-based activities.

Useful Websites

Alaska Travel Industry Association (www.travelalaska.com) Alaska's official tourism site.

Alaska Public Lands Information Centers (www.alaskacenters.gov) Info on parks and activities.

Alaska Wilderness Recreation & Tourism Association (www.awrta.org) Committed to sustainable travel.

Alaska Marine Highway System (www.ferryalaska.com) Booking state ferries.

Lonely Planet (www.lonelyplanet.com) Pre-planning, hotel bookings and more.

Important Numbers

Alaska shares a statewide area code of ☏907, except Hyder, which uses ☏250.

Country code	☏1
International dialing	☏011
Emergency	☏911
Road conditions	☏511 or ☏866-282-7577
Alaska Marine Highway	☏800-642-0066

Exchange Rates

Australia	A$1	$0.93
Canada	C$1	$0.91
Euro Zone	€1	$1.34
Japan	¥100	$0.98
New Zealand	NZ$1	$0.85
UK	£1	$1.68

For current exchange rates see www.xe.com

Daily Costs

Budget: Less than $100

➡ Hostel bed or campground: $10–$30

➡ Cheap restaurant meal: $8–$12

➡ Anchorage–Glennallen bus: $50

Midrange: $100–$250

➡ Double room in a midrange motel: $150

➡ Restaurant mid-afternoon special: $10–$15

➡ Light coffee shop breakfast: $4–$7

Top End: More than $250

➡ Double room in an upscale hotel: $200-plus

➡ Dinner main at a top restaurant: $25–$30

➡ Car rental per day: $55–$70

Opening Hours

Banks 9am to 4pm or 5pm Monday to Friday; 9am to 1pm Saturday (main branches).

Bars & Clubs In cities, bars open until 2am or later, especially at weekends. Clubs stay open to 2am or beyond.

Museums & Sights Large museums and sights usually open virtually every day of the year. Smaller places open daily in the summer, open weekends only or can be completely closed in low season.

Post Offices 9am to 5pm Monday to Friday; noon to 3pm Saturday (main branches open longer).

Restaurants & Cafes Breakfast at cafes and coffee shops is served from 7am or earlier. Some restaurants open only for lunch (about noon to 3pm) or

dinner (about 4pm to 10pm, or later in cities). Asian restaurants often have split hours: 11am to 2pm and from 4pm.

Shops 10am to 8pm/6pm (larger/smaller stores) Monday to Friday; 9am to 5pm Saturday; 10am to 5pm Sunday (larger stores).

Arriving in Alaska

Ted Stevens Anchorage International Airport (p416) People-mover bus to downtown ($2) hourly from South Terminal; 20-minute taxi ride to city ($25).

Alaska Marine Highway terminals (p80) Shuttle vans or taxis greet ferries in the Southeast, except in Juneau.

Fairbanks International Airport (p302) Seven MACS buses daily to downtown transit station ($1.50), 15-minute taxi ride to city ($18).

Getting Around

Most people in Alaska get around in cars, but public transportation is surprisingly abundant if you know where to look.

Train Geared towards tourists, but provide a scenic, if pricey way of traveling between Seward and Fairbanks.

Ferry The standard mode of transportation in the largely road-less southeastern panhandle.

Bus Small shuttles service most of Alaska's interior highways with connections to Canada.

Car The modus operandi for most Americans. Useful for traveling at your own pace. Drive on the right.

Airplane The only way to get to many off-the-grid communities.

For much more on **getting around**, see p418

First Time Alaska

For more information, see Survival Guide (p407)

Checklist

➡ Organize a fishing license if you intend to go fishing

➡ Pre-book rental cars

➡ Study shuttle bus and ferry timetables

➡ Book a ferry cabin on the Alaska Marine Highway

➡ Prebook campgrounds and hotels, especially in and around national parks

➡ Non-Americans should check their entry requirements and, if necessary, purchase travel authorization online through the Electronic System for Travel Authorization (ESTA)

What to Pack

➡ Mosquito repellent

➡ Sun cream and hat

➡ Compass and GPS if hiking

➡ Blindfold for the light summer nights

➡ Binoculars for wildlife viewing

➡ Water filter if camping

➡ Hand sanitizer

➡ Driver's license if renting a car

Top Tips for Your Trip

➡ Alaska is expensive, but some excursions (bear watching, flightseeing over Mt McKinley) are true once-in-a-lifetime experiences and are worth the investment.

➡ Alaska is about wildlife, adventure and the great outdoors. Devote your time and money to these activities and save the posh hotels and fancy restaurants for other climes.

➡ Acquire enough basic physical fitness before setting out to enjoy a day or two in the wilderness.

➡ The Alaskan wilderness is an amazing place, but it doesn't suffer fools. If you intend to travel off the beaten path, do your homework and take all the necessary precautions.

What to Wear

Dress in layers. Alaskan weather can be unpredictable and varies greatly with altitude. Make sure you pack a warm fleece and waterproof jacket even in the summer. Take a hat and gloves year-round in the Far North.

Leave the tux at home. Alaskans dress informally when going out.

Sleeping

Alaska's short summer season (May to September) can get busy, so it is wise to book accommodations at least two months in advance, more in the popular areas.

➡ **Campgrounds** Ubiquitous and occasionally free, but usually cost from $10 for a tent and $30 for an RV.

➡ **Hostels** Small selection in Anchorage and larger towns such as Fairbanks and Juneau.

➡ **Motels** The staple of the US budget-to-midrange market. Comfortable but no-frills.

➡ **B&Bs** Surprisingly widespread and economical.

➡ **Hotels** From small family-run places to large lodges run by cruise lines.

Sourdoughs

During the Klondike and Nome gold rushes, experienced gold prospectors often carried a pouch containing a sourdough bread starter around their necks. The starter was used to make unleavened bread, a key source of nutrition during the tough Arctic winters. Before long, the pouch and its valuable contents became a symbol of a savvy Alaskan old-hand who knew how to live in the wilderness, and the word 'sourdough' entered local parlance to denote someone who had survived an Arctic winter (as opposed to a novice cheechako who hadn't). Although it's unlikely you'll encounter anyone carrying a sourdough pouch these days, the word 'sourdough' is still used to describe a rough-and-ready Alaskan old-timer – an important definition in a state where over 50% of the population was born somewhere else.

Bargaining

Alaska, like the rest of the US, doesn't really have much of a bargaining culture, except perhaps in small markets or at some indigenous craft stalls.

Tipping

Alaska is part of the US, thus tipping is expected in most service industries including restaurants, taxis and hotels. It is also customary to tip guides and bus drivers. In general, 15% is the baseline tip, but 20% is usually more appropriate, and 25% if you enjoyed the service.

MARK CONLIN / GETTY IMAGES ©

Paddling in Tracy Arm-Fords Terror Wilderness (p61)

Etiquette

Although it's part of the US, Alaska is a little more laid-back and less rule-bound than other states.

➡ **Socializing** Informality holds sway. Alaskans are more likely to dress down than up when going out, and high-five greetings are as common as handshakes.

➡ **Politics** Alaska is one of the US's more conservative states. You're less likely to encounter the liberal consensus prevalent in San Francisco or New York up here.

➡ **Go Prepared** Alaskans love the great outdoors, but they're not always overly sympathetic to outsiders who arrive unprepared and fail to treat it with the respect it deserves.

Eating

It isn't usually necessary to pre-book tables in Alaska's restaurants, aside from a handful of posher places in Anchorage and Juneau.

➡ **Food Trucks** Can spring up in the remotest of locations, though they often have sporadic and seasonal opening times.

➡ **Cafes and Diners** Common alongside highways and in smaller towns. They offer standard American fare.

➡ **Restaurants** Wide variety, from cheap ethnic eateries to fancier places in Anchorage.

What's New

Ziplining

In a state where adrenaline adventures have never been in short supply, the Alaskans have manufactured a couple more. Undeterred by the lack of tall trees in parts of the Far North, Alaska has joined the global craze for ziplining with new operators in Seward and Talkeetna shooting daredevils above the forest canopy. The latter claims to be the northernmost zipline in North America. They join established operators in Juneau, Ketchikan and Matanuska. (p226) (p283)

Top of the World Hotel, Barrow

Barrow's Top of the World Hotel relocated to plush new digs in 2014, but it's still the northernmost hotel in the US with a salubrious new restaurant to boot. (p370)

Hoodoo Brewing Co, Fairbanks

Microbreweries, long a feature in the Pacific Northwest, have migrated north to Alaska. Hoodoo in Fairbanks is the state's newest operation – and also one of its best. (p300)

Savage Alpine Trail, Denali National Park

This new trail in Denali National Park takes in 4 miles of steep climbs, colorful wildflowers and expansive taiga-tundra views starting from Savage River on the Park Rd. (p272)

Homeport Eatery, Sitka

Proof that Alaskan eateries aren't all burger and pizza dives is this new gourmet food court where you can grab paninis, crepes and coffee as you pray for the rain to stop. (p114)

Kendesnii Campground, Wrangell-St Elias National Park

The National Park Service has opened up its first official campground in Wrangell-St Elias National Park. Kendesnii is located near the end of the remote Nabesna road and it's free of charge. (p320)

Petersburg Public Library, Petersburg

There's life in books yet. Doubters should check out this cozy new community library in Petersburg, where art adorns the walls and comfy chairs invite relaxation. (p106)

Bubbly Mermaid, Anchorage

Anchorage has developed a penchant for champagne and oysters at this new-ish downtown bar. Grab your share before you venture out into the wilderness with your campfire rations. (p176)

For more recommendations and reviews, see lonelyplanet. com/alaska

If You Like...

Hiking

Alaska is a hiker's heaven, offering paved urban trails, bushwhacking wilderness routes and everything in between. You're rarely far from a hiking trail, even in the state's capital or largest city.

Denali National Park Choose from ranger-led hikes or multi-day backcountry jaunts in this massive wilderness. (p263)

Juneau Dozens of trails climb the lush and vertical mountains behind Alaska's capital city. (p116)

Seward Surrounded by mountains and sparkling Resurrection Bay, Seward's a hiker's paradise, with beach walks and Mt Marathon. (p223)

Anchorage Chugach State Park serves as the dramatic backdrop to Alaska's biggest town, and is filled with stellar hiking. (p158)

Kennicott Glacier walks and hikes to bruised old copper mines in America's largest national park. (p324)

Kodiak Island Verdant, gently crinkled mountains offer rough but spectacular trails on the US's second largest island. (p327)

Paddling

Alaska has more coastline than the rest of the US combined, making kayaking a top choice for outdoor pursuits. Hidden coves, calving glaciers, waterfalls, sea-lion rookeries; the list of photographs you could take from a kayak is seemingly endless.

Prince William Sound A massive green cirque full of deep fjords and quiet coves that covers 15,000 sq miles of wilderness. (p194)

Kenai Fjords National Park Accessible via Seward, Kenai Fjords National Park offers steep fjords, wildlife encounters and tidewater glaciers. (p231)

Glacier Bay National Park Everywhere you turn, a tidewater glacier seems to be calving in this grand park. (p135)

Misty Fiords National Monument Steep mountains and fjords topped by wispy fog, with waterfalls slicing down from beyond sight. (p60)

Kake to Petersburg A 90-mile adventure along the west side of Kupreanof Island that will keep experienced kayakers busy for at least a week. (p104)

Delta River Wilderness paddle off the Denali Hwy that'll suit adventurers with wild-water skills and an ability to portage. (p291)

Bear Watching

Most visitors come to Alaska to see bears, and many are lucky enough to walk away with at least one sighting. Increase your odds by visiting one of these spots.

Katmai National Park & Preserve Best place in the world to see brown bears, preferably snapping jumping salmon mid-flight from Brooks Falls. (p338)

Steep Creek The cheapest place to spot bears is at this salmon-viewing platform outside Juneau. (p120)

Denali National Park Brown and black bears patrol the wilderness beneath North America's tallest mountain. (p263)

Kodiak National Wildlife Refuge It's not hard to spot the world's largest bears (some pushing 1500lb) from a bear-viewing float plane. (p336)

Point Barrow If you're lucky, you just might spot a polar bear close to the US's northernmost settlement. (p368)

Arctic National Wildlife Refuge The hard-to-reach village of Kaktovik on the Beaufort Sea is 'polar bear city' in late summer. (p360)

Izembek National Wildlife Refuge Lots of bears, few tourists and free tours at this remote outpost on the Alaska Peninsula. (p345)

Glacier Viewing

These massive rivers of ice never fail to amaze when you see them up close. Whether they're calving into water or depositing moraines on land, their mighty presence is surprisingly powerful.

Mendenhall A snowball's throw from Juneau, the Mendenhall Glacier is the city's number-one attraction. (p119)

Exit The only glacier in Kenai Fjords National Park that's accessible by road, Exit Glacier is a mere drip from the massive Harding Ice Field. (p233)

Root Walk on it, grip it with your crampons and feel its stealthy chill in Wrangell-St Elias National Park. (p325)

Matanuska Stop to gawk from the Glenn Hwy, or take a tour and walk on the ice. (p315)

Mt McKinley Take a flightseeing tour over Alaska's glacier-encrusted summit and get your bush pilot to land on the ice. (p165)

Scenic Trips

Answer the call of the open road, stare out a train window at homesteaders' cabins or watch glaciers slide by from the deck of a ferry – all are options on Alaska's unique transportation system.

MV Tustumena The slow, 50-year-old ferry that runs from Homer to the remote settlements of the velvet, verdant Aleutian Islands. (p344)

Denali Highway Winding through the foothills of the Alaska Range, the Denali Hwy is full of alpine tundra, braided rivers and massive glaciers. (p290)

CHRISTIAN KOBER / GETTY IMAGES ©

JESSICA LYNN CULVER / GETTY IMAGES ©

Top: Climbing Mt McKinley (p265)
Bottom: Salmon fishers

Hurricane Turn Two-car train from Talkeetna to Hurricane that services homesteaders and adventurers in a wilderness inaccessible by road. (p282)

Denali Star Luxurious train ride through a brawny wilderness between Anchorage and Fairbanks. (p184)

Taylor Highway Rough road to one of Alaska's last frontiers peppered with off-the-grid settlements such as Eagle and Chicken. (p310)

Dalton Highway One of only two opportunities you have of driving north of the Arctic Circle in North America. (p360)

Fishing

Hooking a big one is a major reason why folks visit Alaska, and you can take your pick from salmon, halibut, trout and more.

Russian & Kenai Rivers This is where 'combat fishing' gets its name: hundreds of fisherfolk trying not to hook each other during the salmon run. (p234)

Ship Creek Watch massive salmon run right through downtown Anchorage with the city skyline as a backdrop. (p159)

Homer Take a halibut charter and bring home hundreds of pounds – of one fish. (p248)

Kodiak Alaska's largest fishing fleet resides here, so why wouldn't you charter a halibut boat to bag a big one? (p333)

Copper Center Legendary fishing on the Klutina and Copper Rivers renowned for their salmon. (p318)

River Running

Running Alaska's rivers is a great way to travel and is becoming more and more popular as packrafting takes off. Match your skill (and adrenaline) levels with guided trips or, if you're experienced, head out on an expedition.

Nizina River In Wrangell-St Elias National Park, the highlight of this float is cruising through the vertical-walled Nizina Canyon. (p320)

Denali National Park The Nenana River is the most-rafted river in Alaska, with wet-suited tourists bobbing through a scenic canyon. (p263)

Talkeetna River A placid, scenic float for mellower folks, this one has forget-me-not views of Mt McKinley on a clear day. (p283)

Kenai River A shade of fluorescent glacial blue, the Kenai makes for a great float past bears and anglers on the Kenai Peninsula. (p235)

Sixmile Creek The creek's three canyons with rapids up to class V are often described as a 'death-defying' ride. (p220)

Whale Watching

Catching a whale breach never fails to make a crowd gasp, but seeing belugas bubble to the surface can be equally exciting. Check out the following places for a chance to spot these amazing marine mammals.

Glacier Bay National Park & Preserve Humpback whales performing acrobatics often steal the show on boat tours of Glacier Bay. (p136)

Kenai Fjords National Park Another spot where a boat tour will take you out into whale country. You might see humpbacks, orcas or gray whales. (p231)

Sitka A dozen operators will show you whales and other marine life, or you can view from the shoreline at Whale Park. (p112)

MV Tustumena Breaching whales bring serendipity to this three-day ferry ride to the Aleutian Islands at no extra cost! (p344)

Camping

Peering from a tent out to a view of alpine flowers, glacial rivers or even wildlife is a great way to sleep on a budget. Alaska is full of campsites: public, private, free and nonestablished – take your pick.

Wonder Lake At Mile 84 of the Park Rd in Denali National Park, Wonder Lake reflects Mt McKinley on its surface. (p274)

Golden Sands Beach Stretching a mile outside Nome, this sandy beach allows you to pitch a tent next to miners hoping for a golden nugget. (p354)

Brooks Camp Probably the only place your tent will be behind an electric fence, thanks to all those grizzlies running around. (p338)

Seward Highway This 126-mile scenic road offers more than a half dozen campgrounds, all framed by the Chugach Mountains. (p219)

Kendesnii The only official NPS campground in the 13.2-million-acre Wrangell-St Elias National Park is new, remote and free of charge. (p320)

Month by Month

February

Only the brave venture into Alaska in the winter when temperatures struggle to travel north of 0°F (-17.8°C) in the Interior. But days are getting longer by February when ardent fans of dog mushing can witness the Yukon Quest.

☆ Yukon Quest

The toughest dogsled race in the world (p301) has resurrected a gold-rush-era mail route between Fairbanks and Whitehorse (Canada) covering over 1000 snow-encrusted miles. It starts in odd-numbered years in Whitehorse and in even-numbered years in Fairbanks.

☆ Cordova Iceworm Festival

Arguably Alaska's weirdest festival, this celebration (p209) recognizes the survivalist spirit of the mysterious ice worm. It provides an excuse to celebrate the (near) end of winter with seven days of shenanigans culminating with citizens jumping into the harbor in survival gear. (www.cordovachamber.com)

March

As the sun emerges from hibernation, so do Alaskans. Though the temperatures are still quite low, the sun gives off a welcome hint of warmth and brightness.

☆ Iditarod

Cheer on the dogs and their mushers as they slice by in 'the last great race' (p385). The ceremonial start is in downtown Anchorage, while the official race is from Wasilla or Willow all the way to Nome. (www.iditarod.com)

April

What most folks call spring is 'breakup' in Alaska, and April is full-on breakup season. The air smells of water as snow and ice melt, and the energy level of Alaskans noticeably increases.

☆ Alaska Folk Festival

Musicians from across Alaska and the Yukon descend on Juneau for a week of music and dancing. Who cares if it rains every day? Get wet and dance away. (www.akfolkfest.org)

May

May is shoulder season and a great month to visit, with discounts on tickets, tours and accommodations. The weather's cool and trails are usually snow-covered, but the days are long and the crowds are thin.

🏃 Copper River Delta Shorebird Festival

Birders invade Cordova for four days of workshops, lectures, dinners and exhibitions, all in celebration of some of the greatest migrations in Alaska across one of North America's largest continual wetlands. (www.cordovachamber.com)

🏃 Kachemak Bay Shorebird Festival

If the birders aren't gathering in Cordova, then they're nesting in Homer, enjoying workshops, field trips and birding presentations by keynote speakers. It wouldn't be Homer without an arts and crafts fair too. (www.homeralaska.org)

🎏 Little Norway Festival

Be a Viking for a day in Petersburg and feast on seafood at night at one of Southeast Alaska's oldest festivals. There are parades and pageants, and the entire town appears to be dressed in Norwegian folk costumes. (www.petersburg.org)

🍴 Kodiak Crab Festival

Celebrated since 1958, this festival includes survival-suit races and seafood cook-offs. Grab a plate and dig in to as much of everyone's favorite shellfish as you can fit in your belly. (www.kodiak.org)

June

June marks the height of tourist season in Alaska. The longest day of the year is celebrated in solstice festivities across the state, and salmon begin their runs from sea to spawning grounds.

☆ Spenard Jazz Fest

Alaska is a lightly populated country with a lot of good musicians. Come and see the latest talent improvise with jazz riffs at the rapidly growing Spenard festival in Anchorage. (www.spenardjazzfest.org)

☆ Sitka Summer Music Festival

Since 1972 this festival has been a most civilized gathering, with chamber music, concerts and lots of culture by the sea in beautiful Sitka. You'll need to book tickets in advance. (www.sitkamusicfestival.org)

🎏 Moose Pass Summer Solstice Festival

Join in some small-town fun and games, not to mention a short parade and major boogying, down on the Kenai Peninsula in tiny Moose Pass. (www.moosepasssportsmensclub.com/events.html)

🎏 Midnight Sun Festival

Celebrate summer solstice in Fairbanks with music from 40 bands on three stages, the Yukon 800 Power Boat Races and a baseball game that starts at midnight but doesn't need any lights. Held on the Sunday before the solstice. (www.explorefairbanks.com)

🎏 Nalukataq Festival

Join Barrow residents in late June as they celebrate and give thanks for another successful whaling season with dancing and blanket tosses. You'll even get to taste your first *muktuk* (whale blubber). (www.cityofbarrow.org)

July

The days are still long, the mountains are green, salmon streams are full and everyone is in good spirits. Not surprisingly, this month is the busiest for festivals.

🏃 World Eskimo-Indian Olympics

You have to wait four years in-between the modern Olympic Games, but the indigenous people of the north congregate in Fairbanks annually to display their sporting prowess in esoteric events such as the blanket toss, the ear pull and the two-foot high kick. (www.weio.org)

🎏 Fourth of July in Skagway

Soapy Smith, Alaska's most lovable scoundrel, headed up Skagway's first Fourth of July parade in 1898 and this small town has been staging a great one ever since. It not only includes an egg toss, it holds the Guinness World Record for it. (www.skagway.com)

🎏 Fourth of July in Juneau

Head to the docks with Juneau residents after the cruise ships have slipped away and dress up in your Mardi Gras finest; build a giant sand castle on Douglas Island; or simply enjoy the colorful parade. (www.traveljuneau.com)

🏃 Mt Marathon Race

Take in the exhausting Fourth of July 3.1-mile run up Seward's 3022ft-high peak, which started in 1915.

Join the fans as they crane their necks at the racers, many of whom make it up and back in well under an hour. (www.mmr.seward. com)

✿ Girdwood Forest Fair

Girdwood's magical arts fair is held in the rain forest over the Fourth of July weekend. Come twirl Hula-Hoops to live music, shop for local art and relax in a rainy beer garden by a glacial stream. (www.gird-woodforestfair.com)

✿ Southeast Alaska State Fair

Held in late July in Haines, this unique fair hosts a lively fiddler competition as well as the Ugliest Dog Contest – but make sure you don't miss the pig races. (www.seakfair.org)

August

Summer is in full swing at the beginning of August, but night and chillier temperatures return at the end. Berries are ripe, produce is ready for harvest and you might even spot the northern lights.

✕ Blueberry Festival

Blue tongues aren't the only thing you'll see at this Ketchikan festival: slug races, pie-eating contests, a parade and even a poetry slam are all events held at this celebration of every-one's favorite berry. (www. visit-ketchikan.com)

Top: Blanket tossing at the World Eskimo-Indian Olympics (p29)
Bottom: Competitors in the Iditarod (p28)

 Gold Rush Days

Five days of bed races, canoe races, dances, fish feeds and floozy costumes in Valdez, plus a boat race for dinghies made of cardboard and duct tape. Oh, and a little gold-rush history too. (www.valdezgoldrushdays. org)

Alaska State Fair

Palmer's showcase for 100lb cabbages and the best Spam recipes in the state, plus live music, logging shows and deep-fried Twinkies. It runs from late August through the first weekend in September. (www.alaskastatefair.org)

September

September is another shoulder month for tourism, with discounted prices and fewer crowds. Night is full-on here, but the hiking is still good and you have a good chance of seeing the northern lights.

☆ Seward Music & Arts Festival

This family-friendly festival incorporates artists and more than 20 musical acts and theatrical companies, including circus lessons for the kiddos. Every year the townsfolk get together and paint a mural; come help them. (www.sewardfestival. com)

October

In most of Alaska, winter is on. Winds blow the last of the leaves from trees, snow caps the mountains and days are noticeably long. That doesn't keep Alaskans from having a good time, though.

🍺 Great Alaska Beer Train

All aboard! The *Microbrew Express* is a special run of the Alaska Railroad from Anchorage to Portage; it's loaded with happy passengers sipping the best beer made in Alaska and taking in some of Alaska's finest scenery. (www.alaskarailroad.com)

Alaska Day Festival

Sitka dresses the part in celebrating the actual transfer ceremony when the United States purchased Alaska from Russia in 1867. You'll find community dances, a kayak race and an afternoon tea for kids to learn about life in 1867. (www.sitka.org)

November

Bundle up and put on your bunny boots. You won't find many tourists here this time of year, but the nightlife is vibrant in larger towns and cities and there's a palpable sense of community.

👁 Sitka Whalefest

It's whales galore in Sitka – so many you don't even need a boat to view them. This scientific gathering will teach you everything you need to know about these amazing marine mammals. (www.sitkawhalefest.org)

👁 Alaska Bald Eagle Festival

This is the largest gathering (p142) of bald eagles in the world. There are more birds in Haines than tourists at this festival, when more than 3000 eagles gather along the Chilkat River. Simply spectacular. (www.baldeagles.org/festival)

Itineraries

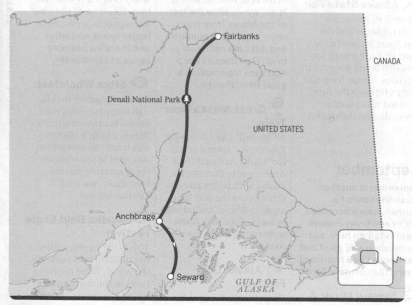

Fairbanks

Denali National Park

CANADA

Anchorage

UNITED STATES

Seward

GULF OF ALASKA

5 DAYS Fairbanks to Seward by Train

This land-based itinerary takes advantage of the scenic Alaska Railroad corridor. Start out in **Fairbanks**, the northernmost point of the Alaska Railroad, where you can spend a day exploring the museums and a night appreciating that the sun barely sets. Hop on the train to **Denali National Park**, and take a good day hike on the Triple Lakes Trail. The next morning, take the extraordinarily scenic, eight-hour ride to **Anchorage**; along this stretch the tracks leave the road and probe into road-less wilderness, paralleling rivers instead of the highway.

Spend two nights and one full day in Anchorage, taking advantage of its surprisingly sophisticated shopping and dining scene. Check out the world-class Anchorage Museum, or work off your salmon belly with a bike ride along the Coastal Trail. Then hop aboard for another scenic journey to **Seward**. Again, the train deviates from the road and takes you 10 miles into the Chugach Mountains. Seward is the southern terminus of the railroad, ending in spectacular Resurrection Bay. Be sure to take a tour of Kenai Fjords National Park to spot sea lions, sea otters and whales.

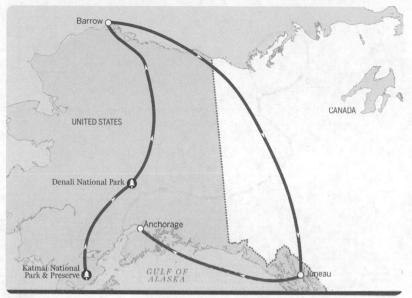

 10 DAYS # Katmai National Park to Anchorage

One of the fastest growing activities in Alaska is bear watching. There's no shortage of bears here, nor tourists wanting to see one – preferably catching and devouring a salmon. Make it to at least one of the following destinations and you're likely to spot one.

One of the most famous bear-viewing sites is Brooks Falls in **Katmai National Park & Preserve**. Here is where you'll catch the ultimate Alaskan photo: a dozen grizzlies perched on the edge of a waterfall, snapping salmon out of the air as they leap upstream. There are so many bears here in July, in fact, that the moment you step out of your float-plane at Brooks Camp you are ushered into the national parks office for a mandatory bear orientation, likely passing a grizzly or two ambling up the shore of Naknek Lake on your way.

A bit more accessible than Katmai National Park & Preserve is **Denali National Park**, which sits on the road system. Here you can jump onto a park shuttle bus and press your face against the glass as you scour the sweeping landscape for both brown and black bears. Though you're likely to spot one of these legendary beasts, you'll probably also catch sight of caribou and moose.

Keep heading north to **Barrow** for a chance to spot a polar bear at the top of the world. Photographing one of these massive white creatures is an experience few will ever have. A guided tour will take you out of town where you might also catch sight of a walrus.

For a more urban experience, fly to **Juneau**. The most affordable bear watching is found here, since you don't have to travel far from the city to catch brown and black bears feasting on salmon at the capital city's Steep Creek near Mendenhall Glacier.

Finally, if you haven't had the luck to be in the right spot at the right time, you can always head to **Anchorage** and see, all in the same hour, a black bear, a grizzly and the magnificent polar bear at the Alaska Zoo. It's not quite as cool as seeing a bear in its natural setting, but you can get much closer to them, and it's a lot safer.

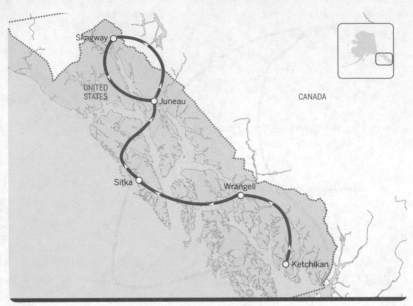

Cruising Southeast Alaska

One of the most exciting trips is taking the Alaska Marine Highway from Bellingham, WA, to Skagway. It's an easy-to-plan journey through a scenic region of Alaska, although you should reserve space on the Alaska Marine Highway ferry if you want a cabin. Board the ferry in Bellingham and enjoy the coastal scenery of Canada – including staffed lighthouses – for a couple of days before disembarking for two days at **Ketchikan**. If it's not raining spend a day climbing Deer Mountain and enjoy lunch on the peak with panoramic views of the Inside Passage. Head out to Totem Bight State Park to see totems and a colorful community house. If it *is* raining, book a flightseeing tour of Misty Fiords National Monument, an almost mystical landscape of steep fjords and waterfalls running off foggy green mountains.

Catch the ferry to **Wrangell** and take a wild jet-boat tour up the Stikine River, North America's fastest navigable river. Be sure to visit Petroglyph Beach, where ancient rock carvings of faces and spirals emerge at low tide. Continue to **Sitka** on the ferry for an afternoon at Sitka National Historical Park and another on a whale-watching cruise.

Head to **Juneau** and sign up for a walk across the beautiful ice of Mendenhall Glacier. Top that off the next day by climbing Mt Roberts and then having a beer (or two) before taking the Mt Roberts tramway back to the city. In the evening enjoy one of the city's salmon bakes and indulge in the tourist trap that is the Red Dog Saloon.

Climb aboard high-speed catamaran MV *Fairweather* for two days in **Skagway**, the historic start of the Klondike Gold Rush. Board the White Pass & Yukon Route Railroad for a day trip to Lake Bennett and in the evening catch the rollicking *Days of '98 Show*. Take a hike in the Dewey Lakes Trail System, which originates right in town. After Skagway you'll need to backtrack to Juneau if you want to fly home. Spend your final day flying through the rainforest like an eagle on one of the city's two ziplines. Fly home from here or extend your trip and take the state ferry back.

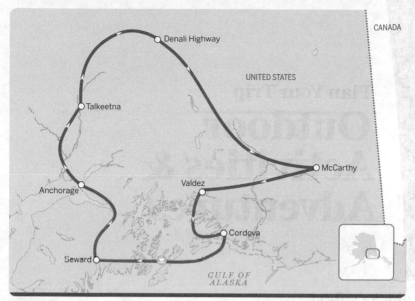

Road Tripping

Driving the very open roads in such a dramatic land is what road tripping is all about. Get yourself a rental vehicle and crank up your tunes: you're in for an amazing ride. Fly into **Anchorage** and pick up your car (make sure you book well in advance). Stop at one of the city's large supermarkets, stock up with road-trip goodies and the local brew and then beat it out of town.

Head north and take the George Parks Hwy through Wasilla. Turn at the Talkeetna Spur Rd and hang out in **Talkeetna**, a laid-back climbers' town. Spend the day on the last flag-stop train in the US, the *Hurricane Turn*. In the evening, be sure to check out the antics at the historic Fairview Inn's bar.

Head back to the Parks Hwy and continue north to the **Denali Highway**. Open only in summer, this 135-mile dirt road traverses the foothills of the Alaska Range. Take your time; the road is rough and the scenery stunning. Pitch a tent along the road wherever it feels right – preferably next to a rushing stream – and then continue heading east in the morning until you hit the Richardson Hwy.

Travel south and then follow the McCarthy Rd east to the Kennicott River, 127 miles from Glennallen. Spend the next day exploring the quaint village of **McCarthy** and the amazing mining ruins at Kennicott. Return to the Richardson Hwy and head south and then west.

Continue into **Valdez** and stay an extra day to splurge on a Columbia Glacier cruise. Drive onto the Alaska Marine Highway ferry (reserve this in advance) and sail across Prince William Sound to **Cordova**. Spend 24 hours dissecting the Sound's most attractive town and its free-thinking locals, incorporating a hike around the Copper River Delta with its many bird species. From Cordova take a ferry to Whittier. On the same day drive 90 miles to **Seward**, passing through scenic Turnagain Pass. Stay two days in Seward; book a boat tour or kayak in Resurrection Bay, but on the afternoon of the second day hightail it back to Anchorage (127 miles) to turn in your car before the dealer closes.

Plan Your Trip

Outdoor Activities & Adventures

Alaska's Best Campgrounds

Blueberry Lake State Recreation Site (p319) Twenty-five sites in a scenic alpine setting north of Valdez.

Fort Abercrombie State Historical Park (p334) Near Kodiak; wooded sites, interesting WWII artifacts and intriguing tidal pools to explore.

Marion Creek Campground (p362) BLM facility along the Dalton Hwy, north of the Arctic Circle, with stunning views of the Brooks Range.

Mendenhall Lake Campground (p127) Near Juneau, a beautiful USFS campground with glacial views from some of the sites.

Ninilchik View State Campground (p245) Lots of sites overlooking Cook Inlet, Old Ninilchik and great clamming beaches.

Get Outside & Play

The Great Land is all about the Great Outdoors with over 350 million acres of land, 28.8 million acres of lakes, rivers and ponds, and an astonishing 6640 miles of coastline.

Because everything is bigger in Alaska, so are the adventures. And unlike many destinations, you need to plan your Alaska adventures well in advance. Really getting into the wilderness can require permits, float planes and months of preparation, while short day-hikes and paddles will provide an enticing glimpse into the wilds of one of the world's last great frontiers.

Hiking

There are a number of trails throughout the state that serve as excellent avenues into the wilderness for unguided, multi-day treks.

➡ Denali National Park (p263)

➡ Chilkoot Trail (p58)

➡ Petersburg Lake Trail (p104)

➡ Iditarod National Historic Trail (p225)

➡ Resurrection Pass Trail (p220)

➡ Dixie Pass Route (p69)

➡ Chena Dome Trail (p303)

➡ Pinnell Mountain Trail (p304)

OVERNIGHT TREKKING GEAR

Double-check your equipment before leaving home. Most towns in Alaska will have at least one store with a wall full of camping supplies, but prices will be high and by mid- to late summer certain items will be out of stock.

Absolutely Essential Equipment...

➡ backpack
➡ lightweight tent with rain fly and bug netting
➡ three-season sleeping bag with a temperature range of -10°F to 40°F (-23°C to 4°C)
➡ sturdy hiking boots that are already broken in
➡ water filter
➡ compass or GPS unit
➡ topo map for your route
➡ multi-tool and knife
➡ lighter/waterproof matches
➡ emergency blanket/first-aid kit
➡ headlamp/torch (it still might get dark, depending on the time of year and latitude)
➡ bug spray

In Your Clothing Bag...

➡ warm gloves
➡ winter hat, sun hat and sunscreen
➡ fleece pullover (it can get cold at night, even in July)
➡ rain gear – both pants and parka (because it will definitely rain)
➡ extra wool socks

Equipment to Consider Packing...

➡ self-inflating sleeping pad
➡ reliable backpacker's stove
➡ small cooking kit
➡ sports sandals for a change of footwear at night or for fording rivers and streams
➡ bear mace
➡ duct tape
➡ extra day's worth of food

Cabins

Every agency overseeing public land in Alaska – from the Bureau of Land Management (BLM) and the National Park Service (NPS) to the Alaska Division of Parks – maintains rustic cabins in remote areas. The cabins are not expensive ($25 to $50 per night), but they are not easy to reach, either. Most of them are accessed via a float-plane charter. Others can be reached on foot, by boat or by paddling.

Most cabins need to be reserved six months in advance – some are so popular that a lottery system has been implemented – while others are available on a first-come-first-served basis. Depending on the cabin, you'll likely need to bring everything you would on an overnight trek (save the tent).

➡ **Tongass National Forest** (☎907-586-8800; www.fs.usda.gov/tongass/) has more than 100 cabins available throughout the Southeast.

➡ Chugach National Forest (p415), a 5.4-million-acre wilderness covering eastern Kenai, the Copper River Delta and Prince William sound, has 40 cabins.

➡ Alaska Division of Parks (p65) has 60 cabins and eight ice huts scattered from Point Bridget

State Park near Juneau to Chena River State Recreation Area east of Fairbanks.

➡ Bureau of Land Management (p415) manages 12 cabins in the **White Mountain National Recreation Area** (☑800-437-7021, 474-2251; www.ak.blm.gov; per night $20-25), north of Fairbanks, and four cabins along the Iditarod National Historic Trail (p225).

➡ Alaska Department of Fish and Game (p240) has four cabins on remote fishing lakes in the Interior.

➡ US Fish & Wildlife Service (p409) has seven cabins on Kodiak Island in the **Kodiak National Wildlife Refuge** (☑487-2600; kodiak.fws.gov; per night $45) and 16 cabins in Kenai.

➡ National Park Service (p59) maintains three cabins in **Kenai Fjords National Park** (☑224-3175; www.nps.gov/kefj; per night $50), which are reached by floatplane or water taxi and are reserved through the **Alaska Public Lands Information Center** (☑907-644-3661; www.alaskacenters.gov).

Camping

Camping is your cheapest lodging solution. It is so popular that many communities have set up facilities on the edge of town, and there are non-official camping areas throughout.

But the best camping is away from towns at the public campgrounds operated by the Alaska Division of Parks, the US For-est Service (USFS) or the BLM in northern Alaska. The state park system maintains the most – more than 70 rustic camp-grounds scattered throughout Alaska – with fees from free to $15 a night in the more popular ones. The majority do not take reservations; some have RV hookups, running water and bathrooms; others are more rustic.

Cycling

With its long days, cool temperatures, a lack of interstate highways and a growing number of paved paths around cities such as Anchorage, Juneau and Fairbanks, Alaska can be a land of opportunity for road cyclists.

Some roads do not have much of a shoulder – and many are quite rough even when paved – so cyclists should utilize the sunlight hours to pedal when traffic is light in such areas. It is not necessary to carry a lot of food, as you can easily restock on all major roads.

Good sources for cycling maps and news on events are Alaska's major bike clubs:

Arctic Bicycle Club (www.arcticbike.org)

Bicycle Anchorage (www.bicycleanchorage.org/wordpress/)

Juneau Freewheelers (www.cycleak.com/juneau-freewheelers)

Fairbanks Cycle Club (www.fairbankscycleclub.org)

BACKCOUNTRY CONDUCT

➡ Check in with the nearest United States Forest Service (USFS) office or National Park Service (NPS) headquarters before entering the backcountry.

➡ Take time to check out the area before unpacking your gear. Avoid animal trails (whether the tracks be moose or bear), areas with bear scat, and berry patches with ripe fruit.

➡ Throughout much of Alaska, river bars and old glacier outwashes are the best places to pitch a tent. If you come along the coast stay well above the high-tide line – the last ridge of seaweed and debris on the shore – to avoid waking up with saltwater flooding your tent.

➡ Do not harass wildlife. Avoid startling an animal, as it will most likely flee, leaving you with a short and forgettable encounter. Never attempt to feed wildlife; it is not healthy for you or the animal.

➡ Use biodegradable soap and do all washing away from water sources.

➡ Finally, be thoughtful when in the wilderness. It is a delicate environment. Carry in your supplies and carry out your trash. Never litter or leave garbage smoldering in a fire pit. In short, leave no evidence of your stay. Only then can an area remain a true wilderness.

Camping on Naknek Lake, Bay of Islands, Savonoski Loop (p75)

Mountain Biking

With a mountain bike you can explore an almost endless number of dirt roads, miner's two tracks and even hiking trails that you would never consider with a road bike.

Always pack a lightweight, wind-and-water-resistant jacket and an insulating layer because the weather changes quickly in Alaska and so can the terrain. Even when renting a bike, make sure you can repair a flat with the proper spare tube and tools. Water, best carried in a hydration pack, is a must, as is energy food.

There is much mountain-bike activity around Anchorage, which has several places to rent bikes. Within the city, mountain bikers head to Kincaid Park (p163) and Far North Bicentennial Park (p162) for their fill of rugged single track. In surrounding Chugach State Park, the Powerline Pass Trail is an 11-mile round-trip adventure into the mountains, while the popular 13.5-mile Lakeside Trail (p187) is a leisurely ride that skirts Eklutna Lake.

The Resurrection Pass (p220), Russian River and Johnson Pass Trails in the Chugach National Forest have become popular among off-road cyclists in the Kenai Peninsula. North of Anchorage, Hatcher Pass is a haven of mountain-biking activity, with riders following Archangel Rd (also known as the Archangel Valley), Craggie Creek Trail and Gold Mint Trail to glaciers and old mines in the Talkeetna Mountains.

The most popular area for riders in Fairbanks is the Chena River State Recreation Area, while in Juneau mountain bikers head to Perseverance Trail (p83) near downtown, and Montana Creek Trail (p124) out Egan Dr near the Mendenhall Glacier.

From Valdez, head out on Mineral Creek Road for excellent views.

If you are able to travel with equipment on your bike (sleeping bag, food and tent), you can partake in a variety of overnight trips or longer bicycle journeys. The 92-mile Denali Park Rd is off-limits to vehicles, but you can explore it on a mountain bike. Another excellent dirt road for such an adventure is the 135-mile Denali Highway from Paxson to Cantwell.

Fishing

Alaska has a fish-every-cast reputation, but serious anglers visiting the state carefully research the areas they plan to fish and arrive equipped with the right gear and tackle. They often pay for guides or book a room at remote camps or lodges where rivers are not fished out by every passing motorist.

Those planning wilderness trips should pack a backpacking rod that breaks down into four or five sections and is equipped with a light reel. In the Southeast and Southcentral backcountry, anglers can target cutthroat trout, rainbow trout and Dolly Varden. Further north, especially around Fairbanks, they can catch grayling, with its sail-like dorsal fin, and arctic char. In August, salmon seem to be everywhere.

An open-face spinning reel with light line – something in the 4lb to 6lb range – and a small selection of spinners and spoons will allow you to fish a wide range of waters, from streams and rivers to lakes. For fly-fishing, a 6-weight rod with a matching floating line or sinking tip is well suited for Dolly Vardens, rainbows and grayling. For salmon, a 7-weight or 8-weight rod and line are better choices. You can purchase the locally used lures and flies after you arrive.

You will also need a fishing license. A nonresident's fishing license costs $145 a year, but you can purchase a one-/three-/seven-/14-day license for $20/35/55/80. Every bait shop in the state sells them;

you can also purchase one online through the **Alaska Department of Fish & Game** (☎907-465-4100; www.state.ak.us/adfg).

Many visiting anglers invest in a fishing charter. Joining a captain on his boat is $170 to $250 per person for four to six hours on the water, and local knowledge is the best investment you can make to put a fish on your line. Communities with large fleets of charter captains include Homer, Seward, Petersburg, Kodiak and Ketchikan, with halibut most in demand among visitors. Head to Soldotna to land a 50lb king salmon in the Kenai River.

If money is no object, fly-in fishing adventures are available from cities such as Anchorage and Fairbanks. These outings use small charter planes to reach wilderness lakes and rivers for a day of salmon and steelhead fishing. It's an expensive day trip – often $400 to $500 per person – but the fishing is legendary, sometimes even a catch per cast.

Glacier Trekking & Ice Climbing

The glaciers may be melting, but glacier trekking is still a popular activity in Alaska. Most first-time glacier trekkers envision a slick and slippery surface, but in reality the ice is very rough and embedded with gravel and rocks to provide surprisingly good traction. There are several roadside-accessible glaciers, the Matanuska Glacier (p315) being the best known.

SEEING ALASKA FROM ABOVE

Most flightseeing is done in small planes, holding three to five passengers, with the tour lasting, on the average, one to two hours. A much smaller number are given in helicopters due to the high costs of operating the aircraft. With the rising price of fuel, expect to pay anywhere from $250 to $350 per person for a one-hour flight.

The following are some of Alaska's most spectacular flights:

Glacier Bay National Park From Haines, glaciers, Fairweather Mountains, maybe a whale or two.

Misty Fiords National Monument Two-hour flights that include a rainforest walk in this wilderness near Ketchikan.

Mt McKinley (p265) The bush pilots who fly climbers to the mountain will also take visitors around it for Alaska's most spectacular flightseeing tour.

Valdez Heli-Ski Take the fun way up (and down) with a helicopter to the top of some of the world's gnarliest ski terrain.

Wrangell-St Elias National Park From McCarthy you can view the stunning peaks and glaciers in the USA's largest national park.

Glaciers are dangerous areas. Not only do they have ice-bridges and crevasses, they also move, meaning the surface changes from time to time. Dry glaciers have no snow on top, and are OK for limited travel without technical equipment. Wet glaciers may have snow bridges. Don't venture beyond the edge without a rope, ice-axe and basic knowledge of glacier travel.

Your best bet is to hook up with a guiding company that offers glacier treks. On such outings you'll be outfitted with a helmet, crampons and an ice axe, and roped up for several miles of walking on the frozen surface.

Glaciers are also the main destination in Alaska for ice climbers in the summer. Icefalls and ice faces, where the glacier makes its biggest vertical descents out of the mountains, are where climbers strap on crampons and helmets and load themselves with ropes, ice screws and anchors. Inexperienced climbers should sign up for a one-day ice-climbing lesson, in which guides lead you to an ice fall and then teach you about cramponing, front pointing and the use of ice tools.

Outfitters that offer glacier trekking or ice-climbing excursions:

➡ Above & Beyond Alaska (p135) in Juneau leads a seven-hour glacier trek and climb on Mendenhall Glacier (p119).

➡ St Elias Alpine Guides (p320) is based in tiny McCarthy and offers half- and full-day treks on Root Glacier (p325) as well as ice climbing.

➡ MICA Guides (p315) of Sutton has fun walks on the Matanuska Glacier (p315).

➡ Ascending Path (p183) of Girdwood offers Midnight Sun Glacier Hikes that start at 8pm and uses Byron Glacier for its ice-climbing outings.

➡ Exit Glacier Guides (p226) is a top operation, based in Seward, for exploring Kenai Fjords National Park's Exit Glacier.

Paddling

The paddle is a way of life in Alaska, and every region has either canoeing or kayaking opportunities or both. Both the Southeast and Prince William Sound offer spectacular kayaking opportunities, while Fairbanks and Arctic Alaska are home to some of the best wilderness canoe adventures in the country.

Great paddling adventures:

Misty Fiords National Monument A kayak adventure near Ketchikan.

Tracy Arm Kayak Route South of Juneau.

Swan Lake Canoe Route In the Kenai Peninsula.

Savonoski Loop In Katmai National Park.

Beaver Creek North of Fairbanks.

Blue-Water Paddling

In Alaska, 'blue water' refers to the coastal areas of the state, which are characterized by extreme tidal fluctuations, cold water and the possibility of high winds and waves. Throughout Southeast and South-central Alaska, the open canoe is replaced with the kayak, and blue-water paddling is the means of escape into coastal areas such as Muir Inlet in Glacier Bay National Park or Tracy Arm-Fords Terror, south of Juneau.

If you do not know how to do a wet entry to a kayak (or know what a wet entry is), it's recommended that you travel with a guide. They know the tides, the wildlife and how to keep you safe.

Tidal fluctuations are the main concern in blue-water areas. Paddlers should always pull their boats above the high-tide mark and keep a tide book in the same pouch as their topographic map. Cold coastal water, rarely above 45°F (7°C) in the summer, makes capsizing worse than unpleasant. With a life jacket, survival time in the water is less than two hours; without one there is no time. If your kayak flips, stay with the boat and attempt to right it and crawl back in. Trying to swim to shore in Arctic water is risky at best.

Framed backpacks are useless in kayaks; gear is best stowed in dry bags or small day packs. Carry a large supply of assorted plastic bags, including several garbage bags. All gear, especially sleeping bags and clothing, should be stowed in plastic bags (or a dry bag if you have one), as water tends to seep in even when you seal yourself in with a cockpit skirt. Over-the-calf rubber boots are the best footwear for getting in and out of kayaks.

White-Water Paddling

Alaska's rivers vary, but they share characteristics not found on many rivers in the Lower 48: water levels tend to change rapidly, while many rivers are heavily braided and boulder-strewn. Take care in picking out the right channel to avoid spending most of the day pulling your boat off gravel. You can survive flipping your canoe in an Alaskan river, but you'll definitely want a plan of action if you do.

Much of the equipment for white-water canoeists is the same as it is for blue-water paddlers. Tie everything into the canoe; you never know when you might hit a whirlpool or a series of standing waves. Wear a life jacket at all times. Many paddlers stock their life jacket with insect repellent, waterproof matches and other survival gear in case they flip and get separated from their boat.

Rafting

White-water and expedition rafting are extremely popular in Alaska. The Nenana River just outside of Denali National Park is a mecca for white-water thrill-seekers with companies like the **Denali Outdoor Center** (☑907-683-1925, 888-303-1925; www.denalioutdoorcenter.com; Mile 240.5 & Mile 247 Parks Hwy; per hr/day $7/40) offering daily raft trips through the summer through Class IV rapids. The season climaxes on the second weekend after the Fourth of July holiday, when the Nenana River Wild-water Festival is staged as two days of river races and a wild-water rodeo. Other rivers that attract white-water enthusiasts include the Lowe River near Valdez, Sixmile Creek with its Class V rapids near Hope, the Matanuska River east of Palmer, and Kennicott River near Kennecott.

Expedition rafting tours are multiday floats through wilderness areas. While some white water may be encountered, the raft is mainly used as transportation. Thanks partly to publicity created by the oil-drilling controversy, the Arctic National Wildlife Refuge (ANWR) is very popular for people seeking this type of remote experience. But it's not cheap. Arctic Treks (p57), for example, offers a 10-day float through the ANWR of the Hulahula River costing $4400 per person. The Tatshenshini–Alsek River system is also a highly regarded wilderness raft trip that begins in the Yukon Territory and ends in Glacier Bay National Park.

Rock Climbing & Mountaineering

Mt McKinley (Denali) and the other high peaks in Alaska draw the attention of mountain climbers from around the world.

PANNING FOR A FORTUNE

There's still gold in them hills. Geologists estimate that only 5% of what the state contains has been recovered. And even short-term visitors can strike it rich.

Alaska has more than 150 public prospecting sites where you can recreationally pan for gold without staking a claim. The best options are in the Interior. They include, on Taylor Hwy, the Jack Wade Dredge at Mile 86 and American Creek at Mile 151; the Petersville State Recreation Mining Area on Petersville Rd off the George Parks Hwy at Trapper Creek; the beach at Nome; and on Glenn Hwy, Caribou Creek at Mile 106.8 and Nelchina River at Mile 137.5.

When panning for gold, you must have one essential piece of equipment: a gravity-trap pan, which can be purchased at most hardware stores. Those who have panned for a while also show up with rubber boots and gloves to protect feet and hands from icy waters; a garden trowel to dig up loose rock; a pair of tweezers to pick up gold flakes; and a small bottle to hold their find.

Panning techniques are based on the notion that gold is heavier than the gravel it lies in. Fill your pan with loose material from cracks and crevices in streams, where gold might have washed down and become lodged. Add water to the pan, then rinse and discard larger rocks, keeping the rinsing in the pan. Continue to shake the contents toward the bottom by swirling the pan in a circular motion, and wash off the excess sand and gravel by dipping the front into the stream.

You should be left with heavy black mud, sand and, if you're lucky, a few flakes of gold. Use tweezers or your fingernails to transfer the flakes into a bottle filled with water.

There's a mountain for every taste, from short alpine-style ascents to longer expedition climbs.

Rock climbing has also been growing in popularity in recent years. On almost any summer weekend, you can watch climbers working bolt-protected sport routes just above Seward Hwy along Turnagain Arm. Canyons in nearby Portage are also capturing the attention of rock climbers. Off Byron Glacier, several routes grace a slab of black rock polished smooth by the glacier. Not far from Portage Lake, a short hike leads to the magnificent slate walls of Middle Canyon.

Fairbanks climbers head north of town to the limestone formations known as Grapefruit Rocks, or else pack a tent and sleeping bag for the Granite Tors Trail (p302) off the Chena Hot Springs Rd. A 7-mile hike from the trailhead leads to the tors, a series of 100ft granite spires in a wilderness setting.

For climbing equipment there's Alaska Mountaineering & Hiking (p178) and Beaver Sports (p301), both in Fairbanks.

For more information, visit www.alaskaiceclimbing.com and www.alaska rockclimbing.com.

Information

➡ For information on scaling the state's loftiest peaks, start with the Anchorage-based **Mountaineering Club of Alaska** (☑907-272-1811; www.mtnclubak.org). On its website is the excellent *Introduction to Alaskan Peaks*.

➡ The best climbing guidebooks to the state are *Alaska: A Climbing Guide*, by Michael Wood and Colby Coombs, and *Alaska Rock Climbing Guide*, by Kelsey Gray.

➡ An excellent website for climbing tips and inspiration is William Finley's **Akmountain.com** (www.akmountain.com).

Outfitters

➡ **Alaska Mountain Guides and Climbing School** (☑800-766-3396; www.alaskamountainguides.com) runs a climbing school in Haines and leads high-altitude climbing expeditions to Mt McKinley, Mt Fairweather and other peaks.

➡ Alaska Mountaineering School (p269) of Talkeetna specializes in Mt McKinley.

➡ St Elias Alpine Guides (p320) tackles Mt Blackburn and other peaks in Wrangell-St Elias National Park.

Surfing

Alaska has more coastline than any other state in the USA, but the last thing most people associate with the frozen north is surfing. Until now. Following a *Surfer* magazine cover story on surfing in Alaska, the state's first surf shop, Icy Waves Surf Shop (p134), opened in Yakutat. That caught the attention of CBS News, which sent a camera crew to the remote town for three days. Yakutat's 20-minute segment on the news show *Sunday Morning* with Charles Osgood propelled it into the limelight and transformed the small town into 'Surf City Alaska.'

Due to its big waves and uncrowded beaches, Yakutat was named one of the five best surf towns in the USA by *Outside* magazine. Today more than 100 surfers from all over the world will visit the surf capital of Alaska every summer to join 20 or so locals for 'surfing under St Elias,' the 18,000ft peak that overshadows the town. The best waves occur from mid-April to mid-June and from mid-August through September, and – to the surprise of non-Alaskan surfers – the water isn't all that cold. The Japanese current pushes summer water temperatures into the mid-60s, while the rest of the surfing season they range from the mid-40s to the mid-50s.

Surfers have also hit the beaches of Sitka and Kodiak. Alaska's 'Big Island' has an almost endless number of places to surf, but the majority of surfers head to the beaches clustered around Pasagshak Point, 40 miles south of town.

An Alaskan-style surfin' safari means packing a wet suit with hood, booties and gloves, and often wearing a helmet. You'll also need to watch for brown bears, which often roam the beaches in search of washed-up crabs, salmon and other meals. Surfers have been known to encounter gray whales, sea otters, and even chunks of ice if they hit the waves too soon after the spring breakup.

Plan Your Trip
Cruising in Alaska

Cruising Alaska's waterways is a singular experience that hits high on many traveler's bucket lists. As you cruise from port to port, you'll surround yourself with precipitous fjords, glaciered peaks, uplifting views that stretch on until tomorrow, mirrored waterways and plenty of remarkable wildlife.

Best Ports of Call

Juneau
The state capital stuns with massive green walls of mountains, a quaint city center and a hulking glacier just out of town.

Skagway
Experience gold-rush history – or at least reenactments – in this Southeast Alaskan town.

Seward
Take a day trip to Kenai Fjords National Park or head up the railway to Denali from this cozy fishing village.

Kodiak
Kodiak's lack of tourist culture makes it a refreshing place to stop. They also have some of the biggest bears on earth.

Ketchikan
Walk the rough-and-ready Creek St or check out the serene Totem Heritage Center, shrouded in pines in this rough-housing waterfront village.

Why Opt to Take a Cruise?

There are plenty of reasons to take an Alaskan cruise, namely the two 'Cs': comfort and convenience. And in a state that could otherwise take months, if not years, to thoroughly explore, you'll have a chance to see many of the top sights in an all-inclusive package.

Most days, you'll disembark at a port for anywhere from four to eight hours, where you can bop around town, take in a hike or an excursion, or even a longer trip inland to places such as Denali National Park, Talkeetna or Eagle. You can also sit on deck and spot bald eagles hunting, humpback whales breaching and glaciers calving: not a bad sightseeing experience. On the smaller cruise lines, there will be more wildlife excursions and more stops.

Backpackers, independent travelers and spendthrifts can always hop on the Alaska Marine Highway ferry. You'll see the same sights, but you won't get a casino, heated pool, hot tub, all-you-can-eat buffet or cruise director.

When to Go & What to Bring

Cruises run from May through to September. You will have the best weather in July and August, but for a bit less traffic and cheaper tickets consider taking a cruise in the shoulder seasons of early May and late September.

It's always colder than you expect. While you may get a few shorts-worthy days, it's worthwhile bringing several warm sweaters, a wool cap and a good waterproof jacket.

Picking Your Ship
Cruise Ships

For the comfort of a floating all-inclusive hotel, you can't beat a large cruise ship. However, these resorts on the sea do have limitations. You won't be able to stop at as many places as you can on a smaller ship, and you'll be sharing your Alaska wilderness experience with around 2000 other vacationers. Most large cruises stop only in the major ports of call, and generally start from Vancouver or Seattle. Excursions range from heli-seeing trips

SUSTAINABLE CRUISING

While all travel causes certain environmental and cultural impacts, by their very size, cruise ships leave a heavy wake.

The Impact
Pollution A large cruise liner such as the *Queen Mary* emits 1lb (0.43kg) of carbon dioxide per mile, while a long-haul flight releases about 0.6lb (0.26kg). In Alaska, an 11-day cruise from Seattle to Juneau on a small boat with around 100 guests will burn around 71 gallons of fuel per passenger, releasing some 0.77 tons of carbon into the air per passenger. The flight from Seattle to Juneau releases 0.17 tons of carbon per passenger. Cruise ships also release around 17% of total worldwide nitrogen oxide emissions, and create around 50 tons of garbage on a one-week voyage. In 2013, the US Environmental and Protection Agency estimated that cruise ships produce about 1 billion gallons of sewage a year.

Cultural impact While cruise lines generate much needed money and jobs for their ports of call, thousands of people arriving at once can change the character of a town in a second. Some towns see five cruise ships a day – that's around 15,000 people. And with such short stays, there is little of that cultural interchange that makes travel an enriching endeavor for both tourist and 'town-y.'

What You Can Do

The cruise industry notes it complies with international regulations, and adapts to stricter laws in places such as Alaska and the US west coast. As consumer pressure grows, more and more ships are being equipped with new wastewater treatment facilities, LED lighting and solar panels. In several Alaska ports (as well as San Francisco, Vancouver and Seattle) 'cold-ironing' allows ships to plug into local power supplies and avoid leaving the engine running while in port. Knowing that customers care about these things has an effect on cruise-ship operations. There are also organizations that review the environmental records of cruise lines and ships. These include the following:

Friends of the Earth (www.foe.org/cruisereportcard) Gives out grades for environmental impact. The most environmentally friendly lines in 2013 were Disney, Holland, Norwegian and Princess, all receiving grades of B or better.

US Centers for Disease Control & Prevention (www.cdc.gov) Follow the travel links to the well-regarded sanitation ratings for ships calling into US ports.

World Travel Awards (www.worldtravelawards.com) Annual awards for the 'World's Leading Green Cruise Line'.

ALASKA MARINE HIGHWAY:
THE INDEPENDENT TRAVELER'S CRUISE

Travel on the state ferries is a leisurely and delightful experience. The midnight sun is warm, the scenery stunning and the possibility of sighting whales, bald eagles or sea lions keeps most travelers at the side of the ship.

Alaska Marine Highway (p418) runs ferries equipped with observation decks, food services, lounges and solariums with deck chairs. You can rent a stateroom for overnight trips – these aren't as 'stately' as they may sound, and are downright spartan compared with what you'll get on a cruise liner – but many travelers head straight for the solarium and unroll their sleeping bags on deck chairs, camping out in the covered, open-air rear deck.

The ferries have cafeterias or snack bars and a few have sit-down restaurants, but budget travelers can save money by bringing their own food (and spirits) and preparing it on board the ship. There are microwaves on every ship. Most ships have onboard naturalists who give a running commentary on the trip. Bring your headphones, warm clothes, some extra snacks and a good book.

Ferry schedules change almost annually, but the routes stretch from Bellingham, WA, to the Aleutian Chain, with possible stops including Prince Rupert, BC, Ketchikan, Wrangell, Petersburg, Sitka, Juneau, Haines and Skagway. From Haines you can drive north and within a couple of hours pick up the Alcan Hwy. A trip from Bellingham to Juneau takes 2½ to four days, depending on the route.

Nine ships ply the waters of Southeast Alaska and once a month the MV *Kennicott* makes a special run from Southeast Alaska across the Gulf of Alaska to Whittier. This links the Southeast routes of the Alaska Marine Highway ferries to the Southcentral portion that includes such ports as Homer, Kodiak, Valdez and Cordova.

Along with the Southeast, the Alaska Marine Highway services Southcentral and Southwest Alaska, with 35 ports in the system. There are ferries nearly daily at the main towns in the Southeast, while routes in Prince William Sound and the Aleutians have limited frequency. Once a month from May through to September the MV *Tustumena* makes a special run along the Alaska Peninsula to Aleutian Islands.

If the Alaska Marine Highway ferries are full in Bellingham, head to Port Hardy at the north end of Vancouver Island, where **BC Ferries** (☑888-223-3779; www.bcferries.com) leave for Prince Rupert, BC. From this Canadian city you can transfer to the Alaska Marine Highway and continue to Southeast Alaska on ferries not as heavily in demand as those in Bellingham.

Reservations & Sample Fares

The ferries are extremely popular during the peak season (June to August). If boarding in Bellingham, you absolutely need reservations for a cabin or vehicle space, and just to be safe you should probably have one even if you're just a walk-on passenger.

The summer cruising schedule comes out in December and can be seen online. Stopovers are not free; rather, tickets are priced on a port-to-port basis.

The complete trip (Bellingham to Haines; $353, 3½ days) stops at ports along the way and should be scheduled in advance.

Trips within the Inside Passage include Ketchikan to Petersburg ($60, 11 hours), Sitka to Juneau ($45, five hours) and Juneau to Haines ($37, two hours). Alaska Marine Highway ferries are equipped to handle cars (Bellingham to Haines $797), but space must be reserved months ahead.

Cruise ships, Skagway (p147)

and zipline tours to guided hikes, kayaks and day trips to inland attractions such as Denali National Park. Cruises cost around $120 a night, but that does not include your flight to the port of embarkation. You can save good money (sometimes as much as 50%) by hopping on a 'repositioning' cruise, which takes the boat back to its home port.

Here's how they break down:

Carnival (☎800-764-7419; www.carnival.com) Young people rule on these ships that receive bad marks for environmental stewardship.

Celebrity (☎877-202-4345; www.celebrity cruises.com; 🛝) Family friendly and laid back.

Disney (☎800-951-3532; www.disneycruise. disney.go.com) Plenty of family fun and activities on a ship with good environmental credentials.

Holland America (☎877-932-4259; www. hollandamerica.com) A classy option.

Norwegian (☎866-234-7350; www.ncl.com) Many modern details make this a top pick for young couples.

Princess (☎800-774-6237; www.princess.com) One of the larger cruise lines to visit Alaska.

Regent Seven Seas (☎844-437-4368; www. rssc.com) Lauded as one of the most luxurious lines.

Royal Caribbean (☎866-562-7625; www. royalcaribbean.com) Despite the name, it offers more than 50 voyages to Alaska each summer.

Small Ships

Just 3% of Alaska cruisers take a small-ship voyage. While you'll have tighter quarters, bumpier seas and fewer entertainment options than on the big boys, these vessels offer better chances of seeing wildlife. There will also be more land and kayak excursions, onboard naturalists (most of the time), good food, a more casual atmosphere (you can leave that blue sports coat at the office where it belongs) and a more intimate portrait of Alaska.

These boats sleep anywhere from eight to 100 and are more likely to depart from within Alaska. While this is probably your best bet if you are looking to match comfort with quality and authentic experience, it does come with a steeper price tag: anywhere from $400 to $1200 a night.

Each small cruise ship is different. Here's a breakdown of some of our favorites:

AdventureSmith Explorations (☑877-620-2875; www.adventuresmithexplorations.com; per person $1795-4500) This company offsets its carbon emissions and focuses on learning and adventure cruises in Southeast Alaska aboard its fleet of small boats, which range from intimate charters (accommodating just 12 people) to larger cruisers that can take around 90 people. The boats have kayaks and small skiffs for numerous excursions that include everything from kayaking in Glacier Bay National Park to wildlife watching near Tracy Arm, the ABC Islands, Icy Straight, Misty Fiords and Frederick Sound. Most trips depart from Juneau.

Adventure Life Voyages (☑800-344-6118; www.adventure-life.com; per person $1595-10,795) Specializes in top-end trips up the Inside Passage. Carries 62 to 128 passengers.

Discovery Voyages (☑800-324-7602; www.discoveryvoyages.com; per person $2200-5550) While the quarters are tight on this small boat, Discovery Voyages offers some interesting five- to eight-day options, with trips focusing on whale watching, hiking and kayaking, photography, or wildlife exploration in Prince William Sound. They have a good environmental record.

Lindblad Expeditions (☑800-397-3348; www.expeditions.com; per person from $8990) Backed by National Geographic, Lindblad offers kayaking, wilderness walks, onboard naturalists and Zodiac excursions during eight-day cruises in the Southeast. Many trips include the airfare from Seattle and take visitors from Juneau through the Inside Passage. Plus you get the unique opportunity of pretending to be a National Geographic explorer for the week.

Un-Cruise Adventures (☑888-862-8881; www.un-cruise.com; per person $2995-8095) Offers themed seven- to 21-day cruises, carrying 12 to 36 passengers, that focus on whale watching, Glacier Bay, wildlife watching or adventure travel. The small boats (they call them yachts) have modern, elegant staterooms, and a naturalist is on board to teach you the ways of the Alaska wilderness. Most trips depart from Juneau, but one leaves from Seattle.

Picking Your Route

Inside Passage

The is the classic route, sailing from Seattle or Vancouver. 'The Great Land' coastal views don't start until Prince Rupert Island. Most trips stop in Ketchikan – with about as many bars as people and some fine totem poles – then continue to Juneau, home to a great glacier and heli-seeing tours; Skagway, a gold-rush port with good hiking close to town; and the granddaddy attraction of Alaska cruises, Glacier Bay, where you'll see 11 tidewater glaciers spilling their icy wares into the sea.

Gulf of Alaska

This trip includes the Inside Passage but then continues to the Gulf of Alaska, with stops in Seward, the Hubbard Glacier and Prince William Sound. While you get a broader picture of coastal Alaska on this one-way cruise, it also comes at a price, as you'll generally need to arrange flights from separate ports.

Bering Sea

These trips are more expensive and generally focus on natural and cultural history. Folks that enjoy learning on their vacations will like this trip, with stops in the Pribilof Islands, Nome and, on the really expensive cruises, King Island.

'Cruisetours'

These trips give you the chance to get off the boat for about half of your trip. Most begin with the Inside Passage cruise, then head out on a tour bus, with stops in Talkeetna, Denali National Park, Fairbanks, Eagle or the Copper River. Most cruise companies have all-inclusive hotels in these destinations (basically cruise ships without the rocking).

Plan Your Trip
Travel with Children

Everybody is a kid in Alaska. Whether it's a stream choking with bright red salmon or a bald eagle winging its way across an open sky, nature's wonders captivate five-year-olds just as much as their parents.

Alaska for Kids

The best that Alaska has to offer cannot be found in stuffy museums or amusement parks filled with heart-pounding rides. It's outdoor adventure, wildlife and scenery on a grand scale, attractions and activities that will intrigue the entire family – whether you're a kid or not.

Outdoor Activities

If your family enjoys the outdoors, Alaska can be a relatively affordable place once you've arrived. A campsite is cheap compared to a motel room, and hiking, backpacking and wildlife-watching are free. Even fishing is free for children, since anglers under 16 don't need a fishing license in Alaska.

The key to any Alaskan hike is to match it to your child's ability and level of endurance. It's equally important to select one that has an interesting aspect to it – a glacier, ruined gold mine, waterfalls or a remote cabin to stop for lunch.

Paddling with children involves a greater risk than hiking due to the frigid temperature of most water in Alaska. You simply don't want to tip at any cost. Flat, calm water should be the rule. Needless to say, all rentals should come with paddles and life jackets that fit your child.

Children marvel at watching wildlife in its natural habitat but may not always

Best Regions for Kids

Anchorage & Around

Packed with parks, urban salmon streams, bike paths and plenty of man-made amusements. Head south to ride the Alyeska Tram or take the whistle-stop train out to Spencer Glacier for unique ways into the backcountry.

Kenai Peninsula

Ice-blue rivers for floating and fishing, boat tours that cruise right up to calving glaciers and sea-lion rookeries, and wilderness cabins for roughing it – but not too much.

Denali & the Interior

A combination of intensely wild lands and the distractions of 'Glitter Gulch' or Fairbanks, the Interior entertains with big animals, huge mountains, hot springs and even an amusement park. Plus there's pizza readily available.

Southeast

Gold mines and glaciers, whales and salmon, hiking trails and boat tours: the Southeast has a little bit of everything but on an Alaskan-sized scale.

have the patience for a long wait before something pops out of the woods. In July and August, however, you can count on seeing a lot of fish in a salmon stream, a wide variety of marine life in tidal pools, and bald eagles where the birds are known to congregate. Marine wildlife boat tours work out better than many park shuttles because, let's face it, a boat trip is a lot more fun than a bus ride. Nature tours that are done in vans are also ideal for children as they stop often and usually include short walks.

Eating Out

Like elsewhere in the USA, most Alaskan restaurants welcome families and tend to cater to children, with high chairs, kids' menus of smaller sizes and reduced prices, and waiters quick with a rag when somebody spills their drink. Upscale restaurants where an infant would be frowned upon are limited to a handful of places in Anchorage. Salmon bakes are a fun, casual and colorful way to introduce Alaska's seafood, especially since they often come with corn and potatoes – familiar items at any barbecue.

Children's Highlights
Hiking Trails

Flattop Mountain Trail (p164) Anchorage's most popular family day hike.

Tonsina (p225) A mellow trail to a beach walk and salmon stream outside Seward.

Perseverance Trail (p83) A path into the heart of Juneau's mining history.

Horseshoe Lake Trail (p271) Near the entrance to Denali National Park, it leads to an oxbow lake where moose are often seen.

For a Rainy Day

Anchorage Museum (p159) Tons of stuff for kids including an Imaginarium Discovery Center and planetarium.

Alaska Sealife Center (p223) Diving seabirds, swimming sea lions and a tide-pool touch tank are found in Seward's marine research center.

Dimond Park Aquatic Center (p121) Flume slides, a bubble bench, tumble buckets and interactive water sprays in Juneau.

NATIONAL PARKS FOR KIDS

America's national park system offers numerous activities specifically geared toward children, and many of them are enshrined in the 'Junior Ranger Program.' This program, designed for kids between the ages of five and 12, provides activity books on parks, which children complete to receive a sew-on patch and certificate.

Parks with active Junior Ranger Programs in Alaska include:
➡ Denali National Park & Preserve (p263)
➡ Wrangell-St Elias National Park (p319)
➡ Glacier Bay National Park & Preserve (p135)
➡ Sitka National Historical Park (p109)
➡ Klondike Gold Rush National Historical Park (p149)

Of all Alaska's parks, Denali is probably the best set up for kids. The **Murie Science & Learning Center** (p274) has a number of hands-on exhibits suitable for children, and a few of the 'Denali-ology' day courses are specifically designed for families with younger children. **Denali Education Center** (p274) also has day and multiday youth programs ranging from 'bug camps' (for budding entomologists) to extended backpacking trips. Look out for free 'Discovery Packs,' available at the visitor center, which include a binder filled with scientific activities and also the tools needed to carry out experiments. Among other fun things, kids can test the water quality of nearby streams and make plaster casts of animal tracks. Other kid-friendly Denali attractions are sled-dog demonstrations, nightly campground talks and a daily ranger-led hike to Horseshoe Lake.

Sitka Sound Science Center (p109) Five aquariums, three touch tanks and a working hatchery.

Outdoor Fun

Pioneer Park (p293) Train rides, salmon bakes and genuine pioneer history entertain the offspring in Fairbanks.

Chena Hot Springs (p303; www.chenahot springs.com) Has swimming pools that are cooled to kid-friendly temps.

Matanuska Glacier (p315) A self-guided trail leads families 200yd onto the ice.

Petroglyph Beach (p95) Search for ancient rock carvings and sea life at low tide in Wrangell.

Planning
When to Go

Summer is by far the best time to visit: the odds of spotting wildlife are good, salmon are swimming upstream, hiking trails are free of snow and the weather is as good as it's going to get. Crowds and lines are rarely a problem, unless everyone is stopped and staring at the same large mammal, so traveling during high season doesn't pose too much of a problem crowd-wise. Festivals abound during the summer, and most are family friendly.

Note that between May and September you're going to have to deal with bugs. A lot of them.

Accommodations

Many independently owned accommodations and lodges in small towns won't offer amenities such as roll-away beds or cribs, but chain motels will. If you absolutely need a crib at night, either check in advance or bring your own travel crib.

Sleeping under the stars – or Alaska's midnight sun – can be a memorable experience and is easy on the budget. Numerous campgrounds are connected to the road system, which means you won't have to lug heavy backpacks around. For toddlers and children younger than five years, the best way to escape into the wilderness is to rent a wilderness cabin. Many are reached by float plane, an exciting start to any adventure for a child. The rustic cabins offer secure lodging in a remote place where children often have a good chance of seeing wildlife or catching fish.

Transportation

Many national car companies have safety seats for toddlers and young children for about $10 extra per day. Unfortunately the smaller, independent agencies away from the airports, which generally offer better rental rates, often do not have car seats.

One of the best ways to see Alaska with toddlers or young children is on a cruise ship. The larger the ship, the more family amenities and activities it will offer. Smaller cruise ships, those that hold fewer than 200 people, do not work as well as they are usually geared more towards adventurous couples. But the Alaska Marine Highway System is well suited to families. Children have the space to move around and large ferries such as the MV *Columbia,* MV *Kennicott,* MV *Malaspina* and MV *Matanuska* feature both current movies and ranger programs on marine life, birds and glaciers.

On the **Alaska Railroad** (www.akrr.com) children can walk between passenger carriages and spend time taking in the scenery from special domed viewing cars.

What to Pack

You'll be able to find almost anything in the larger towns that you forgot to pack. The most important thing to remember is layers – you simply can't pack warm enough. High-quality outerwear, especially rain gear, is important on any hike or camping trip. Don't forget a hat. Finally, sunscreen and insect repellent are indispensable.

Regions at a Glance

The regions you visit in Alaska will depend on your budget and time. The bulk of travelers stick to the few areas that roads reach, as getting off the road can be pricey and plenty of excellent sites are within range of road and ferry, not to mention tourist infrastructure.

The majority of tourists visit Southeast Alaska on a cruise or the Alaska Ferry, fly into Anchorage and explore the Kenai Peninsula or head up to visit North America's tallest mountain. A fair number fly to remote streams and lodges for salmon fishing, bear watching or simply an epic river float.

Juneau & the Southeast

Wildlife
Glaciers
Hiking

Marine Life

The sea is the lifeblood of Southeast Alaska, and it teems with life. You'll have the chance to spot whales, seals, Dall porpoises, sea otters and more.

Rivers of Ice

The massive Mendenhall Glacier outside Juneau is the most visited in Alaska, and for good reason: easily accessible, the half-mile face stretches in a glowing line across an iceberg-studded lake. Further north, Glacier Bay National Park & Preserve is the best place to witness calving tidewater glaciers.

Rainforest Walks

Hiking through the Tongass National Forest or up Mt Roberts, behind Juneau, in the green, sweet-smelling trees can be a divine experience, if a soggy one. Excellent trails meander out of almost every town, offering glimpses into an amazing rainforest ecosystem.

p76

Anchorage & Around

Hiking
Urban Culture
Cycling

The Front Range

Anchorage is backed by the Chugach Mountains, a backyard playground for the state's largest city. Flattop Mountain is the most popular climb, but you can delve into the backcountry or simply take a boardwalk stroll at Potter Marsh.

Bistros & Boutiques

No longer a frontier tent city, Anchorage now serves up fancy cocktails and designer duds, and is home to a world-class museum. Hit the trails, then hit the shower and enjoy an evening on the town.

Rolling Around

With over 120 miles of paved trails, most of them in urban greenbelts, Anchorage is a great place to explore by bike. If you fancy mountain biking, head to Girdwood, where you'll find an excellent mountain-bike course.

p156

Prince William Sound

Kayaking
Hiking
Glaciers

Sea Adventures in the Sound

A 15,000-mile cirque with only three small towns to its name, Prince William Sound is packed with quiet coves, rainy islands, tidewater glaciers and remote wilderness cabins. Kayaking trips from Valdez, Cordova and Whittier are all worthwhile.

Delta Day Trips

The Copper River Delta has more than a half dozen hiking trails originating from the Copper River Hwy, while Valdez has several that originate right out of town and head into the steep peaks. Even more are just outside town off the Richardson Hwy.

Massive Calves

Outside Valdez, the giant Columbia Glacier emits huge chunks of ice, some that release under water and pop to the surface without warning. Outside Cordova, the colossal Childs Glacier rumbles louder than thunder as it releases pieces of ice the size of small houses.

p194

Kenai Peninsula

Paddling
Angling
Road Tripping

Glacial Fjords

Kenai Fjords National Park, outside Seward, and Kachemak Bay, outside Homer, are two excellent kayaking spots, with opportunities for seeing marine life, access to remote hiking trails and cabins, and accessible tidewater glaciers.

Combat Fishing

The Kenai Peninsula is where 'combat fishing' is at its fiercest; here hundreds of anglers lined shoulder to shoulder pull fat, meaty salmon out of icy blue water. The Russian and Kenai rivers are the most popular, but are by no means the only places to hook a salmon.

Highways & Byways

Two main roads splinter across the Peninsula, which is larger than Maryland. Running almost the entire length of both is winding, two-lane scenery overload, with mountains, glaciers and rivers rolling by outside your window.

p217

Denali & the Interior

Mountains
Rivers
Northern Lights

The Big One(s)

This is the home of North America's tallest mountain: Mt McKinley, or Denali. But Foraker and Hunter mountains, perennial bridesmaids to Denali, are stunners too, as is Mt St Elias to the southeast.

Floating & Fishing

Giant mountains have giant glaciers, which in turn create giant rivers, filled with salmon, or perfect for bobbing down in a raft. You can choose between a seemingly endless number of these waterways. The most popular are near Talkeetna and Denali National Park.

Rainbows in the Sky

It doesn't really get dark around Fairbanks during the summer, but when it does you're in for a laser show à la Mama Nature. The northern lights are actually out over 300 days a year here. Head to Chena Hot Springs for an awesome soak and a show.

p262

Kodiak, Katmai & Southwest Alaska

Bears
Wilderness
History

World's Biggest Bruins

Kodiak is home to the world's largest bear, the Kodiak brown bear. It also has the highest concentration of these mighty creatures. In Katmai National Park & Preserve, grizzlies snap salmon as the fish jump up a waterfall, mere feet from where you stand.

Wide Open Spaces

The national park service's least visited outpost (Aniakchak) is found here, as well as the astounding Valley of 10,000 Smokes. There are very few developed trails and getting to these spots requires pricey flights, but the scenery and satisfaction are worth every dollar.

Alaska Natives & WWII

Head out to the Aleutian Chain for forgotten history: you'll see bunkers, pillboxes, Quonset huts and more, all remnants of WWII. Equally intriguing is the Alaska Native history, which is particularly accessible in Unalaska.

p326

The Bush

Wilderness
Culture
Wildlife

Untrodden Tundra

Here, places such as Gates of the Arctic National Park & Preserve don't have trails or even visitor facilities. The Dalton Hwy scrapes through the Brooks Range and on to the North Slope, through mind-boggling space.

Small Towns & Villages

Small Alaska Native villages dot the Bush, some connected by the Yukon River; Kotzebue serves as a hub for many of these. Nome emits a Wild West vibe: a gold-rush town and the end of the Iditarod Trail, it's a good-times scene at the edge of the planet.

Musk Ox & Caribou

The herd of porcupine caribou, whose calving grounds are in the Arctic National Wildlife Refuge, is a stunning sight to behold. Other Arctic animals in the region are musk ox, outside Nome, and polar bears, near Barrow.

p351

On the Road

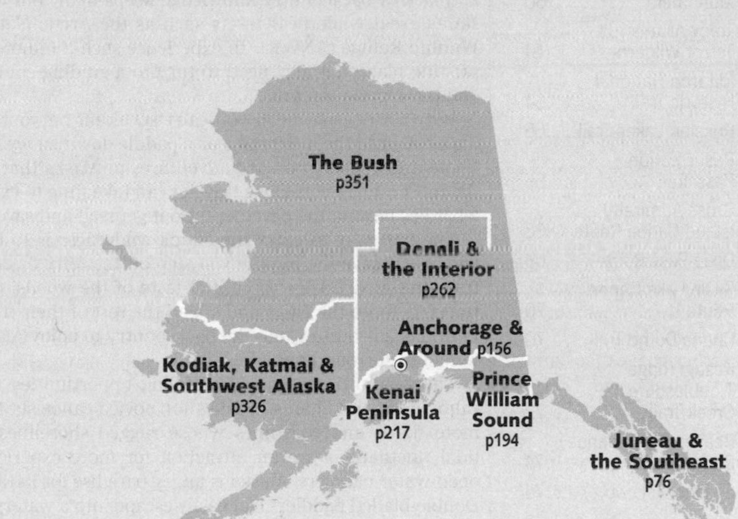

The Bush
p351

**Denali &
the Interior**
p262

**Anchorage &
Around** p156

**Kodiak, Katmai &
Southwest Alaska**
p326

**Kenai
Peninsula**
p217

**Prince
William
Sound**
p194

**Juneau &
the Southeast**
p76

Alaska's Best
Hikes & Paddles

Hiking & Paddling in Alaska

Much of Alaska's wilderness is hard to reach for visitors with limited time or small budgets. The lack of specialized equipment, the complicated logistics of reaching remote areas and lack of backcountry knowledge keeps many out of the state's great wilderness tracts such as the Arctic National Wildlife Refuge (ANWR). To experience such a remote and pristine place you may need to turn to a guiding company and pay a premium price.

But that doesn't mean you can't sneak off on your own for a trek into the mountains or a paddle down an icy fjord. There are so many possible adventures in Alaska that even the most budget-conscious traveler can take time to explore what lies beyond the pavement. Do it yourself and save.

The best way to enter the state's wilderness is to begin with a day hike the minute you step off the ferry or depart from the Alcan. After the initial taste of the woods, many travelers forgo the cities and spend the rest of their trip on multiday adventures into the backcountry to enjoy Alaska's immense surroundings.

There is also a range of paddling opportunities, from calm rivers and chains of lakes for novice canoeists to remote fjords and coastlines whose rugged shorelines and tidal fluctuations are an attraction for more experienced open-water paddlers. Alaska is an icy paradise for kayakers. Double-bladed paddlers can easily escape into a watery wilderness, away from motorboats and cruise ships, and enjoy the unusual experience of gazing at glaciers or watching seal pups snuggle on icebergs from sea level.

Here you'll find 14 popular wilderness excursions. They're either maintained trails or natural paddling routes that backpackers can embark on as unguided journeys provided they have the proper equipment and sufficient outdoor experience.

Hikes in Denali National Park are some of the best in Alaska, but as they are largely trail-less (with no multiday hikes on trails), you'll need to refer to the Denali National Park section (p263) to learn more about hiking there.

RECOMMENDED READS

➡ *Denali National Park Guide to Hiking, Photography & Camping* (2010) Longtime Alaskan Ike Waits has produced the most comprehensive guide to Alaska's best-known national park.

➡ *Klondike Trail: the Complete Hiking and Paddling Guide* (2001) From the legendary Chilkoot Trail to a paddle down the Yukon River, this book by Jennifer Voss will lead you on an adventure of a lifetime.

➡ *55 Ways to the Wilderness in Southcentral Alaska* (2002) Check out this book by Helen Nienhueser and John Wolfe for trails around the Kenai Peninsula, the Anchorage area and from Palmer to Valdez.

➡ *50 Hikes in Alaska's Chugach State Park* (2001) Shane Shepherd and Owen Wozniak cover the state park's best trails and routes near Anchorage. There's a similar guide for Kenai and Anchorage from the same publisher (The Mountaineers Books).

➡ *Hiking with Grizzlies* (2006) Former Denali National Park bear observer Tim Rubbert tells you how to travel into grizzly country to make sure you come back out.

➡ *Hiking Alaska's Wrangell-St Elias National Park* (2008) Greg Fensterman will keep you from getting lost on 50 hikes and backpacking treks in this book, which includes GPS waypoints.

➡ *The Alaska River Guide* (2008) Karen Jettmar provides the complete river guide for Alaska, covering 100 trips, from the Chilkat in the Southeast to Colville on the Arctic slope.

➡ *The Kenai Canoe Trails* (1995) Daniel L Quick's guide to Kenai National Wildlife Refuge's Swan Lake and Swanson River canoe routes, with maps, fishing information and photos.

☞ Tours

If you lack the expertise to head outdoors on your own – or the logistics of visiting remote wilderness, such as the Alaska National Wildlife Refuge, are too daunting – guiding companies will help you get there. Whether you want to climb Mt McKinley, kayak Glacier Bay or pedal from Anchorage to Fairbanks, there's an outfitter willing to put an itinerary together, supply the equipment and lead the way.

Alaska Mountain Guides ADVENTURE TOUR
(☑800-766-3396; www.alaskamountainguides. com) Weeklong kayaking trips in Glacier Bay, big mountain expeditions, mountaineering schools in Haines and heli skiing.

Alaskabike.com CYCLING
(☑907-245-2175, 866-683-2453; www.alaskabike. com) Fully supported cycle tours along the George Parks, Richardson and Glenn Hwys.

Arctic Treks ADVENTURE TOUR
(☑907-455-6502; www.arctictreksadventures. com) Treks and rafting across Arctic Alaska in Brooks Range parks and refuges.

Arctic Wild ADVENTURE TOUR
(☑888-577-8203; www.arcticwild.com) Rafting and backpacking the Arctic National Wild-

life Refuge and Gates of the Arctic National Park, with other trips throughout the state.

**Jody Young
Adventure Travel** ADVENTURE TOUR
(www.jodyyoung.com) Small-scale operation with camping tours and other activities. There's a women's only trip.

Mt Sobek ADVENTURE TOUR
(☑888-831-7526; www.mtsobek.com) There are 14 Alaska trips in all from this trusted operation, ranging from cruises and paddles to wildlife adventures.

St Elias Alpine Guides ADVENTURE TOUR
(☑907-554-4445, 888-933-5427; www.stelias-guides.com) Mountaineering, rafting, trekking and glacier-skiing at Wrangell-St Elias National Park.

Tongass Kayak Adventures KAYAKING
(☑907-772-4600; www.tongasskayak.com) Kayaking LeConte Glacier and Tebenkof Bay Wilderness in Southeast.

ⓘ Useful Websites

Alaska Hike Search (www.alaskahikesearch. com) Includes details on almost 100 trails around Anchorage and Southcentral Alaska.

Alaska Department of Natural Resources (www.dnr.state.ak.us/parks/aktrails) Has details on trails in every corner of the state.

Alaska Department of Fish & Game Wildlife Notebook (www.adfg.alaska.gov/index.cfm?adfg=educators.notebookseries) The excellent *Wildlife Notebook* covers all the state's major species of animals and birds that you may encounter on the trail or while paddling.

Knik Canoers & Kayakers (www.kck.org) With its tips, safety advice and contacts, this website is a great start for anybody thinking about a paddling adventure in Alaska.

SEATrails (www.seatrails.org) SEATrails provides brief descriptions and downloadable maps for more than 80 trails in 19 communities in Southeast Alaska.

Sitka Trail Works (www.sitkatrailworks.org) Detailed-coverage maps on almost 20 trails around Sitka.

Trail Mix (www.juneautrails.org) Helps you find a trail in Alaska's capital city.

Trails of Anchorage (www.trailsofanchorage.com) This site focuses on the great hiking found within the city limits of Anchorage.

Chilkoot Trail

Hiking the Chilkoot Trail

The Chilkoot Trail is the most famous trail in Alaska and often the most popular – more than 3000 people spend three to four days following the historic route every summer.

This was the route used by the Klondike gold miners in the 1898 gold rush, and walking the well-developed trail is not so much a wilderness adventure as a full-on history lesson. The trip is a 33-mile trek and includes the Chilkoot Pass – an extremely steep climb up to 3525ft, where most hikers resort to scrambling on all fours over the loose rocks and boulders.

For many, the highlight of the hike is riding the historic White Pass & Yukon Route (WP&YR) railroad from Lake Bennett to Skagway. Experiencing the Chilkoot and returning on the WP&YR is probably the ultimate Alaska trek, combining great scenery, a historical site and an incredible sense of adventure.

It is possible to hike the Chilkoot Trail starting from either direction but it is easier and safer when you set off from Dyea in the south and climb up the loose scree of the Chilkoot Pass, rather than down it. First stop is the **Chilkoot Trail Center** (☎907-983-9234; www.nps.gov/klgo/planyourvisit/chilkoot

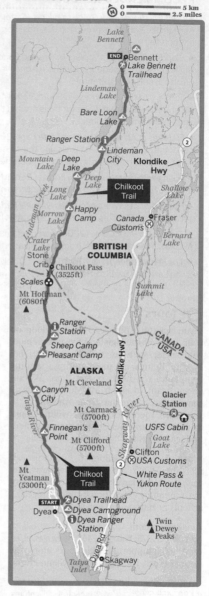

Chilkoot Trail

trail.htm; Broadway St, Skagway) to obtain backpacking permits (adult/child $50/25).

Parks Canada allows only 50 hikers per day on the trail and holds only eight permits to be handed out each day at the trail center. It is definitely wise to reserve your permits ($11.70

per reservation) in advance through Parks Canada (☎867-667-3910, 800-661-0486; www. pc.gc.ca/eng/lhn-nhs/yt/chilkoot/index.aspx) if you intend walking mid-July to mid-August. Also check with the staff at the trail center to make doubly sure you have all the right visas and paperwork to complete the hike into Canada and then return to Skagway in the USA.

SECTION	DISTANCE
Dyea trailhead to Canyon City	7.7 miles
Canyon City to Sheep Camp	5.3 miles
Sheep Camp to Chilkoot Pass	3.5 miles
Chilkoot Pass to Happy Camp	4 miles
Happy Camp to Deep Lake	2.5 miles
Deep Lake to Lindeman City	3 miles
Lindeman City to Bare Loon Lake	3 miles
Bare Loon Lake to Lake Bennett	4 miles

ⓘ Information

Level of Difficulty Medium to hard

Information National Park Service (☎907-983-2921; www.nps.gov/klgo)

Fun Fact The 33-mile-long Chilkoot Trail is considered the world's longest outdoor museum due to all the artifacts that the participants in the Klondike Gold Rush left behind.

ⓘ Getting There & Away

For transport to the Dyea trailhead there's **Frontier Excursions** (☎877 983 2512, 907 983 2512; www.frontierexcursions.com; per person $10). At the northern end of the trail, hikers can return to Skagway via the **White Pass & Yukon Route** (☎800-343-7373; www.whitepass-railroad.com; adult/child $95/47.50; ⊙2pm Mon, Tue & Fri). White Pass & Yukon also offers

hikers a train/bus combination (adult/child $99/44.50; from Sunday to Tuesday and Thursday to Friday) north to Whitehorse in Canada.

Petersburg Lake Trail

Hiking the Petersburg Lake Trail

A short hop across the Wrangell Narrows from the fishing community of Petersburg is Petersburg Lake Trail and Portage Mountain Loop, which can be combined for a trek to two US Forest Service cabins.

The Petersburg Lake Trail is well planked and provides backpackers with a wilderness opportunity and access to a USFS cabin without expensive bush-plane travel. Those planning to continue on to Portage Bay or Salt Chuck along Portage Mountain Loop should keep in mind that the trails are not planked or maintained and, at best, only lightly marked. The 7-mile trek to Portage Bay is very challenging and involves crossing wet muskeg areas or stretches flooded out by beaver dams.

Bring a fishing pole, as there are good spots in the creek for Dolly Varden and rainbow trout. In August and early September there are large coho and sockeye salmon runs through the area that attract anglers and bears.

The trek begins at the Kupreanof Island public dock. From the dock a partial boardwalk heads south for a mile past a handful of cabins and then turns northwest up the tidewater arm of the creek, almost directly across Wrangell Narrows from the ferry terminal. A well planked trail goes from the saltwater arm and continues along the freshwater creek to the Petersburg Lake USFS cabin.

Petersburg Lake Trail

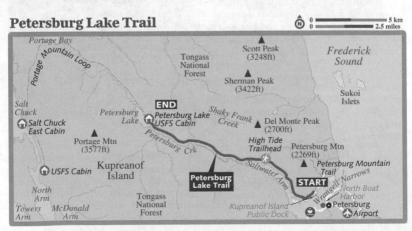

This is one trip on which you'll want to bring good waterproof clothing and rubber boots. Bring a tent or plan on reserving the Petersburg Lake cabin at least two months in advance – even earlier if you want to tackle the route in August during the salmon runs. Reserve the USFS cabin through the **National Recreation Reservation System** (☏877-444-6777, 518-885-3639; www.recreation.gov).

SECTION	DISTANCE
Kupreanof Island dock to Saltwater Arm	2 miles
Saltwater Arm to Petersburg Creek	2.5 miles
Trail by creek to USFS cabin	6 miles
USFS cabin to Portage Bay	7 miles
Portage Bay to Salt Chuck East Cabin	4.5 miles

ℹ Information

Level of Difficulty Medium
Information USFS Petersburg Ranger District (☏907-772-3871; 12 N Nordic Dr; ⊘8am-4:30pm Mon-Fri)

ℹ Getting There & Away

For transportation across Wrangell Narrows to the public dock on Kupreanof Island, contact **Tongass Kayak Adventures** (☏907-772-4600; www.tongasskayak.com; per trip $25).

Misty Fiords National Monument

Paddling Misty Fiords

The Misty Fiords National Monument encompasses 3594 sq miles of wilderness and lies between two impressive fjords – Behm Canal (117 miles long) and Portland Canal (72 miles long). The two natural canals give the preserve its extraordinarily deep and long fjords with sheer granite walls that rise thousands of feet out of the water. Misty Fiords is well named – annual rainfall is 14ft.

The destinations for many kayakers are the smaller but impressive fjords of Walker Cove and Punchbowl Cove in Rudyerd Bay, off Behm Canal. Dense spruce-hemlock rain forest is the most common vegetation type throughout the monument, and sea lions, harbor seals, brown and black bears, mountain goats and bald eagles can all be seen.

Misty Fiords has 15 USFS cabins (p89), which should be reserved in advance. Two paddles – Alava Bay and Winstanley Island in Behm Canal – allow kayakers to end the day at the doorstep of a cabin.

You can't do this trip without good rain gear and a backpacker's stove – wood in the monument is often too wet for campfires. Be

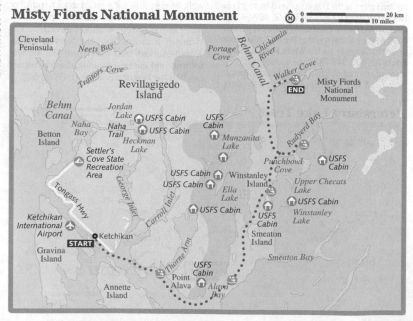
Misty Fiords National Monument

prepared for extended rain periods and make sure all your gear is sealed in plastic bags.

SECTION	DISTANCE
Ketchikan to Thorne Arm	13 miles
Thorne Arm to Alava Bay	9 miles
Alava Bay to Winstanley Island	21 miles
Winstanley Island to Rudyerd Bay	9 miles
Rudyerd Bay to Walker Cove	10 miles

ℹ Information

Level of Difficulty Medium, open water
Information Southeast Alaska Discovery Center (☑ 907-225-3101; www.fs.fed.us/r10/tongass)

ℹ Getting There & Away

Experienced kayakers can paddle out of Ketchikan (a seven- to 12-hour day trip) but most paddlers arrange to be dropped off at Alava Bay or deep in Behm Canal near the protected water of Rudyerd Bay. **Southeast Sea Kayaks** (☑ 907-225-1258, 800-287-1607; www.kayakketchikan.com) has six-day guided tours for $3249 for two people. Southeast Exposure (p88) in Ketchikan rents single/double kayaks for $35/45 per day and has a water-taxi service starting at $100 and ranging up to $500.

Tracy Arm-Fords Terror Wilderness

Paddling Tracy Arm-Fords Terror Wilderness

Endicott Arm, Tracy Arm and Fords Terror form the Tracy Arm-Fords Terror Wilder-

ness, a 653,000-acre preserve, where you can spend weeks paddling to a backdrop of glaciers, icebergs and 2000ft granite walls.

Popular Tracy Arm makes a pleasant two- to three-day (30-mile) paddle, ideal for novice kayakers. Calm water is the norm due to the protection of the steep granite walls. Camping is limited, however; the only spots in the first half are two valleys almost opposite each other, 8 miles north along the arm, and a small island at the head of the fjord.

Tracy Arm attracts cruise ships and tour boats, which detract from the wilderness experience. Experienced kayakers could consider Endicott Arm, a 30-mile fjord created by Dawes and North Dawes glaciers. Extending from Endicott Arm is Fords Terror, a narrow water chasm named after a US sailor who found himself battling whirlpools and grinding icebergs when he tried to row out against the incoming tide in 1899.

SECTION	DISTANCE
Juneau to Sawyer Glaciers drop-off	77 miles
Sawyer Glaciers to mid-fjord camping spots	8 miles
Mid-fjord camping spots to Harbor Island	21 miles
Pick-up to Juneau (tour boat)	48 miles

ℹ Information

Level of Difficulty Easy, open water
Information USFS Juneau Ranger District (☑ 907-225-3101; www.fs.fed.us/r10/tongass)

Tracy Arm-Fords Terror Wilderness

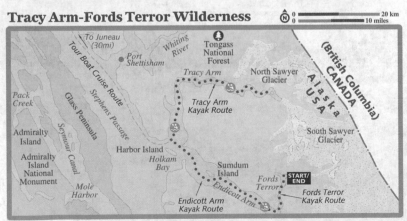

1

2

4

DAVID MADISON / GETTY IMAGES ©

COREY RICH / GETTY IMAGES ©

COREY RICH / GETTY IMAGES ©

3

1. Iditarod National Historic Trail (p64)
Eagle Peak can be seen from a campsite.

2. Cross Admiralty Island Canoe Route (p68)
Calm lakes with a view of snowy peaks.

3. Gates of the Arctic National Park & Preserve (p364)
Hikers in the Brooks Range.

4. West Glacier Trail (p124)
Views of the spectacular Mendenhall Glacier.

ⓘ Getting There & Away

The departure point for Tracy Arm is Juneau, where drop-offs and pickups can be arranged to make the trip considerably easier. Otherwise it's a two- or three-day paddle in open water to reach the fjords. Kayaks can be rented from Alaska Boat & Kayak Shop (p69), which also offers a water-taxi service for drop-offs at the entrance of Endicott Arm. **Adventure Bound Alaska** (☑ 907-463-2509, 800-228-3875; www.adventureboundalaska.com) provides drop-off and pick-up services deep inside Tracy Arm for $193 per person.

Iditarod National Historic Trail

Hiking the Iditarod National Historic Trail

One of the best backpacking adventures near Anchorage is the 26-mile Iditarod National Historic Trail, which was once used by gold miners and mushers. This classic alpine crossing begins at Crow Pass trailhead, 37 miles east of Anchorage, climbs Crow Pass and wanders past Raven Glacier. You then enter Chugach State Park and descend Eagle River Valley, ending north of Anchorage at the Eagle River Nature Center. The trail is well-maintained and well-marked but requires fording Eagle River, which is tricky in rain.

Armed with a decent light backpack and blessed with some reasonably good weather you could potentially cover this trail in one long, challenging, adventurous Alaskan summer day. Heck, they stage a mountain race here every summer with the winner usually smashing it out in less than 3½ hours. But why would you rush? The alpine scenery is remarkable, the mining ruins along the trail are interesting, and the hike is reasonably demanding. Plan on taking two days, or even three, because this is why you come to Alaska – to wander in the mountains.

You must have a stove; campfires are not allowed in the state park. Near Mile 3 of the trail is a USFS cabin (p182) in a beautiful alpine setting. At the other end of the trail are yurts and a cabin ($65) rented out by the Eagle River Nature Center.

SECTION	DISTANCE
Crow Pass trailhead to Crow Pass	4 miles
Crow Pass to Eagle River Ford	9 miles
Eagle River Ford to Icicle Creek	7.3 miles
Icicle Creek to Eagle River Nature Center	5.7 miles

GREAT HIKING NEAR ALASKA'S CITIES

Even if you don't have any desire to hoist a hefty backpack, don't pass up an opportunity to spend a day hiking one of the hundreds of well-maintained and easy-to-follow trails scattered across the state. How good is the day hiking in Juneau? The trailhead for the Mt Roberts Trail (p123) is only five blocks from the state capitol, while the USFS maintains 29 other trails accessible from the Juneau road system. Anchorage is also blessed with numerous close-to-home trails. A 15-minute drive from downtown and you can be at a treeline trailhead in Chugach State Park, where a path quickly leads into the alpine. Skagway, Girdwood, Seward and Sitka also have numerous trails close to main streets.

For the state's best close-to-town day hikes, hit the trail on one of these:

Crow Pass Trail (p64) From Girdwood a round-trip hike of 8 miles takes you past gold-mining artifacts, an alpine lake and Raven Glacier.

Deer Mountain Trail (p82) Just arrived in Alaska? This 2.5-mile trail from downtown Ketchikan to the top of Deer Mountain will whet your appetite to tie up your hiking boots at every stop.

West Glacier Trail (p124) This 3.4-mile-long trail near Juneau hugs a mountainside while providing a bird's-eye view of the Mendenhall Glacier.

Williwaw Lakes Trail (p165) Within minutes of the heart of Anchorage, this easy 13-mile hike leads you to a series of alpine lakes in the Chugach State Park and offers the possibility of seeing Dall sheep.

Mt Marathon Trail (p225) There are several ways to climb 3022ft-high Mt Marathon, which overlooks downtown Seward, but all end at a heavenly alpine bowl just behind the peak.

Iditarod National Historic Trail

0 — 2 km
0 — 1 mile

USFS Glacier Ranger District (☎ 907-783-3242; www.fs.fed.us/r10/chugach)

❶ Getting There & Away

The Crow Pass trailhead is reached 7 miles from Mile 90 Seward Hwy, via Alyeska Hwy and Crow Creek Rd. The northern trailhead is at the end of Eagle River Rd, 12 miles from the Glenn Hwy. There is transportation to Girdwood. To return to Anchorage you can catch bus 102 of the **People Mover** (☎ 907-343-6543; www.peoplemover. org) from the Eagle River Transit Center near Glenn Hwy.

Russian Lakes Trail

Hiking the Russian Lakes Trail

This 21-mile, two-day trek is ideal for hikers who do not want to overextend themselves in Chugach National Forest on the Kenai Peninsula. The trail is well-maintained and well-marked, and most of the hike is a pleasant forest walk broken up by patches of wildflowers, ripe berries, lakes and streams. You can easily connect the trail with the Resurrection Pass Trail to the north and the Russian Rivers Trail to the south.

Highlights of the hike include getting an eyeful of the supremely impressive glaciated mountains that stab the sky across from Upper Russian Lake, the possibility of experiencing a firsthand encounter with moose or bears or both and the chance to catch your own fish-shaped dinner. The trek offers excellent angling opportunities for fishing folk who are willing to carry in a rod and reel. Dolly Varden, rainbow trout and salmon are found in the upper portions of the Russian River; rainbow trout in Lower Russian Lake, Aspen Flats and Upper Russian Lake; and Dolly Varden in Cooper Lake near the Cooper Lake trailhead. Check ahead for restrictions.

There are three USFS cabins (☎ 877-444-6777, 515-885-3639; www.recreation.gov; cabins $35-45) on the trail: one at Upper Russian Lake (9 miles from the Cooper Lake trailhead), another at Aspen Flats (12 miles from the Cooper Lake trailhead) and the third, Barber Cabin, near Lower Russian Lake (3 miles from the western trailhead).

This is serious bear country. It's recommended you take precautions while hiking, setting up camp, and cooking and storing food to prevent any unfortunate encounters with bears.

❶ Information

Level of Difficulty Medium

Information Eagle River Nature Center (☎ 694-2108; www.ernc.org); Alaska Division of Parks (☎ 907-345-5014; www.alaskastateparks.org);

Russian Lakes Trail

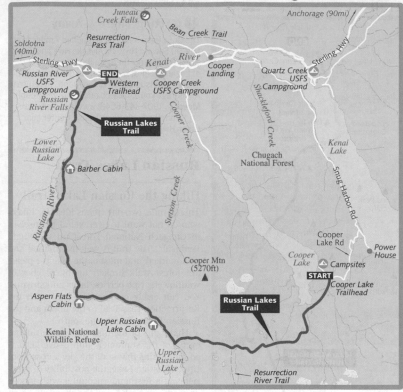

SECTION	DISTANCE
Cooper Lake trailhead to junction of Resurrection River Trail	5 miles
Trail junction to Upper Russian Lake Cabin	4 miles
Upper Russian Lake to Aspen Flats	3 miles
Aspen Flats to Lower Russian Lake	6 miles
Lower Russian Lake to Russian River USFS Campground	3 miles

🛈 Information

Level of Difficulty Easy
Information USFS Seward Ranger District (📞 907-224-3374; www.fs.fed.us/r10/chugach)

🛈 Getting There & Away

It is easiest to begin this trek from the Cooper Lake trailhead, the higher end of the trail. To get there, turn off at Mile 47.8, Sterling Hwy onto Snug Harbor Rd; the road leads south 12 miles to Cooper Lake and ends at a marked parking lot and the trailhead.

The western trailhead is on a side road marked 'Russian River USFS Campground' at Mile 52.7, Sterling Hwy. From there it's just under a mile's hike to the parking lot at the end of the campground road – the beginning of the trail. There is a small fee if you leave a car here. If you're planning to camp at Russian River the night before starting the hike, keep in mind that the campground is extremely popular during the salmon season in June and July.

Resurrection Pass Trail

Hiking the Resurrection Pass Trail

Located in the Chugach National Forest, the 38.5-mile Resurrection Pass Trail (p220) was carved by prospectors in the late 1800s and today is the most popular hiking and cross-country biking route on the Kenai Peninsula. Resurrection Pass Trail's mild climb from 500ft to only 2600ft has made it an increasingly popular trail for mountain bikers, who can ride the entire route in one day. For those on foot, the trip can be done in three days by a strong hiker, but most people prefer to do it in four to five days to make the most of the immense beauty of the region.

The trail is also the first leg of a trek across the Kenai Peninsula. By linking Resurrection Pass, Russian Lakes and Resurrection River Trails in Chugach National Forest, you can hike 71 miles from Hope to Seward and cross only one road.

There are eight **USFS cabins** (☎ 877-444-6777, 518-885-3639; www.recreation.gov; cabins $35-45) along the route but they must be reserved in advance. Most hikers take a tent and stay in designated backcountry campsites at Mile 4, Wolf Creek (Mile 5.3), Caribou Creek (Mile 7), Mile 9.6, Mile 12.6 and East Creek (Mile 14.6). Most sites have bear-resistant food lockers but pack a camp stove, as fallen wood is scarce during summer.

SECTION	DISTANCE
Northern trailhead to Caribou Creek Cabin	6.9 miles
Caribou Creek Cabin to Fox Creek Cabin	4.7 miles
Fox Creek Cabin to East Creek Cabin	2.8 miles
East Creek Cabin to Resurrection Pass	4.9 miles
Resurrection Pass to Devil's Pass Cabin	2.1 miles
Devil's Pass Cabin to Swan Lake Cabin	4.4 miles
Swan Lake Cabin to Trout Lake Cabin	6 miles
Trout Lake Cabin to southern trailhead	6.7 miles

❶ Information

Level of Difficulty Easy
Information USFS Seward Ranger District (☎ 907-224-3374; www.fs.fed.us/r10/chugach)

❶ Getting There & Away

The northern trailhead can be found 20 miles from the Seward Hwy and 4 miles south of Hope on Resurrection Creek Rd. Hope, a historic mining community founded in 1896 by gold seekers, is a charming, out-of-the-way place to visit, but be warned: Hope Hwy is not an easy road for hitchhiking (if you choose to travel in this potentially risky way).

Resurrection Pass Trail

From Hope Hwy, go south at the Resurrection Pass trail signs onto Resurrection Creek Rd, passing the fork to Palmer Creek Rd. The southern trailhead is on the Sterling Hwy, near Cooper Landing.

Cross Admiralty Island Canoe Route

Paddling Cross Admiralty Island Canoe Route

Admiralty Island National Monument, 50 miles southwest of Juneau, is the site of one of the most interesting canoe routes in Alaska. This preserve is a fortress of dense coastal forest and ragged peaks, where brown bears outnumber anything else on the island, including humans. The Cross Admiralty Canoe Route is a 31.7-mile paddle that spans the center of the island from the village of Angoon to Mole Harbor.

Although the majority of it consists of calm lakes connected by streams and portages, the 10-mile paddle from Angoon to Mitchell Bay is subject to strong tides that must be carefully timed. Avoid Kootznahoo Inlet as its tidal currents are extremely difficult to negotiate; instead, paddle through the maze of islands south of it. Leave An-

goon at low tide, just before slack tide so that the water will push you into Mitchell Bay.

The traditional route is to continue on to Mole Harbor via Davidson Lake, Lake Guerin, Hasselborg Lake, Beaver Lake and Lake Alexander, all connected by portages. Because of the logistics and cost of being picked up at Mole Harbor with a canoe, most paddlers stop in the heart of the chain and after a day or two of fishing backtrack to Angoon to utilize the Alaska Marine Highway for a return to Juneau.

There are good camping spots at Tidal Falls on the eastern end of Salt Lake, on the islands at the south end of Hasselborg Lake and on the portage between Davidson Lake and Distin Lake. For those who can plan in advance, there are several USFS cabins (p135) along the route, including those on Hasselborg Lake, Lake Alexander and Distin Lake.

SECTION	DISTANCE
Angoon to Salt Lake Tidal Falls	10 miles
Tidal Falls to Davidson Lake portage	2.5 miles
Portage to Davidson Lake	3.5 miles
Davidson Lake to Hasselborg Lake portage	6 miles

Cross Admiralty Island Canoe Route

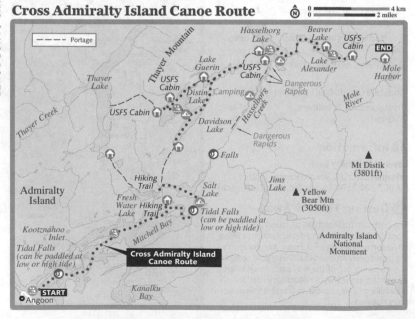

Portage to Hasselborg Lake	1.7 miles
Hasselborg Lake to Beaver Lake portage	2 miles
Portage to Beaver Lake	0.5 miles
Beaver Lake to Mole Harbor portage	3 miles
Portage to Mole Harbor	2.5 miles

ℹ Information

Level of Difficulty Medium; mostly Class 1 water

Information Admiralty Island National Monument (☑ 907-586-8800; www.fs.fed.us/r10/tongass/districts/admiralty)

ℹ Getting There & Away

This adventure begins with a ferry trip to the village of Angoon aboard the Alaska Marine Highway (p133). The one-way fare from Juneau to Angoon is $37, plus another $22 for a canoe. Carefully set up your trip around the ferry schedule; a boat arrives at Angoon roughly every two to three days.

Rent your canoe in Juneau from **Alaska Boat & Kayak Shop** (☑ 907-789-6886; www.juneaukayak.com; single/double per day $50/70), which is conveniently located near the ferry terminal in Auke Bay. Canoes are $50 a day, with discounts for rentals of three days or more.

Dixie Pass Route

Hiking the Dixie Pass Route

Even by Alaskan standards, Wrangell-St Elias National Park is a large tract of wilderness. At 20,625 sq miles, it's the largest US national park, contains the most peaks over 14,500ft in North America and has the greatest concentration of glaciers on the continent.

Within this huge, remote park, Dixie Pass provides the best wilderness adventure that doesn't require a bush-plane charter. The trek from the trailhead up to Dixie Pass and return is 24 miles. Plan to camp there at least one or two additional days to take in the alpine beauty and investigate the nearby ridges. Such an itinerary requires three or four days and is moderately hard.

You reach the Dixie Pass trailhead by hiking 2.5 miles up Kotsina Rd from Strelna and then another 1.3 miles along Kotsina Rd after the Nugget Creek Trail splits off to the northeast. The trailhead is on the right-hand side of Kotsina Rd; look for a marker.

The route begins as a level path for 3 miles to Strelna Creek, and then continues along the west side of the creek for another 3 miles to the first major confluence. After fording the creek, it's 5 to 6 miles to the

Dixie Pass Route

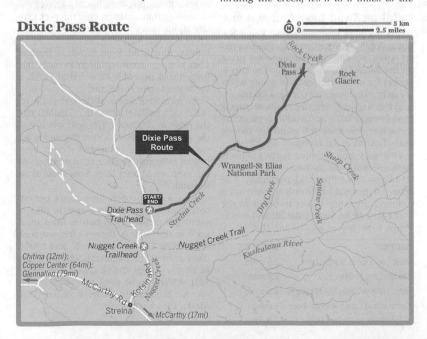

pass; along the way you'll cross two more confluences and hike through an interesting gorge. The ascent to Dixie Pass is fairly easy to spot, and once there you'll find superb scenery and alpine ridges to explore.

SECTION	DISTANCE
McCarthy Rd to Dixie Pass trailhead	3.8 miles
Dixie Pass trailhead to Strelna Creek	3 miles
Strelna Creek to Dixie Pass	8.5 miles

❶ Information

Level of Difficulty Medium to hard
Information Wrangell-St Elias National Park (☑ 907-822-5234; www.nps.gov/wrst)

❶ Getting There & Away

For transportation into the park, there's Kennicott Shuttle (p324), which runs a daily bus from Glennallen to McCarthy. With a round-trip Glennallen-to-McCarthy ticket ($149), the company will also drop off and pick up hikers at the Dixie Pass trailhead. Stop at the park headquarters in Copper Center to complete a backcountry trip itinerary and pick up USGS quadrangle maps.

Swan Lake Canoe Route

Paddling Swan Lake Canoe Route

In the northern lowlands of the Kenai National Wildlife Refuge there is a chain of rivers, lakes, streams and portages that make up the Swan Lake canoe route. The trip is perfect for novice canoeists, as rough water is rarely a problem and portages do not exceed half a mile. Fishing for rainbow trout is good in many lakes, and wildlife is plentiful; padddling this route you could see moose, bears, beavers and a variety of waterfowl.

This easy and popular route connects 30 lakes with forks in the Moose River for 60 miles of paddling and portaging. The entire route would take only a week but a common three-day trip is to begin at the west entrance on Swan Lake Rd and end at Moose River Bridge on Sterling Hwy.

SECTION	DISTANCE
West Entrance to Marten Lake	2.6 miles
Marten Lake to Otter Lake	2.4 miles
Otter Lake to Camp Island Lake	4.5 miles
Camp Island Lake to Moose River	5 miles
Moose River to Sterling Hwy	4.5 miles

❶ Information

Level of Difficulty Easy; Class I water
Information Kenai National Wildlife Refuge (☑ 262-7021; www.fws.gov/refuge/kenai)

❶ Getting There & Away

To reach the Swan Lake canoe route, travel to Mile 84, Sterling Hwy, east of Soldotna, and turn north on Robinson Lake Rd, just west of the Moose River Bridge. Robinson Lake Rd turns into Swanson River Rd, which leads to Swan Lake Rd, 17 miles north of the Sterling Hwy. East on Swan Lake Rd are two entrances for the canoe route. The west entrance for the Swan Lake route is at Canoe Lake, and the east entrance is another 6 miles beyond, at Portage Lake.

Throughout the summer months, Alaska Canoe & Campground (p236) rents canoes and runs a shuttle service for people paddling the Swan Lake canoe route. Alaska Canoe's campground (tent sites/cabins $13/150) is near the takeout along Sterling Hwy and it makes a nice place to stay overnight if you find yourself arriving late on the last day.

Chena Dome Trail

Hiking the Chena Dome Trail

Fifty miles east of Fairbanks in the Chena River State Recreation Area, the 29.5-mile Chena Dome loop trail makes an ideal three- or four-day alpine romp. The trail circles the Angel Creek drainage area, with the vast majority of it along tundra ridgetops above the treeline. That includes climbing Chena Dome, a flat-topped peak near Mile 10, which, at 4421ft, is the highest point of the trail.

An intriguing aspect of the trek is the remains of a military plane that crashed into the ridge in the 1950s. The trail winds past the site near Mile 8.5. Other highlights are views from Chena Dome and picking blueberries in August. In clear, calm weather you can even see Mt McKinley from spots along the trail.

Pack a stove (open fires aren't permitted), and carry at least 3 quarts (3L) of water per person (refill bottles from small pools in the tundra). There's a free-use shelter at Mile 17, while a 1.5-mile and 1900ft descent from the main trail will bring you to **Upper Angel Creek Cabin** (per person $35), which can be used as a place to stay on the third night; reserve online with Alaska Division of Parks.

Swan Lake Canoe Route

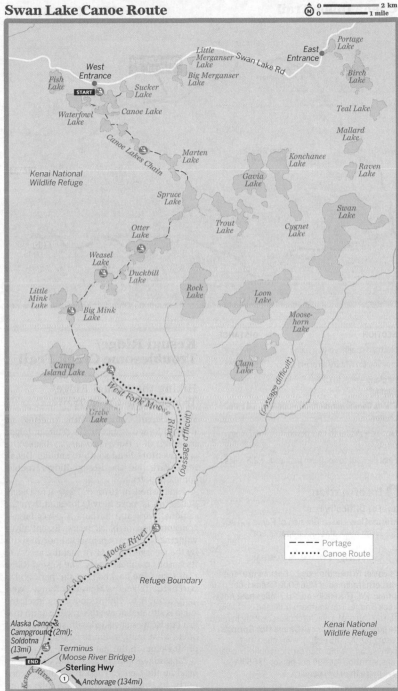

0 — 2 km
0 — 1 mile

Little Merganser Lake
Swan Lake Rd
East Entrance
Portage Lake

West Entrance
Big Merganser Lake
Birch Lake

Fish Lake
START
Sucker Lake
Teal Lake

Waterfowl Lake
Canoe Lake
Mallard Lake

Canoe Lakes Chain
Marten Lake
Konchanee Lake
Raven Lake

Kenai National Wildlife Refuge
Gavia Lake

Spruce Lake
Trout Lake
Cygnet Lake
Swan Lake

Otter Lake

Weasel Lake
Duckbill Lake
Rock Lake
Loon Lake

Little Mink Lake
Big Mink Lake
Moose-horn Lake

Camp Island Lake
West Fork Moose River
(passage difficult)
Clam Lake
(passage difficult)

Grebe Lake

Moose River

Refuge Boundary

Kenai National Wildlife Refuge

Portage
Canoe Route

Alaska Canoe & Campground (2mi); Soldotna (13mi)
END
Terminus (Moose River Bridge)
Sterling Hwy
① Anchorage (134mi)
Kenai River

Chena Dome Trail

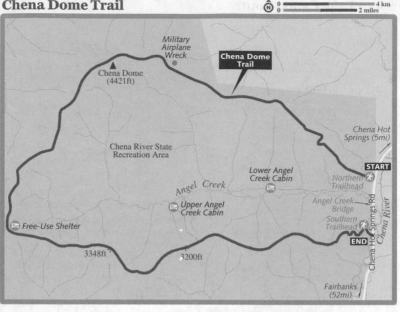

Military Airplane Wreck

Chena Dome Trail

Chena Dome (4421ft)

Chena Hot Springs (5mi)

Chena River State Recreation Area

Lower Angel Creek Cabin

START

Northern Trailhead

Angel Creek

Upper Angel Creek Cabin

Angel Creek Bridge

Southern Trailhead

Free-Use Shelter

END

3348ft

3200ft

Chena Hot Springs Rd

Chena River

Fairbanks (52mi)

SECTION	DISTANCE
Northern trailhead to treeline	3 miles
Treeline to military airplane wreck	5.5 miles
Airplane wreck to Chena Dome summit	2 miles
Chena Dome summit to free-use shelter	6.5 miles
Free-use shelter to final descent off ridge	10 miles
Final descent to southern trailhead	2.5 miles

ⓘ Information

Level of Difficulty Hard
Information Alaska Division of Parks (☑ 907-451-2705; www.alaskastateparks.org)

ⓘ Getting There & Away

It's easier to hike the loop by beginning at the northern trailhead at Mile 50.5, Chena Hot Springs Rd. The trailhead is 0.7 miles past Angel Creek Bridge. The southern trailhead is at Mile 49. You can rent a car, hitchhike (bearing in mind the potential risks) or call **Chena Hot Springs Resort** (☑ 907-451-8104; www.chenahot-springs.com), which can provide round-trip van transportation for $99 per person ($65 if you have more than two people).

Kesugi Ridge/ Troublesome Creek Trail

Hiking the Kesugi Ridge/ Troublesome Creek Trail

With Denali National Park offering no marked long-distance trails, aspiring hikers in search of a three- or four-day backcountry adventure head south to smaller Denali State Park and the Kesugi Ridge/Troublesome Creek trail.

Established in 1970, 325,240-acre Denali State Park is more heavily forested than the national park and harbors Alaska's largest concentration of black bears. Essentially a wilderness, the park is bisected north–south by the George Parks Hwy, making access to its various trailheads easy. The Kesugi Ridge trail forms the backbone of the park and is part of the Talkeetna Mountain Range. Averaging 3000ft to 4000ft above sea level, the ridge is situated above the treeline amid tundra landscapes speckled with small lakes; it offers what many claim to be the best views of Mt Denali in the state.

Most hikers start at Little Coal Creek trailhead on the George Parks Hwy and proceed north to south. The initial 2.5-mile climb to the ridge on the Little Coal Creek trail is steep, but views of Denali will inspire you to dig deep. Once up on the ridge beware of sudden changes in weather. Most of the path is marked by intermittent cairns. After passing Eight-Mile Divide and Stonehenge Hill, you'll encounter the intersection with the Ermine Hill trail, a handy escape hatch if you're tired or weather-beaten. Soon after this the path descends briefly below the treeline before ascending again to open tundra. Many hikers come off the ridge at the Cascade trail intersection, descending 3.4 miles through forest to the Byers Lake campground on the George Parks Hwy (27.4 miles total hike). If you wish to continue, descend on the Troublesome Creek trail, aptly named due to its regular wash-outs and large bear population. The final six miles are in forest. Check ahead for current trail status, and bring bear spray and mosquito repellent.

SECTION	DISTANCE
Little Coal Creek trailhead to top of Coal Creek trail	2.5 miles
Top of Little Coal Creek trail to Ermine Hill trail intersection	14.7 miles
Ermine Hill trail intersection to Cascade trail intersection	6.8 miles
Cascade trail intersection to Upper Troublesome Creek trailhead	11.8 mlles

ℹ Information

Level of Difficulty Medium to hard
Information Denali State Park Visitors Center (http://dnr.alaska.gov/parks/units/denali1.htm)

ℹ Getting There & Away

The four trailheads that give access to the Kesugi Ridge trail are all conveniently located on the arterial George Parks Hwy that runs between Anchorage and Fairbanks. They are Little Coal Creek (Mile 163.9), Ermine Hill (Mile 156.5), Byers Lake (Mile 147) and Upper Troublesome Creek

Kesugi Ridge/Troublesome Creek Trail

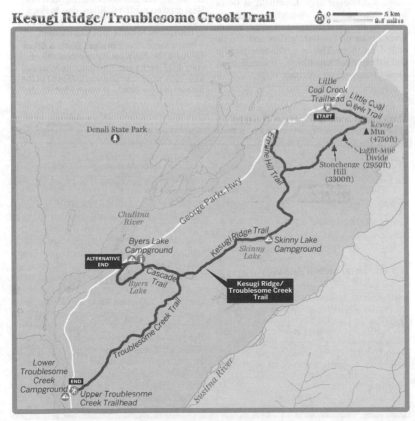

(Mile 137.6). All have parking facilities. **Alaska/ Yukon Trails** (www.alaskashuttle.com) runs a regular shuttle bus along the George Parks Hwy and may be able to help out with transport if you can coordinate times beforehand.

Beaver Creek Canoe Route

Paddling Beaver Creek Canoe Route

Beaver Creek is *the* adventure for budget travelers with time and a yearning to paddle through a roadless wilderness. The moderately swift stream, with long clear pools and frequent rapids, is rated Class I and can be handled by canoeists with expedition experience. The 111-mile creek flows past hills forested in white spruce and paper birch below the jagged peaks of the White Mountains.

A day's paddle beyond Nome Creek, Beaver Creek spills into Yukon Flats National Wildlife Refuge, where it meanders through a marshy area. Eventually it flows north into the Yukon River, where, after two or three days, you'll pass under the Yukon River Bridge on the Dalton Hwy and can be picked up there. This is a 399-mile paddle and a three-week expedition – the stuff great Alaskan adventures are made of.

The scenery is spectacular, the chances of seeing another party remote and you'll catch so much grayling you'll never want to eat another one. You can also spend a night in the Borealis-Le Fevre Cabin, a BLM cabin on the banks of Beaver Creek.

SECTION	DISTANCE
Nome Creek to Beaver Creek	16 miles
Beaver Creek to Victoria Creek	111 miles
Victoria Creek to Yukon River	162 miles
Yukon River to Dalton Hwy	110 miles

ℹ Information

Level of Difficulty Medium, Class I water

Information Bureau of Land Management (BLM; ☎907-474-2200; www.ak.blm.gov)

ℹ Getting There & Away

At Mile 57, Steese Hwy go north on US Creek Rd for 6 miles, then northwest on Nome Creek Rd to Ophir Creek Campground. Put in at Nome Creek and paddle to its confluence with Beaver Creek. Most paddlers plan on six to nine days to reach Victoria Creek, a 127-mile trip; gravel bars are used by bush planes to land and pick up paddlers.

Rent a canoe from **7 Bridges Boats & Bikes** (☎907-479-0751; www.7bridgesboatsbikes. com; 4312 Birch Lane, Fairbanks; daily/weekly $50/150), which can take you to Mile 57 of the Steese Hwy. For pickup at Yukon River Bridge,

Beaver Creek Canoe Route

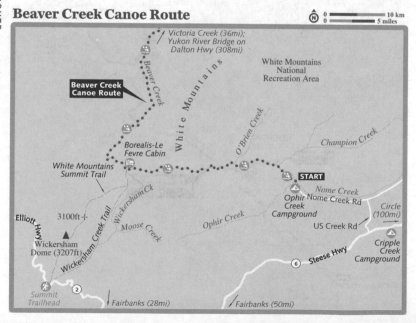

175 miles north of Fairbanks, call Dalton Highway Express (p419).

Savonoski Loop

Paddling Savonoski Loop

This 80-mile, six- to eight-day paddle begins and ends at Brooks Camp and takes paddlers into remote sections of Katmai National Park & Preserve (p338), offering the best in wilderness adventure without expensive bush-plane travel.

Although there's no white water, the trip is still challenging, with the hardest section being the 12-mile run of the Savonoski River, which is braided and has many deadheads and sweepers. The Savonoski is also prime brown-bear habitat and for this reason park rangers recommend paddling the river in a single day and not camping along it.

The first section through Naknek Lake is especially scenic and well protected at the end where you dip in and out of the Bay of Islands. You're then faced with a mile-long portage along a trail (often a mud-hole) before continuing on to Lake Grosvenor and the Grosvenor River. Then head down the Savonoski River, which brings you to the last leg, a 20-mile paddle along the south shore of the Iliuk Arm back to Brooks Camp. Paddlers have to remember that Katmai is famous for its sudden and violent storms, some lasting days. The preferred mode of travel here is a kayak, due to the sudden winds and rough nature of the big lakes.

SECTION	DISTANCE
Brooks Camp to Lake Grosvenor portage	30 miles
Portage to Lake Grosvenor	1 mile
Lake Grosvenor to Grosvenor River	14 miles
Grosvenor River to Savonoski River	3 miles
Savonoski River to Iliuk Arm	12 miles
Iliuk Arm to Brooks Camp	20 miles

ℹ Information

Level of Difficulty Medium to hard, Class I water
Information Katmai National Park (☑ 907-246-3305; www.nps.gov/katm)

ℹ Getting There & Away

See Katmai National Park & Preserve for information on reservations and getting here. Most visitors either fly in with a folding kayak or rent from **Lifetime Adventures** (☑ 800-952-8624; www.lifetimeadventures.net) in Brooks Camp. Folding kayaks are $45/55 a day for a single/double or $245/280 per week. The Anchorage-based outfitter can also arrange an unguided trip that includes airfare from Anchorage to King Salmon, floatplane charter to Brooks Camp and folding kayaks for $950 per person per week.

Savonoski Loop

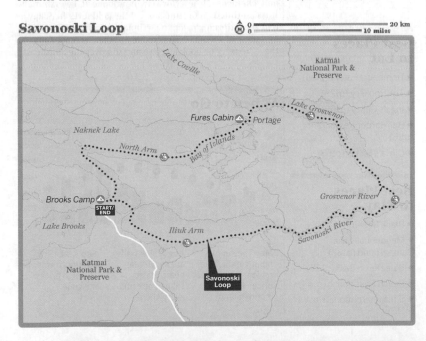

Juneau & the Southeast

Best Places to Eat

➡ Homeport Eatery (p114)

➡ The Rookery (p129)

➡ Inga's Galley (p106)

➡ Bar Harbor Restaurant (p86)

➡ Olivia's Bistro (p153)

Best Places to Stay

➡ Black Bear Inn (p85)

➡ Mendenhall Lake Campground (p127)

➡ Blue Heron B&B (p138)

➡ Beach Roadhouse (p144)

➡ Sitka International Hostel (p113)

Why Go?

Southeast Alaska is so *unAlaska*. While much of the state is a treeless expanse of land with a layer of permafrost, the Southern Panhandle is a slender, long rainforest that stretches 540 miles from Icy Bay south to Portland Canal and is filled with ice-blue glaciers, rugged snowcapped mountains, towering Sitka spruce and a thousand islands known as the Alexander Archipelago.

Before WWII, the Southeast was Alaska's heart and soul, and Juneau was not only the capital but the state's largest city. Today the region is characterized by big trees and small towns. Each community here has its own history and character: from Norwegian-influenced Petersburg to Russian-tinted Sitka. You can feel the gold fever in Skagway and see a dozen glaciers near Juneau. Each town is unique and none of them is connected to another by road. Jump on the state ferry or book a cruise and discover the Southeast.

When to Go
Juneau

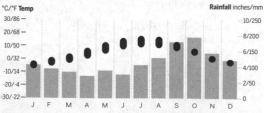

May The sunniest month in this rainy region, with better prices than a month later.

Aug Alpine trails are snow-free; bears are at salmon streams everywhere.

Sep A bit rainy, but the crowds and high prices are gone.

History

Petroglyphs along the shoreline in Wrangell, Petersburg and other locations indicate that human habitation in Southeast Alaska dates back at least 8000 to 10,000 years. The Russians arrived in 1741, entered Sitka Sound and sent two longboats ashore in search of fresh water. The boats never returned, and the Russians wisely departed.

What the unfortunate shore party encountered were members of Tlingit tribes, who over time had developed the most advanced culture – in terms of food gathering, art and the construction of large clan houses – of any Alaska Native group. The Tlingits were still there in 1799 when the Russians returned and established the Southeast's first nonindigenous settlement. Aleksandr Baranov built a Russian fort near the present ferry terminal to continue the rich sea-otter fur trade. He was in Kodiak three years later when Tlingits, armed with guns from British and American traders, overwhelmed the fort, burned it to the ground and killed most of its inhabitants.

Baranov returned in 1804, this time with an imperial Russian warship and, after destroying the Tlingit fort, established the headquarters of the Russian-American Company at the present site of Sitka. Originally called New Archangel, Sitka flourished both economically and culturally on the strength of the fur trade and in its golden era was known as the 'Paris of the Pacific.'

In an effort to strengthen their grip on the region and protect their fur-trading interests, the Russians built a stockade near the mouth of the Stikine River in 1834, but in 1840 the political winds shifted and the Russians leased the entire Southeast coastline to the British. After purchasing Alaska from the Russians, the Americans formally took control of the territory in Sitka in 1867.

In 1880, at the insistence of a Tlingit chief, Joe Juneau and Dick Harris went to Gastineau Channel to try their luck and prospect for gold. They hacked their way through the thick forest to the head of Gold Creek, and there they found, in the words of Harris, 'little lumps as large as peas and beans.' The news spurred the state's first major gold strike, and within a year a small town named Juneau appeared, the first to be founded after Alaska's purchase from the Russians. After the decline in the whaling and fur trades reduced Sitka's importance, the Alaskan capital was moved to Juneau in 1906.

The main gold rush, the turning point in Alaska's history, occurred in Skagway when more than 40,000 gold-rush stampeders descended on the town at the turn of the century as part of the fabled Klondike Gold Rush. Most made their way to the Yukon gold fields by way of the Chilkoot Trail until the White Pass & Yukon Route Railroad was completed in 1900.

In 1887 the population of Skagway was two; 10 years later, it was 20,000; the gold-rush town was Alaska's largest. A center for saloons, hotels and brothels, Skagway became infamous for its lawlessness. For a time, the town was held under the tight control of crime boss Jefferson Randolph 'Soapy' Smith and his gang, who conned and swindled naive newcomers out of their money and stampeders out of their gold dust. In a gunfight between Smith and city engineer Frank Reid, both men died, ending Smith's reign as the 'uncrowned prince of Skagway' after only nine months.

At the time, Wrangell was also booming as the supply point for prospectors heading up the Stikine River to the Cassiar Gold District of British Columbia in 1861 and 1874, and then using the river again to reach the Klondike fields in 1897. Wrangell was as ruthless and lawless as Skagway. With miners holding their own court, it was said 'that a man would be tried at 9am, found guilty of murder at 11:30am and hung by 2pm.'

Just as gold fever was dying out, the salmon industry was taking hold. One of the first canneries in Alaska was built in Klawock on Prince of Wales Island in 1878. Ketchikan was begun in 1885 as a cannery, and in 1897 Peter Buschmann arrived from Norway and established Petersburg as a cannery site because of the fine harbor and a ready supply of ice from nearby LeConte Glacier.

After WWII, with the construction of the Alcan (Alaska Hwy) and large military bases around Anchorage and Fairbanks, Alaska's sphere of influence shifted from the Southeast to the mainland further north. In 1974 Alaskans voted to move the state capital again, this time to the small town of Willow, an hour's drive from Anchorage. The so-called 'capital move' issue hung over Juneau like a dark cloud, threatening to turn the place into a ghost town. The issue became a political tug-of-war between Anchorage and the Southeast, until voters, faced with a billion-dollar price tag to construct a new capital, defeated the funding in 1982.

Juneau & the Southeast Highlights

1 Strapping on crampons and hiking across the icy blue world of Juneau's **Mendenhall Glacier** (p119)

2 Ziplining down a mountain and spending the afternoon viewing bears at Herring Creek, **Ketchikan** (p83)

3 Searching for ancient petroglyphs at low tide on Wrangell's **Petroglyph Beach** (p95)

4 Following the Klondike gold rush by hiking Skagway's **Chilkoot Trail** (p150)

5 Heading deep into **Glacier Bay National Park** (p135) to see seals, sea lions and glaciers calving icebergs the size of small houses

6 Meeting the locals and soothing sore muscles at **Tenakee Springs** (p132)

7 Viewing totems in a mystical rainforest at **Sitka National Historical Park** (p109)

8 Hanging 10 with surfer dudes in **Yakutat** (p134)

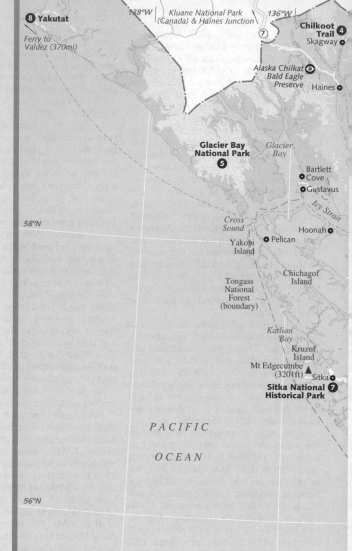

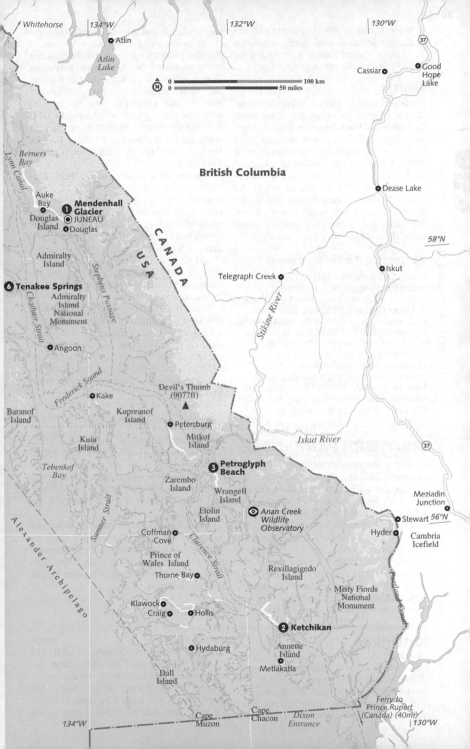

Today Juneau is still the capital and the Panhandle is a road-less, lightly populated area where residents make a living fishing and catering to tourists and cruise ships.

Climate

The Southeast has Alaska's mildest climate. Greatly affected by warm ocean currents, the region has warm summer temperatures averaging 69°F (20°C), with an occasional heat wave that sends temperatures to 80°F (27°C). Winters are also relatively mild, and subzero days are rare. Residents, who have learned to live with an annual rainfall of 60in to 200in, call the frequent rain 'liquid sunshine.' The heavy precipitation creates the dense, lush rainforests and numerous waterfalls most travelers come to cherish.

❶ Getting There & Around

Most of the Southeast may be road-less, but getting there and getting around is easy. Ketchikan is only 1½ hours away from Seattle by air on **Alaska Airlines** (☑ 800-426-0333; www. alaskaair.com) or 37 hours on the **Alaska Marine Highway** (☑ 800-642-0066; www.ferryalaska. com) from Bellingham, WA. The state ferries, North America's longest public ferry system, also provide transportation between the regions, cities, towns and little fishing ports. Separate ferries link Prince of Wales Island with Ketchikan, Wrangell and Petersburg, Haines with Skagway, and Juneau and Glacier Bay.

SOUTHERN PANHANDLE

Residents like to call this region of Alaska 'rainforest islands': lush, green, watery, remote and road-less to the outside world. This is the heart of Southeast Alaska's fishing industry, and the region's best wilderness fishing lodges are scattered in the small coves of these islands. Cruise ships pass through but they only inundate Ketchikan; the other communities receive few if any vessels. Two ferry systems, the Alaska State Marine Highway and the Inter-Island Ferry Authority, serve the area, so island hopping, even in this remote rainforest, is easy.

Ketchikan

POP 13,680

Once known as the 'Canned Salmon Capital of the World,' today Ketchikan settles for 'First City,' the initial port for Alaska Marine ferries and cruise ships coming from the south. Just 90 miles north of Prince Rupert, Ketchikan hugs the bluffs that form the shoreline along the southwest corner of Revillagigedo Island. Several miles long but never more than 10 blocks wide, Ketchikan centers on the single main drag of Tongass Ave, which sticks to the shore of Tongass Narrows like a bathtub ring. Space is so scarce here that the airport had to be built on another island. Extending north and south from the downtown area is Tongass Hwy, which wraps around the south end of Revillagigedo Island.

Founded as a cannery site in 1885, Ketchikan's mainstay for most of its existence was salmon, and then timber when the huge Ketchikan Pulp Mill was constructed at Ward Cove in 1954. But in the 1970s strikes and changes in public policy began to mar the logging industry. Louisiana-Pacific closed its sawmill in the city center after a strike in 1983 and its pulp mill in 1997, resulting in hundreds of workers losing their high-paying jobs.

There is still commercial fishing in Ketchikan and the industry accounts for nearly a third of the local economy, but what rings the local cash registers now is tourism. In the mid-1990s Ketchikan transformed itself into a cruise-ship capital, with up to six ships and 650,000 passengers a day from May to October.

If you stay in Ketchikan longer than an hour, chances are good that it will rain at least once if not several times. The average annual rainfall is 162in, but in some years it has been known to be more than 200in. Local residents never use umbrellas or let the rain interfere with daily activities, even outdoor ones. If they stopped everything each time it drizzled, Ketchikan would cease to exist.

When the skies finally clear, the beauty of Ketchikan's setting becomes apparent. The town is backed by forested hills and faces a waterway humming with floatplanes, fishing boats, ferries and barges hauling freight to other Southeast ports.

◉ Sights

★ **Southeast Alaska Discovery Center**   MUSEUM
(www.alaskacenters.gov; 50 Main St; adult/child $5/free; ⊙8:30am-4pm; ♿) Three large totems greet you in the lobby of the center while a school of silver salmon, suspended from the ceiling, leads you toward a slice of nicely recreated rainforest. Upstairs, the

exhibit hall features sections on Southeast Alaska's ecosystems and Alaska Native traditions. You can even view wildlife here: there's a spotting scope trained on Deer Mountain for mountain goats, while underwater cameras in Ketchikan Creek let you watch thousands of salmon struggling upstream to spawn.

Dolly's House   MUSEUM
(www.dollyshouse.com; 24 Creek St; adult/child $10/free; ☺when cruise ships are in) Departing from Stedman St is Creek St, a boardwalk built over Ketchikan Creek on pilings – a photographer's delight. This was Ketchikan's famed red-light district until prostitution became illegal in 1954. During Creek

Ketchikan

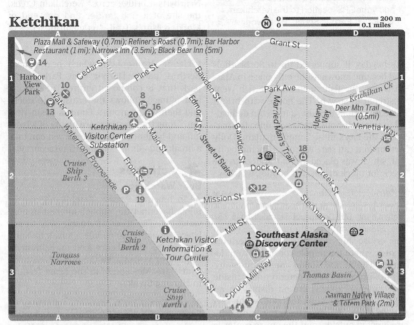

Ketchikan

◉ **Top Sights**
  1 Southeast Alaska Discovery Center C3

◉ **Sights**
  2 Dolly's House D3
  3 Tongass Historical Museum C2

🏛 **Activities, Courses & Tours**
  4 Allen Marine Tours C3
  5 Southeast Sea Kayaks C3

🛏 **Sleeping**
  6 Cape Fox Lodge D2
  7 Gilmore Hotel B2
  8 Ketchikan Hostel B1
  9 New York Hotel D3

🍴 **Eating**
  Annabelle's .... (see 7)
  10 Burger Queen A1
  11 Diaz Café D3

Heen Kahidi Restaurant .... (see 6)
New York Cafe .... (see 9)
12 Pioneer Café C2

🍷 **Drinking & Nightlife**
  13 Arctic Bar A1
  14 First City Saloon A1

🛍 **Shopping**
  15 Alaska Geographic Association Bookstore C3
  16 Main Street Gallery B1
  17 Parnassus Books C2
  18 Soho Coho C2

ℹ **Information**
  Southeast Alaska Discovery Center .... (see 1)
  19 Tongass Trading Company B2

🚍 **Transport**
  20 Promech Air B1

ℹ NOT GETTING LOST

For peace of mind while hiking or paddling in Ketchikan, pick up a free personal locator beacon from the Ketchikan Visitor Information & Tour Center (p87). If you become lost it can be activated to send a distress signal and your GPS location to the Ketchikan Volunteer Rescue Squad. When your adventure is over you simply return it.

St's heyday, it supported up to 30 brothels and became known as the only place in Alaska where 'the fishermen and the fish went upstream to spawn.' The house with bright red trim is Dolly's House, a museum dedicated to this notorious era. It was once the parlor of the city's most famous madam, Dolly Arthur. You can see the brothel, including its bar, which was placed over a trapdoor to the creek for quick disposal of bootleg whiskey.

Totem Heritage Center MUSEUM
(www.city.ketchikan.ak.us/departments/museums/totem.html; 601 Deermount St; adult/child $5/free; ⊙8am-5pm) A 15-minute walk east from the cruise-ship docks is Totem Heritage Center, where totem poles brought from deserted Tlingit and Haida communities are kept to prevent further deterioration. Inside the center, 17 totems are on display in an almost spiritual setting that shows the reverence Alaska Natives attach to them. More are erected outside, and the entire center is shrouded in pines and serenaded by the gurgling Ketchikan Creek.

Tongass Historical Museum MUSEUM
(www.ketchikanmusuems.org; 629 Dock St; adult/child $3/free; ⊙8am-5pm) The Tongass Historical Museum houses a collection of local historical and Alaska Native artifacts, many dealing with Ketchikan's fishing industry. More interesting is the impressive Raven Stealing the Sun totem just outside and an observation platform overlooking the Ketchikan Creek falls.

Thomas Basin HARBOR
If you thought Creek St was photogenic, cross Stedman St and be ready to burn some megapixels. Thomas Basin is home to Ketchikan's fishing fleet and the city's most picturesque harbor. When the boats come in, you can photograph them unloading their catch and then follow the crews to the colorful Potlatch Bar (126 Thomas St) nearby, a classic fishers' pub.

Stairways & Boardwalks LOOKOUTS
All over Ketchikan there are stairways leading somewhere higher; the reward for your exertion is great views from the top. Heading back west along Dock St is Edmond St, also called the Street of Stairs for obvious reasons. Down Park Ave you'll pass the Upland Way stairs that climb to a viewpoint. Nearby is a bridge across Ketchikan Creek, the site of a fish ladder and one end of Married Man's Trail – a delightful series of boardwalks and stairs.

Ketchikan's newest boardwalk is the Waterfront Promenade, which begins near Berth 4, passes Harbor View Park (a city park that is composed entirely of decking and pilings), follows the cruise ship docks and then wraps around Thomas Basin Harbor. Along the way there are plenty of whale-tail and halibut benches where you can take a break and admire the maritime scenery.

🏃 Activities

Bear Watching

As in much of Alaska, Ketchikan's charter pilots have met the public's interest in bear watching. The most affordable way to see bears, though, is to paddle a kayak to Naha Bay, where black bears feed on salmon in August, or visit Alaska Canopy Adventures, which provides access to the bears feeding in Herring Creek.

Alaska Seaplane Tours BEAR WATCHING
(☑907-225-1974,866-858-2327; www.alaskaseaplane tours.com; tour $339) Flies to Prince of Wales Island to watch bruins on a two-hour tour.

Promech Air BEAR WATCHING
(☑907-225-3845, 800-860-3845; www.promechair.com; tours $393) Its three-hour tour includes a flight to the Neet's Bay Hatchery and 1½ hours of watching black bears.

Hiking

Most Ketchikan area trails are either out of town or must be reached by boat.

Deer Mountain Trail HIKING
Within walking distance of downtown is Deer Mountain Trail, Ketchikan's most popular hike. The well-maintained 2.5-mile trail can be reached by taking the Bus' Green Line to the corner of Deermount and Fair Sts and then heading south on Ketchikan Lakes Rd. The trail is a climb to the 3000ft summit of Deer Mountain and along the way overlooks provide panoramic views – the first only a mile up the trail.

Toward the top of the mountain are more trails that extend into the alpine region and a free-use shelter. But keep in mind this is a steady climb and a more challenging hike beyond the shelter.

Rainbird Trail HIKING

Dedicated in 2010, this 1.3-mile trail is within town, stretching from the University of Alaska-Southeast campus off 7th Ave to a trailhead off Third Ave Bypass. You can ride the Bus to UAS and follow this delightful trail as it winds through a rainforest along a bluff before giving way to striking views of the city and Tongass Narrows below.

Ward Lake Nature Walk HIKING

The easy 1.5-mile Ward Lake Nature Walk, an interpretive loop around Ward Lake, begins near the parking area at the lake's north end. Beavers, birds and the occasional black bear might be seen. To reach the lake, follow N Tongass Hwy, 7 miles from downtown to Ward Cove; turn right on Revilla Rd and continue up 1.5 miles to Ward Lake Rd.

Perseverance Trail HIKING

The 2.4-mile (one-way) Perseverance Trail from Ward Lake to Perseverance Lake passes through mature coastal forest and mus-

keg. The view of Perseverance Lake with its mountainous backdrop is spectacular and the hiking is moderately easy. The trailhead is on Ward Lake's east side, just past CCC Campground.

Dude Mountain Trail HIKING

A nice alpine trek is Dude Mountain Trail, which begins in stands of old-growth spruce and becomes a trail as you follow a narrow ridge to the 2848ft peak. It's a 1.5-mile trek and a gain of 1500ft to the top, but once there you're in open alpine and can easily ridge-walk to Diana Mountain (3014ft) or Brown Mountain (2978ft).

Paddling

Ketchikan serves as the base for some of the best kayaking in the Southeast. Possibilities include anything from an easy paddle around the waterfront to a weeklong trip in Misty Fiords National Monument. Pick up charts and topographic maps from the Southeast Alaska Discovery Center, and outdoor supplies from **Tongass Trading Company** (☑ 907-225-5101; 201 Dock St).

For rentals, head to **Southeast Exposure** (☑ 907-225-8829; www.southeastexposure.com; kayak rental $25-35 per day), which will set you up with singles and doubles, or guide

SEEING BEARS IN SOUTHEAST ALASKA

The biggest bears – browns tipping the scale at 1000lbs or more – are seen at such exotic locations as Katmai National Park and the Kodiak National Wildlife Refuge. But for sheer numbers, ease of transportation and affordable bear watching it's hard to pass up Southeast Alaska. Like elsewhere in Alaska, bear watching in the Southeast is best in July and August, and each location corresponds with particular salmon runs:

Fish Creek (Hyder) It may be hard to reach, but once there it's easy to spend an afternoon watching brown bears.

Naha Bay (Ketchikan) It's an 8-mile paddle by kayak to Naha River National Recreation Trail, where in August black bears are snagging salmon at a small waterfall.

Herring Creek (Ketchikan) After ziplining down a mountain you can watch black bears catching salmon.

Margaret Creek (Ketchikan) Bears gather at this creek, located 26 miles north of Ketchikan on Revillagigedo Island, in late August and the first two weeks in September. Most visitors arrive on a charter float plane and then walk a quarter-mile trail to a viewing platform.

Anan Creek (Wrangell) You can rent a USFS cabin and spend your entire day watching black and brown bears.

Pack Creek (Admiralty Island) This wilderness island has one of the highest densities of bears in Alaska; you can see them from the safety of an observation tower.

Steep Creek (Juneau) It's a short hike in Mendenhall Valley to reach Steep Creek Fish Viewing Site and watch black bears feeding on salmon.

'Bear Highway' (Haines) Between Haines and Chilkoot Lake is easily accessible brown bear viewing.

you on a half day tour of the Ketchikan area (adult/child $90/75). It also offers a water taxi and guided trips to Misty Fjords.

Southeast Sea Kayaks (☑907-225-1258; www.kayakketchikan.com; 3 Salmon Landing), located on the boardwalk downtown overlooking Thomas Basin, also offers tours, including a 2½-hour paddle of Ketchikan's waterfront (adult/child $89/59). A much better paddling experience, however, is its Orcas Cove trip (adult/child $159/139), a four-hour adventure that begins with a boat ride across the Tongass Narrows and then paddling among protected islands looking for sea lions, orcas and seals.

Ketchikan Kayak Company (☑907-225-1272; www.ketchikankayakco.com) also offers a two-hour guided tour ($129) along Sea Star Alley (guess what you'll see there?) and other nearby points.

Betton Island   KAYAKING
West of Settler's Cove State Park at the north end (Mile 18.2) of N Tongass Hwy is this island and several smaller islands nearby, making it an excellent day paddle if you're staying at the campground. Although Clover Pass is a highly trafficked area, the backside of Betton Island offers a more genuine wilderness setting. You can turn this into an overnight excursion by camping on the great beaches of the **Tatoosh Islands** on the west side of Betton Island.

Naha Bay   KAYAKING
An 8-mile paddle from Settler's Cove State Park is Naha Bay, the destination of an excellent three- or four-day adventure. At the bay's head is a floating dock; leave your kayak and head down the 5.4-mile Naha River National Recreation Trail. The scenic trail follows the river up to Jordan and Heckman Lakes; both have USFS cabins.

The fishing here is good and black bears are plentiful – in August you might see them catching salmon at a small waterfall 2 miles up the trail from Roosevelt Lagoon.

A narrow outlet connects Naha Bay with Roosevelt Lagoon. You don't have to enter the lagoon to access the trail. Kayakers wishing to paddle into the lagoon must either portage around the outlet or enter it at high slack tide, as the narrow pass becomes a frothy, roaring chute when the tide is moving in or out.

George & Carroll Inlets   KAYAKING
From Hole in the Wall Bar & Marina (p88), 7.5 miles southeast of Ketchikan down the South Tongass Hwy, you can start an easy one- to four-day paddle north into George or Carroll Inlets or both. Each inlet is protected from the area's prevailing southwesterlies, so the water is usually calm (although north winds occasionally whip down George Inlet).

From Hole in the Wall to the top of George Inlet is a 26-mile paddle.

Snorkeling

Snorkel Alaska   SNORKELING
(☑907-247-7782; www.snorkelalaska.com; per person $99) They scuba dive in Alaska, so why not snorkel? This company hands you a wet suit, complete with hood, gloves and boots, and then leads you into the water at Mountain Point for a fascinating underwater wildlife tour that includes sea stars, urchins, sea cucumbers and every fish that swims by. The three-hour tour includes transport from the downtown area.

Ziplining
Ketchikan has everything needed to be the zipline capital of Alaska: lush rainforests and elevation. There are three zipline operations now; more are bound to come.

Alaska Canopy
Adventures   ADVENTURE SPORTS
(☑907-225-5503; www.alaskacanopy.com; 116 Wood Rd; $189 per person) Operates two Ketchikan ziplines. Choose from two sites: **Bear Creek** has seven lines, a skybridge above a waterfall, a 250ft slide and a 4WD vehicle to transport you up the mountain. The **Rainforest Canopy** has similar provisions, and visitors can view wildlife, including salmon runs in Herring Creek and bears that feast on them.

🖝 Tours
The standard tour is a two-hour trip around the city that includes a run out to Totem Bight; a half-dozen operators offer it for around $45 per person. Check the Ketchikan Visitor Information & Tour Center (p87) building on City Dock, where a whole wing is devoted to a gauntlet of tour providers touting their services.

Alaska Amphibious Tours   SCENIC DRIVE
(☑907-225-9899, 866-341-3825; www.akduck. com; tours adult/child $42/25) Uses amphibian vehicles that double as a bus and a boat to provide 1½-hour tours of the downtown area and the harbor. The top-heavy vehicle puts you 8ft above anything on the road for a great view, but the time spent cruising the harbor is shorter than most would like.

Bering Sea Crab Fishermen's Tour BOAT

(📞907-247-2721, 888-239-3816; www.56degrees north.com; tours adult/child $159/99) Ketchikan is far from the Bering Sea and they don't catch many king crabs here, but you can experience both on the *Aleutian Ballad*, which was once featured on the TV show *Deadliest Catch*. It has a 100-seat amphitheater for a 3½-hour tour of commercial fishing; Bering Sea crabbers pull up pots full of tanner, Dungeness and giant king crabs.

This seemingly out-of-place tour is extremely interesting.

✯✯ Festivals & Events

Ketchikan's Fourth of July celebration includes a parade, contests, softball games, an impressive display of fireworks and a logging show. The smaller Blueberry Festival, held at the State Office Building and the Main Street Theater on the first weekend in August, consists of arts and crafts, singers, musicians, and food stalls serving blueberries every possible way. During most of April the Alaska Hummingbird Festival is staged at the Southeast Alaska Discovery Center to celebrate those tiny birds winging their way back to Ketchikan.

🛏 Sleeping

Ketchikan charges 14% on lodging in city and bed taxes. There are no public campgrounds close to town; the closest are 4.5 miles north of the ferry terminal at Ward Lake Recreation Area.

Ketchikan Hostel HOSTEL $

(📞907-225-3319; www.ketchikanhostel.com; 400 Main St; dm $20; ☀Jun-Aug) The best of Ketchikan's two hostels is right downtown, spread out in a Methodist church complex that includes a large kitchen, three small common areas and separate-sex dorm rooms. The friendly hostel is spotlessly clean, but doors are locked after curfew. Reservations are recommended in July.

★ Black Bear Inn B&B $$

(📞907-225-4343; www.stayinalaska.com; 5528 N Tongass Hwy; r $165-235; 🛜) This incredible B&B offers a range of waterfront accommodations 2.5 miles north of the ferry terminal and near a bus stop. There are four bedrooms in the home and a small apartment on the 2nd floor with a private entrance. Outside is a logger's bunkhouse that was floated to Ketchikan and renovated into a

WILDERNESS CABINS

Some 29 USFS cabins (📞877-444-6777, 518-885-3639; www.recreation.gov; cabins $25-45) (and nine public use shelters) dot the Ketchikan area. It's best to reserve them in advance but often early in the summer and midweek something will be available. Some cabins can be reached by boat but most visitors fly to them. Within about 20 miles of Ketchikan are Alava Bay Cabin ($35), on the southern end of Behm Canal in Misty Fiords National Monument; Fish Creek Cabin ($45), connected by a short trail to Thorne Arm; and Patching Lake Cabin ($25), which offer good fishing for cutthroat trout and grayling.

charming honeymooners' cabin. Among the many amenities is a covered hot tub where you can soak while watching eagles soaring and whales swimming in the narrows.

New York Hotel BOUTIQUE HOTEL $$

(📞907-225-0246, 866-225-0246; www.thenewyork hotel.com; 207 Stedman St; r $149-189, ste $229; 🛜) A historic boutique hotel between Creek St and Thomas Basin. The eight rooms are filled with antiques and colorful quilts and have cable TV, small refrigerators and private baths. The hotel also has seven suites a short walk away, five of them on Creek St, which feature comfortable living rooms, small kitchen areas and sleeping accommodations for four. The 2nd-floor perch means you can watch the salmon spawn in Ketchikan Creek below and the seals that follow them.

Narrows Inn LODGE $$

(📞907-247-2600, 888-686-2600; www.narrows inn.com; 4871 N Tongass Hwy; r $145-170, ste $230-245; 🛜) A mile north of the airport ferry on the waterfront, it offers 44 standard rooms that are well kept and very clean. You pay extra for the ocean-view rooms, which feature balconies perched above the namesake narrows. The inn also includes a bar, restaurant and a marina where a fishing charter can be booked.

Gilmore Hotel HISTORIC HOTEL $$

(📞907-225-9423; www.gilmorehotel.com; 326 Front St; d $90-170; 🛜) Built in 1927 as a hotel and renovated several times since, the Gilmore has 34 rooms that still retain a historical flavor. Rooms are 'historically proportioned' (ie small) but comfortable, with cable TV, coffeemakers and hair dryers. It's in a great location across from Berth 3.

Cape Fox Lodge HOTEL $$$
(☎907-225-8001, 866-225-8001; www.capefox-lodge; 800 Venetia Way; r $195-229; ☎) Ketchikan's splashiest lodging. Perched atop the hill behind Creek St, it offers the best views in town and can be reached by a high-tech funicular tram from the Creek St boardwalk. The opulent lodge has 72 amenity-filled rooms and suites and an acclaimed restaurant overlooking the city. There is so much Native art in the lobby it's like walking through a gallery. Also on-site is a coffee shop and gift store, and staff can arrange tours.

✖ Eating

Ketchikan has many places to eat, but the expensive Alaskan prices usually send the newly arrived visitor into a two-day fast. If this is your first Alaskan city, don't fret – it only gets worse as you head north!

New York Cafe FUSION $
(☎ 907-247-2326; 207 Stedman St; breakfast mains $8-10, lunch mains $10-15; ☉ 7am-10pm; ☑) The historic ambience of the New York Hotel spills over into a little cafe. The menu follows the usual seafood trend of fried halibut and chowder, but falafel, tabouleh and mezze are tossed in for some variety.

Burger Queen BURGERS $
(518 Water St; burgers $7-10; ☉ 11am-7pm Tue-Sat, to 3pm Sun & Mon) Ketchikan's favorite burger joint. Ten varieties, including one with a Polish sausage *and* a hamburger patty, plus 30 flavors of milkshake. Order a burger and fries and have it delivered to the Arctic Bar across the street where you can be sipping a beer over the water.

Refiner's Roast CAFE $
(2050 Sea Level Dr; Breakfast $5-7, sandwiches $10; ☉ 7am-5pm Mon-Fri, from 8am Sat) Ketchikan is void of cozy coffee shops for rainy days; Refiner's is an exception. Next to Safeway, the small cafe has light breakfast and sandwiches for lunch, plus free wi-fi and good espresso.

Safeway SUPERMARKET $
(2417 Tongass Ave; ☉ 5am-midnight; ☎) This grocery store on the side of Plaza Mall has a salad bar, Starbucks, deli and ready-to-eat items, including Chinese food, and a dining area overlooking the boat traffic on Tongass Narrows.

Diaz Café ASIAN $$
(335 Stedman St; mains $13-17; ☉ 11:30am-7pm Tue-Sun) Located on the south side of Ketchikan Creek, this longtime cafe dates back to the 1920s, when Filipinos and Japanese weren't allowed to live north of the creek. Today the eatery is a favorite among locals looking for affordable Asian and Filipino dishes ranging from *pansit* (fried noodles) to bowls of green soup heaped with noodles.

Alava's SEAFOOD $$
(Berth 4; mains $12-15; ☉ 11am-6pm) A seafood shack in the shadow of cruise ships, Alava's does excellent fish and chips: everything down to the tartar sauce is homemade. As the sign says, they don't do breakfast 'because we're out catching your lunch.'

Pioneer Café CAFE $$
(619 Mission St; breakfast mains $8-14, lunch mains $9-14, dinner mains $11-20; ☉ 6am-10pm Sun-Thu, 24hr Fri & Sat) One of the few downtown restaurants that was around in the time of the lumber mills, and the only one open 24 hours on Friday and Saturday, it serves the best breakfast in town and serves it all day.

★ Bar Harbor Restaurant MODERN AMERICAN $$$
(☎ 907-225-2813; 2813 Tongass Ave; mains $20-34; ☉ 5-8pm Mon-Sat) A small cozy place between downtown and the ferry terminal with an intriguingly eclectic menu that is constantly changing. Yeah, they serve seafood here, but there are also a lot of things on the menu that didn't start life in the water, such as the signature dish, Ketchikan's best prime rib, and a few surprises: perfect Baja-style tacos. The wine list is nice and so is the back deck with its covered tables and watery view. Reservations strongly recommended.

Annabelle's SEAFOOD $$$
(326 Front St; lunch mains $10-17, dinner mains $23-34; ☉ 10am-10pm) At the Gilmore Hotel, this keg and chowder house has a seafood-heavy menu, a wonderful bar and 1920s decor. The three kinds of homemade chowder are good, and the keg half of the restaurant even better, with its long polished bar, brass footrest and antique slot machine. Where are the spittoons?

Heen Kahidi Restaurant AMERICAN $$$
(800 Venetia Way; breakfast mains $9-15, lunch mains $11-18, dinner mains $19-42; ☉ 7am-9pm Tue-Thu, to 10pm Fri & Sat, to 2pm Sun & Mon) The Cape Fox Lodge restaurant offers hilltop dining with

floor-to-ceiling windows, providing a view of the world below and eagles at eye level. The food is a bit underwhelming, but the experience is pleasant. The dinner menu is split evenly between seafood, steaks and pasta.

Drinking & Nightlife

Arctic Bar   BAR
(509 Water St) Just past the tunnel on downtown's northwest side, this local favorite has managed to survive 70 years by poking fun at itself and tourists. On the back deck overlooking the Narrows is a pair of fornicating bears. And hanging below the wooden bruins, in full view of every cruise ship that ties up in front of the bar, is the sign 'Please Don't Feed the Bears.'

First City Saloon   LOUNGE
(830 Water St) This sprawling club now has two bars, pool tables and comfortable lounge areas with sofas, ottomans and wifi. Its dance floor features a 1970s disco ball and a stripper's pole. This is the one place in Ketchikan that rocks, with live music at least twice a week during the summer, often impromptu when cruise-ship bands are looking to let loose.

Shopping

Ketchikan has a rich artist community and between all the jewelry shops are galleries that display local work.

Main Street Gallery   ARTS & CRAFT
(www.ketchikanarts.org; 330 Main St; ⊙9am-5pm Mon-Fri, 11am-3pm Sat) Operated by Ketchikan Area Arts & Humanities Council, this wonderful gallery stages a reception on the first Friday of every month, unveiling the work of a selected local or regional artist. It's an evening of refreshments and presentations by the artist and extended hours by other galleries downtown.

Soho Coho   ARTS & CRAFT
(www.trollart.com; 5 Creek St) The home gallery of Ketchikan's most noted artist, Ray Troll, whose salmon- and fish-inspired work is seen all around town, including on the sides of buses.

Alaska Geographic Association
Bookstore   BOOKS
(50 Main St; ⊙8:30am-4pm) The Southeast Alaska Discovery Center bookstore offers an extensive selection of Alaska titles and comfortable sitting areas in which to thumb through them.

Parnassus Books   BOOKS
(105 Stedman St; ⊙8am-6pm Mon-Fri, 10am-5pm Sat & Sun) This longtime bookstore is a delightful place to spend a rainy afternoon browsing Alaskan books, cards and local art.

ℹ Information

INTERNET ACCESS
Wi-fi is readily available around town; note the signs in windows advertising it. Ketchikan's new **library** (1110 Copper Ridge Lane ; ⊙10am-8pm Mon-Wed, to 6pm Thu-Sat; 🛜) has free wi-fi and internet computers, a roaring fireplace and an incredible view.

MEDICAL SERVICES
Creekside Family Health Clinic (☑907-220-9982; creeksidehealth.com; 320 Bawden St, Ste 313; ⊙8am-7pm Mon-Fri, 10am 4pm Sat) A walk-in clinic downtown.

Ketchikan General Hospital (☑907-225-5171; 3100 Tongass Ave) Near the ferry terminal.

MONEY
First Bank (☑907-228-4474; 331 Dock St) Has a 24-hour ATM.

Wells Fargo (☑907-225-2184; 409 Dock St) One of a handful of banks mixed in with the gift shops downtown.

POST
Main post office (☑907-225-9601; 3609 Tongass Ave) Near the ferry terminal.

TOURIST INFORMATION
Ketchikan Visitor Information & Tour Center (☑800-770-3300, 907 225 6166; www.visit-ketchikan.com; City Dock, 131 Front St; ⊙7am-6pm) You can pick up brochures and free maps, ask the friendly staff questions, use courtesy phones, and even book tours from here.

Ketchikan Visitor Center Substation Near Berth 3 of the cruise-ship dock and open when ships are in.

Southeast Alaska Discovery Center (☑907-228-6220; www.fs.fed.us/r10/tongass/districts/discoverycenter; 50 Main St; ⊙8:30am-4pm) You don't need to pay the admission to get recreation information at this Alaska Public Lands Information Center. Park passes are also sold here.

ℹ Getting There & Away

AIR
Flights to Ketchikan from Seattle (one way $380, two hours), Anchorage (one way $400, 4½ hours) and major Southeast communities are all possible with **Alaska Airlines** (☑800-252-7522;

www.alaskaair.com). **Promech Air** (📞 907-225-3845, 800-860-3845; www.promechair.com) offers scheduled floatplane flights between Ketchikan and Prince of Wales Island, including Hollis (one way $110), Craig/Klawock ($135) and Thorne Bay ($110). Ketchikan has many bush-plane operators for charter trips, including **Taquan Air** (📞 907-225-8800, 800-770-8800; www.taquanair.com; 4085 Tongass Ave).

BOAT

Northbound Alaska Marine Highway ferries leave almost daily in summer, heading north for Wrangell ($37, six hours), Petersburg ($60, nine hours), Sitka ($83, 20 hours), Juneau ($107, 29 hours) and Haines ($134, 33½ hours). Heading south, the MV *Columbia* departs Ketchikan once a week for Bellingham ($239, 37 hours). The MV *Lituya* provides service to Metlakatla ($21, 1½ hours) Thursday through Monday. For sailing times call the **ferry terminal** (📞 907-225-6182; 3501 Tongass Ave).

Inter-Island Ferry Authority (📞 907-225-4838, 866-308-4848; www.interislandferry. com) vessels are capable of holding vehicles and depart Ketchikan at 3:30pm daily, bound for Hollis on Prince of Wales Island (one way adult/child $49/22.50, three hours). Rates for the ferry vary and are based on your vehicle's length; a subcompact one way costs $50.

❶ Getting Around

TO & FROM THE AIRPORT

The Ketchikan airport is on one side of Tongass Narrows, the city is on the other. A small car-and-passenger **ferry** ($5 for walk-on passengers) runs between the airport and a landing off Tongass Ave, just northwest of the main ferry terminal. From there you can catch the Bus or a taxi.

CAR

For two to four people, renting a car is a good way to spend a day seeing sights out of town. There's unlimited mileage with either of the following but a 16.5% tax.

Alaska Car Rental (📞 800-662-0007; www. akcarrental.com; 2828 Tongass Ave; compacts per day $57) Two locations: one at the airport and one on the town side of the water.

First City Car Rental (📞 907-225-7368; www. firstcitycarrental.com; 1417 Tongass Ave; mid-size per day $60) Will pick up and drop off at major transport areas and many hotels and B&Bs.

PUBLIC TRANSPORTATION

Ketchikan's excellent public bus system is called **the Bus** (📞 907-225-8726; one way $1) but don't worry, there's more than one of them. There are two main lines: the Green Line runs from downtown and then north past the airport ferry. The Silver Line heads south past Saxman Village to Rotary Beach and north all the way past Totem Bight State Park. There's also a free downtown loop. You can't miss the Bus: famed artist Ray Troll painted spawning salmon all over it. The 20-minute loop goes from Berth 4 of the cruise-ship dock to the Totem Heritage Center.

TAXI

Cab companies in town include **Sourdough Cab** (📞 907-225-5544) and **Yellow Taxi** (📞 907-225-5555). The fare from the ferry terminal or the airport ferry dock to downtown is $11 to $15.

BICYCLE

Ketchikan has an expanding system of bike paths that head north and south of downtown along Tongass Ave. Rent Trek hybrids at **Southeast Exposure** (📞 907-225-8829; www.southeastexposure.com; 1224 Tongass Ave; 4hr/full-day rentals $20/30).

Around Ketchikan

South Tongass Highway

On South Tongass Hwy, 2.5 miles south of Ketchikan, is **Saxman Native Village & Totem Park** (📞 907-225-4421; www.capefoxtours. com; admission $5; ☺8am-5pm), an incorporated Tlingit village of 475 residents. The village is best known for its Saxman Totem Park, which holds 24 totem poles brought here from abandoned villages around the Southeast and restored or recarved in the 1930s. Among the collection is a replica of the Lincoln Pole (the original is in the Alaska State Museum in Juneau), which was carved in 1883, using a picture of Abraham Lincoln, to commemorate the first sighting of white people.

You can wander around the Totem Park or, if the cruise ships are in, join an Alaska Native–led two-hour village **tour** (adult/child $37.50/18), which includes a Tlingit language lesson, a traditional drum-and-dance performance, a narrated tour of the totems and a visit to the carving shed. Independent travelers can join this tour by calling the village a day in advance.

From Saxman, South Tongass Hwy continues another 12 miles, bending around Mountain Point and heading back north to George Inlet. This route is more scenic than North Tongass Hwy, but holds little in the way of stores, restaurants or campgrounds. One exception is **Hole in the Wall Bar &**

Marina (7500 S Tongass Hwy; ☺noon-2am), a funky little hangout that feels light years away from the tourist madness of Ketchikan in summer. The bar is in a beautiful location, perched above a small marina in a narrow cove off George Inlet. There's also a good kayaking route that starts here.

The South Tongass Hwy ends at Beaver Falls Hatchery; the Silvis Lake Trail begins nearby.

North Tongass Highway

The closest campgrounds to Ketchikan are in Ward Lake Recreation Area; take North Tongass Hwy 4.5 miles north of the ferry terminal and turn right onto Revilla Rd, then continue 1.5 miles to Ward Lake Rd. CCC Campground (sites $10), basically an overflow area, is on Ward Lake's east shore, while Signal Creek Campground (sites $10) has 24 sites on the south shore. Last Chance Campground (sites $10) is in a beautiful area with four scenic lakes, 19 sites and three trails that run through the lush rainforest.

Ten miles northwest of Ketchikan is Totem Bight State Park (☏907-247-8574; 9883 N Tongass Hwy) FREE, which contains 14 restored or recarved totems and a colorful community house. Just as impressive as the totems are the park's coastline and wooded setting. A viewing deck overlooks Tongass Narrows. Next door to the state park is the equally intriguing Potlatch Park (☏907-225-4445; www.potlatchpark.com; 9809 Totem Bight Rd; ☺7:30am-4pm) FREE. Walk behind its huge gift shop to enter the park; it's home to a dozen totems – one of which is 42ft high – five beautiful tribal houses and an on-site carver who is usually working on a totem in the carving shed. Best of all, the only charge to experience both parks is $1 – for a ride on the Bus' Silver Line.

Six miles beyond Totem Bight is Knudson Cove, where you'll find the best halibut sandwich in Ketchikan, plus homemade pies, at Dockside Galley (☏907-225-4885; Knudson Cove; burgers $10-13; ☺11am-7pm).

Tongass Hwy ends 18 miles north of Ketchikan at Settler's Cove State Recreation Area (sites $10), a scenic coastal area. Its campground has 14 sites, a cabin, a quarter-mile trail to a waterfall and observation deck, and is rarely overflowing like those at Ward Lake.

Misty Fiords National Monument

This spectacular, 3570-sq-mile national monument, just 22 miles east of Ketchikan, is a natural mosaic of sea cliffs, steep fjords and rock walls jutting 3000ft straight out of the ocean. Brown and black bears, mountain goats, Sitka deer, bald eagles and a multitude of marine mammals inhabit this drizzly realm. The monument receives 150in of rainfall annually, and many people think Misty Fiords is at its most beautiful when the granite walls and tumbling waterfalls are veiled in fog and mist. Walker Cove, Rudyerd Bay and Punchbowl Cove – the preserve's most picturesque areas – are reached via Behm Canal, the long inlet separating Revillagigedo Island from the mainland.

Kayaking is *the* best way to experience the preserve. Ketchikan's Southeast Exposure (p83) offers a six-day guided paddle ($1150), with transportation by boat to the fjords and back. It also rents kayaks and provides transport for boats and paddlers.

You can also view the area on sightseeing flights or day cruises. Flightseeing may be the only option if you're in a hurry, and most tours include landing on a lake. Keep in mind that this is a big seller on the cruise ships and when the weather is nice it is an endless stream of floatplanes flying to the same area: Rudyerd Bay and Walker Cove. Throw in the tour boats and one local likened such days to 'the Allied invasion of Omaha Beach.'

If you plan ahead, you can rent one of 10 USFS Cabins (☏877-444-6777, 515-885-3639; www.recreation.gov; cabins $25-45) in the area. The cabins must be reserved in advance, usually several months. An 11th cabin, at Big Goat Lake, is free and available on a first-come, first-served basis, as are four Adirondack shelters (three-sided free-use shelters) in the preserve.

For more on the monument, contact the USFS Ketchikan Ranger District (☏907-225-2148; www.fs.fed.us/r10/tongass).

ℹ Getting There & Around

AIR

There isn't an air charter in Ketchikan that doesn't do Misty Fiords. The standard offering is a 1½-hour flight with a lake landing for $190 to $260, and it's easily booked at the visitors center. The following air charters offer tours and cabin drop-offs.

Alaska Seaplane Tours (☎907-225-1974, 866-858-2327; www.alaskaseaplanetours.com)

Family Air Tours (☎907-247-1305; www.familyairtours.com)

Seawind Aviation (☎907-225-1206, 877-225-1203; www.seawindaviation.com)

Southeast Aviation (☎907-225-2900, 888-359-6478; www.southeastaviation.com)

BOAT

Cruises on a speedy catamaran are another option. **Allen Marine Tours** (☎877-686-8100, 907-225-8100; www.allenmarinetours.com; 5 Salmon Landing, Suite 215; adult/child $180/116) is the main operator, offering four-hour tours on an 80ft catamaran through the monument that include narration, snacks and use of binoculars to look at wildlife.

Prince of Wales Island

POP 3360

For some tourists, the Alaska they come looking for is only a three-hour ferry ride away from the crowds of cruise-ship tourists they encounter in Ketchikan. At 140 miles long and covering more than 2230 sq miles, Prince of Wales Island (POW) is the USA's third-largest island, after Alaska's Kodiak and Hawaii's Big Island.

This vast, rugged island is a destination for the adventurous at heart, loaded with hiking trails and canoe routes, Forest Service cabins and fishing opportunities. The 990-mile coastline of POW meanders around numerous bays, coves, saltwater straits and protective islands, making it a kayaker's delight. And, for anyone carrying a mountain bike through Alaska, a week on the island is worth all the trouble of bringing the two-wheeler north. The island has the most extensive road system in the Southeast, 1300 miles of paved or maintained gravel roads that lead to small villages and several hundred miles more of shot-rock logging roads that lead to who-knows-where.

There are no cruise ships on POW, but there are clear-cuts and you must be prepared for them. Blanketing the island is a patchwork quilt of lush spruce-hemlock forest and fields of stumps where a forest used to be. They are a sign that you have reached real Alaska, a resource-based state where people make a living from fishing, mining and cutting down trees.

The Inter-Island Ferry Authority ferry from Ketchikan lands at Hollis (population 112), which has few visitor facilities and

no stores or restaurants. The towns best set up for tourism are Craig (population 1250) and Klawock (population 800), only 7 miles apart and a 31-mile drive across the island along the paved Hollis–Klawock Hwy. Founded as a salmon-canning and cold-storage site in 1907, Craig is the island's largest and most interesting community, with its mix of commercial fishers and loggers.

Also supporting lodging, restaurants, small grocery stores and other visitor amenities are Thorne Bay (population 490), 38 miles northeast from Klawock, and Coffman Cove (population 180), 55 miles north of Klawock. POW now has 150 miles of paved roads that connect all of these towns.

⊙ Sights

Klawock Totem Park   PARK

(Bayview Blvd) FREE Of the three totem parks on POW, the Klawock Totem Park is by far the most impressive and obviously a great source of community pride. Situated on a hill overlooking the town's cannery and harbor, Klawock's 21 totems comprise the largest collection in Alaska and make for a scenic, almost dramatic setting. Some totems are originals from the former village of Tukekan, the rest are replicas.

Prince of Wales Hatchery   HATCHERY

(☎907-755-2231; www.powha.org; Mile 9, Hollis–Klawock Hwy; ☺8am-4:30pm; 🖐) FREE The Prince of Wales Hatchery was established in 1897 and today is the second-oldest one in Alaska. The present facility was built in 1976 and raises coho, king and sockeye salmon, with many released into the adjacent Klawock River. Inside the visitors center is an aquarium and gift shop where fresh coho is often for sale; outside you can occasionally see black bears feeding across the river.

Fish Ladders   LOOKOUT

On the island's southern half, you can watch salmon attempt to negotiate a couple of fish ladders during the summer spawning season. Both Cable Creek Fish Pass and Dog Salmon Fish Pass have viewing platforms, from which you might also see hungry black bears.

🏃 Activities

Hiking

The USFS maintains more than 20 hiking trails on POW, the majority of them being short walks to rental cabins, rivers or lakes. In the south, a good hike can be made to One Duck Shelter from a trailhead on the road

HYDER

On the eastern fringe of Misty Fiords National Monument, at the head of Portland Canal, is **Hyder** (population 90), a misplaced town if there ever was one. It was founded in 1896 when Captain DD Gailland explored Portland Canal for the US Army Corps of Engineers and built four stone storehouses, the first masonry buildings erected in Alaska, which still stand today. Hyder and its British Columbian neighbor Stewart boomed after major gold and silver mines were opened in 1919, and Hyder became the supply center for more than 10,000 residents. It's been going downhill ever since, the reason it now calls itself 'the friendliest ghost town in Alaska.'

A float plane or a long drive from Prince Rupert are the only options for getting here. Because of Hyder's isolation from the rest of the state, it's almost totally dependent on larger **Stewart** (population 700), just across the Canadian border. Hyder's residents use Canadian money, set their watches to Pacific time (not Alaska time), use Stewart's area code and send their children to Canadian schools. When there's trouble, the famed Canadian Mounties step in. All this can make a sidetrip here a little confusing.

Glacier Inn (☎250-636-9092) The most famous thing to do in Hyder is drink at one of its 'friendly saloons.' The historic Glacier Inn, where you're encouraged to 'get Hyderized,' is the best known and features an interior papered in signed bills, creating the '$20,000 Walls' of Hyder. But the best reason to find your way to this out-of-the-way place is for bear viewing. From late July to September, you can head 6 miles north of town to Fish Creek Bridge and watch brown and black bears feed on chum salmon runs; you might even see a wolf. The USFS has constructed a viewing platform here, and there are interpreters on-site during summer. The entry fee is $5 and you're charged whether or not bears are present.

USFS Office (☎250-636-2367) Has a regularly updated message about bear and other wildlife activity in the area.

Continue along the road and you cross back into British Columbia at Mile 11. At Mile 23 is a point from which to view the impressive **Bear River Glacier**, Canada's fifth largest. For lodging, transport and information, try:

Ripley Creek Inn (☎250-636-2344; www.ripleycreekinn.com; 306 5th Ave, Stewart; r C$115-135; ❧🐾) An inn and several annexes in Stewart.

Bear River RV Park (☎250-636-9205; www.stewartbc.com/rvpark; Hwy 37A, Stewart; tent/RV sites C$22/43; 🐾) Has 68 sites along the Bear River a mile from Stewart.

Taquan Air (☎907-225-8800, 800-770-8800; www.taquanair.com) Makes the run from Ketchikan Monday and Thursday ($310 round-trip), and it's the only way to reach Hyder from Ketchikan.That may seem expensive, but consider that a day trip to Admiralty Island's Pack Creek to see brown bears is around $500.

Stewart/Hyder International Chamber of Commerce (☎250-636-9224, 888-366-5999; www.stewart-hyder.com; 222 5th Ave, Stewart) For information on either town.

to Hydaburg, 2 miles south of Hollis Hwy junction. The trail is steep, climbing 1400ft in 1.2 miles, but it ends at a three-sided free-use shelter that sleeps four. To spend the night in the open alpine area with panoramic views of the Klawock Mountains is worth the knee-bending climb. To the north the **Balls Lake Trail** begins in the Balls Lake Picnic Area just east of Eagle's Nest Campground and winds 2.2 miles around the lake.

Cycling

Mountain bikers have even more opportunities than hikers; unfortunately there are currently no rental facilities so you'll need to bring your own. You can cycle on any road to explore the island. One of the most scenic roads to bike is South Beach Rd (also known as Forest Rd 30) from Coffman Cove to Thorne Bay. It's a 37-mile ride along the narrow, winding dirt road that is often skirting Clarence Strait. Along the way is Sandy Beach Picnic Area (p92), an excellent place to see humpback whales, orcas and harbor seals offshore or examine intriguing tidal pools at low tides.

CAVING ON PRINCE OF WALES ISLAND

One of the most unusual aspects of Prince of Wales' geology is the broad cave system found in the north end of the island. The karst formation is an area of eroded limestone concealing underground streams and caverns, and it includes more than 850 grottos and caves. The caves received national attention in the mid-1990s when paleontologists from the University of South Dakota discovered the remains of a man dating back 9500 years in one cave, and the almost perfect remains of a brown bear that dated back 45,000 years in another. Both allowed scientists to speculate on how the last ice age affected animal and human migration from Asia.

The two most popular caves are northwest of Thorne Bay, a 94-mile drive from Hollis, and can be easily viewed even if you've never worn a headlamp.

El Capitan Cave (Forest Rd 15) is 11 miles west of Whale Pass, you can take a free, two-hour, ranger-led cave tour in summer at 9am, noon and 2:30pm Wednesday through Saturday. Tours are limited to six people and involve a 370-step stairway trail. Contact **Thorne Bay USFS Ranger Station** (☑ 907-828-3304) for reservations (at least two days in advance; no children under seven).

Nearby **Cavern Lake Cave**, on the road to Whale Pass, features an observation deck, allowing visitors to peer into the cave's mouth at the gushing stream inside.

Nearby is the short, wheelchair-accessible **Beaver Falls Karst Trail**, on the main road between the two turnoffs for Whale Pass, which offers an above-ground experience as its boardwalk leads past sinkholes, pits, underground rivers and other typical karst features.

Paddling

Opportunities for paddlers are almost as limitless as they are for mountain bikers. At the north end of POW off Forest Rd 20 is the **Sarkar Lakes Canoe Route**, a 15-mile loop of five major lakes and portages along with a USFS cabin and excellent fishing. For a day of kayaking, depart from Klawock and paddle into **Big Salt Lake**, where the water is calm and the birding is excellent (but be mindful of the inlets at mid-tide, as they can hold treacherous whitewater conditions). Hollis Adventure Rentals (p94) rents single kayaks as well as canoes (one-day/extra day $55/35).

🛏 Sleeping

Much of POW's accommodation is geared towards folks on all-inclusive hunting and fishing tours. There are 18 USFS cabins, one Adirondack shelter and two campgrounds on the island, plus two lovely designated campsites at **Sandy Beach Picnic Area** (Mile 6, Sandy Beach Rd). Two cabins can be reached by rowing across a lake, thus eliminating the floatplane expense required with many others.

Harris River Campground CAMPGROUND $
(sites $8) This campground is near the Hollis Rd junction. The 14-site USFS campground has fire rings, BBQ grills and picnic tables; seven sites have tent pads.

Eagle's Nest Campground CAMPGROUND $
(sites $8) This 12-site campground, 18 miles west of Thorne Bay, overlooks a pair of lakes. It has a canoe-launching site and a half-mile shoreline boardwalk.

USFS Cabins CABINS $
(☑ 518-885-3639, 877-444-6777; www.recreation.gov; cabins $35-45) Control Lake Cabin is reached from State Hwy 929, where a dock and rowboat are kept on the west end of the lake. Red Bay Lake Cabin is at the north end of the POW, off Forest Rd 20, and reached with a half-mile hike to a boat and then a 1.5-mile row across the lake.

Log Cabin Resort & RV Park CABINS $
(☑ 907-755-2205, 800-544-2205; www.logcabinresortandrvpark.com; Big Salt Lake Rd, Klawock; sites tent/RV $10/29, cabins $95-170, ste $180) Located a half-mile up Big Salt Rd in Klawock, this park offers suites, three rustic beachfront cabins and a grassy spot for tents, with showers and a community kitchen. It also rents canoes (per day $25) for use on Big Salt Lake or Klawock Lake.

Inn of the Little Blue Heron B&B $$
(☑ 907-826-3608; www.littleblueheroninn.com; 406 9th St, Craig; r $79-135, ste $155; ☻🛜) This B&B has two waterfront locations: one overlooking South Cove Boat Harbor and the other on Bucareli Bay; each is only a five-minute walk to shops and restaurants in Craig. Between

the two there are nine rooms, all with kitch-enettes, and one apartment suite with a full kitchen. All feature TVs and private baths.

Dreamcatcher B&B
B&B **$$**

(☑907-826-2238; www.dreamcatcherbedandbreak-fast.com; 1405 Hamilton Dr, Craig; s/d $125/135; 🕾) Three guest rooms in a beautiful seaside home. Big picture windows and a wrap-around deck give way to a wonderful view of water, islands, mountains and, of course, clear-cuts. Kayaks and a skiff are available for guests, and you can warm up with a view in either the hot tub or around the firepit.

Shelter Cove
HOTEL **$$**

(☑907-826-2939, 888-826-3474; www.sheltercov-efishinglodge.com; 703 Hamilton Dr, Craig; r $129-139; 🕾) Six of the 10 clean and comfortable rooms here overlook the water; you might never want to leave your room. Most of their guests are part of a fishing package tour, but they take independent travelers if there's space; it's worth the inquiry.

Ruth Ann's Hotel
HOTEL **$$**

(☑907-826-3378; cnr Main & Water Sts, Craig; r $110-157; 🕾🕾) Ruth Ann's hotel has 18 rooms in three buildings, all of which have been renovated and look new. Many come with breakfast bars and/or views.

Coffman Cove Adventures
CABINS **$$$**

(☑907-329-2043; www.coffmancoveak.com; 501 Loggers Lane, Coffman Cove; cabins $225; 🕾) The price may seem steep, but it comes with a car rental and a skiff, plus three meals a day. Cabins are cozy and clean, and there's a firepit and flowers – more of a family environment than some of the very masculine fishing and hunting digs in town.

🍴 Eating

Dockside Restaurant
BREAKFAST **$**

(Front St, Craig; breakfast mains $9-14, lunch mains $10-14; ⊙5:30am-8pm) This wonderful cafe serves the best breakfast on POW, but it's the pies that make it legendary among locals. There's usually a half-dozen different kinds in the cooler, and a $5 slice is money well spent.

The Bread Box
BAKERY **$**

(Westwood Shopping Plaza, Craig; ⊙8am-4pm Mon, 7am-6pm Tue-Fri, 8am-6pm Sat) Part bakery, part natural foods store. There's gourmet coffee and pastries, and you can grab some organic veggies to add to your loaf of fresh bread for a picnic.

The Bait Box
CAFE **$**

(Coffman Cove; burgers $7-13; ⊙7am-6:30pm) In a harbor-front shack; take-out includes homemade burgers and milkshakes, smoked pizzas and pulled pork.

Zat's Pizza
PIZZA **$$**

(420 Port Bagial Blvd, Craig; pizza $20-26; ⊙11:30am-8pm Tue-Sat) A Craig favorite; excellent pizza in a bustling atmosphere. Vegetarian options, including the 'Popeye': garlic and olive oil, spinach, feta, tomatoes and more.

Latitude 55 North
SEAFOOD **$$$**

(☑907-826-2941; www.sheltercovefishinglodge.com; 703 Hamilton Dr, Craig; mains $20-26) At Shelter Cove, this is as upscale as POW gets. Featuring protein from land and sea, with some Asian fusion mixed in. It's best to call ahead for a reservation.

❶ Information

Alicia Roberts Medical Center (☑907-755-4800; Hollis–Klawock Hwy, Klawock; ⊙walk-ins 9am-4pm Mon-Fri) Main medical facility on the island.

Craig Library (☑907-826-3281; 504 3rd St, Craig; ⊙noon-5pm & 7-9pm Mon, 10am-5pm & 7-9pm Tue-Thu, 7-9pm Fri, noon-4pm Sat) Free internet access and used books for sale.

Post Office (Craig–Klawock Hwy, Craig) Next to the supermarket.

Prince of Wales Chamber of Commerce (☑907-755-2626; www.princeofwalescoc.org; ⊙7:30am-4pm Mon & Thu, from 8am Tue & Wed, from 10am Fri; 🕾) Operates a visitors center in Klawock.

USFS Office (⊙8am-5pm Mon-Fri) Head to either the Craig (☑907-826-3271; 900 9th St) or Thorne Bay (☑907-828-3304; 1312 Federal Way) offices for information on trails, cabins and paddling adventures.

Wells Fargo (301 Thompson Rd, Craig) Next to the post office and equipped with a 24-hour ATM.

---

❶ POW MAPS

For a quick visit, the map inside the free *Prince of Wales Island Guide* is sufficient. For an extended stay or if you're planning to explore the logging roads, purchase the *Prince of Wales Island Road Guide* ($10) published by the USFS. Either is available at the POW Chamber of Commerce or USFS Ranger Station.

RAINFOREST ISLANDS FERRY

Presently tourism on Prince of Wales Island is light due to limited ferry service. But that could change with the launch of the Rainforest Islands Ferry. The proposed ferry would restore the Inter-Island Ferry Authority service between Coffman Cove, Wrangell and South Mitkof Island that was discontinued in 2008 and link Coffman Cove directly to Ketchikan. Such a service would allow you to continue north onto Wrangell or Petersburg after visiting POW, eliminating the need to backtrack to Ketchikan.

Contact **City of Coffman Cove** (☑ 907-329-2233; www.ccalaska.com) for the latest news on the new ferry – it should be in service by 2015.

Getting There & Away

The **Inter-Island Ferry Authority** (☑ Hollis Terminal 866-308-4800, Ketchikan Terminal 907-530-4848; www.interislandferry.com) operates a pair of vessels that depart from Hollis at 8am and from Ketchikan at 3:30pm daily (three hours, one way adult/child $49/22.50).

Promech Air (p88) also runs scheduled flights from Ketchikan to Craig/Klawock (one way $115), Hollis ($95) and Thorne Bay ($95).

❶ Getting Around

There are a couple of car rental companies on POW; the best is **Hollis Adventure Rentals** (☑ 907-530-7040; www.hollisadventurerentals. com; 222 Hollis Rd, Craig). You'll be met in Hollis with a car packed with a cooler and some essentials. If staying more than a few days, consider renting a car in Ketchikan and driving it onto the ferry.

Island Ride (☑ 907-401-1414) connects with ferries in Hollis, but you have to call them in advance to reserve a seat. The one-way fare to Craig is $35 per person.

Wrangell & Around

POPULATION 2400

Strategically located near the mouth of the Stikine River, Wrangell is one of the oldest towns in Alaska and the only one to have existed under three flags and ruled by four nations – Tlingit, Russia, Britain and America.

In Wrangell's heyday it was a jumping-off point for three major gold rushes up the Stikine River from 1861 to the late 1890s.

Back then Wrangell was as lawless and ruthless as Skagway, and at one point Wyatt Earp, the famous Arizona lawman, filled in as a volunteer marshal for 10 days before moving on to Nome. Wrangell's most famous visitor, however, was John Muir, who came in 1879 and again in 1880. Muir wrote that 'Wrangell village was a rough place. It was a lawless draggle of wooden huts and houses, built in crooked lines, wrangling around the boggy shore of the island for a mile or so.'

Eventually Wrangell became a fishing and lumber town typical of Southeast Alaska, and when the timber industry crashed in the early 1990s the town was hit harder than most. For years the town was seen as a bitter, dying community, but many believe Wrangell has turned the corner. Unlike Petersburg, the 2010 censuses showed that Wrangell gained residents. Its economy is also more stable, with an emerging dive fishery, which harvests sea urchins, sea cucumbers and geoducks, and the Marine Service Center, a shipyard that provides repair and haul-out for commercial vessels.

Of all the Alaska Marine Highway's major stops, Wrangell is the least gentrified. Cruise ships are only a once-a-week occurrence here, so the town is rarely inundated and isn't ritzy. You don't come to Wrangell for posh luxury hotels or well-developed tourist attractions. Instead, use Wrangell as a home base for exploring the surrounding wilds.

The island offers great mountain biking and bike-camping opportunities; kayakers can explore the Stikine River or myriad islands and waterways around the river's mouth; and local guides lead boat trips to Anan Creek bear observatory and other places of interest.

◉ Sights

★ **Wrangell Museum**   MUSEUM
(296 Campbell Dr; adult/child/family $5/2/12; ⊙ 10am-5pm Mon-Sat) This impressive museum is what the colorful history and characters of Wrangell deserve. As you stroll through the many rooms, an audio narration automatically comes on and explains that chapter of Wrangell's history, from Tlingit culture and the gold-rush era to the time Hollywood arrived in 1972 to film the movie *Timber Tramps*. You can marvel at a collection of Alaskan art that includes a Sidney Laurence painting or be amused that this rugged little town has had two presidential visits.

★ **Chief Shakes Island**   PARK
(Shakes St) FREE The small, grassy and enchanting islet is in the middle of the boat harbor and reached by a pedestrian bridge. With totems, tall pines and the half-dozen eagles usually perched in the branches, the island is a quiet oasis in the hum of the fishing fleet around it. **Shakes Community House**, an excellent example of a high-caste tribal house containing tools, blankets and other cultural items, is open only to accommodate cruise ships (call the Wrangell Museum for times).

Just as impressive are the six totems surrounding the tribal house, all duplicates of originals carved in the late 1930s.

★ **Petroglyph Beach**   ARCHAEOLOGICAL SITE
(Evergreen Ave; 🖐) FREE On Wrangell's north side is a state historic park where you can see primitive rock carvings believed to be at least 1000 years old. Located 0.7 miles from the **ferry terminal**, a sign marks the viewing deck with interpretive displays and replicas. Turn right and walk north on the beach about 50yd. Before you reach the wrecked fishing vessel, look for faint carvings on the large rocks, many of them resembling spirals and faces. There are almost 50 in the area, but the majority are submerged at high tide so check a tide book. Also bring a bottle of water; the carvings are easier to see when wet.

Totems   MONUMENTS
For its size, Wrangell has an impressive collection of totems, with more than a dozen scattered through town. Pick up the free *Wrangell Guide* at the visitors center and spend an afternoon locating them all. Along with Chief Shakes Island, make sure you stop at **Totem Park** (Front St) and **Chief Shakes Grave** (Case Ave) to see the killer-whale totems.

🏃 **Activities**

Bear Watching
Thirty miles southeast of Wrangell on the mainland, Anan Creek is the site of one of the largest pink salmon runs in Southeast Alaska. From the platforms at **Anan Creek Wildlife Observatory** (www.fs.fed.us/r10/ton gass/recreation/wildlife_viewing/ananobserva tory. shtml; permits $10), you can watch eagles, harbor seals, black bears and a few brown bears chowing down gluttonously on the spawning humpies. This is one of the few places in Alaska where black and brown bears coexist (or at least put up with each other) at

the same run. Permits are required from early July through August, or basically when the bears are there, and are reserved online or by calling the USFS Office in Wrangell. Almost half of the daily 60 permits go to local tour operators. Another 18 are available from March 1 for that particular year and 12 permits are issued three days in advance.

The best way to see the bears, if you can plan ahead, is to reserve the USFS **Anan Bay Cabin** (☎877-444-6777; www.recreation.gov; $35), which comes with four permits and is a 1-mile hike from the observation area. This cabin can be reserved six months in advance, and during the bear-watching season it pretty much has to be.

Anan Creek is a 20-minute floatplane flight or an hour boat ride, and almost every tour operator in town offers a trip there. **Alaska Charters & Adventures** (☎907-874-4157, 888-993-2750; www.alaskaupclose.com; 7 Front St) offers an eight-hour boat trip to the observatory ($278), and **Alaska Waters Inc** (☎907-874-2378, 800-347-4462; www.alaskawaters.com; Stikine Ave, Stikine Inn), at the Stikine Inn, has a six-hour boat tour ($285). Sunrise Aviation (p98) will fly up to four passengers in and out for $375 each way.

Hiking
Other than the climb up Mt Dewey and walking the Volunteer Park Trail, all of Wrangell's trails are off the road and often include muskeg, meaning you'll need a car and a pair of rubber boots.

MUSKEG MEADOWS

Completed in 1998 atop the sawdust and wood chips left behind by local sawmill operations, Wrangell's nine-hole golf course (☎907-874-4653; www. wrangellalaskagolf.com; Ishiyama Dr; per round $33), half a mile east of Bennet St, may be the first certified course in the Southeast, but it's uniquely Alaskan. Surrounded by wilderness, members are rarely alarmed when a bear comes bounding across a fairway. Then there is the club's Raven Rule: if a raven steals your ball you may replace it with no penalty provided you have a witness. Finally, the course's narrow fairways and tangled roughs of spruce and muskeg have resulted in this warning posted in the clubhouse: 'You got to have a lot of balls to play Muskeg Meadows.'

Wrangell

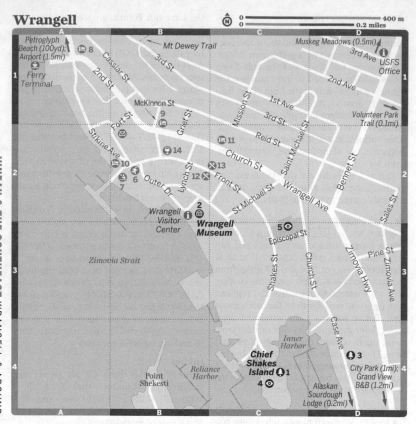

Mt Dewey Trail
HIKING

Mt Dewey Trail is a half-mile climb up a hill to a small clearing in the trees, overlooking Wrangell and the surrounding waterways. From Mission St, walk a block and turn left at 3rd St. Follow the street past the houses to the posted stairway on the right. The hike to the top takes 15 minutes or so, but the trail is often muddy. John Muir fanatics will appreciate the fact that the great naturalist climbed the mountain in 1879 and built a bonfire on top, alarming the Tlingit people living in the village below. Ironically, the only signs on top now say 'No Campfires.'

Volunteer Park Trail
HIKING

A pleasant stroll winding a half-mile through the forest from near Volunteer Park's ball field off 2nd Ave.

Rainbow Falls Trail
HIKING

Signposted 4.7 miles south of the ferry terminal on the Zimovia Hwy is this popular trail across from Shoemaker Bay Recreation Area. It's 0.7 miles to the waterfalls, where you'll find an observation platform above the cascade and great views of Chichagof Pass and Zimovia Strait.

Institute Creek & North Wrangell Trails
HIKING

These trails cross Wrangell Island. Institute Creek Trail begins towards the end of Rainbow Falls Trail and climbs 1500ft in 2.7 miles to the Shoemaker Bay Overlook Shelter.

A half-mile before the shelter, North Wrangell Trail leads 1.3 miles to High Country Shelter and, in 2.3 miles, to Pond Shelter. The trail descends to Spur Rd Extension, on the east side of Wrangell Island 4 miles from town.

The entire hike from the west side to the east is 6.5 miles, passing three-sided shelters along the way for overnight adventures.

Wrangell

◉ Top Sights
1 Chief Shakes Island C4
2 Wrangell Museum B2

◉ Sights
3 Chief Shakes Grave D4
4 Shakes Community
   House C4
5 Totem Park C3

◉ Activities, Courses & Tours
6 Alaska Charters &
   Adventures B2
7 Alaska Vistas B2
   Alaska Waters
   Inc .... (see 10)

Breakaway Adventures .... (see 7)

◉ Sleeping
8 Fennimore's B&B A1
9 Rooney's Roost B1
10 Stikine Inn B2
11 Wrangell Hostel C2

◉ Eating
12 Diamond C Café B2
   Stikine Inn .... (see 10)
13 Zak's Cafe C2

◉ Drinking & Nightlife
   Stikine Inn .... (see 10)
14 Totem Bar B2

Thoms Lake Trail HIKING
A 1.4-mile path to the lake, Thoms Lake Trail is reached by following Zimovia Hwy to its paved end and then turning east on Forest Rd 6267. About halfway across the island, just before crossing Upper Salamander Creek, turn right on Forest Rd 6290 and follow it 4 miles to the trailhead. There is a cabin half a mile from the end of the trail.

Paddling
One look at a nautical chart of Wrangell will have kayakers drooling and dreaming. Islands and protected waterways abound, though many are across the vast Stikine River flats, where experience is a prerequisite due to strong tides and currents. Novices can enjoy paddling around the harbor, over to Petroglyph Beach or to Dead Man's Island.

Alaska Vistas KAYAKING
(☑907-874-3006, 866-874-3006; www.alaskavistas.com; 106 Front St) Inside the Java Junkies espresso shed, a wi-fi hot spot at City Dock, Alaska Vistas rents kayaks (per day single/double $55/65). The company also runs guided kayak tours, including a full-day East West Cove paddle ($200) on the well-protected east side of Wrangell Island.

Vans are used to transport you to the east shore and a jet boat returns you to Wrangell at the end of the day.

★ Festivals & Events

The summer's biggest event is the **Fourth of July** celebration. All of Wrangell gets involved in the festival, which features a parade, fireworks, live music, a logging show, street games, food booths and a salmon bake.

In the third week of April, Wrangell hosts its **Stikine River Birding Festival**, when boat tours head up the river to witness the largest springtime concentration of bald eagles in Alaska.

🛏 Sleeping

Wrangell levies a 13% sales and bed tax on all lodging.

Nemo Point CAMPGROUND
(☑907-874-2323; Forest Rd 6267; sites free) The best camping on Wrangell Island, but unfortunately it is 14 miles from town. Each of the six free wheelchair-accessible sites has a picnic table, outhouse and a stunning view of Zimovia Strait. Take Zimovia Hwy/Forest Hwy 16 south to Forest Rd 6267. The sites stretch along 4 miles of Forest Rd 6267.

City Park CAMPGROUND
(☑907-874-2444; Mile 1.7, Zimovia Hwy; sites free) For those with a tent, the closest campground

---

A CABIN IN THE WOODS

In 2010 the USFS opened **Middle Ridge Cabin** (☑877-444-6777; www.recreation.gov; cabin $35), the first road-accessible cabin of the nearly two dozen in the Wrangell District of Tongass National Forest. Until recently all of them were reached via floatplanes, boats or on foot. It's still an adventurous retreat. The cabin is 20 miles south of Wrangell along Forest Rd 50050, which is recommended for 'high-clearance vehicles.' Once out there you'll feel like you're miles from civilization. And you will be.

is this waterfront park, 1 mile south of town. Within the wooded setting are eight sites, shelters and restrooms. Only tent campers are allowed to stay here and sites are free. There's a one-night limit, but that's overlooked if you arrive on foot.

Shoemaker Bay
Recreation Area   CAMPGROUND $
(☑907-874-2444; Mile 4.5, Zimovia Hwy; tent sites free, RV sites $15-25) This campsite is across from the Rainbow Falls trailhead in a wooded area near a creek. There are 25 sites, 15 with hookups for RVers, and a tent-camping area for everybody sleeping in ripstop nylon. All sites have good views of Zimovia Strait.

Wrangell Hostel   HOSTEL $
(☑907-874-3534; 220 Church St; dm $20) In the First Presbyterian Church, this basic place has separate-sex dorm rooms with inflata-ble mattresses, showers and a large kitchen and dining room. It has no curfew and will graciously let you hang out there during an all-day rain.

★ Grand View B&B   B&B $$
(☑907-874-3225; www.grandviewbnb.com; Mile 1.9, Zimovia Hwy; r $105-135; ☎) Next to City Park, this oceanfront B&B does have the grandest view in town. From the living room a row of picture windows frame Zimovia Strait and the mountains that surround it. The main floor is devoted to guests and includes three rooms, private baths, a large kitchen and an impressive collection of Alaska art and artifacts.

Rooney's Roost   B&B $$
(☑907-874-2026; www.rooneysroost.com; 206 McKinnon St; r $125; ☎) This excellent B&B is within easy walking distance of the ferry,

---

WORTH A TRIP

THE STIKINE RIVER

A narrow, rugged shoreline and surrounding mountains and glaciers characterize the beautiful, wild Stikine River, which begins in the high peaks of interior British Columbia and ends some 400 miles on in a delta called the Stikine Flats, just north of Wrangell. The Stikine is North America's fastest navigable river, and its most spectacular sight is the Grand Canyon of the Stikine, a steep-walled gorge where violently churning white water makes river travel impossible. John Muir called this stretch of the Stikine 'a Yosemite 100 miles long.'

Trips from below the canyon are common among rafters and kayakers. They begin with a charter flight to Telegraph Creek in British Columbia and end with a 160-mile float back to Wrangell.

Travelers arriving in Wrangell with a kayak but insufficient funds to charter a bush plane can paddle from the town's harbor across the Stikine Flats (where there are several USFS cabins) and up one of the Stikine River's three arms. By keeping close to shore and taking advantage of eddies and sloughs, experienced paddlers can make their way 30 miles up the river to the Canadian border – or even further, passing 12 **USFS cabins** (☑877-444-6777; www.recreation.gov), and the two bathing huts at **Chief Shakes Hot Springs** and **Shakes Glacier** inside Shakes Lake along the way. But you must know how to line a boat upstream and navigate a highly braided river and, while in the lower reaches, accept the fact that you'll encounter a lot of jet-boat traffic.

Wrangell's USFS office can provide information on the Stikine River, including two helpful publications: *Stikine River Canoe/Kayak Routes* ($5) and *Lower Stikine River Map* ($5), the latter covering the river up to Telegraph Creek.

Wrangell charter boats that run trips on the Stikine or offer drop-off services for kayakers include the following:

Breakaway Adventures (☑907-874-2488, 888-385-2488; www.breakawayadventures.com; Front St) Day trips up the river by jet boat take in Shakes Glacier and the hot springs ($180).

Alaska Vistas (p97) Provides a water-taxi service for kayakers and rafters.

Sunrise Aviation (☑907-874-2319; www.sunriseflights.com; Wrangell Airport) Has an hour-long flightseeing tour of the Stikine River and LeConte Glacier for $525 for three people (the minimum) or $180 per person for up to five passengers.

just a short way up 2nd St. There are four antique-filled guest rooms with queen-size beds, TV and private baths. In the morning you enjoy a delicious breakfast, and in the afternoon you can relax on the deck with view of Wrangell.

Stikine Inn   MOTEL $$

(☑ 907-874-3388, 888-874-3388; www.stikineinn. com; 107 Stikine Ave; s $150-196, d $168-189; ☜) Wrangell's swankiest lodging is on the waterfront near the ferry dock and comes with a bar, coffee shop, restaurant and 34 clean rooms. The waterview rooms cost more, but they are among the best in town.

Alaskan Sourdough Lodge   LODGE $$

(☑ 907-874-3613; www.akgetaway.com; 1104 Peninsula St; s/d $119/129; @☜) This family-owned lodge is showing some signs of wear; it was hosting visitors when there were still lumber mills in Wrangell. But the 16 rooms are large, there's free transportation to/from the ferry or airport and outdoor decks full of flowers and wicker furniture, some with a view of the harbor. Family-style meals are served in a large eating area.

Fennimore's B&B   B&B $$

(☑ 907-874-3012; www.fennimoresbbb.com; 321 Stikine Ave; r $110; ☜) Trip off the ferry and into your bed; Fennimore's is right across from the ferry terminal. Four rooms, basic but clean, have private bath and private entrances. All have cable, refrigerators, microwave and queen-size beds. There are bikes for guests to tool around town on, and the proprietor is writing a book on the history of the area.

✖ Eating

Zak's Cafe   CAFE $

(316 Front St; breakfast $6-10, lunch $6-12; ⊘ 11am-7pm Mon-Sat, 10am-2pm Sun) Serves diner basics: omelettes, pancakes, BLTs, salads, soups and more. Come for the big portions, stick around for the local gossip.

Stikine Inn   AMERICAN $$

(107 Stikine Ave; lunch mains $14-18, dinner mains $16-30; ⊘ 11am-8pm) Every table at Stikine Inn's restaurant faces the water and the fishing boats passing by. The dinner menu is split between sandwiches, burgers and wraps, and this is as fancy as Wrangell gets.

Diamond C Café   CAFE $$

(223 Front St; breakfast $6-12, lunch $8-17; ⊘ 6am-2pm) Eat what the locals eat – eggs and hash browns, biscuits and gravy, deep-fried fish-

and-chips – and listen to the conservative pulse of the community from the tables around you.

Alaskan Sourdough Lodge   SEAFOOD $$

(☑ 907-874-3613; 1104 Peninsula St; mains $22-27; ⊘ 6-8pm) If you call ahead, the lodge will allow you to join its guests for home-style meals that include a salad bar and often crab, halibut and salmon during the summer.

🍺 Drinking

Stikine Inn   BAR

(107 Stikine Ave) The lounge is adjacent to the the restaurant and has the prettiest view in town. If the evening is nice there's an outdoor patio where you can watch vessels disappear into the mist on Zimovia Strait.

Totem Bar   BAR

(Front St) Wrangell's redneck dive bar.

ℹ Information

First Bank (224 Brueger St) Across from IGA Supermarket, it maintains a 24-hour ATM on Front St.

Irene Ingle Public Library (☑ 907-874-3535; 124 2nd St; ⊘ 10am-noon & 1-5pm Mon & Fri, 1-5pm & 7-9pm Tue-Thu, 9am-5pm Sat; ☜) A wonderful facility for such a small town; has free wi-fi and a paperback exchange, plus a few terminals.

Post Office (112 Federal Way) At the town's north end with an impressive totem out front.

USFS Office (☑ 907-874-2323; 525 Bennett St; ⊘ 8am-4:30pm Mon-Fri) Located three-quarters of a mile north of town; has information on regional USFS cabins, trails and campgrounds.

Wrangell Medical Center (☑ 907-874-7000; 310 Bennett St) For anything from Aspirin to Zoloft.

Wrangell Visitor Center (☑ 907-874-3901; www.wrangell.com; 293 Campbell Dr; ⊘ 10am-5pm Mon-Sat) In the Nolan Center, it stocks the free *Wrangell Guide* and shows a 10-minute film on the area in a small theater.

ℹ Getting There & Around

Daily northbound and southbound flights are available with **Alaska Airlines** (☑ 907-874-3308, 800-426-0333; www.alaskaair.com). Many claim the flight north to Petersburg is the 'world's shortest jet flight,' since the six- to 11-minute trip (one way $126) is little more than a takeoff and landing.

Alaska Marine Highway (☑ 907-874-3711) services run almost daily both northbound and southbound from Wrangell in summer. To the north is Petersburg ($33, three hours) via the scenic, winding Wrangell Narrows, to the south Ketchikan ($37, six hours). There are plans for a new service called Rainforest Islands Ferry to run between Wrangell and Mitkof Island in 2015. Check with the **City of Coffman Cove** (☑907-329-2233; www.ccalaska.com) for the status of it.

Practical Rent-A-Car (☑907-874-3975), at the airport, rents compacts for $65 per day plus 17% rental tax. Running around town in yellow vans is **Northern Lights Taxi** (☑907-874-4646).

Petersburg

POP 2975

From Wrangell, the Alaska Marine Highway ferry heads north to begin one of the Inside Passage's most scenic sections. After crossing over from Wrangell Island to Mitkof Island, the vessel threads through the 46 turns of Wrangell Narrows, a 22-mile channel that is only 300ft wide and 19ft deep in places. So winding and narrow is the channel that locals call it 'pinball alley.' Others refer to it as 'Christmas tree lane' because of the abundance of red and green navigational lights.

At the other end of this breathtaking journey lies Norwegian-influenced Petersburg, one of Southeast Alaska's hidden gems. Peter Buschmann arrived in 1897 and found a fine harbor, abundant fish and a ready supply of ice from nearby LeConte Glacier. He built a cannery in the area, enticed his Norwegian friends to follow him here, and gave his first name to the resulting town. Today, a peek into the local phone book reveals the strong Norwegian heritage that unifies Petersburg.

The waterfront of this busy little fishing port is decorated with working boats and weathered boathouses, while tidy homes and businesses – many done up with distinctive Norwegian rosemaling, a flowery Norwegian art form – line the quiet streets. Petersburg has Alaska's sixth-largest fishing fleet and sends more than 55 million pounds of salmon, halibut, black cod, shrimp and crab annually to the town's four canneries and two cold-storage plants. The canneries sit above the water on pilings, overlooking boat harbors bulging with vessels, barges, ferries and seaplanes. Even at night, you can see small boats trolling the nearby waters for somebody's dinner.

The town lies across Frederick Sound from a spectacular glaciated wall of alpine peaks – including the distinctive Devil's Thumb – that form a skyline of jagged snow-capped summits. Nearby LeConte Glacier discharges icebergs to the delight of visitors.

Without a heavy dependency on timber, Petersburg enjoys a healthier economy than Wrangell or Ketchikan, so it doesn't need to pander to tourists. Thus the lack of a hostel

Petersburg

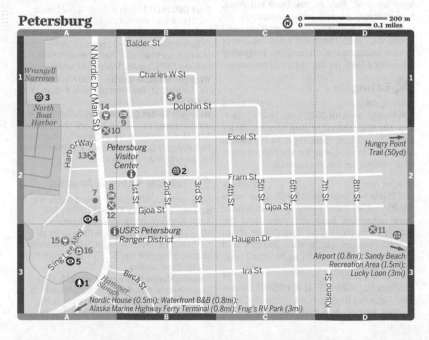

Nordic House (0.5mi); Waterfront B&B (0.8mi);
Alaska Marine Highway Ferry Terminal (0.8mi); Frog's RV Park (3mi)

or even a camping area within town but also the heavy cruise-ship traffic that Juneau and Skagway experience. That makes Petersburg a joy for most independent travelers, who will quickly discover the locals are friendly and their stories interesting.

◉ Sights

Clausen Memorial Museum MUSEUM
(www.clausenmuseum.net; 203 Fram St; adult/child $5/free; ⏰10am-5pm Mon-Sat) This museum holds an interesting collection of artifacts and relics, mostly related to local fishing history. Exhibits include the largest king salmon ever caught (126lbs), a giant lens from the old Cape Decision lighthouse, a Tlingit dugout canoe and the 30-minute film, *Petersburg: The Town Fish Built.* Outside is *Fisk,* the intriguing fish sculpture that was commissioned in 1967 to honor the Alaska Centennial.

Sing Lee Alley HISTORIC SITE
Heading south, Harbor Way passes Middle Boat Harbor and turns into Sing Lee Alley. This was the center of old Petersburg, and much of the street is built on pilings over Hammer Slough. On the alley, **Sons of Norway Hall** is the large white building with the colorful rosemaling built in 1912 and the center for Petersburg's Norwegian culture. Come on down and play bingo at 7pm on Friday.

Also along Sing Lee Alley is **Bojet Wikan Fishermen's Memorial Park**. This deck of-a-park is built on pilings over Hammer Slough and features an impressive statue of a fisher that honors all his fellow crew members lost at sea. Also on display is the Valhalla, a replica of a Viking ship that was built in 1976 and purchased by Petersburg two years later.

North Boat Harbor LANDMARK
(Excel St, at Harbor Way) The North Boat Harbor is the best for wandering the docks, talking to crews and possibly scoring some fresh fish. Begin at the Harbormaster Office; a wooden deck provides a picturesque overview of the commercial fleet and has a series of interpretive panels that will teach you the difference between purse seine and a long liner. Continue north to **Petersburg Fisheries** (Dolphin St, at Nordic Dr), the original outfit founded by Peter Buschmann in 1900; today it's a subsidiary of Seattle's Icicle Seafoods.

Sandy Beach Recreation Area PARK
(Map p122) From downtown, Nordic Dr heads north on a scenic route that ends at Sandy Beach Recreation Area, a beautiful day-use area 2 miles from downtown. There are 2000-year-old Tlingit fish traps snaking the mudflats and a rock with petroglyphs carved on it. Both the traps and the carvings are hard to spot, but the Petersburg Ranger District (p107) organizes guided interpretive walks to them during the summer here. Call for times.

🏃 Activities

Hiking
Hungry Point Trail HIKING
Within town is the 0.7-mile Hungry Point Trail that begins at the ball field at the end of Excel St and cuts across muskeg. The gravel path keeps your feet dry, but surrounding you are stunted trees so short you have a clear view of Petersburg's mountainous skyline. The trail ends at Sandy Beach Rd.

Head right a quarter-mile to reach Outlook Park, a marine wildlife observatory with free binoculars to search Frederick Sound for humpbacks, orcas and sea lions.

Petersburg

RICHARD CUMMINS / GETTY IMAGES ©

1. St Michael's Cathedral (p107), Sitka 2. Juneau (p116)
3. Glaciers near Juneau 4. US Forest Service cabin

DANITA DELIMONT / GETTY IMAGES ©

Juneau & Southeast Alaska Highlights

You can't drive to Juneau, or most of Southeast Alaska, and that seems only proper. This watery, mountainous region, filled with fjords, thousands of islands, impressive glaciers and small but interesting ports, is best explored at the casual pace of a cruise ship or state ferry.

Russian Culture

St Michael's Cathedral not only anchors downtown Sitka but it could be one of the most beloved churches in Southeast Alaska. When the original burnt down in 1966 residents immediately built a replica.

Icing on the Lake

It's big, it's blue and it's still active, tossing icebergs into Mendenhall Lake. No wonder Mendenhall Glacier is Juneau's most popular attraction. View it, hold a piece of it, walk on it; this glacier will amaze you.

Rustic Cabins

The floatplane lands on an isolated lake and you step out to a small A-frame cabin. It's one of the nearly 150 US Forest Service cabins scattered across Southeast Alaska, your personal slice of wilderness for the next three days.

Emerald Maze

The ferry slips into a foggy green labyrinth, sailing past tiny fishing towns with boats hauling the day's catch. The Alaska Marine Highway will introduce you to the most relaxing and scenic form of public transport you'll ever ride.

Raven Trail
HIKING

The 4-mile Raven Trail was relocated to Sandy Beach in 2014. The new mile of trail is wheelchair accessible, crossing muskeg areas on a boardwalk before climbing to beautiful open alpine areas at 2000ft. Some sections are steep and require a little scrambling; continued improvements are planned. The trail eventually leads to the USFS **Raven's Roost Cabin** (☑877-444-6777, 515-885-3639; www.recreation.gov; cabins $35).

The cabin is above the treeline, providing easy access to good alpine hiking and spectacular views of Petersburg, Frederick Sound and Wrangell Narrows.

Petersburg Mountain Trail
HIKING

On Kupreanof Island, the 3.5-mile Petersburg Mountain Trail climbs to the top of Petersburg Mountain (2750ft), which offers views of Petersburg, the Coast Mountains, glaciers and Wrangell Narrows.

To get across the channel, go to the skiff float at the North Boat Harbor and hitch a ride with somebody who lives on Kupreanof Island (warning: it can be tough to find a ride back). Tongass Kayak Adventures also runs hikers across the channel for $25 per trip. On the Kupreanof side, head right on the overgrown road toward Sasby Island. Plan on five hours for the round-trip.

Petersburg Lake Trail
HIKING

This is a 10.5-mile trail in the Petersburg Creek-Duncan Salt Chuck Wilderness on Kupreanof Island; it leads to the USFS **Petersburg Lake Cabin** (☑877-444-6777, 515-885-3639; www.recreation.gov; cabins $35). For more see p59.

Blind River Rapids Boardwalk
HIKING

At Mile 14.5 of the Mitkof Hwy is the mile-long Blind River Rapids Boardwalk that winds through muskeg to the rapids, a scenic area that's busy in June for king salmon fishing.

Three Lakes Loop Trails
HIKING

Along Three Lakes Rd, a USFS road heading east off Mitkof Hwy at Mile 13.6 and returning at Mile 23.8, are Three Lakes Loop Trails, a series of four short trails that total 4.5 miles.

At Mile 14.2 is a 3-mile loop with boardwalks leading to Sand, Crane and Hill Lakes, all known for good trout fishing. Sand Lake has a free-use shelter. From the Sand Lake Trail, a 1.5-mile trail leads to Ideal Cove on Frederick Sound.

Paddling

Petersburg offers interesting possibilities for kayakers, LeConte Glacier and Tebenkof Bay Wilderness among them, but many of the trips require a week or more. Kayak rentals (and anything else you might need, including sleeping bags) are available from **Tongass Kayak Adventures** (☑907-772-4600; www.tongasskayak.com; single/double kayaks $55/65).

Petersburg Creek
KAYAKING

This outstanding steelhead and sockeye stream is across from Petersburg on Kupreanof Island and makes for an easy day paddle, beginning from the South Harbor. During high tide you can paddle more than 4 miles up the creek and reach a trailhead for the Petersburg Lake Trail. Tongass Kayak Adventures offer a guided four-hour paddle up the creek ($95 per person).

LeConte Glacier
KAYAKING

The most spectacular paddle in the region is to LeConte Glacier, 25 miles east of Petersburg. It's North America's southernmost tidewater glacier. From town, it takes one to two days to reach the frozen monument, including crossing Frederick Sound north of Coney Island.The crossing should be done at slack tide, as winds and tides can cause choppy conditions.

If the tides are judged right, and the ice is not too thick, it's possible to paddle far enough into LeConte Bay to camp within view of the glacier.

ADVENTUROUS KAYAKING

One of the best kayaking adventures in Southeast Alaska is the paddle from the Alaska Native village of Kake to Petersburg. This 90-mile route follows Kupreanof Island's west side through Keku Strait, Sumner Strait and up the Wrangell Narrows to Petersburg. The highlight of the trip is Rocky Pass, a remote and narrow winding waterway in Keku Strait that has almost no boat traffic other than the occasional kayaker. This seven- to 10-day trip is easy to put together – kayaks can be rented in Petersburg and transported on the state ferry to Kake – but is not an outing for novice paddlers. Caution has to be used in Sumner Strait, which lies only 40 miles away from open ocean and has its share of strong winds and waves.

Tongass Kayak Adventures offers an easier outing: its 10-hour tour ($285 per person) begins with a cruise to the glacier, then paddling among the icebergs. There's also a six-hour (two paddling) version for $245.

Thomas Bay
KAYAKING

Impressive Thomas Bay is 20 miles from Petersburg and north of LeConte Bay on Frederick Sound's east side. The bay has a pair of glaciers, including Baird Glacier, where many paddlers go for day hikes. The mountain scenery around the bay is spectacular. Paddlers should allow four to seven days for the round-trip out of Petersburg.

The area has three USFS cabins: **Swan Lake Cabin** (per night $35), **Spurt Cove Cabin** (per night $25) and **Cascade Creek Cabin** (per night $35). All require reservations.

Whale Watching
Petersburg offers some of the best whale watching in Southeast Alaska. From mid-May to mid-September humpback whales migrate through, and feed in, Frederick Sound, 45 miles northwest of Petersburg. Other wildlife that can be spotted includes Steller's sea lions, orcas and seals.

Whale Song Cruises (☑907-772-9393; www.whalesongcruises.com; $371 per person), with a two-person minimum, is equipped with a hydrophone so you can listen to the whales as well as see them.

☞ Tours

For a large selection of area tours, head to **Viking Travel** (☑907-772-3818, 800-327-2571, www.alaskaferry.com; 101 N Nordic Dr), which acts as a clearinghouse for just about every tour in town. Possibilities include a four-hour boat tour to LeConte Glacier ($212), an eight-hour whale-watching tour ($371) and a helicopter flightseeing tour with glacier walk ($322).

Most of the charter operators that do whale watching also have sightseeing trips to view LeConte Glacier. **Pacific Wings** (☑907-772-4258; www.pacwing.com) and **Nordic Air** (☑907-772-3535; www.nordicairflying.com) offer flightseeing trips to the glacier ($190 to $215 per person).

✿ Festivals & Events

The community's best event, famous around the Southeast, is the **Little Norway Festival**, held the third full weekend in May. The festival celebrates Norwegian Constitution Day (May 17). The locals dress in traditional costumes, there's a foot race in the morning and Nordic Dr is filled with a string of craft booths and beer tents. But best of all are the fish and shrimp evening feeds, all-you-can-possibly-manage-to-eat affairs.

Other festivals are a lively **Fourth of July** celebration and the **Rainforest Festival** (www.tongassrainforestfestival.org) on the second weekend of September.

🛏 Sleeping

Petersburg already needed budget lodging and campsites in town, and then its only hostel closed in 2011. The city adds 10% sales and bed tax on accommodations.

Ohmer Creek Campground
CAMPGROUND $

(☑information 907-772-3871; Mile 22, Mitkof Hwy; campsites $6) The USFS campground is 22 miles southeast of town, but it's cheap and very scenic. It has 15 sites (for tents or RVs), an interpretive trail and fishing in the creek.

Frog's RV Park
CAMPING

(☑360-482-8589; 126 Scow Bay Loop Rd; tent/RV sites $10/30; ☞) Petersburg's only waterfront campground is two and a half miles past the ferry terminal. It's not much more than a gravel parking lot with seven RV sites and two tent sites, but the views make up for it.

★The Lucky Loon
GUESTHOUSE $$

(☑907-772-2345; www.theluckyloon.com; 181 Frederick Dr; d $150; ☞) If you've had it with the cruise-ship crowds, this is your escape: a beautiful home in its own wooded retreat, 3 miles from downtown Petersburg. From the deck, kitchen and living room you enjoy a spectacular view of Frederick Sound, watching an assortment of wildlife pass by every day – from bald eagles and sea lions to humpback whales.

For what you pay for a room in town, you get the entire home. The only drawback is a five-night minimum, but what a way to spend five days. The owner was also in the process of building a beautiful, self-contained apartment next door.

Scandia House
HOTEL $$

(☑907-772-4281; www.scandiahousehotel.com; 110 Nordic Dr; s/d $110/150 ste $190; ☞) The most impressive place in town, this hotel has 33 bright and modern rooms, some with kitchenettes, and a main-street location. Rates include courtesy shuttle service from the airport/ferry and muffins and coffee in the morning – though it's hard to pass up the jolting espresso in the adjoining Java Hus.

Waterfront B&B   B&B $$
(☑907-772-9300, 866-772-9301; www.waterfront
bedandbreakfast.com; 1004 S Nordic Dr; r $110-145;
☎) The closest place to the ferry terminal –
it's practically next door. It has an outdoor
hot tub where you can soak while watching
the ferry depart. Five bright and comfort-
able rooms have private bath and share a
living room that overlooks the Petersburg
Shipwrights.

For many guests, watching a boat being
repaired on dry dock is far more interesting
than whatever is on TV.

Nordic House   B&B $$
(☑907-772-3620; www.nordichouse.net; 806 S
Nordic Dr; r without bathroom $82-149; ☎) With-
in an easy walk of the ferry terminal, this
place offers seven rooms that are large and
clean. Guests have use of a kitchen/common
area that overlooks the boat harbor.

Tides Inn   MOTEL $$
(☑907-772-4288; www.tidesinnalaska.com; 307 1st
St; s $115-126, d $132-143; ☎) The largest mo-
tel in town has 43 rooms, some with kitch-
enettes. Rates include a light continental
breakfast (with waffles!).

✕ Eating

Petersburg's main supermarket, **Hammer
& Wikan** (1300 Howkan; ☉7am-8pm Mon-Sat,
8am-7pm Sun), is off Haugen Dr on the way
to the airport.

★ Inga's Galley   SEAFOOD $
(104 N Nordic Dr; sandwiches $10, dinner mains $8-
12; ☉11am-8pm Mon-Sat) From this (surpris-
ingly charming) parking-lot shack comes
Petersburg's most creative food. Inga's Mit-
kof sandwich is seasoned and seared halibut
topped with pesto, prosciutto and melted
provolone. The fish 'n' chips is fresh rockfish
rolled in Panko (Japanese breadcrumbs).
There are also nonseafood items on the
menu and a large tent with heaters where
you can mingle with locals while staying dry
and warm.

Coastal Cold Storage   SEAFOOD $
(306 N Nordic Dr; breakfast $4-8, lunch $8-12;
☉7am-2pm Tue-Sat; ☎) You're in Petersburg –
indulge in what they catch. Stop at this
processor/seafood store/restaurant for a
shrimp burger, salmon-halibut chowder or
the local specialty, halibut beer bits. Or pur-
chase whatever is swimming in the tanks:
steamer clams, oysters or Dungeness crab.
In the coolers you find just-made salmon

sandwiches, shrimp salads, halibut cheeks
and even squid bait. Need a beer with those
bits? The staff will deliver your order next
door to the Harbor Bar.

Pappa Bear's Pizza   PIZZA $$
(219 N Nordic Dr; pizzas $18-25; ☉11am-8pm Mon-
Sat) This place hops at lunchtime, serving
pizza whole or by the slice, along with subs
and burger baskets. If you're ready to ditch
your vegetarian ways, order the Carnivore
pizza that comes topped with pepperoni,
Italian sausage, Canadian bacon and an assortment of other animal parts.

🍷 Drinking

Java Hus   COFFEE HOUSE
(Nordic Dr; ☉6am-6pm Mon-Sat, 7am-4pm Sun)
This is where Petersburg gets buzzed first
thing in the morning. Unfortunately, there's
no wi-fi connection.

Harbor Bar   BAR
(310 Nordic Dr; ☎) The classic place of deckhands and cannery workers, with pool tables, free popcorn and an excellent beer
selection.

Kito's Kave   BAR
(Sing Lee Alley; ☎) This bar has regular live
music and dancing and can be a rowdy place
that hops until well after midnight. In the
afternoon it's quieter and you can tap into
its wi-fi for the price of a beer.

🛍 Shopping

Sing Lee Alley Books   BOOKS
(11 Sing Lee Alley; ☉9:30am-5:30pm Mon-Sat,
10am-4pm Sun) In a former 1929 board-
inghouse, this delightful bookstore has five
rooms of books and a well-read proprietor.

ℹ Information

Petersburg Public Library (cnr Haugen Dr &
2nd St; ☉noon-9pm Mon-Thu, 10am-5pm Fri
& Sat; ☎) Petersburg's new library is a beauty
with works of art adorning the walls and a fire
casting a glow over enticing easy chairs.

Petersburg Medical Center (☑907-772-4299;
103 Fram St) Has a 24-hour emergency room,
and on Saturday operates as a drop-in health
clinic.

First Bank (103 N Nordic Dr) 24-hour ATM.

Post Office (1201 Haugen Dr) Half a mile east
of downtown on the way to the airport.

Petersburg Visitor Center (☑907-772-4636;
www.petersburg.org; cnr Fram & 1st Sts; ☉9am-
5pm Mon-Sat, noon-4pm Sun) A good first stop,

with both tourist and USFS information; its free *Petersburg Map* will lead you straight.

USFS Petersburg Ranger District (☑ 907-772-3871; 12 N Nordic Dr; ⊘ 8am-4:30pm Mon-Fri) For information about hiking trails, paddling, camping or reserving cabins.

ℹ️ Getting There & Around

There are daily northbound and southbound flights with **Alaska Airlines** (☑ 907-772-4255, 800-426-0333; www.alaskaair.com). The airport is on Haugen Dr, a quarter-mile east of the post office.

The **Alaska Marine Highway** (☑ 907-772-3855; www.ferryalaska.com) is a mile south of downtown; in the summer there is a ferry passing through in one direction or the other almost daily. On Tuesday the high-speed MV *Fairweather* makes a straight run between Juneau and Petersburg ($66, 4½ hours).

There are plans to begin the Rainforest Islands Ferry service. Check with the **City of Coffman Cove** (☑ 907-329-2233; www.ccalaska.com) for the latest.

Scandia House rents midsize cars for $70 a day. For 24-hour taxi service, there's **Midnight Rides Cab** (☑ 907-772-2222). **Life Cyclery** (☑ 907-650-7387; www.lifecyclery.com; 402 N 2nd Ave; half day $30; ⊘ 10am-5pm Tue-Fri, from noon Sat) rents hybrid bicycles ($30 for four hours).

NORTHERN PANHANDLE

Southeast Alaska gets serious when you enter the northern half of the Panhandle. The mountains get higher, the glaciers are more numerous, fjords seem steeper and there's more snow in the winter that lingers on the mountains longer into the summer. You have the current capital and a former one. You have Alaska's most famous gold rush and two roads that actually go somewhere else. Most of all, the dramatic scenery you witness in the Northern Panhandle leads to great wilderness adventures, whether it's canoeing across Admiralty Island, kayaking in Glacier Bay or hiking on Mendenhall Glacier.

Sitka

POP 9050

Fronting the Pacific Ocean on Baranof Island's west shore, Sitka is a sparkling gem in a beautiful setting. Looming on the western horizon, across Sitka Sound, is the impressive Mt Edgecumbe, an extinct volcano with a graceful cone similar to Japan's Mt Fuji.

Closer in, myriad small, forested islands out in the Sound turn into beautiful ragged silhouettes at sunset, competing for attention with the snowcapped mountains and sharp granite peaks flanking Sitka on the east. And in town, picturesque remnants of Sitka's Russian heritage are tucked around every corner.

Sitka is the heart of the Russian influence in Southeast Alaska. The Russians may have landed here as early as 1741 and they stayed for more than a century – until 1867, when the Americans arrived after purchasing Alaska from them.

Today Sitka's Russian history, the main attraction for tourists, is as interesting and as well preserved as the Klondike Gold Rush era is in Skagway. The heart of Sitka's downtown is St Michael's Cathedral, the city's beloved Russian Orthodox church, with Lincoln St serving as Main St. From here you're within easy walking distance of almost all of Sitka's attractions including Sitka National Historical Park, filled with totems and Russian artifacts.

◉ Sights

Sitka Historical Society Museum   MUSEUM (www.sitkahistory.org; 330 Harbor Dr; admission $3; ⊘ 9am-5pm Mon-Fri, to 4pm Sat & Sun) Within Sitka's **Centennial Building** is this museum, which is one room with a good portion of it a gift shop. The rest is crammed with a collection of relics, a model of the town as it appeared in 1867 and displays on Russian Alaska. Outside between the museum and the library is an impressive handcarved Tlingit canoe, made from a single log.

St Michael's Cathedral   CHURCH (240 Lincoln St; suggested donation $10; ⊘ 9am-4pm Mon-Fri or by appt) Two blocks west of the Centennial Building is the cathedral. Built between 1844 and 1848, the church stood for more than 100 years as Alaska's finest Russian Orthodox cathedral. When a fire destroyed it in 1966, the church had been the oldest religious structure from the Russian era in Alaska. Luckily the priceless treasures and icons inside were saved by Sitka's residents, who immediately built a replica of their beloved church. There's a cathedral-run bookstore across the street.

Castle Hill & Totem Square   HISTORIC SITES Walk west on Lincoln St for the walkway to Castle Hill. Kiksadi clan houses once covered the hilltop site, but in 1836 the Russians built 'Baranov's Castle' atop the hill

Sitka

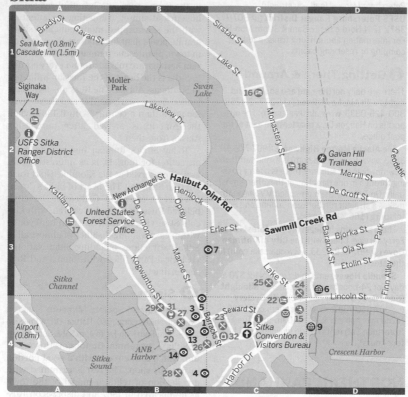

to house the governor of Russian America. It was here, on October 18, 1867, that the official transfer of Alaska from Russia to the USA took place. The castle burned down in 1894.

More Russian cannons and a totem pole can be seen in **Totem Square**, near Lincoln St's end.

Across Katlian St from the square is the prominent, yellow **Alaska Pioneers Home**. Built in 1934 on the old Russian Parade Ground, the home is for elderly Alaskans. The 13ft-tall bronze prospector statue in front of the state home is modeled on long-time Alaska resident William 'Skagway Bill' Fonda.

Blockhouse & Princess Maksoutoff's Grave
HISTORIC SITES

Sitka's Russian background guards the hill north of the Alaska Pioneers Home. The **blockhouse** (cnr Kogwanton & Marine Sts) is a replica of what the Russians used to protect their stockade from the Indian village.

Across Marine St, at the top of Princess St, is **Princess Maksoutoff's Grave** (Lutheran Cemetery), marking the spot where the wife of Alaska's last Russian governor is buried. A strategically placed chain-link fence and a bright and shiny sign proclaims this tiny three-grave site as the Lutheran Cemetery.

Cynics might postulate that the princess probably lost her status as a bona fide Lutheran when she married the Russian Orthodox governor, but now that she's a bona fide tourist attraction the Lutherans want her back. More old headstones and Russian Orthodox crosses can be found in the overgrown and quintessentially creepy **Russian Cemetery** (located at the north end of Observatory St, or just squeak through the gap in the chain-link fence behind the princess' grave), where the drippy verdure seems poised to swallow up the decaying graves.

home to a small but excellent collection of indigenous Alaska artifacts gathered between 1888 and 1898 by Dr Sheldon Jackson, a minister and federal education agent in Alaska.

Among the artifacts are Native masks, hunting tools and baskets, and a collection of boats and sleds used in Alaska – from reindeer sleds and dogsleds to *umiaks* (kayaks).

Sitka Sound Science Center HATCHERY, AQUARIUM
(www.sitkascience.org; 801 Lincoln St; admission $5; ⊙9am-4pm; ⊛) Sitka's best children's attraction is this hatchery and science center. Outside, the facade is being restored to its original appearance. Inside the science center are five aquariums, including the impressive 800-gallon 'Wall of Water' and three touch tanks where kids can get their hands wet handling anemones, sea cucumbers and starfish. Watch feedings on Tuesday and Friday at 2pm. Outside is a working hatchery where tanks are filled with 60,000 salmon fryling.

Sitka National Historical Park HISTORIC SITE
(www.nps.gov/sitk/index.htm; Lincoln St; ⊙8am-5pm) FREE Lincoln St ends at this 113-acre park, Alaska's smallest national park, at the site where the Tlingits were finally defeated by the Russians in 1804.

Totem Trail leads you one mile past 18 totems first displayed at the 1904 Louisiana Exposition in St Louis and then moved to the park. It is these intriguing totems, standing in a beautiful rainforest setting by the sea and often enveloped in mist, that have become synonymous with the national park and even the city itself.

Eventually you arrive at the site of the Tlingit fort near Indian River, where its outline can still be seen. You can either explore the trail as a self-guided tour or join the ranger-led 'Battle Walk.'

The **visitors center** displays Russian and indigenous artifacts, and a 12-minute video in the theater provides an overview of the Tlingit and Russian battle. You can also dial into a cell phone tour that will guide you through the park and center.

Here, the Tlingits defended their wooden fort for a week. The Russians' cannons did little damage to the walls of the Tlingit fort and, when the Russian soldiers stormed the structure with the help of Aleuts, they were repulsed in a bloody battle. It was only when the Tlingits ran out of gunpowder and flint, and slipped away at night, that the Russians were able to enter the deserted fort.

Russian Bishop's House HISTORIC BUILDING
(☑907-747-0135; Lincoln St; adult/child $4/free; ⊙9am-5pm) East of downtown along Lincoln St, the Russian Bishop's House is the oldest intact Russian building in Sitka. Built in 1843 out of Sitka spruce, the two-story log house is one of the few surviving examples of Russian colonial architecture in North America. The National Park Service (NPS) has restored the building to its condition in 1853, when it served as a school, bishop's residence and chapel. The 1st-floor museum is free, while the tours to the 2nd floor are well worth the price of admission.

Sheldon Jackson Museum MUSEUM
(104 College Dr; adult/child $5/free; ⊙9am-5pm) East along Lincoln St on the former campus of Sheldon Jackson College is Sheldon Jackson Museum. The college may be gone, but this fine museum survived because the state of Alaska purchased it in 1983. The unusual building, the first concrete one in Alaska, is

Sitka

Alaska Raptor Center WILDLIFE RESERVE
(☎907-747-8662; www.alaskaraptor.org; 101 Sawmill Creek Rd; adult/child $12/6; ☺8am-4pm; ⊞) The raptor center is reached by turning left on the first gravel road after crossing Indian River. The 17-acre center treats 200 injured birds a year, with its most impressive facility being a 20,000-sq-ft flight-training center that helps injured eagles, owls, falcons and hawks regain their ability to fly. In the center eagles literally fly past you, only 2ft or 3ft away, at eye level; it's so close you can feel the wind from their beating wings – amazing.

🏃 Activities

Hiking
Sitka offers superb hiking in the beautiful and tangled forest surrounding the city. A complete hiking guide is available from the USFS Sitka Ranger District office. **Sitka Trail Works** (www.sitkatrailworks.org), a nonprofit group that raises money for trail improvements, has additional trail information on its website and arranges hikes on weekends throughout the summer.

Indian River Trail HIKING
This easy trail is a 4.5-mile walk along a clear salmon stream to Indian River Falls, an 80ft cascade at the base of the Three Sis-

ters Mountains. The hike takes you through typical Southeast rainforest and offers the opportunity to view brown bears, deer and bald eagles. Plan on four to five hours round-trip to the falls.

The new trailhead is a short walk from the town center, off Sawmill Creek Rd, just east of Sitka National Cemetery. Turn onto Indian River Rd, and go a short ways to the end, where you'll find the new parking lot and trailhead.

Gavan Hill Trail HIKING
Close to town is this popular mountain climb, a trail that ascends almost 2500ft over 1.6 miles to Gavan Hill ridge. The trail offers excellent views of Sitka and the surrounding area. From the trail's end, the adventurous can continue to the peaks of the Three Sisters Mountains.

Gavan Hill is linked to **Harbor Mountain Trail**. Halfway across the alpine ridge is a free-use emergency shelter available on a first-come, first-served basis; it's 3 miles from the Gavan Hill trailhead, a hike of three to four hours.

The trailhead and a small parking area are just before the cemetery gate at the end of Baranof St. Camping is good in the trail's alpine regions, but bring drinking water as it is unavailable above the treeline.

Sitka Cross Trail   HIKING

This easy, well-used, 3-mile trail runs roughly from one end of town to the other. The west end starts at Kramer Ave but you can pick it up off of Verstovia Rd. The trail heads east, crossing Gavan Hill Trail and ending at Indian River Trailhead. Make an 8-mile loop by going up Harbor Mountain and down Gavan Hill.

Along the way you'll pass peat bogs and old-growth forests.

Harbor Mountain Trail   HIKING

This trail ascends in a series of switchbacks to alpine meadows, knobs and ridges with spectacular views. It follows the tundra ridge to the free-use shelter between Harbor Mountain and Gavan Hill, where you can pick up Gavan Hill Trail. Plan on spending two to four hours if you are just scrambling through the alpine area above Harbor Mountain Rd.

The USFS recently applied a major restoration to the trail; steep grades have been rerouted and the tread smoothed with gravel. Several rock benches make great picnic spots.

This trail is reached from Harbor Mountain Rd, one of the few roads in the Southeast providing access to a subalpine area. Head 4 miles northwest from Sitka on Halibut Point Rd to the junction with Harbor Mountain Rd. A parking area and picnic shelter are 4.5 miles up the rough dirt road. Another half-mile further is the parking lot at road's end, where an unmarked trail begins on the lot's east side.

Mosquito Cove Trail   HIKING

At the northwest end of Halibut Point Rd, 0.7 miles past the ferry terminal, Starrigavan Recreation Area offers a number of short but scenic trails. One of them, Mosquito Cove Trail, is an easy and scenic 1.5-mile loop over gravel and boardwalk, with a little beach-walking as well.

Mt Verstovia Trail   HIKING

This 2.5-mile (one-way) trail is a challenging climb of 2550ft to the 'shoulder,' a compact summit that is the final destination for most hikers, although it is possible to continue climbing to the peak of Mt Verstovia – also called Mt Arrowhead (3349ft). The panorama from the shoulder on clear days is spectacular, undoubtedly the area's best.

The trailhead is 2 miles east of Sitka, along Sawmill Creek Rd and is posted across from Jamestown Bay. The Russian charcoal pits (signposted) are reached within a quarter-mile, and shortly after that the trail begins a series of switchbacks. It's a four-hour round trip to the shoulder, from where a ridgeline leads north to the peak (another hour each way).

Beaver Lake–Herring Cove Loop   HIKING

Dedicated in 2010, the Herring Cove Trail is a 1.3-mile route that extends north to Beaver Lake Trail, which loops around the lake from Sawmill Creek Campground. Together the two trails make for a 3.6-mile hike from the Herring Cove Trailhead, featuring three waterfalls, outstanding views of the surrounding mountains and boardwalks that wind through an interesting muskeg.

It begins just past the gate at the eastern end of Sawmill Creek Rd, and is a popular trail for families.

Mt Edgecumbe Trail   HIKING

The 6.7-mile trail begins at the USFS Fred's Creek Cabin (📞877-444-6777, 518-885-3639; www.recreation.gov; cabins $35) and ascends to the crater of this extinct volcano. Views from the summit are spectacular on a clear day. About 4 miles up the trail is a free-use shelter.

Mt Edgecumbe (3201ft) is on Kruzof Island, 10 miles west of Sitka, and is only reached by boat.

Hiking time is five to six hours one way, but by securing Fred's Creek Cabin you can turn the walk into a three-day adventure with two nights spent in shelters. That would be Sitka's best backpacking adventure by far.

Sitka Sound Ocean Adventures offers a water-taxi service to the USFS cabin for $320 round-trip for two passengers.

Kayaking

Sitka also serves as the departure point for numerous blue-water trips along the protected shorelines of Sitka Sound, Baranof and Chichagof Islands. You can rent kayaks in town at Sitka Sound Ocean Adventures (📞907-752-0660; www.kayaksitka.com), which operates from a blue bus in the parking lot near Crescent harbor. Kayaks are available for experienced paddlers (single/double $75/95 per day), as are guided trips. The company's most popular is a 'paddle and cruise,' a 4½-hour tour that includes lunch and one-way boat transportation back so you can paddle further into the Sound ($159).

JUNEAU & THE SOUTHEAST SITKA

Katlian Bay
KAYAKING

This 45-mile round-trip from Sitka Harbor to scenic Katlian Bay (on Kruzof Island's north end) and back is one of the area's most popular paddles. The route follows narrow straits and well-protected shorelines in marine traffic channels, making it an ideal trip for less experienced blue-water paddlers, who will never be far from help.

A scenic sidetrip is to hike the sandy beach from Katlian Bay around Cape Georgiana to Sea Lion Cove on the Pacific Ocean. Catch the tides to paddle the Olga and Neva Straits on the way north and return along Sukot Inlet, staying overnight at the USFS Brent's Beach Cabin (☑877-444-6777, 518-885-3639; www.recreation.gov; cabins $35). Plan on four to six days for the paddle.

Shelikof Bay
KAYAKING

You can combine a 10-mile paddle to Kruzof Island with a 7-mile hike across the island from Mud Bay to Shelikof Bay along an old logging road and trail. Once on the Pacific Ocean side, you'll find a beautiful sandy beach for beachcombing and the USFS Shelikof Cabin (☑877-444-6777, 518-885-3639; www.recreation.gov; cabins $35).

On the northern side of Shelikof Bay, a 7.5-mile hike along old logging roads from Mud Bay, is the North Beach Cabin ($35).

West Chichagof
KAYAKING

Chichagof Island's western shoreline is one of Southeast Alaska's best blue-water destinations for experienced kayakers. The arm is the southern end of a series of straits, coves and protected waterways that shield paddlers from the ocean's swells and extend over 30 miles north to Lisianski Strait. With all its hidden coves and inlets, the trip is a good two-week paddle.

Unfortunately, the trip often requires other transportation, because few paddlers have the experience necessary to paddle the open ocean around Khaz Peninsula (which forms a barrier between Kruzof Island's north end and Slocum Arm, the south end of the West Chichagof-Yakobi Wilderness). For most paddlers that means a water-taxi service to take you there.

Travelers with more time and a sense of adventure could continue another 25 miles through Lisianski Strait to the fishing village of Pelican, where the ferry stops twice a month in summer. Such an expedition would require at least two to three weeks.

Whale Watching

Many companies in Sitka offer boat tours to view whales and other marine wildlife, and most of them swing past St Lazaria Island National Wildlife Refuge, home to 1500 pairs of breeding tufted puffins.

Allen Marine Tours
CRUISE

(☑907-747-8100; www.allenmarinetours.com; adult/child $99/69; ⏱1:30-4:30pm Sat) Offers wildlife cruises whenever cruise ships are in. On Saturday the three-hour tour (adult/child $99/69) departs 1:30pm from the Crescent Harbor dock to view whales, sea otters, puffins and other wildlife. Reservations are not needed for the Saturday special.

Whale Park
WHALE WATCHING

(Sawmill Creek Rd) If you can't afford a wildlife cruise, try Whale Park, 6 miles south of downtown, which has a boardwalk and spotting scopes overlooking the ocean. Best of all is listening to whale songs over the 'hydrophone.' Fall is the best time to sight cetaceans; as many as 80 whales – mostly humpbacks – can gather between mid-September and year's end.

☞ Tours

Sitka Tours
BUS

(☑907-747-8443; www.sitkatoursalaska.com; adult/child $20/10) If you're only in Sitka for as long as the ferry stopover, don't despair: Sitka Tours runs a two-hour bus tour just for you. The tour picks up and returns passengers to the ferry terminal, making brief visits to Sitka National Historical Park and St Michael's Cathedral. Time is allotted for obligatory T-shirt shopping.

Fortress of the Bear
BEAR WATCHING

(☑907-747-3550; www.fortressofthebear.com; adult/child $10/5) If you haven't seen a bear in the wild – or don't want to – this attraction offers an opportunity to observe brown bears that were abandoned as cubs. The walls of the 'fortress' are actually wastewater treatment pools left over after the lumber mill near the end of Sawmill Creek Rd closed in 1993.

The setting is a little strange and these are captive bears, but they are incredibly active – swimming, wrestling and just being bears. Bus transportation from downtown included.

Sitka Tribal Tours
CULTURAL

(☑907-747-7137; www.sitkatours.com) A wide array of local tours with an Alaska Native perspective. Tribal Tours' 3½-hour bus tour includes Sitka National Historical Park, Alaska Raptor Center and a Tlingit Native dance performance. Custom tours that include hiking Starrigavan Trail may be available as well.

Festivals & Events

Sitka Summer Music Festival (☎907-747-6774; www.sitkamusicfestival.org; ☉ Jun) extends Sitka's reputation as the Southeast's cultural center at this three-week event in June, which brings together professional musicians for chamber-music concerts and workshops. The evening concerts are truly a treat for the senses: classical music filling Centennial Hall, where the glass backdrop of the stage gives way to views of the harbor, snow-covered mountains and eagles soaring in the air. The highly acclaimed event is so popular you should purchase tickets in advance of your trip.

The first weekend in August is the Sitka Seafood Festiva (www.sitkaseafoodfestival.org; ☉early Aug), which sees chefs, food lovers and fisher folk come together to enjoy Alaska's favorite natural resource: wild salmon.

On the weekend nearest October 18, the Alaska Day Festival sees the city re-enact – in costumes and even beard styles of the 1860s – the transfer of the state from Russia to the USA.

The city stages WhaleFest (☎907 747 7964; www.sitkawhalefest.org; ☉early Nov) in the first weekend of November to celebrate the large fall gathering of humpbacks, with whale-watching cruises, lectures, craft shows and more.

Sleeping

Sitka levies a 12% city and bed tax on all lodging. Two USFS campgrounds are in the area, but neither is close to town.

Southeast of town, via Sawmill Creek Rd and Blue Lake Rd, is a free campground (Blue Lake Rd; campsites free) that features mountain scenery, the Beaver Lake Trail and fishing opportunities. However, when we visited it was being renovated with tentative plans to reopen in 2015. Contact the Forest Service (USFS; ☎907-747-6671; 204 Siginaka Way; ☉8am-4:30pm Mon-Fri) for updated information.

★ Sitka International Hostel HOSTEL $
(☎907-747-8661; sitkahostel.org; 109 Jeff Davis St; dm $24-69, r $65; 🖥) Sitka's top-notch hostel

is downtown in the historic Tillie Paul Manor, which once served as the town's hospital. The building has been totally renovated and now features a men's room with its own kitchen and several women's rooms, along with a family room, another small kitchen and a lovely sun porch with a mountain view.

Beds are comfortable and are made up with soft flannel sheets. The hostel is locked from 10am to 6pm, but hostel managers are good about greeting late-night arrivals who call ahead.

Ann's Gavan Hill B&B B&B $
(☎907-747-8023; www.annsgavanhill.com; 415 Arrowhead St; s/d $75/95; @🖥) An easy walk (or two minute bus ride) from downtown is this Alaskan home, with a wraparound deck that includes two hot tubs. There are six bedrooms with shared baths that are comfortable and equipped with TV and DVD. The proprietor is delightfully informative, and serves up a full breakfast.

Starrigavan Recreation Area CAMPGROUND $
(☎518-885-3639, reservations 877-444-6777; www.recreation.gov; Mile 7.8, Halibut Point Rd; campsites $12-16) Sitka's finest campground has 35 sites for three types of campers: RVers, car-and-tenters, and backpackers and cyclists. You're 7 miles north of town, but the coastal scenery is beautiful and nearby is Old Sitka State Historic Site. There are bird- and salmon-viewing decks, several hiking trails and (for mountain bikers) Nelson Logging Rd. Sites can be reserved in advance.

On-site is also a USFS cabin ($50), and there are plans to add a yurt.

WILDERNESS CABINS

Nearly two dozen USFS cabins lie within 30 minutes' flying time of Sitka. Among the most popular cabins are **Baranof Lake Cabin**, which enjoys a scenic (though reportedly buggy) mountainous setting on the island's east side; barrier-free **Lake Eva Cabin**, also on Baranof Island's east shore, north of the Baranof Lake Cabin; and **White Sulphur Springs Cabin**, on the west shore of Chichagof Island, which is popular with locals because of the adjacent hot-springs bathhouse.

All cost $35 to $45 per night and should be reserved in advance through the **USFS** (☎518-885-3639, 877-444-6777; www.recreation.gov; 204 Siginaka Way). For air-taxi service, try Harris Aircraft Services.

Fly-in Fish Inn   BOUTIQUE HOTEL $$
(☎907-747-7910; www.flyinfishinn.com; 485 Katlian St; r $179-225; @) In the middle of Katlian's bustling harbors and canneries is Sitka's best inn. Fly-in Fish Inn is gracious luxury, with 10 large rooms featuring refrigerators, wet bars, microwaves, cable TV – you name it. There's also a restaurant (serving guests a full breakfast), a small bar and a seaplane dock. Arranging a flightseeing or fly-in fishing trip is as easy as calling the front desk and then stepping out of your room.

Hannah's B&B   B&B $$
(☎907-747-8309; www.hannahsbandb.com; 504 Monastery St; r $115-125) This long-time B&B proprietor believes that if you're coming to Alaska you're trying to escape, so there are no phones, no TVs and no computers. What she does have is location – only four blocks from Lincoln St – and two beautiful rooms with private baths that include microwaves, mini-refrigerators and private entrances.

Cascade Inn   INN $$
(☎907-747-6804, 800-532-0908; www.cascadeinnsitka.com; 2035 Halibut Point Rd; r $125-160; @) Perched right above the shoreline, all 10 rooms in this inn face the ocean and have a private balcony overlooking it. There are four top-floor rooms with kitchettes. Sure, you're 2.5 miles north of town, but the inn's oceanfront deck is worth the ride on the downtown bus. It's just past the Sea Mart grocery store.

Totem Square Inn   HOTEL $$$
(☎907-747-3693, 866-300-1353; www.totemsquareinn.com; 201 Katlian St; r $225-245; @) This is Sitka's largest hotel, with 68 comfortable rooms featuring the traditional (Alaska Native art and prints on the walls) and the modern (flat-screen TVs, hair dryers and wi-fi). There's a work-out facility, laundry, business center and free airport shuttle. The rooms overlook either the historic square or a harbor bustling with boats bringing in the day's catch.

Westmark Sitka Hotel   HOTEL $$$
(☎907-747-6241, 800-544-0970; www.westmarkhotels.com; 330 Seward St; r/ste $279/299; @) The business traveler's favorite, it has 106 rooms and suites, a central location, a fine restaurant and bar with views of the harbor and room service.

✖ Eating

★ Homeport Eatery   CAFE $
(www.homeporteatery.com; 209 Lincoln St; paninis & crepes $6-10; ◷7:30am-6pm Mon-Sat) ✦ A gourmet, indoor food court with stalls that serve crepes, paninis and espresso – and there's even a little tavern serving wine and a beer bar in the back. Mix and match, then sit at a big wood table and watch the rain outside.

Back Door Café   COFFEE HOUSE $
(104 Barracks St; snacks $1-5; ◷6:30am-5pm Mon-Frit, to 2pm Sat) Enter this small coffee house through either Old Harbor Books on Lincoln St or the...you guessed it...which is off Barracks St. The cruise-ship hordes parading endlessly down Lincoln St can't immediately see it so they go elsewhere. As a result, this cafe is as local as it gets.

Kenny's Wok & Teriyaki   CHINESE $
(210 Katlian St; lunch $7-10, dinner $9-12; ◷11:30am-9pm Mon-Fri, from noon Sat & Sun) This Chinese restaurant always seems packed. That's because it has only nine tables, and the locals love the portions and the prices. You might have to share a table, but the lunch-bowl specials ($8) are the best meal deal in Sitka.

Highliner Coffee   CAFE $
(www.highlinercoffee.com; 327 Seward St, Seward Sq Mall; light fare under $5; ◷6am-5pm Mon-Sat, 7am-4pm Sun) At the Highliner they like their coffee black and their salmon wild, which explains why the walls are covered with photos of local fishing boats or political

stickers like 'Invest in Wild Salmon's Future: Eat One!' Sip a warming latte and indulge in a bagel sandwich.

Sea Mart SUPERMARKET $
(1867 Halibut Point Rd; ⊘24hr) Sitka's main supermarket is northwest of town and never closes. Inside it has an ATM, bakery, deli, ready-to-eat items and a dining area overlooking Mt Edgecumbe. The Bus' red line stops here.

Larkspur Café CAFE $$
(2 Lincoln St; sandwiches $8-12, dinner mains $8-20; ⊘8am-10pm Tue-Sat, 9am-2pm Sun) In the back of the Raven Radio Building is this cozy cafe that has beer on tap, wine by the glass, great desserts and occasional live music at night. It has a blackboard menu that changes daily, but if the smoked salmon soup is listed, order it and then enjoy a bowl of it on the pleasant outdoor porch.

Bayview Pub PUB FOOD $$
(www.sitkabayviewpub.com; 407 Lincoln St; sandwiches $12-16; ⊘11am-late) Head upstairs in the MacDonald Bayview Trading Company Building for the best view of any restaurant in town. Recently remodeled and expanded, the Bayview has house-smoked turkey and pastrami on their sandwiches, and a nice list of wines, and daily specials that feature locally caught fish. Local beer and pool tables also available for later-night fun.

Ludvig's Bistro MEDITERRANEAN $$$
(☑907-966-3663; www.ludvigsbistro.com; 256 Katlian St; tapas $14-18, mains $20-40; ⊘4.30-9:30pm Mon-Sat) Sitka's boldest restaurant has only seven tables and a few stools at its brass-and-blue-tile bar. Described as 'rustic Mediterranean fare,' almost every dish is local, even the sea salt. If seafood paella is on the menu, order it. The traditional Spanish rice dish comes loaded with scallops, king crab, salmon, calamari, prawns and whatever else the local boats netted that day.

An evening here is well worth the wait or even a reservation and you can wait for your table upstairs at their new wine bar.

🍷 Drinking

⭐**Ludvig's Wine Bar & Gallery** WINE BAR
(www.ludvigsbistro.com; 256 Katlian St; ⊘5-9pm Mon-Sat) Follow the stairs next to Ludvig's Bistro up to a wood-floored art gallery furnished with tall bar tables. You'll find excellent tapas, homemade ice cream and a diverse wine list. Enjoy live music three

times per week and occaisionally salsa dancing. It's a great place to have dessert after dinner downstairs or appetizers while you're waiting for a table.

Baranof Island Brewing Co BREWERY
(www.baranofislandbrewing.com; 215 Smith St; ⊘noon-8pm) Off Sawmill Creek Rd, past the main post office, is Sitka's microbrewery and taproom, producing such beers as Halibut Point Hefeweisen and Redoubt Red Ale. Order a sampler of their beers to wash down a slice of pizza or salmon dip.

Pioneer Bar BAR
(212 Katlian St) The 'P-Bar' is Alaska's classic maritime watering hole. The walls are covered with photos of fishing boats and their crews, big fish and a blackboard with messages like, 'Experienced deckhand looking for scine job.' Don't ring the ship's bell over the bar unless you're ready to buy every crew-member a drink.

⭐ Entertainment

New Archangel Russian Dancers DANCE
(☑907-747-5516; www.newarchangeldancers.com; adult/child $10/5) Whenever a cruise ship is in port, this troupe of more than 30 dancers in Russian costumes takes the stage at Centennial Hall for a half-hour show. A schedule is posted in the hall.

**Sheet'ka Kwaan Naa
Kahidi Dancers** DANCE
(☑907-747-7137; sitkatours.com; 204 Katlian St; adult/child $10/5) These dancers perform traditional Tlingit dances when the cruise ships are in at the Tlingit Clan House, next to the Pioneers' Home.

🛍 Shopping

Old Harbor Books BOOKS
(201 Lincoln St; ⊘Mon-Sat) A fine bookstore with a large Alaska section.

ℹ Information

INTERNET ACCESS
Using a head tax on cruise-ship passengers, the city of Sitka has set up free wi-fi throughout the downtown area. It can be picked up in most cafes, stores, bars and hotels along Lincoln St and Harbor Dr.

Kettleson Memorial Library (320 Harbor Dr; ⊘10am-9pm Mon-Fri, 1-9pm Sat; 🖥) Next door to the Centennial Building, this waterfront building has one of the best library views in Alaska. There are 10 computers for internet access, free wi-fi and tables overlooking the harbor.

MEDICAL SERVICES

Sitka Community Hospital (☑907-747-3241; 209 Moller Dr) By the intersection of Halibut Point Rd and Brady St.

MONEY

First National Bank of Anchorage (318 Lincoln St) Downtown, with a 24-hour ATM.

POST

Pioneer Substation (338 Lincoln St)

TOURIST INFORMATION

Sitka Convention & Visitors Bureau (☑907-747-5940; www.sitka.org; 303 Lincoln St, Suite 4; ⊙8am-5pm Mon-Fri) Across the street from St Michael's cathedral. The bureau also staffs a visitor-information desk in the Centennial Building next to Crescent Harbor.

USFS Sitka Ranger District Office (☑907-747-6671, recorded information 907-747-6685; 204 Siginaka Way, at Katlian St; ⊙8am-4:30pm Mon-Fri) Has information about local trails, camping and USFS cabins.There are tentative plans to move the office, so call before heading there.

❶ Getting There & Away

AIR

Alaska Airlines (☑800-252-7522; www.alaskaair.com) Alaska Airlines has flights to/from Juneau (45 minutes) and Ketchikan (one hour). Its airport is on Japonski Island, 1.8 miles west, or a 20-minute walk, of downtown. The Bus' green line runs to the island but stops short of the airport; a taxi is the easiest way to reach downtown.

Harris Aircraft Services (☑907-966-3050, 877-966-3050; www.harrisair.com) Floatplane air-taxi service to small communities, USFS cabins as well as larger SE towns such as Juneau.

BOAT

The Alaska Marine Highway **ferry terminal** (☑907-747-8737) is 6.5 miles northwest of town; ferries depart in both directions almost daily to Juneau ($45, nine hours), Angoon ($35, six hours), Petersburg ($45, 11 hours) and Tenakee Springs ($35, nine hours).

❶ Getting Around

BOAT

For water-taxi service to USFS cabins, contact **Esther G Sea Taxi** (☑907-738-6481, 907-747-6481; www.puffinsandwhales.com) or Sitka Sound Ocean Adventures (p111).

BUS

Sitka's public bus system, **Community Ride** (☑907-747-7103; adult/child $2/1; ⊙6:30am-7:30pm Mon-Fri), has expanded significantly in recent years and now offers hourly service from downtown to as far south as Whale Park and as far north as the ferry terminal. **Sitka Tours** (☑907-747-5800; one way/round-trip $6/10) meets ferries year-round (one-way/round trip $8/12) and Alaska Airlines flights (one-way/round trip $6/10) in summer for the trip to and from town.

CAR

At the airport, **Northstar Rent-A-Car** (☑907-966-2552, 800-722-6927) rents compacts for $55 per day, but there is a 20% tax. Hey, you get unlimited mileage (like you need that in Sitka).

TAXI

For a ride around Sitka, try **Hank's Taxi** (☑907-747-8888) or **Baranof Taxi** (☑907-738-4722).

BICYCLE

Yellow Jersey Cycle Shop (☑907-747-6317; www.yellowjerseycycles.com; 329 Harbor Dr; per 2hr/day $20/30), across the street from the library, rents quality mountain bikes.

Juneau

POP 33,060

Juneau is a capital of contrasts and conflicts. It borders a waterway that never freezes but lies beneath an ice field that never melts. It was the first community in the Southeast to slap a head tax on cruise-ship passengers but draws more of them (almost a million) than any other town. It's the state capital but since the 1980s Alaskans have been trying to move it. It doesn't have any roads that go anywhere, but half its residents and its mayor opposed a plan to build one that would.

Welcome to America's strangest state capital. In the winter it's a beehive of legislators, their loyal aides and lobbyists locked in political struggles. They no sooner leave than, in May, the cruise ships arrive with swarms of passengers. It's the most geographically secluded state capital in the country, the only one that cannot be reached by car – only boat or plane. And in 2014, it surpassed Fairbanks to become Alaska's second-largest city.

But Juneau is also the most beautiful city in Alaska and arguably the nation's most scenic capital. The city center, which hugs the side of Mt Juneau and Mt Roberts, is a maze of narrow streets running past a mix of new structures, old storefronts and slanted houses, all held together by a network of staircases. The waterfront is bustling with cruise ships, fishing boats and floatplanes buzzing in and out. High above the city is the Juneau Ice Field, covering the Coastal Range and sending glaciers down between the mountains like marshmallow syrup on a sundae.

The state's first major gold strike and the first town to be founded after Alaska's purchase from the Russians, Juneau became the territorial capital in 1906. Juneau's darkest hour occurred in the late 1970s after Alaskans voted to move the state capital again. The so-called 'capital move' put a stranglehold on the growth of Juneau until Alaskans defeated its billion-dollar price tag in a statewide vote in 1982. The referendum gave Juneau new life and the town burst at its seams, booming in typical Alaskan fashion.

While the downtown area clings to a mountainside, the rest of the city 'officially' sprawls over 3100 sq miles to the Canadian border, making it one of the largest cities (in area) in the USA. The city center is the busiest and most popular area among visitors in summer. From downtown, Egan Dr, the Southeast's only four-lane highway, heads northwest to Mendenhall Valley, home to the city's growing residential section, much of its business district and world-famous Mendenhall Glacier. In the Valley, Egan Dr turns into Glacier Hwy, a two-lane road that leads to Auke Bay, site of the Alaska Marine Highway terminal. Across Gastineau Channel is Douglas, a small town that was once the major city in the area.

Considering it's still a state capital, Juneau isn't the hive of cultural activity you might expect. But many find it a refreshing haven of liberalism in a state that is steadily marching to the right. Spend a morning eavesdropping in cafes and coffee houses and you'll hear the environmental and social conscience of Alaska.

For visitors who come to Alaska for outdoor adventure, what really distinguishes the capital from other Alaskan towns – and certainly other state capitals – is the superb hiking. Dozens of great trails surround the city; some begin downtown, just blocks from the capitol. Juneau also serves as the departure point for several wilderness attractions, including paddling paradises such as Glacier Bay National Park, Tracy Arm-Fords Terror Wilderness Area and Admiralty Island National Monument.

 Sights

 In Juneau

State Library, Archives & Museum MUSEUM
(SLAM; Map p118; www.museums.state.ak.us; 395 Whittier St; adult/child $7/free; ⊙8:30am-5:30pm; ♿) The Alaska State Museum was being demolished and rebuilt when we visited, with plans to reopen in 2016. Called SLAM (State Library, Archives and Museum), the new $140 million building will have four times the floor space as the old museum and will house a gift store, cafeteria, auditorium, classroom, reading room, museum galleries, research room, historical library, and state archives.

Juneau-Douglas City Museum MUSEUM
(Map p118; www.juneau.org/parkrec/museum; 114 W 4th St; adult/child $6/free; ⊙9am-6pm Mon-Fri, 10am-4:30pm Sat & Sun) This museum focuses on gold with interesting mining displays and the video *Juneau: City Built On Gold*. If you love to hike in the mountains, the museum's 7ft-long relief map is the best overview of the area's rugged terrain. Tuesday to Thursday the staff leads a historical walking tour (adult/child $25/20) of the downtown area beginning 1:30pm at the museum.

Alaska State Capitol HISTORIC BUILDING
(Map p118; 120 4th St; ⊙8:30am-5pm Mon-Fri, 9:30am-4pm Sat & Sun) Built from 1929 to 1931 as the territorial Federal Building, the capitol looks more like an overgrown high school. Stuffed inside are legislative chambers, the governor's office, and offices for the hundreds of staff members who arrive in Juneau for the winter legislative session.

Free 30-minute tours are held every half-hour and start from the visitor desk in the lobby; a self-guided tour pamphlet is also available.

Last Chance Mining Museum HISTORIC SITE
(Map p118; ☎907-586-5338; 1001 Basin Rd; adult/child $5/free; ⊙9:30am-12:30pm & 3:30-6:30pm) Amble out to the end of Basin Rd, a beautiful half-mile walk from the north end of Gastineau Ave, to the intriguing Last Chance Mining Museum. The former Alaska-Juneau Gold Mining Company complex is now a museum where you can view remains of the compressor house and examine tools of what was once the world's largest hard-rock gold mine.

Juneau

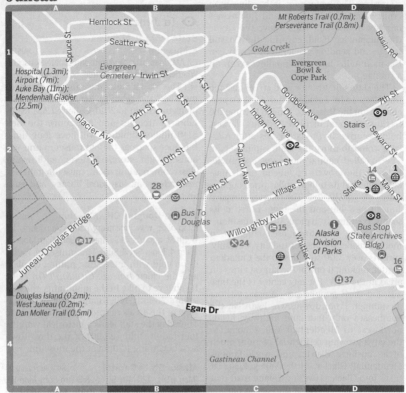

There is also a re-created mining tunnel and a 3D glass map of shafts that shows just how large it was. Nearby is the Perseverance Trail, and combining the museum with a hike to more mining ruins is a great way to spend an afternoon.

Mt Roberts Tramway   CABLE CAR
(Map p122; www.goldbelttours.com; 490 S Franklin St; adult/child $32/16; ☺11am-9pm Mon, 8am-9pm Tue-Sun; 🚹) As far as trams go, this tramway is rather expensive for a five-minute ride. But from a marketing point of view its location couldn't be better. It whisks you right from the cruise-ship dock up 1800ft to the treeline of Mt Roberts, where you'll find a restaurant, gift shops and a small theater with a film on Tlingit culture.

Or skip all that and just use the tram to access the stunning Mt Roberts alpine area, marked with trails and wildflowers. Alternatively, you could hike up the Mt Roberts Trail and take the tram down.

Waterfront Area & South Franklin Street   PLAZA
Between the cruise ships and Willoughby Ave, **Marine Park** is an open space where kids practice skateboard tricks, state workers enjoy a sack lunch and tired tourists occasionally take a sunny nap. The dock has a **sculpture of Patsy Ann** (Map p118), the late faithful Fido, the 'Official Greeter of Juneau,' thanks to her tendency to rush to meet cruise ships.

Spotting scopes let you search Mt Juneau for mountain goats. A block inland from the waterfront is **South Franklin Street**, a refurbished historical district where many buildings date from the early 1900s and have since been turned into bars, gift shops and restaurants.

Museums & Historic Sites   HISTORIC BUILDINGS
Overlooking downtown Juneau is **Wickersham State Historical Site** (Map p118; 213 7th St; ☺10am-5pm Sun-Thu), which preserves

From the outdoor court on the 8th floor there is a spectacular view of the channel and Douglas Island, while in the lobby is a massive Kimball organ dating back to 1928. Every Friday at noon a performance is given, a good reason to join state workers for a brown-bag lunch. West of the SOB along 4th Ave is the pillared **Governor's Mansion** (Map p118; 716 Calhoun Ave). Built and furnished in 1912 at a cost of $44,000, the mansion is not open to the public.

⊙ Around Juneau

Alaskan Brewing Company   BREWERY
(Map p122; www.alaskanbeer.com; 5429 Shaune Dr; ⊙11am-6pm) **FREE** Established in 1986, Alaska's largest brewery is in the Lemon Creek area and reached from Anka St, where the city bus will drop you off, by turning right on Shaune Dr. The beermaker's gift shop downtown, **Alaskan Brewing Co Depot** (Map p118; 219 S Franklin St), also runs a van out to the brewery every hour for $15 per person round trip.

The guided tasting includes viewing the small brewery and a free sampling of lagers and ales plus an opportunity to purchase beer in the gift shop, even 5-gallon party kegs. The brewery's beer-bottle collection from around the world is amazing. So many beers, so little time to drink them.

Mendenhall Glacier   GLACIER
The most famous of Juneau's ice floes, and the city's most popular attraction, is Mendenhall Glacier, Alaska's famous drive-in glacier. The glacier flows 13 miles from its source, the Juneau Ice Field, and has a half-mile-wide face. It ends at Mendenhall Lake, the reason for all the icebergs, but naturalists estimate that within a few years it will retreat onto land and within 25 years retreat out of view entirely from the observation area.

On a sunny day it's beautiful, with blue skies and snowcapped mountains in the background. On a cloudy and drizzly afternoon it can be even more impressive, as the ice turns shades of deep blue.

The river of ice is 13 miles from downtown, at the end of Glacier Spur Rd. From Egan Dr at Mile 9 turn right onto Mendenhall Loop Rd, staying on Glacier Spur Rd when the loop curves back toward Auke Bay.

Near the face of the glacier is the Mendenhall Glacier Visitor Center, which houses various glaciology exhibits, including a fabricated ice face of the glacier along with

the 1898 home of pioneer judge and statesman James Wickersham. In 2011, the museum was closed for extensive renovation. Call to see if it has reopened.

Two blocks downhill is **St Nicholas Russian Orthodox Church** (Map p118; ☏907-586-1023; 326 5th St; admission by donation; ⊙noon-5pm Mon-Fri, to 4pm Sat & Sun). Built in 1893 against the backdrop of Mt Juneau, the onion-domed church is the oldest original one in Alaska. From a small gift shop filled with *matreshkas* (nestling dolls) and other handcrafted items from Russia, you enter the church where, among the original vestments and religious relics, a row of painted saints stare down at you. Playing softly in the background are the chants from a service. If you weren't spiritual before, you probably are now.

Across from the Juneau-Douglas City Museum is the **State Office Building** (Map p118; 400 Willoughby Ave), known locally as the SOB.

Juneau

a large relief map of the ice field, spotting scopes that let you look for mountain goats, and a theater that shows the 11-minute film *Landscape of Change*.

Outside you'll find seven hiking trails (see p123), from a 0.3-mile photo-overlook trail to a trek of several miles up the glacier's west side. The newest is the Nugget Falls Trail that leads a half-mile to the impressive cascade near the face of the glacier. For many the most interesting path is Steep Creek Trail, a 0.3-mile boardwalk that winds past viewing platforms along the stream. From July through September you'll not only see sockeye and coho salmon spawning from the platforms but also brown and black bears feasting on them. This is Southeast Alaska's most affordable bear-viewing site (though it can be partially closed due to heavy bear traffic in summer).

The cheapest way to see the glacier is to hop on a Capital Transit bus, but that leaves you a mile short of it. It's easier to jump on a bus from Mendenhall Glacier Transport/M & M Tours (p126), which picks up from the cruise-ship docks downtown for the glacier,

with a run every 30 minutes. The last bus of the day depends on the cruise-ship schedule.

One of the most unusual outdoor activities in Juneau is glacier trekking: stepping into crampons, grabbing an ice axe and roping up to walk on ice 1000 years old or older. The scenery and the adventure is like nothing you've experienced before as a hiker. The most affordable outing is offered by Above & Beyond Alaska (p135). Utilizing a trail to access Mendenhall Glacier, it avoids expensive helicopter fees on its guided seven-hour outing. The cost is $209 per person and includes all mountaineering equipment and transportation.

Shrine of St Terese SHRINE

(Map p122; ⊙8:30am-10pm) FREE At Mile 23.3 Glacier Hwy is the Shrine of St Terese, a natural stone chapel on a beautifully wooded island connected to the shore by a stone causeway. As well as being the site of numerous weddings, the island lies along the Breadline, a well-known salmon-fishing area in Juneau. It is perhaps the best place to shore fish for salmon.

Point Bridget State Park　　　PARK
(Mile 39, Glacier Hwy) Juneau's only state park is 2850-acre Point Bridget State Park, which overlooks Berners Bay and Lynn Canal; salmon fishing is excellent off the Berners Bay beaches and in Cowee Creek. Hiking trails wander through rainforest, along the park's rugged shoreline and past three rental cabins. The most popular hike is Point Bridget Trail, a 3.5-mile, one-way walk from the trailhead on Glacier Hwy to Blue Mussel Cabin at the point. Here, you can often spot sea lions and seals playing in the surf. Plan on six to seven hours for the round-trip with lunch at the cabin.

🏃 Activities

Cycling

Bike paths run between Auke Bay, Mendenhall Glacier and downtown, and from the Juneau-Douglas Bridge to Douglas. Because most of Juneau's trails are steep, mountain biking is limited, but the Windfall Lake, Perseverance Trail and Peterson Lake trails are popular with off-road cyclists.

Cycle Alaska　　　BICYCLE RENTAL
(Map p118; ☑907-780-2253; www.cycleak.com; 1107 W 8th St; per 4/8hr $35/45; ☺10am-6pm Mon-Sat, 9am-5pm Sun) Rents quality road and mountain bikes along with children's bikes and tandems. The company offers a Bike & Brew (adult/child $99/75), a four-hour bicycle tour that includes Auke Bay, Mendenhall Glacier and finishes off at the Flight Deck.

Gold Panning

Juneau was built on gold or, more realistically, the tailings from its gold mines, and for many visitors that's the most fascinating part of its history. Two of the Juneau area's most successful historic mines were the Alaska-Juneau Mine, on the side of Mt Roberts, and the Treadwell Mine, across Gastineau Channel near Douglas. During its heyday at the turn of the 20th century, the Treadwell made Douglas the channel's major city, with a population of 15,000. For more information about these mines and what you can see of them today, stop by the Juneau-Douglas City Museum.

AJ/Gastineau Mill Enterprises　　　MINE
(☑907-463-5017; adult/child $59/30) Offers a two hour tour of the Gastineau Mill ruins at Sheep Creek, once the world's largest gold mill. The highlight of the tour is following a 360-foot-long conveyor tunnel carved into

---

JUNEAU FOR CHILDREN

Macauley Salmon Hatchery (☑907-463-4810, 877-463-2486; www.dipac.net; 2697 Channel Dr; adult/child $3.25/1.75; ☺10am-6pm Mon-Fri, to 5pm Sat & Sun) The best attraction for kids visiting Juneau is this hatchery, 3 miles northwest of downtown, in the Mendenhall Valley. The visitors center has huge seawater aquariums loaded with local marine life from tanner crabs to octopus, while the interpretive displays explaining the life cycle of salmon are museum quality. Underwater viewing windows and a 450ft fish ladder allow children to witness, from July to September, the amazing sight of thousands of salmon fighting their way upstream to spawn. You can also wander the outside grounds and pier to watch people catching lunker salmon. A behind-the-scenes tour is $10.50.

Twin Lakes Park (Map p122; Old Glacier Hwy) The City of Juneau maintains a wonderful system of parks including Twin Lakes Park, just past the hospital. The heart of the park is Project Playground, an amazing playscape that includes a mini climbing wall, a four-story Swiss chalet and a stairway that makes kids feel like they're salmon spawning upstream. There's also a solar-system trail around the lake that provides a realistic idea of how far each planet is from the sun.

Dimond Park Aquatic Center (☑907-586-2782; www.juneau.org/parkrec; 3045 Riverside Dr; adult/child $8.50/4.50; ☺ 6am-10:30am Mon, to 8pm Tue-Fri, 9am-6pm Sat, noon-6pm Sun) Juneau's newest attraction is this wonderful aquatic center that has flume slides, bubble benches, tumble buckets and interactive water sprays for children – and a hot tub for their parents.

Chum Fun (☑907-398-2486; www.chumfun.com; $99) A salmon fishing charter catering to families with an emphasis on fun, Chum Fun offers three-hour shore fishing tours from the docks at Macauley Hatchery (free tour included). Transportation and all gear are provided, and though they'll take care of your fishing license for you, the $20 fee is not included.

Around Juneau

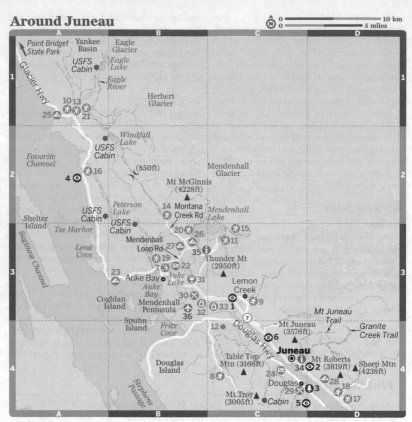

the mountainside where a miner demonstrates the equipment that was used. Gold panning at the end of course.

Hiking

Few cities in Alaska have such a diversity of hiking trails as Juneau. A handful of these trails are near the city centre, the rest are out the road. All five USFS cabins (see p125) should be booked in advance.

Juneau Parks & Recreation (Map p118; 907-586-0428; www.juneau.org/parksrec) offers volunteer-led hikes every Wednesday (adults) and Saturday (kids OK) in 'rain, shine or snow.' Call or check the website for a schedule and the trails. **Gastineau Guiding** (907-586-8231; www.stepintoalaska. com) does guided hikes for small groups that include snacks, ponchos if needed and transportation. Among the offerings is West Glacier Trail (per person $89), a four-and-a-half-hour tour which includes Steep Creek Trail to look for bears.

City Center Trails

Perseverance Trail off Basin Rd is Juneau's most popular. The trail is a path into Juneau's mining history but also provides access to two other popular treks, **Mt Juneau Trail** and **Granite Creek Trail**, and together the routes can be combined into a rugged 10-hour walk for hardy hikers, or an overnight excursion into the mountains surrounding Alaska's capital city.

To reach Perseverance Trail, take 6th St one block southwest to Gold St, which turns into Basin Rd, a dirt road that curves away from the city into the mountains as it follows Gold Creek. The trailhead is at the road's end, at the parking lot for Last Chance Mining Museum. The trail leads into Silverbow Basin, an old mining area that still has many hidden and unmarked adits and mine shafts; be safe and stay on the trail.

From the Perseverance Trail, you can pick up Granite Creek Trail and follow it

Around Juneau

to the creek's headwaters basin, a beautiful spot to spend the night. From there, you can reach Mt Juneau by climbing the ridge and staying left of Mt Olds, the huge rocky mountain. Once atop Mt Juneau, you can complete the loop by descending along the Mt Juneau Trail, which joins Perseverance Trail a mile from its beginning. The hike to the 3576ft peak of Mt Juneau along the ridge from Granite Creek is an easier but longer trek than the ascent from the Mt Juneau Trail. The alpine sections of the ridge are serene, and on a clear summer day you'll have outstanding views. From the trailhead for the Perseverance Trail to the upper basin of Granite Creek is 3.3 miles one-way. Then it's another 3 miles along the ridge to reach Mt Juneau.

Mt Roberts Trail is a 4-mile climb up Mt Roberts. The original trail head has moved from downtown at the northeast end of 6th street to Basin Rid, close to the start of the Perseverance Trail. It starts with a series of switchbacks, then breaks out of the trees at Gastineau Peak and comes to the tram sta-

tion. From here it's a half-mile to the Cross, where you'll have good views of Juneau and Douglas. The Mt Roberts summit (3819ft) is still a steep climb away through the alpine brush. If you hike up, you can ride down the Mt Roberts Tramway to S Franklin St for only $10. And if you purchase $10 worth of food or drink at the visitors center on top, like a beer that you well deserve, the ride down is free.

Dan Moller Trail is a 3.3-mile trail leading to an alpine bowl at the crest of Douglas Island, where you'll find the recently rebuilt Dan Moller Cabin. Just across the channel in West Juneau, the public bus conveniently stops at Cordova St and from there, you turn left onto Pioneer Ave and follow it to the end of the pavement to the trailhead. Plan on six hours for the round-trip.

Mendenhall Glacier Trails
East Glacier Loop (Map p122) is one of many trails near Mendenhall Glacier, a 3-mile round-trip providing good views of the glacier from a scenic lookout at the halfway

point. Pick up the loop along the **Trail of Time**, a half-mile nature walk that starts at the Mendenhall Glacier Visitor Center.

Nugget Creek Trail (Map p122) begins just beyond the East Glacier Loop's scenic lookout. The 2.2-mile trail climbs 500ft to Vista Creek Shelter, a free-use shelter that doesn't require reservations, making the round-trip to the shelter from the Mendenhall Glacier Visitor Center an 8-mile trek. Hikers who plan to spend the night at the shelter can continue along the creek toward Nugget Glacier, though the route is hard to follow at times.

West Glacier Trail (Map p122) was one of the most spectacular hikes in the area, but, while still beautiful with stunning panoramas, the glacier's retreat means you won't have good views until a couple of miles in. The 3.4-mile trail begins off Montana Creek Rd past Mendenhall Lake Campground and hugs the mountainside above the glacier. Within 1.2 miles is a spur to a small shelter and bench now half-hidden in brush. From here an unmaintained trail, marked by cairns, heads for the face of the glacier. It involves more scrambling over rocks but is as popular as the main trail. Allow four to five hours for the West Glacier Trail.

Juneau Area Trails

Point Bishop Trail (Map p122) is at the end of Thane Rd, 7.5 miles southeast of Juneau. This 8-mile trail leads to Point Bishop, a scenic spot overlooking the junction of Stephens Passage and Taku Inlet. The trail is flat but can be wet in many spots, making waterproof boots the preferred footwear. The hike makes for an ideal overnight trip, as there is good camping at Point Bishop.

Montana Creek Trail (Map p122) and **Windfall Lake Trail** (Map p122) connect at Windfall Lake and can be combined for an interesting 11.5-mile overnight hiking trip. It is easier to begin at the trailhead at Montana Creek and follow the Windfall Lake Trail out to the Glacier Hwy. The 8-mile Montana Creek Trail, known for its high concentration of bears, begins near the end of Montana Creek Rd, 2 miles from its junction with Mendenhall Loop Rd. The 3.5-mile Windfall Lake Trail begins off a gravel spur that leaves the Glacier Hwy just before it crosses Herbert River, 27 miles northwest of Juneau. The trail features the popular USFS cabin, **Windfall Lake Cabin**, which sleeps six and is open as a warming shelter during the day.

Spaulding Trail (Map p122) is primarily used for cross-country skiing, but can be hiked in summer (prepare for mud). The 3-mile route provides access to the Auke Nu Trail, which leads to the **John Muir Cabin**. The trailhead is off Glacier Hwy just past and opposite Auke Bay Post Office, 12.3 miles northwest of Juneau.

Peterson Lake Trail (Map p122) is a 4-mile route along Peterson Creek to its namesake lake, a favorite among hike-in anglers for the good Dolly Varden fishing. The trailhead is 20ft before the Mile 24 marker on Glacier Hwy, north of the Shrine of St Terese. Wear rubber boots, as it can be muddy during summer. The **Peterson Lake Cabin** turns this trail into a delightful overnight adventure.

Herbert Glacier Trail (Map p122) extends 4.6 miles along the Herbert River to Herbert Glacier, a round-trip of four to five hours. The trail is easy with little climbing, though wet in places, and begins just past the bridge over Herbert River at Mile 28 of Glacier Hwy.

Amalga Trail (Map p122), also known as the Eagle Glacier Trail, is a level route that winds 7.5 miles to the lake formed by Eagle Glacier and the **Eagle Glacier Cabin**. Less than a mile from the glacier's face, the view from the cabin is well worth the effort of reserving it in advance. The trailhead is beyond the Glacier Hwy bridge, across Eagle River, 0.4 miles past the trailhead for the Herbert Glacier Trail. Plan on a round-trip of seven to eight hours (15 miles) to reach the impressive Eagle Glacier and return to the trailhead.

Paddling

Day trips and extended paddles are possible out of the Juneau area in sea kayaks.

Alaska Boat & Kayak Center　　KAYAKING
(Map p122; ☑ 907-364-2333; www.juneaukayak. com; 11521 Glacier Hwy; s/d kayak $50/70; ⊙ 9am-5pm) Kayak rentals are available from this place, which is based in the Auke Bay Harbor and offers transportation services and multiday discounts. The company also offers half-day and full-day guided paddles.

Mendenhall Lake　　KAYAKING
This lake at the foot of Mendenhall Glacier is an excellent destination for a paddle. Alaska Boat & Kayak offers a self-guided package to Mendenhall Lake ($115), which includes kayaks, transportation and a waterproof map that leads you on a route among the

icebergs. It also shows you where to land for a short hike for close glacier views.

Auke Bay
KAYAKING

The easiest trip is out to and around the islands of Auke Bay. You can even camp on the islands to turn the adventure into an overnight trip.

Taku Inlet
KAYAKING

This waterway is an excellent four- to five-day trip, with close views of Taku Glacier. Total paddling distance is 30 to 40 miles, depending on how far you travel up the inlet. It does not require any major crossing, though rounding Point Bishop can be rough at times.

You can camp at Point Bishop and along the grassy area southwest of the glacier, where brown bears are occasionally seen.

Berners Bay
KAYAKING

At the western end of Glacier Hwy, 40 miles from Juneau, is Echo Cove, where kayakers can paddle Berners Bay's protected waters. The bay, which extends 12 miles north to the outlets of the Antler, Lace and Berners Rivers, is ideal for an overnight trip or longer excursions up Berners River.

The delightful USFS Berners Bay Cabin is an 8-mile paddle from Echo Cove. Alaska Boat & Kayak charges $150 round-trip for transporting two kayaks to Echo Cove.

Whale Watching

The whale watching in nearby Stephens Passage is so good that some tour operators will refund your money if you don't see at least one. The boats depart from Auke Bay, and most tours last three to four hours. Some operators offer courtesy transportation from downtown.

Orca Enterprises
WHALE WATCHING

(Map p122; ☎907-789-6801, 888-733-6722; www.alaskawhalewatching.com; adult/child $119/89) Uses fully wheelchair-accessible jet boats to look at sea lions, orcas and harbor seals as well as humpback whales. Lower prices for infants and kids under 6.

Gastineau Guiding
WHALE WATCHING

(☎907-586-8231; www.stepintoalaska.com; adult/child $199/139) Five-hour tours that combine whale watching with an hour-long hike in the rainforest. Gastineau caters to small groups.

Harv & Marv's
WHALE WATCHING

(☎907-209-7288, 866-909-7288; www.harvandmarvs.com; per person $149) Small, personalized tours with no more than six passengers in the boat.

Ziplining

Juneau has a two zipline courses where you can harness up and fly through 100ft trees like an eagle on the prowl.

WILDERNESS CABINS

Numerous **USFS cabins** (☎877-444-6777, 518-885-3639; www.recreation.gov; cabins $35) are accessible from Juneau, but all are heavily used, requiring advance reservations. If you're just passing through, check with the USFS Juneau Ranger District Office for a list of what's available. The following cabins are within 30 minutes' flying time from Juneau; air charters will cost around $500 to $600 round-trip from Juneau, split among a planeload of up to five passengers. Alaska Seaplane Service (p133) can provide flights on short notice.

West Turner Lake Cabin (cabins $35) is one of the most scenic and is by far the Juneau area's most popular cabin. It's 18 miles east of Juneau on the west end of Turner Lake, where the fishing is good for trout, Dolly Varden and salmon. A skiff is provided.

Admiralty Island's north end has three popular cabins, all $35 a night. **Admiralty Cove Cabin** is on a scenic bay and has access to Young Lake along a rough 4.5-mile trail. Brown bears frequent the area. The two **Young Lake Cabins** have skiffs to access a lake with good fishing for cutthroat trout and landlocked salmon. A lakeshore trail connects the two cabins.

There are also three rental cabins in Point Bridget State Park that rent for $45 a night. **Cowee Meadow Cabin** is a 2.5-mile hike into the park, **Blue Mussel Cabin** is a 3.4-mile walk and **Camping Cove Cabin** a 4-mile trek. Both Blue Mussel and Camping Cove overlook the shoreline and make a great destination for kayakers.

There are three cabins available at Eagle Beach State Recreation Area campground. Reserve them through the **DNR Public Information Center** (☎907-269-8400; www.dnr.state.ak.us/parks/cabins).

Alaska Zipline Adventures   ZIPLINING
(Map p122; ☑907-321-0947; www.alaskazip.com; adult/child $149/99) Located at beautiful Eaglecrest Ski Area on Douglas Island, this course includes seven ziplines and a sky bridge that zigzags across Fish Creek Valley. Transportation is included.

☞ Tours

The easiest way to book a tour in Juneau is to head to the cruise-ship terminal, near the Mt Roberts Tram, where most of the operators will be hawking their wares from a line of booths like sideshow barkers at a carnival.

☞ City & Glacier

Juneau Tours   CITY TOUR
(☑907-523-6095; www.juneautours.com; per person $25) A trolley tour that departs from the Mount Roberts Tram Station and in a 45-minute loop includes the Capitol, Governor's Mansion and even Douglas Island. It also offers a 2½-hour tour that includes the above and a trip to Mendenhall Glacier ($35) and a shuttle to the glacier (round trip $20).

**Mendenhall Glacier Transport/
M & M Tours**   BUS
(☑907-789-5460; www.mightygreattrips.com; per person $35) Offers a city-and-glacier tour ($35) and glacier shuttle (round-trip $20).

☞ Juneau Ice Field

The hottest tour in Juneau is a helicopter ride to the Juneau Ice Field for a 20-minute ride in the basket of a dogsled. These tours last less than two hours and are $500 a pop, but when the weather is nice, people (primarily cruise-ship passengers) are waiting to hand over their money.

NorthStar Trekking   HIKING
(☑907-790-4530; www.northstartrekking.com; per person $409) Skip the dogsled and strap on the crampons. NorthStar offers several glacier treks of varying levels that begin with a helicopter ride and include all equipment and training. On its two-hour glacier trek ($409), you cross 2 miles of frozen landscape riddled with crevasses for a hike that is as stunning as it is pricey.

Era Helicopters   SCENIC FLIGHTS
(Map p122; ☑800-843-1947; www.eraflightseeing.com) You spend an hour on the glacier as part of Era's glacier dogsled adventure

($519). For something more affordable, book its hour-long, four-glacier tour ($299), which includes a 20-minute glacier landing and cruising over the Juneau Icefield.

☞ Tracy Arm

This steep-sided fjord, 50 miles southeast of Juneau, has a pair of tidewater glaciers and a gallery of icebergs floating down its length. Tracy Arm makes an interesting day trip, far less expensive and perhaps even more satisfying than a visit to Glacier Bay. You're almost guaranteed to see seals inside the Arm, and you might spot whales on the way there.

Adventure Bound Alaska   BOAT
(Map p118; ☑907-463-2509, 800-228-3875; www.adventureboundalaska.com; 76 Egan Dr; adult/child $160/95) This longtime tour operator uses a pair of boats that leave daily from the Juneau waterfront. Reserve a seat in advance if you can – the full-day tour is popular with cruise ships – and pack a lunch (you can bring beer or wine!) along with your binoculars.

✯✰ Festivals & Events

Alaska Folk Festival   MUSIC
(www.alaskafolkfestival.org; ⊙mid-Apr) Attracts musicians from around the state for a week of performances, workshops and dances at Centennial Hall in mid-April.

Juneau Jazz & Classics Festival   MUSIC
(www.jazzandclassics.org; ⊙early May) Jazz and classical music concerts and workshops during the first half of May.

Gold Rush Days   CULTURAL
(⊙mid-Jun) Two days of logging and mining events mid-June in Douglas.

Fourth of July   CULTURAL
(⊙Jul 4) Parades, carnival, outdoor food booths and a huge fireworks show over the Gastineau Channel.

⨿ Sleeping

Juneau tacks on 12% in bed and sales taxes to the price of lodging.

★ **Juneau International Hostel**   HOSTEL $
(Map p118; ☑907-586-9559; www.juneauhostel.net; 614 Harris St; dm adult/child $12/5; @ ☜) Alaska's best hostel and certainly its most affordable. One of the eight bunk rooms is a family room, while amenities include laundry, storage and free internet access and wi-

fi. In the lounge area, the overstuffed sofas are strategically placed around a large bay window with a view of snowy peaks and Douglas Island.

Best of all is the downtown location. You're only a few blocks from the Mt Roberts Trail. The only gripes are a strict locking-up (9am to 5pm) and chores.

★ Mendenhall Lake Campground   CAMPGROUND $
(Map p122; ☑ 518-885-3639, reservations 877-444-6777; www.recreation.gov; Montana Creek Rd; tent sites $12, RV sites $23) One of Alaska's most beautiful USFS campgrounds. The 69-site area (17 sites with hookups) is on Montana Creek Rd, off Mendenhall Loop Rd, and has a separate seven-site walk-in area. The campsites are alongside Mendenhall Lake, and many have spectacular views of the icebergs or even the glacier that discharges them.

All the sites are well spread out in the woods, and 20 can be reserved in advance.

Auke Village Campground   CAMPGROUND $
(Map p122; Glacier Hwy; sites $10) Located 2 miles from the ferry terminal on Glacier Hwy, this first-come, first-served USFS campground has 11 sites in a beautiful wooded location overlooking Auke Bay.

Eagle Beach State Recreation Area   CAMPGROUND $
(Map p122; ☑ 907-586-2506; Mile 28, Glacier Hwy; sites $10) This state campground, 15 miles from the ferry terminal and 28 miles from downtown Juneau, is worth the drive. Eagle Beach includes a ranger station, wildlife viewing area and 17 wooded campsites ideal for tents. It's within walking distance of three trails: Amalga (Eagle Glacier), Herbert Glacier and Windfall Lake.

Spruce Meadow RV Park   CAMPGROUND $
(Map p122; ☑ 907-789-1990; www.juneaurv.com; 10200 Mendenhall Loop Rd; tent sites $22-28, RV sites $34-38; ☎) Practically next door to Mendenhall Lake Campground but not nearly as nice is this full-service campground with laundromat, cable TV and tent sites as well as full hookups. It's right on the city bus route.

Alaskan Hotel   HOTEL $
(Map p118; ☑ 907-586-1000, 800-327-9347; www.thealaskanhotel.com; 167 S Franklin St; r with/without shared bath $90/$70, ste $100; ☎) The smallish rooms in this historical hotel are a little worn, but you accept that for the price and the gold-rush ambiance. Most rooms have small refrigerators, sinks and cable TV, but avoid the ones overlooking Franklin St unless you plan to join the revelry below.

Thane Public Campground   CAMPGROUND $
(Map p122; ☑ 907-586-0617; 1585 Thane Rd; tent sites $5) Located a mile south of downtown on Thane Rd is the city-operated, tent-only place that tends to draw transients and seasonal workers; it feels a little rough around the edges.

Auke Lake B&B   B&B $$
(Map p122; ☑ 907-790-3253, 800-790-3253; www.aukelakebb.com; 11595 Mendenhall Loop Rd; r $125-165; ☎) Located 10 minutes from Mendenhall Glacier, this valley B&B has five luxurious rooms with phone, TV, refrigerator and coffeemaker. In the living room is a stuffed giant brown bear, while outside is a beautiful deck and hot tub overlooking Auke Lake. A kayak, a canoe, and a BBQ in a gazebo are available. So Alaskan.

Driftwood Hotel   MOTEL $$
(Map p118; ☑ 907-586-2280; www.driftwoodalaska.com; 435 Willoughby Ave; r $115-125, ste $145-165; ☎) Near the Alaska State Museum, this lodge is the best value in accommodations downtown. The 63 rooms are clean and updated regularly, the motel offers 24-hour courtesy transportation to the airport and the ferry, and it's hard to top the location unless you're willing to spend twice as much.

Beachside Villa Luxury Inn   B&B $$
(Map p122; ☑ 888-879-0858, 907-463-5531; www.beachsidevilla.com; 3120 Douglas Hwy; r $169-279; ☎) This luxurious B&B has five rooms with amenities that range from balconies and private entrances to fireplaces and in-room Jacuzzis. But best of all is its Douglas Island location and views. Perched on the Gastineau Channel, its porches and neatly landscaped backyard overlook downtown Juneau, Mt Roberts and the parade of floatplanes and vessels entering the capital city harbors.

Juneau Hotel   HOTEL $$
(Map p118; ☑ 907-586-5666; www.juneauhotels.net; 1200 W 9th St; ste $174-189; ☎) Located within easy walking distance of downtown attractions, this all-suites hotel is Juneau's best deal in top-end accommodations. The 73 suites have full kitchens, sitting areas, two TVs each and even washers and dryers.

★ **Alaska's Capital Inn**   B&B $$$
(Map p118; ☎907-586-6507, 888-588-6507; www.alaskacapitalinn.com; 113 W 5th St; r incl breakfast $259-$339; @⊜) Political junkies will love this place: it's across the street from the state capitol. In the gorgeously restored home of a wealthy gold rush–era miner, this inn has seven rooms with private bath, phone and TV, and hardwood floors covered by colorful Persian rugs.

In the morning there's a full breakfast, all day there's a bottomless cookie jar, and in the evening wine and cheese is served on the back deck, which overlooks the city. The backyard has multiple decks, gardens and a secluded hot tub that even the governor can't spy on. A Mount Roberts Tram pass comes with every room.

Silverbow Inn   BOUTIQUE HOTEL $$$
(Map p118; ☎907-586-4146; www.silverbowinn.com; 120 2nd St; r $189-219; @⊜) A swanky (for Alaska) boutique inn with 11 rooms. The 100-year-old building is filled with antiques and rooms come with private bath, king and queen beds and flat-panel TVs. A 2nd-floor deck features a hot tub with a view of Douglas Island's mountains. Breakfast is served in the morning, wine and cheese in the new wine bar in the evening.

Goldbelt Hotel Juneau   HOTEL $$$
(Map p118; ☎907-586-6900, 888-478-6909; www.goldbelthotel.com; 51 Egan Dr; r $199-209; ☻@⊜) Alaska Native–owned and centrally located downtown, the Goldbelt has excellent rooms with big, comfortable beds and such amenities as cable TV and courtesy pickup from the airport. The waterfront rooms are $20 extra but face a view of the cruise ships sailing in and the floatplanes taking off.

 ## Eating

Once a culinary desert in a rainforest setting, Juneau is finally beginning to serve up a restaurant scene worthy of a state capital. Several new bistros and bars are catering to an increasingly savvy crowd who want more than fried fish for dinner.

Paradise Café   BAKERY $
(Map p122; 9351 Glacier Hwy; breakfast mains $5-9, lunch mains $7-9; ⊙7am-4pm Tue-Fri, 8am-5pm Sat & Sun) This colorful bakery cafe is filled with the aroma of freshly baked scones, hot pressed sandwiches and croissants. Its menu features delicate pastries, salads and soups, and the cafe's proximity to the airport makes it a great place to while away a layover; it's worth the 10-minute walk, even in a downpour.

Silverbow Bagel Bakery   BAKERY $
(Map p118; 120 2nd St; bagel sandwiches $8-9; ⊙6:30am-6pm Mon-Fri, to 5pm Sat, 7am-4:30pm Sun; ⊜☑) This downtown place bakes bagels daily, serving them au naturel, with a variety of spreads and toppings, or using them as bookends for breakfast and lunch sandwiches. Lots of seating.

Southeast Waffle Co   BREAKFAST $
(Map p122; 11806 Glacier Hwy; waffles $5-8; ⊙6am-10pm Mon-Fri, from 7am Sat, from 9am Sun; ⊜) All you campers in the Mendenhall Valley and out on the road, here's where you head to in Auke Bay for a latte, free wi-fi and a blackboard menu of great waffles, stuffed

---

DON'T MISS

TAKU GLACIER LODGE

The most popular tours in Juneau are flightseeing, glacier viewing and salmon bakes, and a trip to **Taku Glacier Lodge** (☎907-586-6275; www.wingsairways.com; adult/child $297/250) allows you to combine all three. Built in 1923 as a hunting and fishing camp, the lodge is classic Alaska – a sturdy log structure with a front porch overlooking its namesake glacier.

Wings Airways (Map p118; ☎907-586-6275; www.wingsairways.com; Suite 175, 2 Marine Way; adult/child $299/260) flies along the edge of the Juneau Ice Field and across a half-dozen glaciers to the lodge. Once there you enjoy an incredible meal of wild king salmon caught in the nearby Taku River and then can wander the grounds, where visitors occasionally see black bears pop out of the woods. The tour lasts three hours and includes 45 minutes of flying, making it a much better and cheaper experience than taking a helicopter to the ice field. Sign up at the Wings Airways office behind Merchant's Wharf on Juneau's waterfront.

with ham, cheese, sausage, blueberries, even chocolate chip and peanut butter.

Hot Bite
BURGERS $

(Map p122; ☎907-790-2483; 11465 Auke Bay Harbor Dr; hamburgers $10-14; ☉11am-10pm) The best milkshakes and burgers in Juneau are in Auke Bay Harbor. It's housed in the one-time ticket office of Pan American Airways and has seating outside in nice weather. It offers up almost 40 flavors of milkshake and, as if three scoops of ice cream wasn't enough, its cheesecake shake also has cream cheese and graham-cracker crumbs mixed in.

Pel'Meni
DUMPLINGS $

(Map p118; Merchant's Wharf, Marine Way; dumplings $7; ☉11:30am-1:30am Sun-Thu, 11:30am-3:30am Fri & Sat) There's no menu here – just authentic, homemade Russian dumplings, filled with either potato or beef, spiced with hot sauce, curry and cilantro. The perfect end to a night of drinking – Pel'Meni is open until the wee hours. Record buffs will be amazed by the wall full of LPs and the turntable that provides the proper late-night atmosphere.

Rainbow Foods
HEALTH FOOD $

(Map p118; ☎907-586-6476; www.rainbow-foods. org; 224 4th St; food bar per lb $8; ☉9am-7pm Mon-Fri, noon-6pm Sat & Sun) Practically right next door to the dig-and-drill politicians in the state capitol is this natural-food store, a hangout for liberals and environmentalists. Along with a large selection of fresh produce and bulk goods, the store has a hot-and-cold food bar for lunch, espresso and fresh baked goods and a bulletin board with the latest cultural happenings.

★ The Rookery
CAFE $$

(Map p118; ☎907-463-3013; wwwtherookerycafe. com; 111 Seward St; breakfast $6-8 lunch $9-14 dinner mains $15-24) Laid-back coffee shop by day, hip bistro by night. The Rookery serves Portland, Oregon's Stumptown coffee and original breakfasts, lunch and dinners. Buttermilk corncakes, sandwiches on homemade foccacia, and breakfast rice bowls are just some of the daytime offerings. At 4pm, the wi-fi is turned off and a daily-changing menu that includes charcuterie, house-ground burgers, and salads is served.

★ Saffron
INDIAN $$

(Map p118; ☎907-586-1036; www.saffronalaska. com; 112 N Franklin St; lunch $14, dinner $8-19; ☉11am-9:30 Mon-Sat, noon-8pm Sun; ☕) Saffron serves up hot, chewy *naan* bread and complex yet delicate curries for dinner, and *thalis* (plates with a little bit of everything) for lunch. All dishes are made from scratch and the dinner menu is à la carte so you can sample many items. Curries are just spicy enough that you'll leave feeling warm on the inside.

Tracy's King Crab Shack
SEAFOOD $$

(Map p118; www.kingcrabshack.com; 406 S Franklin St; crab $13-45; ☉10:00am-8pm) The best of the food shacks along the cruise ship berths is Tracy's shack. On a boardwalk surrounded by a beer shack and a gift shop, she serves up outstanding crab bisque, crab rolls and mini crab cakes. Grab an outdoor table with friends and split a 3lb bucket of king crab pieces ($110); the sweetest seafood you'll ever have.

Island Pub
PIZZA $$

(Map p122; www.theislandpub.com; 1102 2nd St; large pizza $13-20; ☉11:30am-10pm) Across the channel from the capital city, this relaxing, unhurried restaurant serves firebrick-oven focaccia and the best pizza in town, with a side of channel and mountain views. Before the pie arrives you can enjoy a drink from an impressive list of cocktails. Don't worry about a Red Dog Saloon mob scene. You're on Douglas Island.

Sandpiper
BREAKFAST $$

(Map p118; 429 Willoughby Ave; breakfast mains $10-17, lunch mains $11-14; ☉6am-2pm) Juneau's best breakfast. Skip the eggs and try one of their Belgian waffles, blueberry buttermilk pancakes or specialty French toasts such as mandarin orange and mascarpone cheese.

Douglas Café
CAFE $$

(Map p122; 916 3rd St, Douglas; breakfast mains $11-13, burgers $12-16, dinner mains $19-24; ☉11am-8:30pm Tue-Fri, 8:30am-8:30pm Sat, 9am-12:30pm Sun) This casual eatery (one of two restaurants on Douglas Island) serves up 15 different types of burgers, including a Boring Burger. But if it's dinner, skip the bun and go for one of its tempting mains, which range from tarragon-lime chicken to Cajun prawn fettuccine. Brunch on weekends.

Rockwell
AMERICAN $$

(Map p118; www.rockwelljuneau.com; 109 S Franklin St; sandwiches $9-14, dinner mains $13-18; ☉11am-midnight Mon-Fri, from 9am Sat & Sun) Is this a hip bar or a casual restaurant? Rockwell doesn't seem to know yet, but as one of Juneau's newer establishments it's still figuring out its identity. The meat-heavy menu features hand-cut steaks and excellent burgers, hardly a whiff of the usual Alaska seafood, and the bar serves a decent list of cocktails and wines.

Salt
MODERN AMERICAN $$$
(Map p118; ☑907-780-2221; www.saltalaska.com; 200 Seward St; mains $24-34; ⊙4-10pm) A new and excellent restaurant, Salt is run by Tracy of Tracy's Crab Shack and the dedication is evident. High quality, creative Alaskan cuisine is the highlight, accompanied by a long wine list and fresh desserts, as well as attention to locals with un-Alaskan seafood. It's swanky (but still Juneau), with candlelit tables and muted colors. Reservations are recommended.

Drinking

Nightlife centers on S Franklin and Front Sts, a historic, quaint (but not quiet) main drag, attracting locals and tourists alike.

Coppa
COFFEE
(Map p118; ☑907-586-3500; 917 Glacier Ave; ⊙6:30am-5pm Mon-Thu, to 9pm Fri, 8am-6pm Sat) So much more than a coffee shop (though it does serve locally-roasted Sentinel Coffee), Coppa serves fresh-baked pastries, loose leaf teas and house-made gelato – if you can't handle the caramelized onion flavor, try local favorite rhubarb. Located at the foot of the Douglas Bridge.

McGivney's Sports Bar & Grill
PUB
(Map p122; 9101 Mendenhall Mall Rd; ⊙11am-10pm Sun-Thu, to midnight Fri & Sat) This isn't your typical sports bar: with a menu that includes a flat iron steak salad, miso black cod, and a veggie wrap, you can eat well AND watch the game. There's more than a dozen beers on tap and fancy-time cocktails to boot. Happy hour for appetizers is 3pm to 5pm.

Red Dog Saloon
BAR
(Map p118; 278 S Franklin St) A sign at the door says it all – 'Booze, Antiques, Sawdust Floor, Community Singing' – and the cruise-ship passengers love it! Most don't realize, much less care, that this Red Dog is but a replica of the original, a famous Alaskan drinking hole that was across the street until 1987. Now *that* was a bar.

The duplicate is interesting, but the fact that it has a gift shop should tell you who the clientele is during summer.

Viking Lounge
LOUNGE
(Map p118; 218 Front St; ☏) In this classic tin-ceiling building are actually three bars. At street level is a sports pub with four giant TV screens and almost 20 beers on tap, while half-hidden in the back is a lounge featuring a small dance floor and DJs on Friday and Saturday. Upstairs is a billiards hall with seven tables, sofas and free wi-fi.

Hangar on the Wharf
BAR
(Map p118; www.hangaronthewharf.com; 2 Marine Way) Housed in Merchant's Wharf (also called Fisherman's Wharf), a renovated floatplane hangar that sits on pilings above Juneau's waterfront, the Hangar is mediocre and overpriced for food but a great place for a beer...or two. Your table is perched right over a seaplane dock, and the unobstructed channel view channel includes all the activity buzzing and floating downtown.

Heritage Coffee Co & Café
COFFEE
(Map p118; www.heritagecoffee.com; 174 S Franklin St; ⊙6:30am-7pm Mon-Fri, 7am-6pm Sat & Sun; ☏) ✔ A coffee house popular with tourists and cruise ship employees who come for locally roasted coffee and free wi-fi. The company also has a cafe at 216 2nd St that is a bit quieter and features outdoor seating.

☆ Entertainment

Food Truck Fridays
LIVE MUSIC
(Map p118; www.jahc.org; 350 Whittier St; ⊙4-7pm Fri) FREE Kick off your summer weekends with live music, an arts and flea market and, of course, food trucks. Held outside the JACC every Friday from June through August.

Gold Town Nickelodeon
CINEMA
(Map p118; ☑907-586-2875; www.goldtownnick.com; 171 Shattuck St; adult/child $9/5) This delightful art-house theater presents small-budget and foreign films and documentaries. Seating arrangements include velour couches.

Perseverance Theater
THEATER
(Map p122; ☑907-364-2421; www.perseverancetheatre.org; 914 3rd St, Douglas) Founded in 1979, this is Alaska's only genuine full-time professional theater company. Sadly the theater season begins in September and ends in May, though they do host events throughout the summer – check their website for info.

🔒 Shopping

Despite all the cruise-ship jewelry stores and gift shops, the Juneau art scene is alive and vibrant. The best time to sample it is during First Friday (www.jahc.org; ⏰ 4:30-7pm 1st Fri of the month), a free event when a reception is held for a local artist at the Juneau Arts & Culture Center while the Alaska State Museum (when it reopens) and a dozen local art galleries are also open late.

★ Juneau Arts & Culture Center   ARTS & CRAFTS

(JACC; Map p118; www.jahc.org; 350 Whittier St; ⏰ 9am-6pm) The impressive JACC gallery features the work of a local artist every month, while the adjacent Lobby Shop is a place for Southeast Alaskans to sell their artworks, including jewelry, paintings and books. Its website is an excellent resource for Juneau happenings.

Juneau Artists Gallery   ARTS & CRAFTS

(Map p118; www.juneauartistsgallery.com; Senate Bldg, 175 S Franklin St) Downtown is the Juneau Artists Gallery, a co-op of 27 local artists who have filled the store with paintings, etchings, glass work, jewelry and pottery. The person behind the counter ready to help you is that day's 'Artist On Duty.'

Rie Munoz Gallery   ARTS & CRAFTS

(Map p122; www.riemunoz.com; 2101 Jordan Ave; ⏰ 9:30am-3.30pm Tue-Sat) Out in the Valley, near Nugget Mall, is the Rie Munoz Gallery, featuring a large selection of Rie Munoz prints as well as some by Dale DeArmond, Byron Birdsall and several other noted Alaskan artists.

Second Wind Sports   OUTDOOR EQUIPMENT

(Map p122; www.secondwindsportsak.com; 8363 Old Dairy Rd) In a strip mall near the airport, Second Wind Sports is the place to get quality used outdoor clothing and gear, from warm jackets to bicycle tubes to backpacks.

Foggy Mountain Shop   OUTDOOR EQUIPMENT

(Map p118; www.foggymountainshop.com; 134 N Franklin St) For packs, outdoorwear, USGS topo maps and anything else you need for backcountry trips, stop at Foggy Mountain Shop. This is the only outdoor shop in town with top-of-the-line equipment, and the prices reflect that.

Hearthside Books   BOOKS

(Map p118; www.hearthsidebooks.com; 254 Front St) Juneau's best bookstore also has a store in Nugget Mall in the Valley.

ℹ Information

INTERNET ACCESS

Juneau Library (292 Marine Way; ⏰ 11am-8pm Mon-Thu, 1-5pm Fri, from noon Sat & Sun; 🛜) Juneau's main public library sits atop a four-story parking structure and offers free internet access and wi-fi. It's worth a stop here just for the views of downtown Juneau.

MEDICAL SERVICES

Bartlett Regional Hospital (☎ 907-796-631; 3260 Hospital Dr) Southeast Alaska's largest hospital is off Glacier Hwy between downtown and Lemon Creek.

Juneau Urgent Care (☎ 907-790-4111; 8505 Old Dairy Rd; ⏰ 8am-7pm Mon-Fri, 9am-5pm Sat & Sun) A walk-in medical clinic near Nugget Mall in the Valley.

MONEY

There's no shortage of banks in Juneau. Most have ATMs and branches both downtown and in the Valley.

First Bank (605 W Willoughby Ave)
Wells Fargo (123 Seward St)

POST

Post Office (Map p118; cnr 9th St & Glacier Ave) On the 1st floor of the Federal Building.

Postal Contract Station (Map p118; 145 S Franklin St) Conveniently located downtown in the Seward Building.

TOURIST INFORMATION

Alaska Accessible Travel (☎ 907-321-3154; www.alaskaaccessibletravel.com) A website dedicated to accessible travel in Juneau and beyond.

Alaska Division of Parks (Map p118; ☎ 907-465-4563; 400 Willoughby Ave; ⏰ 8am-4:30pm Mon-Fri) Head to the 5th floor of the Natural Resources Building for state park information, inlcuding cabin rentals.

Juneau Visitor Center (Map p122; ☎ 907-586-2201, 888-581-2201; www.traveljuneau.com; 470 S Franklin St; ⏰ 8am-5pm) The new visitors center is in the cruise ship terminal right next to the Mt Roberts Tram, and has all the information you need to explore Juneau, find a trail or book a room. The center also maintains smaller information booths at the airport, the marine ferry terminal and downtown near the library.

USFS Juneau Ranger District Office (Map p122; ☎ 907-586-8800; 8510 Mendenhall Loop Rd; ⏰ 8am-4:30pm Mon-Fri) This impressive

SECONDARY PORTS

For an unusual sidetrip into rural Southeast Alaska you can board the Alaska Marine Highway for a cruise to seven small villages. Most stopovers by the ferry last an hour, enough time to walk around. But for a better cultural experience, spend a night or two, even if it means paying for a charter flight back to Juneau or Ketchikan. Here are three of the most interesting:

Tenakee Springs

Since the late 19th century when it served as a winter retreat for fishers and prospectors, Tenakee Springs (population 130) has evolved into a village known for its relaxed pace. On the east side of Tenakee Inlet, the settlement is basically a ferry dock, a row of houses on pilings, and the hot springs, which bubble out of the ground at 107°F (41.6°C). Tenakee's alternative lifestyle centers on the free public bathhouse at the end of the ferry dock. The building encloses the principal spring, which flows through the concrete bath at 7 gallons per minute. Bath hours, separate for men and women, are posted, and most locals take at least one good soak per day.

The ferry MV *LeConte* stops at Tenakee Springs twice a week (six hours; $35), allowing you to arrive on Friday from Juneau and depart on Sunday. Tenakee Hot Springs Lodge (☑ 907-364-3640, 907-736-2400; www.tenakeehotspringslodge.com; 801 E Tenakee Ave ; s/d $90/150; ☎) is the place to stay, or pitch a tent at the rustic campground on the beach a mile east of town, at the mouth of the Indian River. For more information on lodging and services check the website for the Tenakee Springs Business Association (www.tenakeespringsak.com).

Pelican

Juneau's has a twice-monthly state ferry to Pelican (population 90), a lively little fishing town on Chichagof Island. The cruise through Icy Straits is scenic, with regular humpback spottings, and the two hours in port is enough to see one of Southeast Alaska's last boardwalk communities. Pelican is a photographer's delight. Most of it is built on pilings over tidelands, and its main street, dubbed Salmon Way, is a mile-long wooden boardwalk.

The town was established in 1938 by a fish packer and named after his boat. Fishing is Pelican's raison d'être. It has the closest harbor to Fairweather's salmon grounds – the reason its population swells during the summer. You can mingle with trollers, long-liners and Pelican seafood workers at Rose's Bar & Grill, a classic Alaskan fishers' bar, while Highliner Lodge (☑907-735-2476, 877-386-0397; www.highlinerlodge.com; Boat Harbor; s/d with shared bath $175/225) is a good place to lay your head. Seaplane Service (☑888-350-8277, in Juneau 907-735-2244, in Pelican 907-789-3331; www.akseaplanes.com) fly people back to Juneau for $170. For more contact Pelican Visitors Association (www.pelican.net).

Metlakatla

Founded in 1887 when Anglican missionary William Duncan arrived at Annette Island with 823 Tsimsheans from British Columbia, Metlakatla became a federally recognized Indian Reservation four years later and today is the only one in Alaska. The 20-mile-long island is reserved for the Metlakatla Indians, whose village (population 1624) is the antithesis to Ketchikan just across the Tongass Narrows, where much is made for cruise ships. Metlakatla is an authentic slice of Native Alaska, from its totems scattered throughout the town and its artists' village to its award-winning Tsimshean dancers.

Its heart is Annette Island Packing Company, perched on stilts overlooking a beautiful harbor dotted with small islands. Graveyard and Yellow Hill Trails lead to overlooks. The MV *Lituya* makes two runs to the new ferry terminal 15 miles north of Metlakatla, Annette Bay, and Ketchikan ($23, 45min) Thursday to Monday. If day-tripping, taking the ferry leaves you only two hours to explore, so it's best to arrange a personally narrated tour through MIC Tourism (☑907-886-8687; per person $40). Tuckem Inn (☑907-886-1074; winter@atpalaska.net; Western Ave; r $95; ☎) is a decent choice for lodging, with 31 rooms. Promech Air (☑907-225-3845, 800-860-3845; www.promechair.com) will fly you back to Ketchikan for $55.

office is in Mendenhall Valley and is the place for questions about cabins, trails, kayaking and Pack Creek bear- watching permits.

❶ Getting There & Away

AIR

Alaska Airlines (☑ 800-252-7522; www.alaskaair.com) Offers scheduled jet service to Seattle (two hours), all major Southeast cities, Glacier Bay (30 minutes), Anchorage (two hours) and Cordova (2½ hours) daily in summer.

Alaska Seaplane Service (Map p122; ☑ 907-789-3331; www.flyalaskaseaplanes.com) Flies floatplanes from Juneau to Angoon ($135), Elfin Cove ($175), Pelican ($175) and Tenakee Springs ($135).

Wings of Alaska (☑ 907-789-0790; www.wingsofalaska.com) Flies to Glacier Bay/Gustavus ($65), Haines ($85), Hoonah ($55) and Skagway ($105), with dozens of options per day.

BOAT

Alaska Marine Highway (☑ 800-642-0066; www.ferryalaska.com) Ferries dock at Auke Bay Ferry Terminal, 14 miles northwest of downtown. In summer, the main line ferries traversing the Inside Passage depart daily southbound for Sitka ($45, nine hours), Petersburg ($66, eight hours) and Ketchikan ($107, 18 hours).

You can shorten the sailing times on the high-speed MV *Fairweather*, which connects Juneau to Petersburg once a week and to Sitka five times a week. Several shorter routes also operate in summer. The smaller MV *LeConte* regularly connects Juneau to the secondary ports of Hoonah ($33, four hours), Tenakee Springs ($35, eight hours) and Angoon ($37, 12 hours). Two times a month, the MV *Kennicott* departs Juneau for a trip to Yakutat ($85, 15½ hours) then across the Gulf of Alaska to Whittier ($221, 39 hours); reservations are strongly suggested.

❶ Getting Around

TO/FROM THE AIRPORT & FERRY

A taxi to/from the airport costs around $25. The city bus express route runs to the airport, but only from 7:30am to 5:30pm Monday to Friday. On weekends and in the evening, if you want a bus you'll need to walk 10 minutes to the nearest 'regular route' stop behind Nugget Mall. The regular route headed downtown stops here regularly from 7:15am until 10:45pm Monday to Saturday, and from 9:15am until 5:45pm Sunday. The fare on either route is $2/1 per adult/child.

Unbelievable but true: no buses or regularly scheduled shuttles go to the ferry terminal in Auke Bay, an ungodly long 14-mile distance from

downtown. A few taxis, including **Glacier Taxi** (☑ 907-796-2300), show up for most ferry arrivals, charging $35 for downtown. You can stick out your thumb (hitchhiking is commonplace) or take the city bus to/from the end of the line, which is 1.6 miles south of the ferry terminal at DeHart's Store in Auke Bay.

BUS

Juneau's sadistic public bus system, **Capital Transit** (☑ 907-789-6901; www.juneau.org/capitaltransit; adult/child $2/1), stops way short of the ferry terminal and a mile short of the Mendenhall Glacier Visitor Center. Even getting to/from the airport can be problematic: only the 'express' route goes right to the terminal, and it only runs during business hours on weekdays. At other times, you'll have to schlep your bags between the airport and the 'regular' route's stop at Nugget Mall, a 10-minute walk. The 'regular' route buses start around 7am and stop before midnight, running every half-hour after 8am and before 6:30pm. The main route circles downtown then heads out to the Valley and Auke Bay Boat Harbor via Mendenhall Loop Rd, where it travels close to Mendenhall Lake Campground. Routes 3 and 4 make stops in the Mendenhall Valley either from downtown or Auke Bay, while a bus runs every hour from city stops to Douglas. Fares are $2/1 each way per adult/child, and exact change is required. Major stops downtown include the Federal Building and the Main St Parking Garage, the closest thing to a bus terminal in Juneau, at the corner of Egan Hwy and Main St.

CAR

Juneau has many car-rental places, and renting a car is a great way for two or three people to see the sights out of the city or to reach a trailhead. For a $59 special, call **Juneau Car Rental** (☑ 907-957-7530, 907-789-0951; www.juneaucarrentals.com), which is a mile from the airport but provides pickups and has a designated airport parking spot for when you drop the car off. You can also rent a car at the airport, but will have to stomach a 26% tax as opposed to a 15% tax elsewhere.

Admiralty Island & Pack Creek

Only 15 miles southeast of Juneau is Admiralty Island National Monument, a 1493-sq-mile preserve, of which 90% is designated wilderness. The monument has a wide variety of wildlife – from Sitka black-tailed deer and nesting bald eagles to harbor seals, sea lions and humpback whales – but more than anything else, Admiralty Island is known for **bears**. The 96-mile-long island has one of the highest populations of bears in Alaska, with an estimated 1500 brown bears, more than all the lower 48 states combined. It's the reason the Tlingit called Admiralty Kootznoowoo, 'the Fortress of Bears.'

The monument's main attraction for visitors is Pack Creek, which flows from 4000ft mountains before spilling into Seymour Canal on the island's east side. The extensive tide flats at the mouth of the creek draw a large number of bears in July and August to feed on salmon, making the spot a favorite for observing and photographing the animals.

Bear viewing at Pack Creek takes place at **Stan Price State Wildlife Sanctuary**, named for an Alaskan woodsman who lived on a floathouse here for almost 40 years. The vast majority of visitors to the sanctuary are day-trippers who arrive and depart on floatplanes. Upon arrival, all visitors are met by a ranger who explains the rules and then each party hikes to an observation tower – reached by a mile-long trail – that overlooks the creek.

Pack Creek has become so popular that the area buzzes with planes and boats every morning from early July to late August. Anticipating this daily rush hour, most resident bears escape into the forest, but a few bears hang around to feed on salmon, having long since been habituated to the human visitors. Seeing five or six bears would be a good viewing day at Pack Creek. You might see big

---

WORTH A TRIP

YAKUTAT: ON THE EDGE OF NOWHERE

Isolated on the strand that connects the Southeast to the rest of Alaska, Yakutat – of all places – is now something of a tourist destination, admittedly a minor one. The main reason is improved transportation. You still can't drive to the most northern Southeast town, but in the late 1990s, it became a port for the Alaska Marine Highway (p133) when the MV *Kennicott* began its cross-Gulf trips. Now the ferry stops twice a month during the summer, headed to either Juneau or Whittier, while Alaska Airlines (p133) stops daily both northbound and southbound.

What does Yakutat have to offer curious tourists? Big waves, a big and very active glacier and a lot of USFS cabins next to rivers with big salmon.

The waves rolling in from the Gulf of Alaska have made Yakutat the surf capital of the Far North. This town of 668 people even has its own surf shop, the **Icy Waves Surf Shop** (☑907-784-3226; www.icywaves.com).

Just 30 miles north of Yakutat is **Hubbard Glacier**, the longest tidewater glacier in the world. The 76-mile-long glacier captured national attention by galloping across Russell Fjord in the mid-1980s, turning the long inlet into a lake. Eventually Hubbard receded, reopening the fjord, but in 2002 it again surged across Russell Fjord and came close to doing it a third time in 2011. The 8-mile-wide glacier is easily Alaska's most active. The rip tides and currents that flow between Gilbert Point and the face of the glacier, a mere 1000ft away, are so strong that they cause Hubbard to calve almost continuously at peak tides. The entire area, part of the 545-sq-mile **Russell Fjord Wilderness**, is one of the most interesting places in Alaska and usually visited through flightseeing or boat tours.

Yakutat Charter Boat Co (☑888-317-4987; www.alaska-charter.com) runs a four-hour tour of the area for $170 per person.

Yakutat has a dozen lodges and B&Bs, including the **Glacier Bear Lodge** (☑907-784-3202, 866-425-6343; www.glacierbearlodge.com; r $195; ☎), which has 31 comfortable rooms, a restaurant and lounge, and provides a shuttle to and from the airport.

There are eight USFS cabins (p125) in the area, four of them accessible by hiking from the Forest Hwy 10, which extends east from Yakutat. Many are near rivers and lakes that are renowned, even by Alaskan standards, for sport fishing for salmon, steelhead trout and Dolly Varden trout.

For more information contact the **Yakutat Chamber of Commerce** (www.yakutatalaska.com) or **USFS Yakutat Ranger Station** (☑907-784-3359). Thrumming with the fishing energy and general pulse of Yakutat is **Situk River Fly Shop** (www.situk.net; Yakutat; ⊙10am-7pm), where you'll find tackle and other gear but also area information. The website and blog are excellent sources of news and happenings.

boars during the mating season from May to mid-June; otherwise it's sows and cubs the rest of the summer.

Above & Beyond Alaska (☑907-364-2333; www.beyondak.com) offers one- and multi-day kayak rental packages that include round-trip floatplane transport; a one-day rental package is $595 per person while a two-day/one-night trip is $695. You'll need to arrange your own permits.

Some visitors fly into the monument to stay at one of the 14 **USFS cabins** (☑877-444-6777, 518-885-3639; www.recreation.gov; cabins $25-35) or to paddle the **Cross Admiralty Island canoe route**, a 32-mile paddle that spans the center of the island from the village of Angoon to Mole Harbor. Although the majority of the route consists of calm lakes connected by streams and portages, the 10-mile paddle from Angoon on Admiralty Island's west coast to Mitchell Bay is subject to strong tides that challenge even experienced paddlers.

Angoon (population 460) is the only community on Admiralty Island and serves as the departure point for many kayak and canoe trips into the heart of the monument, including the Cross Admiralty canoe route. Because of the difficulty getting a canoe out of Mole Harbor, many people are content to just spend a few days exploring and fishing Mitchell Bay and Salt Lake or paddling to a USFS cabin and then backtracking.

From June to mid-September, the USFS and Alaska Department of Fish and Game operate a permit system for Pack Creek and only 24 people are allowed per day from July to the end of August. Guiding and tour companies receive half the permits, leaving 12 for individuals who want to visit Pack Creek on their own. **National Recreation Reservation Service** (☑877-444-6777, 518-885-3639; www.recreation.gov), the people who handle USFS cabin reservations, are also handling Pack Creek permits. For the latest on the permit changes, particularly the date they become available each year (usually early February), contact the **Admiralty Island National Monument office** (Map p122; ☑907-586-8800; www.fs.fed.us/r10/tongass/districts/admiralty) in Juneau.

There are no kayak or canoe rentals in Angoon. You can rent kayaks from Alaska Boat & Kayak (p124) at Auke Bay near Juneau and then place it on the Alaska Ferry.

There is also no tourist office; call the **City of Angoon** (☑907-788-3653) for info.

🛏 Sleeping

Most accommodation around Angoon is all-inclusive fishing lodges. Services are limited as tourism seems to be tolerated only because the village is a port of call for the ferry. It's also important to remember Angoon is a dry community.

Eagle's Wing Inn   B&B $$
(☑907-788-3234; catherine.quinn@usw.salvationarmy.org; s/d/tr $169/179/189; 🐾) A great place to stay; this large, rambling log home is two miles from the ferry terminal. Three of the five rooms have views of the bay, and all come with a hearty breakfast that includes fresh-baked goods.

❶ Getting There & Away

PACK CREEK

Most visitors arrive at Pack Creek via a guided air-charter trip from Juneau.

Pack Creek Bear Tours (☑907-789-3331; www.packcreekbeartours.com) holds permits and offers a guided 7-hour fly-in tour ($689). Alaska Seaplane Service (p133) has charters for between $430 and $662 each way for the plane; they can hold up to four or five people depending on weight. **Admiralty Air Service** (☑907-796-2000; www.admiraltyairservice.com) can fly you to Pack Creek on a charter; the plane carries up to four people and costs $450 an hour – about how long it takes to get out there.

ANGOON

Alaska Marine Highway (☑800-642-0066; www.ferryalaska.com) provides ferry service between Juneau and Angoon ($37, five hours) on Thursday and Saturday and from Sitka on Monday. **Alaska Seaplane Service** (☑907-789-3331, 888-350-8277; www.flyalaskaseaplanes.com) offers four flights a day between Juneau and Angoon ($135 one way).

Glacier Bay National Park & Preserve

Eleven tidewater glaciers that spill out of the mountains and fill the sea with icebergs of all shapes, sizes and shades of blue have made Glacier Bay National Park and Preserve an icy wilderness renowned worldwide.

When Captain George Vancouver sailed through the ice-choked waters of Icy Strait in 1794, Glacier Bay was little more than a dent in a mountain of ice. In 1879 John Muir made his legendary discovery of Glacier Bay and found that the end of the bay had retreated 20 miles from Icy Strait. Today, the glacier that bears his name is more than 60 miles from Icy Strait, and its rapid retreat has revealed plants and animals that continue to fascinate modern-day naturalists.

Apart from its high concentration of tidewater glaciers, Glacier Bay is the habitat for a variety of marine life, including whales. The humpbacks are by far the most impressive and acrobatic, as they heave their massive bodies in spectacular leaps (called 'breaching') from the water. Adult humpbacks often grow to 50ft and weigh up to 40 tons. Other marine life seen at Glacier Bay includes harbor seals, porpoises, killer whales and sea otters, and other wildlife includes brown and black bears, wolves, moose, mountain goats and more than 200 bird species.

Glacier Bay is also where the cruise-ship industry and environmentalists have squared off. After the number of whales seen in the park dropped dramatically in 1978, the NPS reduced ship visits to 79 during the three-month season. But the cruise-ship industry lobbied the US Congress and the NPS in 1996 to OK a 30% increase in vessels allowed in the bay – almost 200 cruise ships a season. Environmentalists sued, and eventually a compromise of two large cruise ships per day was hammered out.

But the whales aren't the only area of concern here. Glacier Bay's ice, like glaciers all over Alaska, is rapidly melting. This is particularly true in Muir Inlet, or the East Arm as it's commonly called. Twenty years ago it was home to three active tidewater glaciers, but now there is only one, McBride. Only two glaciers in the park are advancing; Johns Hopkins and Lamplugh. The rest are receding and thinning.

Still, Glacier Bay is the crowning jewel of the cruise-ship industry and the dreamy destination for anybody who has ever paddled a kayak. The park is an expensive sidetrip, even by Alaskan standards. Plan on spending at least $400 for a trip from Juneau, but remember that the cost per day drops quickly after you've arrived. Of the more than 300,000 annual visitors, more than 90% arrive aboard a ship and never leave the boat. The rest are a mixture of tour-group members who head straight for the lodge and backpackers who wander toward the free campground.

Although the park headquarters, campground and visitors centers are located in Bartlett Cove, the gateway to Glacier Bay is Gustavus (gus-*tay*-vus), located nine miles away. This interesting backcountry community (population 440) is where the state ferry and Alaska Airlines lands, but it has no downtown. Most of the area businesses are either spread out along the Salmon River or half-hidden in the woods. Electricity only arrived in the early 1980s, and residents still maintain a self-sufficient lifestyle. For visitors who rush through to see the glaciers, Gustavus is little more than an airstrip left over from WWII and a road to Bartlett Cove. For those who spend a little time poking around and meeting locals, Gustavus can be an interesting place and a refreshing break from cruise-ship ports such as Skagway.

◉ Sights & Activities

Glaciers

The glaciers are 40 miles up the bay from Bartlett Cove. If you're not on a cruise ship or don't want to spend a week or two kayaking, the only way to see them is onboard a tour boat.

★ **Glacier Bay Lodge & Tours**   BOAT TOUR
(☏ 888-229-8687; www.visitglacierbay.com; adult/child $195/97.50) The *Fairweather Express* operated by Glacier Bay Lodge & Tours is a high-speed catamaran that departs at 7:30am for an eight-hour tour into the West Arm and returns by 4pm. The tour includes lunch and narration by an onboard park naturalist.

Hiking

Glacier Bay has few trails and in the backcountry foot travel is done along riverbanks, on ridges or across ice remnants of glaciers. The only developed trails are in Bartlett Cove.

The new **Nagoonberry Loop** is an accessible 2.2-mile trail that begins and ends at the terminus of Glen's Ditch Rd. Along the way you'll pass through all stages of a forest, from meadow to old growth, and on to the beach. There are benches, two viewing areas and more wildflowers than you can take photos of.

The mile-long **Forest Trail** is a nature walk that begins and ends near the Bartlett Cove dock and winds through the pond-studded spruce and hemlock forest near the campground. Rangers lead walks on this trail daily in summer; inquire at the Glacier Bay Visitor Center.

Bartlett River Trail, a 1.5-mile trail, begins just up the road to Gustavus, where there is a posted trailhead, and ends at the Bartlett River estuary. On the way, it meanders along a tidal lagoon and passes through quite a few muddy spots. Plan on two to four hours for the 3-mile round-trip.

The **Point Gustavus Beach Walk**, along the shoreline south of Bartlett Cove to Point Gustavus and Gustavus, provides the only overnight trek from the park headquarters. The total distance is 12 miles, and the walk to Point Gustavus, an excellent spot to camp, is 6 miles. Plan on hiking the stretch from Point Gustavus to Gustavus at low tide, which will allow you to ford the Salmon River, as opposed to swimming across it. Point Gustavus is an excellent place to sight orcas and whales in Icy Strait.

Paddling

Glacier Bay offers an excellent opportunity for people who have some experience on the water but not necessarily as kayakers, because the **Fairweather Express** ([☎]907-264-4600, 888-229-8687; www.visitglacierbay.com; one way adult/child $105/52.50) drops off and picks up paddlers at two spots, usually at the entrance of the Muir Inlet (East Arm) and inside the West Arm. By using the tour boat, you can skip the long and open paddle up the bay and enjoy only the well-protected arms and inlets where the glaciers are located. The most dramatic glaciers are in the West Arm, but either one will require at least four days to paddle to glaciers if you are dropped off and picked up. With only a drop-off, you need a week to 10 days to paddle from either arm back to Bartlett Cove.

Paddlers who want to avoid the tour-boat fares but still long for a kayak adventure should try the **Beardslee Islands**. While there are no glaciers to view, the islands are a day's paddle from Bartlett Cove and offer calm water, protected channels and pleasant beach camping. Wildlife includes black bears, seals and bald eagles, and the tidal pools burst with activity at low tide.

Glacier Bay Sea Kayaks   KAYAKING
([☎]907-697-2257; www.glacierbayseakayaks.com; s/d kayaks per day $60/45) Glacier Bay rents kayaks as well as leads guided trips to the Beardslee Islands (half-/full-day $95/150).

Alaska Mountain Guides   KAYAKING
([☎]800-766-3396; www.alaskamountainguides.com) Has a field office in Gustavus to run several guided kayak trips into Glacier Bay.

A seven-day paddle to the West Arm, which includes tour transportation as well as all equipment and food, is $2350 per person, and an eight-day paddle up the East Arm that begins from Bartlett Cove is $2650.

Spirit Walker Expeditions   KAYAKING
([☎]907-697-2266, 800-529-2537; www.seakayakalaska.com) Spirit Walker runs paddling trips to Point Adolphus where humpback whales congregate during the summer. Trips begin with a short boat ride with the kayaks across Icy Strait to Point Adolphus and run $435 for a day paddle ($375 per person for four or more) and $1085 for a three-day paddle.

Whale Watching

Cross Sound Express   WHALE WATCHING
([☎]888-698-2726; www.taz.gustavus.com; tours adult/child $120/60) Its 50ft MV *Taz* carries up to 23 passengers and departs the Gustavus dock daily during the summer at 8:30am and 12:30pm for a 3½-hour whale-watching tour.

☞ Tours

You can see Glacier Bay in a hurry, though you have to ask yourself if that is a wise use of your travel funds. For a quickie flightseeing tour, Haines is the closest community and thus offers cheaper flights.

Glacier Bay Lodge & Tours   BOAT
([☎]907-264-4600, 888-229-8687; www.visitglacierbay.com) Has an inclusive package that includes one night at Glacier Bay Lodge and a day tour to see the glaciers up bay on the *Fairweather Express*. The cost is $595 for two people but does not include air transportation from Juneau.

Gray Line   BOAT
([☎]907-586-3773, 800-544-2206; www.graylineofalaska.com) Offers a two-day package from Juneau that includes round-trip flight to Gustavus, a night at Glacier Bay Lodge and an eight-hour boat tour of the bay ($769 per person).

🛏 Sleeping & Eating

Most of the accommodations are in Gustavus, which adds a 7% bed-and-sales tax.

🛏 Bartlett Cove

NPS Campground   CAMPGROUND $
This NPS facility 0.25 miles south of Glacier Bay Lodge is set in a lush forest just off the shoreline, and camping is free. There's no

need for reservations; there always seems to be space. It provides a bear cache and warming shelter. Coin-operated showers are available in the park, but there's no place to buy groceries or camping supplies.

Glacier Bay Lodge LODGE $$$

(☑888-229-8687; www.visitglacierbay.com; 199 Bartlett Cove Rd; r $199-224) This is the only hotel and restaurant in Bartlett Cove. The lodge has 55 rooms, a crackling fire in a huge stone fireplace and a dining room that usually hums in the evening with an interesting mixture of park employees, backpackers and locals from Gustavus. Nightly slide presentations, ranger talks and movies held upstairs cover the park's natural history.

⨳ Gustavus

Seaside Campground CAMPING $

(☑907-697-2214; sites $20) On the edge of the Fairweather golf course, this basic campground is in a grassy field and has room for a few tents and RVs. Shower and restroom access across the road.

★Blue Heron B&B B&B $$

(☑907-697-2293; www.blueheronbnb.net; State Dock Rd; r/cottages $154/190; ☎) The B&B is surrounded by 10 acres of wildflowers and surround-sound views of the Fairweather mountains. The two rooms and two cottages (with kitchenettes) are modern, bright and clean, and each has a TV/VCR and private bath. In the morning everybody meets in the sun room for a full breakfast ranging from organic rolled oats with blueberries to omelets.

The wonderful proprietor Deb has everything you need to enjoy Gustavus – rubber boots, rain pants, bikes, and transportation. Check out the giant eagle's nest outside.

Aimee's Guest House GUESTHOUSE $$

(☑907-697-2330; www.glacierbayalaska.net; Gustavus Rd; ste $105-160; ☺) A former smokehouse on the Salmon River (the reason for the colorful fish mural outside) has been converted into three bright, airy and comfortable vacation rentals featuring one or two bedrooms, full kitchens, and everything you would need to spend a few days in Gustavus. The upper-level deck, with its hammock, wicker furniture and bed outside, is classic Alaska.

Annie Mae Lodge LODGE $$

(☑907-697-2346; www.anniemae.com; Grandpa's Farm Rd; s $160-220, d $170-230; ☎) This large rambling lodge has wraparound porches and 11 rooms, most with private bath. On the 2nd level all seven rooms have a private entrance off the porch. Continental breakfast is served in a large dining room and common area; lunches, dinners and hot breakfast items are available for an additional charge. Your stay includes ground transfers and free bicycles.

Gustavus Inn INN $$$

(☑907-697-2254, 800-649-5220; www.gustavusinn.com; Mile 1, Gustavus Rd; r $225, with shared bath $215; ☺☎) This longtime Gustavus favorite is a charming family homestead lodge mentioned in every travel book on Alaska, with good reason. It's thoroughly modern and comfortable but without being sterile or losing its folksy touch. The all-inclusive inn is well known for its gourmet dinners, which feature homegrown vegetables and fresh local seafood served family-style.

Guests have free use of bicycles, and courtesy transportation to/from Bartlett Cove and the airport is cheerfully provided. Packages with Glacier Bay tours and kayaking trips are avaialbe. Even if you can't afford to stay at the inn, book a seat at its dinner table one night.

Sunnyside Market CAFE $

(☑907-697-3060; Dock Rd; ☺9am-6pm; ☑) ∅ This bright market and cafe is your one-stop choice for organic sundries, deli sandwiches and breakfast burritos. There are two tables inside and plenty outside under a sunny overhang. On Saturday there's an artsy market.

Clove Hitch Cafe CAFE $

(Gustavus Rd, at Wilson Rd; Breakfast $8-12, lunch $10-13) This little nautical-themed cafe is a local hangout, serving breakfast, lunch and pizzas on the weekend.

Fireweed Gallery COFFEE SHOP $

(4 Corners, Gustavus Rd; pastries $3-6) You're there because it's the best coffee in Gustavus (and a whole lot of Southeast) and serves freshly baked goods, but the local art is definitely easy on the eyes.

❶ Information

The best source of information is the NPS in Bartlett Cove.

Glacier Bay Visitor Center (☑ 907-697-2661; www.nps.gov/glba; ◷ 11am-8pm) On the 2nd floor of Glacier Bay Lodge, it has exhibits, a bookshop and an information desk. There are also daily guided walks from the lodge, park films and slide presentations.

Gustavus Visitors Association (☑ 907-697-2454; www.gustavusak.com) Has loads of information on its website.

Visitor Information Station (☑ 907-697-2627; ◷ 7am-7pm) Campers, kayakers and boaters can stop at the park's Visitor Information Station at the foot of the public dock for backcountry and boating permits, logistical information and a 20-minute orientation video.

❶ Getting There & Around

TO & FROM THE AIRPORT

If you arrive at the Gustavus airport, you're still 9 miles from Bartlett Cove. The Glacier Bay Lodge bus meets all Alaska Airlines flights; it's free for guests and $15 for folks on Glacier Bay tours.

TLC Taxi (☑ 907-697-2239) meets most ferry arrivals and also charges $15 per person for a trip to Bartlett Cove.

AIR

Alaska Airlines (☑ 800-252-7522; www.alaskaair.com) Offers the only jet service, with a daily 25-minute trip from Juneau to Gustavus.

Alaska Seaplanes (☑ 907-789-3331; www.flyalaskaseaplanes.com) Has several flights per day between Gustavus and Juneau for $99 one way.

Wings of Alaska (☑ in Gustavus 907-697-2201, in Juneau 907-789-0790; www.wingsofalaska.com) Scheduled flights to Juneau for $54 one way.

BOAT

The cheapest way to reach Gustavus is via the **Alaska Marine Highway** (☑ 800-642-0066; www.ferryalaska.com). Several times a week the MV *LeConte* makes the round-trip run from Juneau to Gustavus (one way $33; 3½ hours) along a route that often features whale sightings.

Haines

POP 2510

Heading north of Juneau on the state ferry takes you up Lynn Canal, North America's longest and deepest fjord. Along the way, Eldred Rock Lighthouse stands as a picturesque sentinel, waterfalls pour down off the Chilkoot Range to the east, and the David-

son and Rainbow Glaciers draw 'oohs' and 'aahs' as they snake down out of the jagged Chilkat Mountains to the west. You end up in Haines, a scenic departure point for Southeast Alaska and a crucial link to the Alaska Hwy. Every summer thousands of travelers, particularly RVers, pass through this slice in the mountains on their way to Canada's Yukon Territory and Interior Alaska.

Haines is 75 miles north of Juneau on a wooded peninsula between the Chilkat and Chilkoot Inlets. Originally a stronghold of the wealthy Chilkat Tlingit Indians, it was put on the map by a gun-toting entrepreneur named Jack Dalton. In 1897 Dalton turned an old Indian trade route into a toll road for miners seeking an easier way to reach the Klondike. The Dalton Trail quickly became such a heavily used pack route to mining districts north of Whitehorse that the army arrived in 1903 and established Fort William H Seward, Alaska's first permanent post. For the next 20 years it was Alaska's only army post and then was used as a rest camp during WWII.

WWII led to the construction of the Haines Hwy, the 159-mile link between the Southeast and the Alcan. Built in 1942 as a possible evacuation route in case of a Japanese invasion, the route followed the Dalton Trail and was so rugged it would be 20 years before US and Canadian crews even attempted to keep it open in winter. By the 1900s, the 'Haines Cut-off Rd' had become the paved Haines Hwy, and now more than 50,000 travelers in cars and RVs follow it annually.

After logging fell on hard times in the 1970s, Haines swung its economy towards tourism and it's still surviving. And it should. Haines has spectacular scenery, quick access to the rivers and mountains where people like to play, and is comparatively dry (only 53in of rain annually). All of this prompted *Outside* magazine to plaster a photo of Haines on its cover in 2004 and call it one of the country's '20 best places to live and play.'

You'll immediately notice that this town is different from what you've experienced elsewhere in the Southeast. Maybe it's the relative lack of cruise-ship traffic that gives Haines a tangible sense of peace and tranquility; as a port Haines receives less than 40,000 cruise-ship passengers in a season – it is lucky to reach the number that Juneau sees in a good weekend. Or maybe it's the fact that there isn't a restaurant, gift shop or tour operator along Main St that is owned by a corporate conglomerate. Haines' businesses are uniquely Haines, and most likely the person behind the counter is the one who owns the store. The town isn't especially well developed for tourism: you won't find a salmon bake here and, no doubt for many travelers, that's part of its charm.

◉ Sights

Sheldon Museum   MUSEUM
(www.sheldonmuseum.org; 11 Main St; adult/child $5/free; ⊙10am-5pm Mon-Fri, 1-4pm Sat) The Sheldon Museum houses a collection of indigenous artifacts upstairs, including a par-

ticularly interesting display on rare Chilkat blankets. Downstairs is devoted to Haines' pioneer and gold-rush days and even includes the sawed-off shotgun that Jack Dalton used to convince travelers to pay his toll.

Hammer Museum   MUSEUM
(www.hammermuseum.org; 108 Main St; adult/child $5/free; ⊙10am-5pm Mon-Fri, to 2pm Sat) The Hammer Museum is a monument to Dave Pahl's obsession with hammers. He has 1500 on display, a 20ft-high one outside and several hundred more in storage. In the world's only hammer museum you learn world history through the development of

Haines

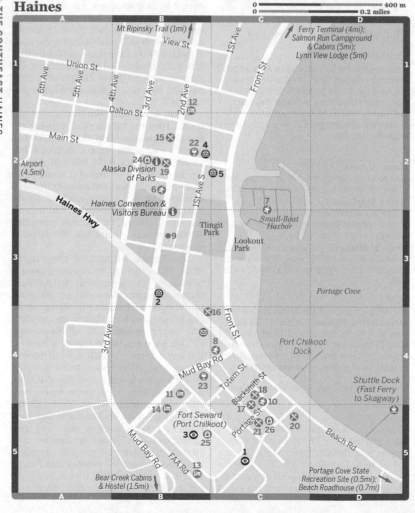

the hammer, from one less than ¼oz to another weighing more than 40lb.

American Bald Eagle Foundation MUSEUM
(www.baldeagles.org; 113 Haines Hwy; adult/child $10/5; ☉9am-5pm Mon-Fri, from 1pm Sat; ⊞) An impressive wildlife diorama is featured at the American Bald Eagle Foundation – it displays more than 180 specimens and almost two dozen eagles. Two live raptors are always on display, with handlers giving demonstrations.

Fort Seward HISTORIC BUILDINGS
Alaska's first permanent military post is reached by heading uphill (east) at the Front St–Haines Hwy junction. Built in 1903 and decommissioned after WWII, the fort is now a national historical site, with a handful of restaurants, lodges and art galleries in the original buildings. A walking-tour map of the fort is available at the visitors center, or you can just wander around and read the historical panels that have been erected there.

Alaska Indian Arts Center ARTS CENTER
(www.alaskaindianarts.com; 24 Fort Seward Dr; ☉9am-5pm Mon-Fri) Indigenous culture can be seen in Fort Seward in the former military post hospital, home of the Alaska Indian Arts Center. During the week you can watch artists carve totems, weave Chilkat blankets or produce other works of art. You can even order a totem.

Kroschel's Wildlife Center WILDLIFE RESERVE
(☑907-766-2050; www.kroschelfilms.com; $50 per person) Twenty-eight miles north of Haines is Kroschel's Wildlife Center, run by an ex-Hollywood animal trainer. There are 15 species of Alaska wildlife here, including bears, lynx and wolves, and the feeling is definitely less zoo and more wild. Tours are by appointment only; you won't be able to enter if you simply show up. Add $25 extra for round-trip transport.

⭐ Activities

Cycling
You can discover some great road trips or what little single-track mountain biking there is in Haines by visiting **Sockeye Cycle** (☑907-766-2869, 877-292-4154; www.cycle alaska.com; 24 Portage St; bicycles per 2/4/8hr $14/25/35; ☉9am-5:30pm Mon-Fri, to 4pm Sat), which rents a variety of top-of-the-line bicycles. The most popular road trip is the scenic 22-mile ride out to Chilkoot Lake. The shop also offers bicycle tours, with its best being an eight hour ride on dirt roads through the alpine of the newly created Tatshenshini-Alsek Provincial Park. The cost is $206 per person and includes mountain bikes, guide, transport and lunch. **Mike's Bikes & Boards** (☑907-766-3232; Mud Bay Rd & Beach St; ☉9am-6pm Mon-Tue & Thu-Sun; from 8am Wed) also rents mountain bikes (half/full day $20/30).

Haines

Hiking

Two major trail systems are within walking distance of Haines. South of town are the Chilkat Peninsula trails, including the climb to Mt Riley. North of Haines is the path to the summit of Mt Ripinsky. Stop at the visitors bureau and pick up the brochure *Haines is for Hikers,* which describes the trails in more detail. For outdoor gear or a guided hike, stop by **Alaska Backcountry Outfitter** (☑907-766-2876; 111 2nd Ave; ☉10am-5pm).

Mt Ripinsky Trail   HIKING

The trip to Mt Ripinsky's summit offers a sweeping view of Lynn Canal and the land from Juneau to Skagway. The route, which includes South Summit (3573ft), Peak 3920 and a descent from 7 Mile Saddle to Haines Hwy, is either a strenuous 10-hour journey for experienced hikers or an overnight trip.

To reach the trailhead, follow 2nd Ave north to where Young Rd, posted with a Mt Ripinsky Trail sign, splits from Lutak Rd (the road to the ferry terminal) and heads up the hill. Signs will direct you to the old pipeline road, where parking and the trail are clearly posted.

You can camp in the alpine area between Mt Ripinsky and the South Summit and then continue the next day west along the ridge to Peak 3920. From here you can descend to 7 Mile Saddle and then to the Haines Hwy, putting you 7 miles northwest of town. In recent years the trail has been greatly improved, but this is still a challenging overnight hike with spectacular views. For a 3-mile day hike, trek to the AT&T tower on Ridge Trail, a spur off the east end of the main trail.

Battery Point Trail   HIKING

This 2-mile trail has had recent improvements and is a pleasant, flat walk along the shore to Kelgaya Point; cut across to a pebble beach and follow it to Battery Point for excellent views of Lynn Canal. The trail begins a mile beyond Portage Cove Recreation Site at the end of Beach Rd and has been extensively updated; soon it should be completely accessible.

A VALLEY FULL OF EAGLES

The **Alaska Chilkat Bald Eagle Preserve** was created in 1982 when the state reserved 48,000 acres along the Chilkat, Klehini and Tsirku Rivers to protect the largest known gathering of bald eagles in the world. Each year from October to February, more than 4000 eagles congregate here to feed on spawning salmon. They come because an upwelling of warm water prevents the river from freezing, thus encouraging the late salmon run. It's a remarkable sight – hundreds of birds sitting in the bare trees lining the river, often six or more birds to a branch.

The best time to see this wildlife phenomenon is during the **Alaska Bald Eagle Festival** (www.baldeagles.org/festival). The five-day event in the second week of November attracts hundreds of visitors from around the country to Haines for speakers and presentations at the Sheldon Museum and the American Bald Eagle Foundation Center. But the basis of the festival is trooping out to the Chilkat River on 'expedition buses' with naturalists on board and encountering numbers of eagles that you cannot see anywhere else in the country at any other time of the year.

If the rain, snow and sleet of November is not on your Alaskan agenda, then you can still see eagles during the summer from the Haines Hwy, where there are turnouts for motorists to park and look for birds. The best view is between Mile 18 and Mile 22, where you'll find spotting scopes, interpretive displays and viewing platforms along the river. The numbers are not as mind-boggling as in early winter but 400 eagles live here year-round and more than 80 nests line the rivers.

There are several operators who tour the area by boat and land.

Alaska Nature Tours (p143) Conducts four-hour tours (adult/child $78/63) daily in summer. The tours cover much of the scenery around the Haines area but concentrate on the river flats and river mouths, where you usually see up to 40 eagles, many of them nesting.

River Adventures (☑907-766-2050, 800-478-9827; www.jetboatalaska.com) Uses jet boats for its Eagle Preserve River Adventure. The tour includes bus transportation 24 miles up the river to the jet boats and then a 1½-hour boat ride to look for eagles and other wildlife. The price is $100 per person.

Mt Riley Trails HIKING

This climb to a 1760ft summit provides good views in all directions, including vistas of Rainbow and Davidson Glaciers. One trail up the mountain begins at a junction about a mile up the Battery Point Trail out of Portage Cove Recreation Site. From here, you hike 3 miles over Half Dome and up Mt Riley.

Another route, closer to town, begins at the end of FAA Rd, which runs behind Officers' Row in Fort Seward. From the road's end, follow the water-supply access route for 2 miles to a short spur that branches off to the right and connects with the trail from Mud Bay Rd. The hike is 3.9 miles one way and eliminates the need to find a ride out to the third trailhead to Mt Riley, 3 miles out on Mud Bay Rd. The trailhead off Mud Bay Rd is posted, and this 2.8-mile route is the steepest but easiest to follow and the most direct to the summit. Plan on a five- to six-hour round-trip.

Seduction Point Trail HIKING

This trail begins at Chilkat State Park Campground and is a 6.8-mile (one-way) hike to the point separating Chilkoot and Chilkat Inlets. The sometimes-swampy and definitely rooty trail swings between forest and beaches, and provides excellent views of Davidson Glacier.

If you have the equipment, this trail can be turned into an excellent overnight hike by setting up camp at the cove east of Seduction Point. Carry in water and check the tides before departing, as the final stretch along the beach after David's Cove should be walked at low- or mid-tide. The entire round-trip takes nine to 10 hours.

River Running

Haines is a departure point for numerous raft trips. **Chilkat Guides** ($\square$907-766-2491; www.raftalaska.com; adult/child $94/65) offers a four-hour float daily down the Chilkat River through the bald-eagle preserve, with opportunities to view eagles and possibly brown bears; there is little or no white water.

On a much grander scale of adventure is the exciting nine- to 10-day raft trip down the Tatshenshini-Alsek River system, from Yukon Territory to the coast of Glacier Bay. This river trip is unmatched for its scenic mix of rugged mountain ranges and dozens of glaciers. Chilkat Guides and **Alaska Discovery/Mt Sobek** ($\square$888-687-6235; www.mtsobek.com) both run the trip, which costs between $3000 and $3300 per person.

$\square$ Tours

Other than Gustavus, Haines is the closest community to Glacier Bay National Park, making flightseeing tours much more reasonable here than in Skagway or Juneau. There's good bear watching between Haines and Chilkoot Lake.

Alaska Nature Tours NATURE

($\square$907-766-2876; www.alaskanaturetours.net; adult/child $78/63; $\square$) Offers environmentally focused tours with knowledgeable guides for activities that range from birding and bear watching to easy hikes to Battery Point. Its Twilight Wildlife Watch is a 2½-hour tour (adult/child $78/63) that departs at 6pm and heads up the Chilkoot River, stopping along the way to look for eagles, mountain goats and brown bears who emerge at dusk.

Jilkaat Kwaan Cultural Tours CULTURAL

($\square$907-767-5581, 907-767-5485; www.chilkat-nsn. gov; Mile 22, Haines Hwy; adult/child $104/52) Two tours take place in Klukwan, a Native village north of Haines: a four-hour one that includes everything from cultural dances and songs to meeting artists and watching villagers preparing fish using centuries-old methods. This tour coincides with cruiseships; call ahead to join. A one-hour tour includes history and storytelling inside a replica clan house (by appointment; $50 per person).

Klukwan is also home of the future **Jilkaat Kwaan Cultural Heritage Center**. The center is due to be finished in 2016 and will include a museum housing the village's treasured artworks, including the famous whale house collection, an arts studio, a replica tribal house and an eagle observatory along the Chilkat River. The current traditional knowledge camp has a carving shelter, replica clan house with totems, a fish processing area and hospitality house.

Fjord Express TOUR

($\square$800-320-0146; www.alaskafjordlines.com; Small Boat Harbor; adult/child $165/135) Don't have time to make it to Juneau? The Fjord Express zips you down Lynn Canal in a catamaran, will stop for whales, sea lions and other marine wildlife, and then rumbles around Juneau's top sights in a motorcoach before dropping you back off in Haines. A light breakfast and dinner are included.

Haines–Skagway Fast Ferry BOAT

(☑907-766-2100, 888-766-2103; www.hainesskagwayfastferry.com; Beach Rd) If you don't have time to overnight in Skagway, the Fast Ferry has a Rail & Sail Tour (adult/child $178/89) that includes round-trip transportation to the Klondike city and the Summit Excursion on the White Pass & Yukon Railroad.

Mountain Flying Service SCENIC FLIGHTS

(☑907-766-3007, 800-954-8747; www.mountainflyingservice.com; 132 2nd Ave) Offers an hour-long tour of the Glacier Bay's East Arm for $170 per person and an 80-minute tour of the more dramatic West Arm for $199. The two-hour outer coast flight lands on beach; it costs $299. On a clear day, it's money well spent.

✴ Festivals & Events

Haines stages the **Great Alaska Craft Beer & Home Brew Festival** in the third week of May when most of the state's microbrews compete for the honor of being named top suds.

Like every other Alaskan town, Haines has a festive celebration for **Fourth of July**, but the town's biggest event is the **Southeast Alaska State Fair**. Staged at the end of July, the fair is five days of live music, an Ugliest Dog Contest, logging and livestock shows and the famous pig races that draw participants from all Southeast communities.

🛏 Sleeping

Haines tacks a 9.5% tax onto the price of lodging.

Chilkat State Park Campground CAMPGROUND $

(Mud Bay Rd; sites $10) Seven miles southeast of Haines toward the end of Chilkat Peninsula, this campground has good views of Davidson and Rainbow Glaciers spilling out of the mountains into the Lynn Canal. There are 15 woodsy drive-in campsites and, a bit lower, three walk-ins on the beach.

Chilkoot Lake State Recreation Site CAMPGROUND $

(Lutak Rd; sites $10) Five miles north of the ferry terminal and nine miles north of town, the campground has 32 sites and picnic shelters. The fishing for Dolly Varden is good on Chilkoot Lake, a turquoise blue body of water surrounded by massive mountains.

Bear Creek Cabins & Hostel HOSTEL $

(☑907-766-2259; www.bearcreekcabinsalaska.com; Small Tract Rd; dm/cabins $20/68; ☎) A 20-minute walk outside town – follow Mud Bay Rd and when it veers right, continue straight onto Small Tract Rd for 1½ miles – this hostel is comprised of a number of cabins arround a grassy common area. A restroom/shower building also has laundry facilities, and there is a common, fully equipped kitchen reminiscent of a mess hall.

Portage Cove State Recreation Site CAMPGROUND $

(Beach Rd; campsites $5; ⊙mid-May–Aug) Half a mile southeast of Fort Seward or a 2-mile walk from downtown, this scenic campground overlooks the water and has nine sites on a circle of grass that are for backpackers and cyclists only. Follow Front St south; it becomes Beach Rd near Fort Seward.

Salmon Run Campground & Cabins CABINS $

(☑907-766-3240; Mile 6.5, Lutak Rd; sites $17, cabins $65-85; ☎) About a mile past the ferry terminal is this private campground on a hillside above Lynn Canal. There are 17 tent sites and 18 RV sites, plus two small cabins that come with heating and bunks but no indoor plumbing or kitchen facilities.

★ Beach Roadhouse B&B $$

(☑907-766-3060, 866-741-3060; www.beachroadhouse.com; 717 Beach Rd; r/cabins $115/145; ☎) This B&B is what Alaska is all about. The large cedar home is perched above Lynn Canal and surrounded by impressive pines for a tranquil, woodsy setting. Four rooms are large and include kitchenettes. The three cabins are even larger with full kitchens and lofts that sleep three to four persons.

Perhaps the best amenity of this roadhouse is just a few yards away: the start of scenic Battery Point Trail.

Alaska Guardhouse Lodging B&B $$

(☑907-766-2566, 866-290-7445; www.alaskaguardhouse.com; 15 Seward Dr; s/d $115/145; ☎) What used to jail misbehaved soldiers is now housing visitors in comfort and luxury. Four large bedrooms, a pleasant living room and an enclosed sun porch with rocking chairs all give way to views of mountains and water. When we visited they were restoring the old Ft Seward firehall next door; you'll recognize it by the giant tower.

Hotel Halsingland
HOTEL $$
(☏907-766-2000, 800-542-6363; www.hotel-halsingland.com; 13 Fort Seward Dr; r $79-119; ⊜@�) The grand dame of Haines hotels is the former bachelor officers' quarters and overlooks Fort Seward's parade ground. A National Historic Landmark, the hotel's rooms are slowly being renovated and a couple more are added each year; to date there are 35. Many still have fireplaces and classic claw-foot bathtubs.

Room No 4, a corner room on the 2nd floor, has unbelievable views.

Fort Seward B&B
B&B $$
(☏766-2856, 877-615-6676; www.fortsewardalaska.com; Ft Seward; $122-160; �) Built in 1902, this grand and roomy place was the commanding officer's house and the walls are adorned with historic photos. There are four rooms upstairs with private baths, three downstairs, and one lovely penthouse apartment ($175) with perhaps the best views in Haines. Rooms come with a large continental breakfast and use of the kitchen.

Lynn View Lodge
LODGE $$
(☏907-766-3713; www.lynnviewlodge.com; Mile 6.5, Lutak Rd; r $105-145, cabins $109; �) A mile past the ferry terminal northeast of town, this basic lodge has a great view of Lynn Canal and a long, covered porch to relax on and soak up the scenery. Accommodations range from one room with shared bath and two suites with private bath to three small cabins. Cars are also available for $79 a day.

Captain's Choice Motel
MOTEL $$
(☏907-766-3111; www.capchoice.com; 108 2nd Ave N; s/d $127/137) Haines' largest motel has the best view of the Chilkat Mountains and Lynn Canal and a huge sundeck to enjoy it on. The wood-paneled rooms are simple but spacious enough to include a microwave, small refrigerator, coffee-maker and TV. A light breakfast is offered in the morning, and courtesy transportation to the ferries and airport is available.

✖ Eating
If you're craving fresh seafood, check the bulletin boards around town to see if any commercial fishers are selling fish or Dungeness crab off their boats in the harbor. For fresh veggies, there's the **Haines Farmer's Market** held every other Saturday and some Wednesdays during the summer at the Southeast Alaska State Fairground from 10am to noon. **Howsers IGA** (211 Main St) is the main supermarket in Haines.

Sarah J's
CAFE $
(25 Portage St; breakfast $6-9, sandwiches $9-10; ☉6:30am-5pm Mon-Fri, 7am-3pm Sat & Sun; ☑) In a little shed that started out as a pigeon coop, Sarah J whips up two types of breakfast burritos, homemade granola, organic smoothies, baked goods, excellent coffee and more. Check out the burled spruce bar she made – would you expect anything less from an Alaskan?

Mountain Market & Cafe
DELI $
(3rd Ave, at Haines Hwy; breakfasts $6-9, sandwiches $7-9; ☉7am-7pm Mon-Sat, 8am-6pm Sun; ☑) The center of Haines hipness and healthy eating. The market stocks health foods, while its deli is loaded with vegetarian options, baked goods, great homemade soup, espresso drinks and indoor seating. Adjoining the store is **Mountain Spirits**, the best wine shop in town.

Big Al's
SEAFOOD $
(Mile 0 Haines Hwy; mains $10-13, ☉11am-7pm) Run by a local fisherman, all the seafood at this food truck is locally caught, probably that day. There are three kinds of fish and chips: halibut, rockfish and salmon. Get a combo and sample them all.

★ Fireweed Restaurant
BISTRO $$
(37 Blacksmith St; pizza $14-30, salads $10-19; ☉11:30am-3pm Wed-Sat & 4:30-9pm Tue-Sat, ☑) This clean, bright and laid-back bistro is in an old Fort Seward building and its salads are an antidote to Southeast's penchant for fried food. On its menu are words such as 'organic', 'veggie' and 'grilled' as opposed to 'deep fried' and 'captain's special'.

Vegetarians and canivores alike can indulge in sandwiches, burgers and the town's best pizza, all washed down with beer served in icy mugs.

Mosey's Cantina
MEXICAN $$
(www.moseyscantina.com; 31 Tower Rd; lunch $8-14, dinner $16-24; ☉11:30am-2:30pm Mon & Wed-Fri, 5:30-8:30pm Wed-Mon) This may be Haines, but Mosey's offers some of the best Mexican fare outside of Anchorage. The mole sauce is outstanding, the salsa is fire roasted and the tacos are filled with everything from applewood-grilled chicken and carne asada to locally caught rockfish. There is a delightful deck and garden seating as well as nine tables inside.

Bamboo Room
CAFE $$

(2nd Ave; breakfasts $7-15, lunch mains $8-15, dinner mains $15-25; ☺7am-10pm) CBS newsman Charles Kuralt once ate breakfast at this cafe and loved it. No doubt he had the blueberry pancakes with whipped cream. The Bamboo likes to claim it has the best fish 'n' chips in the world, but it's hard to pass up a plate of steamed Dungeness crabs served whole.

Dejon Delights
SEAFOOD $$

(☑907-766-2505; 37 Portage St; ☺10am-6pm Mon-Fri, to 4pm Sat & Sun) This shop in Fort Seward turns out some of the best smoked fish in the Southeast, such as salmon that is first marinated in stout beer.

Commander's Room
MODERN AMERICAN $$$

(☑907-766-2000; 13 Fort Seward Dr; mains $27-32; ☺5:30-9pm Wed-Mon) Located in Hotel Halsingland is Haines' most upscale restaurant. Begin the evening with a drink (and maybe some duck confit) in its cozy Officer's Club Lounge and then venture into the Commander's Room, where you'll find white tablecloths, a fine wine list and a chef who has a herb garden out back.

In July and August the salmon and halibut are flown in daily, or try Moroccan-spiced braised lamb shank served on a bed of Israeli couscous.

DON'T MISS

HAINES BREWING COMPANY

Haines' Dalton City was the movie set built for the 1991 film *White Fang*. After Hollywood left Haines, the set was relocated to the Southeast Alaska State Fairgrounds, and is now a destination for beer lovers. Among the false-front buildings and wooden sidewalks is the **Haines Brewing Company** (www. hainesbrewing.com; Dalton City; ☺1-6pm Mon-Sat), the maker of such beer as Dalton Trail Ale, Elder Rock Red and the potent Black Fang (9% alcohol content). Tours are short – hey this is a one-room brewery – but pints are available and you can have a half-gallon growler ($10 to $13) filled for later. Most of the restaurants in town also serve the local brew and, frankly, why drink anything else? As local author Heather Lende says on a sign in the brewery, 'Life is too short to waste my alcohol consumption on cheap beer.'

Drinking

Pioneer Bar
BAR

(www.bamboopioneer.net; 2nd Ave) The cheapest beer in town, and where to go to hear live music. It's connected to the Bamboo Room.

Fort Seward Lodge Restaurant & Saloon
BAR

(39 Mud Bay Rd) Tucked away upstairs in the Fort Seward Lodge's two-level restaurant is this small bar that's popular with heli-skiers in winter. Dangling from the ceiling in the middle is the original red-velvet swing that ladies swung on to the delight of the soldiers.

Captain's Lounge
BAR

(Captain's Choice Motel, 108 2nd Ave) A small, half-hidden bar in the back of a motel. It offers casual atmosphere, cheap bar snacks and one of the best mountainous views of any bar in Southeast Alaska.

Fogcutter Bar
BAR

(Main St) Haines is a hard-drinking town, and this is where a lot of them belly up to the bar and spout off.

Shopping

Despite a lack of cruise-ship traffic, or maybe because of it, Haines supports an impressive number of local artists and has enough galleries to fill an afternoon.

Extreme Dreams Fine Arts
ARTS & CRAFTS

(www.extremedreams.com; Mile 6.5, Mud Bay Rd) At the Chilkat State Park entrance is this wonderful gallery packed with the work of 20 local artists, from watercolors and weavings to hand-blown glass, cast silver and beautiful beads. The gallery also has a climbing wall because it's the studio of artist John Svenson, a renowned mountain climber who has scaled the highest peak on almost every continent.

Wild Iris
ARTS & CRAFTS

(22 Tower Rd) This art gallery is the most impressive of a growing number on the edge of Fort Seward. Outside the home is a beautiful Alaskan garden; inside, a fine selection of original jewelry, silk-screened prints, cards, pastels and other local art.

Sea Wolf Art Studio
ARTS & CRAFTS

(www.tresham.com; Ft Seward Parade Ground) Housed in a log cabin is Tresham Gregg's gallery. Gregg is one of Haines' best-known Alaska Native artists, and he combines the imagery of the spiritism, animism and shamanism of Northwest Coast Indians to create wood carvings, totems, masks, bronze sculpture and talismanic silver jewelry.

Babbling Book BOOKS
(☑907-766-3356; 223 Main St; ☺11am-5pm Mon-Sat, from noon Sun) Stocks a great selection of Alaska books, cards and calendars, while its walls serve as the notice board for Haines' cultural scene.

ℹ Information

Alaska Division of Parks (☑907-766-2292; 219 Main St, Suite 25; ☺8am-5pm Mon-Fri) For information on state parks and hiking; above Howser's IGA (there's no sign).
First National Bank of Anchorage (123 Main St) For all your presidential-portrait needs.
Post Office (Haines Hwy)
Haines Borough Public Library (111 S 3rd Ave; ☺10am-9pm Mon-Fri, 12:30-4:30pm Sat & Sun; 🖥) The cultural jewel of the community. This impressive facility has a book exchange, six computers for internet access (by donation), a beautiful reading area with rocking chairs and a two-story window overlooking the mountains. Curl up and read before the majestic view.
Haines Convention & Visitors Bureau (☑907-766-2234; www.haines.ak.us; 122 2nd Ave; ☺8am-5pm Mon-Fri, 9am-4pm Sat & Sun) Has restrooms, free coffee and racks of free information for tourists. There is also a lot of information on Canada's Yukon for those heading up the Alcan.
Haines Health Center (☑907-766-6300; 131 1st Ave S)

ℹ Getting There & Around

AIR
There is no jet service to Haines, but **Wings of Alaska** (☑907-766-2030; www.wingsofalaska.com) has daily flights to Juneau ($103) and Skagway ($63). **Alaska Seaplanes** (☑907-766-3800, 907-789-3331; www.flyalaskaseaplanes.com) will also take you to Juneau seven times a day ($110).

BOAT
State ferries depart daily from the **ferry terminal** (☑907-766-2111; 2012 Lutak Rd) 4 miles north of town for Skagway ($31, one hour) and Juneau ($37, 5½ hours). **Haines-Skagway Fast Ferry** (☑907-766-2100, 888-766-2103; www.hainesskagwayfastferry.com; one-way adult/child $35/18; ☺Jun-Sep) uses a speedy catamaran to cruise down Taiya Inlet to Skagway in 45 minutes. The 80ft cat departs Haines from the **Fast Ferry shuttle dock** at 6am, 1pm and

7pm and more often if cruise ships are packing Skagway. One-way fares are adult/child $36/18, round-trip $70/35.

BUS
Amazingly no buses serve Haines. You'll need to either thumb it north or take the ferry to Skagway and get a bus north from there.

CAR
To visit Alaska Chilkat Bald Eagle Preserve on your own, you can rent a car at **Captain's Choice Motel** (☑907-766-3111, 800-478-2345), which has compacts for $79 a day with unlimited mileage.

TAXI
You can also arrange for a ride out to the ferry terminal. **Any Time Taxi** (☑907-303-9246, 907-303-8984) will pick you up – you guessed it – any time! Rides from the airport into town are $6; from the ferry terminal $12. They'll even take you to the village of Klukwan for $45.

Skagway
POP 920

Situated at the head of Lynn Canal is Skagway, one of the driest places in an otherwise soggy Southeast. While Petersburg averages more than 100in of rain a year and Ketchikan a drenching 154in, Skagway gets only 26in annually.

At first sight, Skagway appears to be solely an amusement park for cruise ship daytrippers. But its easily accessed trails, historic railway and excellent dining options make this a a good place to stay a few days. You need only to wander a block or two away from Broadway St before you're away from the tourist bustle.

Much of Skagway is within Klondike Gold Rush National Historical Park, which comprises downtown Skagway, the Chilkoot Trail, the White Pass Trail corridor and a visitors center. Beginning in 1897, Skagway and the nearby ghost town of Dyea were the starting places for more than 40,000 gold-rush stampeders who headed to the Yukon primarily by way of the Chilkoot Trail. The actual stampede lasted only a few years, but it produced one of the most colorful periods in Alaskan history, that of a lawless frontier town controlled by villainous 'Soapy' Smith who was finally removed from power in a gunfight by town hero Frank Reid.

At the height of the gold rush, Michael J Heney, an Irish contractor, convinced a group of English investors that he could build a railroad over the White Pass Trail to Whitehorse. The construction of the White Pass & Yukon Route was nothing short of a superhuman feat, and the railroad became the focal point of the town's economy after the gold rush and during the military build-up of WWII.

The line was shut down in 1982 but was revived in 1988, to the delight of cruise-ship tourists and backpackers walking the Chilkoot Trail. Although the train hauls no freight, its rebirth was important to Skagway as a tourist attraction. Today Skagway survives almost entirely on tourism, and bus tours and more than 400 cruise ships a year turn this village into a boomtown again every summer. Up to five ships a day stop here and, on the busiest days, more than 9000 tourists – 10 times the town's resident population – march off the ships and turn Broadway into something of an anthill. It's the modern-day version of the Klondike

Gold Rush and the reason why Skagway has more jewelry shops per capita than any place in Alaska and possibly the country.

Unlike the majority of Southeast towns, Skagway is a truly delightful place to arrive in by sea. Cruise-ship and state-ferry passengers alike step off their boats and are funneled to Broadway St, Skagway's main avenue and the heart of Klondike Gold Rush National Park Historic District. Suddenly you find yourself in a bustling town, where many people are dressed as if they are trying to relive the gold-rush days and the rest are obviously tourists from the luxury liners.

⊙ Sights

Several changes are in store for some of Skagways sites in 2016; the National Park Service plans to move the Junior Ranger Acivity Center, change all of the exhibits at the Visitors Center, and open Soapy Smith's Parlor across the street.

Skagway

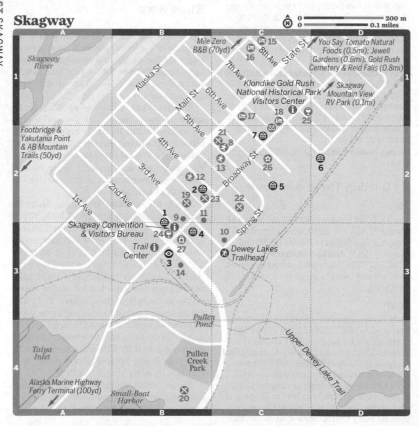

Klondike Gold Rush National Historical Park HISTORIC SITE
(☎907-983-9200; www.nps.gov/klgo; Visitor Center, Broadway St, at 2nd Ave; ☉8am-6pm, to 7pm Fri) FREE The **NPS center** is in the original 1898 White Pass & Yukon Route depot. The center features displays – the most impressive being a replica of the ton of supplies every miner had to carry over the Chilkoot Pass – ranger programs and a small bookstore. The 25-minute film *Gold Fever: Race to the Klondike,* an excellent introduction to the gold rush, is shown on the hour.

Rangers lead a 50-minute walking tour of the historic district on the hour from 9am to 11am and at 2 & 3pm; call to see if there are extra tours that day.

Skagway Museum MUSEUM
(☎907-983-2420; cnr 7th Ave & Spring St; adult/child $2/1; ☉9am-5pm Mon-Fri, 10am-5pm Sat, noon-4pm Sun) Skagway Museum is not only one of the finest in a town filled with museums but one of the finest in the Southeast. It occupies the entire 1st floor of the venerable century-old McCabe Building, a former college, and is devoted to various aspects of local history, including Alaska Native baskets, beadwork and carvings, and, of course, the Klondike Gold Rush. The display that draws the most looks is the small pistol Soapy Smith kept up his sleeve.

Mascot Saloon Museum MUSEUM
(Broadway St, at 3rd Ave; ☉8am-6pm) FREE The only saloon in Alaska that doesn't serve booze – but it did during the gold rush, and plenty of it. Built in 1898, the Mascot was one of Skagway's 80 to 100 saloons in its heyday as 'the roughest place in the world.' The NPS has turned it into a museum that looks into the vices – gambling, drinking, prostitution – that followed the stampeders to the gold-fields, encouraging visitors to belly up to the bar for a shot of sinful history.

Junior Ranger Activity Center MUSEUM
(Broadway St, at 4th Ave; ☉10am-3pm Mon-Fri; ☻) FREE At the Pantheon Saloon, built in 1903, kids are the customers. The historic bar is now home to the park's Junior Ranger Program where children and their parents examine artifacts that they can touch, dress up as stampeders and shoulder a miner's pack on their way to earning a Junior Ranger badge. The NPS has plans to move the ranger station in 2016; check at the visitor center for info.

Moore's Cabin HISTORIC BUILDING
(5th Ave, at Spring St; ☉10am-5pm) A block southeast of the city museum is Skagway's oldest building, Moore's Cabin. Captain William Moore and his son, Bernard, built the cabin in 1887, when they staked out their homestead as the founders of the town. The NPS has since renovated the building and,

in doing so, discovered that the famous Dead Horse Trail that was used by so many stampeders actually began in the large lawn next to the cabin.

Adjacent to the cabin is the restored **Bernard Moore House**, which features exhibits and furnishings depicting family life during the gold rush.

Wells Fargo Bank
HISTORIC BUILDING

(Broadway St, at 6th Ave; ⊘ 9:30am-5pm Mon-Fri) FREE This bank dates back to 1916 when a group of East Coast businessmen founded the National Bank of Alaska and built the bank a year later. Today it is an interesting place to visit even if you're not short on cash. Two of the five brass teller gates are originals, there are spittoons in case you're chewing tobacco, and on display everywhere are banking artifacts, from a classic 'Cannonball' safe to an old coin machine.

Arctic Brotherhood Hall
HISTORIC BUILDING

(Broadway St, at 2nd Ave) The most outlandish building of the seven-block historical corridor along Broadway St, and possibly the most photographed building in Alaska, is this defunct fraternal hall that was a club for prospectors, now home of the Skagway Convention & Visitors Bureau. The original driftwood, nearly 9000 pieces of it, that covers the facade were attached in 1899 and extensively renovated, piece-by-piece, in 2005.

Gold Rush Cemetery & Reid Falls
CEMETERY

Visitors who become infatuated with Smith and Reid can walk out to this cemetery, a 1.5-mile stroll northeast on State St. Follow State until it curves into 23rd Ave and just before crossing the bridge over the Skagway River. The cemetery is the site of many stampeders' graves, including Soapy's, as well as the plots of Reid and Smith. From Reid's gravestone, it's a short hike uphill to lovely Reid Falls, which cascades 300ft down the mountainside.

Jewell Gardens
GARDENS

(☑ 907-983-2111; www.jewellgardens.com; Klondike Hwy; adult/child $12.50/6; ⊘ 9am-5pm) If the crowds are overwhelming you, cross the Skagway River to Jewell Gardens. Located where Henry Clark started the first truck farm in Alaska, the garden is a quiet spot of flowerbeds, ponds, giant vegetables and a miniature train. There is also a pair of glass-blowing studios where artists give fascinating demonstrations while making beautiful glassware. Call for times of the glassblowing

and then hop on a SMART bus that will drop you off at the entrance.

Dyea
HISTORIC SITE

In 1898 Skagway's rival city, Dyea (die-yee), at the foot of the Chilkoot Trail, was the trailhead for the shortest route to Lake Bennett, where stampeders began their float to Dawson City. After the White Pass & Yukon Route was completed in 1900, Dyea quickly died. Today it's a few old crumbling cabins, the pilings of Dyea Wharf and Slide Cemetery, where 47 men and women were buried after perishing in an avalanche on the Chilkoot Trail in April 1898.

To explore the ghost town, you can pick up the Dyea Townsite Self-Guided Walking Tour brochure from the NPS center. The guide will lead your along a mile loop from the townsite parking area past what few ruins remain. Or join a ranger-led walk, which meets at the parking area at 2pm Monday to Thursday.

Dyea is a 9-mile drive along winding Dyea Rd, whose numerous hairpin turns are not for timid RVers. But it's a very scenic drive, especially at Skagway Overlook, a turnoff with a viewing platform 2½ miles from Skagway. The overlook offers an excellent view of Skagway, its waterfront and peaks above the town. Just before crossing the bridge over the Taiya River, you pass the Dyea Campground.

🏃 Activities

Hiking

The 33-mile Chilkoot Trail (p58) is Southeast Alaska's most popular hike, but there are a couple of excellent trails that originate downtown and more that you can reach by train. There is no USFS office in Skagway, but the NPS Visitor Center has a free brochure entitled *Skagway Trail Map*. You can also get backcountry information and any outdoor gear you need (including rentals) at the excellent **Mountain Shop** (www.packerexpeditions.com; 355 4th Ave).

Dewey Lakes Trail System
HIKING

This series of trails leads east of Skagway to a handful of alpine and subalpine lakes, waterfalls and historic sites. From Broadway, follow 3rd Ave southeast to the railroad tracks. On the east side of the tracks are the trailheads to Lower Dewey Lake (0.7 miles), Icy Lake (2.5 miles), Upper Reid Falls (3.5 miles) and Sturgill's Landing (4.5 miles).

Plan on taking an hour round-trip for the hike to Lower Dewey Lake, where there are picnic tables, camping spots and a trail circling the lake. At the lake's north end is an alpine trail that ascends steeply to Upper Dewey Lake, 3.5 miles from town, and Devil's Punchbowl, another 1.25 miles south of the upper lake. If you want to stay the night, Skagway Recreation Center has a new **cab in** (☎907-983-2679; www.skagwayrecreation.org; $35) at Upper Dewey Lake, and there is also a run-down free-use shelter that does not require reservations.

The hike to Devil's Punchbowl is an all-day trip or an ideal overnight excursion; stay at the Dewey Lake cabins. There are also campsites at Sturgill's Landing.

Yakutania Point & AB Mountain Trails   HIKING
The Skagway River footbridge, at the foot of the airport runway on 1st Ave, leads to two trails of opposite caliber. For an easy hike turn left from the bridge and follow the mile-long trail to picnic areas and lovely views at Yakutania Point and Smugglers Cove.

The AB Mountain Trail ascends 5.5 miles to the 5100ft summit of AB Mountain.

Also known as the Skyline Trail, it's official name comes from the 'AB' pattern that appears on its south side when the snow melts every spring. The first 30 minutes is along a well-defined trail through a hemlock forest to a view of Skagway. After that the trail is considerably more challenging, especially above the treeline, requiring a full day to reach the summit. Watch the weather and consider something lower if the summit is obscured.

Denver Glacier Trail   HIKING
(round-trip adult/child $31/16) This trail begins at Mile 6 of the White Pass & Yukon Route, where the USFS has renovated a WPYR caboose into the **Denver Caboose** (☎877-444-6777; www.recreation.gov; cabins $35), a rental cabin of sorts. The trail heads up the east fork of Skagway River for 2 miles, then swings south and continues another 1.5 miles up the glacial outwash to Denver Glacier.

Most of the trail is overgrown with brush, and the second half is particularly tough hiking. White Pass & Yukon Route will drop hikers off at the caboose.

Laughton Glacier Trail   HIKING
(round-trip adult/child $66/33) At Mile 14 of the White Pass & Yukon Route is a 1.5-mile hike to the USFS **Laughton Glacier Cabin** (☎877-444-6777; www.recreation.gov; cabins $35). The cabin overlooks the river from Warm Pass but is only a mile from Laughton Glacier, an impressive hanging glacier between the 3000ft walls of the Sawtooth Range.

The alpine scenery and ridge walks in this area are well worth the ticket on the White Pass & Yukon Route. There are two excursion trains from Skagway, so this could be a possible day hike. But it's far better to carry a tent and spend a night in the area.

Cycling

Sockeye Cycle   MOUNTAIN BIKING
(☎907-983-2851; www.cyclealaska.com; 381 5th Ave; bikes per 2/8hr $20/40) Rents hybrids and mountain bikes and offers several bike tours from Skagway. Its three-hour Rainforest Tour ($87) begins with transportation to Dyea, followed by a guided tour of the area. The Klondike Tour takes you up to Klondike Pass (elevation 3295ft) on the Klondike Hwy. Ride the 15 miles down to town, stopping to view waterfalls.

The same trip is also offered with a ride up on the White Pass & Yukon Route ($191).

Alcan Outfitters   MOUNTAIN BIKING
(☎907-612-0745, www.alcanoutfitters.com; 380 State St; bikes per 1/2/24hr $15/25/40; ⏱9am-6pm) A small shop that rents fat bikes (good for beaches and snow) and mountain bikes and has a small collection of camping supplies. Guided tours available; open year round.

Rafting

Skagway Float Tours   RAFTING
(☎907-983-3688; www.skagwayfloat.com) Offers a three-hour tour of Dyea that includes a 45-minute float down the placid Taiya River (adult/child $75/55); there are two per day at 9am and 1:30pm. Its Hike & Float Tour ($90/70) is a four-hour outing that includes hiking 2 miles of the Chilkoot Trail then some floating back; there are several per day.

⚐ Tours

★White Pass & Yukon Route Railroad   TRAIN
(☎800-343-7373; www.wpyr.com; 231 2nd Ave; ⏱Jun-Aug) Without a doubt the most spectacular tour from Skagway is a ride aboard the historic railway of the White Pass & Yukon Route (WPYR). Two different narrated

SUMMIT & CITY TOURS

The 'Summit & City Tour' is the standard tour in Skagway and includes Gold Rush Cemetery, White Pass Summit and Skagway Overlook, including a lively narration that might be historically accurate. The cost is $40 to $50 per person for a three-hour outing. Check out the Sockeye Cycle (p151) rail/bike combo tour for a workout. The following all offer such a tour, among others.

Frontier Excursions (☑907-983-2512, 877-983-2512; www.frontierexcursions.com; cnr Broadway St & 3rd Ave)

Gray Line (☑907-983-6088; cnr Spring St & 3rd Ave, at Westmark Inn)

Klondike Tours (☑907-983-2075, 866-983-2075; www.klondiketours.com; cnr Broadway St & 2nd Ave)

sightseeing tours are available; reservations are recommended for both. Remember your passport, as some of the tours cross into Canada and back.

Running Tuesday through Saturday, the eight-hour Bennett Scenic Journey is the premier trip. At Skagway's railroad depot you board parlor cars for the trip to White Pass on the narrow-gauge line built during the 1898 Klondike Gold Rush. This segment is only a small portion of the 110-mile route to Whitehorse, but it contains the most spectacular scenery, including crossing Glacier Gorge and Dead Horse Gulch, viewing Bridal Veil Falls and then making the steep 2885ft climb to White Pass, only 20 miles from Skagway. You make a whistle stop at the historic 1903 Lake Bennett Railroad Depot for lunch and then board the train to follow the shoreline of stunning Lake Bennett to Carcross. At this small Yukon town, buses take you back to Skagway. The Bennett Scenic Journey departs from Skagway at 7:30am on Wednesday, Thursday and Saturday, and 8:30am (bus up, train back – the reverse of the other days) on Tuesday and Friday; the fare is $229/115 per adult/child.

The White Pass Summit Excursion (three to 3½ hours, adult/child $122/56) is a shorter tour to White Pass Summit and back. The tour is offered at 8:15am and 12:45pm daily mid-May to mid-September and at 4:30pm Tuesday and Wednesday until early September.

Red Onion Saloon TOUR
(☑907-983-2222; www.redonion1898.com; cnr Broadway St & 2nd Ave) Skagway's beloved saloon was once a house of sin, the reason for its tours of the upstairs bedrooms, now a brothel museum. 'The Quickie' is $10 for 20 minutes and offered throughout the day, while the 30-minute 'Happy Endings Brothel Tour' is $17 and includes a grown-up beverage upon completion. Now that's a happy ending.

Klondike Gold Dredge Tours TOUR
(☑907-983-3175; www.klondikegoldfields.com; Mile 1.7, Klondike Hwy; 2hr tours $50) Offers tours of a former working gold dredge that was in Dawson before being moved to Skagway, where it has hit the mother lode. There is also a gold-panning show with a crack at finding dust yourself, and a brewpub onsite.

Gold Rush Trail Camp GOLD PANNING
(☑907-983-3333; Mile 3, Klondike Hwy; adult/child $55/37) Offers a miners' show, a turn at gold panning and Skagway's salmon bake. You book it and pick up the bus at Skagway Mountain View RV Park.

✫ Festivals & Events

Skagway's **Fourth of July** celebrations feature a footrace, parade, street dance and the Ducky Derby, when a thousand plastic ducks are raced down a stream. But the town's most unusual celebration is **Soapy Smith's Wake**, on July 8. Locals and the cast of the *Days of '98 Show* celebrate with a hike out to the grave and a champagne toast, with champagne often sent up from California by Smith's great-grandson.

🛏 Sleeping

Skagway levies an 8% sales and bed tax on all lodging.

Alaskan Sojourn Hostel HOSTEL $
(☑907-983-2040; www.alaskansojourn.net; 488 8th Ave; dm/r $32/70) Skagway's only hostel is comfortable and friendly, in a large converted house shared with the welcoming owners. There are mixed and single-sex dorms, as well as a private room and even a cute and very cozy two-person cabin. This is a relaxed and pleasant place away from the hustle of Broadway and across from the library.

Dyea Campground CAMPGROUND $
(☑907-983-2921; sites $10) Located near the Chilkoot trailhead in Dyea, about 9 miles north of Skagway, this 21-site campground

is operated by the NPS on a first-come, first-served basis. There are vault toilets and tables but no drinking water. A mile away past the Dyea Townsite, the city of Skagway operates a **free eight-site campground** – register at the **police station** (1st Ave & Main St) in Skagway.

Skagway Mountain View
RV Park   CAMPGROUND **$**
(☑907-983-3333; 12th Ave, at Broadway St; tent/RV sites $30/49; ☏) The town's best campground for tenters. It has 34 RV sites and a limited number of tent sites. Amenities include firepits, laundry facilities, coin-operated showers, and dump stations for both humans and RVs. It's easy walking distance from downtown, but you won't feel trampled by tourists.

At the White House   INN **$$**
(☑907-983-9000; www.atthewhitehouse.com; cnr 8th Ave and Main St; r incl breakfast $125-165; ☏) A large, historic nine-room inn filled with antiques, remembrances of the Klondike and colorful comforters on every bed. Rooms are spacious and bright, even on a rainy day, and have cable TV and phone. In the morning you wake up to a breakfast of fresh-baked goods and fruit served in a sun-drenched dining room.

Mile Zero B&B   B&B **$$**
(☑907-983-3045; www.mile-zero.com; 901 Main St; r $135-145; ☏☏) This B&B is more like a motel with the comforts of home, as the six large rooms have their own private entrance on the wraparound porch. If you hook the fish of your dreams, there's a BBQ area where you can grill it for dinner.

Skagway Inn   INN **$$**
(☑907-983-2289, 888-752-4929; www.skagwayinn.com; Broadway St, at 7th Ave; r incl breakfast $129-229; ☏☏) In a restored 1897 Victorian building that was originally one of the town's brothels – what building still standing in Skagway wasn't? – the beautiful inn is downtown and features 10 rooms, four with shared baths. All are small but filled with antique dressers, iron beds and chests. Breakfast is included, as is ferry/airport/train transport.

Sgt Preston's Lodge   MOTEL **$$**
(☑907-983-2521, 866-983-2521; www.sgtprestonslodge.com; 370 6th Ave; s $90-115, d $100-151; ☏) This motel is the best bargain in Skagway and the 38 rooms are nicer than outside appearances indicate. It's just far enough from Broadway St to escape most of the cruise-ship crush. Courtesy transportation and complimentary coffee provided.

Chilkoot Trail Outpost   CABINS **$$**
(☑907-983-3799; www.chilkoottrailoutpost.com; Mile 8.5, Dyea Rd; cabins $155-185; ☏) Hitting the 'Koot? Start with a good night's sleep at this excellent resort located a half-mile from the trailhead. The cabins are comfortable and equipped with microwaves, refrigerators and coffee-makers. In the morning you can fuel up on a buffet breakfast at the main lodge (included). There are bicycles available, and the screened-in gazebo is strategically located at a waterfall.

✖ Eating

Skagway has more than 20 restaurants operating during the summer, and there's a higher per capita rate of excellent ones than elsewhere in Southeast.

You Say Tomato Natural Foods   ORGANIC **$**
(21st Ave, at State St; ☒10:30-7:30pm Mon-Fri, noon-6:30 Sat & Sun) This natural-foods store with organic produce is located in a replica of the Whitehorse Railroad Depot.

Lemon Rose Bakery   BAKERY **$**
(cnr of State St & 5th Ave; light fare $3-10; ☒8am-4pm Mon-Fri, 10am-3pm Sat, 10am-2pm Sun) This bakery is so small, the line in the morning for its giant cinnamon rolls covered with glaciers of icing ($3) snakes out to the sidewalk. They're worth the wait.

Glacial Smoothies
& Espresso   COFFEE HOUSE **$**
(336 3rd Ave; breakfasts $4-7, sandwiches $8-10; ☒6am-5pm Mon-Sat, 7am-4pm Sun; ☒) Skagway's favorite for breakfast bagels, healthy sandwiches and smoothies. This is where you come to idle away a rainy afternoon.

★Olivia's Bistro   SEAFOOD **$$**
(Broadway St, at 7th Ave; breakfast & lunch mains $9-15, dinner mains $14-27; ☒10am-9pm; ☒) A charming bistro in the Skagway Inn. The menu features wild game and seafood and whatever is growing in the lovely garden outside. How can you top that? With a serving of homegrown rhubarb crisp for dessert.

Poppies   ORGANIC **$$**
(Klondike Hwy; mains $8-16; ☒11am-3pm; ☒) Located inside a greenhouse at Jewell Gardens, this restaurant has the best salads in town

because the greens are grown just outside and probably picked that afternoon. Most of the other dishes also begin with organic ingredients and, best of all, are served with a view of the gardens in full bloom and AB Mountain looming overhead.

Starfire
THAI $$
(☑907-983-3663; 4th Ave, at Spring St; lunch $12-15, dinner $14-19; ⊘11am-10pm; ☑) Skagway's Thai restaurant is authentic and good, with a small lunch menu and a large, varied dinner menu. Order spicy drunken noodles or curry dishes in five colors (purple is *Fire with Flavor!*) and enjoy it with a beer on the outdoor patio – so pleasant and secluded you would never know Skagway's largest hotel is across the street.

Harbor House
SEAFOOD $$
(☑907-983-3463; 205 Congress Way; breakfast $7-14, lunch $6-16, dinner $12-25; ⊘10am-10pm) Skagway's newest restaurant is in a little house above the harbor. Its menu covers three squares a day, and includes breakfast basics, a boatful of seafood, and non-Alaskan options such as ribs and smoked fried chicken.

Sweet Tooth Cafe
CAFE $$
(315 Broadway St; breakfast $8-13; ⊘6:30am-2:30pm) Skagway's diner is open early and serves up full, if general, breakfasts. At lunch, sandwiches are served on homemade bread.

Skagway Fish Company
SEAFOOD $$$
(☑907-983-3474; Congress Way; lunch mains $10-17, dinner mains $18-40; ⊘11am-9pm) Located above the harbor is this restaurant overlooking the harbor, with crab traps on the ceiling. You can certainly feast on fish, such as halibut stuffed with cream cheese, shrimp and veggies or king-crab bisque, but surprisingly, what many locals rave about are its baby back ribs. Its bar has the best view in town.

🍷 Drinking & Nightlife

★ Skagway Brewing Company
BREWERY
(www.skagwaybrewing.com; cnr 7th Ave & Broadway; burgers $15; ⊘10am-10pm Mon-Fri, 11am-10pm Sat & Sun) Skagway's microbrewery offers stampeders such choices as Prospector Pale Ale, Boomtown Brown and Chilkoot Trail IPA. There's a full menu with nightly dinner specials and a quiet outdoor deck in the back to escape the rowdiness at the front. It's the best place in town to relax after a long hike.

Red Onion Saloon
BAR
(Broadway St, at 2nd Ave) Skagway's beloved brothel at the turn of the century is now its most famous saloon. The 'RO' is done up as a gold-rush saloon, complete with mannequins leering down at you from the 2nd story to depict pioneer-era working girls. When bands are playing here, it'll be packed, noisy and rowdy. It also has the best pizza in town.

☆ Entertainment

Days of '98 Show
THEATER
(☑907-983-2545; www.thedaysof98show.com; Eagle's Hall, 598 Broadway, at 6th Ave; adult/child $22/11) This is Southeast Alaska's longest-running melodrama. The evening show begins with 'mock gambling,' then moves on to a show focusing on Soapy and his gang. Up to four shows are offered daily, but call as the schedule is heavily dependent on cruise ships.

🔒 Shopping

Skaguay News Depot
BOOKS
(www.skagwaybooks.com; 264 Broadway St; ⊘9am-6pm) A small bookstore with an excellent selection on the Klondike Gold Rush.

ℹ Information

Dahl Memorial Clinic (☑907-983-2255; 350 14th Ave; ⊘7am-7pm Mon, Tue & Fri, 8am-5pm Wed & Thu, 10am-2pm Sat) If gold fever strikes, head to this clinic. Has a 24-hour on-call doctor.

Klondike Gold Rush National Historical Park Visitors Center (☑907-983-9200; www.nps.gov/klgo; 154 Broadway St; ⊘8am-6pm) For everything outdoors – local trails, public campgrounds, NPS programs – head to this center.

Post Office (641 Broadway St)

Skagway Convention & Visitors Bureau (☑907-983-2854; www.skagway.com; cnr Broadway St & 2nd Ave; ⊘8am-6pm Mon-Fri, to 5pm Sat & Sun) For information on lodging, tours, restaurant menus or what's new, visit this bureau housed in the can't-miss Arctic Brotherhood Hall (think driftwood).

Skagway Library (8th Ave, at State St; ⊘noon-9pm Mon-Fri, 1-5pm Sat & Sun; ☎) One of the few places in town for internet. Wi-fi access is free, but its two internet computers are heavily used.

Skagway Port of Call (221 2nd Ave; internet per hr $5; ⊘9am-6:30pm Mon-Thu, 9am-5pm Fri, 10am-4pm Sat, 8:30am-4pm Sun) Makes a living, and probably a decent one, selling cruise-ship workers high-speed internet access on 16 computers, along with phone cards and every brand of instant noodles made in Asia.

Trail Center (☑ 907-983-9234; www.nps.gov/klgo; Broadway St, at 2nd Ave; ⊙ 8am-5pm) If you're stampeding to the Chilkoot Trail, first stop here in the restored Martin Itjen House at the foot of Broadway. The center is a clearinghouse for information on permits and transportation.

Wells Fargo (Broadway St, at 6th Ave) Occupies the original office of National Bank of Alaska.

❶ Getting There & Away

AIR

Regularly scheduled flights to Juneau ($93) and Haines ($39) are available from **Wings of Alaska** (☑ 907-983-2442; www.wingsofalaska.com). **Alaska Seaplanes** (☑ 907-983-2479, 907-789-3331; www.flyalaskaseaplanes.com) also offers services at roughly $20 more and flies to smaller communities throughout the Southeast.

BOAT

There is a daily run of the **Alaska Marine Highway** (☑ 800-642-0066, 907-983-2229; www.ferryalaska.com) from Skagway to Haines ($31, one hour), Juneau ($50, 6½ hours) and back again. In Skagway, the ferry departs from the terminal and docks at the southwest end of Broadway St. Haines-Skagway Fast Ferry (p419) provides speedy transportation on a catamaran to Haines. The boat departs from the Skagway small-boat harbor between one and seven times per day. Alaska Fjordlines runs the **Fjord Express** (☑ 800-320-0146; www.alaskafjordlines.com), which departs Skagway at 8am and arrives in Juneau at 11am and includes a bus to the Juneau airport or downtown. A one-way ticket is $120.

BUS

Yukon-Alaska Tourist Tours (p419) offers a minibus service to Whitehorse (one way $65), departing the train depot in Skagway at 2pm daily.

TRAIN

It's possible to travel part way to Whitehorse, Yukon Territory, on the White Pass & Yukon Route (p151), then complete the trip with a bus connection at Carcross, Yukon Territory. The

❶ THUMBING NORTH

Hitchhiking the Klondike Hwy out of Skagway is best just after a state ferry pulls in, and even then it's challenging. Backpackers thumbing north would do better buying a $31 ferry ticket to Haines and trying the Haines Hwy instead, as it has considerably more traffic.

northbound train departs from the Skagway depot at 7:30am Wednesday, Thursday and Saturday in summer, and passengers arrive in Whitehorse by bus at 5pm Yukon time. There's a stop for lunch in Bennett. The one-way fare is adult/child $185/92.50; it's three times what the Yukon Alaska Tourist Tours bus costs, but many feel the ride on the historic, narrow-gauge railroad is worth it.

❶ Getting Around

CAR

Sourdough Car Rental (☑ 907-983-2523; 6th Ave, at Broadway St) has cars for $69 a day with unlimited miles. In Skagway, there's a 14% tax on rental cars.

PUBLIC TRANSPORTATION

The city operates the **SMART bus** (☑ 907-983-2743; single ride/day pass $2/5) that moves people (primarily cruise-ship passengers) from the docks up Broadway St and to Jewell Gardens and the Klondike Gold Dredge on the edge of town. Call ahead for an airport or ferry pickup.

TAXI

Frontier Excursions (☑ 907-983-2512, 877-983-2512; www.frontierexcursions.com; Broadway St, at 7th Ave) runs a one-way backpacker shuttle to Dyea for $10 per person.

BICYCLE

Several places in town rent bikes, but Sockeye Cycle (p151) has the best bikes.

Anchorage & Around

Best Places to Eat

➜ Snow City Café (p172)

➜ Jack Sprat (p184)

➜ Bear Tooth Grill (p173)

➜ Turkey Red (p192)

➜ Spenard Food Truck Festival (p173)

Best Places to Stay

➜ Copper Whale Inn (p170)

➜ Hatcher Pass Lodge (p191)

➜ Wildflower Inn (p167)

➜ Eklutna Lake State Recreation Area (p189)

➜ Alyeska Hostel (p183)

Why Go?

Once you realize that Anchorage isn't simply a big city on the edge of the wilderness, but rather a big city in the wilderness, it starts to make sense. The town manages to mingle hiking trails and traffic jams, small art galleries and Big Oil, like no other city. Among big chain stores and mini-malls, there are more than 100 miles of city trails meandering in hidden greenbelts and a creek splitting downtown where anglers line up to catch trophy salmon.

Towering behind the municipality is the nation's third-largest state park, the half-million-acre Chugach. The wilderness is never far away, which is why Anchorage's young population (the average age is 33) is an active one. Stay for a few days, explore the cycle trails, patronize the art galleries and dine in Alaska's best restaurants, and you'll understand why half the state's population chooses to live in and around this city.

When to Go

Anchorage

Mar Anchorage comes alive for the Iditarod Sled Dog Race and Fur Rendezvous festival.

May The weather is nice, and the crowds and high prices are yet to arrive.

Jul The best month to see or catch a king salmon in Anchorage's Ship Creek.

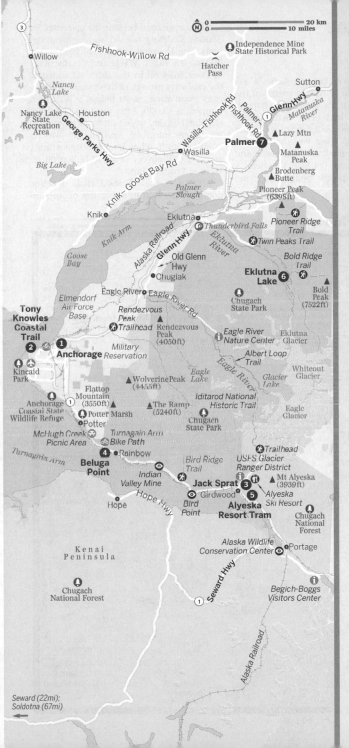

Anchorage & Around Highlights

1 Spending an afternoon at the **Anchorage Museum** (p159), soaking up Alaskan culture and art

2 Pedaling the scenic **Tony Knowles Coastal Trail** (p163), with views of the Alaska Range, on the way to Kincaid Park

3 Enjoying a fine, fresh meal while taking in the mountains on the deck of **Jack Sprat** (p184) in Girdwood

4 Watching the amazing bore tide fill Turnagain Arm in one swoop near **Beluga Point** (p182)

5 Riding the **Alyeska Resort Tram** (p182) for an alpine hike and lunch above the treeline

6 Exploring **Eklutna Lake** (p188) by combining a day of kayaking and mountain biking

7 Seeing 100lb cabbages and softball-sized radishes at the **Alaska State Fair** (p190) in Palmer

ANCHORAGE

POP 298,610

History

The British explorer Captain James Cook sailed past the site in 1779 in search of the elusive Northwest Passage, and hopeful gold prospectors had been visiting Ship Creek since the 1880s, but Anchorage wasn't founded until 1915. That was the year the Alaska Railroad called the area home and the 'Great Anchorage Lot Sale' was held. A tent city of 2000 people popped up in no time.

Anchorage soon became the epicenter for Alaska's fledgling rail, air and highway systems. The Depression-era colonizing of the Matanuska Valley, WWII and the discovery of Cook Inlet oil in the 1950s all added to the explosive growth of these years. Anchorage's population, 8000 before WWII, then jumped to 43,000. After the 1964 Good Friday Earthquake, which dumped more than 100 homes into Knik Arm, the city was rebuilding itself when another opportunity arose: the discovery of a $10 billion oil reserve in Prudhoe Bay.

Although the Trans-Alaska Pipeline doesn't come within 300 miles of Anchor-

Greater Anchorage

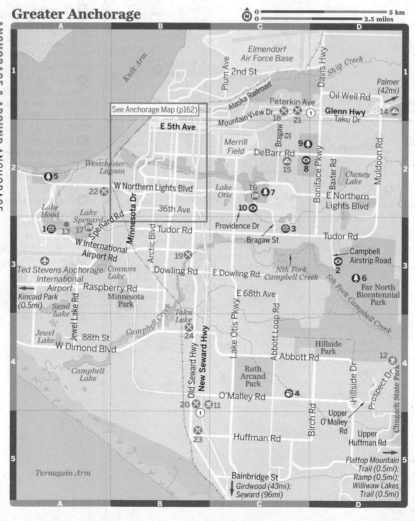

age, the city took its share of the wealth, growing a further 47% between 1970 and 1976. As the headquarters of various petroleum and service companies, Anchorage still manages to gush with oil money.

This city of stage plays and snowy peaks also has serious pork-barrel power. During the late 1970s, when a barrel of crude oil jumped more than $20 and Alaska couldn't spend its tax revenue fast enough, Anchorage received the lion's share. It used its political muscle to revitalize downtown Anchorage with the Sullivan Arena, Egan Civic Center and stunning Alaska Center for the Performing Arts.

◉ Sights

◉ Downtown Anchorage

★ **Anchorage Museum** MUSEUM
(Map p168; www.anchoragemuseum.org; 625 C Street; adult/child $15/7; ⊙ summer 9am-6pm; ⊕) What was once simply Alaska's best museum is now a world-class facility thanks to the $106 million expansion of Anchorage's cultural jewel in 2010. The West Wing, a four-story, shimmering, mirrored facade, added 80,000 sq ft to what was already the largest museum in the state. Its flagship exhibit is the Smithsonian Arctic Studies Center with more than 600 Alaska Native objects – art, tools, masks and household implements – that was previously housed in Washington DC.

It's the largest Alaska Native collection in the state and it's surrounded by large video screens showing contemporary Native life. Nearby is the Listening Space where you can listen to storytellers and natural sounds from Arctic Alaska.

The museum also contains the Imaginarium Discovery Center, a hands-on science center for children that was previously housed in a separate downtown location. On the 1st floor of the original East Wing you will still find the Art of the North gallery, with entire rooms of Alaskan masters Eustace Ziegler and Sydney Laurence. On the 2nd floor, the Alaska History Gallery is filled with life-size dioramas that trace 10,000 years of human settlement, from early subsistence villages to modern oil dependency.

There are also galleries devoted to traveling art exhibits, a planetarium and the Kid-Space Gallery designed for young children (and their parents) to explore the worlds of art, history and science through hands-on play. Clearly, this is a place where you can spend an entire afternoon.

Ship Creek Viewing Platform LOOKOUT
(Map p162) FREE From mid- to late summer, king, coho and pink salmon spawn up Ship Creek, the historical site of Tanaina Indian fish camps. At the overlook you can cheer on those love-starved fish humping their way toward destiny, and during high tide see the banks lined with anglers trying to hook them in what has to be one of the greatest urban fisheries anywhere in the

Greater Anchorage

◉ Sights
1 Alaska Aviation Heritage
   Museum A3
2 Alaska Botanical Garden D3
3 Alaska Native Medical Center C3
4 Alaska Zoo C4
5 Earthquake Park A2
6 Far North Bicentennial Park D3
7 Goose Lake C2
8 Mann Leiser Memorial
   Greenhouses C2
9 Russian Jack Springs Park C2
10 University of Alaska Anchorage C2

◉ Activities, Courses & Tours
11 H2Oasis B4
12 Prospect Heights Trailhead D4
13 Regal Air A3
   Rust's Flying Service .... (see 1)

◉ Sleeping
14 Centennial Park Campground D1
15 Golden Nugget RV Park C2
16 Goose Lake Lodge B&B C2
   Lake Hood Inn .... (see 17)
   Long House Alaskan Hotel .... (see 17)
17 Millennium Hotel A3
   Puffin Inn .... (see 17)
   Spenard Hostel .... (see 17)

◉ Eating
18 Alaska Pho Restaurant C1
19 Arctic Roadrunner B3
20 Fromagio's O'Malley B4
21 Hula Hands C1
22 Rustic Goat A2
23 Southside Bistro B5
24 Terra Bella B4

◉ Shopping
   ANC Auxiliary Craft Shop .... (see 3)

① CULTURE PASS JOINT TICKET

Anchorage's top two attractions, the Alaska Native Heritage Center and the Anchorage Museum, can both be enjoyed at a discount with a special joint-admission ticket. The **Culture Pass Joint Ticket** is $29.95 per person and includes admission to both museums as well as shuttle transportation between them. You can purchase the joint pass from the ticket offices at either location.

USA. Follow C St north as it crosses Ship Creek Bridge and then turn right on Whitney Rd. Nearby is the **Bait Shack** (Map p162; ☎522-3474; www.thebaitshackak.com; 212 N Whitney Rd; ☉6am-10pm), which will rent you the rod, reel, waders and tackle needed to catch a trophy king.

Oscar Anderson House HISTORIC BUILDING
(Map p168; www.aahp-online.net; 420 M St; adult/child $10/5; ☉noon-4pm Tue-Sun Jun–mid-Sep) Housed in the city's oldest wooden-framed home, this little museum overlooks the delightful Elderberry Park. Anderson was the 18th person to set foot in Anchorage, and he built his house in 1915. Today it's the only home museum in Anchorage, and despite past budget problems, it's open as a reminder that there's not a single building in this city a century old.

4th Avenue Market Place/ Village of Ship Creek Center MARKET
(Map p168; 333 W 4th Ave; ☉8am-8pm Mon-Fri, 9am-9pm Sun) FREE This shopping mall contains an array of native and crafty gift shops; in a few, you can watch artists at work. There is also a lot of history. Painted on the walls outside is a historic timeline of Anchorage, while inside are displays devoted to the 1964 Good Friday Earthquake.

Resolution Park PARK
(Map p168) At the west end of 3rd Ave, this small park is home to the **Captain Cook Monument**, built to mark the 200th anniversary of the English captain's 'discovery' of Cook Inlet. If it's not overrun by tour-bus passengers, this observation deck has an excellent view of the surrounding mountains.

Delaney Park PARK
(Map p168) Known locally as the Delaney Park Strip, this narrow slice of well-tended grass stretches from A to P Sts between W 9th and W 10th Aves; there's an impressive playground near the corner of E St. The park was the site of the 50-ton bonfire celebrating statehood in 1959 and Pope John Paul II's 1981 outdoor mass. Today it hosts festivals like Summer Solstice and Pridefest, not to mention Frisbee games any time the weather is nice.

◉ Midtown Anchorage & Spenard

Alaska Heritage Museum MUSEUM
(Map p162; www.wellsfargohistory.com/museums/anchorage/; 301 W Northern Lights Blvd; ☉noon-4pm Mon-Fri) FREE Inside the midtown Wells Fargo bank, this museum is home to the largest private collection of Alaska Native artifacts in the state and includes costumes, baskets and hunting weapons. There are also original paintings covering the walls, including several by Sydney Laurence, and lots of scrimshaw. The museum's collection is so large that there are displays in the elevator lobbies throughout the bank.

Alaska Aviation Heritage Museum MUSEUM
(Map p158; www.alaskaairmuseum.org; 4721 Aircraft Dr; adult/child $10/6; ☉9am-5pm) On the south shore of Lake Hood, the world's busiest floatplane lake, this museum is a tribute to Alaska's colorful bush pilots and their faithful planes. Housed within are 25 planes along with historic photos and displays of pilots' achievements, from the first flight to Fairbanks (1913) to the early history of Alaska Airlines.

You can view early footage of bush planes in the museum's theater or step outside to its large observation deck and watch today's pilots begin their own quest for adventure with a roar on Lake Hood.

◉ Greater Anchorage

★**Alaska Native Heritage Center** CULTURAL CENTER
(☎800-315-6608, 330-8000; www.alaskanative.net; 8800 Heritage Center Dr; adult/child $25/17; ☉9am-5pm) To experience Alaska Native culture firsthand, you can travel to the Bush or come to this 26-acre center and see how humans survived – and thrived – before central heating. This is much more than just a

museum: it represents a knowledge bank of language, art and culture that will survive no matter how many sitcoms are crackling through the Alaskan stratosphere. It's a labor of love, and of incalculable value.

The main building houses meandering exhibits on traditional arts and sciences – including kayaks and rain gear that rival outdoors department store REI's best offerings. It also features various performances, among them the staccato Alaghanak song, lost for 50 years: the center collected bits and pieces of the traditional song from different tribal elders and reconstructed it. Outside, examples of typical structures from the Aleut, Yupik, Tlingit and other tribes are arranged around a picturesque lake. Docents explain the ancient architects' cunning technology: check out wooden panels that shrink in the dry summers (allowing light and air inside) but expand to seal out the cold during the wet winter. Dog cart rides and private and audio tours are all available for an extra charge.

Alaska Botanical Garden   GARDENS
(Map p158; www.alaskabg.org; 4601 Campbell Airstrip Rd; adult/child $7/5; ☺daylight hours) The garden is a colorful showcase for native species, where gentle paths lead you through groomed herb, rock and perennial gardens in a wooded setting. The mile-long Lowenfels Family Nature Trail – built for tanks during WWII – is a great place to learn your basic Alaskan botany or just to stroll and watch the bald eagles pluck salmon from Campbell Creek. Guided tours are offered daily at 1pm.

Alaska Native Medical Center   GALLERY
(Map p158; www.anmc.org; 4315 Diplomacy Dr; ☺24hr) FREE This hospital has a fantastic collection of Alaska Native art and artifacts: take the elevator to the top floor and wind down the staircase past dolls, basketry and tools from all over Alaska.

Earthquake Park   PARK
(Map p158) For decades after the 1964 earthquake, this park remained a barren moonscape revealing the tectonic power that destroyed nearby Turnagain Heights. Today Earthquake Park, at the west end of Northern Lights Blvd on the Knik Arm, is being reclaimed by nature; you'll have to poke around the bushes to see evidence of tectonic upheaval.

University of Alaska Anchorage   UNIVERSITY
(Map p158; www.uaa.alaska.edu; Providence Dr; ☐1, 3, 13, 36, 45, 102) UA Anchorage is the largest college campus in Alaska, but there is far less to do here than at its sister school, UA Fairbanks. The Campus Center is home to a small art gallery and the bookstore, which has a good selection of Alaskana, clothing that says 'Alaska' on it and used microbiology texts. There are trails from the campus that connect UA to Goose Lake, Chester Creek Greenbelt and Earthquake Park.

Goose Lake   PARK
(Map p158; UAA Dr; ☐3, 45) You'll stop complaining about global warming once you export ence an 85°F (29°C) Anchorage afternoon at Goose Lake. Just off Northern Lights Blvd,

DON'T MISS

THE MOST DIVERSE NEIGHBORHOOD IN THE USA

New York, San Francisco...Anchorage? With its lack of a port, relatively short history and somewhat inconvenient location, Anchorage does not at first glance appear to be the type of place that caters to a diverse population. But over 90 languages are spoken in the city's schools and, as of 2010, Anchorage's Mountain View neighborhood is the most diverse census tract in the US. After Native Alaskans, Asians and Pacific Islanders make up the bulk of the neighborhood's diversity.

The northeast Mountain View neighborhood is not necessarily set up for tourists, but it's worth a visit to sample one of the many restaurants that reflect its diversity. Cycle the Ship Creek Bike Trail (p163) to its end in Mountain View, and wander along Mountain View Dr and its ethnic grocery stores and small restaurants until you find a place that sounds appetizing. Here a couple of suggestions:

Alaska Pho Restaurant (Map p158; 4011 Mountain View Dr) One of dozens of pho restaurants in Anchorage reflecting the city's Southeast Asian population, including the Hmong minority group.

Hula Hands (Map p158; 4630 Mountain View Dr; ☺11am-10pm Mon-Sat, noon-8pm Sun) Represents Anchorage's large Polynesian population.

Anchorage

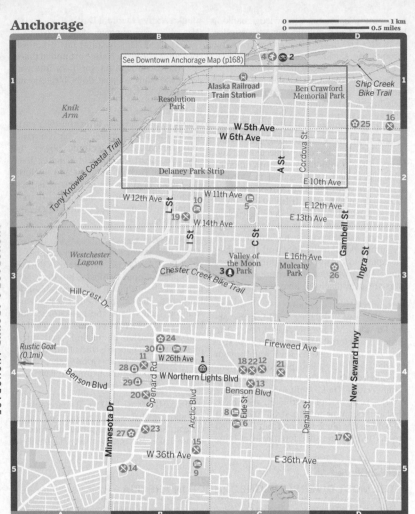

See Downtown Anchorage Map (p168)

this is the city's most developed lake for swimming, with lifeguards, paddleboat rentals and a small cafe, which serves fresh-baked pizza.

Russian Jack Springs Park PARK
(Map p158; 8, 45, 15) Named after the original homesteader of the site, this 300-acre park is south of Glenn Hwy on Boniface Pkwy. The park has tennis courts, hiking and cycling trails, and a picnic area. Near the DeBarr Rd entrance, you'll find the **Mann Leiser Memorial Greenhouses** (Map p158; 343-4717; 8am-3:30pm), a toasty oasis of tropical plants, exotic birds and fish.

Far North Bicentennial Park PARK
(Map p158) Comprising 4000 acres of forest and muskeg in east central Anchorage, this park features 20 miles of trails. In the center of the park is the Bureau of Land Management's (BLM's) Campbell Tract, a 700-acre wildlife preserve where it's possible to see moose and bears in the spring, and brilliant fall colors in mid-September. There is an active grizzly population, so it's wise to steer clear of salmon streams during the twilight hours.

Take O'Malley Rd east to Hillside Dr and follow the signs, or take Campbell Airstrip Rd off of Tudor Rd.

Anchorage

⊙ Sights
1 Alaska Heritage Museum.......................B4
  Heritage Library Museum..............(see 1)
2 Ship Creek Viewing Platform.................C1
3 Valley of the Moon Park.......................C3

🏃 Activities, Courses & Tours
4 Bait Shack...C1

🛏 Sleeping
5 11th Avenue B&B...................................C2
6 Arctic Adventure Hostel.......................C5
7 Base Camp Anchorage Hostel..............B4
8 Bent Prop Inn Midtown C4
9 Qupqugiaq Inn......................................B5
10 Wildflower Inn.......................................B2

🍴 Eating
11 Bear Tooth Grill.....................................B4
12 Charlie's Bakery....................................C4
13 Crossbar..C4
14 Fromagio's B5
15 Jen's Restaurant B5
16 Lucky Wishbone.....................................D1
  Middle Way Cafe ....(see 29)
17 Moose's Tooth Brewpub........................D5

18 New Central Market...............................C4
19 New Sagaya City Market.......................B2
20 Pho Lena..B4
  Ray's Place ....(see 11)
  Spenard Food Truck
  Festival...(see 30)
21 Taco King...C4
22 VIP Restaurant C4
23 Yak & Yeti..B5
  Yak & Yeti Cafe ....(see 29)

🎭 Entertainment
  Bear Tooth Theatrepub.................(see 11)
24 Chilkoot Charlie's B4
25 Raven D1
26 Sullivan Arena......................................D3
27 Tap Root B5

🛍 Shopping
  Alaska Mountaineering &
  Hiking..(see 24)
28 Dos Manos...B4
29 REI B4
30 Spenard Farmers Market B4
  Title Wave Books...........................(see 29)

Kincaid Park
PARK

At the western 'nose' of the peninsula and southern terminus of the Tony Knowles Coastal Trail is this beloved 1400-acre park populated by mountain bikers in the summer and Nordic skiers in the winter. Trails wind through a rolling terrain of forested hills where there are views of Mt Susitna and Mt McKinley on a clear day and fiery sunsets in the evening. From certain spots on the coastal trail you can stand directly under incoming jets.

Follow Raspberry Rd west to the parking lot and trailheads.

🏃 Activities

Cycling

Anchorage has 122 miles of paved paths that parallel major roads or wind through the greenbelts, making a bicycle the easiest and cheapest way to explore the city. If you run out of gas before the end of the ride, all People Mover buses are equipped with bike racks.

Anchorage is also a haven for mountain biking, with the most popular areas being Kincaid Park, Far North Bicentennial Park and Powerline Pass Trail in Chugach State Park.

Downtown Bicycle Rental
BICYCLE RENTAL

(Map p168; www.alaska-bike-rentals.com; 333 W 4th Ave, 3/24hr rental $16/32; ⊙8am-10pm) Has road, hybrid and mountain bikes as well as tandems, trailers and even clip-in pedals and shoes. Locks, helmets and bike maps are free, and the staff is a wealth of information on where to ride.

Pablo's Bicycle Rental
BICYCLE RENTAL

(Map p168; www.pablobicyclerentals.com; 501 L St; per 3/24hr $15/40; ⊙8am-8pm) Bicycles (including tandems, kids' trailers and hybrids) and hotdogs to go.

Tony Knowles Coastal Trail
CYCLING

Anchorage's favorite trail is the scenic 11-mile Tony Knowles Coastal Trail. It begins at the west end of 2nd Ave downtown and reaches Elderberry Park a mile away, before winding through Earthquake Park, around Point Woronzof and finally to Point Campbell in Kincaid Park. There are good views of Knik Arm and the Alaska Range along the way, and the Anchorage Lightspeed Planet Walk.

Ship Creek Bike Trail
CYCLING

The newest ribbon of asphalt for cyclists runs 2.6 miles from the Alaska Railroad depot along the namesake creek and into the

Mountain View neighborhood. Here you can watch aggressive anglers fish for salmon as you wind through woods and industry.

Chester Creek Bike Trail CYCLING
This scenic 4-mile path through the Chester Creek Greenbelt connects with the coastal trail at Westchester Lagoon and follows a mountain-fed stream to Goose Lake.

Campbell Creek Trail CYCLING
Campbell Creek Trail features some of the newest paved path in Anchorage, stretching 7 miles from Far North Bicentennial Park, under the Seward Hwy, to Dimond Blvd, with most of the ride in the Campbell Creek Greenbelt.

Hiking
Though there are dozens of trails in town, outdoors enthusiasts head to 773-sq-mile Chugach State Park for the mother lode. You can access an array of trails from the Glen Alps and Prospect Heights (Map p158) entrances; parking at each is $5.

Flattop Mountain Trail HIKING
This very popular 3-mile round-trip hike to the 3550ft peak is easy to follow, though you'll scramble at the summit. It begins at Glen Alps and climbs steeply from there. Another trail continues 3 miles more along the ridgeline to Flaketop Peak, and the 2-mile Blueberry Loop at the base is great for kids.

ANCHORAGE FOR CHILDREN

Anchorage is exceptionally kid-friendly – more than 40 city parks boast playscapes. Close to downtown, Frontierland Park (Map p168; 10th Ave & E St) is a local favorite, while Valley of the Moon Park (Map p162; Arctic Blvd & W 17th St) makes a delightful picnic spot. Entice your family to the Anchorage Museum by promising to first explore Imaginarium (Map p168; ☑907-929-9200; 625 C St; adult/child $5.50/5; ⊙10am-6pm Mon-Sat, noon-5pm Sun), the wonderful hands-on science center for children.

Alaska Zoo (Map p158; www.alaskazoo.org; 4731 O'Malley Rd; adult/child $15/7; ⊙9am-9pm; ⑭) The unique wildlife of the Arctic is on display at this zoo, the only one in North America that specializes in northern animals, including snow leopards, Amur tigers and Tibetan yaks. Alaskan native species, from wolverines and moose to caribou and Dall sheep, are abundant. What kids will love watching, however, are the bears. The zoo has all four Alaskan species (brown, black, glacier and polar), but the polar bears are clearly the star attraction.

Bear & Raven Adventure Theatre (Map p168; www.bearsquare.net; 315 E St; per group $8.50; ⊙10am-6pm) This mini-amusement park is a cheesy but easy downtown break from shopping. It offers three 'special effects' movies (think snow falling from the ceiling) about the Iditarod, the Alaska Earthquake and bears (adult/child $10/8, discount for two movies). Virtual 'rides' (reeling in a salmon, for example) ought to satisfy the little ones.

Alaska Wild Berry Park (www.alaskawildberryproducts.com; 5525 Junau St; ⊙10am-8pm Mon-Thu, to 9pm Fri & Sat, 11am-8pm Sun) If the Flattop Mountain hike is overly ambitious for your kids, head to this giant jam and gift shop with chocolate falls. It's definitely a tourist trap, but who can resist a 20ft chocolate waterfall? Outside there's a short nature trail leading to a handful of reindeer that kids can feed and pet.

Anchorage Lightspeed Planet Walk (Map p168) A massive sun sits at the corner of 5th Ave and G St, marking the start of this built-to-scale model of the solar system. There are colorful interpretive displays for each of the planets; the first four planets can be reached within a few blocks of the sun but Pluto is out in Kincaid Park. The scale is set so that walking pace mimics the speed of light, but it'll take you all day to reach marble-sized Pluto at that pace. Travel faster than the speed of light by renting a mountain bike.

H2Oasis (Map p158; www.h2oasiswaterpark.com; 1520 O'Malley Rd; adult/child $25/20; ⊙10am-8pm) Qualifying as surreal, Anchorage's original water park is a $7 million, three-level amusement zone with palm trees, water slides, a wave pool and the 505ft Master Blaster, one very wet roller coaster. Feel free to just watch from the grown-ups-only hot tubs.

For transportation there's **Flattop Mountain Shuttle** (☑ 279-3334; www.hike-anchorage-alaska.com; round trip $22), which leaves Downtown Bicycle Rental (p163) on 4th Ave at 1pm and 7pm daily.

In Los Angeles, you cruise the Sunset Strip; in Paris, you stroll the Champs-Élysées; and in Anchorage, you climb Flattop Mountain. This is the first mountain every Anchorage youth scales on the way to higher things.

Ramp   HIKING

The 14-mile round-trip hike starts at Glen Alps and takes you past alpine summits and through tranquil tundra. Hike half a mile to the Powerline Pass Trail. Turn right and follow the power line 2 miles, turn left and head downhill across the south fork of Campbell Creek.

Continue to a valley on the other side. Hike up the alpine valley to Ship Lake Pass, which lies between the 5240ft Ramp and the 4660ft Wedge.

The camping and climbing are great in the area.

Williwaw Lakes Trail   HIKING

This easy 13-mile hike also begins at Glen Alps, leading to the handful of alpine lakes at the base of Mt Williwaw.

Walk half a mile to the Powerline Pass Trail and turn right, continuing 300yd to the Middle Fork Loop Trail. Follow it across the south fork of Campbell Creek, then north for 1.5 miles to the middle fork of the creek. At the junction, make a right on Williwaw Lakes Trail.

The trail makes a pleasant overnight hike and many consider it the most scenic outing in the Hillside area of Chugach State Park. You can make this an overnight trek or a long day hike.

Wolverine Peak Trail   HIKING

This strenuous but rewarding 9.5-mile round-trip ascends the 4455ft triangular peak, visible from Anchorage. The trail begins at an old homesteader road that crosses the south fork of Campbell Creek. Head east; the road becomes a footpath that ascends above treeline and eventually fades out (mark it for the return trip). From there, it's 3 miles to Wolverine Peak.

From Seward Hwy, go 4 miles east on O'Malley Rd, turn left on Hillside Dr and follow signs to Prospect Heights.

Rendezvous Peak Route   HIKING

A 4-mile trek to the top of this 4050ft peak. From the parking lot, a short trail leads along the right-hand side of the stream up the valley to the northwest. It ends at a pass where a short ascent to Rendezvous Peak is easily seen and climbed.

From Glenn Hwy, exit Arctic Valley Rd (Fort Richardson) and follow signs to Arctic Valley; a 7-mile gravel road leads to the Alpenglow Ski Area parking lot. Parking costs $5.

This climb rewards hikers with incredible views of Mt McKinley, Cook Inlet and the city far below.

McHugh Lake Trail   HIKING

This 13-mile trail originates at McHugh Creek Picnic Area, 15 miles south of Anchorage at Mile 111.8 of the Seward Hwy. The route follows the McHugh Creek valley, and in 7 miles reaches Rabbit and McHugh Lakes, two beautiful alpine pools reflecting the 5000ft Suicide Peaks.

The first 3 miles feature some good climbs, and the round-trip trek makes for a long day. It's better to haul in a tent and spend the afternoon exploring the open tundra country and nearby ridges.

☞ Tours

City Tours

Anchorage City Trolley Tours   BUS

(Map p168; ☑ 775-5603, 888-917-8687; www.alaskatrolley.com; 546 W 4th Ave; adult/child $20/10; ☺ tours 9am-7pm) One-hour rides in a bright-red trolley past Lake Hood, Earthquake Park and Cook Inlet, among other sights. Tours depart on the hour.

Gray Line   BUS

(Map p168; ☑ 888-425-1737; www.graylineofalaska.com; Hilton Anchorage, 500 W 3rd Ave) The narrated half-day Experience the City historical tour (adult/child $65/40) covers downtown plus the Anchorage Museum and Alaska Wild Berry Park.

Flightseeing Tours

They're costly and never as long as you wish, but they're a stunning way to spend an hour or two. If you've got the cash – lots of it – flightseeing tours provide an eagle-eye view of the wilderness and mountains, imparting a sense of scale that's difficult to appreciate from the ground.

GHOSTLY TOURS OF ANCHORAGE

In Anchorage you can sign up for a city tour, a tour on a trolley or a walking tour with a guide dressed (somewhat) like Captain Cook. Or you can be really brave and join a ghost tour. Oooooh! Now that's scary.

These tours are a hit with out-of-towners who can't seem to get enough grizzly Alaskan tales of murder and mayhem.

On the **Ghost Tours of Anchorage** (☎274-4678; www.ghosttoursofanchorage.com; per person $15; ☉7:30pm Tue-Sun) of the stops during the 90-minute downtown walk is the Anchorage Club, where the staff will only go into the basement in pairs; the Gaslight Lounge with its unexplained noises, seismic activity and a jukebox that kicks on by itself; and the Historic Anchorage Hotel, which is said to have at least 32 'entities' as permanent guests.

The ghost tours take place nightly from mid-May to mid-September. To join, just show up in front of Snow City Café at 4th Ave and L St – site of perhaps the most notorious murder in Anchorage's history.

Regal Air
SCENIC FLIGHTS
(Map p158; ☎243-8535; www.regal-air.com) Flying out of Lake Hood, this has some of the best rates for flightseeing. Its three-hour Mt McKinley tour is only $405, while a 1½-hour tour of Knik Glacier is $245. There are several more stunning tours on offer.

Rust's Flying Service
SCENIC FLIGHT
(Map p158; ☎243-1595, 800-544-2299; www.flyrusts.com; 4525 Enstrom Circle) Offers a three-hour Mt McKinley flight that includes flying the length of Ruth Glacier ($415) and a three-hour Prince William Sound tour ($355 to $395). All flights have a 3% transportation fee.

Day Tours
Have a leftover day? Go on an adventure. There are few places in Alaska that somebody in Anchorage isn't willing to whisk you off to in a day.

Alaska Railroad
TRAIN
(Map p168; ☎800-544-0552, 265-2494; www.akrr.com; 411 W 1st Ave) Has many one-day tours from Anchorage that begin with a train ride. Its nine-hour Spencer Glacier Float Tour (per person $220) trundles to Spencer Lake and includes a gentle raft trip among icebergs. The Glacier Quest Cruise ($203) rumbles to Whittier and includes a four-hour boat cruise in Prince William Sound; watch glaciers calve while feasting on king crab cakes.

Alaska Photo Trek
PHOTOGRAPHY
(☎350-0251; www.ttlalaska.com) Unleash your wildlife paparazzi with a tour that caters specifically to shutter snappers. Led by professional photographers, tours range from the two-hour Anchorage PhotoWalk (adult/

child $45/20) to a one-day brown bear flightseeing tour ($1185), to a multiday trek in Denali ($1785). Optimum light and wildlife sighting probability are all taken into account.

Phillips Cruises & Tours
BOAT
(Map p168; ☎276-8023, 800-544-0529; www.phillipscruises.com; 519 W 4th Ave) Takes you by bus to Whittier and then on a boat past 26 glaciers in Prince William Sound. The five-hour cruise (adult/child $169/106) is offered daily and includes lunch. Bus service from Anchorage tacks on a couple of hours on either side and costs an extra $55/30, but it's worth it.

Alaska's Finest Tours
BUS
(☎764-2067; www.akfinest.com) Several companies will take you on a six-hour tour of Turnagain Arm that will include a boat cruise to the face of Portage Glacier and the Alaska Wildlife Conservation Center. This one will do it for $99 per person.

✫ Festivals & Events

These are just a few of Anchorage's more popular events; contact **Visit Anchorage** (☎276-3200; www.anchorage.net/events) to see what's on while you're here.

Anchorage Fur Rendezvous
CULTURAL
(www.furrondy.net; ☉late Feb & early Mar) The place to get fresh-trapped furs is still the 'Rondy,' but most folks prefer to sculpt ice, ride the Ferris wheel in freezing temperatures, or watch the 'Running of the Reindeer.' When Rondy ends, the famed 1049-mile Iditarod Trail sled-dog race to Nome begins. Better stay another week.

Three Barons Renaissance Fair CULTURAL
(www.3barons.org; 3400 E Tudor Rd; adult/child
$6/3; ⊙early Jun) Duchesses, counts, knights
and wenches gather for revelry, merriment
and drinking at the Crooked Toad Tavern for
a week at Tozier Track.

Spenard Jazz Fest MUSIC
(www.spenardjazzfest.org; ⊙early Jun) For three
days cool, trendy and local jazz musicians
stage concerts and workshops throughout
Anchorage. A grand centennial festival will
be held in 2015.

🛏 Sleeping

Several new hostels in town are helping
bring the cost of sleeping down, but Anchorage is expensive. Note that most of the
hostels rent to long-term tenants in the
off season and aren't always available for
travelers.

Chugach State Park has several public
campgrounds, but none are close to town.

Tack on the city's 12% sales-and-bed tax to
the prices given here.

🛏 Downtown Anchorage

Bent Prop Inn HOSTEL $
(Map p168; ☑276-3635; www.bentpropinn.com;
700 H St; dm/r $35/72; @🛜) This excellent
downtown hostel is friendly and relaxed,
with eight private rooms that share bathrooms, and 14 dorm rooms with either four
or eight bunks as well as lockers. Key-card

access, a large kitchen and eating area, city-
center location and super-friendly management make this hostel one of the best
budget sleeps in Anchorage.

Alaska Backpackers Inn HOSTEL $
(Map p168; ☑277-2770; www.alaskabackpackers.
com; 409 Eagle St; dm/s/d $28/60/70; 🛜) Tak-
ing up two city blocks, his hostel is roomy
but showing some wear. Most rooms have
four or two beds and the dayroom has a
50in TV, a foosball table and a massive clean
kitchen. A bit east of central downtown,
it's still within walking distance of restaurants and bars. There's a large annex with
one-bedroom suites.

Wildflower Inn B&B $$
(Map p162; ☑274-1239; www.alaska-wildflower-inn.
com; 1239 I St; r incl breakfast $149-159; @🛜)
Housed in a historic home, a duplex built
in 1945 for Federal Aviation Administra-
tion (FAA) families, this B&B offers three
large rooms, pleasant sitting areas and a full
breakfast in the morning featuring treats
such as caramelized French toast. For any
body who packed their walking shoes, the
location is ideal, just three blocks south of
Delaney Park.

Arctic Fox B&B $$
(Map p168; ☑274-1239, 877-693-1239; www.arctic-
foxinn.com; 327 E 2nd Ct; r $109-139, ste $149-249)
Built as a seven-unit apartment complex,
this downtown B&B now has six rooms and

ANCHORAGE & AROUND ANCHORAGE

OFFBEAT ANCHORAGE

The wildest salmon in Anchorage are nowhere near Ship Creek. They're found spawning
along downtown streets as part of the Wild Salmon on Parade, an annual event in
which local artists turn fiberglass fish into anything but fish. The first run of fish art was
organized in 2003 and modeled after Chicago's Cows on Parade and Seattle's Pigs on
Parade – Anchorage doesn't have too many cows or pigs, but it does have plenty of
salmon.

Over the years this art competition has spawned an 'Alaska Sarah Salmon'; a fish with
boxing gloves titled 'Socked Eye Salmon'; 'Marilyn MonROE' and 'Vincent Van Coho.' The
30 or so colorful fish appear on the streets in early June and stick around until September. To see them all, pick up a fish tour map at the Log Cabin Visitors Center.

Most of us would rather avoid the police. But who can resist a museum dedicated
solely to the state's troopers? Displays at Fraternal Order of Alaska State Troopers
Law Enforcement Museum (Map p168; www.alaskatroopermuseum.com; 245 W 5th Ave;
⊙10am-4pm Mon-Fri, from noon Sat) are dedicated to law enforcement, starting from when
Alaska was a territory. The storefront museum has exhibits that range from a beautifully
restored 1952 Hudson Hornet cop car to state-issued sealskin cop boots. Stop by its gift
shop to buy a T-shirt that proclaims 'Alaska: 367 Troopers, 570,000 square miles.' That
will impress the next cop who pulls you over at home.

Downtown Anchorage

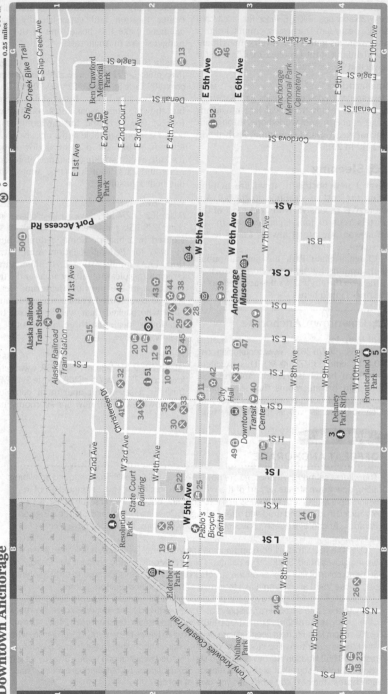

500 m
0.25 miles

Ship Creek Bike Trail
E Ship Creek Ave

Ben Crawford
Memorial
Park

Eagle St

E 5th Ave
E 6th Ave

Fairbanks St

Anchorage
Memorial Park
Cemetery

E 10th Ave

E 9th Ave

Eagle St

Denali St

E 2nd Ave
E 3rd Ave
E 4th Ave

Denali St

Cordova St

13

46

52

Quvana
Park

E 1st Ave

E 2nd Court

16

A St

W 5th Ave

W 6th Ave

6

B St

W 7th Ave

Port Access Rd

50

W 1st Ave

4

C St

Anchorage
Museum
1

48

Alaska Railroad
Train Station

9

15

43
44
38

D St

39

27
29
45

28

37

Christensen Dr

32

51

10
53
11

2

20
21
12

42

31
40

34
35
30
33

E St

F St

City
Hall

Downtown
Transit
Center

G St

47

W 8th Ave

W 9th Ave

Delaney
Park Strip

3

W 10th Ave

Frontierland
Park

5

49

17

H St

I St

State Court
Building

W 2nd Ave
W 3rd Ave
W 4th Ave

22
25

W 5th Ave

Pablo's
Bicycle
Rental

8

Resolution
Park

36

K St

L St

14

19

7

Elderberry
Park

N St

26

N St

24

W 8th Ave

W 9th Ave

W 10th Ave

Tony Knowles Coastal Trail

Nuthay
Park

18 23

P St

Downtown Anchorage

five apartment-style suites. About half have been remodeled into sleek, modern digs, but even the older rooms are bright and well-maintained. There are several decks with views of the port and a full hot breakfast each morning. It's one of Anchorage's best midrange deals.

11th Avenue B&B   B&B $$
(Map p162; ☑646-1410, 855-446-1410; www .11thavenue.net; 334 W 11th Ave; r $159-195) The reason to stay here is not (just) the memory foam mattresses, private bathrooms, downtown location, lifelong Alaskan owner or even the large, south-facing deck. No, stay for the plentiful gourmet breakfasts.

Oscar Gill House   B&B $$
(Map p168; ☑279-1344; www.oscargill.com; 1344 W 10th Ave; r $120-140; ☎; ☐7A) This historic clapboard home was built in 1913 in Knik by former Anchorage Mayor Oscar Gill and later moved to its midtown location. The quaint and friendly B&B offers three guest rooms (two that share a bath), a fantastic breakfast that ranges from sourdough French toast to smoked salmon quiche, and free bicycles. There's parking.

City Garden B&B

B&B $$

(Map p168; ☑ 276-8686; www.citygarden.biz; 1352 W 10th Ave; r $125-175; ☎; ☐7A) One of several B&Bs located on a two-block stretch of 10th Ave, this is an open, sunny, gay- and lesbian-friendly place with more cutting-edge art than antiques. The nicest of the three rooms has a private bath, which has recently been remodeled.

Susitna Place

B&B $$

(Map p168; ☑ 274-3344; www.susitnaplace.com; 727 N St; r $115-145, ste $175-200; ☎) On the edge of downtown, this 4000-sq-ft home sits on a bluff overlooking Cook Inlet and Mt Susitna in the distance. Four rooms have shared baths while the Susitna suite comes with fireplace, hot tub and private deck.

Anchorage
Downtown Hotel

BOUTIQUE HOTEL $$

(Map p168; ☑ 886-928-7669, 258-7669; www.theanchoragedowntownhotel.com; 826 K St; r $179-199; ☎) Recently remodeled with fun murals on the walls, this not-so-downtown hotel is a very pleasant place to stay, with 16 colorful and comfortable rooms that feature private baths, coffeemakers and small refrigerators. It offers a light continental breakfast, parking and a free shuttle.

★Copper Whale Inn

INN $$$

(Map p168; ☑ 258-7999, 866-258-7999; www.copperwhale.com; cnr W 5th Ave & L St; r $189-229, ste $259; @☎) An ideal downtown location and a bright and elegant interior make this inn one of the best top-end places in Anchorage. The suite has a full kitchen. Two relaxing waterfall courtyards make it easy to consume that novel, while many rooms and the breakfast lounge give way to views of Cook Inlet. Are those beluga whales out there?

Historic Anchorage Hotel

BOUTIQUE HOTEL $$$

(Map p168; ☑ 272-4533, 800-544-0988; www.anchoragehistorichotel.com; 330 E St; r/ste from $219/269; ☻@☎) This boutique hotel was established in 1916, only a year after the city was founded, though the current building is from 1936. It's luxurious, loaded with amenities ranging from an excellent continental breakfast to free newspapers, and has an ideal downtown location.

Hilton Anchorage

HOTEL $$$

(Map p168; ☑ 272-7411; www.hiltonanchorage.com; 500 W 3rd Ave; r $310; @☎) The Hilton has the best location of any of the luxury hotels, right in the heart of the downtown scene. Two restaurants, a fitness center with a pool, two 1000lb bears in the lobby, 606 rooms and lots of elegance. If you're going to pay this much, ask for a room with a view of Cook Inlet.

Anchorage Grand Hotel

LUXURY HOTEL $$$

(Map p168; ☑ 929-8888, 888-800-0640; www.anchoragegrand.com; 505 W 2nd Ave; r $199; @☎) This converted apartment building rests on a quiet street with 31 spacious suites that include full kitchens and separate living and bedroom areas. Many overlook Ship Creek and Cook Inlet, and its downtown location is convenient to everything.

Hotel Captain Cook

HOTEL $$$

(Map p168; ☑ 276-6000, 800-843-1950; www.captaincook.com; 939 W 5th Ave; s/d $295/315; @☎⛨) The grand dame of Anchorage accommodations still has an air of an Alaskan aristocrat right down to the doormen with top hats. There are plenty of plush services and upscale shops: hot tubs, a fitness club, beauty salon, jewelry store and four restaurants, including the famed Crow's Nest bar on the top floor. Rooms have been updated with new mattresses.

Voyager Hotel

HOTEL $$$

(Map p168; ☑ 277-9501, 800-247-9070; 501 K St; r $210; @☎) A 40-room hotel that has a great location downtown and was recently completely remodeled. Each room comes with a kitchenette, and some have peek-a-boo inlet views. Guests also have access to the fitness center at the Hotel Captain Cook across the street.

⌣ Midtown Anchorage & Spenard

★Bent Prop Inn Midtown

HOSTEL $

(Map p162; ☑ 222-5220; www.bentpropinn.com; 3104 Eide St; dm $30-35; ☎) The micro-dorms here are the best deal in town: in converted one-bedroom apartments, these come with four beds, a private kitchen and a living room – it's like dorms meet the suite life. Regular dorms are co-ed and have six beds. There are two kitchens, coin-op laundry and a big-screen TV. The one private apartment goes for $149.

Base Camp Anchorage Hostel

HOSTEL $

(Map p162; ☑ 274-1252; www.basecampanchorage.com; 1037 W 26th Ave; dm/r $25/66; @☎; ☐3, 7) The former 26th Street Hostel has undergone a remodel and has a new owner. Conveniently located in the thick of midtown action, it has a coin-op laundry, a kitchen, lockers, luggage storage and bicycle rental ($10 per day). The large, light dorm rooms (including female-only) have two bunk beds, so you're never crowded. Buses stop on Spenard Rd, a block away.

Spenard Hostel   HOSTEL $
(Map p158; ☎907-248-5036; www.alaskahostel. org; 2845 W 42nd Ave; sites/dm/r $20/29/116; @ ☎; ➡7, 36) Two blocks from Spenard Rd, this relaxed hostel has been an Anchorage mainstay for more than 20 years. It has a laundry, no lockout and three kitchens. Campsites are a little cramped, but you can rent a tent if you're without. Also for rent: mountain bikes ($4 per hour) and store bags ($1/15 per day/month). Reservations necessary for July and August.

Qupqugiaq Inn   INN $
(Map p162; ☎563-5633; www.qupq.com; 640 W 36th Ave; pod $45, s/d $90/100, without bathroom $75/85; ☎) This colorful establishment was a construction zone when we visited, but once complete the curved hallways and tiled bathroom floors should instill a sense of calm. Six small sleeping 'pods' (like adult-sized cubbyholes) have one thin mattress, outlets and a window; private rooms vary in quality and size. It has a small kitchen and a sunny deck.

Arctic Adventure Hostel   HOSTEL $
(Map p162; ☎562-5700; www.arcticadventurehostel.com; 337 W 33rd Pl; dm/r $25/50; ☎) The welcome isn't always the warmest, but in a city with so few budget options Arctic Adventure Hostel is a decent standby. The private rooms (with shared bath) are a screamin' deal for two people, and the kitchen is huge – a great place to cook a big spread.

Goose Lake Lodge B&B   B&B $$
(Map p158; ☎252-3958; www.gooselakelodge. com; 3040 Widgeon Ln; r $150-250) A large, warm home filled with light, right on Goose Lake and near the university. There are four bedrooms of varied sizes, including one suite with a double soaking tub. Lofty wood ceilings, large windows and an open sitting area make this house a comfortable place to relax.

Lake Hood Inn   B&B $$
(Map p158; ☎258-9321, 866-663-9322; www.lakehoodinn.com; 4702 Lake Spenard Dr; r $169-189;

☺☎) This spotless upscale home, with four guest rooms, is adorned with airplane artifacts, from a Piper propeller that doubles as a ceiling fan to a row of seats from a Russian airline. Outside are decks where you can watch a parade of floatplanes lift off the lake. Headsets on the lakeside deck even let you listen to radio control.

Long House Alaskan Hotel   HOTEL $$
(Map p158; ☎888-243-2133, 243-2133; www.longhousehotel.com; 4335 Wisconsin St; s/d $163/173; ☎) Near Spenard Rd, this log hotel has large rooms that have been recently updated. It offers continental breakfast, guest laundry facilities, in-room fridges, microwaves, TV, coffee service and 24-hour shuttle to the airport. And to top it off, the staff are really friendly.

Puffin Inn   MOTEL $$
(Map p158; ☎907-243-4044; www.puffininn.net; 4400 Spenard Rd; r $125-229; ☎) Anchorage's best late-night-airport-arrival motel. It has four tiers of fine rooms, from 26 sardine-can economy rooms ($119) to full suites with hot tubs and hideaway kitchens, all recently updated and accessible via free 24-hour airport shuttle.

Millennium Hotel   HOTEL $$$
(Map p158; ☎243-2300, 800-544-0553; 4800 Spenard Rd; r $249-340; ☎) A large, 248-room resort with a woodsy lodge feel overlooking Lake Spenard. PETA members take note: there are stuffed animals, trophy mounts and large fish everywhere. All rooms are large with king or queen beds and a 2015 renovation has been scheduled. There's a decent pub with a great deck for imbibing on sunny evenings.

🛏 Greater Anchorage

Golden Nugget RV Park   CAMPGROUND $
(Map p158; ☎800-449-2012, 333-5311; www.goldennuggetcamperpark.com; 4100 DeBarr Rd; RV sites $42-48; ☎; ➡15) If you're pulling a trailer or driving an RV, this is Anchorage's largest commercial campground, with 215 sites in all. Everything you could possibly need is there: showers, a laundry, a souvenir shop and a bus stop.

Centennial Park Campground CAMPGROUND $
(Map p158; ☎343-6986; 8300 Glenn Hwy; sites $25; ➡3, 75) It's 5 miles from downtown, but pleasant, with 100 sites, good rates and 'the hottest showers in town.'

✖ Eating

Anchorage's dining scene has stepped it up several notches the past few years. You'll still find lots of fast food, espresso stands and more fried halibut and grilled salmon than you can shake a rod and reel at, but the bustling city also boasts a variety of international cuisines, from Polynesian to Mexican to Vietnamese. Best of all, Anchorage restaurants and bars are smoke-free.

Scattered along 4th Ave downtown are so many pushcart vendors selling brats and reindeer sausage ($5) the road ought to be renamed Hot Dog Blvd.

✖ Downtown Anchorage

Brown Bag Sandwich Co   SANDWICHES $
(Map p168; www.akbrownbag.com; 400 D St; sandwiches $9; ⊘7am-3pm) Delicious, funky and popular, Brown Bag has a diverse selection of creative and loaded sandwiches. Go hungry, leave full.

Lucky Wishbone   AMERICAN $
(Map p162; 1033 E 5th Ave; mains $12, burgers $6-8; ⊘10am-10pm Mon-Thu, to 11pm Sat) Down home, pan-fried chicken is the main draw at this busy diner. No frills, just deep-fried goodness, cheap and delicious burgers, and massive milkshakes.

New Sagaya City Market   MARKET $
(Map p162; www.newsagaya.com; 3900 W 13th Ave; ⊘6am-10pm Mon-Sat, 8am-9pm Sun) Eclectic and upscale, this is a grocery store with lots of organic goodies, a great deli specializing in Asian fare and seating indoors and outdoors. There's also a midtown branch at 3700 Old Seward Hwy.

10th & M Seafoods   MARKET $
(Map p168; www.10thandmseafoods.com; 1020 M St; ⊘8am-6pm Mon-Fri, from 9am Sat) This market sells the freshest seafood in a city that loves its seafood fresh. Staff will also butcher and ship your freshly killed moose or 200lb halibut.

Side Street Espresso   COFFEE HOUSE $
(Map p168; 412 G St; light fare $4-7; ⊘7am-3pm Mon-Sat) Serves espresso, bagels and muffins within walls covered in art.

★ **Snow City Café**   CAFE $$
(Map p168; www.snowcitycafe.com; 1034 W 4th Ave; breakfast $8-15, lunch $10-15; ⊘7am-3pm Mon-Fri, to 4pm Sat & Sun; 🕾) Consistently voted best breakfast by *Anchorage Press* readers, this busy cafe serves healthy grub to a clientele that ranges from the tattooed to the up and coming. For breakfast, skip the usual eggs and toast and try a bowl of Snow City granola with dried fruit, honey and nuts.

Ginger   FUSION $$
(Map p168; ☑929-3680; www.gingeralaska.com; 425 W 5th Ave; lunch $9-16, dinner $17-28; ⊘11:30am-2pm & 5-10pm) Sleek and trendy, Ginger's menu is a fusion of Pacific Rim cuisine and classic Asian dishes. The end result is an artistic endeavor like banana and lemongrass soup or spicy tuna tower, served in surroundings that are elegant but still Alaskan casual. The bar stocks fine wines and locally brewed beer, as well as a wide selection of sake.

Glacier Brewhouse   BREWERY $$
(Map p168; www.glacierbrewhouse.com; 737 W 5th Ave; lunch $12-19, dinner $18-30; ⊘11am-9:30pm Mon, to 10pm Tue-Thu, to 11pm Fri & Sat, 10am-9:30pm Sun) Grab a table overlooking the three giant copper brewing tanks and enjoy wood-fired pizzas and rotisserie-grilled ribs and chops with a pint of oatmeal stout. But be prepared to wait for that table, as this place is unbelievably (and deservedly) popular.

Orso   MEDITERRANEAN $$
(Map p168; ☑222-3232; www.orsoalaska.com; 737 W 5th Ave; lunch $9-16, dinner $16-27; ⊘11:30am-9:30pm Sun-Thu, to 11pm Fri & Sat) The walls are a smoked salmon color and the wooden floors are covered with Asian rugs, there's modern art all around and soft jazz floating into both dining levels and the bar. Mains are Mediterranean grill with an Alaskan twist, and the lamb osso buco served with creamy polenta has stayed on the menu from the day Orso opened.

Humpy's Great Alaskan Alehouse   PUB $$
(Map p168; www.humpys.com; 610 W 6th Ave; mains $15-21; ⊘11am-2am Mon-Thu, 11am-2:30am Fri, 10am-2:30am Sat, 10am-2am Sun; 🕾) Anchorage's most beloved beer place, with almost 60 beers on tap. It also has ale-battered halibut, gourmet pizzas, outdoor tables and live music most nights.

Sack's Café   FUSION $$$
(Map p168; ☑274-4022; www.sackscafe.com; 328 G St; lunch mains $12-16, dinner $19-36; ⊘11am-2:30pm & 5-9pm Sun-Thu, to 10pm Fri & Sat) An upscale, chic restaurant serving elegant fare that is consistently creative. It is always bustling (reservations recommended) and has the best weekend brunch in town.

Marx Bros Café   MODERN AMERICAN **$$$**

(Map p168; 278-2133; www.marxcafe.com; 627 W 3rd Ave; dinner $36-38; 5:30-10pm Tue-Sat) Some of Anchorage's most innovative cooking and a 500-bottle wine list are the reasons this 14-table restaurant (located in an historic home built in 1916) is so popular. The menu changes nightly, but the beloved halibut macadamia always stays put. In the summer, book your table a week in advance.

Club Paris   STEAKHOUSE **$$$**

(Map p168; 277-6332; www.clubparisrestaurant. com; 417 W 5th Ave; lunch $12-14, dinner $20-42; 11am-midnight Mon-Sat, from 4pm Sun) This longtime restaurant – it survived the 1964 earthquake – is old-school fine dining and serves the best steaks in Anchorage. If there's room on your credit card, try the 4in-thick filet mignon.

✖ Midtown Anchorage & Spenard

Yak & Yeti   TIRFTAN **$**

(Map p162, www.yakandyetialaska.com; 3301 Spenard Rd; mains $9-13; 11am-2:30pm Mon-Fri, 5-9pm Wed-Sat) Billing itself as 'Himalayan' cuisine, Yak & Yeti serves delicious Indian, Nepalese and Tibetan dishes, including momos (Tibetan dumplings), curries and spiced meats. No alcohol is served, but you can bring your own. The homemade chai is perfect on a rainy day. The owners also run a cafe (Map p162, www.yakandyetialaska.com; 1360 W Northern Lights Blvd, mains $8-13; 10am-8pm Mon-Thu, to 9pm Fri & Sat, 11am-7pm Sun;) in the Northern Lights mall.

Spenard Food Truck Festival   FAST FOOD **$**

(Map p162; cnr 26th Ave & Spenard Rd; 11am-2pm Thu) If you're in town on Thursday, check out the Food Truck Festival in Spenard, in the Chilkoot Charlie's parking lot (p177). An eclectic mix of Asian cuisine, sandwiches, ice cream and Alaskan seafood as well as live music.

Pho Lena   ASIAN **$**

(Map p162; www.pholena.com; 2904 Spenard Rd; mains $9-14; 11am-10pm Mon-Fri, from 10am Sat) An Anchorage favorite, Pho Lena serves up more than the namesake soup: Thai, Laos and other Vietnamese specialties are all available in the tiny Spenard restaurant.

Taco King   MEXICAN **$**

(Map p162; www.tacokingak.com; 113 W Northern Lights Blvd; dinner $7-9; 11am-10pm) Anchor-

age's beloved taco shop is so good and so affordable there are now five more locations, including one on Spenard near the airport. The original is still the busiest.

Ray's Place   VIETNAMESE **$**

(Map p162; 279-2932; www.raysplaceak.com; 32412 Spenard Rd; mains $8-15; 10am-3pm & 5-9pm Mon-Fri;) This Vietnamese restaurant does great cold noodle salads and stir-fries, huge bowls of pho, and stocks Vietnamese beer.

New Central Market   MARKET **$**

(Map p162; www.newcentralmarket.com; 555 W Northern Lights Blvd; 9am-8pm) A touch of Asia in the heart of Anchorage.

Middle Way Cafe   CAFE **$$**

(Map p162; www.middlewaycafe.com; 1200 W Northern Lights Blvd, Suite G; lunch & brunch $8-13; 7am-6pm Mon-Fri, from 8am Sat & Sun;) This veggie-friendly cafe serves healthy breakfasts and organic salads, soups and sandwiches in a cozy, artsy atmosphere. Many vegan and gluten-free options, and really, it's one of the best brunch spots in town.

Bear Tooth Grill   TEX-MEX **$$**

(Map p162; www.beartoothgrill.freshalepubs.com; 1230 W 27th St; burgers $10-16, mains $12-20; 11am-11pm Mon-Fri, 10am-11:30pm Sat & Sun) A popular hangout with an adjacent theater. It serves excellent burgers and seafood as well as Mexican and Asian fusion dishes. The microbrews are fresh and the cocktails are the best in town – if you're up for a splurge, lash out on el Cielo (the sky) margarita. Has an excellent Mexican-leaning brunch menu (with matching cocktails).

Moose's Tooth Brewpub   PIZZA **$$**

(Map p162; www.moosestooth.net; 3300 Old Seward Hwy; large pizza $16-25; 10:30am-midnight Mon-Fri, from 11am Sat & Sun;) An Anchorage institution serving two dozen custom-brewed beers, including monthly specials. This is *the* place to refuel after climbing Flattop, with 40 gourmet pizzas on the menu, including 10 veggie pies.

Rustic Goat   BISTRO **$$**

(Map p158; 334-8100; www.rusticgoatak.com; 2800 Turnagain St; small plates $7-14, mains $17-29; 6am-10pm Mon-Thu, to 11pm Fri, 7am-11pm Sat, 7am-10pm Sun) Anchorage's newest bistro is in the suburban Turnagain neighborhood, but it feels like a city loft. Old-growth timbers support two stories of windows that look out to the Chugach Mountains. Oh, and

1. Anchorage Museum
A world-class facility (p159) and the cultural jewel of Anchorage.

2. Crossroads of Alaska
Signposts in downtown Anchorage.

3. Totems
Artwork outside the Anchorage courthouse.

4. Dog Sledding
Dogs pulling through the snow outside Anchorage.

the food's good, too. The menu specializes in local ingredients, whether they're on wood-fired pizzas or in sandwiches and salads. Dinner reservations recommended; coffee only in the morning.

Fromagio's   SANDWICHES $$
(Map p162; www.fromagioscheese.com; 3701 Spenard Rd; sandwiches $10-13; ⊙10am-6pm Mon-Sat) A cheesemonger that serves gourmet sandwiches. Stop in for lunch, sample some exotic cheeses and then grab some for a picnic while on your hike. There's a **second location** (Map p158; 10950 O'Malley Center Dr; ⊙10am-6pm Tue-Sat, noon-5pm Sun) on the south side, and both sell boxed lunches to take on the road.

Crossbar   AMERICAN $$
(Map p162; www.crossbaralaska.com; 2830 C St; appetizers $8-12, mains $14-22; ⊙11am-10pm Sun & Mon, to midnight Tue-Sat) This isn't your run-of-the-mill sports bar. Sure, there are giant monitors broadcasting the game and hockey decor throughout, but the food is decidedly 'upscale pub grub': think organic blue corn dogs, locally raised bison chili, and house-cured pastrami sandwiches. There are gluten-free dishes as well. Score!

VIP Restaurant   KOREAN $$
(Map p162; 555 W Northern Lights Blvd; barbecue $17-22; ⊙11am-10pm) Of the many Korean restaurants in Anchorage, VIP is the most popular. Try the barbecue, which comes with your choice of sizzling tender meat and about 20 side dishes, and then follow all that spice with an imported beer.

Charlie's Bakery   CHINESE $$
(Map p162; 2729 C St; mains $10-15; ⊙11am-8:30pm Mon-Sat) The most authentic Chinese food you'll find in Anchorage, sold next to French baguettes and wedding cakes. There's dim sum on Saturdays.

Jen's Restaurant   EUROPEAN $$$
(Map p162; ☎561-5367; www.jensrestaurant. com; 701 W 36th Ave; lunch $13-26, dinner $18-40; ⊙11:30am-2pm Mon-Fri, 6-10pm Tue-Sat) This fine restaurant in midtown has dazzled the critics with innovative, Scandinavian-accented cuisine emphasizing fresh ingredients and elaborate presentation. The dining room features a constantly changing exhibition of Alaskan artists while the wine bar stays open to midnight with music and a menu of tapas. You can make reservations online.

✖ Greater Anchorage

Arctic Roadrunner   BURGERS $
(Map p158; 5300 Old Seward Hwy; burgers $5-7; ⊙10am-9:30pm Mon-Sat) Since 1964 this place has been turning out beefy burgers and great onion pieces and rings. If your timing is right, you can eat outdoors while watching salmon spawn up Campbell Creek.

Terra Bella   CAFE $
(Map p158; www.terrabellacoffee.com; 601 E Dimond Blvd; mains $10-12; ⊙7:30am-6pm; 🛜🚲) 🌿 Specializing in organic and gluten-free baked goods as well as vegetarian wraps and sandwiches, Terra Bella also has organically roasted coffee. Don't worry – meat eaters will find a few items on the menu as well. Makes boxed lunches to take on the road, but also has a cozy fireplace to eat your brunch next to.

Southside Bistro   MODERN AMERICAN $$$
(Map p158; ☎348-0088; www.southsidebistro. com; 1320 Huffman Park Dr; lunch $11-20, dinner $18-34; ⊙11:30am-10pm Tue-Thu, to 11pm Fri & Sat) On the south side of town, this trendy bistro is beloved by all those living in the hills above it. The menu incorporates Alaskan seafood, wood-oven pizzas and a massive wine list, along with Mat-Su veggies and Anchorage-area berries. Freshness never tasted so good, at least not in Alaska.

🍷 Drinking & Nightlife

With its young and lively population, Anchorage has a lot to do after the midnight sun finally sets. The free *Anchorage Press* has events listings.

★Bubbly Mermaid   WINE BAR
(Map p168; 417 D St; ⊙noon-late) Perch like a mermaid (or mer-man) at the prow of the boat the Bubbly Mermaid uses for a bar as you pour champagne and local oysters down your throat. It's small, intimate and unique. Bubbly is $7 to $12; oysters $3 a pop.

Crush   WINE BAR
(Map p168; www.crushak.com; 343 W 6th Ave; ⊙11:30am-10pm Mon-Thu, to midnight Fri & Sat) This swanky wine bar serves 'bistro bites,' a menu of appetizers, salads and small plates, as well as more than 40 wines by the glass. Nibble and sip.

McGinley's Pub   IRISH PUB
(Map p168; www.mcginleyspub.com; 645 G St; ⊙11am-2am) We're all Irish, at least on St Pat-

rick's Day, and in Anchorage this is where you come for corned beef and cabbage, bangers and mash, shepherd's pie and a pint of Smithwick's.

SubZero
COCKTAIL BAR

(Map p168; 610 W 6th Ave; ☺11am-2am; 🛜) Cool and jazzy, this hot spot has two pages of cocktails, including almost a dozen martinis and affordable 'Microlounge Micro-plates,' nibbles that range from crab-cake sliders to macadamia-seared goat cheese. Good discounts on food during happy hour.

Snow Goose Restaurant
BREWERY

(Map p168; www.alaskabeers.com; 717 W 3rd Ave; ☺3-10pm Tue-Thu, to 11:30pm Fri & Sat) The outdoor deck on the 2nd floor looks onto Cook Inlet, Mt Susitna and the sunsets whenever they occur. The menu ranges from pizza and local fish to reindeer meatloaf, but there are few things nicer than simply enjoying the homebrewed IPA on a sunny evening.

Crow's Nest
LOUNGE

(Map p168; 939 W 5th Ave; ☺5 11:30pm Tue-Sat) There's upscale dining at the Crow's Nest, at the top of the Hotel Captain Cook, but most come for a drink made by the award-winning bartenders and the million-dollar view of Cook Inlet.

Bernie's Bungalow Lounge
LOUNGE

(Map p168; www.berniesak.com; 626 D St; ☺2:30pm-2am) Pretty people, pretty drinks: this is the place to see and be seen. Its outdoor patio, complete with a water-spewing serpent, is the best in Anchorage and on the summer weekends it rocks late into the night with DJs up in the VIP room.

☆ Entertainment

Live Music

Chilkoot Charlie's
LIVE MUSIC

(Map p162; www.koots.com; 2435 Spenard Rd; ☺11:30am-2am) More than just Anchorage's favorite meat market, 'Koots,' as the locals call it, is a landmark. The sprawling, wooden edifice has 22 beers on tap, 10 bars, four dance floors and a couple of stages where almost every band touring Alaska ends up.

Tap Root
LIVE MUSIC

(Map p162; www.taprootalaska.com; 3300 Spenard Rd; ☺11am-1am Mon-Thu, to 2am Fri, 10am-2am Sat, 10am-1am Sun) With the addition of Tap Root, Spenard cemented its reputation as the heart of Anchorage nightlife. The lively bar has 20 microbrews on tap, an impressive list of single malt Scotch whiskeys and more than 25 types of bourbon. Live music every night of the week.

Cinemas

Bear Tooth Theatrepub
CINEMA

(Map p162; ☐276-4200; www.beartooththeatre. net; 1230 W 27th Ave) Cruise into this very cool venue (check out the mural on the lobby ceiling) where you can enjoy great microbrews, wine or even dinner while watching first-run movies as well as foreign and independent films ($4).

Alaska Experience Center
CINEMA

(Map p168; ☐272-9076; www.alaskaexperiencetheatre.com; 333 W 4th Ave; adult/child $9/8; ☺10am-7pm) More a tourist trap than a movie house, with IMAX nature films and a 15-minute theatrical simulation of the 1964 Good Friday Earthquake.

Theater & Performing Arts

Anchorage had an orchestra before it had paved roads, which says a lot about priorities around here.

Alaska Center for the Performing Arts
PERFORMING ARTS

(Map p168; ☐263-2900, tickets 263-2787; www.myalaskacenter.com; 621 W 6th Ave) Impresses tourists with the film *Aurora: Alaska's Great Northern Lights* (adult/child $11.75/8.75), screened on the hour from 9am to 9pm during summer in its Sydney Laurence Theatre. It's also home to the Anchorage Opera (☐279-2557; www.anchorageopera.org), Anchorage Symphony Orchestra (☐274-8668; www.anchoragesymphony.org), Anchorage Concert Association (☐272-1471; www.anchorageconcerts.org) and Alaska Dance Theatre (☐277-9591; www.alaskadancetheatre.org).

Egan Civic Center
CONCERT VENUE

(Map p168; ☐263-2800; www.anchorageconventioncenters.com; 555 W 5th Ave) Try this place for top-drawer musical groups and other big events.

Sullivan Arena
CONCERT VENUE

(Map p162; ☐279-0618; www.sullivanarena.com; 1600 Gambell St) Also hosts musical events.

Cyrano's Theatre Company
THEATER

(Map p168; ☐274-2599; www.cyranos.org; 413 D St) This off-center playhouse is the best live theater in town, staging everything from *Hamlet* to *Archy and Mehitabel* (comic characters of a cockroach and a cat), Mel

GAY & LESBIAN ANCHORAGE

The week-long **Pridefest** (mid-June) is a gay-pride celebration that includes a Queer Film Festival, Drag Queen Bingo, a parade through downtown and a party at Delaney Park.

It's not West Hollywood, but Anchorage does have a handful of gay- and lesbian-friendly bars and lodgings, and several straight bars are regarded as gay and lesbian friendly: try Bernie's Bungalow Lounge (p177) and the Moose's Tooth Brewpub (p173).

Identity Center of Anchorage (GLCCA; Map p168; 929-4528; www.identityinc.org; 336 E 5th Ave; 3-9pm Mon-Fri, noon-6pm Sat & Sun) Has a community bulletin board and lots of info, including gay-friendly doctor recommendations. It also helps organize Pridefest.

Gay & Lesbian Helpline (258-4777, 888-901-9876; 6-11pm) Provides information on services, referrals for assistance, and a listening ear.

Mad Myrna's (Map p168; www.madmyrnas.com; 530 E 5th Ave; 4pm-2am) A fun, cruisy bar with two dance floors, Drag Diva shows, a cabaret, and dance music most nights after 9pm.

Raven (Map p162; 708 E 4th Ave; 1:30pm-2am) One of a small handful of gay and lesbian bars in Anchorage.

Brooks' jazz musical based on the poetry of Don Marquis and an ever-changing lineup of original shows. Only in Anchorage. Shows typically run Thursday to Sunday.

Sports

Anchorage Bucs BASEBALL
(561-2827; www.anchoragebucs.com; general admission $5) This semipro team of the Alaska Baseball League plays at Mulcahy Ball Park, where living legend Mark McGuire once slammed a few homers. Also taking the same field is archrival **Anchorage Glacier Pilots** (274-3627; www.glacierpilots.com).

🛍 Shopping

Dos Manos ARTS & CRAFTS
(Map p162; 1317 W Northern Lights Blvd; 11am-6pm Mon-Sat, to 5pm Sun) Billing itself as a 'funktional' art gallery, Dos Manos sells locally crafted art and jewelry, and very cool Alaska-themed T-shirts. A recent expansion allows room for large works of fine art.

Oomingmak Musk Ox Producers Co-op CLOTHING
(Map p168; www.qiviut.com; 604 H St; 10am-6pm Mon-Sat) Handles a variety of very soft, very warm and very expensive garments made of arctic musk-ox wool, hand-knitted in isolated Inupiaq villages.

Alaska Mountaineering & Hiking OUTDOOR EQUIPMENT
(AMH; Map p162; www.alaskamountaineering.com; 2633 Spenard Rd; 9am-7pm Mon-Fri, to 6pm Sat, noon-5pm Sun) Staffed by experts and stocked with high-end gear, AMH is the place for serious adventurers.

REI OUTDOOR EQUIPMENT
(Map p162; 1200 W Northern Lights Blvd; 10am-9pm Mon-Fri, 9am-7pm Sat, 10am-6pm Sun) Anchorage's largest outdoor store has everything you might ever need, from wool socks to backpacks to kayaks to camp chairs. Besides being able to repair your camp stove or bicycle tire, it will also rent canoes, bear containers, tents and bicycles.

Title Wave Books BOOKSTORE
(Map p162; www.wavebooks.com; 1360 W Northern Lights Blvd; 10am-8pm Mon-Thu, to 9pm Fri & Sat, 11am-7pm Sun;) A fabulous used bookstore, with more than 30,000 sq ft of books, including many on Alaska.

Spenard Farmers Market MARKET
(Map p162; www.spenardfarmersmarket.org; cnr 26th Ave & Spenard Rd; 9am-2pm) Handmade arts and crafts, plus locally grown produce and Alaska seafood. A festive vibe with live music on Saturday mornings in Chilkoot Charlie's parking lot.

Alaska Native Arts Foundation Gallery ARTS & CRAFTS
(Map p168; www.alaskanativearts.org; 500 W 6th Ave) The gallery showcases Native art in a bright, open space.

ANC Auxiliary Craft Shop ARTS & CRAFTS
(Map p158; 4315 Diplomacy Dr; 10am-2pm Mon-Fri, 1st & 3rd Sat of month) Located on the 1st floor of the Alaska Native Medical Center, it has some of the finest Alaska Native arts and crafts available to the public. But it has limited hours and does not accept credit cards.

Alaska Native Heritage Center ARTS & CRAFTS
(www.alaskanative.net; 8800 Heritage Center Dr) Stocks a gift shop with jewelry, carvings and other 'artifacts,' and features booths where craftspeople make fresh knickknacks while you watch.

Anchorage Market & Festival ARTS & CRAFTS
(Map p168; www.anchoragemarkets.com; cnr W 3rd Ave & E St; ⊙10am-6pm Sat & Sun; 🖷) This was called the 'Saturday Market' until it became so popular it opened on Sundays. A fantastic open market with live music and more than 300 booths stocked with cheap food, Mat-Su Valley veggies and souvenirs from birch steins to birch syrup and T-shirts that proclaim your love of Alaska.

Ulu Factory HANDICRAFTS
(Map p168; www.theulufactory.com; 211 W Ship Creek Ave) The *ulu* (oo-loo) is to Alaska what the rubber alligator is to Florida: everybody sells them. Still, this shop is interesting, with demonstrations that will teach you how to use the cutting tool.

ℹ Information

INTERNET ACCESS
Internet access and wi-fi are widely available all over Anchorage at hotels, restaurants, bars and even gift shops.

ZJ Loussac Public Library (☑343-2975; 3600 Denali St; ⊙10am-9pm Mon-Thu, to 6pm Fri & Sat, 1-5pm Sun) Has free internet terminals (one hour per day) as well as wi-fi.

MEDIA
Tourist freebies are available everywhere: the *Official Anchorage Visitors Guide* and *Anchorage Daily News' Alaska Visitor's Guide* are all packed with useful information.

Alaska Dispatch News (www.alaskadispatch.com) In 2014, the independent, online-only news site Alaska Dispatch bought the long-running, award-winning *Anchorage Daily News* and named the combined outlet *Alaska Dispatch News*. Anchorage-centric events are published in Thursday's *Play* insert.

MEDICAL SERVICES
Alaska Regional Hospital (☑276-1131; www.alaskaregional.com; 2801 DeBarr Rd; ⊙24hr; 🚍13, 15) Near Merrill Field.

First Care Medical Center (☑248-1122; 3710 Woodland Dr, Suite 1100; ⊙7am-11pm; 🚍7) Walk-in clinic just off Spenard Rd in midtown.

Providence Alaska Medical Center (☑562-2211; www.alaska.providence.org; 3200 Providence Dr; ⊙24hr; 🚍1, 3, 13, 36, 45, 102) The largest medical center in the state.

MONEY
Key Bank (☑257-5502; 601 W 5th Ave; ⊙10am-5pm Mon-Fri) Downtown.

Wells Fargo (☑265-2805; 301 W Northern Lights Blvd; ⊙10am-6pm Mon-Sat) The main bank is in midtown.

POST
Post Office (Map p168; 320 W 5th Ave; ⊙10am-2pm & 3-6pm Mon-Fri) This one's downtown in the 5th Avenue Mall, but there are nearly a dozen more in town.

TOURIST INFORMATION
Alaska Public Lands Information Center (Map p168; ☑644-3661, 866-869-6887; www.alaskacenters.gov; 605 W 4th Ave, Suite 105; ⊙9am-5pm) In the Federal Building (you'll need photo ID). The center has handouts for hikers, mountain bikers, kayakers, fossil hunters and just about everyone else, on almost every wilderness area in the state. There are also excellent wildlife displays, free movies, fun dioramas, and guided walks including ones about Captain Cook (11am and 4pm) and the 1964 earthquake (2:45pm).

Log Cabin Visitor Center (Map p168; ☑257-2363; www.anchorage.net; 524 W 4th Ave; ⊙8am-7pm) Has pamphlets, maps, bus schedules, city guides in several languages and a lawn growing on its roof

Visitors Center (☑266-2860; Anchorage International Airport; ⊙8am-7pm) Several are located in the baggage-claim areas of both terminals; the south-terminal desk is staffed 9am to 4pm daily in summer.

ℹ Getting There & Away

AIR
Ted Stevens Anchorage International Airport (p416), Alaska's largest airport, is 6.5 miles west of the city center and handles more than 130 domestic and international flights daily from more than a dozen major airlines.

Alaska Airlines (☑800-252-7522; www.alaskaair.com) Provides the most intrastate routes to travelers, generally through its contract carrier, Ravn Air (formerly Era Aviation), which operates services to Valdez, Homer, Cordova, Kenai, Iliamna and Kodiak. You can book tickets either online or at the airport.

Pen Air (☑800-448-4226; www.penair.com) Flies smaller planes to 27 difficult-to-pronounce destinations in Southwest Alaska, including Unalakleet, Aniak and Igiugig.

❶ MORE AFFORDABLE CAR RENTALS

Avoid renting a car at the Anchorage Airport if at all possible, as you will be hit with a 34% rental tax. Rental agencies within Anchorage will tack on only an 18% tax and generally have cheaper rates. And while they can't pick you up at the airport, if you drop the car off during business hours some rental places will provide you with a ride to the airport.

Also keep in mind that if you can rent a vehicle in May or September as opposed to June, July or August, you will usually save an additional 30%.

BUS

Anchorage is a hub for various small passenger and freight lines that make daily runs between specific cities. Always call first; Alaska's volatile bus industry is as unstable as an Alaska Peninsula volcano.

Alaska Park Connection (☎800-266-8625; www.alaskacoach.com) Offers daily service from Anchorage north to Talkeetna ($65, 2½ hours) and Denali National Park ($90, six hours), and south to Seward ($65, three hours).

Alaska/Yukon Trails (☎888-5659, 479-2277; www.alaskashuttle.com) Runs a bus up the George Parks Hwy to Denali ($75, six hours) and Fairbanks ($99, nine hours).

Homer Stage Lines (☎868-3914; http://stagelineinhomer.com) Will take you to Homer ($90, 4½ hours) and points in between.

Interior Alaska Bus Line (☎800-770-6652; www.alaskadirectbusline.com) Has regular services between Anchorage and Glennallen ($75, three hours), Tok ($130, eight hours) and Fairbanks ($185, 17 hours), and points in between.

Seward Bus Line (☎563-0800; www.sewardbuslines.net) Runs between Anchorage and Seward ($40, three hours) twice daily in summer. For an extra $5, you can arrange an airport pickup/drop-off.

TRAIN

From its downtown depot, **Alaska Railroad** (☎265-2494; www.akrr.com) sends its *Denali Star* north daily to Talkeetna (adult/child $89/45), Denali National Park ($146/73) and Fairbanks ($210/105). The *Coastal Classic* stops in Girdwood ($59/30) and Seward ($75/38), while the *Glacial Discovery* connects to Whittier ($65/33). You can save 20% to 30% traveling in

May and September. See the Riding the Alaska Railroad boxed text on p184.

❶ Getting Around

TO/FROM THE AIRPORT
People Mover bus 7 offers hourly service between downtown and the airport (adult/child $2/1, 6:15am to 10:40pm Monday to Friday, 8:35am to 8:35pm Saturday, 10:35am to 6:05pm Sunday). Pickup is at the south (domestic) terminal. You can call **Alaska Shuttle** (☎694-8888, 338-8888; www.alaskashuttle.net) for door-to-door service to downtown and South Anchorage ($90 per hour; fill that van!) or Eagle River ($55). Plenty of the hotels and B&Bs also provide a courtesy-van service. Finally, an endless line of taxis will be eager to take your bags and your money. Plan on a $25 fare to the downtown area.

BUS
Anchorage's excellent bus system, **People Mover** (☎343-6543; muni.org/Departments/transit/PeopleMover; adult/child $2/1; ⊗6am-11:30pm Mon-Fri, 8am-9pm Sat, 10am-7pm Sun), runs from 6am to 11:30pm Monday to Friday, 8am to 9pm Saturday and 10am to 7pm Sunday. Pick up a schedule ($1) at the **Downtown Transit Center** (Map p168; cnr W 6th Ave & G St) or call for specific route information. One-way fares are $2/1 per adult/child; an unlimited day pass ($4) is available at the transit center. Valley Mover (p193) offers 14 round-trips a day between Eagle River, the Mat-Su Valley and Anchorage (one-way/day pass $7/10)

CAR & MOTORCYCLE
All the national concerns (Avis, Budget, Hertz, Payless, National etc) have counters in the airport's south terminal.

Midnight Sun Car & Van Rental (☎243-8806, 855-543-8806; www.ineedacarrental.com; 4211 Spenard Rd) The best of the Spenard cheapies, with compacts for $80/480 per day/week in July, a little bit less in June and August.

House of Harley-Davidson (☎246-5300; www.harleyalaska.com; 4334 Spenard Rd) Rents out Harley-Davidsons (per day $200 to $250) and even offers a Fly-Buy-Ride program so you can hit the road in the Last Frontier on your new Harley. Sure, it's pricey, but it's still much better value than traditional psychotherapy.

TAXI
If you need to call a cab, try either **Anchorage Yellow Cab** (☎222-2222) or **Anchorage Checker Cab** (☎276-1234).

SOUTH OF ANCHORAGE

The trip out of Anchorage along Turnagain Arm is well worth the price of a train ticket or rental car. Sure, it might be quicker (and probably cheaper) to fly, but staying on the ground will help you to appreciate just how close to the wilderness Anchorage really is.

Seward Highway

Starting at the corner of Gambell St and 10th Ave in Anchorage, Seward Hwy parallels the Alaska Railroad south 127 miles to Seward. Once it leaves Anchorage proper, the highway winds along massive peaks dropping straight into Turnagain Arm. Expect lots of traffic, a frightening percentage of which involves folks who have (1) never seen a Dall sheep before, and (2) never driven an RV before; it's a frustrating and sometimes deadly combination. Mile markers measure the distance from Seward.

If you're lucky (or a planner), you'll catch the bore tide, which rushes along Turnagain Arm in varying sizes daily.

Potter Marsh (Mile 117) was created in 1916, when railroad construction dammed several streams; at the time of writing, it was in the process of being filled with eroded earth. You can stretch your legs along the 1500ft boardwalk while spying on ducks, songbirds, grebes and gulls.

Chugach State Park Headquarters (☑ 345-5014; Mile 115, Seward Hwy; ☺ 10am-4pm Mon-Fri) is housed in the Potter Section House, a historic railroad workers' dorm with a snowplow train outside.

Turnagain Arm Trail, an easy 11-mile hike, begins at Mile 115. Originally used by Alaska Natives, the convenient route has since been used by Russian trappers, gold miners and happy hikers. The trail, with a mountain goat's view of Turnagain Arm, alpine meadows and beluga whales, can also be accessed at the McHugh Creek Picnic Area (Mile 112), Rainbow (Mile 108) and Windy Corner (Mile 107).

Indian Valley Mine (www.indianvalleymine.com; Mile 104, Seward Hwy; admission $1; ☺ 9am-6pm), a lode mine originally blasted out in 1901, still produces gold. You can buy bags of ore ($10 to $50) and see for yourself. The wonderful proprietors are extremely knowledgeable on the history and science of Alaskan gold mining; ask about the potato retort.

Indian Valley Trail (Mile 103) is a mellow 6-mile path that starts 1.3 miles along the gravel road behind Turnagain House. You can also access Powerline Pass Trail for much longer hiking or cycling. Nearby is the **Brown Bear Motel** (☑ 653-7000; Mile 103, Seward Hwy; r $60) with six clean rooms and plenty of cheap beer in the adjoining Brown Bear Saloon, which can get hopping at night. There are also two cabins out back ($100 and $120) with kitchens.

Bird Ridge Trail starts with a wheelchair-accessible loop at Mile 102, then continues with a steep, popular and well-marked path that reaches a 3500ft overlook at Mile 2; this is a traditional turnaround point for folks in a hurry. Or you can continue another 4 miles to higher peaks and even better views from sunny Bird Ridge, a top spot for rock climbing.

Bird Creek State Campground (☑ 269-8400; Mile 101, Seward Hwy; campsites $15) is popular for fishing, hiking and, best of all, the sound of the bore tide rushing by your tent. Remind children and morons to stay off the deadly mud flats, which act as quicksand and are subject to extremely strong tides.

Girdwood

POP 1817

Some 37 miles south of Anchorage, Alyeska Hwy splits off at Mile 90 Seward Hwy and heads 3 miles east to Girdwood, a small hamlet with a city-like list of things to do and see. Encircled by mighty peaks brimming with glaciers, Girdwood is a laid-back antidote to the bustle of Anchorage. Home to the luxurious Alyeska Ski Resort and the fabled **Girdwood Forest Fair** (www.girdwoodforestfair.com), Girdwood is a dog-and-kid kind of town with excellent hiking, fine restaurants and a feel-good vibe that will have you staying longer than anticipated.

◉ Sights

Crow Creek Mine   MINE
(www.crowcreekmine.com; Mile 3.5 Crow Creek Rd; adult/child $10/free; ☺ 9am-6pm; ⊞) Girdwood was named for James Girdwood, who staked the first claim on Crow Creek in 1896. Two years later the Crow Creek Mine was built and today you can still see some original buildings and sluices at this working mine. You can even learn how to pan for gold and then give it a try yourself (adult/child $20/10) or pitch the tent and spend the

CATCHING THE BORE TIDE

One attraction along the Turnagain Arm stretch of the Seward Hwy is unique among sights already original: the bore tide. The bore tide is a neat trick of geography that requires a combination of narrow, shallow waters and rapidly rising tides. Swooping as a wave sometimes 6ft in height (and satisfyingly loud), the tide fills the arm in one go. It travels at speeds of up to 15mph, and every now and then you'll catch a brave surfer or kayaker riding it into the arm.

So, how to catch this dramatic rush?

First, consult a tide table, or grab a schedule, available at any Anchorage visitor center. The most extreme bore tides occur during days with minus tides between -2ft and -5.5ft, but if your timing doesn't hit a huge minus, aim for a new or full moon period. Once you've determined your day, pick your spot. The most popular is Beluga Point (Mile 110), and a wise choice. If you miss the tide, you can always drive further up the arm and catch it at Bird Point (Mile 96).

ANCHORAGE & AROUND GIRDWOOD

night ($10). It's a peaceful little place and worth a visit just to walk around.

Girdwood Center for Visual Arts GALLERY (www.gcvaonline.org; Olympic Circle; ⊙10am-6pm) **FREE** In town this center serves as an artisan cooperative during the summer and is filled with the work of those locals who get inspired by the majestic scenery that surrounds them.

Alyeska Resort Tram CABLE CAR (☎754-2275; www.alyeskaresort.com; adult/child $25/15; ⊙9:30am-9:30pm; ⊕) The Alyeska Ski Resort Tram offers the easiest route to the alpine area during the summer. The resort offers a Tram & Lunch Combo (adult/child $35/25) that lets you wander the alpine terrain and then grab a bite at the Glacier Express Restaurant located in the Upper Tram Terminal.

🏃 Activities

Hiking

Take the Alyeska Resort Tram to the easy, 1-mile **Alyeska Glacier View Trail**, in an alpine area with views of the tiny Alyeska Glacier. You can continue up the ridge to climb the so-called summit of Mt Alyeska, a high point of 3939ft. The true summit lies further to the south, but is not a climb for casual hikers.

Winner Creek Gorge is an easy, pleasant hike that winds 5.5 miles through lush forest, ending in the gorge itself, where Winner Creek becomes a series of cascades. The first half of the trail is a boardwalk superhighway, but toward the end it can get a bit muddy. From the gorge you can connect to the **Iditarod National Historic Trail** for

a 7.7-mile loop. Either way, you'll cross the gorge on an ultrafun hand-tram. The most popular trailhead is near Arlberg Rd: walk along the bike path past the Alyeska Prince Hotel, toward the bottom of the tram. Look for the footpath heading into the forest.

The highly recommended **Crow Pass Trail** is a short but beautiful alpine hike that has gold-mining relics and an alpine lake, and often there are Dall sheep on the slopes above. It's 4 miles to Raven Glacier, the traditional turnaround point of the trail, and 3 miles to a **USFS cabin** (☎877-444-6777, 518-885-3639; www.recreation.gov; cabins $35). Or you can continue on the three-day, 24-mile route along the Iditarod National Historic Trail to the Eagle River Nature Center. The trailhead is 5.8 miles north of Alyeska Hwy on Crow Creek Rd.

Cycling

The Indian–Girdwood Trail – a paved path that leads out of the valley and along the Seward Hwy above Turnagain Arm, dubbed Bird-to-Gird – is the most scenic ride here. The fabulous route extends to Mile 103 of the highway, linking Alyeska Resort with Indian Creek, 17 miles away. **Girdwood Ski & Cyclery** (☎783-2453; www.girdwoodskicyclery. com; 1553 Alyeska Hwy; bicycles per half/full day $20/30; ⊙10am-7pm Wed-Sun) will rent you the bikes to enjoy it.

Alyeska Resort has installed elevated tread single-tracks for mountain bikers, suitable for beginners as well as adrenaline addicts. The tram and chairs 3, 4 and 6 will carry cyclists and their wheels all the way up to Glacier Bowl if they choose and then a variety of intermediate and advanced trails lead them downhill. Easier trails depart from the resort itself. A day pass for the lifts is $30. You can purchase it or rent downhill bikes with pads and helmet at **Alyeska Day-lodge Rental Shop** (☑754-2553; bikes per day $100).

👉 Tours

Ascending Path   HIKING
(☑783-0505, www.ascendingpath.com) This climbing-guide service has a three-hour glacier hike on Alyeska Glacier ($139), and tours that combine guided hikes with an Alaska Railroad trip to Spencer Glacier ($279). The company also offers a three-hour rock-climbing outing designed for beginners ($189), or summer ice climbing ($250).

Alpine Air   SCENIC FLIGHTS
(☑783-2360; www.alpineairalaska.com; Girdwood airport) Has a 30-minute glacier tour ($230) and an hour-long tour in which the helicopter lands on the ice ($345).

Hotel Alyeska   TOURS
(☑754-2111; www.alyeskaresort.com; 1000 Arlberg Ave) Whether you want to golf, paraglide, photograph brown bears or do a yoga session in the alpine, this resort has the (expensive) tour for you.

Spencer Whistle Stop Train   GLACIER
(☑265-2494, 800-544-0552; www.akrr.com) Ride the Alaska Railroad to Spencer Glacier, where you can hike a 3.4-mile trail to the face of the glacier or join a guided walk with a USFS Ranger. Whistle Stop hikers have from 1:45pm to 4:30pm to complete the hike and meet the train for the return. Or you can camp overnight at a group campsite. The round-trip fares from Girdwood and Anchorage include transport (adult/child $109/55); save money by catching the train directly at Portage station (adult/child $70/35).

🛏 Sleeping

At the Alyeska Ski Area, **Alyeska Accommodations** (☑783-2000, 888-783-2001; www.alyeskaaccommodations.com; 203 Olympic Mountain Loop; r $120-450) sublets massive, privately owned (and decorated) condos, many with full kitchens, hot tubs and saunas. If you need something smaller, it also rents out rooms and cabins.

B&Bs make up the bulk of Girdwood's lodging and are the only midrange option. The **Alyeska/Girdwood Accommoda-tions Association** (☑222-4858; alyeskagirdwoodaccommodations.net) can find last-minute rooms. Girdwood has a 12% bed tax.

⭐ Alyeska Hostel   HOSTEL $
(☑783-2222; www.alyeskahostel.com; 227 Alta Dr; dm/s/d $25/56/67; 🕿) A cozy, no-shoes guesthouse with a private cabin ($84), private room, eight bunks and killer mountain views. The one dorm room sleeps eight; make sure you book ahead. A small expansion is planned for 2015.

Girdwood Campground   CAMPGROUND $
(☑343-8373; tent sites $10) Eighteen walk-in sites in the woods with an excellent, in-town location. It has a cooking pavilion, outhouses and a bear-proof locker. From the Alyeska Highway, turn right on Egloff Drive and follow the road past the ballfield.

Bud & Carol's B&B   B&B $$
(☑783-3182; www.budandcarolsbandb.com; 211 Brighton Rd; r $130; 🕿🕿) Located at the base of the ski hill, this B&B offers two very clean rooms with private bath and a fully equipped kitchen stocked with all you need for a hearty continental breakfast.

Glacier View B&B   B&B $$
(☑350-0674; www.glacierviewbnb.com; Alpina Way; r $130-180; 🕿) An upscale B&B with four guest rooms along with an extra-large hot tub, a brand new deck to soak in the sunshine, and a common area where you can view the mountains and see six glaciers. Rooms come with full breakfast.

Hotel Alyeska   RESORT $$$
(☑754-2111; www.alyeskaresort.com; 1000 Arlberg Ave; d $279-299, ste $349; 🕿🕿🕿🕿) This place earned four stars from AAA because it deserved them – from the whirlpool with a view to bathrobes and slippers in every room, this place is swanky. For something less swanky you can park your RV in the day lodge for $10 a night and then ride the resort shuttle to use the pool or take a shower.

🍴 Eating

For such a tiny place, Girdwood has an amazing selection of restaurants that often pull their patrons in from Anchorage. Since it's part of the municipality of Anchorage, all restaurants and bars are refreshingly smoke-free.

Bake Shop BAKERY $
(www.thebakeshop.com; Olympic Circle; breakfast $6-10, lunch $7-8; ☺ 7am-7pm) Always busy, this bright and art-filled place serves wholesome omelets with fresh-baked breads and sourdough pancakes, all of which you can enjoy at one of the large wooden tables. One of the giant cinnamon rolls is big enough to share with a friend – or not.

Crow Creek Mercantile MARKET $
(Nightower Rd; ☺ 7am-midnight Mon-Fri, from 8am Sat & Sun) Girdwood's tiny grocery store also has some ready-to-eat items.

Chair 5 Restaurant PIZZA $$
(www.chairfive.com; 5 Lindblad Ave; medium pizza $14-18, dinner $17-30; ☺ 11am-11pm) The kind of bar and restaurant skiers love after a long day on the slopes. It features more than 60 beers, including a dozen on tap, 16 types

of gourmet pizzas, big burgers and a lot of blackened halibut. The bar closes late.

★ **Jack Sprat** MODERN AMERICAN $$$
(☎ 783-5225; www.jacksprat.net; Olympic Circle Dr; brunch $9-17, dinner $20-35; ☺ 5-10pm Mon-Fri, 10am-2:30pm & 4-10pm Sat & Sun; ✎) ✐ Creative fresh cuisine at the base of the ski hill. Many dishes are vegetarian-friendly and made from organically grown ingredients. Homemade almond milk lattes and the constant favorite *bibimbap* (a Korean-influenced bowl with kimchi, rice, pork and eggs) are only two of the many reasons to eat here. It has a wine list and outdoor seating. Reservations are recommended.

Seven Glaciers Restaurant SEAFOOD $$$
(☎ 754-2237; dinner $32-52; ☺ 5-9pm Thu, noon-9pm Fri & Sat, to 10pm Sun) Sitting 2300ft above sea level is the best of Alyeska Resort's six restaurants and bars. The hotel tram will take

---

RIDING THE ALASKA RAILROAD

In a remote corner of the Alaskan wilderness, you stand along a railroad track when suddenly a small train appears. You wave a white flag in the air – actually yesterday's dirty T-shirt – and the engineer acknowledges you with a sound of his whistle and then stops. You hop onboard to join others fresh from the Bush: fly-fishermen, backpackers, a hunter with his dead moose, locals whose homestead cabin can be reached only after a ride on the *Hurricane Turn*, one of America's last flag-stop trains.

This unusual service between Talkeetna and Hurricane along the Susitna River is only one aspect that makes the Alaska Railroad so unique. At the other end of the rainbow of luxury is the railroad's Gold Star Service, two lavishly appointed cars that in 2005 joined the *Denali Star* train as part of the Anchorage–Fairbanks run. The 89ft double-decked dome cars include a glass observation area on the 2nd level with 360-degree views and a bartender in the back serving your favorite libations. Sit back, sip a chardonnay and soak in the grandeur of Mt McKinley.

Take your pick, rustic or relaxing, but don't pass up the Alaska Railroad. There's not another train like it.

The railroad was born on March 12, 1914, when the US Congress passed the Alaska Railroad Act, authorizing the US president to construct and operate the line. With the exception of the train used at the Panama Canal, the US government had never before owned and operated a railroad.

It took eight years and 4500 men to build a 470-mile railroad from the ice-free port of Seward to the boomtown of Fairbanks, a wilderness line that was cut over what were thought to be impenetrable mountains and across raging rivers. On a warm Sunday afternoon in 1923, President Warren Harding – the first US president to visit Alaska – tapped in the golden spike at Nenana.

The Alaska Railroad has been running ever since. The classic trip is to ride the railroad from Anchorage to Fairbanks, with a stop at Denali National Park. Many believe the most scenic portion, however, is the 114-mile run from Anchorage to Seward, which begins by skirting the 60-mile-long Turnagain Arm, climbs an alpine pass and then comes within a half-mile of three glaciers.

There are far cheaper ways to reach Seward, Fairbanks or points in between. But in the spirit of adventure, which is why many of us come to Alaska, a van or bus pales in comparison to riding the Alaska Railroad.

you to an evening of gourmet dining and absolutely stunning views that include Turnagain Arm and, yes, seven glaciers. The menu is dominated by seafood; even the meat mains are offered with a side of king crab.

Double Musky Inn   CAJUN $$$
(www.doublemuskyinn.com; Crow Creek Rd; dinner $22-45; ⊙5-10pm Tue-Thu, from 4:30pm Fri-Sun) Folks drive down from Anchorage for the French pepper steak – New York strip encrusted in cracked pepper and covered with a spicy burgundy sauce – the reason you might have to wait two hours on weekends (reservations are not accepted). The cuisine is Cajun accented, hence the masks and mardi-gras beads hanging from the ceiling. The desserts are divine.

ℹ Information

There are ATMs at the Tesoro Station, Laundromall, Alyeska Resort and Crow Creek Mercantile.
Girdwood Chamber of Commerce (www.girdwoodchamber.com) No visitor center, but has a great website for pretrip planning.
Girdwood Clinic (📞783-1355; Hightower Rd; ⊙10am-6pm Mon-Sat) Offers basic medical care. Call for urgent care on Sunday.
Girdwood Laundromall (158 Holmgren Pl; ⊙8am-9:30pm; 🛜) Voted the number-one laundromat in the US by *American Coin Op* magazine, this place also has themed coin-op showers ($7) complete with nature sounds, plus Internet access (per minute 6.5¢, free wi-fi) and an ATM.
Scott & Wesley Gerrish Library (250 Egloff Dr; ⊙1 6pm Tue & Thu, 1 8pm Wed, 10am 6pm Fri & Sat; 🛜) Girdwood's library has 10 terminals for free internet access, as well as wi-fi.
USFS Glacier Ranger Station (📞783-3242; Ranger Station Rd; ⊙8am 5pm Mon Fri) Has topo maps, a viewing scope, and information on area hikes, campgrounds and public-use cabins.

ℹ Getting There & Around

Alaska Railroad (📞265-2494, 800-544-0552; www.akrr.com) Although the fare is steep, you could hop on the Alaska Railroad in Anchorage for a day trip to Girdwood (one way adult/child $65/33). On its way to Seward, the *Coastal Classic* train arrives at Girdwood at 8am daily during the summer and again at 9pm for the return journey to Anchorage.
Glacier Valley Transit (📞754-2547; www.glaciervalleytransit.com) Known simply as 'The Shuttle,' Girdwood's bus service operates from Alyeska Resort to the Seward Hwy at $1 a ride.

Magic Bus (📞230-6773; www.themagicbus.com) An accommodating charter-bus service that leaves Anchorage at 9:30am and departs from Girdwood for the return trip at 6:30pm (one way/round-trip $30/50). Also travels to Whittier; it's $55 whether you're going one way or both.
Seward Bus Lines (📞563-0800, 888-420-7788; www.sewardbuslines.net) Can arrange transport to Seward and Anchorage from Girdwood ($30 to $40).

South of Girdwood

Seward Hwy continues southeast past Girdwood and a few nifty tourist attractions to what's left of Portage, which was destroyed by the 1964 Good Friday Earthquake and is basically a few structures sinking into the nearby mud flats.

The Wetland Observation Platform (Mile 81) features interpretive plaques on the ducks, arctic terns, bald eagles and other wildlife inhabiting the area.

Alaska Wildlife Conservation Center (📞783 2025; www.alaskawildlife.org; Mile 79, Seward Hwy; adult/child $12.50/9; ⊙8am-8pm) is a nonprofit wildlife center where injured and rescued animals are on display. Particularly of interest are the wood bison, which are the only herd in the US, and are part of a program to reintroduce the extinct-in-Alaska breed. It's also a good spot to see a bear or moose if you haven't yet.

Portage Glacier

Portage Glacier Access Rd leaves Seward Hwy at Mile 79, continuing 5.4 miles to the **Begich-Boggs Visitors Center** (📞783 2326; adult/child $5/free; ⊙9am-6pm; 🛜) en route to Whittier (on the other side of the Anton Memorial Tunnel).

The building, with its observation decks and telescopes, was designed to provide great views of Portage Glacier. But ironically (and to the dismay of thousands of tourists) the glacier has retreated so fast you can no longer see it from the center. Still, inside are neat high-tech wildlife displays and the excellent movie, *Voices from the Ice.*

Most people view the glacier through **Gray Line** (📞888-425-1737; www.graylinealaska.com; adult/child $34/17), whose cruise boat MV *Ptarmigan* departs from a dock near the Begich-Boggs Center five times daily during summer. The one-hour (adult/child $34/17) tour cruises up to Portage Glacier's face. If you have a pair of hiking boots, Portage Pass Trail, a mile-long trek to the pass, will provide a good view of Portage Glacier. The trail begins near the tunnel on the Whittier side, so it's a $12-per-car fare to drive through and then return.

The multi-use **Trail of Blue Ice** parallels Portage Glacier Access Rd and meanders through forest on a wide gravel (and occasionally boardwalk) trail, connecting Portage Lake to the Seward Hwy. Another interesting hike is **Byron Glacier View Trail**, a single, flat mile to an unusually ice-worm-infested snowfield and grand glacier views.

There are two USFS campgrounds. **Black Bear Campground** (Mile 3.7 Portage Glacier Access Rd; tent & RV sites $14) is beautiful and woodsy – and caters more to tent campers – while **Williwaw Campground** (www.recreation.gov; Mile 4.3 Portage Glacier Access Rd; tent & RV sites $18-28) is stunningly located beneath Explorer Glacier and receives more of an RV crowd. Both campgrounds are extremely popular, although sites at Williwaw can be reserved in advance through **National Recreation Reservation Service** (☎877-444-6777; www.recreation.gov).

NORTH OF ANCHORAGE

As you drive out of Anchorage, you'll soon parallel Knik Arm, while the Chugach Mountains stay to your right. Small communities dot either side of the road, but Eagle River and Eklutna offer the best access to the mountains. Both communities are worthy of a day trip from Anchorage, but to escape the hustle of the city, you can use these small towns as a base for exploring both Anchorage and the wilds around it.

Glenn Highway

In Anchorage, 5th Ave becomes Glenn Hwy, running 189 miles through Palmer, where it makes a junction with the George Parks Hwy, to Glennallen and the Richardson Hwy. Milepost distances are measured from Anchorage.

At Mile 11.5 of Glenn Hwy is **Eagle River Campground** (☎694-7982; Hiland Rd exit; tent sites $15), with beautiful walk-in sites. The river runs closest to the shady sites in the 'Rapids' section. Keep in mind this is one of the most popular campsites in the state and half the sites can be reserved up to a year in advance through **Lifetime Adventures** (☎764-4644, 800-952-8624; www.lifetimeadventures.net).

Eagle River

POP 25,770

At Mile 13.4 of Glenn Hwy is the exit to Old Glenn Hwy, which takes you through the bedroom communities of Eagle River and Chugiak. Eagle River has something of a city center; the Eagle River Town Square is off Business Blvd, and just about every business you'll need. The Bear Paw Festival, held here in July, is worth the trip just for the 'Slippery Salmon Olympics,' which involves racing with a hula hoop, a serving tray and, of course, a large dead fish. Most people, however, come here for the drive down Eagle River Rd.

🏃 Activities

Eagle River Road DRIVING TOUR
This stunning sidetrip into the heart of the Chugach Mountains follows the Eagle River for 13 miles. The road is paved and winding, and at Mile 7.4 there is a put-in for rafts to float the Class I and II section of the river. The road ends at the **Eagle River Nature Center** (☎694-2108; www.ernc.org; 32750 Eagle River Rd; vehicles $5; ⏰10am-5pm; 🚗). The log-cabin center offers wildlife displays, telescopes for finding Dall sheep, guided hikes on most Saturdays and Sundays, and heaps of programs for kids.

Rodak Nature Trail HIKING
Several trails depart from the Eagle River Nature Center, with Rodak Nature Trail being the easiest. Children will love the mile-long interpretive path, as it swings by an impressive overlook straddling a salmon stream and a huge beaver dam. **Albert Loop Trail** is a slightly more challenging 3-mile hike through boreal forest and along Eagle River.

Iditarod National Historic Trail HIKING
(Mile 1.7) The National Historic Iditarod Trail is a 24-mile trek used by gold miners and sled-dog teams until 1918, when the Alaska Railroad was finished. It's a three-day hike through superb mountain scenery to Girdwood (where it's known as the Crow Pass Trail), and the region's best backpack adventure. For more see p70.

Pitch a tent at Rapids Camp or Echo Bend (Mile 3), or rent one of two yurts ($65 per night) close by. For a shorter outing you can turn around at the Perch, a very large rock in the middle of wonderland, then backtrack to the Dew Mound Trail at Echo Bend and loop back to the Nature Center, making this a scenic 8-mile trip.

Thunderbird Falls HIKING
Thunderbird Falls, closer to Eklutna, is a rewarding 2-mile round-trip walk with a gorgeous little waterfall for the grand finale. Anchorage's People Mover bus 102 stops at the trailhead, off the Thunderbird Falls exit of Glenn Hwy.

🛏 Sleeping & Eating
Eagle River has a 12% bed tax, and all restaurants are smoke-free.

Alaska Chalet B&B B&B $$
(☑ 694-1528; www.alaskachaletbb.com; 11031 Gulkana Cr; r/ste $105/135; ❀ @) This excellent value European-style B&B is within walking distance of downtown Eagle River. The clean guest quarters are separate from the main house and include kitchenettes, and the host speaks German.

Microtel MOTEL $$
(☑ 622-6000; www.microtelinn.com; 13049 Old Glenn Hwy; r $130-170, ste $160; ☎) A nondescript motel on a nondescript stretch of road, but it's clean and has all the amenities – including continental breakfast. There are 60 rooms, plus suites

Jitters COFFEE HOUSE $
(www.jitterseagleriver.com; 11401 Old Glenn Hwy, snacks $5-10; ❀ 5:30am-9pm Mon-Fri, 6am-7pm Sat, 7am-7pm Sun; ☎) The best place to stop after a rainy hike. Jitters serves up soup, sandwiches and pastries in a warm environment.

Pizza Man PIZZA $$
(16410 Brooks Loop; medium pizza $18-23; ❀ 11am-midnight Mon-Sat, from noon Sun) An Eagle River establishment, Pizza Man is the place to go to replace those carbs you burned off on the nearby trails. There are 24 beers on tap to wash the pizza down.

ℹ Information
Acute Family Medicine Clinic (☑ 622-4325; 11470 Business Blvd; ❀ 8am-5pm Mon-Fri, 9am-4pm Sat) Offers walk-in service.
Chugiak-Eagle River Chamber of Commerce (☑ 694-4702; www.cer.org; 12001 Business Blvd; ❀ 9am-4pm Mon-Fri)

Chugiak-Eagle River Library (12001 Business Blvd; ❀ noon-7pm Tue, from 11am Wed & Thu, 10am-6pm Fri & Sat)
Key Bank (10928 Eagle River Rd; ❀ 10am-5pm Mon-Thu, 10am-5:30pm Fri, 11am-2pm Sat) Has an ATM.

Eklutna
POP 335
This 350-year-old Alaska Native village is just west of the Eklutna Lake Rd exit, Mile 26.5 of Glenn Hwy. One of the most interesting anthropological sites in the region is preserved at **Eklutna Village Historical Park** (☑ 688-6026; www.eklutnahistoricalpark.org; tour adult/child $5/2.50; ❀ 10am-5pm Mon-Sat), where the uneasy marriage of the Athabascan and Russian Orthodox cultures is enshrined. The interior of St Nicholas Church is modeled after Noah's ark while outside, outdoor altars abound, including a heartfelt lean-to for St Herman, patron saint of Alaska. The most revealing structures, however, are the 80 brightly colored spirit boxes in the nearby Denáina Athabascan cemetery. Invest your time in one of the half-hour tours.

🏃 Activities
Eklutna Lake is 10 long, bumpy miles east on Eklutna Lake Rd. It's worth every minute once the sky suddenly opens, unveiling a stunning valley with glacier-and-peak-ringed Eklutna Lake, the largest body of water in Chugach State Park, at its center. This slice of Chugach State Park is a recreational paradise with more than 27 miles of hiking and mountain-biking trails.

Lakeside Trail MOUNTAIN BIKING, HIKING
This trail is a flat 13 miles to the end of the lake, passing two excellent free backcountry camping areas: Eklutna Alex Campground (Mile 9) and Kanchee Campground (Mile 11). East Fork Trail diverts from the main trail at Mile 10.5 and runs another 5.5 miles to a great view of Mt Bashful, the tallest mountain (8005ft) in the park.

Keep going past the Lakeside Trail terminus to view the receding Eklutna Glacier. ATVs can use the trails Sunday through Wednesday, hikers and cyclists anytime.

Bold Ridge Trail HIKING
To reach the alpine treeline, hike this steep 3.5-mile trail that begins 5 miles along the Lakeshore Trail and continues to a saddle below Bold Peak (7522ft), where there are

SARAH PALIN'S WASILLA

For years Wasilla (population 7831) was a quick stop for most visitors to either pick up supplies at the state's largest Wal-Mart before heading to Denali National Park or to visit the town's main attractions: **Iditarod Trail Headquarters** (📞376-5155; www.iditarod. com; 2100 Knik-Goosebay Rd; ⊙8am-7pm) FREE or the **Dorothy Page Museum** (www. cityofwasilla.com/museum; 323 Main St; adult/child $3/free; ⊙9am-5pm Tue-Fri).

Then the nation discovered Sarah Palin during the 2008 presidential campaign and this town, or Alaska for that matter, hasn't been the same since.

Palin was only three when her father, a science teacher, moved his family from Idaho to Alaska in 1964 to accept a teaching position. Eventually he relocated to Wasilla, where senior point-guard Palin led her high-school girls' basketball team to the Alaska state championship. Over the next few years, Palin finished third in the 1984 Miss Alaska pageant, worked as a sports reporter for an Anchorage TV station and married her high-school sweetheart.

Then, in 1992, the self-described 'hockey mom' won a seat on the Wasilla City Council and four years later, at 32, she was elected Wasilla's mayor. But the turning point for Palin was in 2004 when she resigned as the head of the Alaska Oil and Gas Conservation Commission over ethical violations by another commissioner. Two years later, when Palin ran for governor, promising 'transparency and trust' in Alaska politics, she struck a chord with many residents disillusioned with the career politicians, corruption and cronyism. The results were stunning. In the Republican primary she crushed incumbent Governor Frank Murkowski by more than 30 percentage points. In the general election, she handily beat former Democratic Governor Tony Knowles to not only become Alaska's first female governor but also, at age 42, its youngest.

Two years later Republican presidential candidate John McCain tapped Palin as his running mate, making her the first Alaskan and only the second woman to run on a major US party ticket. The national campaign was rough for Palin: there was the announcement of her unwed teenage daughter's pregnancy and an interview with CBS News anchor Katie Couric in which she stumbled badly over foreign policy questions. But Palin's prolife views on abortion, strong advocacy of gun ownership and conservative fiscal beliefs excited the right wing of the Republican party, while her trademark 'you betcha' phrase became a rallying cry for the so-called Joe Six-Packs of America.

Even though the Republicans lost the presidential campaign, Palin became a Tea Party favorite. She shocked the political world in 2009 by resigning as Alaska governor and then shocked the literary world when her first book, *Going Rogue: An American Life,* became one of only four political memoirs to sell more than a million copies in its first two weeks. Almost immediately a movement was organized to position Palin for the Republican nomination in 2012, but in October 2011 she announced that she would not run.

Today Palin is recognized more as a national political celebrity than she is as an Alaskan, evident in her purchasing a second home in Arizona in 2011. Still, in Alaska nobody has more full-size cutouts gracing the doors of gift shops and restaurants. And a day doesn't go by in Wasilla without a tourist asking a local, 'Where's Sarah Palin?'

views of the valley, Eklutna Glacier and even Knik Arm. People with the energy can scramble up nearby ridges. To actually climb Bold Peak requires serious equipment.

Twin Peaks Trail   HIKING
This route to the mountains is 2.5 miles from the parking lot, but steep. It takes you through lush forest into alpine meadows presided over by the imposing eponymous peaks. Berries, wildlife and great lake views make scrambling toward the top downright enjoyable.

Eklutna Lake   KAYAKING
(single/double kayaks per half-day $40/45, full day $55/60) This 7-mile-long lake makes for great paddling. Lifetime Adventures rents kayaks and mountain bikes (half-/full day $20/30). It also offers a fun Paddle & Pedal rental where you kayak down the lake and then ride a mountain bike back ($75 per person).

Sleeping

**Eklutna Lake State Recreation
Area** CAMPGROUND $
(dnr.alaska.gov; tent sites $10) Has a rustic campground at the west end of the lake and is a beautiful place to spend a night. But even with 60 sites it's often filled. There's also a rustic cabin ($50).

Alaska Wilderness Cabins CABIN $
(☑688-6201; www.goalaskan.com; Eklutna Lake Rd; cabin/r $50/70) Offers accommodations ranging from its cozy Eklutna room with a view of the lake to a pair of cabins without electricity or running water.

Palmer

POP 6335

Filled with old farming-related buildings, Palmer at times feels more like the Midwest than Alaska, except that it's ringed by mountains. Many downtown venues exude 1930s ambience, with antique furniture and wood floors. Sure, Palmer is subjected to the same suburban sprawl as anywhere else, but its charm lies in its unique history and living agricultural community. For those who want to skip the city hassles and high prices of Anchorage, Palmer is an excellent option with just enough choices in lodging, restaurants and sights to keep you satisfied for a day or two.

From Eklutna Lake Rd, Glenn Hwy continues north, crossing Knik and Matanuska Rivers at the northern end of Cook Inlet, and at Mile 35.3 reaching a major junction with the George Parks Hwy. At this point, Glenn Hwy curves sharply to the east and heads into Palmer, 7 miles away. If you're driving, a much more scenic way to reach Palmer is to leave Glenn Hwy just before it crosses Knik River and follow Old Glenn Hwy into town.

History

Born during President Roosevelt's New Deal, Palmer was one of the great social experiments in an era when human nature was believed to be infinitely flexible. The mission was to transplant 200 farming families, who were refugees from the Depression-era dustbowl (the worst agricultural disaster in US history), to Alaska, where they would cultivate a new agricultural economy.

Trainloads of Midwesterners and their Sears & Roebuck furniture were deposited in the Matanuska and Susitna valleys, both deemed suitable by the government for such endeavors. Nearly everything was imported, from building materials (and plans) to teachers. Soil rich by Alaskan standards enjoyed a growing season just long enough for cool-weather grains and certain vegetables. There was little margin for error, however, and any unexpected frost could destroy an entire year of seed and sweat.

Original buildings stand throughout Palmer, many of which have been refurbished, and maintain their hearty wooden farm feel. Descendents of the original colonists, who refer to themselves as Colony children or grandchildren, still inhabit Palmer and have wonderful stories to tell.

Sights & Activities

If you have a vehicle, cruise through Palmer's back roads past original Colony farms. Go northeast 9 miles on Glenn Hwy and hop on Farm Loop Rd; look for vegetable stands if you're passing through here from mid- to late summer.

There is some great hiking in the Mat-Su area and a more complete list of hikes is available from the **Mat-Su Trails & Parks Foundation** (www.matsutrails.org).

Palmer Museum of History & Art MUSEUM
(723 S Valley Way; ⊙9am-6pm) FREE The log cabin that used to be just a visitor center is now more museum than brochures with local art and interesting displays on Palmer's agricultural past.

Matanuska Valley Agricultural Showcase GARDENS
(723 S Valley Way; ⊙8am-7pm Jun-Aug) FREE A garden featuring flowers and the area's famous oversized vegetables. But you have to be passing through in August if you want to see a cabbage bigger than a basketball. Every Friday during summer is **Friday Fling** (723 S Valley Way; ⊙11am-6pm Jun-Aug), an open-air market with local produce, art, crafts, food and live music.

Colony House Museum MUSEUM
(☑745-1935; 316 E Elmwood Ave; adult/child $2/1; ⊙10am-4pm Tue-Sat) This friendly museum is run by Colony descendents, and their enthusiasm for Palmer's history is evident. Take the time for a guided tour, and you'll leave with an appreciation of the enormity of the colonizing project. The museum itself was a 'Colony Farm House' built during the original settlement of Palmer, and its eight rooms are still

furnished with artifacts and stories from that era. To bring the living-room piano to Alaska, members of one pioneer family left behind their luggage and stuffed their clothes in it, the only way to make their weight allotment.

Knik Glacier — GLACIER

Trekkies take note: Knik Glacier is best known as the setting where a portion of *Star Trek VI* was filmed. You can get a partial view of the ice floe at Mile 7 of Knik River Rd off Old Glenn Hwy, but the best way to experience it is on an airboat ride up the Knik River. **Knik Glacier Tours** (☑745-1577; www.knikglacier.com; adult/child $100/50) has four-hour tours departing at 10am and 2pm daily.

Pyrah's Pioneer Peak Farm — FARM

(www.pppfarm.net; Mile 2.8 Bodenberg Loop Rd; ☺10am-5pm Mon-Sat) South of Palmer, Pyrah's Pioneer Peak Farm is the largest pick-your-own-vegetables place in the Mat-Su Valley, with would-be farmers in the fields from July to early October picking everything from peas and potatoes to carrots and cabbages.

Reindeer Farm — FARM

(www.reindeerfarm.com; Mile 11.5 Old Glenn Hwy; adult/child $8/6; ☺10am-6pm) The Reindeer Farm is one of the original Colony farms and a great place to bring the kids. Here they will be able to pet and feed the reindeer, and are encouraged to think the reindeer are connected to Santa. There are also elk, moose and bison to take photos of. Rubber boots are provided. There's a small snack shack for munchies on the picnic tables.

Musk Ox Farm — FARM

(☑745-4151; www.muskoxfarm.org; Mile 50 Glenn Hwy; adult/child $11/5; ☺10am-6pm) The Musk Ox Farm is the only domestic herd of these big, shaggy beasts in the world. These ice-age critters are intelligent enough to have evolved a complex social structure that allows survival under incredibly harsh conditions. Qiviut (pronounced 'kiv-ee-oot'), the incredibly warm, soft and pricey ($40 per ounce) material made from the musk ox's soft undercoat, is harvested here; fine sweaters and hats are for sale in the gift shop. Tours are given every 45 minutes.

Yes, you'll probably get to pet them, too.

Lazy Mountain Trail — HIKING

The best hike near Palmer is the berry-lined climb to the top of 3720ft Lazy Mountain.

The 2.5-mile trail is steep at times, but makes for a pleasant trek that ends in an alpine setting with good views of Matanuska Valley farms. Take Old Glenn Hwy across the Matanuska River, turn left onto Clark-Wolverine Rd and then right onto Huntley Rd; follow it to the Equestrian Center parking lot and trailhead, marked 'Foot Trail.'

Plan on three to five hours for the round-trip.

Matanuska Peak Trail — HIKING

The 8-mile Matanuska Peak Trail is steep, traversing the south slope of Lazy Mountain. As you ascend Matanuska Peak, you'll climb 5670ft in 4 miles – be prepared for a long day. You'll be richly rewarded for your hard work, however, by the views of the Knik and Matanuska Rivers, and Cook Inlet. Take Old Glenn Hwy from Palmer toward Butte and turn left onto Smith Rd at Mile 15.5. Drive 1.4 miles until it ends at the parking lot.

Pioneer Ridge Trail — HIKING

Pioneer Ridge Trail is a 5.7-mile route that climbs the main ridge extending southeast from Pioneer Peaks (6400ft). You'll climb through forest until you reach alpine tundra at 3200ft. From the ridge, South Pioneer Peak is a mile to the northwest, and North Pioneer Peak is 2 miles. Don't scale any peaks without rock-climbing experience and equipment. Follow Knik River Rd 3.8 miles; the trailhead is on the right.

✦ Festivals & Events

Palmer becomes the state's hottest ticket during the **Alaska State Fair** (www.alaskastatefair.org; adult/child per day $13/9), a rollicking 12-day event that ends on Labor Day, the first Monday in September. The fair features live music and prized livestock from the surrounding area, as well as horse shows, a rodeo, a carnival and, of course, the giant cabbage weigh-off to see who grew the biggest one in the valley (the 2010 winner was the largest ever: 127lb!). If greased pigs, Spam-sponsored recipe contests and the Great Alaskan Husband Holler contest aren't enough to get you here, try this: berry pie cook-offs.

The fairground is also home to the **Mat-Su Miners** (☑745-6401; www.matsuminers.org; adult/child $4/2), another semipro team of the Alaska Baseball League that plays against clubs like Fairbanks Goldpanners and the Anchorage Bucs. Until 1980 the

Palmer players were the Valley Green Giants but changed their name for obvious reasons.

Celebrate the first farmers arriving in Palmer at **Colony Days** (www.palmerchamber. org) with a bed race down Main St, a dunk tank with the mayor, and a good old home-town parade. There's also lots of yummy food, naturally.

🛌 Sleeping

If you arrive late, the Palmer Visitor Center has a courtesy phone outside with direct lines connected to area accommodations. There is also the **Mat-Su B&B Association** (www.alaskabnbhosts.com), which lists almost 30 B&Bs in the area, including 10 in Palmer. Add 8% tax to the prices here.

DON'T MISS

HATCHER PASS

A sidetrip from Palmer (or even a base) is the photogenic Hatcher Pass. This alpine passage cuts through the Talkeetna Mountains and leads to meadows, ridges and glaciers. Gold was the first treasure people found here; today it's footpaths, abandoned mines and popular climbs that outshine the precious metal.

The main attraction of Hatcher Pass is **Independence Mine State Historical Park** (Mile 18, Hatcher Pass Rd; admission per vehicle $5), a huge 272-acre abandoned gold mine sprawled out in an alpine valley. The 1930s facility, built by the Alaska-Pacific Mining Company (APC), was for 10 years the second-most-productive hardrock gold mine in Alaska. At its peak, in 1941, APC employed 204 workers here, blasted almost 12 miles of tunnels and recovered 34,416oz of gold, today worth almost $18 million. The mine was finally abandoned in 1955. Today you can explore the structures, hike several trails and take in the stunning views at Hatcher Pass.

At the **Visitors Center** (745-2827; 11am-6pm) you'll find a map of the park, a simulated mining tunnel, displays on the ways to mine gold (panning, placer mining and hardrock) and guided tours (adult/child $6/3) at 1pm and 3pm. From the center, follow Hardrock Trail past the dilapidated buildings, which include bunkhouses and a mill complex that is built into the side of the mountain and looks like an avalanche of falling timber. Make an effort to climb up the trail to the water tunnel portal, where there is a great view of the entire complex and a blast of cold air pouring out of the mountain.

Hatcher Pass also offers some of the best alpine hiking in the Mat-Su areas. The easy, beautiful **Gold Mint Trail** begins at a parking lot across from Motherlode Lodge, at Mile 14 Fishhook–Willow Rd, where you'll find a small campground (tent sites $10). The trail follows the Little Susitna River into a gently sloping mountain valley and within 3 miles you spot the ruins of Lonesome Mine. Keep hiking and you'll eventually reach Mint Glacier.

With two alpine lakes, lots of waterfalls, glaciers and towering walls of granite, the 7-mile **Reed Lakes Trail** (9 miles to the upper lake) is worth the climb, which includes some serious scrambling. Once you reach upper Reed Lake, continue for a mile to **Bomber Glacier**, where the ruin of a B-29 bomber lies in memorial to six men who perished there in a 1957 crash. A mile past Motherlode Lodge, a road to Archangel Valley splits off from Fishhook–Willow Rd and leads to the Reed Lakes trailhead, a wide road. If you've got a 4WD, you can (theoretically) drive the first 3 miles of the **Craigie Creek Trail**, posted along the Fishhook–Willow Rd just west of Hatcher Pass. It's better, however, to walk the gently climbing old road up a valley and past several abandoned mining operations to the head of the creek. It then becomes a very steep trail for 3 miles to Dogsled Pass, where you can access several wilderness trails into the Talkeetna Mountains.

If the weather is nice and you have the funds, it's hard to pass up spending the night at the pass. The **Hatcher Pass Lodge** (745-5897; www.hatcherpasslodge.com; Mile 17.5, Hatcher Pass Rd; r/cabins $95/127.50;) is inside the state park, and is a highly recommended splurge. Aside from spectacular views at 3000ft, the lodge has seven cabins, three rooms, a (pricey) restaurant and bar, and a sauna built over a rushing mountain stream.

ANCHORAGE & AROUND PALMER

Matanuska River Park CAMPGROUND $
([📞]745-9690; Mile 17.5 Old Glenn Hwy; tent/RV sites $15/25) A delightful and very affordable campground less than a half-mile east of town. Some of the 80 sites are wooded, while winding around ponds and the Matanuska River are a series of short foot trails.

Valley Hotel HOTEL $
([📞]Alaska only 745-3330; 606 S Alaska St; r $89; 🌐🛜) This longtime hotel has small but serviceable rooms. On the 1st floor its Caboose Lounge is a friendly pub at which to end a day, while the 24-hour cafe is a great place to start one.

★Colony Inn HISTORIC HOTEL $$
([📞]745-3330; 325 E Elmwood Ave; r $100; 🌐@) What was constructed in 1935 as the Matanuska Colony Teacher's Dorm is now a quaint inn. The 12 rooms are spacious, especially the corner rooms, well kept and equipped with TVs, pedestal sinks and whirlpool tubs. There's an inviting parlor for reading, furnished with antiques. Check in at the Valley Hotel.

Hatcher Pass B&B B&B $$
([📞]745-6788; www.hatcherpassbb.com; Mile 6.6 Palmer-Fishhook Rd; cabin s/d $139/179; 🌐🛜) If you have wheels, you can rent a cabin at several places on the way to Hatcher Pass. This B&B, 6 miles from Palmer, offers five button-cute log cabins with kitchenettes and fridges stocked with everything you need to make breakfast. The prices go down the longer you stay.

Alaska's Harvest B&B B&B $$
([📞]745-4263; www.alaskasharvest.com; 225 Love Dr; r $95-145; 🛜) This grand home sits on 15 acres and has uninterrupted views of Pioneer Peak over the trees. There are trails in the woods – and a sheep farm! Rooms range from the Fox Hole (a cozy closet-turned-bunk-bed) to the Pioneer Suite (sleeps nine). Each has a kitchenette and comes with continental breakfast. The prices are an amazing bargain.

✖ Eating

Hearty cuisine, often utilizing locally grown produce, makes Palmer's expanding restaurant scene unique in Alaska.

Vagabond Blues COFFEE HOUSE $
(www.vagblues.com; 642 S Alaska St; light meals $4-7; ⊙7am-9pm Mon-Sat, 8am-6pm Sun; 🛜) 🍴

The cultural heartbeat of Palmer is this cozy coffee shop, with local art on the walls and often live music at night. It has healthy sandwiches, soups and salads.

★Turkey Red FUSION $$
(www.turkeyredak.com; 550 S Alaska St; lunch $8-12, dinner $14-28; ⊙7am-9pm Mon-Sat; 🍴) A bright and colorful cafe serving fresh dishes made from scratch, including wonderful fresh-baked breads and desserts. Vegetarians won't go hungry here, and much of the produce is organic and locally grown. Lunch is good but the menu really shines at dinner.

Inn Café CAFE $$
(325 E Elmwood Ave; sandwiches $9-10, brunch $16; ⊙10am-3pm Tue-Fri, 9:30am-2:30pm Sun) This former teachers' dorm houses a pleasant restaurant with the kind of creaky wood-floored ambience expected in Palmer. Sandwiches and salads are served on weekdays, and brunch is on Sunday.

Colony Kitchen BREAKFAST $$
(1890 Glenn Hwy; breakfast $8-13, dinner $12-22; ⊙6am-10pm) If you like your breakfast big, you'll be stoked: not only is your most important meal huge, but it's served all day. You'll eat beneath stuffed birds suspended from the ceiling (hence its other name, the Noisy Goose Café).

Palmer City Alehouse AMERICAN $$
(320 E Dahlia St; mains $13-19; ⊙11am-10pm Sun-Thu, to 11pm Fri & Sat) Housed in the renovated Palmer Trading Post, this is basically a sports bar in a cool building. If you're not into the game, head out to the delightful outdoor area, where every seat has a view of the mountains. The menu includes beer, pizza and hearty apps.

ℹ Information

Gateway Visitors Center ([📞]746-5000; 7744 Visitors View Ct) Currently next to Mat-Su Regional Medical Center, but a grand new one is planned to open 2016. Billed as the 'Gateway to Denali,' the two-story center will be located at mile 36 of the Glenn Hwy, just before Palmer if you're coming from Anchorage. You'll find info on Palmer and Wasilla and all the adventure between there and Denali.

Mat-Su Regional Hospital ([📞]861-6000; 2500 S Woodworth Loop) Gleaming on a hill near the intersection of the Parks and Glenn Hwys.

Palmer Library (655 S Valley Way; ⊙10am-8pm Mon & Wed, to 6pm Tue & Thu, to 2pm Fri & Sat) An excellent library with free internet access.

Palmer Visitor Center (✆745-2880; www.palmerchamber.org; 723 S Valley Way; ⊙9am-6pm) Within the Palmer Museum of History & Art; has a booking phone outside and pamphlets, books, maps and free coffee inside.

Post Office (500 S Cobb St; ⊙10am-5:30pm Mon-Fri, 9am-noon Sat) Where to mail your mountain-themed postcards.

Wells Fargo (705 S Bailey St; ⊙10am-6pm Mon-Fri, Sat 10am-5pm) Lets you drain that account.

ⓘ Getting There & Around

The Mat-Su Community Transit system, **Mascot** (✆376-5006; www.matsutransit.com; single ride/day pass $2.50/6), makes several trips daily between Wasilla and Palmer. If staying in Anchorage, you can use **Valley Mover** (✆892-8800; valleymover.org; 1-way/day pass $7/10) for a cheap day trip to Palmer, or vice versa. All buses stop at Carrs.

Alaska Cab (✆746-2727) and **R & B Taxi** (✆775-7475) both provide service around town, as well as to Wasilla ($35) and Anchorage ($85).

Prince William Sound

Best Hikes

➡ Shoup Bay Trail (p197)

➡ Crater Lake (p208)

➡ Portage Pass Trail (p212)

Best Places to Stay

➡ USFS Cabins out of Cordova (p210)

➡ Robe Lake Lodge (p201)

➡ Orca Adventure Lodge (p210)

Why Go?

This 15,000-sq-mile region is home to precipitous fjords, impossibly steep coastal mountains, 150 boom-crashing glaciers, remarkable bird and animal life, and three very unique villages that provide your jumping off point to adventure.

Connected to the highway system (and the Trans-Alaska Pipeline), Valdez has dramatic mountain views, and helicopter skiing and blue-water paddling that is out of this world. The rough-neck city is flat, industrial and stark. Earthy Cordova is only accessed by boat or plane. This fun-loving fishing town has a quaint and compact city center, excellent bird watching and access to great hikes in the Chugach Mountains. On the western edge of the Sound, Whittier is easily reached by car from Anchorage. It is a bizarre city born out of war-time necessity that's hideous, gorgeous, evocative and eerie. There are fun glacier cruises and paddles out here, but the geography limits your land-bound adventures.

When to Go
Valdez

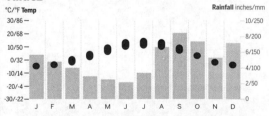

Apr–May Tail end of the heli-skiing season, massive bird migrations and pre-season discounts.

Jun Things dry out (kind of), hotels open and the wildlife kicks into overdrive.

Jul Whale watching picks up, the salmon are running and the sun shines bright.

History

Prince William Sound was long a crossroads of Alaska Native cultures; the region has been inhabited at various times by coastal Chugach Inuit people, Athabascans originally from the Interior, and Tlingits who traveled up from Alaska's panhandle. The first European to arrive was Vitus Bering, a Danish navigator sailing for the tsar of Russia, who anchored his ship near Kayak Island, east of Copper River, in 1741.

Prince William Sound's three major towns have rather divergent modern histories. Valdez was settled in 1897, when 4000 gold prospectors took what had been billed as the 'All-American Route' to the Klondike goldfields. It turned out to be one of the most dangerous trails, with hundreds of

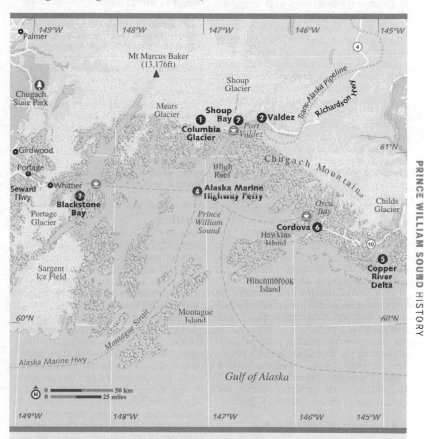

Prince William Sound Highlights

1 Listening to the snap-crackle-and-pop of icebergs from your blue-water paddle near **Columbia Glacier** (p199)

2 Taking a helicopter ride above and around the vertical peaks of **Valdez** (p196)

3 Cruising out to **Blackstone Bay** (p213) from Whittier for good kayaking and wildlife watching

4 Scanning the horizon for whales, seals, sea otters and more aboard the **Alaska Marine Highway ferry** (p196)

5 Exploring the birds and bears of the **Copper River Delta** (p209) by boat, raft, car and bike

6 Boasting about the salmon that got away with the genuine-article fishermen of **Cordova** (p203)

7 Kayaking out to McAllister Creek Cabin on **Shoup Bay** (p199)

poorly provisioned dreamers dying on the trek across two glaciers and through the uncharted Chugach Mountains.

Over the next 60 years the community largely languished until catastrophe struck again, in the form of the 1964 Good Friday Earthquake, which killed over 30 locals and forced the wholesale relocation of the town. However, Valdez' fortunes turned in the 1970s when it was selected as the terminus of the Trans-Alaska Pipeline. The $9 billion project was a windfall beyond those early miners' wildest dreams; the population grew by 320% and the town never looked back.

Cordova's past is somewhat less fraught with catastrophe. A cannery village since the late 1800s, it was chosen a century ago as the port for a railway from the Kennecott copper mines near McCarthy. By 1916 it was a boomtown, with millions of dollars worth of ore passing through its docks. The railroad and town prospered until 1938, when the mine closed and the railroad ceased operations. Cordova then turned to fishing, its main economic base today.

The Sound's third community, Whittier, is of more recent origin, having been built as a secret military installation during WWII, when the Japanese were assaulting the Aleutian Islands. The army maintained the town until 1968, after which, as in Cordova, fishing became the main industry. Tourism now puts food on many residents' plates.

In recent decades, the most monumental event in the Sound has been the *Exxon Valdez* oil spill, which dumped at least 11 million gallons of petroleum into the sea, killing countless birds and marine mammals, and devastating the fishing industry for several years. Though fishing – and the environment – has largely rebounded, oil is still easy to find beneath the surface of beaches, and certain species are not expected to recover.

ⓘ Dangers & Annoyances

By definition, glaciers move at a glacial pace, so you'd think they'd be harmless. In glacier-strewn Prince William Sound, however, they can be a real hazard. Not only have trekkers and mountaineers been killed when they've plunged into crevasses in the ice, but glaciers can also wreak havoc when they calve. Massive chunks often crack free from Childs Glacier, outside Cordova, and occasionally they're big enough to create mini tsunamis in the river. In recent years, Columbia Glacier has been retreating rapidly (the source of all those icebergs glowing on the horizon) and giant underwater bergs have broken free only to pop to the surface in a random location. Use caution if you're in a kayak. The rule of thumb is to provide a buffer twice the size as the glacier is tall.

ⓘ Getting There & Around

Prince William Sound is all about the sea, and by far the best way to get around is on water. The **Alaska Marine Highway ferry** (☏ 800-642-0066; www.ferryalaska.com) provides a fairly convenient, fairly affordable service, linking Valdez and Cordova daily and making three runs per week between Valdez, Cordova and Whittier. But the ferry is more than just transport: it's an experience. There's something transcendent about bundling up on deck and watching the mountain-riddled, fjord-riven, watery world unfold.

Both Valdez and Whittier are highway accessible; the former is the beginning of the Richardson Hwy and the latter is connected to the Seward Hwy via the continent's longest automobile–rail tunnel.

Finally, planes are an option in Cordova and Valdez, where daily scheduled flights provide service to Anchorage and other major centers.

Valdez

POP 4020

Surrounded on three sides by steep snow-capped mountains, this blue-water port town, best known as the southern terminus of the Trans-Alaska Pipeline, offers the most dramatic mountain views you'll see in any of the Prince Williams Sound towns.

Wilderness and adventure lovers will want to set aside a few days to explore the glaciers, wildlife and Norman Rockwell-style harbor cradled by some of the highest coastal mountains (topping 7000ft) in the world. The city itself isn't all that attractive: it's flat, industrial and barren. But get outside of town, and you'll enjoy some of the best paddling, hiking and other outdoor adventures Alaska has to offer. There are plenty of high-quality museums in town, largely due to the black gold that flows through the pipeline.

◉ Sights

Maxine & Jesse Whitney Museum   MUSEUM
(☏ 907-834-1690; 303 Lowe St; ◷ 9am-7pm; ♿)
FREE If you only have time for one museum, this is your spot. The high-quality museum is devoted to Alaska Native culture and Alaskan wildlife, and features ivory and baleen artwork, moose-antler furniture, and natural-

history displays, including some very creative taxidermy. Kid-delighting exhibits include fossils and arrowheads in cool pull-out drawers.

Valdez Museum   MUSEUM
(🖉 907-835-2764; www.valdezmuseum.org; 217 Egan Dr; adult/child $7/free; ⊘9am-5pm) This gargantuan museum includes an ornate, steam-powered antique fire engine, a 19th-century saloon bar and the ceremonial first barrel of oil to flow from the Trans-Alaska Pipeline.

There are arresting photos of the six minutes when Valdez was shaken to pieces by the 1964 Good Friday Earthquake, and an exhibit featuring correspondence from stampeders attempting the grueling All American Route from Valdez to the inland goldfields. A new oil spill exhibit shows the daily oil usage around the world, and a compelling video about those affected by the spill.

'Remembering Old Valdez' Annex   MUSEUM
(🖉 907-835-5407; Hazelet Ave; admission $7, free with Valdez Museum ticket; ⊘9am-5pm) This annex is dominated by a scale model of the Old Valdez township. Each home destroyed in the Good Friday Earthquake has been restored in miniature, with the family's name in front. In the theater, stick around to check out the award-winning film *Between the Glacier and the Sea*, a collection of first-hand accounts of the 1964 earthquake.

The exhibits on the earthquake and subsequent tsunamis and fires are moving, and there is a decent collection of pioneer-era artifacts.

Small-Boat Harbor   HARBOR
Valdez' harbor is a classic: raucous with gulls and eagles; reeking of fish guts, sea salt and creosote; and home to all manner of vessels. The benches and long boardwalk are ideal for watching lucky anglers weighing in 100lb or 200lb halibut, and for taking in the fairy-tale mountainscape in the background.

Nearby is the civic center (Fidalgo Dr), which has more picnic tables and panoramic vistas.

Old Valdez   HISTORIC SITE
Valdez has been unduly blessed by nature, but at 5:46pm on March 27, 1964, came payback time. Some 45 miles west of town and roughly 14 miles under the ground, a fault ruptured, triggering a magnitude 9.2 earthquake – the most powerful ever in American

history. The land rippled as though it was water as Valdez slid into the harbor; tsunamis destroyed what was left. More than 30 people died.

After the quake, survivors labored to relocate and rebuild Valdez at its present site. But if you drive out on the Richardson Hwy you can see the ghostly and overgrown foundations of Old Valdez. The Earthquake Memorial, listing the names of the dead, is reached by turning off the highway onto the unsigned gravel road just south of Mark's Repair. On the day of the quake, Valdez' post office was here; in mere moments the ground sank so far that nowadays high tides reach the spot.

Trans-Alaska Pipeline Terminal   LANDMARK
Across the inlet from town, Valdez' ever-pumping heart once welcomed visitors, but since September 11, 2001, stricter security protocols have closed it to the public.

From the end of Dayville Rd you can still get a peek at the facility, including the storage tanks holding nine million barrels of oil apiece. But heed the dire warnings: plenty of septuagenarian RVers have been pulled over and interrogated for getting too close. Those truly interested in the terminal can learn more about it at the Maxine & Jesse Whitney Museum, which offers a pipeline 'video tour,' featuring great photography and a narrative that amounts to little more than Big Oil hype, and the Valdez Museum, which has a newer pipeline exhibit.

🏃 Activities

Hiking
Valdez has a number of scenic and historic trails to get you away from town and up into the surrounding slopes. For a winter trails map, head to the civic center on Fidalgo Dr.

Shoup Bay Trail   HIKING
This verdant stunner has views of Port Valdez, Shoup Glacier and the impressive Gold Creek Delta. Turn around when you reach Gold Creek Bridge at Mile 3.5 to make this a somewhat challenging day, or go another seven steep, difficult and not always perfectly maintained miles along the water (and sometimes through it), bearing right to follow Shoup Bay to its tidewater glacier.

A free campsite and two reservable public-use cabins, Kittiwake and Moraine (🖉 907-269-8400; www.alaskastateparks.org; $70), are at the end of the trail, near a noisy kittiwake rookery. McAllister Creek Cabin

Valdez

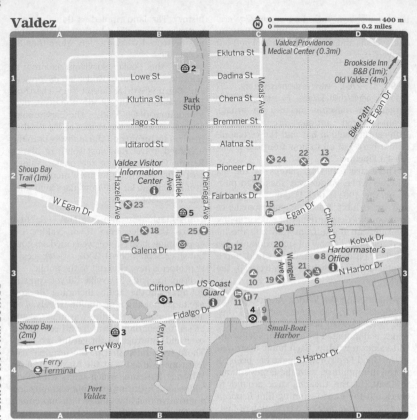

(✆907-269-8400; www.dnr.alaska.gov; $70) is accessible by boat only. The trailhead is at a parking lot at the western terminus of Egan Dr.

Dock Point Trail   HIKING
Not so much a hike as an enjoyable stroll through Dock Point Park beside the small-boat harbor, this mile loop offers views of the peaks and the port, proximity to eagle nests, and salmonberry and blueberry picking.

Mineral Creek Trail   HIKING
A great walk away from town is the trek to the old Smith Stamping Mill. Built by WL Smith in 1913, the mill required only two men to operate it and used mercury to remove the gold from the ore. To reach the trailhead, turn onto Mineral Creek Rd from Hanagita St.

The marginal road bumps along for 5.5 miles and then turns into a mile-long trail to the old mill. Bears and mountain goats are often visible on this hike.

Solomon Gulch Trail   HIKING
A mile past the Solomon Gulch Fish Hatchery on Dayville Rd, this 1.7-mile trail is a steep uphill hike that quickly leads to splendid views of Port Valdez and the city below. It ends at Solomon Lake, which is the source of 80% of Valdez' power.

Goat Trail   HIKING
The oldest hike in the area is the Goat Trail, originally an Alaska Native trade route and later used by Captain Abercrombie in his search for safe passage to the Interior. Today, you can pick up the posted trailhead at Mile 13.5 of the Richardson Hwy, just past Horsetail Falls in Keystone Canyon.

A few spots have been washed out; don't try to cross any rushing streams.

Valdez

Paddling

This is a kayaker's paradise. Folks sticking to the bay will be rewarded with views of seagulls fighting over cannery offal for the first hour or so and it's worthwhile heading out with a guided outfit or watertaxi. Independent kayakers should be aware of no-go zones around the pipeline terminal and moving tankers; contact the **US Coast Guard** (☑907-835-7222; 105 Clifton Dr) for current regulations.

★ **Anadyr Adventures**   KAYAKING
(☑907-835-2814;   www.anadyradventures.com; 225 N Harbor Dr) You may wish to check here for rental kayaks, though they are unlikely to rent to anybody who isn't a true expert. Better yet, go with one of their hilarious and super fun guides (Ilene is the best) for trips ranging from a day at Columbia Glacier ($249) to several days on the water aboard a 'mothership' (two days $1550).

A unique and very popular tour is of the Valdez Glacier ice caves, which includes both hiking and kayaking on and in the magnificent blue ice of this freshwater glacier ($120).

Pangaea Adventures   KAYAKING
(☑907-835-8442; www.alaskasummer.com; 107 N Harbor Dr) Pangaea Adventures has guided tours, costing from $69 for a three-hour trip on Duck Flats, to $249 for a day trip to Columbia Glacier. It also does longer custom tours and rents kayaks (single/double $55/75) to capable paddlers.

Shoup Bay

Protected as a state marine park, this bay off Valdez Arm makes for a great kayaking trip, overnighting at McAllister Creek Cabin (p197). The bay is home to a retreating glacier, which has two tidal basins and an underwater moraine that protects harbor seals and other sea life. It's about 10 miles to the bay and another 4 miles up to the glacier. You must enter the bay two hours before the incoming tide to avoid swift tidal currents.

Columbia Glacier

A mile wide and rising 300ft from the waterline at its face, this is the largest tidewater glacier in Prince William Sound, and a spectacular spot to spend a few days kayaking and watching seals and other wildlife. In recent years the glacier has been in 'catastrophic retreat,' filling its fjord with so many calved bergs that it's difficult to get within miles of the face. The retreat is slowing according to locals, and you can expect changing iceberg conditions. Only experienced paddlers should attempt to paddle the open water from Valdez Arm to the glacier, a multiday trip. Others should arrange for a drop-off and pickup; Anadyr Adventures is a good one to call.

Lowe River

This glacial river, 12 miles from Valdez, cuts through impressive Keystone Canyon. The popular float features Class III rapids, sheer canyon walls and cascading waterfalls. The highlight is Bridal Veil Falls, which drops

900ft from the canyon walls. Pangaea Adventures offers a three-hour raft down the river for $89.

Tours

Columbia Glacier is the second-largest tidewater glacier in North America, spilling forth from the Chugach Mountains and ending with a face as high as a football field. Several tour companies can take you into Columbia Bay, west of Port Valdez, but it's difficult for any boat to get close to the face as the water is too clogged with ice. You're more likely to see calving further west in Unakwik Inlet, where the more accessible Mears Glacier, a smaller ice-tongue, dumps bergs from a snout just half the height of Columbia's.

Columbia is great for icebergs, but you generally only get 10 miles from the glacier because of the huge iceberg field from this rapidly retreating glacier that has gone back 18 miles since 1980. On the Mears' tour you get closer to the glacier itself and have better wildlife watching opportunities.

**Lu-Lu Belle Glacier
Wildlife Cruises** BOAT
(☑ 800-411-0090; www.lulubelletours.com; Kobuk Dr; per person $125; ☺ tours depart 1pm daily) The dainty and ornately appointed MV *Lu-Lu Belle* is all polished wood, leather and oriental rugs. Cruise into Columbia Bay where, unless winds have cleared away the ice, wildlife is more the attraction than glacier-calving.

Vertical Solutions SCENIC FLIGHTS
(☑ 907-831-0643; www.vshelicopters.com) An awesome way to see the glaciers and peaks around Valdez is on a helicopter. Tours are $220 to $400 for up to an hour for three people or less and well worth every penny: you'll be up close to wildlife (including bears and goats), glaciers and historic mines. Custom and aerial photography trips are also available.

HELI-SKIING

Valdez is legend. It has some of the steepest, deepest, gnarliest and burliest snow-riding terrain anywhere in the world.

At inland ski resorts in, say, Colorado, dry powder barely clings to 50-degree inclines; here in the coastal Chugach Mountains, the sopping-wet flakes glue to angles of 60-plus-degrees, creating ski slopes where elsewhere there'd be cliffs. Factor in 1000in of snow per winter and mountains that descend 7000ft from peak to sea, and you've got a ski bum's version of Eden.

The season lasts only from February to the end of April. And because helicopters often get grounded due to poor weather (or you need to find safe terrain because of avalanche danger), it's recommended that you schedule at least five days for a trip, expecting that you'll get three or four days of great turns.

The operations will provide you with a knowledgeable guide, along with avalanche equipment including a beacon, shovel, probe and air-bag pack. Expect an average of six runs a day. That's more than enough to leave your quads pulverized.

Heli-skiing is for advanced and expert skiers only. And while your guides know this terrain well, avalanches do happen (though the heavy maritime snow generally creates consistent, stable snow pack). It still pays to know how to use your beacon and have some understanding of safe backcountry travel – your guides will give you tutorials when you get there. Get up-to-date avalanche information at www.avalanche.org.

Points North Heli Adventures (p209) runs trips out of Cordova. And there are rumors that a heli or snowcat operation may make its way to Seldovia.

H2O Heli-Guides (☑ 907-835-8418; www.alaskahelicopterskiing.com) in Valdez offers a six-run day for $1333, and has five- and seven-day helicopter-plus-lodging packages for $4675 and $7655. It has concessions for 4000 sq miles of terrain and take just four groups per week. Check out fishing, hiking, glacier trekking and ice climbing adventures during the summer.

Valdez Heli-Ski Guides (☑ 907-835-4528; www.valdezheliskiguides.com) offers a day of heli-skiing (usually six runs) for $1100, plus lodge-ski packages for three to seven days for $4451 to $10,390. It rusn a snowcat on down days.

Stan Stephens Glacier & Wildlife Cruises
BOAT

(☑907-835-4731, 866-867-1297; www.stanstephenscruises.com; 112 N Harbor Dr) The biggest tour operator in town runs large vessels on seven-hour journeys to Columbia Glacier (adult/child $125/62) and nine-hour trips (adult/child $160/80) to Mears Glacier. Lunch and lots of tummy-warming tea are included.

Festivals & Events

Gold Rush Days
CULTURAL

(www.valdezgoldrushdays.org; ☺Jul/Aug) A five-day festival in late July or early August, this hometown rocker includes a parade, bed races, dances, a free fish feed and a portable jailhouse that's pulled throughout town by locals, who arrest people without beards and other innocent bystanders.

Sleeping

As Valdez doesn't have a hostel, devout budgeteers will have to settle for a campsite. The visitor center has a 24-hour hotline outside, where you can book last-minute rooms. Valdez' 6% bed tax is not included in the rates quoted here.

Valdez Glacier Campground
CAMPGROUND $

(☑907-835-2282; Airport Rd; tent sites $15, RV sites $20-40) Located 6 miles out of town, this spot has 101 pleasant wooded sites and a nice waterfall. Though it's privately owned, it has a noncommercial feel. Recently added hot showers (free for campers) are a huge bonus.

Keystone Hotel
HOTEL $

(☑835-3851, 888-835-0665; www.keystonehotel.com; 401 W Egan Dr; s/d $95/105; ☺☜☒) A modular relic of the pipeline boom years with lots of clean, cramped, prefab rooms, plus continental breakfast.

Downtown B&B Inn
B&B $

(☑907-835-2791; www.valdezdowntowninn.com; 113 Galena Dr; r with/without bath $110/95; ☺☜) This threadbare place has bowed beds and stained carpets and is more hotel than B&B, though you do get breakfast with your basic room. Some are dorm-style; one holds a party of eight.

Bear Paw RV Campground
CAMPGROUND $

(☑907-835-2530; www.bearpawrvpark.com; 101 N Harbor Dr; tent sites $20-25, RV sites $40-45; ☜) Conveniently located right downtown in a big barren parking lot, this campground

has two locations. The RV lot is downtown and has showers and friendly service, and the tent-camping only site on Wyatt Way sits right on the water (and offers easy access to the ferry). The tent site is reserved for adults only.

Eagle's Rest RV Park
CAMPGROUND $

(☑800-553-7275; www.eaglesrestrv.com; 139 E Pioneer Dr; tent sites $27, RV sites $37-49, cabins $135-155; ☜) On the edge of town, this RV site has nice views, plus showers and laundry, though the cabins are too small for the price.

Robe Lake Lodge
LODGE $$

(☑907-831-2339; www.robelakelodge.com; Mile 6 Richardson Hwy; d/q $179/199; ☺☜) Brand new and immaculate, this large home has six rooms (all with shared bath) available. The place is built out of full scribe logs, with massive beams crossing the vaulted ceilings. The hot tub has a view of the absurdly pretty Robe Lake – as does the wraparound balcony – but you can also warm up in the sauna.

Continental breakfast is served in the great room, and if you rent the whole place out ($998) you have access to the full kitchen. There are also trails to the lake, and a canoe for paddling around.

Brookside Inn B&B
B&B $$

(☑907-835-9130; www.brooksideinnbb.com; 1465 Richardson Hwy; r $160; ☺☜) This 100 year old home from Fort Liscum was moved to Old Valdez and then to its present location after the earthquake. Even though it's about a mile from downtown, it's a clean and cozy option with four rooms. Breakfast is served on a gorgeous sun porch.

Best Western Valdez Harbor Inn
HOTEL $$

(☑907-835-3434; www.valdezharborinn.com; 100 Harbor Dr; r $169-179, ste $209-194; ☜☒) This is a strong pick if you are looking for comfort on the waterfront. The independently owned hotel has the standard business-savvy rooms you'd expect from the Best Western chain, with a few pictures of jumping orcas to remind you you're in Alaska. There are a few rooms with harbor views (request a corner unit).

Mountain Sky Hotel
HOTEL $$

(☑907-835-4445; www.mountainskyhotel.com; 101 Meals Ave; r/ste $179/199; ☜) This business hotel is set in an inordinately large parking lot, but has pretty nice rooms and good views (if you can see past the parking

PRINCE WILLIAM SOUND VALDEZ

THE EXXON VALDEZ 25 YEARS LATER

It's been a quarter of a century since the *Exxon Valdez* crashed into Bligh Reef in 1989, spilling some 11 million gallons of oil into the delicate ecosystem of Prince William Sound. To this day, the communities, industries and environment in the area have yet to fully recover from one of modern history's worst man-made environmental disasters ever.

It is getting better, but most experts say the ecosystem has suffered permanent damage. According to CNN, as of 2010 'only 13 of the 32 wildlife populations, habitats and resource services are fully recovered or very likely to recover.' The disaster financially crippled the commercial fisheries and tourism industries in places such as Valdez and Cordova. And while commercial salmon and halibut fishing have returned to the region, the herring population remains at risk.

There is some positive news. Many studies show rebounds in animal populations decimated by the spill, which stretched over 1000 miles and killed anywhere from 100,000 to 250,000 sea birds, 2800 sea otters, and obliterated huge populations of salmon and herring. Sea otter populations are at pre-spill levels, but a pod of orcas is at risk of extinction, and you can still find oil just below the surface on many beaches in the Sound.

Exxon claims to have spent some $4.3 billion in cleanup costs and legal settlements. In 2008, the US Supreme Court took a knife to the original jury award of $5 billion, cutting it to just $507 million plus $470 million in interest due.

And whatever happened to the captain, Joseph Hazelwood? He was acquitted from the drunken-boating charges and slapped with 1000 hours of community service and a $50,000 fine. Most onlookers argue, however, that it was really Exxon's lack of security protocols and onboard collision avoidance radar that led to the disaster.

Other legacies of the disaster are more inspiring. Long-recommended security measures have finally been enacted at oil-processing facilities across the nation. Double-hulled tankers, once a pipe dream of environmentalists, will be a pipeline requirement by 2015; some are already in service. Tugs must once again escort tankers passing through Prince William Sound. And the *Exxon Valdez* itself, now renamed the *SeaRiver Mediterranean*, has been banned from ever returning to Valdez.

lot). For comfort, it's not the top midrange choice, but the staff are friendly, it's modern and clean, and the spa suites have awesome tubs (*muy romántico*).

Totem Inn HOTEL $$
(☑835-4443, 888-808-4431; www.toteminn.com; 144 E Egan Dr; r $189; ⊜🐾) You can probably do better than this aging hotel complex with upper-scale suites, plain rooms and tin-box cabins. The rooms can be quite stale and smoky, but do have fridges and microwaves for the self-catering set. There's a large restaurant and gift shop at the main lodge.

✖ Eating

Alaska Halibut House FAST FOOD $
(☑907-835-2788; 208 Meals Ave; fish $8-12; ⊗lunch & dinner) Frying up fresh local fish, this home-spun fish shack is what every fast-food joint should be. The halibut basket is delish.

Old Town Burgers BURGERS $
(E Pioneer Dr; burgers $8-15; ⊗11am-10pm) This super-popular burger and breakfast joint often has a line out the door. Set in a modular home with plastic tables and slightly ineffective (yet friendly) service, it has plenty of greasy spoon favorites, but the burgers are the real star.

Fu Kung CHINESE $
(☑907-835-5255; 207 Kobuk Dr; lunch $7-10, dinner $13-18; ⊗11am-10pm Mon-Fri, 4-10pm Sat & Sun) Fantastic Chinese food. Lunch specials include egg rolls and quality wonton soup.

Rogue's Garden MARKET $
(354 Fairbanks Dr; sandwiches $8-10; ⊗7:30am-6pm Mon-Fri, 9am-5pm Sun) This health food market has a tip-top deli where you can customize your sandwich or smoothie. There's a small seating area.

Safeway GROCERY $
(185 Meals Ave; ⊗4:30am-midnight) With its impressive sandwich and salad bar, this grocery store is among Valdez' best places for a bite.

Fat Mermaid PIZZA $$
(143 N Harbor Dr; sandwiches $12-13, pizza $14-24; ⊗10am-2am) With good views and scrump-

tious pizza pies, this smallish bar and restaurant is quite popular. The patio is great on summer days, and the eclectic menu features funked-out sandwiches such as a taste-bud-popping wasabi chicken, inventive pizzas and a standard assortment of seafood.

Mike's Palace ITALIAN $$
(201 N Harbor Dr; mains $14-34; ⊙11am-11pm) This locals' favorite specializes in Italian fare, but also serves up well-conceived fresh catch specials and a massive seafood platter sampler. The high-backed chairs and moose horns just add to the rich ambience of a *ristorante* in the rough.

Ernesto's Taqueria MEXICAN $$
(☑907-835-2519; 328 Egan Dr; meals $11-16; ⊙dinner) Locally loved, this place serves large portions of serviceable Mexican food on the cheap – go for the blackened shrimp or halibut tacos – and has a cold selection of Mexican beer.

Totem Inn Restaurant AMERICAN $$
(144 E Egan Dr; breakfast $8-13, lunch & dinner $10-20, ⊙5am-11pm) In the morning, tourists and locals flock here for the Alaska-sized breakfasts. Lunch is all about burgers and sandwiches, while dinner has decent seafood.

Drinking & Nightlife

Standard opening hours are approximately 7am to 2am, though some places may stay open later for crowds.

Wheelhouse Bar BAR
(100 N Harbor Dr) Located at the Best Western, this bar has excellent harbor views in a smoke-free setting. You can also get good grub from the Off the Hook (the Harbor Cafe's sister restaurant), located next door.

Pipeline Club BAR
(112 Egan Dr) If you've ever hugged a tree in your life, this crowd may not be for you. But this smoky lounge is the watering hole where the locals like to hang out.

❶ Information

Crooked Creek Information Site (☑907-835-4680; Mile 0.9 Richardson Hwy) Staffed by US Forest Service (USFS) naturalists in a brand new building, this place offers great advice about all manner of outdoorsy activities. The nearby viewing platform is an excellent place to park yourself while watching chum and pink salmon spawn in July and August, and there's a cool waterfall.

Harbormaster's Office (☑907-835-4981; 300 N Harbor Dr) Has showers ($4).

Post Office (cnr Galena Dr & Tatitlek Ave)

Valdez Consortium Library (☑907-835-4632; 212 Fairbanks Dr; ⊙10am-6pm Mon & Fri, 10am-8pm Tue-Thu, noon-5pm Sat, 1-5pm Sun; ☜) Head here for free internet access.

Valdez Medical Clinic (☑907-835-4811; 912 Meals Ave) Provides walk-in care.

Valdez Providence Medical Center (☑907-835-2249; 911 Meals Ave) Has an emergency room.

Wells Fargo (☑907-835-4381; 337 Egan Dr) Bank and ATM.

Valdez Visitor Information Center (☑907-835-2984; www.valdezalaska.org; 309 Fairbanks Dr; ⊙8am-7pm Mon-Fri, noon-6pm Sat, noon-5pm Sun) There are a few interesting historic photos and plenty of free maps and brochures. There's an unstaffed information booth at the airport.

❶ Getting There & Around

AIR
There are flight services with **Ravn Alaska** (☑907-835-2030, www.flyravn.com) from Valdez to Anchorage, Aniak, Bethel, Fairbanks, Homer, Kenai, Kodiak, St Mary's and Unalakleet. One-way tickets start from around $185 to $200, depending on how early you make your reservations. The **Valdez Airport** (Airport Rd) is 3 miles from town, off the Richardson Hwy.

BICYCLE
Bikes can be rented (per half/full day $15/25) through the outdoorsy folk at Anadyr Adventures (p199).

BOAT
Within Prince William Sound, the **Alaska Marine Highway Ferry** (☑907-835-4436, 800-642-0066; www.ferryalaska.com) provides daily services from Valdez to Cordova ($50) and Whittier ($89). The newer, speedier ferry halves the old times, but on the older, slower ferry you are more likely to see whales and sea lions as you amble pleasantly along.

Cordova
POP 2260
Cut off from Alaska's road system, this quaint cluster of rainforest-rotted homes on a hillside overlooking the busy harbor is the prettiest city in Prince William Sound. It's also an excellent jumping off point for hikes, bikes and paddles into the surrounding wilderness, which lacks the snow-capped grandeur of Valdez but is impressive nonetheless. Spread thinly between Orca Inlet and Eyak

Cordova

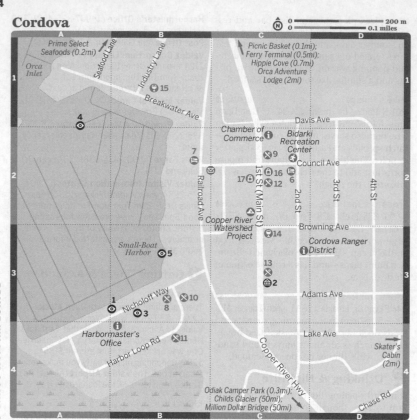

Prime Select
Seafoods (0.2mi)

Orca
Inlet

Seafood Lane

Industry Lane

⊗15

Breakwater Ave

4 ⊙

Picnic Basket (0.1mi);
Ferry Terminal (0.5mi);
Hippie Cove (0.7mi);
Orca Adventure
Lodge (2mi)

Davis Ave

Chamber of
Commerce ❶

Bidarki
Recreation
Center

⊗9

Council Ave

7
✉

Railroad Ave

✉

17⊗ ⓤ16
⊗12

ⓤ 6

2nd St

3rd St

4th St

1st St (Main St)

Copper River
Watershed
Project

⊙14

Browning Ave

Cordova Ranger
❶ District

Small-Boat
Harbor ⊙5

13

🏛2

Adams Ave

1 ⊙
⊙3

Nicholoff Way

⊗10
⊗8

Lake Ave

❶
Harbormaster's
Office

⊗11

Harbor Loop Rd

Copper River Hwy

Skater's
Cabin
(2mi)

Odiak Camper Park (0.3mi);
Childs Glacier (50mi);
Million Dollar Bridge (50mi)

Chase Rd

0 ━━━━ 200 m
0 ━━━━ 0.1 miles

Lake, and overshadowed by Mt Eccles, this unassuming and slightly eccentric fishing village has yet to sell its soul to tourism. All the more reason to visit today.

This is quintessential Alaska, full of ruggedly independent freethinkers, unconcerned with image or pretense, and friendly as hell. They seem to revel in their isolation. In recent years, pro-development politicians have proposed connecting the community to the state highway system. Judging from the ubiquity of 'No Road' bumper stickers in town, it's a prospect the locals abhor. And with a bridge washing out on the Copper River Hwy, the chances of a road coming any time soon are pretty slim.

Visitors will be enthralled by what lies beyond the town limits. Just outside the city, along the Copper River Hwy (still open to the Mile 36 Bridge), is one of the largest wetlands in Alaska, with more than 40 miles of trails threading through spectacular gla-

ciers, alpine meadows and the remarkable Copper River Delta. Into that delta run some of the world's finest salmon. Local operators are still running boat and car trips to the Childs Glacier and Million Dollar Bridge at Mile 40 of the highway.

Cordova's main north–south drag is officially 1st St but is often called Main St – the names are used interchangeably. It becomes the Copper River Hwy as it leaves town, connecting Cordova to the airport at Mile 12.

⊙ Sights

Cordova Museum
MUSEUM

(☏ 907-424-6665; 622 1st St; $1 donation; ⊙ 10am-5pm Tue-Sat) Adjacent to the Cordova Library, this museum is a small, grassroots collection worth seeing. Displays cover local marine life, relics from the town's early history – including a captivating lighthouse lens – and a three-seater *bidarka* (kayak) made from spruce pine and 12 sealskins.

Cordova

Want your heart wrenched? Peruse the museum's coverage of the *Exxon Valdez* oil spill. The amateur photos and local newspaper headlines revive the horror more vividly than any slick documentary. Then there's the jar of oily sediment collected in 2006 – nearly 20 years after the spill.

The museum will have a new home across the street in the Cordova Center Auditorium, which has faced numerous delays, but is slated to open in summer 2015.

Ilanka Cultural Center CULTURAL CENTER
(☑907-424-7903; 110 Nicholoff Way; ☺10am-5pm Mon-Fri) **FREE** This excellent museum, operated by local Alaska Natives, has a small but high-quality collection of Alaska Native art from all over the state. Don't miss the intact killer-whale skeleton – one of only five in the world – with flippers that could give you quite a slap.

Also on display is artist Mike Webber's Shame Pole, a totem pole that tells the grim tale of the oil spill, spitting back Exxon's then top official Don Cornett's famous words, 'We will make you whole again.' This place also has a wonderful gift shop and offers classes on such crafty subjects as scrimshaw and spruce-root weaving. Call for a schedule.

**Prince William Sound Science
Center** SCIENCE CENTER
(☑907-424-5800; www.pwssc.org; 300 Breakwater Ave; ☺8:30am-5:30pm Mon-Fri; 👶) **FREE** This dockside research facility offers themed 'Discovery Packs' for kids, which include information on the birds, flora and geology of Cordova. Inside the facility there's not much for visitors save a few interesting brochures.

The researchers always seem happy to answer questions about local ecology.

Small-Boat Harbor HARBOR
In Cordova, the standard greeting among locals is 'Been fishing?' Unsurprisingly, the harbor is the community's heart, humming throughout the season as fishers frantically try to meet their quota before the runs are closed. Watching over the hubbub is the **Cordova Fisherman's Memorial**, a quiet place dominated by artist Joan Bugbee Jackson's sculpture *The Southeasterly* (1985), and spotted with flower bouquets.

The fishing fleet is composed primarily of seiners and gill-netters, with the method used by the fishers determining the species of salmon they pursue. The former primarily target pink salmon, while the latter, generally one-person operations, go for kings and reds early in the season and silvers later on.

Salmon Canneries BUILDINGS
Every summer Cordova's population swells with young idealists, opportunists and stragglers hoping to make a mint canning salmon on 16-hour shifts.

Whether you're curious about the effects of sleep deprivation on adventurous teenagers or just want to see how some of the finest salmon in the world is processed, ask at the chamber of commerce about canneries offering tours. You can watch your own catch get processed at **Prime Select Seafoods** (☑907-424-7750, 888-870-7292; www.pssifish.com; 210 Seafood Lane), a smaller-scale operation that packs salmon and ships it to your home.

PRINCE WILLIAM SOUND CORDOVA

MICHAEL DEYOUNG / DESIGN PICS / GETTY IMAGES ©

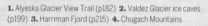

1. Alyeska Glacier View Trail (p182) **2.** Valdez Glacier ice caves
(p199) **3.** Harriman Fjord (p215) **4.** Chugach Mountains

MARC MUENCH / GETTY IMAGES ©

2

PIRIYA PHOTOGRAPHY / GETTY IMAGES ©

Prince William Sound Wild Explorer

Prince William Sound is massive. It's wild. It's everything Alaska is meant to be. Beyond the villages of Cordova, Valdez and Whittier, out-of-this-world terrestrial and maritime adventures await. Grab your backpack, put on your rain jacket and hold on tight for some of the best hiking and paddling around.

Shoup Bay

You can do this as a day hike, overnight backpack or paddle out of Valdez. At the end, two public-use cabins and a campsite await. The paddle takes you past seals, otters and a retreating glacier.

Copper River Delta

Just outside Cordova, the mountains step back and make room for the sky. Here you'll find the 700,000-acre Copper River Delta, a wildlife-rich wilderness with amazing opportunities for birding, fishing, hiking and rafting. Along the 60-mile Copper River Highway, you can trek up the Sheridan Mountain Trail, Saddlebag Glacier Trail and more. Join a tour to take you past the downed bridge to the end of the road, where you can camp for the night on the edge of the Million Dollar Bridge and the massive Childs Glacier, which calves at high-water right into the river.

4

MARK NEWMAN / GETTY IMAGES ©

Harriman Fjord

Hire a guide in Whittier to take you on a multiday paddle through spectacular nearby fjords. Camp with all the creature comforts afforded by boat travel, while seeing truly wild terrain. Plan to get wet.

Chugach National Forest

Basically all the mountains, islands, fjords and glaciers of Prince William Sound fall within the boundaries of this 5.9-million-acre forest, the second largest in the US, after Tongass National Forest in Southeast Alaska. Hire a floatplane, trek or paddle to corners seldom visited.

✦ Activities

Drop by the **Bidarki Recreation Center** (☑907-424-7282; www.cityofcordova.org; cnr 2nd St & Council Ave; $10; ☺6am-8pm Mon-Fri, 9am-2pm Sat, noon-5pm Sun) for a suana, pool, basketball and hot showers.

Hiking

More than 35 miles of trails are accessible from Cordova roads. Several of these paths lead to USFS cabins. As in much of the Southeast, the hiking in this area is excellent, combining lush forest with alpine terrain, great views and glaciers.

Note that the Copper River Hwy to **Childs Glacier** and the **Million Dollar Bridge** is closed at the Mile 36 Bridge. Orca Adventure Lodge (p210) runs a boat-and-car tour to the glacier ($240 from Cordova, $175 from Mile 36).

Heney Ridge Trail   HIKING
Cordova's most popular trail – as it's accessible without a car – is this scenic, fairly easy 3.7-mile route beginning at Mile 5.1 of Whitshed Rd. The first stretch winds around Hartney Bay, followed by a mellow 2-mile climb through forests and wildflowers (and, in rainy weather, lots of mud – rubber boots are recommended) to the treeline. It's another steep mile up to the ridge, where you'll enjoy a gorgeous view.

Crater Lake & Power Creek Trails   HIKING
The 2.4-mile Crater Lake Trail begins on Eyak Lake across from Skater's Cabin. The trail ascends steeply but is easy to follow as it winds through lush forest. At the top it offers panoramic views of both the Copper River Delta and Prince William Sound. Plan on two to four hours for the round trip.

Once at the lake you can continue with a 4.5-mile ridge route to Alice Smith Intertie, which descends to the Power Creek Trail. The entire 12-mile loop makes for an ideal overnight backpacking trip. Halfway along the ridge is a free-use shelter, while at Mile 4.2 of the Power Creek Trail is the USFS Power Creek Cabin. Arrange to be dropped off at the Power Creek trailhead and hike all the way back into town via the Mt Eyak Trail.

McKinley Lake & Pipeline Lakes Trails   HIKING
The 2.5-mile McKinley Lake Trail begins at Mile 21.6 of the Copper River Hwy and leads to the head of the lake and the remains of the Lucky Strike gold mine. There are two

USFS cabins (☑518-885-3639, 877-444-6777; www.recreation.gov; $35): McKinley Lake Cabin, just past the trailhead, and McKinley Trail Cabin, at Mile 2.4.

The abandoned Lucky Strike mine is accessible via an unmaintained trail behind McKinley Trail Cabin. Departing from the midway point of the McKinley Lake Trail is the Pipeline Lakes Trail, which loops back to the Copper River Hwy at Mile 21.4. Almost all of this marshy 2-mile trail has been boardwalked to provide easier access to several small lakes packed with grayling and cutthroat trout, but if it's rainy consider bringing rubber boots.

Sheridan Mountain Trail   HIKING
This trail starts near the picnic tables at the end of Sheridan Glacier Rd, which runs 4.3 miles from the turnoff at Mile 13 of Copper River Hwy. Most of the 2.9-mile route is a moderate climb, which passes through mature forests before breaking out into an alpine basin.

From there, the view of mountains and the Sheridan and Sherman Glaciers is stunning, and it only gets better when you start climbing the surrounding rim. This trail isn't the best maintained, putting it into the 'difficult' category.

Saddlebag Glacier Trail   HIKING
You reach this trail via a firewood-cutting road at Mile 25 of Copper River Hwy. It's an easy 3-mile walk through cottonwoods and spruce, emerging at Saddlebag Lake. Outstanding views of surrounding peaks and cliffs (and maybe mountain goats) are made even more fabulous by the namesake glacier, which litters the lake with icebergs.

Cycling

Most of Cordova's trails are too muddy and steep to ride; an exception is the Saddlebag Glacier Trail. However, if you have a few days, the Copper River Hwy itself is a remarkable mountain-bike route. Inquire at the Orca Adventure Lodge (p210) about passage across the river at the downed Mile 36 Bridge.

Skiing

Mt Eyak Ski Area   SKIING
(☑907-424-7766; www.mteyak.org; 6th St; $30; ☺mid-Nov–mid-May) The small but much-loved Mt Eyak ski area, just a quick walk from town, features an 800ft drop, an average of 118in of natural snow annually, and runs that accommodate everyone from novice snowboarders to world-class skiers. The

PRINCE WILLIAM SOUND CORDOVA

most famous attraction is the vintage ski lift from Sun Valley, Idaho (which doesn't operate in summer).

Points North Heli Adventures SKIING
(☑907-424-7991; www.alaskaheliski.com; Orca Adventure Lodge; 7-day all-inclusive $5575) This all-inclusive heli-ski operation works out of the Orca Adventure Lodge. Packages include rooms, food and unforgettable rides in the steep-and-deep Chugach Mountains. It's like Valdez, only chiller. Ski season is normally February to April.

Birdwatching

The **Copper River Delta** and the rich waters of Prince William Sound attract an astonishing number and variety of birds. Spring migration is the busiest, and that is when the town hosts the Copper River Delta Shorebird Festival. Stop at the Cordova Ranger District visitor center (p212) for a birding checklist and advice about where to break out the binoculars.

A favorite birding area is **Hartney Bay**, 6 miles southwest of town along Whitshed Rd, where as many as 70,000 shorebirds congregate during spring migration. Bring rubber boots and plan to be there two hours before or after high tide for the best fall and spring viewing conditions. **Sawmill Bay**, at Mile 3 of Whitshed Rd, is also a prime birdwatching spot.

Another good place for bird and wildlife watching is **Alaganik Slough**. Turn south on Alaganik Slough Rd at Mile 17 of Copper River Hwy and travel 3 miles to the end, where a picnic area and boardwalk offer great views of dusky Canada geese, bald eagles and other feathered friends.

Paddling

The Copper River flows for 287 miles, beginning at Copper Glacier near Slana in the Interior and ending in the Gulf of Alaska, east of Cordova. Most of the river is for experienced rafters, as rapids, glaciers and narrow canyons give it a white-water rating of Class II–III much of the way. The 20-mile stretch between Million Dollar Bridge and Flag Point, at Mile 27 of the Copper River Hwy, is considerably wider and slower. Below Flag Point, the river becomes heavily braided, which inevitably means dragging your boat through shallow channels.

For skiff rentals to remote lodges check at the small-boat harbor. For blue-water paddlers, Orca Adventure Lodge (p210) is the only kayak operation currently working in town. Rent kayaks (rental/guided $65/95) here for a fun day trip up the coast to Nelson Bay.

⭐ Festivals & Events

**Copper River Delta
Shorebird Festival** BIRDWATCHING
(☺early May) On the first weekend of May, this festival celebrates the largest migration in the USA, as some five million shorebirds throng the delta – the biggest contiguous wetland on the Pacific coast – en route to their Arctic breeding grounds.

The festival draws birders from the world over, and features presentations and workshops by international experts and field trips to the prime viewing areas. Nonbirders, don't scoff: this event fills every hotel room in town.

PRINCE WILLIAM SOUND CORDOVA

CORDOVA ICEWORM FESTIVAL

They're real, and every February Cordovans celebrate them. Ice worms spend their entire lives on ice, and if they warm up too much they disintegrate (read: melt). These little critters feed on snow algae, and thread through tiny cracks in the ice. Their coloring tends to mimic glacial ice: white or blue. They're just mysterious enough that not only did they became the topic of a Robert Service poem, *Ballad of the Ice Worm Cocktail,* but they've also captured the attention of NASA, which has been studying what makes the worms such excellent survivors.

Towards the end of a Cordovan winter, it might feel as if you, too, have spent your entire life on ice, which is why, in 1961, Cordova residents got together and decided to break the monotony of the winter (and celebrate their survival of it, no doubt) with the **Iceworm Festival** (www.cordovachamber.com).

This tongue-in-cheek celebration includes the crowning of a Miss Iceworm; the Survival Suit Race, in which participants don survival suits and plunge into the harbor; and a parade that culminates with a giant iceworm float. The festivities last a full week, which might be what it takes to snap out of a long winter.

WILDERNESS CABINS

There are 15 **USFS cabins** (☑518-885-3639, 877-444-6777; www.recreation.gov; $25-45) located in the Cordova area, and they're much easier to reserve than those in other Southcentral Alaskan parts. Three are best accessible by boat or plane: Tideman Slough bunks six in the wilderness of the Copper River flats; Softuk Bar sleeps six on a remote beach 40 miles southeast of Cordova; and popular Martin Lake, 30 minutes east of town by floatplane, has a rowboat and sleeps six people. Two others are along the McKinley Lake Trail and a third is on the Power Creek Trail. Hinchinbrook Island, 20 minutes from Cordova by plane and, at most, two hours by boat, has three more cabins: Shelter Bay, Double Bay and Hook Point. The other cabins are further afield. Check at the Cordova Ranger District (p212) for more details.

Copper River Wild Salmon Festival MUSIC (www.copperriverwild.org; ☉mid-Jul) This newish festival happens in the middle of July and features a fun run, salmon-themed jam session, the taste of Cordova and other family activities.

🛏 Sleeping

Cordova tacks on 12% in bed-and-sales tax to the rates listed here.

Skater's Cabin CABIN $ (☑907-424-7282; Eyak Lake; cabin 1st/2nd/3rd night $25/35/50) In a beautiful setting on Eyak Lake, 2 miles east of town on Lake Ave, with a nice gravel beach and a woodstove, this one-room cabin can be booked through the Bidarki Recreation Center. There are no bunks, but a few tables and chairs, so bring your sleeping pad, food and water. There's an outhouse onsite and a fire pit with a grill on the beach.

You'll have to scavenge your own wood. The escalating prices are to deter multiday use so more people can enjoy it.

Copper River Watershed Project CAMPGROUND $ (☑907-424-7282; www.copperriver.org; Hippie Cove; tent sites $5) Several raised tent platforms set back in the woods near Hippie Cove, a half-mile north of the ferry terminal, are a good option for those leaving on an early-morning ferry. Pay at the Bidarki Recreation Center. There are no showers or sinks, just an outhouse.

Odiak Camper Park CAMPGROUND $ (☑907-424-7282; Whitshed Rd; tent/RV sites $5/22) A half-mile from town, this is basically a gravel parking lot with a rest room and a view. Make reservations at the Bidarki Recreation Center.

Cordova Rose Lodge INN $$ (☑907-424-7673; www.cordovarose.com; 1315 Whitshed Rd; r $145; ⊜@) This spot has a higgledy-piggledy assortment of structures, including a lighthouse and rooms in a large barge, docked – sort of – on Odiak Slough. All come with breakfast and have use of a communal living room and kitchen.

Orca Adventure Lodge LODGE $$ (☑907-424-7249, 866-424-6722; www.orcaadventurelodge.com; Orca Rd; s/d/ste $139/165/196; P⊜⊜) Housed in the historic Orca Cannery 2 miles north of downtown, this waterfront lodge caters to adventurers with daily adventure-tour packages. All the rooms have ocean views. And though they are sparse, they are clean and homey. There are fullboard options.

Reluctant Fisherman Inn HOTEL $$ (☑907-424-3272, 800-770-3272; www.reluctantfisherman.com; cnr Railroad & Council Aves; r $135-185; ⊜⊜) As close to luxurious as Cordova gets, this place overhangs Orca Inlet and has a restaurant and lounge. Some of the tidy rooms have been remodeled; all are shipshape. Pay a little extra for a harbor view.

Prince William Motel MOTEL $$ (☑907-424-3201; www.princewilliammotel.com; 501 2nd St; r/ste $140/160; ⊜) There are eight rooms with kitchenettes, and eight more with full kitchens at this utilitarian motel. Some of the units were remodeled recently with flat-screen TVs, but be sure to ask for a nonsmoking room.

🍴 Eating

⭐ **Baja Taco** MEXICAN $ (☑907-424-5599; Harbor Loop Rd; tacos $4.25, mains $12-17; ☉7am-9pm) Graft a bus onto a cabin, add flowers, cattle skulls and nautical implements, and what do you have? The best fish-taco stand north of San Diego. It also serves beer, espressos and great Mexican-flavored breakfasts – try the *migas*.

Harborside Pizza
PIZZA $

(📞 907-424-3730; 131 Harbor Loop Rd; pizza & pasta $6-17, per slice $3.50-7; ⊙ 11am-9pm) Ask anyone where to eat in town, and this friendly pizzeria is bound to be one of the first places listed. A wood-fired oven and hand-tossed dough ensure cheesy goodness. There's no seating, so you'll need to take it with you (or hope they add some picnic tables). Though pizza is definitely their specialty, the pasta and salads are worthwhile.

Picnic Basket
FAST FOOD $

(Railroad Ave; meals $3-9; ⊙ lunch & dinner Tue-Sun) This spot does the cheapest (and best) halibut and chips in town, in addition to homemade desserts, wraps and shakes.

AC Value Center
SUPERMARKET $

(106 Nicholoff Way; ⊙ 7:30am-10pm Mon-Sat, 8am 9pm Sun) A supermarket with a deli, espresso bar, ATM and Western Union. It also sells camping and fishing gear.

Reluctant Fisherman Restaurant
SEAFOOD $$

(📞 907-424-3272, 800-770-3272; cnr Railroad & Council Aves; meals $19-32; ⊙ 11am-10pm) This is the classiest restaurant in town with excellent harbor views and a decent bar scene. The seafood is fresh and fused wonderfully into Asian dishes.

Killer Whale Cafe
AMERICAN $$

(📞 907-424-7733; 1st St; mains $12-19; ⊙ 7am-4pm Sun-Thu, to 7pm Fri & Sat) This locally loved cafe has daily lunch specials, substantial breakfasts (try the homemade sticky buns) and a cozy wood stove in the middle.

OK Restaurant
CHINESE $$

(616 First St; lunch $13-15, dinner $15-23; ⊙ noon-10pm) If you have a hankering for Chinese... or Japanese...or Korean...or American, the catch-all menu at this dark restaurant is your perfect bullet. The Mongolian beef is excellent, and you can wash it all down with pie à la mode. It's O-Tay.

Ambrosia
ITALIAN $$

(413 1st St; dinner $11-19, pizza $14-22; ⊙ 4-10pm) Nothing pretentious here, but the Italian food comes out steaming hot, there's fake grapes on the ceiling, and wine by the carafe is just $14.

Drinking & Nightlife

There's not much of a formal entertainment scene in Cordova, but with scads of young cannery workers thronging the place in the summertime, there always seems to be a jam session going on somewhere.

Powder House Bar
BAR

(Mile 2, Copper River Hwy; ⊙ 10am-late Mon-Sat, from noon Sun) Overlooking Eyak Lake on the site of the original Copper River & Northwestern Railroad powder house, this is a fun place with live music, excellent beer, soup and sandwiches for lunch, and quality steak and seafood dinners (mains $8 to $20). Friday is sushi day – it starts at noon and goes till the sushi's all gone.

Reluctant Fisherman Bar
BAR

(cnr Railroad & Council Aves) The best part about this bar, besides a healthy selection of microbrews on tap, is its harborview deck. You'll be rubbing shoulders and jockeying for a table with all the locals on a sunny evening.

Alaskan Hotel & Bar
BAR

(600 1st St) This raucous old salt's bar offers wine tastings 5pm to 7pm on Wednesday.

Anchor Bar
BAR

(Breakwater Ave) Across from the small-boat harbor, this is your basic watering hole that's open 'as long as there are fish.'

Shopping

Fill up your backpack with a couple of unique souvenirs from Cordova.

Orca Book & Sound
BOOKS

(📞 424-5305; 507 1st St; ⊙ 7am-5pm Mon-Sat; 📶) Besides being your best source for locally oriented literature, there's a Buddhist lending library upstairs and the owners are friendly, helpful and knowledgeable about the area. There's also espresso, outdoor clothing and some gifts.

Copper River Fleece
CLOTHING

(📞 800-882-1707; www.copperriverfleece.com; 504 1st St) You'll see folks around town sporting these high-quality, unique fleece jackets, vests and hats. Colorful trim is the company's signature, and most of the sewing is done upstairs from the shop.

❶ Information

Chamber of Commerce (📞 907-424-7260; www.cordovachamber.com; 404 1st St; ⊙ 10am-4pm Mon-Fri) If you find it open, you can get visitor info here, or just call and leave a message – the friendly folks will call you back. **Cordova Community Medical Center** (📞 907-424-8000; 602 Chase Rd) Emergency services.

Cordova Library (☎907-424-6667; 622 1st St; ☉10am-8pm Tue-Fri, to 5pm Sat; ☏) In the same building as the Cordova Museum (and also set to move across the street whenever they finish the big new town hall), this library is your best bet for information. It also has free internet.

Cordova Ranger District (USFS Office; ☎877-444-6777; 612 2nd St; ☉8am-5pm Mon-Fri) This excellent office has the latest on trails, campsites and Forest Service cabins, and wildlife in the Copper River basin.

Harbormaster's Office (☎907-424-6400; Nicholoff Way) Has excellent $5 showers and a small book swap.

Post Office (cnr Railroad & Council Aves) Near the small-boat harbor.

Wells Fargo (☎907-424-3258; 515 1st St) Has fresh cash in its 24hr ATM.

ⓘ Getting There & Around

Compact Cordova can be easily explored on foot, but the major problem for travelers exploring the outlying Copper River area is finding transportation. Hitchhiking along the Copper River Hwy is possible, though you might not encounter many passing motorists, even in the summer months.

AIR

Ravn Alaska (p219) flies two or three times daily between Cordova's Merle K 'Mudhole' Smith Airport to Anchorage, Homer, Kenai, Kodiak and Saint Mary's. **Alaska Airlines** (☎800-252-7522; www.alaskaair.com) comes here on a milk run from Anchorage to Yakutat and Juneau once per day. To Juneau, an advance-purchase one-way/round-trip ticket is $223/450.

BOAT

Alaska Marine Highway (☎907-424-7333, 800-642-0066; www.ferryalaska.com) Runs ferries daily to Valdez ($50, four hours) and Whitter ($89, 6½ hours).

CAR

Cordova Taxi (☎907-253-5151) The town's taxi service only runs 3pm to midnight.

Whittier

POP 220

Whittier is weird. It's outlandish and vexing. And it's unlike any other place on the planet.

Founded in World War II as a secret military installation, the town has a stark industrial cityscape that's dominated by the sky-scraping WWII-era Begich Towers, which houses about 80 percent of the town's 200 or so permanent residents, or Whittiots as they

lovingly refer to themselves. From the towers, an underground walkway takes you below the railyard to the ferry terminal and waterfront, where most of the action takes place.

Located on the hood of the Kenai Peninsula and the westernmost edge of Prince William Sound on Passage Canal, this unruly dystopia with its dilapidated military complexes seems out of place amidst the unabashed natural beauty that surrounds it.

But the impossibly remote location provides access to an almost unspoiled wilderness of water, ice and granite, and there's decent hiking right out of town. Kayaking and scuba diving are superb, and the docks are packed with cruise ships and water-taxis waiting to take you out into the wildlife-rich waters, making this a popular day-trip from Anchorage.

Ask any Alaskan about the weather here, and you'll likely learn that 'the weather is probably shittier in Whittier.' And it seems to be true.

🏃 Activities

Hiking

Portage Pass Trail   HIKING

Whittier's sole USFS-maintained trail is a superb afternoon hike, providing good views of Portage Glacier (where Alaska Natives once portaged goods between Turnagain Arm and Prince William Sound), Passage Canal and the surrounding mountains and glaciers. Even better, hike up in the late afternoon and spend the evening camping at Divide Lake.

The Portage Pass Trail is along an old roadbed and is easy to follow. To reach it, head west of town toward the tunnel, then follow the signs to the left onto a road crossing the railroad tracks. You'll find a parking area at the trailhead. Proceed along the right fork as it begins to climb steeply along the flank of the mountain. There's a steady ascent for a mile, finishing at a promontory (elevation 750ft) that offers views of Portage Glacier and Passage Canal to the east.

The trail then descends for a half-mile to Divide Lake and Portage Pass. At this point the trail ends, and a route through alder trees continues to descend to a beach on Portage Lake. It's a 2-mile hike one way from the trailhead to the lake, and it's well worth bashing some brush at the end. There are great views from the shores of Portage Lake and plenty of places to set up camp on the alluvial flats.

BORN IN WORLD WAR II

Understanding how the town of Whittier was born is key to unraveling the complexities of this odd non sequitur.

Shortly after the Japanese attack on the Aleutian Islands during WWII, the US began looking for a spot to build a secret military installation. The proposed base needed to be not only an ice-free port, but also as inaccessible as possible, lost in visibility-reducing cloud cover and surrounded by impassable mountains. They found it all right here.

And so, in this place that would be considered uninhabitable by almost any standard, surrounded by 3500ft peaks and hung with sloppy gray clouds most of the year, Whittier was built. A supply tunnel was blasted out of solid granite, one of Alaska's true engineering marvels, and more than 1000 people were housed in a single tower, the Buckner Building. It wasn't picturesque, but it was efficient.

The army maintained Whittier until 1968, leaving behind not only the Buckner Building, now abandoned, but also the 15-story Begich Towers.

A labyrinth of underground tunnels connects the apartment complex with schools and businesses, which certainly cuts down on snow-shoveling time. The structure has also given rise to a unique society, where 150-odd people, though virtually isolated from the outside world, live only a few feet from one another – high-rise living in the middle of the wilderness. It's a must-see attraction for cultural anthropologists.

For years Whittier was accessible only by train or boat, despite being only 11 miles from the most traveled highway in Alaska. But in 2000, the Anton Anderson Memorial Tunnel was overhauled for auto traffic and, since then, one of the most abnormal places imaginable has been easily accessible – though normalization seems yet to happen.

Shotgun Cove Trail
HIKING

This 1.5-mile walk along a dirt road leads to the First Salmon Run Picnic Area, so named because of the king and silver salmon runs during June and late August. The forest and mountains en route are scenic and the picnic area, with its little lookout platform, is a great lunch spot.

From the northeast corner of the Buckner Building, follow Salmon Run Rd up the mountain, staying to the right at the first fork and to the left at the second fork.

At the picnic area you can cross a bridge over the stream and continue another 3 miles to Second Salmon Run. This walk, along what is known as Shotgun Cove Rd, is exceptionally scenic, with views of Billings Glacier most of the way. At Second Salmon Run, trails on each side of the creek lead down to the waterfall and beach. From there you can continue east through the forest and uplands following a series of boardwalks and trails.

Horsetail Falls Trail
HIKING

East of town off Reservoir Rd, this short trail has wonderful views of Passage Canal and the falls.

Paddling

Whittier is a prime location for sea kayakers as it's practically surrounded by glaciated fjords and inlets. The most common overnight trip from Whittier is **Blackstone Bay**, which contains a pair of tidewater glaciers, Blackstone and Beloit. Many kayakers utilize charter boats to access the dramatic fjords to the north, including Harriman Fjord, College Fjord and Unakwik Inlet.

★ Sound Paddler
KAYAKING

(Prince William Sound Kayak Center; ☑ 907-472-2452; www.pwskayakcenter.com; Eastern Ave; ⊙ 7am-7pm) This well-run operation has been outfitting kayakers since 1981. Perry and Lois Solmonson rent kayaks including outer rain gear (single/double/triple $70/120/150, discounted for multiple days) and run guided tours. The day-long excursion to Blackstone Bay (for two people $625; hefty discount if you can get six folks together) are top flight.

They also have escorts for multiday trips. These aren't guided tours: while escorts will suggest camping spots and routes, you're in charge of your own trip, including food and gear. It's a neat option for independent-minded folks who don't have the experience to feel comfortable spending a week on the water solo.

Lazy Otter Charters
KAYAKING

(☑ 907-694-6887, 800-587-6887; www.lazyotter.com; Harbor View Rd; ⊙ 6:30am-7pm) Offers escorted four-hour day trips to Blackstone Bay (per person $185) and a longer eight-hour trip around the Sound ($250 per person) for a minimum of four people. It also runs a water-taxi and rents out fiberglass kayaks (per day singles/doubles $55/95).

Alaska Sea Kayakers   KAYAKING
(☑ 907-472-2534, 877-472-2534; www.alaska-seakayakers.com; The Triangle; ⊘ 7am-7pm) Rents out kayaks (single/double $65/80 per day), arranges water-taxis and takes multi-day tours to places such as Harriman Fjord, Nellie Juan Glacier and Whale Bay. It has booking offices at the harbor and Triangle. Guided trips include a three-hour tour for $85, half-day trips for $125 to $225 and a Blackstone Bay full-day trip for $345.

Epic Charters   KAYAKING
(☑ 907-242-4339; www.epicchartersalaska.com; Harbor Loop Rd; kayak per day s/d $45/55; ⊘ 8am-6pm) Rents out kayaks and also offers guided kayak charters and glacier viewing from $195, whether you have one or two people.

Diving

Whittier is a top spot for (involuntary shiver) Alaskan scuba diving – it's one of the wildest places easily accessible to human beings. The best time to dive is March through June. Bring your own gear.

Popular dive sites include the Dutch Group islands, known for high visibility offshore and for the kittiwake rookery. In this spot, a combination of steep cliffs and fresh fertilizer from the birds above has created a gently

---

WANDERING THROUGH WHITTIER

Whittier's raw townscape is perversely intriguing, and thus well worth a stroll. Start at **Begich Towers**, visible from anywhere in town, where the 1st, 14th and 15th floors are open to nonresidents. Watching children playing in the cinder-block corridors, you can't help contemplating how much of your private business would be common knowledge if you'd grown up here.

From the southwest corner of Begich Towers, you can look west to Whittier Creek, while above it, falling from the ridge of a glacial cirque, is picturesque **Horsetail Falls**. Locals use the cascade to gauge the weather: if the tail is whipping upwards, it's too windy to go out in a boat. There are also great views of dozens of other waterfalls streaking from the snowfields to the Sound.

Heading back toward the waterfront along Eastern Ave, you'll come to the rather extravagantly named **Prince William Sound Museum** (100 Whittier St; admission $5; ⊘ 10am-8pm), which occupies an ill-lit room beside the Anchor Inn Grocery Store. The space has lots of tidy displays about Whittier's military history. It's long on storytelling and short on artifacts, and the in-depth tales of the pilots, surveyors and early engineers that built this town are quite evocative.

Climbing Blackstone Rd from the museum, the **Buckner Building** dominates the otherwise picture-postcard view. Once the largest structure in Alaska, the 'city under one roof' looms dismal and abandoned above town; the use of asbestos in the structure has complicated attempts to remodel or tear down the eerie edifice.

From here, walk along the **Shotgun Cove Trail** (p213), which winds through blueberry and salmonberry thickets to First Salmon Run Picnic Area, and then head a quarter mile down the road to your right (northeast) to get to **Smitty's Cove**.

Returning to town, you can take the tunnel from near the Prince William Sound Museum to the area known as **The Triangle**. This clutter of restaurants, tour outfits and quirkier-than-average gift shops is fun; don't miss **Log Cabin Gifts** (☑ 907-472-2501; The Triangle; ⊘ 11am-6pm), Whittier's best stab at adorable. The knickknacks, including lots of high-quality leatherwork, are handmade by owner Brenda Tolman, but the live reindeer outside are the real crowd-pleasers. If it's wet out, though, they'll be back in their pen in front of the Begich Towers. Apparently, they don't like rain – which makes it tough to live in Whittier.

Continue along the water to the **small-boat harbor**, where you'll find local commercial fishing boats and a whole lot of pleasure vessels owned by Anchorage-based weekenders. After checking out the fleet, finish up your tour with a meal at any of the good, inexpensive eateries lining the water. At low tide you can comb the beach westward, following the water's edge past the ferry terminal.

swaying rainbow of nudibranchs. Good places to view giant Pacific octopuses, wolf eels and crabs the size of manhole covers can be found in Esther and Culross Passages, close to South Culross Passage cabin (☑877-444-6777, 518-885-3639; www.recreation.gov; $45). Divers also often head to Smitty's Cove, which is east of the ferry terminal and is the only dive spot accessible by foot. Lazy Otter Charters (p213) can provide water-taxi service to the best underwater locations. It charges a minimum of $185 for the boat plus additional fees that are based on mileage.

👉 Tours

Various tour boats sail from the small boat harbor into a rugged, icy world that's unbelievably rich in wildlife. On the way to Harriman Fjord, ships pass so close to a kittiwake rookery that you can see the eggs in the nests of the black-legged birds.

Major Marine Tours   BOAT
(☑800-764-7300,907-274-7300;www.majormarine.com; Harbor Loop Rd) Has a USFS ranger on every cruise. It does a five hour tour of glacier-riddled Blackstone Bay for $119/59.50 per adult/child. A slightly longer tour visits Surprise Glacier and cruises through the Esther Passage for $149/74 adult/child.

Phillips Tours   BOAT
(☑907-276-8023, 800-544-0529; www.26glaciers.com; Harbor View Rd) Packs in 26 glaciers on a speedy boat ride for $169/109 per adult/child. There's a slightly less harried Blackstone cruise for $114/74 per adult/child.

🛏 Sleeping

Those wishing to stay overnight in Whittier face unappealing options: camping in puddles, flopping at a dive of a hotel or paying through the nose for something nicer. Ask around and locals will point you to informal (and free) camping spots along Salmon Run Rd. Also note that a 5% sales tax will be added to the prices listed here.

Whittier Camping   CAMPGROUND $
(☑907-382-0276; Glacier St; tent/RV sites $10/20) There's only one official campground in Whittier: the horrid Whittier Camping, which is basically a mud-soaked, clear-cut gravel quarry in the middle of town.

June's Whittier Condo Suites   VACATION RENTAL $$
(☑907-841-5102, 888-472-6001; www.juneswhittiercondosuites.com; Lot 7, Harbor View Rd; con-

WILDERNESS CABINS

There are six USFS cabins (☑518-885-3639, 877-444-6777; www.recreation.gov; $35) accessible by boat from Whittier. Pigot Bay and Paulson Bay are the closest, with excellent salmon fishing and good views; Harrison Lagoon has the best access for mobility-impaired folk, plus some great tide pools; Shrode Lake comes with a boat; Coghill Lake is a scenic spot with good fishing and berry-picking; and South Culross Passage is on a picturesque cove on Culross Island.

dos $135-295; 🖥📶) This business offers an insight into the local lifestyle, putting you up in comfortable, homey suites on the 14th and 15h floors of Begich Towers. There are 10 suites in all, and occasionally owner June rents out an economy suite on the ground floor. With full kitchens and living rooms these are more suited to longer stays.

Anchor Inn   MOTEL $$
(☑907-472-2354; www.anchorinnwhittier.com; 100 Whittier St; s/d $85/120; 🖥📶) This multipurpose venue has cinder-block walls, and overlooks a junkyard on one side and the railyard on the other. The rooms smell like gasoline, but it'll do in a pinch. There's an attached restaurant, bar, laundry and grocery store, and this is the only hotel open outside the summer season.

Inn at Whittier   HOTEL $$$
(☑907-472-3200; www.innatwhittier.com; Harbor Loop Rd; r $169-299; 🖥📶) This Cape Cod stylized inn on a secluded end of the harbor is the best in town. The rooms are rather plain, but the views more than make up for it – make sure you spend the $20 extra for a water view. Families can rent a two-story townhouse suite or cozy junior suites with fireplaces and peaked ceilings.

Attached is a high-end restaurant and Whittier's best stab at a swank bar.

🍴 Eating

Cafe Orca   CAFE $
(The Triangle; light meals $8-12; ⊙11am-7pm) Gourmet sandwiches, some of the best chowder on the Sound, and a great little waterfront deck are the perfect combination for the best lunch in town. If it's raining, sit inside with a hot espresso.

Anchor Inn Grocery Store SUPERMARKET $
(100 Whittier St; ⊙ 9am-10pm) A bigger grocery store across town.

Harbor Store SUPERMARKET $
(Harbor View Rd; ⊙ 8am-8pm) This store has groceries and snacks for your hike.

Varly's Swiftwater Seafood Cafe SEAFOOD $$
(www.swiftwaterseafoodcafe.com; The Triangle; mains $10-18; ⊙ 11:30am-9pm Mon-Fri, 11:30am-10pm Sat & Sun) This tiny hole in the wall is a top spot on the Triangle. Skip the sandwiches, opting instead for the halibut and chips, signature red seafood chowder, topping things off with rhubarb crisps for dessert. You can peruse the photos of famous Alaskan shipwrecks or sit outside on the patio overlooking the harbor.

China Sea CHINESE $$
(The Triangle; lunch buffet $13, dinner $13-18; ⊙ 11am-10pm) Serving up Chinese and Korean food, this place has a generous lunch buffet featuring fresh 'halibut à la Peking,' and nice views onto the boat harbor.

Inn at Whittier Restaurant SEAFOOD $$$
(☑ 907-472-3200; Harbor Loop Rd; breakfast & lunch $8-18, dinner $23-36; ⊙ 7am-9pm) This dining room has glorious views of the Sound and cooks up steaks, seafood and a spicy cajun shrimp alfredo that's out of this world. Have a martini at the posh lounge attached to the restaurant.

 Drinking

There are two good spots in town for drinks. The Inn at Whittier Restaurant has friendly bartenders and outstanding views. Above the Anchor Inn, there's a karaoke bar on the third story that has pool tables and a beatdown ambience that perfectly befits this odd berg.

ⓘ **Information**

The post office is in Begich Towers, along with the police and fire stations, a medical clinic – even a church.

Anchor Inn (☑ 907-472-2354; www.anchorinnwhittier.com; 100 Whittier St; ⊙ 9am-10pm; 🛜) Has an ATM, wi-fi, a coin-op laundry and showers.

Harbor Store (☑ 472-2277; Harbor View Rd; ⊙ 8am-8pm) Has an ATM and sells phone cards.

Harbormaster's Office (Harbor View Rd; ⊙ 7am-7pm) Has pay phones and showers ($4). Pay here for boat launches and overnight parking.

ⓘ **Getting There & Around**

Whittier is one of those places where getting there is half the fun. Sometimes, leaving can be even better.

BOAT

Alaska Marine Highway (☑ 800-642-0066; www.ferryalaska.com; The Triangle) Departure times and schedules vary, but in the height of the summer, they have daily sailings to Valdez (adult/child $89/44, 3½ to seven hours depending on if you go direct or make an hour layover in Cordova). There are also daily departures for the same price to Cordova. The ferry terminal is beside the Triangle.

Both trips are super-scenic – think Dall porpoises, Stellar sea lions and a kittiwake rookery. Twice per month a ferry departs from Whittier, crosses the Gulf of Alaska and docks in Juneau (adult/child $221/110, 39 hours).

BUS

If you are taking a glacier tour on a day trip from Anchorage, check with the tour company about bus/boat tour combos.

Magic Bus (☑ 907-230-6773; www.themagicbus.com) This bus line has a daily bus between Anchorage and Whittier (one-way/same-day round trip $50/55, 1½ hours one way), which leaves Anchorage at 9:30am and departs Whittier for the return trip at 5:30pm. You'll have plenty of time to catch the 12:45pm ferry.

CAR

Whittier Access Rd, also known as Portage Glacier Access Rd, leaves the Seward Hwy at Mile 79, continuing to Whittier through the claustrophobic Anton Anderson Memorial Tunnel (www.dot.state.ak.us/creg/whittiertunnel/index.shtml), which at 2.7 miles long is the longest 'railroad-highway' tunnel in North America. Negotiating the damp one-lane shaft as you skid across the train tracks is almost worth the steep price of admission (per car/RV $12/20) which is charged only if you're entering Whittier; if you bring your car into town on the Alaska Marine Highway you can exit through the tunnel for free. Eastbound and westbound traffic alternate every 30 minutes, with interruptions for the Alaska Railroad. Bring a magazine.

Avis (☑ 907-440-2847; www.avis.com; Lot 8 Small Boat Harbor) This chain rents cars and has a kiosk in the Harbor Store.

TRAIN

The **Alaska Railroad** (☑ 907-265-2494, 800-544-0552; www.akrr.com) operates the *Glacier Discovery* train between Anchorage and Whittier (one way/round trip $74/89, two hours) daily June through September 14. It departs Anchorage at 9:45am and Whittier at 6:45pm.

Kenai Peninsula

Best Places to Paddle

➡ Sixmile Creek near Hope (p220)

➡ Kachemak Bay State Park (p261)

➡ Aialik Bay (p232)

➡ Kenai Fjords National Park (p231)

Best Places to Hike

➡ Lost Lake Trail (p225)

➡ Russian Lakes Trail (p235)

➡ Resurrection Pass Trail (p220)

➡ Glacier Lake Trail (p260)

➡ Harding Ice Field Trail (p231)

Why Go?

The Kenai Peninsula offers some of the most accessible wilderness adventures in Alaska. There are multiday hikes through the snow-capped Kenai Mountains and mind-blowing paddles through glaciated fjords. You'll camp on never-seen-before lost coves in remote corners of Kenai Fjords National Park and Kachemak Bay State Park, and battle some of the biggest fish around. And in every forgotten corner you'll be close to the natural world, the mountains, the lakes, the rivers and the people that make Alaska wild.

Approximately the size of Belgium, the eastern Peninsula is dominated by large ice fields, the jutting Kenai Mountains and the icy waters of Resurrection Bay. To the west it flattens out, with rolling hills, large lakes and a long coastline.

This is a top pick for first-time Alaska explorers. The wilderness is accessible by a good network of trails and navigable rivers, and there are several worthwhile towns, such as Seward, Hope and Homer that provide interesting cultural attractions and rip-roaring nightlife.

When to Go
Hope

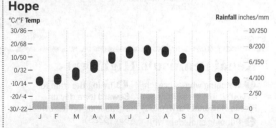

°C/°F Temp												Rainfall inches/mm

May Beat the crowds for the best deals and excursions into the desolate wilderness.

Jul Hook a salmon as they jump upstream at the height of the summer season.

Sep The cruise crowds thin, and it's time for berry picking.

History

For millennia, Dena'ina people made the Kenai Peninsula their home, as did Alutiiqs in the south and Chugaches in the east. They largely subsisted as many modern residents do – by pulling fish from the area's bountiful waterways. In 1741 Vitus Bering, a Dane sailing for the Russians, was the first European to lay eyes on the peninsula; in 1778 British explorer Captain James Cook sailed up the inlet that would bear his name, landing north of the present-day city of Kenai and claiming the area for England. Despite that, the first white settlement on the peninsula was Russian – St Nicholas Redoubt, founded at the mouth of the Kenai River as a fur trading post in 1791. Russian Orthodox missionaries arrived soon thereafter and many

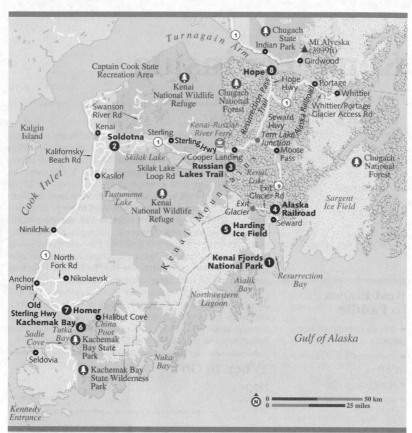

Kenai Peninsula Highlights

❶ Watching whales breach as you sit in a kayak in **Kenai Fjords National Park** (p231)

❷ Rubbing shoulders with hundreds of other anglers outside **Soldotna** (p240)

❸ Hiking from cabin to cabin past splendiferous mountain scenes on the **Russian Lakes Trail** (p235)

❹ Taking the train to **Seward** for a day of sightseeing on Resurrection Bay (p223)

❺ Hiking up to one of the last remnants of the ice age, the **Harding Ice Field** (p231)

❻ Escaping across **Kachemak Bay** (p259) for

berry picking and mountain biking

❼ Feasting on art, culture and home brews in peace-loving **Homer** (p245)

❽ Rafting outside **Hope** (p220) before a night of waterfront bluegrass

of the local Alaska Natives were converted to that faith.

When Alaska came under American rule in 1867, the US established Fort Kenay near where the redoubt had stood. The surrounding settlement endured as a commercial fishing village until 1957, when the nearby Swanson River became the site of the state's first major oil strike. The city of Kenai has been an oil town ever since.

The Alaska Railroad made its start in Seward in 1903, where Resurrection Bay was the closest ice-free port. The Kenai Peninsula was officially on the map as the main thoroughfare for goods to Anchorage, and eventually for coal leaving the state.

The 1964 Good Friday Earthquake hit the peninsula really hard. After the earth finally stopped churning, oil tanks exploded and tsunamis rolled through Seward, ravaging the town. With the bridges, railroad and boat harbor gone, Seward was suddenly cut off from the rest of the state. Homer suffered badly too: the quake dropped the Spit by 6ft and leveled most of the buildings. It took six years and almost $7 million to rebuild.

Since then tourism has boomed on the Kenai Peninsula, turning the region into Alaska's premier playground for visitors and locals, and becoming a key engine of the region's economy.

⊙ Getting There & Around

If you have ever been stuck in a Soldotna traffic jam or inhaled the fumes spewing out from behind a string of Seward-bound RVs, you'll know the Kenai Peninsula is a place of vehicles. Two busy, paved highways extend through this region. The Seward Hwy runs south from Anchorage to Seward, while the Sterling Hwy spurs westward off the Seward Hwy to Soldotna, then drops down to Homer. If you don't have your own wheels, you could rent some in Anchorage. Alternatively, hop aboard a long-haul bus. **Homer Stage Line** (📞 907-868-3914; www.stagelineinhomer.com) operates daily between Anchorage, Homer and Seward. Sticking out a thumb to hitch a ride is also common practice here.

Another excellent transport possibility is rail; the southern terminus of the **Alaska Railroad** (📞 907-265-2494, 800-544-0552; www.akrr.com) is at Seward, which is visited daily by trains from Anchorage.

If you want to fly, Homer and the city of Kenai are served by **Ravn Alaska** (📞 907-266-8394, 800-866-8394; www.flyravn.com); many of the peninsula's other towns also have airstrips and scheduled flights.

SEWARD HIGHWAY

The Seward Hwy is a road-trip-lover's delight, with smooth, winding turns through mountains that have you craning your neck around every corner. The 127 miles of highway is all Scenic Byway, and there are plenty of turnoffs for gawking and snapping photos. Keep in mind that the mileposts along the highway show distances from Seward (Mile 0) to Anchorage (Mile 127). The first section of this road is from Anchorage to Portage Glacier (Mile 79).

Turnagain Pass & Around

After it leaves Turnagain Arm, Seward Hwy heads for the hills. Near Mile 68 it begins climbing into the alpine region of **Turnagain Pass**, where there's a roadside stop with garbage cans and toilets. In early summer, this area is a kaleidoscope of wildflowers and there's good skiing here in the winter.

Bertha Creek Campground (Mile 65, Seward Hwy; campsites $14) is just across Bertha Creek Bridge. This primitive first-come, first-served campground is understandably popular - site No 6 even has a waterfall view. You can spend a day climbing the alpine slopes of the pass here, or head to Mile 64 and the northern trailhead of both the 23-mile **Johnson Pass Trail** and the paved **Six-Mile Bike Trail**, which runs 9 miles not six - along the highway.

Granite Creek Campground (📞 907-522-8368; www.reserveamerica.com; Mile 63, Seward Hwy; campsites $14) is reminiscent of Yosemite Valley: wildflower meadows, dramatic mountains - the works. Reserve ahead, sites fill up fast.

The Seward Hwy heads south of this junction to **Upper Summit Lake**, surrounded by neck-craning peaks. The lakeside **Tenderfoot Creek Campground** (📞 907-522-8368; www.reserveamerica.com; Mile 46, Seward Hwy; sites $18) has 27 sites that are open enough to catch the view but wooded enough for privacy. There's a boat ramp here too.

Within walking distance of the campsite is **Summit Lake Lodge** (📞 907-244-2031; www.summitlakelodge.com; Mile 45.8, Seward Hwy; r/cabin $135/185; ⊛ 🐾). This lakeside complex has refined log cabins, more basic motel accommodation and a bustling restaurant. We only wish it were a bit further from the road.

The **Devil's Pass Trail** (Mile 39.4 Seward Hwy) is a very well signed, difficult 10-mile hike over a 2400ft gap to the Resurrection Pass Trail.

Tern Lake Junction (Mile 37 Seward Hwy) – also known as 'The Y' – is the turnoff for the Sterling Hwy, which runs another 143 miles to Homer.

Hope

POP 147

Hope has beautiful views of Turnagain Arm, a quaint and historic downtown, wonderful restaurants and gold rush–era relics, and incredible camping and hiking opportunities.

Life here moves slower. It's rural Alaska at its best. Authentic, pioneering, friendly and esoteric. Expect town to fill up on weekends with day-trippers from Anchorage. Most tourist services close October to May.

◉ Sights & Activities

Hope-Sunrise Mining Museum   MUSEUM
(☑907-782-3740; Old Hope Rd; admission by donation; ☺noon-4pm) **FREE** This small grouping of log cabins preserves relics from early miners and homesteaders with a great deal of respect. Creaky buildings give a feel for life at the turn of the 20th century; a quick guided tour is worth the tip for history buffs and anyone with a little extra time.

You might learn that the town got its name when early prospectors decided to name the town after the next person off the boat. That man turned out to be Percy Hope.

Gold Panning

There are about 125 mining claims throughout the Chugach National Forest. Some of the more serious prospectors actually make money, but most are happy to take home a bottle with a few flakes of gold in it.

The Hope area provides numerous opportunities for the amateur panner, including a 20-acre claim that the US Forest Service (USFS) has set aside near the Resurrection Pass trailhead for recreational mining.

Hiking

The northern trailhead of the legendary 39-mile **Resurrection Pass Trail** (see p66) is near the end of Resurrection Creek Rd.

From Porcupine Campground, two fine trails lead to scenic points overlooking Turnagain Arm.

Gull Rock Trail   HIKING
A flat 5-mile (one-way), four- to six-hour walk to Gull Rock, a rocky point 140ft above the Turnagain shoreline. The trail follows an old wagon road built at the turn of the 19th century, and along the way you can explore the remains of a cabin and sawmill.

Hope Point   HIKING
This is a steep trail, following an alpine ridge 5 miles for incredible views of Turnagain Arm. Begin at an unmarked trail along the right-hand side of the small Porcupine Creek. Except for an early-summer snowfield, you'll find no water after Porcupine Creek.

Paddling

Sixmile Creek is serious white water, with thrilling – and dangerous – rapids through deep gorges that survivors describe as 'the best roller coaster in Alaska.' The first two canyons are rated Class IV; the third canyon is a big, bad Class V. It's a four- to five-hour round-trip. Dress warm and bring extra clothes.

Chugach Outdoor Center   RAFTING
(☑907-277-7238; www.chugachoutdoorcenter. com; Mile 7.5, Hope Hwy) Offers guided trips down Sixmile twice daily during summer. The two-canyon run is $112 per person; to defy death on all three canyons it's $163 per person. It offers a float on Turnagain Arm for $93.

Nova River Runners   RAFTING
(☑800-746-5753; www.novalaska.com) Does twice-daily trips down the river, at $99 for the Class III–IV canyons, and $149 if you continue for the Class V.

🛏 Sleeping

Near the end of Resurrection Creek Rd, just before and just after the Resurrection Pass trailhead, are many underdeveloped camping spots beneath a verdant canopy. The town charges a 3% lodging tax.

Discovery Cabins   CABIN $
(www.advenalaska.com/cabins.htm; Bear Creek Rd; r $95) Set above gurgling Bear Creek, this cozy collection of spruce cabins brings you closer to the zen-entranced forest surrounding Hope. There's a hot tub on-site. You have to share bathrooms, but with little porches looking onto the creek, it doesn't matter.

Hope

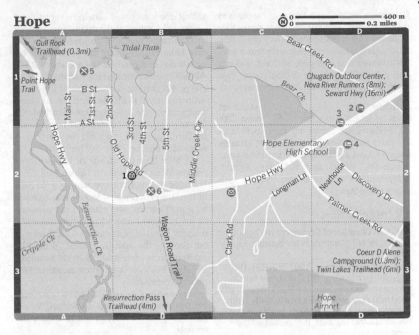

Hope

◎ Sights

1 Hope-Sunrise Mining Museum B2

🛏 Sleeping

2 Alaska Dacha Motel D1
3 Bowman's Bear Creek Lodge.............D1
4 Discovery Cabins D2

✴ Eating

Bowman's Bear Creek
  Lodge.......................................(see 3)
5 Seaview Cafe A1
6 Tito's Discovery Cafe B2

Porcupine Campground   CAMPGROUND $
(☑ 907-224-3374; www.reserveamerica.com; Mile 17.8, Hope Hwy; campsites $18) This highly recommended waterfront campground is set in a shimmering birch forest at the trailhead for Hope Point and Gull Rock. Its transcendent views (especially from sites 4, 6, 8 and 10) of Turnagain Arm ensures it books up quickly.

Coeur d'Alene Campground   CAMPGROUND $
(Mile 6.4, Palmer Rd; campsites free) A gorgeous informal campground at the end of a narrow, winding back road in an alpine valley.

Alaska Dacha Motel   MOTEL $
(☑ 907-782-3223; www.alaskadacha.com; Mile 15.8, Hope Hwy; campsite $20-35, r $99-120, cabin $145; ⏰9am-9pm; 🛜) At the entrance to town, this sundry store also has RV campsites, four passable rooms with minifridges, microwaves, pine walls and quaint appointments, plus two cabins that are often rented by long-term tenants. The rooms smell a bit propancy, but it's cozy enough.

Bowman's Bear Creek Lodge   CABIN $$$
(☑907-782-3141; www.bowmansbearcreeklodge. com; Mile 15.9, Hope Hwy; cabins $225 incl dinner; ⏰🛜) This place has seven hand-hewn log cabins (with shared baths except one) surrounding a beautiful pond and burbling creek. You'll love the cozy fires and suana. Room rates include a five-course meal at the excellent restaurant.

✴ Eating

Tito's Discovery Cafe   AMERICAN $
(Mile 16.5, Hope Hwy; breakfast $6-13, wraps $7-14; ⏰7am-7pm) This is a very popular eatery that serves homemade soups, seafood wraps and local gossip. It's best for breakfast and pie – go for the triple-berry pancakes and the strawberry rhubarb pie.

Bowman's Bear Creek Lodge AMERICAN **$$**
(☑907-782-3141; Mile 15.9, Hope Hwy; dinner $45; ☺dinner) This creekside lodge features a fabulous Alaska-casual-cuisine prix-fixe menu with homemade desserts, seafood specials and a friendly, intimate dining room. Two seatings per night; reservations are required.

Seaview Cafe SEAFOOD **$$**
(www.seaviewcafealaska.com; B St; mains $10-20; ☺11am-2am) Serves up good beer and chowder with views of the Arm. It attracts some of Alaska's best acts for weekend jams (Thursday, Friday and Saturday nights). They rent RV and tent sites ($6/18) with views of the Arm.

❶ Information

The Hope **Chamber of Commerce** has a good website for pre-plannning (www.hopealaska. info).

Hope Sunrise Library (☑907-782-3121; Old Hope Rd; by donation; 🛜) This library is in a one-room 1938 schoolhouse. Don't miss its gift shop next door, which sells locally made crafts to help support this grassroots facility. It also has an internet machine. It's open when the neon sign says 'open.'

Post Office (Palmer Rd)

❶ Getting There & Away

Hope remains idyllic in part because of its isolation. Though the **Seward Bus Line** (☑907-224-3608; www.sewardbuslines.net) and **Homer Stage Line** (☑907-868-3914; www.stagelineinhomer.com) will drop you off at the junction of the Hope and Seward Hwys, the only way to get to the town proper is by driving, hitching, pedaling or plodding.

Moose Pass & Around

POP 201

Traveling south on the Seward Hwy after Tern Lake Junction, you'll pass a number of worthwhile hikes, roadside inns and view points.

Set on nine gorgeous acres, the **Tern Lake Inn** (☑907-288-3667; www.ternlakeinn.com; Mile 36 Seward Hwy; r $175-200; 🛜) has four guest rooms and a patio with lovely lake views. The rooms are folksy and warm, and there's a separate living area for guests. There's a golf practice hole (on the airstrip) and a tennis court, and canoes are available.

Four miles south of the junction is the trailhead for the **Carter Lake Trail** (Mile 33 Seward Hwy), a steep 1.9-mile 4WD track providing quick access to subalpine terrain and Carter Lake, where you can continue another mile to some excellent campsites and Crescent Lake. Sturdy hikers can press on another 4 miles to **Crescent Lake Cabin** (☑877-444-6777; www.recreation.gov; cabins $45). If you're not driving, Seward-bound buses can drop you here. You'll also find the southern trailhead for the **Johnson Pass Trail** (Mile 33 Seward Hwy), a 23-mile trail that heads north to Turnagain Pass, and can be done as a single-day bike or a two-day backpack.

At Mile 29.4 the village of **Moose Pass** relaxes along the banks of Upper Trail Lake. Founded during the Hope-Sunrise gold rush of the late 19th century, Moose Pass (named by a mail carrier who couldn't get past one of the critters) came into its own when the original Iditarod National Historic Trail was cut around the lake in 1910–11. Today the small town is known for its lively **Summer Solstice Festival** (www.moosepasssportsmensclub.com/events.html).

Just south of Moose Pass are a few sleeping options close enough to Seward to use as a base, but far enough out to escape the crowds.

Renfro's Lakeside Retreat (☑907-288-5059; www.renfroslakesideretreat.com; 27177 Seward Hwy; RV sites from $30, cabins $170; ☺) has mediocre RV sites but fabulous lakeside cabins with fire pits and lofts with views. Nearby, the USFS-run **Trail River Campground** (www.recreation.gov; Mile 24, Seward Hwy; campsites $18) has 91 lovely sites among tall spruce trees along Kenai Lake and Lower Trail River.

After departing Moose Pass, the highway winds through national forest. At Mile 23, the **Ptarmigan Creek Trail** leads 3.5 miles from the campground to Ptarmigan Lake. Here you'll find turquoise, trout-filled waters that reflect the mountains. A 4-mile trail continues around the north side of the lake, which is brushy in places and wet in others; plan on five hours for the round-trip.The **Ptarmigan Creek Campground** (☑907-522-8368; www.reserveamerica.com; Mile 23 Seward Hwy; campsites $18) has 16 sites that were once shady but now resemble a clear-cut in places due to the spruce beetle.

The **Victor Creek Trail** (Mile 19.7, Seward Hwy) on the east side of the highway is a fairly steep path that ascends 3 miles to good views of the surrounding mountains.

If everywhere else is full, head to the Snow River Hostel (p227) or **Primrose Landing**

Campground (Mile 17.2, Seward Hwy; sites $10), which is a quiet and wooded spot with wonderful views of Kenai Lake, plus a rushing creek. It's also where the Primrose Trail (Mile 17 Seward Hwy) begins. This trail leads south to Lost Lake, and traverses to Mile 5 of the Seward Hwy. About 2 miles up the path is an unmarked side trail to the right, which leads to a magnificent waterfall – the source of that roaring you can hear as you hike.

The Grayling Lake Trail (Mile 13.2 Seward Hwy), accessed from a parking lot at Mile 13.2, leads walkers for two pleasant miles to Grayling Lake, a beautiful spot with views of Snow River and excellent grayling fishing. Side trails connect Grayling Lake with Meridian and Leech lakes. This is an excellent hiking trail for the kids.

Seward

POP 2737

Seward is at the crossroads of everything. Perched on the edge of Resurrection Bay, it offers out-of-this-world views of water, sky, mountain and forest, and is easily accessed by road, boat and rail. Because of its size (and its history as a railroad port), there is plenty of nightlife, good shopping and quality restaurants in the picturesque old-time downtown area.

Just a jump from town, you have access to Kenai Fjords National Park, superb sea kayaking, birding and whale watching, and hikes and bikes that can take you to the top of the Harding Ice Field or across the whole Kenai Peninsula.

The body of the city is divided into two centers: the newer, touristy harbor and the historic downtown. Lowell Point stretches to the south of town, and other amenities can be found just north along the Seward Hwy.

History

Seward got its start in 1903, when settlers arrived and plotted construction of a northbound rail line. Once the Alaska Railroad was completed two decades later, this ice-free port would become the most important shipping terminal on the Kenai Peninsula. The city also served as the start of the 1200-mile Iditarod National Historic Trail to Nome, along a major dogsled thoroughfare via the Interior and Bush. In WWII the town got another boost when the US Army built Fort McGilvray at Caines Head, just south of town.

⊙ Sights

★ **Alaska Sealife Center** AQUARIUM
(Map p224; ☑ 800-224-2525; www.alaskasealife. org; 301 Railway Ave; adult/child $20/10; ⊙ 9am-9pm Mon-Thu, 8am-9pm Fri-Sun; ⊕) A fitting legacy of the *Exxon Valdez* oil-spill settlement, this $56-million marine research center is more than just one of Alaska's finest attractions. As the only coldwater marine-science facility in the Western Hemisphere, it serves as a research and educational center and provides rehabilitation for injured marine animals.

Kids will love the tidepool touch tank, where they can hold sea anemones and starfish, as well as the ship's helm and the massive two-story tanks where you can see seals, birds and more both above and below the water.

An outdoor observation platform offers a fabulous view of the mountains ringing Resurrection Bay where you can watch salmon thrash their way up a fish ladder. Plan to spend the better part of one of your best afternoons here.

It's worth including an Encounter tour (adult/child $79/59); you'll get face to face with the creatures you normally only see behind the glass and delve more deeply into the lives of octopus, puffins or marine mammals.

Seward Community Library & Museum MUSEUM
(Map p224; 239 6th Ave; adult/child $5/free; ⊙ 10am-5pm Tue-Sat, 1-5pm Sun) This eclectic museum has an excellent Iditarod exhibit; a rare 49-star US flag; and relics of Seward's Russian era, the 1964 Good Friday Earthquake and the 1989 oil spill. There are also lots of amusing antiques, including an ancient electric hair-curling machine.

The staff are enthusiastic and knowledgeable, and worth engaging. The library is a good place to relax on a rainy day.

Benny Benson Memorial MONUMENT
(Map p224) This humble monument at the corner of the Seward Hwy and Dairy Hill Lane honors Seward's favorite son, Benny Benson. In 1926 the orphaned 13-year-old Alaska Native boy submitted his design for the Alaska state flag, arguably the loveliest in the Union.

His stellar design (you can see one of his first at the library) includes the North Star, symbolizing the northernmost state, the Great Bear constellation for strength, and a

Seward

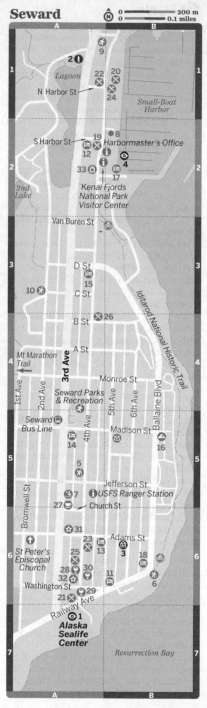

0 ___ 200 m
0 ___ 0.1 miles

Seward

blue background for the sky and the forget-me-not, Alaska's state flower.

Small-Boat Harbor   HARBOR
(Map p224) The small-boat harbor at the northern end of 4th Ave hums during the summer with fishing boats, charter vessels,

cruise ships and a number of sailboats. At its heart is the harbormaster's office (p231). Look for the huge anchors outside. Radiating outward from the docks are seasonal restaurants, espresso bars and tourist services.

Murals

Seward is the undeniable mural capital of Alaska. There are more than two dozen public paintings in town – mostly on buildings in the downtown area. Enjoy historic treatments of Exit Glacier (it really was that big), tributes to the Mt Marathon Race and more politically charged pieces. See www.seward-muralsociety.com.

🏃 Activities

There are excellent hikes from Exit Glacier in nearby Kenai Fjords National Park (p231). The park offers the best blue-water paddling you could imagine.

Hiking

★ **Lost Lake Trail**   HIKING
(Map p228) This challenging 7-mile trail to an alpine lake is one of the most scenic hikes the Kenai Peninsula has to offer in midsummer. The trailhead is in Lost Lake subdivision, at Mile 5.3 of the Seward Hwy.

Clemens Memorial Cabin (p226) is 4.5 miles up the trail (book way ahead). It has amazing views of Resurrection Bay and is also a good winter destination. The final 2 miles are above the treeline, making the shores of Lost Lake a wondrous place to pitch a tent.

If you'd rather not return the same way, continue around the east side of Lost Lake to the Primrose Trail, an 8-mile alpine trek ending at Primrose Landing Campground at Mile 17.2 of the Seward Hwy. Plan on seven to 10 hours for the round-trip to Lost Lake, and bring a camp stove, as wood is hard to come by.

Mt Marathon Trail   HIKING
(Map p228; www.mmr.seward.com) According to local legend, grocer Gus Borgan wagered $100 in 1909 that no one could run Mt Marathon in an hour, and the race was on. Winner James Walters clocked in at 62 minutes, losing the bet but becoming a legend.

The 3.1-mile suffer-fest quickly became a celebrated Fourth of July event and today is Alaska's most famous footrace, pitting runners from all over the world against the 3022ft-high peak. You can trek to the top several ways. At the end of Monroe St, the so-called Jeep Trail provides easier (though not drivable) access to the peak and a heavenly bowl behind the mountain. At the west end of Jefferson St, you can access either a trailhead with switchbacks to mellow the ascent, or the official route, which begins at a nearby cliff face behind the water tanks. Be careful: the runner's trail is painful – think Stairmaster with a view – and every summer several tourists who didn't know what they were in for have to be rescued.

Iditarod National Historic Trail   HIKING
(Map p224) Though the Iditarod Race to Nome currently departs from Anchorage, the legendary trail actually begins in Seward (see p64). A far more interesting segment of the trail for hikers, however, can be reached by heading east 2 miles on Nash Rd, which intersects the Seward Hwy at Mile 3.2.

From here you can follow the Iditarod National Historic Trail through woods and thick brush for a 4-mile hike to Bear Lake. Nearby is the unmarked trailhead for the Mt Alice Trail, a fairly difficult and highly recommended 3.5-mile climb to the alpine summit. Bald eagles, blueberries and stunning views can be had elsewhere, but it's the solitude – this trail is relatively unused – and afternoon light that make Mt Alice great. Back at Bear Lake, you can either backtrack to town or forge on another 11 miles to rejoin the Seward Hwy. At the foot of Ballaine Blvd, a memorial marks Mile 0 and a paved bike path heads 2 miles north along the beach.

Two Lakes Trail   HIKING
(Map p224; cnr 2nd Ave & C St) This easy 1-mile loop circumnavigates pleasant Two Lakes Park, through woods and picnic grounds, across a creek and around the two promised lakes at the base of Mt Marathon. Unsatisfied hikers can access the Jeep Trail nearby, which climbs Mt Marathon, for a much more intense climb.

Caines Head State Recreation Area HIKING
(Lowell Point; 5 miles south of Seward) This 6000-acre preserve, 5.5 miles south of Seward on Resurrection Bay, contains WWII military facilities (bring a flashlight for exploring), a 650ft headland, trails to Tonsina Beach (2.3 miles), North Beach (5 miles) and Fort Gilvany (7.8 miles) and two public-use cabins. There's a $5 day-use fee for the recreation area, paid at the trailhead.

Time your trips with low tide.

Glacier Trekking

Exit Glacier Guides   HIKING

(Map p224; ☑ 907-224-5569; www.exitglacier-
guides.com; 405 4th Ave) ✆ Exit Glacier Guides
gives you the chance to tread upon Seward's
backyard glacier. Its five-hour ice-hiking trip
costs $130 per person, gears you up with ice
axes and crampons, ascends partway up the
Harding Ice Field Trail and then heads out
onto the glacier for crevasse exploration and
interpretive glaciology. It also offers helicopter tours, hiking tours and a historic downtown tour.

Mountain Biking

Popular with hikers, the Lost Lake Trail is
sometimes steep and technical, but highly rewarding, single-track riding. Local cyclists say
the Iditarod National Historic Trail and the
Resurrection River Trail are also good rides.

Seward Bike Shop   BIKE

(Map p224; 411 Port Ave; per half cruisers $18,
mountain bikes full/half-day $38/25; ⊙ 9:30am-
6pm) Rents out bikes and has the latest details on local biking trails.

Seward Adventure Company MOUNTAIN BIKING

(☑ 907-362-7433; www.sewardbiketours.com) Run
by cycling aficionado Karl, Seward Adventure Company offers guided day trips ($80
to $145) to Devil's Pass and the Iditarod
Trail, to name a few. Bikes are provided, and
multiday custom trips can include meals
and lodging. Winter tours on fat-tire snow
bikes are also available.

Paddling

It's better to go to Kenai Fjords National
Park (p231), but it costs more. Otherwise
you can kayak right outside Seward in Resurrection Bay. It lacks tidewater glaciers
and ample wildlife but can still make for a
stunning day on the water. Sunny Cove Sea
Kayaking (Sunny Cove Sea Kayaking; Map p224;
☑ 800-770-9119; www.sunnycove.com; small-boat
harbor) offers a big Kenai Fjord day trip for
$425, trips to Fox Island with a paddle and
salmon bake ($149, but the salmon bake is
not worth your time), and a hike and paddle
combo for $135. Kayak Adventures World-
wide (Map p224; ☑ 907-224-3960; www.kayakak.
com; 328 3rd Ave) runs half-day kayak adventures for $70 or longer trips to Aialik Bay for
$399 to $505. Adventure 60 North (p232)
and Miller's Landing (Map p228; ☑ 866-541-
5739, 907-224-5739; www.millerslandingak.com;
cnr Lowell Rd & Beach St) rent kayaks.

Ziplining

Stoney Creek Canopy Adventures   ZIPLINE

(Map p228; ☑ 907-224-3662; 13037 Knotwood St,
accessed from Mile 6.5, Seward Hwy; child/adult
$119/149) This three-hour canopy zipline takes
you whizzing past giant Sitka spruce and mirror ponds. There are eight zip runs in all, plus
three suspension bridges and two rappels.

Dogsledding

Godwin Glacier Dog Sled Tours   DOGSLED

(☑ 888-989-8239; www.alaskadogsled.com; tours
per person $300) Transports you by helicop-
ter to an alpine glacier, where you'll be met
by lots of dogs and a genuine snow-sledding
adventure, even in July.

Wilderness Cabins

You can paddle, fly or hike to a remote, rustic lodging administered by the Alaska Division of Parks, USFS or even the National
Park Service, as Kenai Fjords National Park
has several boat-accessible public-use cabins. Cabins close to town book up six months
in advance.

Orca Island Cabins   YURT

(☑ 907-491-1988; www.orcaislandcabins.com; yurt
per person $239) In Humpy Cove, 9 miles
southeast of Seward, this privately owned
place has three onshore yurts with private baths and kitchens. All have propane-
powered ranges and water-heaters but no
electricity. These are a great choice for those
who want to rough it without roughing it
too much. The price includes water-taxi and
kayak rentals.

Clemens Memorial Cabin   CABIN

(☑ 907-224-3374; www.recreation.gov; cabins
$45) Located 4.5 miles up the Lost Lake
Trail, this renovated public-use cabin sleeps
eight and is located at the treeline, providing spectacular views of Resurrection Bay.
It's always booked so reserve at least six
months ahead.

Derby Cove Cabin   CABIN

(www.alaskastateparks.org; cabins $65) This is just
off the tidal trail between Tonsina Point and
North Beach in Caines Head State Recreation
Area, 4 miles from the Lowell Point trailhead.
This public-use cabin can be accessed on foot
at low tide, or by kayak any time.

Callisto Canyon Cabin   CABIN

(www.alaskastateparks.org; cabins $65) A public-
use cabin located just off the tidal trail, a
half-mile before you reach Derby Cove. It
can be reached on foot or by kayak.

Resurrection River Cabin
CABIN

(☑ 518-885-3639, 877-444-6777; www.recreation.
gov; cabins $35) This public-use cabin is 6.5
miles from the southern trailhead of the
Resurrection River Trail.

Gym

Seward Parks & Recreation
GYM

(Map p224; ☑ 907-224-4054; 519 4th Ave; adult/
child $4/2; ☺ 2-9pm Mon-Fri) Has a gym and
sauna as well as showers. Inquire here about
swimming at the high school.

✯ Festivals & Events

Seward knows how to party, and these are
just a few of the more popular events. The
Fourth of July celebration is huge.

Polar Bear Jumpoff Festival
CULTURAL

A favorite of costumed masochists who
plunge into frigid Resurrection Bay with a
smile in mid-January, all to raise money for
cancer.

Mt Marathon Race
CULTURAL

(www.mmr.seward.com) This Fourth of July
race attracts runners who like to test themselves by running up a near vertical peak,
and fans who like to drink beer and yell.

Silver Salmon Derby
CULTURAL

An event held in mid-August that gets even
bigger crowds, all vying for prizes in excess
of $150,000.

Seward Music & Arts Festival
MUSIC

(www.sewardfestival.com) Held the last weekend in September, this summer's-end celebration brings together an eclectic mix of
local artists and musicians, and is particularly kid-friendly, with circus training and
mural-painting.

🛏 Sleeping

Above and beyond the listed rates you have
to add 11% in Seward sales and bed taxes.
Kenai Fjords National Park maintains a
free, drive-up campground near Exit Glacier.
There are lots of informal campsites along
Exit Glacier Rd.

Among Seward's midrange places, dozens
are B&Bs and vacation rentals; you can book
through **Alaska's Point of View** (☑ 907-224-
2424; www.alaskaspointofview.com), even at the
last minute.

Resurrection Campground
CAMPGROUND $

(Map p224; ☑ 907-224-3331; Ballaine Blvd; tent
sites $10, RV sites $15-30) Perfectly situated between the city center and boat harbor, with
stunning views of Resurrection Bay, this
semi-urban campground gets windy, but
there's a compact skateboard park, a massive playground and a paved bicycle path
running through. Hot showers are only $2.

Moby Dick Hostel
HOSTEL $

(Map p224; ☑ 907-224-7072; www.mobydickhostel.
com; 430 3rd Ave; dm $25, r $72-89; ☺ 🖥) Right
in the middle of the town, this rambling hostel has a great big kitchen table for sharing
tales, plus four dorm rooms sleeping up to
six, with decent bunks and enough room to
move about. It will help book tours. The private rooms are pricey, but a decent buy for
couples.

Nauti Otter
HOSTEL $

(Map p228; ☑ 907-491-2255; www.nautiotterinn.
com; Mile 6, Seward Hwy; dm $30, r $45-80, Cabin
$70; 🖥) This relaxed hostel 5 miles outside
town has nightly bonfires and good vibes.
There are only two bathrooms in the entire
place (yikes) and it can get a little messy, but
the hostel rooms are surprisingly clean and
cheery. It rents mountain bikes for $20.

Snow River Hostel
HOSTEL $

(☑ 907-440-1907; www.alaskahostels.org; Mile 16,
Seward Hwy; dm/r $30/60; ☺) Nestled beside
the forest and a burbling creek, this cord-
wood place is some distance from town, but
worth the trip for the idyllic atmosphere and
easy access to challenging Primrose Trail.
There's a cool common area and picnic/fire
spots outside, perfect for hanging out. It often closes (call ahead).

Kayaker's Cove
HOSTEL $

(☑ 907-224-8662; www.kayakerscove.net; across
from Fox Island Spit; dm/cabins $20/60; ☺) Lo-
cated 12 miles southeast of Seward near Fox
Island in a lush little cove, this place is accessible by kayak or water-taxi only. There's
a shared kitchen, and you'll need to bring
your own food. It rents out single/double
kayaks for $20/30.

Miller's Landing
CAMPGROUND $

(Map p228; ☑ 866-541-5739; www.millerslandin-
gak.com; cnr Lowell Rd & Beach St; tent/RV sites
$27/37, cabins $50-150) This touristplex –
offering everything from campsites to kayak
rentals to fishing charters – isn't very clean
or organized, but the waterfront location is
hard to beat. It's a good mile-long slog south
of downtown.

KENAI PENINSULA SEWARD

Around Seward

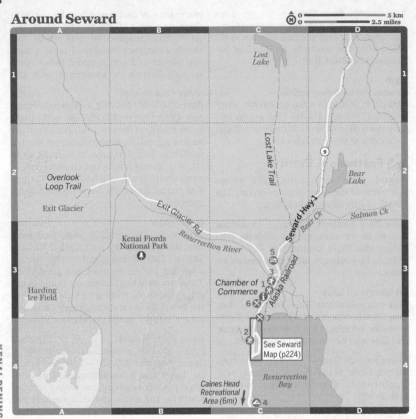

Forest Acres Campground CAMPGROUND $
(☑ 907-224-4055; cnr Hemlock St & Seward Hwy;
tent sites $10, RV sites $15-30) Located 2 miles
north of town just off the Seward Hwy on
Hemlock St. It has quiet sites shaded by towering spruce.

Seward Front Row B&B B&B $$
(Map p224; ☑ 907-224-3080; swannest@seward.
net; 227 Ballaine Blvd; r $199, house $700; ☎)
This waterfront B&B has fabulous two-sto-
ry views of Resurrection Bay from the large
living room. There are two well-done rooms
(neither with ocean views). Next door is a
six-person vacation rental perfect for fami-
lies. Book six months ahead.

Stoney Creek Inn B&B $$
(☑ 907-224-3940; www.stoneycreekinn.net; Ston-
ey Creek Ave; d $149-164; ⊜☎) This secluded
place has five rooms sharing a common
area, and comes with a fantastic sauna and
hot tub next to a deliciously icy-cold salmon

stream. The barbecue area is a great place
to grill up your catch. Continental breakfast
is included.

Best Western Edgewater Hotel HOTEL $$
(Map p224; ☑ 907-224-2700; www.hoteledgewater.
com; 202 5th Ave; d $229-299; ☎) Some of the
most comfortable rooms in town are found
in this chain hotel that faces the bay. There's
a slightly odd configuration for the baths
(with the sink in the room), but the bay
views are spectacular. The handsome wood
furniture and jumping orca photos provide
a fleeting glimpse of Alaska.

Hotel Seward HISTORIC HOTEL $$
(Map p224; ☑ 907-224-8001, 800-440-2444; www.
hotelsewardalaska.com; 221 5th Ave; standard r
with/without bathroom $159/109, deluxe $229-289;
⊜☎) This historic hotel is very Alaskan, a
bit stinky and a decent splurge depending
on your tastes. The historic wing has low-
slung ceilings, smallish rooms and will give

Around Seward

you the sense of living in a fisherman's flophouse. The deluxe rooms in the new wing have expansive views, and some even come with fireplaces.

In all, it feels a bit rundown, but you'll love the taxidermy.

Murphy's Alaskan Inn MOTEL **$$**
(Map p224; 📞 800-686-8191; www.murphysmotel.com; 911 4th Ave; r $149-189; ❄🛜) You'll find nice harbor views from private decks at this surprisingly nice spot on the edge of downtown. There are some smaller rooms without views and deluxe kitchen units. It can get a bit musty and the comforters are dated.

Breeze Inn MOTEL **$$**
(Map p224; 📞 907-224-5283; www.breezeinn.com; 303 3rd Ave; r $159-259; ❄🛜♿) If you can't get a harbor-view annex room (ask for no 33), this sprawling industrial-stylized business hotel probably isn't worth your time.

★Alaska Paddle Inn B&B **$$$**
(📞 907-362-2628; www.alaskapaddleinn.com; 13745 Beach Dr; r from $209; ❄🛜) Two custom-built rooms overlook a private beach and Resurrection Bay on Lowell Point. Arched ceilings, walk-in tiled showers and gas fireplaces make this place one of the coziest and classiest in Seward. It offers discounts for stays of multiple days.

Safari Lodge LODGE **$$$**
(Map p224; 📞 907-224-5232, 800-832-1564; www.saltwatersafari.com; 120 4th Ave; d $199-289; ❄🛜) Facing the small boat harbor, these modern rooms are probably the best waterfront spots in town. All rooms have bay views, cushy beds, large bathrooms and tasteful Alaskan appointments, including

the occasional deer head on your own patio.

🍴 Eating

Sea Bean Cafe CAFE **$**
(Map p224; 225 4th Ave; light meals $7-11; ⏰ 7am-6pm Mon-Fri, 9am-6pm Sat & Sun; 🛜) Serves hot paninis, wraps, Belgian waffles, ice cream, smoothies and espressos.

Smoke Shack BARBECUE **$**
(Map p228; 📞 907-224-7427; 411 Port Ave; breakfast & lunch $6-11, dinner $10-16; ⏰ 6am-8pm) Housed in a rail car, this joint oozes blue-collar atmosphere. It has the best breakfast in town (biscuits and gravy made from scratch) and pulled pork for dinner.

Ranting Raven BAKERY **$**
(Map p224; 238 4th Ave; light meals $3-4; ⏰ 7am-6pm) In the back of a gift store, you'll find this little bakery with excellent pastries and cookies (seriously, you have to try the lemon shortbread) and equally awesome soups at lunchtime.

Railway Cantina MEXICAN **$**
(Map p224; www.railwaycantina.com; 1401 4th Ave; light meals $6-12; ⏰ 11am-10pm) Near the small-boat harbor, this spot offers unorthodox quesadillas, burritos and tacos. Try the blackened halibut burrito, with your choice of salsa (we like the pineapple-ginger).

Bakery at the Harbor BAKERY **$**
(Map p224; 1210 4th Ave; breakfast & lunch $3-8, dinner $5-12; ⏰ 7am-2pm) This busy joint is a bargain: breakfast is delish and lunch includes half-pound burgers on homemade buns. Also sells box lunches for those going out on the bay for the day.

Safeway SUPERMARKET **$**
(Map p228; Mile 1.5, Seward Hwy; ⏰ 5am-midnight) Has sushi, espressos, a sandwich bar and all the groceries you need.

★Chinooks SEAFOOD **$$**
(Map p224; 📞 907-224-2207; www.chinooksbar.com; 1404 4th Ave; $14-35; ⏰ 11am-11pm) The most innovative of Seward's waterfront eateries, this airy, steel-walled spot features a good selection of small plates such as pacific cod ceviche, Jakolof Bay Oysters and crispy razon clams. The entrees are equally creative and the chili-crusted rockfish and walnut-crusted sable fish are not to be missed. Take advantage of cheaper sandwiches (even on the dinner menu).

...0, dinner $18-22; ... – 'cheap beer and ... on the second count. ...on sandwich, which you ...ckles from a barrel. It's a ...m the Seward Hwy turnoff.

...n Roadhouse PIZZA **$$**
(w... ...rdwindsong.com; Exit Glacier Rd; breakfast & ...nch $9-14, dinner $18-46; ☺6am-10pm) This local favorite is home to the 'Buddha Belly' pizza, sweet-potato fries that are well worth traveling for, and the best deck in town. It also has a vast range of on-tap brews. It's about 1 mile west of the Seward Hwy on Exit Glacier Rd.

Christo's Palace PIZZA **$$**
(Map p224; 133 4th Ave; dinner $11-32; ☺11am-9pm) Has a huge dining room dominated by a 1950s Brunswick bar (featuring a great selection of beer on tap). The pizza gets rave reviews.

Woody's Thai Kitchen THAI **$$**
(Map p224; ☎907-422-0338; 800 4th Ave; $13-15; ☺noon-9pm) Near the baseball diamond, this little Thai bistro gives a welcome break from the bucket o' halibut. And while the ambience is a little too spartan, you'll love the excellent thai dishes, with perfectly cooked fresh veggies and generous portions.

Ray's Waterfront SEAFOOD **$$$**
(Map p224; ☎907-224-5606; small-boat harbor; mains $22-45; ☺11am-10pm) Vying for the top dining spot in Seward, Ray's has amazing views, carefully crafted seafood dishes and attentive service in a fine-dining atmosphere that retains its Alaskan vibe.

🍷 Drinking & Nightlife

Seward has no shortage of welcoming watering holes, most featuring a mix of young and old, locals and tourists. Almost all the bars are downtown.

★ Resurrect Art Coffee House Gallery CAFE
(Map p224; 320 3rd Ave; ☺8am-5pm) Located in an old high-ceilinged church, this place serves espressos, Italian sodas and bagels, displays great local art and hosts live jazz on Tuesday nights. The best place to read the paper and check out the view is from the airy choir loft. Stop by here for first-friday art walks.

Thorn's Showcase Lounge LOUNGE
(Map p224; 208 4th St) This curio-bedecked plush leather lounge serves the strongest drinks in town – try its white Russians – and is said to have the best halibut around (mains $14 to $18). The Jim Beam collection is valued at thousands of dollars; can you spot the pipeline bottle?

Seward Brewing Company BREWERY
(Map p224; ☎907-422-0337; 139 4th Ave; ☺11:30am-11pm) The homecrafted brew at this expansive restaurant and taphouse is some of Alaska's hoppiest best. They also have a great list of other Alaska craft beers, alluring waitstaff and decent meals ($12 to $19) that depart from standard pub grub to include Alaskan faves such as salmon poke, clams and a lamb mac and cheese.

Seward Alehouse BAR
(Map p224; 215 4th Ave) This fun pub has a good selection of beers on tap and a dance-party-starting jukebox.

Yukon Bar BAR
(Map p224; ☎907-224-3063; 201 4th Ave) There are hundreds of dollars pinned to this bar's ceiling and almost nightly live music in the summer. It's festive.

Pit Bar BAR
(Mile 3.5, Seward Hwy; ☺to 5am) Just past Exit Glacier Rd; this is where the crowd heads when the bars close in town.

☆ Entertainment

Liberty Theatre THEATER
(Map p224; ☎907-224-5418; 304 4th Ave; admission $7) A delightful little WWII-era cinema showing first-run flicks daily.

🛍 Shopping

Fish House OUTDOOR EQUIPMENT
(True Value; Map p224; 1303 4th Ave; ☺7am-7pm) This hardware store sells fishing licenses, quality camping gear and has the town's best collection of rubber boots.

ℹ Information

There is free internet and wi-fi at the Seward Community Library & Museum (p223).
First National Bank of Anchorage (☎907-224-4200; 303 4th Ave; ☺10am-5pm Mon-Thu, 9am-6pm Fri) One of two banks in town. There are ATMs in Safeway and the Yukon Bar.

Post Office (Map p224; cnr 5th Ave & Madison St) The informal community gathering place.
Providence Seward Medical Center (☑ 907-224-5205; 417 1st Ave) At the west end of Jefferson St.
Suds N' Swirl (335 3rd Ave; laundry per wash $3.25; ☺7am-8:30pm) Attached to a wonderful cafe, the Sip-N-Spin.

TOURIST INFORMATION

Chamber of Commerce (Map p228; ☑ 907-224-8051; www.seward.com; 2001 Seward Hwy/3rd Ave; ☺9am-4pm Mon-Fri) At the entrance to town, this helpful place provides everything from trail maps to local menus, plus lots of good advice.
Harbormaster's Office (Map p224; ☑ 907-224-3138; ☺8am-5pm) Has showers for $2 (24 hours). Boat launches start at $10.
Kenai Fjords National Park Visitor Center (Map p224; ☑ 907 224-3175; www.nps.gov/kefj; ☺8:30am-7pm) Beside the small-boat harbor.
USFS Ranger Station (Map p224; ☑ 907-224 3374; 334 4th Ave; ☺8am-5pm Mon-Fri) Has maps and information about Seward's outstanding selection of trails, cabins and campgrounds.

❶ Getting There & Around

BUS

Seward Bus Line (Map p224; ☑ 907-224-3608; www.sewardbuslines.net) Departs at 9:30am and 2pm daily en route to Anchorage ($40). It also offers service at 9:30am to Whittier ($60, minimum two passengers).
Homer Stage Line (☑ 907-868-3914; www.stagelincinhomer.com) Runs Monday, Wednesday and Friday from Seward (9am) to Homer ($90), with stops in Soldotna ($75) and Cooper Landing ($65).
Park Connection (☑ 800 266 8625; www.alaskacoach.com) Has a daily service from Seward to Denali Park (one-way $155) via Anchorage (one-way $55 to $65).

SHUTTLE

Seward Shuttle When cruise ships are in town, the free shuttle runs between the ferry terminal and downtown every 15 to 20 minutes.

TRAIN

Alaska Railroad (☑ 907-265-2494, 800-544-0552; www.akrr.com; 408 Port Ave; one-way/round-trip $85/135) Offers a daily run to Anchorage from May to September. It's more than just public transportation; it's one of the most famous rides in Alaska, complete with glaciers, steep gorges and rugged mountain scenery.

Kenai Fjords National Park

Seward is the gateway to **Kenai Fjords National Park** (☑ 907-224-2125; www.nps.gov/kefj), created in 1980 to protect 587,000 acres of Alaska's most awesome, impenetrable wilderness. Crowning the park is the massive Harding Ice Field; from it, countless tidewater glaciers pour down, carving the coast into dizzying fjords.

With such a landscape – and an abundance of marine wildlife to boot – the park is a major tourist attraction. Unfortunately, it's also an expensive one. That is why road-accessible Exit Glacier is its highlight attraction, drawing more than 100,000 tourists each summer. Hardier souls can ascend to the Harding Ice Field from the same trailhead, but only experienced mountaineers equipped with skis, ice axes and crampons can investigate the 900 sq miles of ice.

The vast majority of visitors either take a quick trip to Exit Glacier's face or splurge on a tour-boat cruise along the coast. For those who want to spend more time in the park, the coastal fjords are a blue-water kayaker's dream; to reach the area, though, you either have to paddle the sections exposed to the Gulf of Alaska or pay for a drop-off service. The park is free.

✦ Activities

Hiking

Exit Glacier Nature Center   HIKING
(☺9am-8pm) At the Exit Glacier trailhead; the center has interpretive displays, sells postcards and field guides, and is the starting point for ranger-guided hikes. At 10am, 2pm and 4pm daily, rangers at the Exit Glacier Nature Center lead free one-hour hikes to the glacier, providing information on the wildlife and natural history of the area.

For a more strenuous outing, show up at the nature center on a Wednesday or Saturday at 9am for the guided ascent of the Harding Ice Field Trail. The trek lasts eight hours; pack a lunch and rain gear.

Harding Ice Field Trail   HIKING
This strenuous and yet extremely popular 4-mile trail (six- to eight-hour round-trip) follows Exit Glacier up to Harding Ice Field. The 936-sq-mile expanse remained undiscovered until the early 1900s, when a map-surveying team discovered that eight

coastal glaciers flowed from the exact same system.

Today you can rediscover it via a steep, roughly cut and sometimes slippery ascent to 3500ft. Beware of bears; they're common here. Only experienced glacier-travelers should head onto the ice-field proper.

The trek is well worth it for those with the stamina, as it provides spectacular views of not only the ice field but Exit Glacier and the valley below. The upper section of the route is snow-covered for much of the year; bring a jacket and watch for ice-bridges above creeks. Camping up here is a great idea, but the free, tiny public-use cabin at the top is for emergencies only.

Resurrection River Trail   HIKING
This 16-mile trail accesses a 72-mile trail system connecting Seward and Hope. The continuous trail is broken only by the Sterling Hwy and provides a wonderful wilderness adventure through streams, rivers, lakes, wooded lowlands and alpine areas.

It's difficult and expensive to maintain, so expect to encounter natural hassles such as downed trees, boggy patches and washed-out sections. Resurrection River Cabin is 7 miles from the trailhead.

The southern trailhead is at Mile 8 of Exit Glacier Rd. The northern trailhead joins the Russian Lakes Trail 5 miles from Cooper Lake or 16 miles from the Russian River Campground off the Sterling Hwy. The hike from the Seward Hwy to the Sterling Hwy is a 40-mile trip, including Exit Glacier.

Paddling
Blue-water paddles out of Resurrection Bay along the coastline of the park are for experienced kayakers only; others should invest in a drop-off service. You'll be rewarded, however, with wildlife encounters and close-up views of the glaciers from a unique perspective.

With several glaciers to visit, Aialik Bay is a popular arm for kayakers. Many people hire water-taxis to drop them near Aialik Glacier, then take three or four days to paddle south past Pedersen Glacier and into Holgate Arm, where they're picked up. The high point of the trip is Holgate Glacier, an active tidewater glacier that's the main feature of all the boat tours.

Northwestern Lagoon is more expensive to reach but much more isolated, with not nearly as many tour boats. The wildlife is excellent, especially the seabirds and sea

otters, and more than a half-dozen glaciers can be seen. Plan on three to four days if you're being dropped inside the lagoon.

Most companies can arrange drop-off and pickup; it's about $250 for the round-trip to Aialik Bay and $275 to $300 for the more remote Northwestern Lagoon.

Kayak Adventures Worldwide   KAYAKING
(☑ 907-224-3960; www.kayakak.com) ⌀ A highly respected, eco-oriented operation that guides educational half- and full-day trips out of Seward. Trips to Aialik Bay cost from $399 to $505.

Sunny Cove Sea Kayaking   KAYAKING
(☑ 907-224-8810, 800-770-9119; www.sunnycove. com) It doesn't rent out kayaks, but does arrange a multitude of different trips, including a $425 Kenai Fjords day trip.

Miller's Landing   KAYAKING
(☑ 907-224-5739, 866-541-5739; www.millerslandin gak.com) Rents out kayaks (single/double $45/50) and equipment, and also provides a water-taxi service as far as Aialik Bay.

Adventure 60 North   KAYAKING
(☑ 907-224-2600; www.adventure60.com; Mile 3, Seward Hwy) This is a reputable kayaking and adventure outfitter.

☞ Tours

The easiest and most popular way to view the park's dramatic fjords, glaciers and abundant wildlife is from a cruise ship. Several companies offer the same basic tours: wildlife cruises (three to five hours) take in Resurrection Bay without really entering the park. Don't bother taking the short cruise, unless you are really trying to avoid seasickness. Much better tours (eight to 10 hours) explore Holgate Arm or Northwestern Lagoon. Some offer a buffet lunch on beautiful Fox Island, which basically means spending an hour picking at trays of overcooked salmon when you could instead be whale watching. Eat on the boat.

Kenai Fjords Tours   BOAT
(Map p224; ☑ 888-478-3346; www.kenaifjordstours .com; small-boat harbor, Seward) A long-running operation offering a wide variety of options, including an all-inclusive overnight on Fox Island at the Kenai Fjords Wilderness Lodge (per person $488 based on double occupancy). Instead of having a naturalist on board, the captain rocks the mic. The big difference from the other tours is they have a lunchtime salmon bake on standard tours at Fox Island.

EXIT GLACIER

The marquee attraction of Kenai Fjords National Park is Exit Glacier, named by explorers crossing the Harding Ice Field who found the glacier a suitable way to 'exit' the ice and mountains.

From the Exit Glacier Nature Center (p231), the **Outwash Plain Trail** is an easy half-mile walk to the glacier's alluvial plain – a flat expanse of pulverized silt and gravel, cut through by braids of gray meltwater. The **Edge of the Glacier Trail** leaves the first loop and climbs steeply to an overlook at the side of the glacier before returning. Both trails make for a short hike that will take one or two hours; you can return along the half-mile **nature trail** through cottonwood forest, alder thickets and old glacial moraines before emerging at the ranger station. Note how the land becomes more vegetated the further you get from the ice, the result of having had more time to recover from its glacial scouring. Signs indicate how far the glacier extended.

Prices range from $89 to $184 for four- to nine-hour tours. Children are half price. Smaller vessels are available for more intimate tours, often adapted to the interests of the group.

Major Marine Tours BOAT
(Map p224; ☑907-224-8030, 800-764-7300; www.majormarine.com; small-boat harbor, Seward) Major Marine Tours includes a national park ranger on every boat. It has a half-day Resurrection Bay tour (adult/child $79/39), a full-day viewing Holgate Arm ($149/74), and an assortment of semicustomized trips for birders, whale-watchers and more. With most tours, you can add a prime rib and salmon buffet feast for $15.

Scenic Mountain Air SCENIC FLIGHTS
(☑907-362-6205; www.sewardair.com) For flightseeing trips, contact Scenic Mountain Air at Seward airport for flights over the fjords. Flights cost about $99 per hour per person.

🛌 Sleeping

Public-Use Cabins CABIN $
(☑907-224-3175; www.nps.gov/kefj/planyourvisit/publicusecabins_summer.htm; cabins $50) There are three cabins along the fjords, as well as countless other informal campsites that line the kayak-accessible beaches of Aialik Bay and Northwestern Lagoon.

Aialik Cabin is on a beach that's perfect for hiking, beachcombing and whale watching; Holgate Arm Cabin has a spectacular view of Holgate Glacier; and North Arm Cabin is actually much closer to Homer. You'll want to reserve these well in advance through the **Alaska Public Lands Information Center** (☑907-271-2742).

Exit Glacier Campground CAMPGROUND $
(Exit Glacier Rd; tent sites free) The only formal campground in the park. It has great walk-in sites for tents only and a bear-proof food-storage area. Other campsites are dotted along Exit Glacier Rd – look for small turnoffs in the alders.

Kenai Fjords Glacier Lodge CABIN $$$
(☑800-334-8730; www.kenaifjordsglacierlodge.com; cabins per person from $725) 🌿 On gorgeous Pedersen Lagoon, this lodge has 16 rustic-chic cabins (with private baths and electricity) connected by a network of boardwalks. The all-inclusive price is a better deal for longer stays and includes transportation from Seward, gourmet meals, glacier cruises and guided kayaking.

ℹ️ Information

Kenai Fjords National Park Visitor Center (1212 4th Ave, Seward; ⊙8:30am-7pm) In Seward's small-boat harbor; has information on hiking and camping, and issues free backcountry permits.

ℹ️ Getting There & Around

To reach the coastal fjords, you'll need to take a tour or catch a water-taxi with **Miller's Landing** (☑907-224-5739, 866-541-5739; www.millerslandingak.com). Getting to Exit Glacier is a bit easier. If you don't have a car, Exit Glacier Guides (p226) runs an hourly shuttle to the glacier in its recycled-vegetable-oil van between 8:30am and 4:30pm. The van departs from the Holiday Inn Express at the small-boat harbor ($10 roundtrip). **Glacier Taxi** (☑907-224-5678; www.glaciertaxicab.com) charges $60 for as many people as you can squeeze in. Hitching here is pretty easy too.

STERLING HIGHWAY

At Tern Lake Junction, the paved Sterling Hwy turns off from the Seward Hwy, heading westward through the forests and mountains of the Kenai National Wildlife Refuge (p240) to Soldotna and then bending south along Cook Inlet toward Homer.

Tern Lake Junction to Cooper Landing

From **Tern Lake Junction** (Mile 37, Seward Hwy) it's only 58 miles to Soldotna, not much more than an hour's drive. Yet this stretch contains so many hiking, camping and canoeing opportunities that it would take you a month to enjoy them all. Surrounded by the Chugach National Forest and Kenai National Wildlife Refuge, the Sterling Hwy and its side roads pass a dozen trails, 20 campgrounds and an almost endless number of lakes, rivers and streams.

Mileposts along the highway show distances from Seward, with Tern Lake Junction at Mile 37 the starting point of the Sterling Hwy.

During July and August, be prepared to stop at a handful of campgrounds before finding an available site.

At the roadside **Sunrise Inn & Cafe** (☏907-595-1222; www.alaskasunriseinn.com; Mile 45 Sterling Hwy; d/tr $120/170; ⏰7am-10pm; 🛜) there are 10 cozy rooms facing the parking lot. The bar and restaurant – with its gorgeous patio – are worth a stop.

Around the corner on Quartz Creek Rd, **Alaskan Horsemen Trail Adventures** (☏907-595-1806; www.alaskahorsemen.com; Mile 45 Sterling Hwy; cabin $125-175) gives you the full cowpoke treatment, with big stetsons and trail coats for guests, a mess hall, basic

spruce cabins and horseback rides along Quartz and Crescent Creeks (per half-/full day $129/229. Pricier guided overnight trips include rafting (called the 'Saddle Paddle') and/or flightseeing or custom fishing trips.

Just past Sunrise Inn, **Quartz Creek Campground** (www.recreation.gov; Mile 0.3 Quartz Creek Rd; tent/RV sites $18/28) on the shores of Kenai Lake is crazily popular with RVs and anglers during salmon runs. The campground is so developed that the sites are paved.

The **Crescent Creek Trail**, about half a mile beyond the **Crescent Creek Campground** (7 miles along Quartz Creek Rd from Alaska Horsemen), leads 6.5 miles to the outlet of Crescent Lake and the USFS's **Crescent Saddle Cabin** (☏877-444-6777; www.recreation.gov; cabins $45). It's an easy walk or bike ride and has spectacular autumn colors in September. Anglers can fish for Arctic grayling in the lake during the summer. The **Carter Lake Trail** connects the east end of the lake to the Seward Hwy, with a rough path along the south side of the lake between the two trails.

Cooper Landing & Around
POP 395

After skirting the north end of Kenai Lake, you enter scenic **Cooper Landing** (Mile 48.4). The picturesque outpost, named for Joseph Cooper, a miner who worked the area in the 1880s, is best known for its rich and brutal combat salmon fishing along the Russian and Kenai Rivers. While rustic log-cabin lodges featuring giant fish freezers are still the lifeblood of this town, the trails and rafting opportunities attract a very different sort of tourist.

COMBAT FISHING

In a place that's mostly natural and wild, there are few sights more unnatural than what happens each summer wherever Alaska's best salmon rivers meet a busy road. When the fish are running, the banks become a human frenzy – a ceaseless string of men, women and children hip-to-hip, hundreds of fishing rods whipping to and fro, the air filled with curses and cries of joy. This is combat fishing.

As with any form of combat, there are subtle rules that guide the chaos. Among them: don't wade out in front of other anglers, or snap up their spot on the bank if they briefly step away. (On the other hand, don't let the glares of the earlier arrivals dissuade you from taking your proper place in the fray.) Try to give your neighbor space – and whatever you do, don't foul your line with theirs. Most importantly, if you get a bite, shout, 'Fish on!' so others can reel in their lines and give you room to wrestle your catch. In combat fishing, you don't 'play' a fish; you land it fast, so others can rejoin the fight.

⊙ Sights & Activities

K'Beq Interpretive Site   ARCHAEOLOGICAL SITE
(☑907-398-8867; www.kenaitze.org; Mile 52.6, Sterling Hwy; ⊙10am-4pm) **FREE** This riverfront site, run by the local Kenaitzie tribe, is a refreshing reminder of what this area was like before the flood of sport fishermen. A quarter-mile boardwalk winds past an ancient house pit and other archaeological relics, while interpretive panels address berry picking, steam-bath building and more traditional methods of catching fish on the Kenai. Several guided tours depart throughout the day.

Fishing
Most of the fishing on the Upper Kenai is for rainbow trout, Dolly Varden, and silver and sockeye salmon. Expect to pay at least $150 for a half-day on the water and more than $200 for a full day.

Alaska River Adventures   FISHING
(☑888-836-9027; www.alaskariveradventures.com; Mile 47.9, Sterling Hwy) Guided fishing for $275 per day.

Alaska Rivers Company   FISHING
(☑888-595-1226; www.alaskariverscompany.com; Mile 49.9, Sterling Hwy) Offers half-day and full-day fishing for $120/220.

Hiking
Cooper Landing is the starting point for two of the Kenai Peninsula's loveliest multiday trails: the 39-mile Resurrection Pass Trail (p235) to Hope; and the 21-mile Russian Lakes Trail (p65), a favorite for fishers and families. This is serious bear country. It is recommended that you bring good bear protection and make a lot of noise while hiking in the area.

Paddling
Alaska River Adventures   RAFTING
(☑888-836-9027; www.alaskariveradventures.com; Mile 48, Sterling Hwy) Runs scenic three-hour floats on the Kenai (per person $59). Extend the trip with an intro to gold prospecting for $289 per person.

Alaska Rivers Company   RAFTING
(☑888-595-1226; www.alaskariverscompany.com; Mile 49.9, Sterling Hwy) Runs guided raft trips down the Kenai River (per half-/full day $55/150). These are mostly float trips, but the longer paddle bumps over some Class III rapids.

Kenai Lake Sea Kayak Adventures   KAYAKING
(☑907-595-3441; www.kenailake.com; Mile 0.3, Quartz Creek Rd) Has guided three-hour sea-kayak trips on Kenai Lake ($73) that are a good introduction to paddling in a stunning setting.

🛏 Sleeping

Russian River Campground   CAMPGROUND $
(www.recreation.gov; Mile 52.6, Sterling Hwy; s/d sites $18/28) Located where the Russian and Kenai Rivers merge, this place is beautiful and incredibly popular when red salmon are spawning; you'll want to reserve one of the 83 sites. It costs $11 just to park here and there's a three-day limit for stays.

Hutch B&B   B&B $
(☑907-598-1270; www.arctic.net/~hutch; Mile 48.5, Sterling Hwy; incl breakfast r $95-109, cabins $225; ⊛@) In a three-story, balcony-ringed lodge, the big, simple, clean rooms are the best deal in town, and its mini mess hall the cutest. Nightly campfires add a social angle.

Cooper Creek Campground   CAMPGROUND $
(☑907-522-8368; www.reserveamerica.com; Mile 50.7, Sterling Hwy; sites $18-28) This campground, nestled in a cottonwood and spruce grove, has 29 sites on both sides of the highway, including some right on the Kenai River. Good luck hooking one of those.

Kenai Riverside Campground & RV Park   CAMPGROUND $
(☑888-536-2478; www.kenairiversidecampground.com; 16918 Sterling Hwy; tent/RV sites $18/35, r $69) Has wooded campsites along the river and six clean and bright rooms with shared baths.

Drifters Lodge   CABIN $$
(☑907-595-5555; www.drifterslodge.com; Mile 48.3, Sterling Hwy; cabins $335-375, r $100-230; ☎) Six tidy and fresh cabins come with memory-foam mattresses, river views and kitchenettes, while five smaller rooms share bathrooms and leafy views. A brook babbles next to the sauna, and there's a nightly campfire. Drifters also takes folks out on the river – a float costs $50 to $75 and fishing trips are $175 to $275.

🍴 Eating

Cooper Landing Grocery   SELF-CATERING $
(Mile 48.2, Sterling Hwy; ⊙10am-8pm) Has scads of snacks and souvenirs.

Gwin's Lodge   AMERICAN **$$**
(☑907-595-1266; www.gwinslodge.com; Mile 52,
Sterling Hwy; $10-30) Established way back in
1952 (that's ancient for Alaska), this chunky-
log roadhouse serves up generous portions
with the friendliest waiters in Cooper's
Landing. The Mexican dishes are a special
treat, and they can make you a bag lunch to
take on the river ($13).

Sackett's Kenai Grill   CAFE **$$**
(16201 Sterling Hwy; sandwiches $6-10, pizza $12-
18; ☺7am-10pm Tue-Sun) Everything here is
made from scratch: from the buns to the
barbecued pork and the pizza dough. It's a
local favorite and a great place to stop before
and after a day on the river.

Kingfisher Roadhouse   SEAFOOD **$$**
(www.letseat.at/kingfisherak; Mile 47.4, Sterling
Hwy; mains $15-30; ☺4:30-10:30pm) Overlook-
ing Kenai Lake, this steak and seafood place
has the best atmosphere in town. If you've
had enough fish, try the organic Kingfisher
Bleus burger; it's the perfect replenishment
after a long hike.

❶ Information

Chamber of Commerce (☑907-595-8888;
www.cooperlandingchamber.com; 19194 Sterling
Hwy) The doors are unlocked when volunteer
staff aren't around; you'll find a few brochures
but the website is actually more informative.
Cooper Landing Library (☑907-595-1241;
www.cooperlandinglibrary.webs.com; Bean
Creek Rd; ☺Mon-Sat) Close to Mile 47.7,
Sterling Hwy; it offers free internet access. It's
worth it just to enjoy the wood stove. Open late
mornings and afternoons.
Wildman's (☑907-595-1456; www.wildmans.
org; Mile 47.5, Sterling Hwy; ☺6am-11pm) Your
basic backcountry superstore, with snacks,

booze, espresso beverages, an ATM, a laundry
and showers ($4).

❶ Getting There & Around

If you're without wheels, your best option for
reaching Cooper Landing is **Homer Stage Line**
(☑907-868-3914; www.stagelineinhomer.com),
which runs daily buses through here from both
Anchorage and Homer. From either end, it's $65
per person one-way.

Kenai National Wildlife Refuge

Once west of the Resurrection Pass trail-
head, you enter the Kenai National Wildlife
Refuge, managed by the US Fish & Wildlife
Service. Originally called the Kenai Nation-
al Moose Range, 1.73 million acres was set
aside by President Roosevelt in 1941, and
the 1980 Alaska Lands Act increased that
acreage to the almost 2 million acres that
it now encompasses. It supports impressive
populations of Dall sheep, moose, caribou
and bear, and has attracted hunters from
around the world since the early 1900s.

Highlights of the area include camping
along Skilak Lake, canoeing through the
Kenai National Wildlife Canoe Trail Sys-
tem and flying or boating in for a weekend
on Tustumena Lake. A massive forest fire
burned more than 300 square miles in the
refuge in 2014, including much of the north-
ern shore of Tustumena Lake.

◉ Sights & Activities

Russian River Ferry   FERRY
(Mile 55, Sterling Hwy; per passenger $10.25) This
ferry, west of the confluence of the Kenai
and Russian Rivers, transports more than

EXPLORING THE REFUGE CANOE TRAIL SYSTEM

One of only two wilderness canoe systems established in the US (the other is the Bound-
ary Waters, Minnesota), the **Kenai National Wildlife Refuge Canoe Trail System**
(www.fws.gov) offers yet another unique experience for the Alaskan visitor. Divided into
two areas, the Swan Lake and the Swanson River routes, the system connects 120 miles
of lakes and water trails in an undulating landscape. Expect there to be as much portag-
ing as paddling.

Swan Lake is the more popular area, covering 60 miles and 30 lakes, and connecting
to the Moose River. The Swanson River route requires longer portages and isn't as well
marked as Swan Lake, but you'll be rewarded for effort with solitude and excellent trout
fishing. This route covers 80 miles, 40 lakes and 46 miles of the Swanson River.

Several outfitters can rent you canoes and paddles: try **Alaska Canoe & Camp-
ground** (☑907-262-2331; www.alaskacanoetrips.com; 35292 Sterling Hwy; canoe per 12/24hr
$45/55, kayak $35/40), which also rents out rafts and kayaks.

30,000 anglers across the water every summer to some of the finest fishing anywhere. It costs $11.25 just to park there; the ferry fee is in addition to that.

Hiking

As the highway heads southwest toward Soldotna, the mountains will fade back. You can still hit up a few good hiking trails before that happens, though.

Fuller Lakes Trail   HIKING

(Mile 57, Sterling Hwy) This 3-mile hike leads to Fuller Lake just above the treeline. The well-marked trail begins with a rapid ascent to Lower Fuller Lake, where you cross a stream over a beaver dam and continue over a low pass to Upper Fuller Lake.

At the lake, the trail follows the east shore and then branches; the fork to the left leads up a ridge and becomes a route to the Skyline Trail.

Skyline Trail   HIKING

(Mile 61, Sterling Hwy) This route ascends above the treeline and then follows a ridge on an unmarked and unmaintained route for 0.5 miles before connecting with the Fuller Lakes Trail. Those who want to hike both trails should plan to stay overnight at Upper Fuller Lake, where there are several good campsites.

Skilak Lake Road

Skilak Lake Rd, a scenic 19-mile loop off the Sterling Hwy, is a bit too rough for low-clearance vehicles outside summer. It provides access to an assortment of popular recreational opportunities.

Kenai River Trail   HIKING

(Mile 0.6, Skilak Lake Rd) A half mile down this trail are wonderful views of the Kenai River Canyon.

Skilak Lookout Trail   HIKING

(Mile 5.5, Skilak Lake Rd) Ascends 2.6 miles to a knob (elevation 1450ft) that has a panoramic view of the mountains and lakes. Plan on four to five hours for the round-trip.

Seven Lakes Trail   HIKING

(Engineer Lake, Mile 9.5, Skilak Lake Rd) A 4.4-mile hike to the Sterling Hwy. The trail is easy walking over level terrain and passes Hidden and Hikers lakes before ending at Kelly Lake Campground.

🛏 Sleeping

There are five campgrounds along Skilak Lake Rd. Some, such as Hidden Lake and Upper Skilak, cost $10 to $14. The campgrounds are well marked, running from east to west:

CAMPGROUND	SITES	LOCATION
Hidden Lake	44	Mile 3.6
Upper Skilak Lake	25	Mile 8.4
Lower Ohmer Lake	3	Mile 8.6
Engineer Lake	4	Mile 9.7
Lower Skilak Lake	14	Mile 14

If you choose to stay on the Sterling Hwy past the Skilak Lake Rd junction, a side road at Mile 69 leads south to the Peterson Lake Campground (www.recreation.gov; campsites free) and Kelly Lake Campground (campsites free), near one end of the Seven Lakes Trail. Watson Lake Campground (Mile 71.3 Sterling Hwy; campsites free) has three sites. Four miles down the highway is the west junction with Skilak Lake Rd.

At Mile 81, the Sterling Hwy divides into a four-lane road, and you soon arrive in the small town of Sterling (population 1800), where Moose River empties into the Kenai. Izaak Walton Recreation Site (www.dnr. alaska.gov; Mile 82 Sterling Hwy; campsites $10), at the confluence of the Kenai and Moose Rivers, is popular among anglers during the salmon runs and with paddlers ending their Swan Lake route canoe trip at the Moose River Bridge.

Swanson River Road, at Mile 85 of the Sterling Hwy, heads north for 18 miles, with Swan Lake Rd heading east for 12 miles at the end of Swanson River Rd. The roads offer access to the Swanson River and Swan Lake canoe routes, and three campgrounds: Dolly Varden Lake Campground (Mile 14 Swanson River Rd; campsites free), Rainbow Lake Campground (Mile 16 Swanson River Rd; campsites free) and Swanson River Campground (www.alaska.org/detail/swanson-river-campground; campsites free) at the very end of the road. Even without a canoe, you'll enjoy exploring the trails that connect prized fishing holes.

Across the Sterling Hwy from Swanson River Rd is the entrance to Scout Lake Rd, where you'll find the Scout Lake Campground (campsites $10) and Morgans Landing State Recreation Area (www.dnr.alaska. gov/parks/aspunits/kenai/morgldcamp.htm; campsites $10). This is a particularly scenic

KENAI PENINSULA KENAI NATIONAL WILDLIFE REFUGE

NICK HALL / GETTY IMAGES ©

1. Salmon fisher 2. Roasting marshmallows, Homer (p245)
3. Seward Highway

LUCAS PAYNE / DESIGN PICS / GETTY IMAGES ©

Kenai Peninsula Highlights

With mountains, glaciers, ice fields, fjords, rivers and lakes, there are at least a summer's worth of recreational opportunities in the rugged and accessible Kenai Peninsula. The friendly villages of Homer, Hope and Seward provide shelter before you head into the wilds in a land the size of a small European country. Here are a few of our favorite sights and activities.

Road Tripping

A 126-mile road trip that could last all day – or all week! Driving the Seward Highway gives you the chance to spot Dall sheep, beluga whales, moose, glacial streams and even a bore tide. Stop along the way to hook sockeye salmon, head out for a day hike or jaw drop at the wonders of the Great Land.

Into the Fjords

Witness calving tidewater glaciers, toppling icebergs, breaching whales, whispering waterfalls, and about a million birds and playful sea otters on a boat or kayak tour of Kenai Fjords National Park. Most visitors only see a tiny percentage of this vast wilderness.

Arctic Art

Explore the cozy cafes, spirited jam sessions, uproarious bonfires and thoughtful galleries of the peninsula's arts capital in the lyrical fairyland of Homer. Glaciers, lost trails and watery adventures await out your door on the other side of Kachemak Bay.

The Resurrection

The maritime village of Seward offers easy access to remarkable hikes that take you to precipitous heights above Resurrection Bay. Test your lungs with a run to the top of Mt Marathon, home to Alaska's most famous footrace.

area on the bluffs overlooking the Kenai River, a 3.5-mile drive from the Sterling Hwy.

There are 14 public use cabins in the refuge. Get more information at Refuge Headquarters in Soldotna.

ℹ️ Information

Kenai National Wildlife Refuge Visitor Contact Station (Mile 58 Sterling Hwy; ⊗10am-4pm), near the junction of Skilak Lake Rd, has up-to-date information on camping, hiking, canoeing and fishing throughout the refuge. They may close the station, in which case, you'll want to contact Refuge Headquarters in Soldotna.

Soldotna

POP 4359

With its strip malls and fast-food chains, Soldotna is ugly as ugly gets, and its flat nearby topography offers very little for hikers, bikers or adventurers. But the Kenai River runs right through town, making this one of the Peninsula's premier fishing outposts.

Most years, you'll be competing with hundreds of anglers for prime shoreline. But the opportunity to hook some of the biggest salmon in the state make it worthwhile – note that recent King Salmon closures have serious anglers looking elsewhere.

Situated where the Sterling Hwy crosses the Kenai River, Soldotna sprawls in every direction, including practically to the city of Kenai, some 12 miles northwest along the Kenai Spur Hwy. The intersection of the Spur Hwy and the Sterling Hwy is referred to as the 'Y.'

◉ Sights

Soldotna Homestead Museum　　MUSEUM
(☑907-262-3832; 44790 Sterling Hwy; entry by donation; ⊗10am-4pm Tue-Sat, from noon Sun) **FREE** This museum includes a wonderful collection of homesteaders' cabins spread through six wooded acres in Centennial Park. Ask for a free guided tour to discover the stories of early homesteaders who were awarded plots here after WWII.

There's also a one-room schoolhouse, a torture-chamber collection of early dental tools, an excellent natural history display with archaeological finds and a replica of the $7.2-million check the US paid Russia for Alaska.

Kenai National Wildlife Refuge Headquarters　　PARK
(☑907-262-7021; www.kenai.fws.gov; 1 Ski Hill Rd, Soldotna) Opposite Kalifornsky Beach Rd near the Kenai River is the junction with Funny River Rd. Follow signs to Ski Hill Rd, following it for a mile to reach this excellent, kid-friendly information center that has an exhibit hall, bookstore and 2.2 miles of trails that wrap around the nearby lake.

It features displays on the life cycles of salmon, daily wildlife films and naturalist-led outdoor programs.

🏃 Activities

Fishing

From mid-May through September, runs of red, silver and king salmon make the lower Kenai River among the hottest sportfishing spots in Alaska. King Salmon levels on the Kenai River have been lower than normal since 2009, and the **Alaska Department of Fish & Game** (☑907-465-4180; www.adfg.alaska.gov) heavily restricted king salmon fishing on the river in 2013 and 2014. Check ahead for openings, bank closures and the latest news.

If you're green to the scene but want to wet a line, first drop by the visitors center where staff members will assist you in determining where to fish and what to fish for. They can also hook you up with a guide, who'll charge you up to $300 a day but vastly improve your chances of catching dinner – and of not violating the river's multilayered regulations.

Rather go it alone? From the shore, you've still got a shot at catching reds (from mid-July to early August) and silvers (late July through August). Try casting from the 'fishwalk' below the visitors center, or from city campgrounds. If you don't have your own rod, you can pick up inexpensive gear from **Trustworthy Hardware** (☑907-262-4655; 44370 Sterling Hwy; ⊗8am-8pm Mon-Fri, 9am-6pm Sat, 10am-6pm Sun), right across the highway from PJ's Klondike Diner.

🛏️ Sleeping

Spending the night in Soldotna is a catch-22. Outside fishing season there's no reason to stay here; in season, there's nowhere to stay – just about every campsite and room is taken. What's left will cost you dearly. Make reservations. The chamber of commerce can locate last-minute rooms. The **Kenai Penin-**

sula B&B Association (www.kenaipeninsula bba.com) has listings for the entire peninsula.

Diamond M Ranch
RESORT $

(☎ 866-283-9424; www.diamondmranch.com; Mile 16.5, Kalifornsky Beach Rd; RV sites $30-40, r $70-149, cabins $99-159; ☺ 🛜) Fifteen years ago, this was just the Martin family farm – but with fishermen constantly asking to camp in their field, the Martins converted it to a tourist megaplex, complete with kids' programs, walking tours, movie nights and horse rides.

If you get up early enough, you can help milk the cows that share the 80 acres with an extensive campground, cabins and full B&B.

Centennial Park Campground
CAMPGROUND $

(☎ 907-262-5299; www.ci.soldotna.ak.us; cnr Sterling Hwy & Kalifornsky Beach Rd; tent & RV sites $17) Maintained by the city, this 176-site campground has boardwalked fishing access to the Kenai River. The day-use fee is $6.

Swiftwater Park Campground
CAMPGROUND $

(☎ 907-262-5299; www.ci.soldotna.ak.us; cnr E Redoubt Ave & Rinehart St; tent & RV sites $17) Run by the city; it doesn't have a boardwalk but is still a good place for pulling in prized salmon. If you just want to fish, it's $6 to park for the day.

Kenai River Lodge
HOTEL $$

(☎ 907-262-4292, www.kenairiverlodge.com; 393 Riverside Dr; r $149-189; ☺ 🛜) Has a private fishing hole right outside and delicious river views – though the road noise can be a bit much. All rooms come with coffee, microwave and fridge. It's worth it to splurge for the river-facing rooms.

Soldotna B&B Lodge
B&B $$$

(☎ 877-262-4779; www.alaskafishinglodges.us; 399 Lovers Lane; r $99-357; ☺ 🛜) This is the town's top luxury spot, drawing blue-chip anglers and honeymooners. It has plush rooms, custom adventure and fishing packages, and some rooms without baths. There's breakfast in a riverfront sunroom and a private fishing hole for reds.

✕ Eating & Drinking

Odie's Deli
DELI $

(44315 Sterling Hwy; sandwiches $9-11; ☺ 7am-4pm) Try whimsical cupcakes (like the Breakfast in Bed: maple and bacon) and build-your-own-sandwiches on homemade bread.

Moose is Loose
CAFE $

(44278 Sterling Hwy; snacks $2-7; ☺ 7am-4pm Tue-Sun) This Moose comes with coffee and goodies galore, including a huge array of fresh doughnuts.

Fred Meyer
SELF-CATERING $

(43843 Sterling Hwy) This supermarket has a deli, a salad bar, a bakery, espresso and any camping gear that you forgot.

PJ's Klondike Diner
DINER $

(44619 Sterling Hwy; breakfast & lunch $5-9, dinner $9-14; ☺ 24hr) Soldotna's best stab at a tourist trap, this diner is jammed with weary travelers, gabbing locals and frantic waitresses. The meals aren't as tasty as they are ample.

St Elias Brewing Company
PIZZA $$

(434 Sharkathmi Ave; dinner $8-14; ☺ 11am-11pm) Stone-fired pizzas and sandwiches served in an echoing brewery with a big patio. Delicious. Beer-lovers should order the sampler. Expect the service to be poor.

Mykel's
SEAFOOD $$$

(☎ 907-262-4305; www.mykels.com; dinner $18-34; ☺ 11am-11pm) This is Soldotna's fanciest place, with high-backed leather booths and dishes such as walnut-crusted salmon with a raspberry beurre blanc.

ⓘ Information

Central Peninsula General Hospital (☎ 907-262-4404; Marydale Dr) Just west of the Kenai Spur Hwy.

Joyce Carver Memorial Library (235 S Binkley St; ☺ 9am-8pm Mon-Thu, noon-6pm Fri, from 9am Sat; 🛜) Near the post office; has free internet access with an ID.

Post Office (175 S Binkley St) Just west of the Kenai Spur Hwy and north of the Soldotna 'Y.'

Soldotna Chamber of Commerce & Visitors Center (☎ 907-262-9814; www.visitsoldotna. com; 44790 Sterling Hwy; ☺ 9am-7pm; 🛜) Has internet plus up-to-date fishing reports and a nice boardwalk along the river.

Wash & Dry (121 Smith Way; ☺ 24hr summer; 🛜) Near the intersection of the Kenai Spur and Sterling Hwys at the Soldotna 'Y'; has showers ($5), laundry and free wi-fi.

Wells Fargo (44552 Sterling Hwy) Has cash and an eclectic collection of historical exhibits.

ⓘ Getting There & Around

Homer Stage Line (☎ 907-868-3914; www. stagelineinhomer.com) buses pass through daily en route to Anchorage ($70) and Homer ($50).

KENAI PENINSULA SOLDOTNA

Kenai & Around

POP 7452

At first blush, Kenai is a sorry sight – an object lesson in poor city planning. It's not convenient – 10 miles northwest of Soldotna and the Sterling Hwy – or especially picturesque, existing primarily as a support community for the drilling operations at Cook Inlet.

It's long been a rare bird: a major Alaskan city with minimal tourism. Lately, though, this faded boomtown has taken some hesitant steps toward wooing visitors – especially those tantalized by the excellent salmon fishing that takes place at the mouth of the Kenai River.

The first Russian Orthodox Church on mainland Alaska today presides over a replica of the 1867 fort, which hasn't fully realized its potential as adorable tourist magnet. And then there's the view: Mt Redoubt (the volcano that erupted steam and ash in December 1989) to the southwest, Mt Iliamna at the head of the Aleutian Range and the Alaska Range to the northwest. Nice.

North of town, around Mile 19 of the Kenai Spur Hwy, is Alaska's largest concentration of oil infrastructure outside Prudhoe Bay.

◉ Sights & Activities

Kenai Visitors & Cultural Center
CULTURAL CENTER

(☑ 907-283-1991; www.visitkenai.com; 11471 Kenai Spur Hwy; ⊙ 9am-5pm Tue-Fri, 10am-4pm Sun) **FREE** This excellent visitors center is among Kenai's main attractions. The museum features historical exhibits on the city's Russian heritage, offshore drilling and a room full of stuffed wildlife staring down from the rafters. It also has quality Alaska Native art from around the state. Free movies about the city's strange history are screened, and docents offer summer interpretive programs.

Old Town Kenai
HISTORIC SITE

From the visitors center, follow Overland Ave west to what locals refer to as 'Old Town' – an odd amalgam of historic structures and low-rent apartments, all stupendously situated high above the mouth of the Kenai River. You can pick up a free *Walking Tour* pamphlet at the visitors center.

Near Cook Inlet, the US military established **Fort Kenay** in 1867 and stationed more than 100 men here. What stands today is a replica constructed as part of the Alaska Centennial in 1967. It's not open to the public.

Across Mission St from the fort is the ornate **Russian Orthodox Church**, a white-clapboard structure topped with baby blue onion domes. Built in 1895, it's the oldest Orthodox church on mainland Alaska. It was renovated in 2009. Staff at the visitor center can call to check the hours for you. West of the church overlooking the water is **St Nicholas Chapel**, built in 1906 on the burial site of Father Igumen Nicolai, Kenai's first resident priest.

Head southeast on Mission St, and you'll be traveling along the **Bluff**, a good vantage point to view the mouth of the Kenai River or the mountainous terrain on the west side of Cook Inlet. Look for belugas in the late spring and early summer.

Kenai Beach
BEACH

Down below the bluffs is an oddity in Alaska: a sweeping, sandy beach, ideal for picnicking, Frisbee-chucking and other waterfront fun. There are stellar views of the volcanoes across the inlet, and from July 10 to 31 you can watch hundreds of frantic fishermen dip-net for sockeye salmon at the mouth of the Kenai River. Sadly, unless you've lived in Alaska for the past year, you can't participate.

Captain Cook State Recreation Area
PARK

By following the Kenai Spur Hwy north for 36 miles, you'll first pass the trailer parks and chemical plants of the North Kenai industrial district before reaching this uncrowded state recreation area that encompasses 4000 acres of forests, lakes, rivers and beaches along Cook Inlet.

The area offers swimming, camping and the beauty of the inlet in a setting that is unaffected by the stampede for salmon to the south.

The Kenai Spur Hwy ends in the park after first passing Stormy Lake, where you'll find a bathhouse and a swimming area along the water's edge. **Discovery Campground** (☑ 907-522-8368; www.dnr.alaska. gov; campsites $10) has 53 sites on the bluff overlooking Cook Inlet, where some of the world's greatest tides ebb and flow. The fishing in Swanson River is great, and this is a fine place to end the Swan Lake canoe route (p70).

Kenai River Estuary
BIRDWATCHING

(Boat Launch Rd, 1 mile south of town) This beautiful estuary with its own viewing platform is an excellent spot for birdwatching. Get here by heading 1 mile south of town along the bike path on Bridge Access Rd, then turning west onto Boat Launch Rd.

🛏 Sleeping

Finding last-minute rooms during summer's salmon runs can be more challenging than hauling in a 70-pounder, but for help log onto the website of Kenai Peninsula B&B Association (www.kenaipeninsulabba.com). If you're on a tight budget, head north along the Kenai Spur Hwy, where several motels cater to oil workers and offer lower rates. Kenai adds 10% in bed-and-sales tax.

Beluga Lookout Lodge & RV Park
CAMPGROUND $

(☑907-283-5999; www.belugalookout.com; 929 Mission St; tent sites $30, RV sites $45-75, r $129-149; 🐾) This campground expanded into a 'lodge' in 2009 and now has superclean (if a bit small) rooms that have either ocean or river views. The campground is little more than a parking lot with a nice view. There's also a gift shop, as well as a laundry, showers and a nice covered sitting area for gazing at the ocean.

Uptown Motel
MOTEL $$

(☑907 283 3660; www.uptownmotel.com; 47 Spur View Dr; r $169-179; @🐾) The rooms here are clean and the very cool lobby is full of antiques, including an old barber's chair and cash register.

🍴 Eating & Drinking

Veronica's Coffee House
CAFE $

(604 Peterson Way; light meals $3-8; ⊙7am-4pm) In an Old Town log building dating from 1918, Veronica's serves espressos and healthy sandwiches and hosts open mics, folk jams and live bands. There's a warm wooden sun porch filled with flowers – the best place in town to relax with a sandwich.

Charlotte's Restaurant
CAFE $

(115 Willow St; ⊙7am-3pm) Grab sandwiches or just some fresh-baked goodies for your beach picnic.

Safeway
SELF-CATERING $

(10576 Kenai Spur Hwy; ⊙24hr) Offers the usual groceries, plus it has a deli and salad bar.

Louie's Restaurant
STEAKHOUSE $$$

(☑907-283-3660; 47 Spur View Dr; dinner $19-29; ⊙5am-10pm) Under stuffed moose and elk heads in the Uptown Motel, Louie's serves the best surf-and-turf in the city.

ℹ Information

Alaska USA Bank (☑800-525-9094; 230 Kenai Spur Hwy; ⊙10am-6pm Mon-Sat) Has a 24-hour ATM.

Central Peninsula General Hospital (☑907-262-4404; Marydale Dr) Just west of the Kenai Spur Hwy.

Kenai Community Library (☑907-283-4378; 163 Main St Loop; ⊙10am-8pm Mon-Thu, to 5pm Fri & Sat; 🐾) Has free internet access; bring an ID.

Post Office (140 Bidarka St) Just north of the Kenai Spur Hwy.

Wash-n-Dry (☑907-283-8473; 502 Lake St; ⊙8am-10pm) Has a laundry and showers ($5.30).

ℹ Getting There & Around

Kenai has the main airport on the peninsula and is served by Ravn Alaska (p219), which offers multiple daily flights between Anchorage and Kenai. The round-trip fare is between $170 and $210 with ongoing service to other rural destinations.

Homer Stage Line (☑907-868-3914; www.stagelineinhomer.com) buses make daily trips departing from Kenai to Seward ($50).

For taxis, Alaska Cabs (☑907-283-6000) serves Kenai and Soldotna.

South to Homer

After you pass Soldotna, traffic thins out as the Sterling Hwy rambles south, hugging the coastline and opening up to grand views of Cook Inlet. This stretch is 78 miles long and it passes through a handful of small villages near some great clamming areas, ending at the charming town of Homer.

Heading south from Soldotna, stop for an afternoon of fishing, boating and hiking at the 332-acre Johnson Lake State Recreation Area (www.dnr.alaska.gov/parks/aspunits/kenai/johnsonlksra.htm). There's an excellent campsite here, too, with 51 lakeview sites.

Take your time in this area; the coastline and Homer are worth every day you decide to spend here.

Ninilchik

POP 883

This appealing little village is well worth spending a night. The community is among the oldest on the Kenai Peninsula, having been settled in the 1820s by employees of the Russian-American Company. Many stayed even after imperial Russia sold Alaska to the US, and their descendants form the heart of the present community.

◉ Sights & Activities

The main event held in Ninilchik is the **Kenai Peninsula State Fair** (www.kenaipeninsulafair.com), the 'biggest little fair in Alaska,' which takes place annually in mid-August.

Old Ninilchik Village   HISTORIC SITE

The site of the original community, this is a postcard scene of faded log cabins in tall grass and beached fishing boats against the spectacular backdrop of Mt Redoubt.

Old Russian Church   CHURCH

Reached via a posted footpath behind the Village Cache Gift Shop, the historic bluff-top structure was built in 1901. It sports five golden onion domes, and commands an unbelievable view of Cook Inlet and the volcanoes on the other side. Adjoining it is a prim Russian Orthodox cemetery of white-picket cribs.

DIGGING FOR CLAMS

Almost all the beaches on the west side of the Kenai Peninsula (Clam Gulch, Deep Creek, Ninilchik and Whiskey Gulch) have a good supply of razor clams, considered by mollusk connoisseurs to be a true delicacy. Not only do razors have the best flavor, but they're also among the largest of the mollusks. The average razor clam is 3.5in long.

To clam, you first have to purchase a sportfishing license (one-/seven-day visitor's license $20/55). The daily bag limit is 60 clams, but that's an awful lot of clams to clean and eat. Two dozen per person is more than enough for a meal. While the clamming is good from April to August, the best time is July, right before spawning. And though you can dig for clams any time the tide is out, the best clamming is during extra-low, 'minus,' tides. Consult a tide book – and count on hundreds of other clammers to do the same.

Equipment You'll need a narrow-bladed clam shovel that can either be purchased or rented at many lodges and stores near the clamming areas. You'll also want rubber boots, rubber gloves, a bucket and a pair of pants to which you're not terribly attached.

Finding clams Play detective. Look for the clam's 'footprint,' a dimple mark left behind when it withdraws its neck. That's your clue to the clam's whereabouts, but don't dig directly below the imprint or you'll break its shell. You have to be quick, as a razor clam can bury itself and be gone in seconds.

Preparation Once you're successful, leave the clams in a bucket of seawater or better yet beer, for several hours to allow them to 'clean themselves.' Many locals say a handful of cornmeal helps this process. The best way to cook clams is right on the beach over an open fire while you're taking in the mountain scenery. Use a large covered pot and steam the clams in saltwater or, for more flavor, in white wine with a clove of garlic.

Here's where to go:

Clam Gulch This is the most popular and, many say, most productive spot by far. The Clam Gulch State Recreation Area is a half-mile from Mile 118 of the Sterling Hwy, where there's a short access road to the beach from the campground.

Ninilchik The best bet is to camp at Ninilchik View State Campground, located above the old village of Ninilchik. From there, you can walk to beaches for clamming.

Deep Creek Just south of Ninilchik is the Deep Creek State Recreation Site, where there's camping and plenty of parking along the beach.

Whiskey Gulch Look for the turnoff at about Mile 154 of the Sterling Hwy. Unless you have a 4WD, park at the elbow-turn above the beach.

Mud Bay On the east side of Homer Spit is Mud Bay, a stretch abundant with eastern soft-shells, cockles and blue mussels. Some surf clams (rednecks) and razor clams can also be found on the Cook Inlet side of the Spit.

Clamming

OUTDOORS

(clamming license $16) Clamming is Ninilchik's number-one summer pastime. At low tide, go to **Ninchilik Beach State Recreation Site**, across the river from the old village, or **Deep Creek State Recreation Site**. It costs $5 to park at the state recreation areas. You need a fishing license. You can purchase a shovel and bucket ($5) and a sportfishing license ($20) at the Ninilchik General Store.

🛏 Sleeping & Eating

Ninilchik View State Campground   CAMPGROUND $

(www.dnr.alaska.gov/parks/aspunits/kenai/ninil-vwcamp.htm; Mile 135.5, Sterling Hwy; tent & RV sites $10) By far the best of Ninilchik's public campgrounds, it's set atop a wooded bluff with a view of the old village and Cook Inlet. A stairway leads down to the beach.

Ninilchik River Campground   CAMPGROUND $

(www.dnr.alaska.gov/parks/aspunits/kenai/ninilrv-camp.htm; Mile 134.9, Sterling Hwy; tent & RV sites $10) Across the Sterling Hwy from Coal St; this campground has great river access and some pleasant trails.

Alaskan Angler RV Resort   CABIN $$

(☑800-347-4114; www.afishhunt.com; Kingsley Rd; tent/RV sites $15/42, cabins $150-185) A privately owned place with on-site fish processing. There is a tenting area back in the trees, and guests who are traveling without their own gear onboard are able to rent rods and reels ($10), hip boots ($5) and clam shovels ($5).

Roscoe's Pizza   PIZZA $$

(15915 Sterling Hwy; pizza $12-25; ⊘ lunch & dinner) Hand-tossed dough made from scratch makes this a perfect place to fill up after a day of clam slamming.

ℹ Information

Alaskan Angler RV Resort (☑800-347-4114; Kingsley Rd) For a shower ($2) or laundry.

Ninilchik General Store (☑907-567-3378; Mile 135.7, Sterling Hwy; ⊘9am-10pm) Has an ATM, lots of fishing and camping gear, and you will find a few tourist-oriented brochures posted out the front of the store.

Homer

POP 5310

Lucky is the visitor who drives into Homer on a clear day. As the Sterling Hwy descends into town, a panorama of mountains sweeps across the horizon in front of you. The Homer Spit slowly comes into view, jutting into a glittering Kachemak Bay, and just when you think the view might unwind forever, it ends with the dramatic Grewingk Glacier.

Hearing travelers' tales of Homer, you half expect to find lotus-eaters and mermaids lounging about. At first blush, though, Homer's decidedly feminine appeal might not be evident. The city isn't overhung with mountains like Seward, nor does it have the quaint townscape of Cordova. It sprawls a bit and is choked with tourists; it isn't lushly forested, it lacks legendary hikes, and it has a windswept waterfront that makes kayaking a bitch. And then there's the Homer Spit – a tourist trap you may love to hate.

Stick around for a bit, however, and Homer will make you a believer. There's the panorama, and the promise that it holds. Across Kachemak Bay, glaciers and peaks and fjords beckon – a trekkers' and paddlers' playground to which Homer is the port of entry.

And then there's the vibe: the town is a magnet for radicals, artists and folks disillusioned with mainstream society, who've formed a critical mass here, dreaming up a sort of utopian vision for their city, and striving – with grins on their faces – to enact it. Because of that, this is the arts capital of Southcentral Alaska, with great galleries, museums, theater and music.

Homer lies at the end of the Sterling Hwy, 233 road miles from Anchorage. For tourists, there are two distinct sections of town. The 'downtown' area, built on a hill between high bluffs to the north and Kachemak Bay to the south, lies along – or near – busy Pioneer Ave. Heading eastward, Pioneer Ave becomes rural East End Rd, with a number of other lodging and eating options. The second section of Homer, and certainly the most notorious, is the Homer Spit, a skinny tongue of sand licking halfway across Kachemak Bay.

History

Homer was founded, and picked up its name, when Homer Pennock, an adventurer from Michigan, landed on the Spit with a crew of gold-seekers in 1896, convinced that Kachemak Bay was the key to their riches. It wasn't, and Pennock was soon lured to the Klondike, where he also failed to find gold. Three years later the Cook Inlet Coal Field Company established the first of a succession of coal mines in the area. It was fishing, though, that would come to dominate the town's economy for most of the 1900s.

Homer

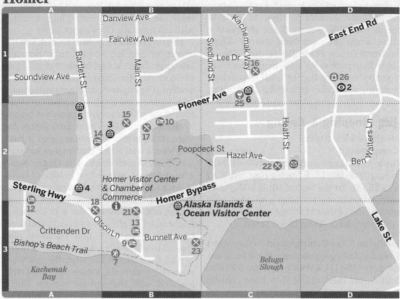

KENAI PENINSULA HOMER

Homer

◎ Sights

Homer Spit NEIGHBORHOOD
(Map p250) Generally known as 'the Spit', this long needle of land – a 4.5-mile sand bar stretching into Kachemak Bay – is viewed by some folks as the most fun place in Alaska. Others wish another earthquake would come along and sink the thing. Regardless, the Spit throbs all summer with tourists.

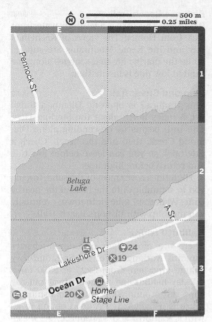

rods ($10 to $20) as well as rakes and shovels (each $5) for clamming.

⭐ **Alaska Islands &**
Ocean Visitor Center   MUSEUM

(Map p246; ☏ 907-235-6961; www.islandsand-ocean.org; 95 Sterling Hwy; ⊙ 9am-5pm) FREE More a research facility and museum than a visitor center, this impressive place has numerous cool interactive exhibits. The best is a room that's a replica seabird colony, complete with cacophonous bird calls and surround-view flocking.

There's also a decent film about ship-based marine research, a hands-on discovery lab, a pole that shows Homer's tides in real time, and a slate of daily educational programs and guided walks (they even have loner binoculars for free).

Pratt Museum   MUSEUM

(Map p246; ☏ 907-235-8635; www.prattmuseum.org; 3779 Bartlett St; adult/child $8/4; ⊙ 10am-6pm) There's lots of local art and Alaska Native artifacts, but a more impressive feature is the interactive displays on the area's wild life, designed to mesmerize both kids and ex-kids. More sobering is the Storm Warning Theater, with harrowing tales about fishing on Kachemak Bay, where making a living can end your life.

More light-hearted and whimsical, and perhaps the coolest aspect of the museum, is the Forest Ecology Trail, where artists can contribute to the 'Facing the Elements' exhibit. Paths wind through the trees, and you'll stumble upon small exhibits, be they mirrors, rocks or pottery. A must-do.

The Pratt also offers 1½-hour **harbor tours** (Map p250; tours $10) throughout summer at 3pm Friday and Saturday, leaving from the Salty Dawg Saloon (p254).

Alaskan Coastal
Studies Center   CULTURAL CENTER

(Map p246; ☏ 907-235-6667; www.akcoastalstudies.org; 708 Smokey Way; ⊙ 9am-5pm Mon-Fri) FREE This nonprofit organization devoted to promoting appreciation of Kachemak Bay's ecosystem, runs the Carl E Wynn Nature Center and the Peterson Bay Field Station ($140 day tour), both of which offer guided hikes and educational programs throughout the summer.

It also operates the **Yurt on the Spit** (Map p250; Homer Spit Rd; ⊙ noon-5pm), right behind Mako's Water-Taxi, which does a daily 'Creatures of the Dock' tour at 1pm and 4pm ($5).

They mass here in unimaginable density, gobbling fish-and-chips, purchasing alpaca sweaters, arranging bear-watching trips, watching theatrical performances and – oh yeah – going fishing in search of 300lb halibut. The hub of all this activity is the small-boat harbor, one of the best facilities in Southcentral Alaska and home to more than 700 boats. Close by is the **Seafarer's Memorial** (Map p250), which, amid all the Spit's hubbub, is a solemn monument to residents lost at sea.

Beachcombing, bonfiring, bald-eagle watching (they seem as common here as pigeons in New York City) and observing recently docked fishermen angling for cute tourist chicks at the Salty Dawg Saloon are all favorite activities. You can also go clamming at Mud Bay, on the east side of the Spit. Blue mussels, an excellent shellfish overlooked by many people, are the most abundant.

If you'd rather catch your dinner than buy it, try your luck at the **Fishing Hole**, just before the Pier One Theater. The small lagoon is the site of a 'terminal fishery,' in which salmon are planted by the state and return three or four years later to a place where they can't spawn. **Sportsman's Supply & Rental** (Map p250; ☏ 907-235-2617; 1114 Freight Dock Rd; ⊙ 6am-midnight), close by, rents out

KENAI PENINSULA HOMER

Carl E Wynn Nature Center
NATURE RESERVE

(Skyline Dr; adult/child $7/5; ⊙10am-6pm) Situated on the bluffs above Homer, this moose-ridden 140-acre reserve is highly recommended for families and anyone interested in the area's ethnobotany – though the price tag is a little steep.

With a few short interpretive nature trails, one of them boardwalked and wheelchair accessible, this is a grand place to learn which plants can be used to heal a cut, condition your hair or munch for lunch. Naturalist-led hikes leave at 10am and 2pm daily in summer. It also has a slate of lectures and other programs; call the center for a schedule.

🏃 Activities

Hiking

For all its natural beauty, Homer has few good public trails (though hiking across the Bay is awesome). For a map of short hiking routes around town, pick up the *Walking Guide to the Homer Area* at the visitor center.

Homestead Trail
HIKING

(Map p250) This 6.7-mile trek from Rogers Loop Rd (accessed one mile north of town on the Sterling Hwy) is probably the best in town, taking you via boardwalk and singletrack to large meadows with panoramic views of Kachemak Bay, and Mt Iliamna and Mt Redoubt on the other side of Cook Inlet.

They maintain cross-country trails here in winter.

Bishop's Beach Trail
HIKING

(Map p246) This hike is a leisurely waterfront trek from Homer. The views of Kachemak Bay and the Kenai Mountains are superb, while the marine life that scurries along the sand at low tide is fascinating.

Diamond Creek Trail
HIKING

This trailhead is opposite Diamond Ridge Rd, 5 miles north along the Sterling Hwy. The trail begins by descending along Diamond Creek, then hits the beach. Check a tide book so you can leave before low tide and return before high tide.

High tides cover most of the sand, forcing you to scramble onto the base of the nearby cliffs. Walk the 7 miles into town; eventually you meet up with Bishop's Beach Trail.

Halibut Fishing

There are more than two dozen charter captains working out of the Spit, and they charge anywhere from $225 to $350 for a full-day halibut and salmon trip – half-day trips run around $150 and your fishing license is usually extra. A good option to go with is **Rainbow Tours** (Map p250; ☎907-235-7272; www.rainbowtours.net; Homer Spit Rd), but peruse the board beside the Halibut Derby Office; it lists the biggest fish caught that summer, along with who captained the boat. Other than that, the biggest distinction between the charter operations is vessel size: bigger boats bounce around less when the waves kick, meaning greater comfort and

KENAI PENINSULA HOMER

HOMER ART GALLERIES

The cold, dark season of unemployment has inspired a saying in these parts: 'If you're starving, you might as well be an artist.' Just browsing these great galleries is a treat, and on the first Friday of the month, many break out the wine and cheese, and stay open late for a series of openings all over town. This is just the tip of the iceberg – grab a free *Downtown Homer Art Galleries* flyer at the visitors center with many more gallery listings, or stop by the **Homer Council of the Arts** (Map p246; ☎907-235-4288; www.homerart.org; 355 W Pioneer Ave; ⊙1-5pm Mon-Fri), with its own awesome gallery and information on various tours, artist-in-residence programs and guerilla installations throughout town.

Art Shop Gallery (Map p246; www.artshopgallery.com; 202 W Pioneer Ave; ⊙10am-7pm Mon-Sat, 11am-5pm Sun) Alaskan art.

Bunnell Street Gallery (Map p246; ☎907-235-2662; www.bunnellstreetgallery.org; 106 W Bunnell Ave; ⊙11am-6pm Mon-Sat, noon-4pm Sun) The town's best gallery.

Fireweed Gallery (Map p246; ☎907-235-3411; www.fireweedgallery.com; 475 E Pioneer Ave; ⊙10am-6pm Mon-Sat, 11am-5pm Sun) This gallery can get good local wares.

Ptarmigan Arts (Map p246; ☎907-235-5345; www.ptarmiganarts.com; 471 E Pioneer Ave; ⊙10am-7pm Mon-Sat, to 6pm Sun) Local cooperative gallery.

NIKOLAEVSK & NORMAN LOWELL STUDIO

Tucked inconspicuously down a winding road from Anchor Point sits one of several Russian Old Believer Villages on the Kenai Peninsula. The Old Believers are members of a sect that split from mainstream Russian Orthodoxy in the 1650s, defending their 'old beliefs' in the face of what they considered heretical reforms. Long considered outcasts in Russia, they fled communism in 1917, ending up in Brazil, then Oregon, and then – in 1968 – Alaska, where they finally felt they could enjoy religious freedom while avoiding the corruptive influences of modernity.

Alaska's Old Believers are hardcore traditionalists, speaking mainly Russian, marrying in their teens, raising substantial broods of children, and living simply. The men – usually farmers or fishermen – are forbidden from trimming their beards; the women typically cover their hair and are garbed in long dresses. The Old Believers tend to keep to themselves, inhabiting a handful of isolated villages on the Kenai Peninsula, of which Nikolaevsk is the most prominent.

To get there, head 10 miles east on North Fork Rd, which departs from the Sterling Hwy in the heart of Anchor Point and winds through hillbilly homesteads and open, rolling forest. Right before the pavement ends, hang a left at Nikolaevsk Rd. Two miles later, you'll enter the village.

One recommended stop is the **Samovar Café & B&B** (☑907-235-6867; www.russian-giftsnina.com; mains $5-12; ☺10am-10pm Mon-Fri, to 8pm Sat) where the owner Nina is pretty hilarious, and provides good insights into the life and times of Old Believers

On your way back, consider stopping at the **Norman Lowell Studio** (www.normal-lowellgallery.net; Normal Lowell Rd, Anchor Point; 9am-5pm) in Anchor Point. This spacious gallery features the work of the self-taught homesteading painter. While it can get a little cheesy, many of the Alaskan wildland paintings are quite powerful – and certainly masterfully crafted.

less mal de mer. Make sure you buy a derby ticket.

Cycling & Mountain Biking

Though Homer lacks formal mountain biking trails, the dirt roads in the hills above town lend themselves to some great rides, especially along Diamond Ridge Rd and Skyline Dr. For an easy tour, head out on E End Rd, which extends 20 miles east to the head of Kachemak Bay. There's also good biking to be had in Seldovia, an easy day or overnight trip from Homer by water-taxi.

Paddling

Though, theoretically, you could spend a wavy day paddling in the vicinity of the Spit, you'll find infinitely better scenery, more varied wildlife and far more sheltered waters across the bay in the **Kachemak Bay State Park**. Due to fast currents and massive waves, attempting the wide-open crossing is a poor idea; you're better off taking your kayak across on a water-taxi or renting one from the various companies that maintain fleets of kayaks on the far side, such as True North Kayak Adventures (p261).

Bear Viewing

Due largely to the density of tourists visiting Homer, the town has become a major departure point for bear-watching trips to the famed bruin haven of Katmai National Park, located on the Alaska Peninsula 100-plus miles southwest by floatplane. Due to the distances involved, these trips cost a pretty penny: expect to pay between $600 and $700 per person for a day trip. However, that may be a small price to pay for the iconic Alaskan photo: a slavering brown bear, perched atop a waterfall, snapping its fangs on an airborne salmon.

Bald Mountain Air   BEAR WATCHING
(Map p250; ☑907-235-7969; www.baldmountain-air.com; Homer Spit Rd; per person $615) Runs trips to the park headquarters at Brooks Camp, where countless bears converge to snag salmon ascending Brooks River – and where countless tourists converge to watch them. Also flies 'where no-one else goes' in June and August to spot bears when they aren't at Brooks Camp.

Emerald Air Service   BEAR WATCHING
(Map p246; ☑907-235-4160; www.emeraldair-service.com; 2144 Lakeshore Dr; per person $675)

Around Homer

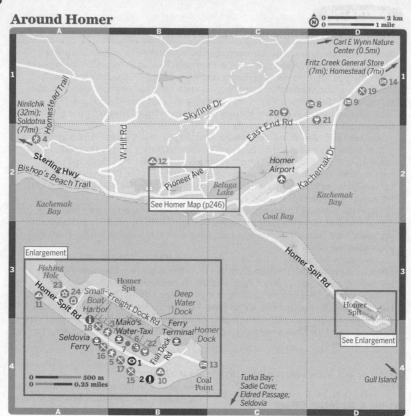

See Homer Map (p246)

Run by respected naturalists this offers a more wilderness-oriented experience, by-passing Brooks Camp and seeking out bears along isolated Katmai beaches and salmon streams. Expect about 4 miles of walking.

⭐ Festivals & Events

There's always something happening in Homer, especially in May – check to see what's on at the visitors center.

Homer Jackpot Halibut Derby CULTURAL
(www.homerhalibutderby.com) May 1 marks the beginning of the five-month, $200,000-plus contest to catch the biggest fish (300-pounders are the norm). Tickets cost $10, are good for one day of fishing, and can be bought at numerous places in Homer, including the derby office on the Spit.

Kachemak Bay Shorebird Festival CULTURAL
(www.homeralaska.org/visit-homer/events-homer/kachemak-bay-shorebird-festival) Brings hun-dreds of birders and 100,000 shorebirds to Mud Bay in early May, making it the largest bird migration site along the Alaskan road system. The tidal flats of Homer become the staging area for thousands of birds, including one-third of the world's surfbirds.

Kachemak Bay Wooden Boat Festival CULTURAL
(www.kbwbs.org) Held in September, this boater's fest celebrates the craft, design and history of wooden boatbuilding, and is rounded out by tall tales of drama on the high seas.

🛏 Sleeping

Homer has B&Bs galore. Homer adds a 7.5% sales tax to lodging.

Homer Spit Public Camping CAMPGROUND $
(Map p250; Homer Spit Rd; tent/RV sites $8/15) On the west beach of Homer Spit, a catch-as-catch-can tent city springs up every night of the summer. It's a beautiful spot, though

Around Homer

often windy (make sure you add weight to your tent if you leave). It can get crowded and sometimes rowdy. The self-registration stand is right across the road from Sportsman's Supply (p247).

Karen Hornaday Memorial Campground   CAMPGROUND $
(Map p250; tent/RV sites $8/15) Below the bluffs just north of downtown, this is the best family camping option in Homer. It has private, wooded sites with impressive views of the Bay and baseball field.

Seaside Farm   HOSTEL $
(Map p250; ☑ 907-235-7850; www.seasidealaska.com; E End Rd; sites/dm/r/cabins $10/20/65/75) Located 5 miles from the city center, this is more like Burning Man than a regulation youth hostel. Run by Mossy Kilcher, pop star Jewel Kilcher's aunt, Seaside Farm has a meadow campground with views of Grewingk Glacier, somewhat dingy dorms and basic cabins.

The outdoor cooking pavilion is patrolled by roosters and impromptu jam sessions often spark up around the campfire.

Homer Spit Campground   CAMPGROUND $
(Map p250; ☑ 907-235-8206; Homer Spit Rd; tent sites $20, RV sites $30-50; 🐾) Catering to the RV crowd, this Spit-end place has coin-operated laundry facilities, showers ($5) and about 150 bald eagles. Tent campers should head to the public campground.

★ **Driftwood Inn**   INN $$
(Map p246; ☑ 907-235-8019; www.thedriftwood inn.com; 135 W Bunnell Ave; RV sites $34-49, r $99-199, cottage $295; 🐾🛜) This joint has cheery European-style rooms with or without baths, snug, cedar-finished 'ships' quarters,' two sprawling vacation houses with remarkable waterfront views, and a great patio area. It's an excellent deal for the price, and larger groups can have an entire cottage (complete with kitchen and living area) all to themselves.

Old Town B&D   B&B $$
(Map p246; ☑ 907-235-7558; www.oldtownbandb.com; 106 W Bunnell Ave; d $110-130; 🐾🛜) Built in 1937, this historic B&B has just three rooms. The Mabel Suite has ocean views and a private bath. All come with hardwood floors, great paintings from artists in residence and a fresh feel that makes this a top pick in downtown. Breakfast is served downstairs at Maura's.

Homer Floatplane Lodge   LODGE $$
(Map p246; ☑ 907-235-4160; www.floatplanelodge.com; 2144 Lakeshore Dr; r from $125; 🐾🛜) Aviation buffs will love the waterfront rooms at this cozy grouping of log cabins right on Beluga Lake. Spruce walls, ample porches and kitchenettes make this a great spot for families.

Room at the Harbor   B&B $$
(Map p250; ☑ 907-235-4921; www.spitsisterscafe.com; Homer Spit Rd; r $120; 🐾) Upstairs from

KENAI PENINSULA HOMER

Spit Sisters, this establishment has one beautiful room; cozy up with a scone and a book. Though the shower is in the room, one of the beds is in its own nook overlooking the boat harbor.

Glacier View Cabins
CABIN $$

(Map p250; ☑907-299-1519; www.glacierview cabins.com; 59565 E End Rd; cabins $125-160; ⊝🛜🐕) These log cabins sit in a sort of suburban utopia: a wide expanse of lawn has views of Kachemak Bay over neighborhood rooftops. While they feel a bit modular, the spruce cabins have nice kitchens, and there are grills on every porch and plenty of firepits.

Ocean Shores Motel
MOTEL $$

(Map p246; ☑800-770-7775; www.oceanshores alaska.com; 451 Sterling Hwy; d $169-209; ⊝🛜) This motel-style lodge has spacious rooms, many with flatscreens and modern bed treatments. The decks and awesome views make this a strong contender in the mid-range motel category. Those down by the ocean cost the most; the cheaper ones are up on the hill and lack good views. They have plans to build a new lodge.

Beluga Lake Lodge
HOTEL $$

(Map p246; ☑907-235-5995; www.belugalakel odging.com; 204 Ocean Dr Loop; d $54-174; ⊝🛜) This lodge overlooks its namesake lake (where floatplanes take off) and is pleasant and clean. Some of the sizeable rooms have kitchens, and there's a hopping bar and grill on site.

Pioneer Inn
MOTEL $$

(Map p246; ☑907-235-5670; www.pioneerinn homerak.com; 244 W Pioneer Ave; r $129-149; ⊝🛜) A little overpriced for what you get, this motel complex has run-of-the-mill rooms (save for the beautiful handmade quilts). A few have larger kitchenettes and living rooms – and you can get at least partial ocean views from much of the motel.

Land's End Resort
HOTEL $$

(Map p250; ☑800-478-0400; www.lands-end -resort.com; r $169-289; ⊝🛜🏊) Located at the end of the Spit, it's considered a luxury hotel for its grand views, but only the pricier rooms in this aging complex really fit that description. There's a spa, a hot tub and an endless pool. You can do better on ambience and location, but the views are spectacular.

Heritage Hotel
HOTEL $$

(Map p246; ☑907-235-7787; www.alaskaherit agehotel.com; 147 E Pioneer Ave; r $119; ⊝🛜) Housed in a 1948 log cabin, it has an older section with small, rustically decorated rooms, plus a newer wing with rooms that are larger but less charming. The lobby is a bit smelly.

Bear Creek Lodging
B&B $$$

(Map p250; ☑907-235-8484; www.bearcreekwin ery.com; Bear Creek Dr; ste $275; ⊝) 🌿 On a hillside at the Bear Creek Winery, this place has two suites (each with a kitchenette), a hot tub overlooking the fruit vineyard and koi pond, and a complimentary bottle of vino beside each bed. No kids allowed.

🍴 Eating

Two Sisters Bakery
BAKERY $

(Map p246; ☑907-235-2280; www.twosistersbak ery.net; 233 E Bunnell Ave; light meals $4-7, dinner mains $15-18; ☺7am-6pm Mon-Tue, 7am-9pm Wed-Sat, 9am-2pm Sun) This quintessential Homer institution has great fresh-baked bread and light snacks. There is a lilting air to the open-kitchen that seems pulled straight from Johnny Depp's classic *Chocolat*. The gorgeous waitstaff all exude the cool hippie chic you would expect from this uniquely feminine bakery, and staying for dinner is highly recommended.

Cosmic Kitchen
MEXICAN $

(Map p246; 510 E Pioneer Ave; burritos & sandwich es $6-11; ☺9am-8pm Mon-Sat, to 3pm Sun; 🛜) With excellent burritos, burgers and a salsa bar, this joint is the place to go for a filling meal on the cheap; it's probably the best bargain in town. It also serves breakfast until 3pm and has a deck for sunny evenings.

Fresh Sourdough Express
ORGANIC $

(Map p246; ☑907-235-7571; 1316 Ocean Dr; breakfast $6-10, lunch & dinner $6-11; ☺7am-10pm) 🌿 This is the first official 'green' restaurant in Alaska, and you can taste it. Almost everything is organic and as much as possible locally raised or grown. Come here for ample breakfasts. Box lunches are also available.

Homer Farmers Market
MARKET $

(Map p246; www.homerfarmersmarket.org; Ocean Dr; snacks $2-10; ☺3-6pm Wed, 10am-3pm Sat) Pick up fresh produce, peruse homemade crafts kiosks or just chow down on kettle corn.

Fritz Creek General Store
DELI $

(Mile 8.2, E End Rd; snacks $3-8; ☉7am-9pm Mon-Sat, 10am-6pm Sun) What is an excellent deli doing all the way out on East End Rd? This place serves some of the best takeout food in Homer – it's worth the drive for the veggie burritos alone, but you shouldn't leave without dessert.

Duncan Diner
CAFE $

(Map p246; 125 E Pioneer Ave; breakfast & lunch $6-11; ☉7am-2pm) This busy downtown spot fries up home-style breakfast among home-style decor.

Spit Sisters
BAKERY $

(Map p250; ☑907-235-4921; www.spitsisterscafe.com; Homer Spit Rd; pastries $2-5; ☉7am-7pm) There's a great view overlooking the small-boat harbor, and delicacies to enjoy (apricot scones, blackberry muffins, sticky buns) made by the revered Two Sisters Bakery in town. Gourmet boxed lunches are perfect for a day on the water.

Safeway
GROCERY $

(Map p246; Mile 90, Sterling Hwy; ☉5am-midnight) On the way to the Spit, this is the best place in town for groceries, fresh-baked breads, deli sandwiches and salads.

Maura's Cafe
DELI $$

(Map p246; www.maurascafe.com; 248 W Pioneer Ave; mains $9-14; ☉8am-5pm) Homerites consistently recommend this place, which serves up hearty – yet civilized – breakfasts, sandwiches and salads. Get some imported meat and cheese for a picnic on Bishop's Beach. If animal products aren't your thing, don't despair – in true Homer fashion, Maura's is vegan friendly.

Boardwalk
SEAFOOD $$

(Map p250; Homer Spit Rd; fast food $5-15; ☉11am-10pm) This waterfront spot is widely viewed as the best place on the Spit for halibut – tempura-battered, fried and served kebab-style (its motto is 'Where the fish comes on a stick').

Cafe Cups
FUSION $$

(Map p246; ☑907-235-8330; 162 W Pioneer Ave; dinner $11-30; ☉dinner Tue-Sat) In a charming little building (you'll know it by the cups outside) with a changing menu that includes excellent curries and fresh fish. Though the food is delicious, the service can be quite harried.

Fat Olives
ITALIAN $$

(Map p246; ☑907-235-8488; www.fatolivesrestaurant.com; 276 Ohlson Lane; dinner $16-29; ☉11am-10pm) Housed in the old 'bus barn,' this chic and hyperpopular pizza joint and wine bar serves affordable appetizers such as prosciutto-wrapped Alaskan scallops and delicious mains such as wood-oven-roasted rack of lamb. Almost everything is fresh and homemade. You can also grab a huge slice of pizza to go ($5).

Finn's Pizza
PIZZA $

(Map p250; Homer Spit Rd; slice $5-6, pizza $14-22; ☉noon-9pm) Finn's wood-fired pizzas are best enjoyed with a pint of ale in the sunny upstairs solarium. Is there anything better than an excellent pizza and unobstructed views of the bay? We don't think so. You can also get soup, salad and polenta.

Mermaid Cafe
CAJUN $$

(Map p246; ☑907-235-7649; 3487 Main St; mains $5-20; ☉11am-2pm Mon-Tue, to 8pm Wed-Sat) Specializing in charcuterie, this log-cabin cajun cafe has a wondrous patio, savory shrimp po boys and gumbo, plus a wide selection of tapas and the signature Monkey Fist meat platters. The attached Old Inlet Book Shop is a bibliophile's dream.

Captain Pattie's
SEAFOOD $$

(Map p250; Homer Spit Rd; mains $10-34; ☉11am-9pm) This oceanfront eatery has become a Spit institution by selling overpriced seafood to a constant stream of landlubbers. It claims its halibut is Alaska's best, but those in the know always order crab.

Homestead
FUSION $$$

(☑907-235-8723; www.homesteadrestaurant.net; Mile 8.2, E End Rd; dinner $26-32; ☉dinner) One of Homer's oldest and priciest restaurants, with mains such as the Chelsea Duck and the Seafood Duet (wild shrimp and Alaskan scallops). Though the waiters wear black ties, patrons can come as they are (hey, this is Homer, after all).

Wasabi's
JAPANESE $$$

(Map p250; ☑907-226-3663; www.wasabisrestaurant.com; 57217 East End Ave; mains $8-32; ☉5-10pm) With some of the best views in town, this playful and modern sushi house offers innovative cocktails, finely constructed rolls and some of the freshest fish you could imagine.

KENAI PENINSULA HOMER

Drinking & Nightlife

The bumper sticker says it all: 'Homer, Alaska: A quaint drinking village with a fishing problem.'

Kharacters   BAR
(Map p246; Pioneer Ave) Pure Alaskana, this smoke-filled juke joint has live music, boisterous crowds and is fun as hell.

Salty Dawg Saloon   BAR
(Map p250; Homer Spit Rd) Maybe the most storied bar on the Kenai Peninsula, the Salty Dawg isn't just a tourist trap. Locals love the cavernous lighthouse tavern, back patio and pool table. Come evening, the sea shanties start in earnest.

Down East Saloon   BAR
(Map p250; 3125 E End Rd) This spacious bar is where locals head to listen to live music. The view is killer, but you'll likely be paying more attention to whichever Homer talent is on stage and the sexy hippies.

The Alibi   BAR
(Map p246; www.alibihomer.com; 453 E Pioneer Ave; ⊙4pm-4am) Catering to a younger crowd, the Alibi has DJs, karaoke and occasional dance parties. The large picture windows reveal the bay and locals say the food isn't bad.

Homer Brewing Company   BREWERY
(Map p246; www.homerbrew.com; 1411 Lakeshore Dr; ⊙noon-7pm Mon-Sat, to 6pm Sun) This tasting room has picnic tables and fresh Jakalof Bay oysters Friday and Saturday. Try the broken birch bitter ale and then grab a growler to go.

Bear Creek Winery   WINE BAR
(Map p250; www.bearcreekwinery.com; Bear Creek Dr; ⊙10am-6pm) Wineries are scarcer than vineyards in Alaska, but this impressive family-run operation bottles some fine berry-based wines. Tastings are $5 (credited to your purchase), and they do tours at 11am Monday, Wednesday and Friday.

Entertainment

Pier One Theatre   THEATER
(Map p250; ☑907-235-7333; www.pieronetheatre.org; Homer Spit Rd) Live drama and comedy are performed in a 'come-as-you-are' warehouse next to the Fishing Hole on the Spit. Shows start at 8:15pm Friday and Saturday, and 7:30pm Sunday during summer.

Shopping

Chain Reaction Sports   SPORTS
(Map p246; 5 Lake St; ⊙8am-7pm Mon-Fri, to 5pm Sat & Sun) This outfitter sells camping, hunting and fishing supplies.

Information

INTERNET
Homer Public Library (500 Hazel Ave; ⊙10am-6pm Mon, Wed, Fri & Sat, to 8pm Tue & Thu; 🛜 ♿) Homer's excellent library is arty and airy, with a decidedly Homer-esque selection of magazines. Internet access is free, and they have a great kids section for rainy days.

LAUNDRY
East End Laundry (Mile 2.9, E End Rd; ⊙10am-8pm Mon-Sat) Convenient to Seaside Farm.

Sportsman's Supply & Rental (1114 Freight Dock Rd; ⊙6am-midnight) Offers showers ($7) and laundry right on the Spit.

Washboard Laundromat ($6) The showers come with towels and last as long as you want.

MEDICAL SERVICES
Homer Medical Clinic (☑907-235-8586; 4136 Bartlett St) Next door to South Peninsula Hospital; for walk-in service.

South Peninsula Hospital (☑866-235-0369; Bartlett St) North of the Pratt Museum.

MONEY
Wells Fargo (88 Sterling Hwy) ATM.

POST
Post Office (Map p246; 3658 Heath St)

TOURIST INFORMATION
Halibut Derby Office (Map p250; ☑907-235-7740; www.homerhalibutderby.com; Homer Spit Rd; ⊙5:30am-8am & 3-7pm) Has a few pamphlets and is the official weigh-in station for the Homer Halibut Derby.

Homer Visitor Center & Chamber of Commerce (Map p246; ☑907-235-7740; www.homeralaska.org; 201 Sterling Hwy; ⊙9am-6pm Mon-Fri, 10am-5pm Sat & Sun) Has countless brochures and a funky mosaic on the floor. It's operated by the chamber of commerce, however, and only provides info on members.

Getting There & Around

AIR
Ravn Alaska (p219) provides daily flights between Homer and Anchorage from Homer's airport, 1.7 miles east of town on Kachemak Dr. The advance-purchase fare runs at about $140 one-way, or $250 for the round-trip. **Smokey Bay Air** (☑907-235-1511; www.smokeybayair.

com) ...

ACROSS THE BAY

Opposite Homer, but outside Kachemak Bay State Park, is a handful of compelling destinations easily accessible by water-taxi.

Gull Island

Halfway between the Spit and Halibut Cove, the 40ft-high Gull Island attracts some 16,000 nesting seabirds: puffins, kittiwakes, murres, cormorants and many more species. If you can cope with the stench, you'll enjoy photographing the birds up close, even if you don't have a 300mm lens.

Mako's Water-Taxi (p256) has a one-hour island tour (per person $40, three-person minimum) and a two-hour tour that includes adorable sea otters (per person $75, four-person minimum). Several other companies do Gull Island tours as well.

Halibut Cove

Halibut Cove is an absurdly quaint village of 30 permanent residents. In the early 1920s the cove had 42 herring salteries and more than 1000 residents. Today it's home to the noted Saltry restaurant, several art galleries and a warren of boardwalks – but no roads.

The Danny J (☑907-226-2424; www.halibut-cove-alaska.com/ferry.htm; per person noon/evening tour $58/35) travels to the cove twice daily. It departs from Homer at noon, swings past Gull Island and arrives at 1:30pm. You have 2½ hours to explore and have lunch. The ferry returns to the Spit by 5pm and then makes an evening run to the cove for dinner, returning to Homer at 10pm.

For many couples, dining at the Saltry (☑906-226-2424; lunch $17-20, dinner $23-28; ☺lunch 1:30pm & 3pm; dinner 6pm & 7:30pm) makes for the ultimate date, with an outdoor deck over the aquamarine inlet and excellent seafood and vegetarian cuisine. After eating, check out the galleries.

North of Seldovia

In Tutka Bay, Sadie Cove and Eldred Passage are a selection of quality lodges accessed only by water-taxi.

Otter Cove Resort (☑800-426-6212; www.ottercoveresort.com; cabins $100) Located on Eldred Passage, Otter Cove Resort has affordable camping-style cabins (with electricity) near the Sadie Knob Trail. It rents out kayaks ($70 to $85) and guides single- and multi-day paddling trips. Round-trip transportation is $70 to $85.

Tutka Bay Wilderness Lodge (☑907-274-2710; www.withinthewild.com; r per person from $1000) Tutka Bay Wilderness Lodge is an all-inclusive resort with chalets, cottages and rooms surrounding the lodge house, where guests enjoy meals with a sweeping view of the inlet and Jakolof Mountain. The accommodations are very comfortable, the food is excellent, and the amenities include a sauna, deepwater dock, boathouse and hiking trails. Activities range from clamming to sea kayaking to a maritime cuisine cooking school.

Sadie Cove Wilderness Lodge (☑888-283-7234, 907-235-2350; www.sadiecove.com; r per person $550) Located just to the north of Tutka Bay in Sadie Cove. This wilderness lodge offers cabins, a sauna, an outdoor hot tub and Alaskan seafood dinners – but it's not quite as elegant or pricey as some other options in the area.

KENAI PENINSULA HOMER

com; 2100 Kachemak Dr) offers flights to Seldovia for $66 each way.

BICYCLE

Homer Saw & Cycle (☑907-235-8406; 1532 Ocean Dr; ☺9am-5:30pm Mon-Fri, 11am-5pm Sat) Rents out mountain bikes and hybrids ($25 per day).

Cycle Logical (☑907-226-2925; www.cyclelogicalhomer.com; 3585 E End Rd; ☺9am-6pm Tue-Sat, by appointment Mon) Has disc-brake-equipped mountain bikes, fat bikes and city bikes for $27 to $55 per day.

BOAT

The Alaska Marine Highway provides a thrice-weekly service from Homer to Seldovia (each way $33, 1½ hours) and Kodiak ($74, 9½ hours), with a connecting service to the Aleutians. The **ferry terminal** (Map p250; ☑907-235-8449; www.ferryalaska.com) is found at the end of Homer Spit. **Rainbow Tours** (☑907-235-7272; Homer Spit Rd; one-way/round-trip $30/45) offers the inexpensive Rainbow Connection shuttle from Homer to Seldovia. It departs at 9am, gets to Seldovia an hour later, and then returns to take you back to Homer at 5pm. It'll transport your bike for $5 and your kayak for $10. The **Seldovia Ferry** (Map p250; ☑907-435-3299; www.seldoviabayferry.com; Lot 21, Freight Dock Rd; one way $38) takes passengers to Seldovia twice a day, with departures from Homer at 9am and 11am.

Many water-taxi operations shuttle campers and kayakers between Homer and points across Kachemak Bay. Though the companies are good and work closely together, the most respected by far is **Mako's Water-Taxi** (Map p250; ☑907-235-9055; www.makoswatertaxi.com; Homer Spit Rd). It usually charges $65 to $85 per person round-trip with a two-person minimum.

BUS

Homer Stage Line (Map p246; ☑907-868-3914; www.stagelineinhomer.com) Runs from Homer to Anchorage, and between Homer and Seward.

Homer Trolley (☑907-235-2228; www.homertrolley.com; $12 day pass; ⊘Wed-Sun) Hop-on-hop-off bus trolley between downtown and the spit.

CAR

Polar Car Rental (☑907-235-5998; airport) For an affordable rental car, this small dealer has subcompacts for $67 a day.

TAXI

Kostas Taxi (☑907-399-8008) and **Kachecab** (☑907-235-1950) are fierce rivals, and can get you anywhere around town for a reasonable fare.

Seldovia

POP 262

Normally visited as a quick overnight from Homer, this bewitching waterfront village is just 15 miles from Homer by boat. While touring the boardwalk and compact center will take less than a day, the nearby adventures in Kachemak Bay could well extend your trip for a week.

The town is sleepy and secluded, esoteric and at-times frustrating – plan for an extra day to get in or out. A new generation of end-of-the-worlders are moving in and making it theirs. Today it relies in part on fishing but is making its best stab at becoming a tourist destination. It's a process that's happening in fits and starts: the hiking, skiing, paddling and biking possibilities here are excellent. And while the accommodations are plush, the culinary offerings are limited and the galleries feel a bit desperate.

All in all you'll find a village with quaintness to spare, but little tourist infrastructure, which may be the best thing about the place.

History

One of the oldest settlements on Cook Inlet, Russians founded the town in the late 18th century and named it after their word *seldevoy*, meaning 'herring bay.' By the 1890s Seldovia had become an important shipping and supply center for the region, and the town boomed right into the 1920s with salmon canning, fur farming, a theater, and, of course, a (short-lived) herring industry.

But then the highway came, stretching only as far as the tip of the Homer Spit. After it was completed in the 1950s, Seldovia's importance as a supply center began to dwindle.

◉ Sights

Seldovia Village Tribe Visitor Center   MUSEUM
(☑907-234-7898; www.svt.org; cnr Airport Ave & Main St; ⊘9am-5pm) This visitor center and museum showcases Seldovia's Alaska Native heritage – a unique blend of Alutiiq and Tanaina cultures. The small, tidy museum covers the history of Alaska Natives in the area, and its subsistence display is informative and interesting. This is also the place to buy souvenirs.

St Nicholas Orthodox Church   CHURCH
(tinetteh@ptialaska.net; ⊘services 6pm Sat, 10am Sun) Seldovia's most popular attraction is this onion-domed church, which overlooks the town from a hill just off Main St. Built in 1891 and restored in the 1970s, the church is open only during services and by appointment. Though there is no resident clergyman, occasionally the priest from Nanwalek travels here to conduct services.

Outside Beach   BEACH
(Jakolof Bay Rd) This beach is an excellent place for wildlife sightings and a little beachcombing. To reach it, follow Anderson Way

out of town for a mile, then head left at the first fork to reach the picnic area at Outside Beach Park.

You stand a good chance of spotting eagles, seabirds and possibly even otters here. At low tide, you can explore the sea life among the rocks, and on a clear day the views of Mt Redoubt and Mt Iliamna are stunning.

Historic Boardwalk   WATERFRONT

(Main St) Continue 200ft south of the boat harbor to Seldovia's historic boardwalk. Overlooking the slough, this atmospheric collection of shops and inns is worth a quick stroll.

🏃 Activities

Berry Picking

Seldovia is known best for its blueberries, which grow so thick just outside town that from late August to mid-September you often can rake your fingers through the bushes and fill a two-quart bucket in minutes. You'll also come across plenty of low-bush cranberries and salmonberries, a species not found around Homer. Be aware, however, that many of the best berry areas are on tribal land; before setting out, stop at the Seldovia Native Association (☑907-234-7625; www.snai.org; Main St; day-use/camping permits $5/10), which will sell you a day-use permit for a nominal fee.

Hiking

The Otterbahn Trail was famously created by local high-school students, who dubbed it the 'we-worked-hard-so-you-better-like-it trail.' The trailhead lies behind Susan B English School, off Winfred Ave. Lined with salmonberries and affording great views of Graduation Peak, it skirts the coastline most of the way and reaches Outside Beach in 1.5 miles. Make sure you hike it at tides below 17ft, as the last stretch runs across a slough that is only legally passable when the water is out (property above 17ft is private). At press time, a boardwalk across the slough was impassable.

Two trails start from Jakolof Bay Rd. You can either hike down the beach toward the head of Seldovia Bay at low tide, or you can follow a 4.5-mile logging road to reach several secluded coves. There is also the Tutka/Jakolof Trail, a 2.5-mile trail to a campsite on the Tutka Lagoon, the site of a state salmon-rearing facility. The posted

trail departs from Jakolof Bay Rd about 10.5 miles east of town.

The town's steepest hike is the rigorous Rocky Ridge Trail, where 800ft of climbing will be rewarded with remarkable views of the bay, the town and Mt Iliamna. The trail starts (or ends) on Rocky St and loops back to the road to the airport, covering about 3 miles.

Cycling

Seldovia's nearly carless streets and outlying gravel roads make for ideal biking; mountain bikes can be brought over from Homer. Those looking for a fairly leisurely ride can pedal the 10-mile Jakolof Bay Rd, which winds along the coast nearly to the head of Jakolof Bay. For a more rigorous experience, continue on for another 6 miles beyond the end of the maintained road, climbing 1200ft into the alpine country at the base of Red Mountain.

In the past, fit cyclists could also depart from Jakolof Bay Rd for an epic 30-mile round-trip ride along the rough Rocky River Rd, which cuts across the tip of the Kenai Peninsula to Windy Bay. In recent years washouts have made the road largely impassable; inquire about current conditions.

Thyme on the Boardwalk   OUTDOORS

(☑907-443-2213; www.thymeontheboardwalk.com; Main St) This flower shop on the old Boardwalk rents bikes and kayaks for $5 per hour. They have a nice vacation rental upstairs.

Paddling

There are some excellent kayaking opportunities in the Seldovia area. Just north, Eldred Passage and the three islands (Cohen, Yukon and Hesketh) that mark its entrance are prime spots for viewing otters, sea lions and seals, while the northern shore of Yukon Island features caves and tunnels that can be explored at high tide. Even closer are Sadie Cove, and Tutka and Jakolof Bays, where you can paddle in protected water amid interesting geological features, row up to oyster farmers to buy straight from the source, and camp in secluded coves.

Kayak'Atak   KAYAKING

(☑907-234-7425; www.alaska.net/~kayaks; single/double kayaks 1st day $50/80, subsequent days $35/50) Rents out kayaks and can help arrange transportation throughout the bay. It also offers various guided tours starting

from $80, some including a 'gourmet lunch.'
Make reservations in advance.

Tours

Smokey Bay Air   AIR
(☑ 888-482-1511; www.smokeybayair.com; 2100 Kachemak Dr; one-way $66) Offers a scenic 12-minute flight from Homer, over the Kenai Mountains and Kachemak Bay to Seldovia.

Mako's Water-Taxi   BOAT
(☑ 907-235-9055; www.makoswatertaxi.com; drop-off at Homer Spit Rd; round-trip $135) Has an excellent tour that takes you by boat, car and plane. Mako's drops you at Jakolof Bay, from where you'll be driven to Seldovia. You return to Homer via a short flightseeing trip.

Central Charters   BOAT
(☑ 907-235-7847; www.centralcharter.com; drop-off at Homer Spit Rd, one-way/round-trip $30/59) Does a daily seven-hour tour from Homer, leaving at 11am, circling Gull Island, and dropping you in Seldovia to enjoy the village for the afternoon. Also ask about sailing trips.

🛏 Sleeping

For free camping head to Sandy Beach, accessed north of town on the Otterbahn Trail. Be sure to camp in the grass above the high-tide line.

★ Across the Bay Tent & Breakfast CABIN $
(☑ summer 907-350-4636, winter 907-345-2571; www.tentandbreakfastalaska.com; tent/cabin per person $80/90; 🌐🖥) Located 8 miles from town on Jakolof Bay, this is something a little different. Its cabin-like tents include a full breakfast, and for $115 per day you can get a package that includes all your meals – dinner could consist of fresh oysters, beach-grilled salmon or halibut stew with a side of garden-grown greens. Bring your sleeping bag.

The offbeat resort also organizes guided kayak trips ($95 to $105).

Seldovia Wilderness RV Park CAMPGROUND $
(☑ 907-234-7643; tent/RV sites $5/10) About a mile out of town, this is a city-maintained campground on spectacular Outside Beach. You can pay for your site at the ferry terminal or harbormaster's office.

Seldovia Rowing Club B&B   B&B $$
(☑ 907-234-7614; www.seldoviarowingclubinn. wordpress.com; 343 Bay St; r $135) Located on the Old Boardwalk, this place (the first B&B

in Southcentral Alaska) has homey suites decorated with quilts, antiques and owner Susan Mumma's outstanding watercolors. She serves big breakfasts and often hosts in-house music concerts.

Even if you aren't staying here, stop by in the afternoon to see the artist at work or inquire about drawing classes.

Seldovia Boardwalk Hotel   HOTEL $$
(☑ 907-234-7816; www.seldoviaboardwalkhotel. com; 234 Main St; r $149-159; 🌐🖥) While these are the best hotel digs in town, you lose some of the flavor of a cottage rental. The 12 bright and cheery rooms have brand new everything, expansive windows and flatscreen TVs. Spring the extra 10 bucks for a harbor view.

Bridgekeeper's Inn B&B   B&B $$
(☑ 907-234-7535; www.thebridgekeepersinn.com; 223 Kachemak Dr; r $140-150; 🌐) A cozy place with private baths and full breakfasts; one room has a balcony overlooking the salmon-filled slough.

Sea Parrot Inn   INN $$
(☑ 907-234-7829, 907-632-6135; www.seaparrotinn.com; 226 Main St; r $99-145; 🌐🖥🐾) They aren't the best rooms in town, but they are affordable, and you get fine harbor views, a nice deck, wood floors, a continental breakfast and a social atmosphere (thanks to a shared great room). Laundry and showers are also available for campers.

Dancing Eagles   CABIN $$$
(☑ 907-360-6363; www.dancingeagles.com; Main St; d $195; 🖥) Large windows look onto the harbor from this weather-beaten waterfront cabin just south of the harbor. It sleeps up to four in its cramped loft and private bedroom. There's a full kitchen, great decks and a wood-burning stove.

Harbor's Edge
Vacation Rental   VACATION RENTAL $$$
(☑ 901-399-3195; www.seldovia.us; 194 Main St; r/apt $175/300; 🖥) This gorgeous house right across from the harbor offers plenty of room for a large family to spread out. There are great views from the nautically themed upstairs kitchen and living area. Downstairs, the large rooms are super comfy, each offering a private bath. Ask about a more affordable apartment for rent nearby.

✕ Eating

Restaurants are packed when the ferry gets in. Time your visit well.

Amon's Coffee House   CAFE $
(230 Kachemak St) For homemade baked goods, local art, daily food specials and friendly talk, head to Amon's (right by the bridge on your way to the airport). With a patio dangling over the slough and large picture windows, this is the best cafe in town.

Linwood Bar & Grill   PUB $$
(257 Main St; mains $10-17; ⊘grill 11am-2am) The only bar in town has an awesome deck that overlooks the harbor. The playful and uproarious owner, Stephanie, keeps everybody in check and shows everyone a good time. The food is simple and well prepared, making this place just north of the harbor a must.

Tidepool Cafe   CAFE $$
(267 Main St; breakfast $6-11, lunch $9-16, dinner $16-30; ⊘7am-4pm) In a sunny space overlooking the harbor, this eclectic eatery was slated to reopen at press time.

❶ Information

The post office is on the corner of Main St and Seldovia St. There's an ATM at Linwood Bar & Grill but no banks in town.

Harbormaster's Office (☑907-234-7886; Harbor; ⊘8am-9pm) Has toilets and pamphlets.

Information Stand (Main St) Close to the small-boat harbor, this gorgeous timber-frame structure was just being completed at press time.

Library (☑907-234-7662; 250 Seldovia St; ⊘afternoon Tue, Thu & Sat; 🖥) Has computer-based internet access as well as free wi-fi.

Sea Parrot Inn (226 Main St; ⊘9am-9pm) Offers showers (10 minutes $7.50) with soap and towel, as well as laundry (wash and dry $10.50).

Seldovia Chamber of Commerce (www.seldoviachamber.org) Its website is great for pre-trip planning.

Seldovia Medical Clinic (☑907-234-7825; 250 Seldovia St; ⊘Mon, Wed & Fri 9am-noon & 1-4pm) By appointment.

Seldovia Village Tribe Visitor Center (☑907-234-7898; www.svt.org; cnr Airport Ave & Main St; ⊘7am-5pm) Book the Seldovia Bay Ferry here.

❶ Getting There & Around

AIR
Homer Air (☑907-235-8591; www.homerair.com; $66) Flights to Seldovia hourly.

ATV
The Sea Parrot Inn rents ATVs for $107 per day.

BOAT
Alaska Marine Highway ferries provide twice-weekly service between Homer and Seldovia ($33, 1½ hours) with connecting service throughout the peninsula and the Aleutians. The Seldovia ferry terminal is at the north end of Main St.

Rainbow Tours (☑907-235-7272; drop-off at Homer Spit Rd; one-way/round-trip $30/45) Offers the inexpensive Rainbow Connection shuttle from Homer to Seldovia. It departs at 10:30am, gets to Seldovia about two hours later, and then returns to take you back to Homer at 5pm. It'll transport your bike for $5 and your kayak for $10.

Seldovia Bay Ferry (☑907-435-3299; www.seldoviabayferry.com; cnr Airport Ave & Main St; $38) The newest addition to ferry services, with two departures per day, from Seldovia at 9am and 4:30pm.

TAXI
For rides out to Jakolof Bay Rd or to the airport, try **Halo Cab** (☑907-399-4229; halocab@yahoo.com).

Kachemak Bay State Park

Stand on Homer Spit and look south, and an alluring wonderland sprawls before you: luxuriantly green coastline, sliced by fjords and topped by sparkling glaciers and rugged peaks. This is Kachemak Bay State Park, which, along with Kachemak Bay State Wilderness Park to the south, includes 350,000 acres of wilderness accessible only by bush plane or boat. It was Alaska's first state park, and according to locals, it remains the best.

The most popular attraction is Grewingk Glacier, which can be seen across the bay from Homer. Viewing the glacier at closer range means a boat trip to the park and a very popular one-way hike of 3.5 miles. Outside the glacier, you can easily escape into the wilds by either hiking or kayaking. With more than 40 miles of trails, plenty of sheltered waterways, numerous campsites, good backcountry skiing, and a few enclosed accommodation options, this is a highly recommended outing for a day or three.

◉ Sights & Activities

Peterson Bay Field Station   NATURE RESERVE
(☑ 907-235-6667; www.akcoastalstudies.org)
Though technically it's outside the park,
this field station operated by the Center for
Alaskan Coastal Studies provides an excellent introduction to the ecology and natural
history of the area.

In summer, staff members lead day-long
educational tours of the coastal forest and
waterfront tidepools; the best intertidal
beasties are seen during extremely low, or
'minus,' tides. Inside the station, too, you can
get up close and personal with a touch tank
full of squishy sea creatures. It costs $140,
which includes the boat ride over from the
Spit. If you want to overnight here, the station has bunks and yurts.

Hiking

Glacier Lake Trail   HIKING
The most popular hike in Kachemak Bay
State Park is this 3.5-mile, one-way trail that
begins at the Glacier Spit trailhead, near the
small Rusty Lagoon Campground.

The level, easy-to-follow trek proceeds
across the glacial outwash and ends at a
lake with superb views of Grewingk Glacier.
Camping on the lake is spectacular, and often the shoreline is littered with icebergs
(and day-trippers). At Mile 1.4 you can connect to the 6.5-mile Grewingk Glacier Trail,
with a hand-tram and access to the face of
the glacier. If you don't have time for the entire hike, there are excellent views less than
a mile from the tram.

Saddle Trail   HIKING
A mile-long trail starting in Halibut Cove; it
connects to the Glacier Lake Trail for a nice
loop.

Alpine Ridge Trail   HIKING
At the high point of the Saddle Trail you will
reach the posted junction for this 2-mile
climb to an alpine ridge above the glacier.
The climb can be steep at times but manageable for most hikers with day packs. On a
nice day, the views of the ice and Kachemak
Bay are stunning.

Lagoon Trail   HIKING
Departing from the Saddle Trail is this 5.5-mile
route that leads to the ranger station at the
head of Halibut Cove Lagoon. Along the way it
passes the Goat Rope Spur Trail, a steep 1-mile
climb to the alpine tundra. You also pass the
posted junction of Halibut Creek Trail.

If Grewingk Glacier is too crowded for
you, follow this trail a half-mile to Halibut
Creek to spend the night in a beautiful, but
much more remote, valley.

The Lagoon Trail is considered a difficult
hike and involves fording Halibut Creek,
which should be done at low tide. At the
ranger station, more trails extend south to
several lakes, as well as Poot Peak and the
Wosnesenski River.

Poot Peak   HIKING
Poot Peak is a difficult, slick, rocky ascent of
2600ft. The trailhead begins at the Halibut
Cove Lagoon, where a moderate 2.6-mile
climb along the China Poot Lake Trail takes
you to a campsite on the lake.

From there, the trail to the peak diverges
after the Wosnesenski River Trail junction.
For a little over a mile you'll clamber upward
through thinning forest until you reach the
Summit Spur, where the route climbs even
more precipitously to the mountain's lower summit, 2100ft in elevation. From here,
reaching the very top involves scaling a
shifting wall of scree, a feat that should be
attempted only by those who have some
rock-climbing experience. In wet weather, it
should be avoided altogether. Getting from
the lake to the summit and back will take
the better part of a day.

Grace Ridge Trail   HIKING
This is a 7-mile trail that stretches from a
campsite at Kayak Beach trailhead to deep
inside Tutka Bay in the state park. Much of
the hike runs above the treeline along the
crest of Grace Ridge, where, needless to say,
the views are stunning. There's also access
from the Sea Star Cove public-use cabin. You
could hike the trail in a day, but it makes a
great two-day trek with an overnight camp.

Emerald Lake Trail   HIKING
This steep, difficult 6.4-mile trail begins at
Grewingk Glacial Lake and leads to Portlock
Plateau. You'll witness firsthand the recla-
mation of the wasted forest (due to spruce
bark beetle damage) by brushy alder and
birch, considered delicacies by local wildlife.

At Mile 2.1 a spur trail reaches the scenic
Emerald Lake, and there are great views of
the bay from the plateau. In spring, stream
crossings can be challenging.

Paddling
You can spend three or four days paddling
the many fjords of the park, departing from
Homer and making overnight stops at Gla-

cier Spit or Halibut Cove. Think twice before crossing Kachemak Bay from the Spit, however; the currents and tides are powerful and can cause serious problems for inexperienced paddlers.

Seaside Adventures
KAYAKING

(☑907-235-6672; www.seasideadventure.com; half-/full-day trip incl water-taxi $110/150) A tiny family-run outfit, Seaside Adventures will show you the bay on kayak, complete with running commentary about local flora and fauna.

St Augustine Charters
KAYAKING

(☑907-299-1894; www.homerkayaking.com; half-/full-day paddles incl water-taxi $105/145) Offers many guided tours from its Petersen Bay office, including multiday paddling and trekking trips through state parks, camping at seaside sites. 'Paddle Hike Dine' ($210) is a popular day of kayaking and hiking, ending with dinner at Saltry (p255) in Halibut Cove.

True North Kayak Adventures
KAYAKING

(Map p250; ☑907-235-0708; www.truenorthkayak.com) Based on Yukon Island and with an office on Homer Spit, it runs half-day paddles amid the otters, with eagles overhead, for $105 (water-taxi included). Once you've spent all that time crossing the bay, however, it makes more sense to spring for the full day paddle ($150), or at least the three-quarter-day ($130).

There are also several multiday options that cross Eldred Passage into Tutka Bay or Sadie Cove. For experienced kayakers, it rents rigid single/double kayaks for $40/65 per day.

🛏 Sleeping

Camping is permitted throughout Kachemak Bay State Park. Moreover, numerous free, primitive camping areas have been developed, usually at waterfront trailheads or along trails. Consult **Alaska State Parks** (☑907-269-8400; www.dnr.alaska.gov/parks) for the locations and facilities.

Center for Alaskan Coastal Studies
YURT $

(☑907-235-6667; www.akcoastalstudies.org; Heath St; ⊙9am-5pm Mon-Fri) This organization reserves bunks ($25) or yurts ($80) close to its Peterson Bay Field Station, just outside the park. Lodgers can use the kitchen at the field station.

Public-Use Cabins
CABIN $

(☑907-262-5581; www.alaskastateparks.org; cabins $65) There are six cabins that can be reserved in the park.

Three are in Halibut Cove: Lagoon Overlook, with a pair of bunk-beds; Lagoon East Cabin, which has disabled access; and Lagoon West Cabin, a half-mile west of the public dock. China Poot Lake Cabin is a 2.4-mile hike from Halibut Cove on the shore of what's also called Leisure Lake. Moose Valley Cabin is about 2.5 miles from the Halibut Cove Lagoon Ranger Station and only sleeps two ($35). Sea Star Cove Cabin, on the south shore of Tutka Bay, is convenient to the Tutka Lake Trail. China Poot Cabin is accessible by kayak or water-taxi. Make reservations for any of them months in advance.

Yurts
YURTS $

(☑907-299-6879; www.alaskanyurtrentals.com; yurts $77.25) There are eight of these for rent in the park, maintained by a private operator. All are near the ocean and equipped with bunks and woodstoves.

Their locations include: at the mouth of Humpy Creek, at the mouth of Halibut Cove, in China Poot Bay, near the North Eldred Passage Trailhead, near the northwest and southeast Grace Ridge Trailheads, in Tutka Bay and on Quarry Beach at the mouth of Sadie Cove.

ℹ Information

Center for Alaskan Coastal Studies (☑907-235-6667; www.akcoastalstudies.org) Has maps and information about the park, both at its downtown Homer headquarters at Lake St and at its yurt on the Spit behind Mako's Water-Taxi. National Geographic's *Trails Illustrated* map of the park is an excellent resource, depicting hiking routes, public-use cabins, docks and campsites, and it's available here.

ℹ Getting There & Around

A number of water-taxis offer drop-off and pick-up service (round-trip $50 to $80). Because boat access to some of the trailheads is tidally dependent, you'll need to work with them to establish a precise rendezvous time and location – and then be sure to stick to it.

Ashore Water Taxi (☑907-235-2341; www.ashorewatertaxi.com) Charges $75 per person with a two-person minimum to any place in the park.

Mako's Water-Taxi (☑907-235-9055; www.makoswatertaxi.com) For most cross-bay destinations from Homer Spit, it costs $75 with a two-person minimum. To Seldovia, the boat costs $250 one-way, so grab all your friends and fill 'er up. It can also give you the lowdown on possible hikes and paddles in the park – and about the logistics of getting over and back.

Denali & the Interior

Best Places for a Microbrewed Beer

➡ 49th State Brewing Company (p279)

➡ Hoodoo Brewing Co (p300)

➡ Denali Brewing Company (p285)

➡ Silver Gulch Brewery (p300)

Best Frontier Towns

➡ Chicken (p310)

➡ Eagle (p312)

➡ McCarthy (p322)

➡ Manley Hot Springs (305)

Why Go?

Adventures are served up raw in this part of the state, or barbecued with a pint of handcrafted beer. It's your choice. The best of the Interior can be found by forging a trail alone down a braided riverbed, but once-in-a-lifetime encounters with natural wonders can also be had from the seat of a rumbling park bus.

The big name in this region is Denali National Park, blessed with the continent's mightiest mountain, abundant megafauna and easy access. But don't miss the small towns, with their clapboard facades, quirky museums and tales from the days of working some of the biggest mineral finds in history.

Compared to most places in the developed world, the Interior is a trackless hinterland. For Alaska, however, it's got roads galore. With most routes so scenic they've become destinations in themselves, it's best to have an open schedule when you head out.

When to Go

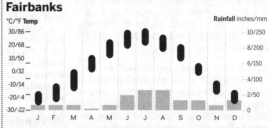

May The best month to visit Denali National Park for clear views of Mt McKinley.

Jun The tundra comes alive with millions of migratory birds.

Sep High probability of seeing the northern lights in Fairbanks.

History

If archaeologists are correct, Interior Alaska was the corridor through which the rest of the continent was peopled, as waves of hunter-gatherers migrated across the Bering land bridge to points south. Ancestors of the region's present Alaska Native group, the Athabascans, are thought to have been here at least 6000 years.

It wasn't until the 1800s that the first white people began to trickle in. The newcomers were mainly traders: Russians, who established posts along the lower Yukon and Kuskokwim Rivers; and Britons, who began trading at Fort Yukon, on the upper Yukon River, in the 1840s. Later came prospectors, whose discoveries transformed this region, beginning with the first major gold rush in the Fortymile district in the 1880s. Similar rushes, for gold and also copper, subsequently gave rise to many Interior communities.

Transportation projects brought the next wave of growth. In 1914 Congress agreed to fund the building of the USA's northernmost railroad, from Seward to Fairbanks. At the peak of construction, 4500 workers labored along the route, and their base camps became boom towns.

Three decades later, during WWII, the building of the Alcan had the same effect on the eastern Interior. Tok and Delta Junction got their starts as highway construction camps, while Fairbanks saw a second boom in its economy and population. Another three decades after that came the biggest undertaking the Interior has ever seen: the laying of the $8 billion Trans-Alaska Pipeline, which transects Alaska, running from Valdez to the Arctic Ocean at Prudhoe Bay.

Dangers & Annoyances

Getting lost in the backcountry is a real possibility, as national and state parks, national forest and Bureau of Land Management (BLM) areas have few marked trails. Come prepared with a compass, topographic map, GPS (optional), enough food and water to get you by for a few extra days and, most importantly, the skills to use your equipment properly. Long sleeves and light pants will help fend off mosquitoes, while our bear tips (p410) should prevent any unpleasant encounters with these creatures. Glacier travel and mountaineering are dangerous endeavors. If you don't know how to self-arrest and perform a crevasse rescue (or don't know what these things are), you should go with a qualified guide.

ℹ Getting There & Around

With scenic highways such as the George Parks, Alcan, Richardson, Glenn, Denali and Taylor criss-crossing this region, consider renting a vehicle if you want to get around at your own pace.

However, most places can – surprisingly – be reached by bus. Interior Alaska Bus Line (p419) travels the Glenn Hwy, Tok Cutoff and bits of the Alcan and Richardson Hwys. Soaring Eagle Transit (p419) plies the Glenn Hwy from Anchorage to Glennallen and the Richardson Hwy from Glennallen down to Valdez. **Alaska/Yukon Trails** (☑ 800-770-7275; www.alaskashuttle.com) covers the George Parks and Taylor Hwys, and the Alcan Hwy into Canada. Both Denali and Wrangell-St Elias National Parks are penetrable by summer shuttles.

Alaska Railroad (☑ 907-265-2494; www.alaskarailroad.com) runs daily between Anchorage and Fairbanks. The train is a mellow, scenic alternative to driving, with depots at two of the Interior's most-visited destinations: Talkeetna and Denali National Park.

For much of Alaska's heartland, bush plane is the only way to get around. Even small Interior villages usually have airstrips and scheduled flights.

DENALI NATIONAL PARK

For many travelers, **Denali National Park & Preserve** (☑ 907-683-2294; www.nps.gov/dena) is the beginning and end of their Alaskan adventure. And why shouldn't it be? Here is probably your best chance in the Interior (if not in the entire state) of seeing a grizzly bear, moose or caribou, and maybe even a fox or wolf. And unlike most wilderness areas in the country, you don't have to be a hiker to view this wildlife. The window of the park bus will do just fine for a close look at these magnificent creatures roaming free in their natural habitat.

For those with a bit more time and the desire to get further into the wild, there are vast expanses of untracked country to explore – more than 6 million acres of it, to be exact. That's more landmass than the US state of Massachusetts. At the center of it all is the icy behemoth of Mt McKinley, known to most Alaskans as Denali and to native Athabascans as the Great One. This is North America's highest peak and rightly celebrated as an icon of all that is awesome and wild in the state.

There's only one road through the park: the 92-mile unpaved Park Rd, which is closed to private vehicles after Mile 14. The

Denali & the Interior Highlights

1 Viewing caribou against the backdrop of Mt McKinley from Denali National Park's **Park Road** (p265)

2 Hiking or birdwatching off **Denali Highway** (p290)

3 Circling the highest mountain in North America on a **flightseeing tour** (p283) out of Talkeetna

4 Stepping into the great expanse of untouched wilderness in **Wrangell-St Elias National Park** (p319)

5 Riding the luxurious **Denali Star** (p184) train between Anchorage and Fairbanks

6 Exploring mountains, glaciers and massive copper mine remains around **Kennecott** (p324) and **McCarthy** (p322)

7 Beholding the northern lights from **Fairbanks** (p292)

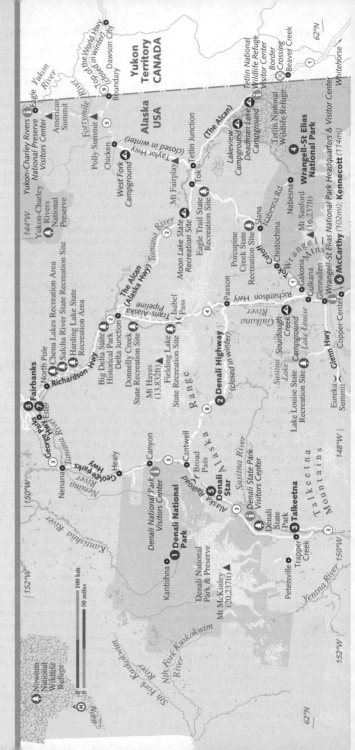

park entrance area, where most visitors congregate, extends a scant 4 miles up Park Rd. It's here you'll find the park headquarters, visitor center and main campground, as well as the Wilderness Access Center (WAC), where you pay your park entrance fee and arrange campground and shuttle-bus bookings to take you further into the park. In a trailer across the lot from the WAC sits the Backcountry Information Center (BIC), where backpackers get backcountry permits and bear-proof food containers.

There are few places to stay within the park, excluding campgrounds, and only one restaurant. The majority of visitors base themselves in the nearby communities of Canyon, McKinley Village, Carlo Creek and Healy.

History

The Athabascan people used what is now Denali National Park as hunting grounds, but it wasn't until gold was found near Kantishna in 1905 that the area really began to see development. With the gold stampede came the big-game hunters, and things weren't looking very good for this amazing stretch of wilderness until a noted hunter and naturalist, Charles Sheldon, came to town.

Sheldon, stunned by the destruction, mounted a campaign to protect the region. From this, Mt McKinley National Park was born. Later, as a result of the 1980 Alaska National Interest Lands Conservation Act, the park was enlarged by 4 million acres, and renamed Denali National Park and Preserve.

In 1923, when the railroad arrived, 36 visitors enjoyed the splendor of the new park. Nowadays some 400,000 visitors are received annually. A number of unique visitor-management strategies have been created to deal with the masses, and generally they've been successful. The Denali National Park of today is still the great wilderness it was decades ago.

◉ Sights & Activities

◉ Park Road

Park Rd begins at George Parks Hwy and winds 92 miles through the heart of the park, ending at Kantishna, an old mining settlement and the site of several wilderness lodges. Early on, park officials envisaged the onset of bumper-to-bumper traffic along this road and wisely closed almost all of it to private vehicles. With few exceptions, motorists can drive only to a parking area along the Savage River at Mile 14, 1 mile beyond the Savage River Campground. To venture further along the road you must walk, cycle, be part of a tour or, most popularly, take a park shuttle or camper bus.

If you're planning to spend the day riding the buses (it's an eight-hour round trip to the Eielson Visitor Center, the most popular day trip in the park), pack plenty of food and drink. It can be a long, dusty ride, and in the park there are only limited services at the Toklat River Contact Station and Eielson Visitor Center. Carry a park map so you know where you are and can scope out ridges or riverbeds that appeal for hiking.

Mt McKinley   MOUNTAIN
What makes 20,237ft Mt McKinley (Denali) one of the world's great scenic mountains is the sheer independent rise of its bulk. McKinley begins at a base of just 2000ft, which means that on a clear day you will be transfixed by over 18,000ft of ascending rock, ice and snow. By contrast, Mt Everest, no slouch itself when it comes to memorable vistas, only rises 12,000ft from its base on the Tibetan Plateau.

Despite its lofty heights, the mountain is not visible from the park entrance or the nearby campgrounds and hotel. Your first glimpse of it comes between Mile 9 and Mile 11 on Park Rd, if you're blessed with a clear day. The rule of thumb stressed by the National Park Service (NPS) rangers is that Mt McKinley is hidden two out of every three days, but that's a random example – it could be clear for a week and then hidden for the next month. While the 'Great One' might not be visible for most of the first 15 miles of Park Rd, this is the best stretch to spot moose because of the proliferation of spruce and especially willow, the animal's favorite food. The open flats before Savage River are good for spotting caribou and sometimes brown bears.

◉ Savage River to Eielson Visitor Center

From Savage River, the road dips into the Sanctuary and Teklanika valleys, and Mt McKinley disappears behind the foothills. Igloo Creek Campground (p275) is the unofficial beginning of 'bear country.'

After passing through the canyon formed by the Igloo and Cathedral Mountains, the road ascends to 3880ft **Sable Pass** (Mile

Denali National Park – Park Road

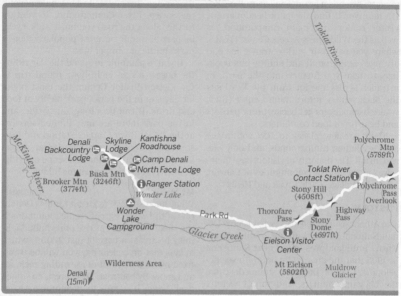

38.5). The canyon and surrounding mountains are excellent places to view Dall sheep, while the pass is known as a prime habitat for Toklat brown bears.

Given the prevalence of big brown bears and other wildlife, the area around Sable Pass is permanently closed to hikers and backpackers. From here, the road drops to the bridge over the **East Fork Toklat River** (Mile 44). Hikers can trek from the bridge along the riverbanks both north and south.

Polychrome Pass Overlook (Mile 47) is a rest stop for the shuttle buses. This scenic area, at 3500ft, has views of the Toklat River to the south.

Passengers on the shuttle bus normally stop at the **Toklat River Contact Station** (Mile 53; ⊘9am-7pm) on the way back. There are a few displays and some books for sale, as well as scopes to check out Dall sheep on the neighboring hills.

Eielson Visitor Center (Mile 66; ⊘9am-7pm Jun–mid-Sep), on the far side of Thorofare Pass (3900ft), is the most common turning-around point for day-trippers taking the shuttle or tour buses into the park. This remote outpost is built directly into the tundra slopes and Mt McKinley seems to almost loom over you from the observation decks. Inside there's a massive panorama to give

you an idea of the mountain's topography, as well as more utilitarian features such as toilets and potable water. Note that there's no food available here.

Two ranger-led hikes are offered daily in summer: a two-hour 'tough' hike, starting at noon and heading up the ridge behind the facilities; and an easier one-hour hike down to the river, starting at 1pm.

⊙ Eielson to Kantishna

Past Eielson, Park Rd drops to the valley, passing a sign for **Muldrow Glacier** (Mile 74.4). At this point, the glacier lies about a mile to the south, and the terminus of the 32-mile flow of ice is clearly visible, though you might not recognize it because the ice is covered with a mat of plant life. If the weather is cloudy and Mt McKinley and the surrounding peaks are hidden, the final 20 miles of the bus trip are still an enjoyable ride through rolling tundra, passing small glacier-made lakes known as kettle ponds. Study the pools of water carefully to spot beavers or waterfowl.

Wonder Lake Campground (p274), only 26 miles from Mt McKinley, sees the beauty of the mountain doubled on a clear day as the peak reflects off the lake's surface. Sad-

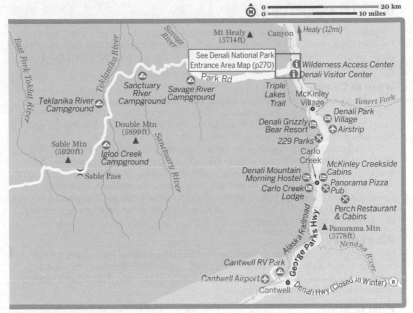

ly, the heavy demand for the 28 campsites and the numerous overcast days caused by Mt McKinley itself prevent the majority of visitors from ever seeing this remarkable panorama. If you do experience the reddish sunset on the summit reflecting off the lake's still waters, cherish the moment.

The campground is on a low rise above the lake's southern end. The famous McKinley reflected-in-the lake photos are taken along the northeast shore, 2 miles beyond the campground.

Kantishna (Mile 90) is mainly a destination for people staying in the area's private lodges. The buses turn around here after a 40-minute rest, and begin the long trip back to the WAC.

Wildlife Watching

Because hunting has never been allowed in the park, professional photographers refer to animals in Denali as 'approachable wildlife.' That means bear, moose, Dall sheep and caribou aren't as skittish here as in other regions of the state. For this reason, and because Park Rd was built to maximize the chances of seeing wildlife by traversing high open ground, the national park is an excellent place to view a variety of animals.

On board the park shuttle buses, your fellow passengers will be armed with binoculars and cameras to help scour the terrain for animals, most of which are so accustomed to the rambling buses that they rarely run and hide. When someone spots something and yells 'Stop!' the driver will pull over for viewing and picture taking. The best wildlife watching is on the first morning bus.

Bears

In the area of the park that most people visit (north of the Alaska Range), there are an estimated 350 grizzly bears and an unknown number of black bears. Grizzlies tend to inhabit tundra areas, while black bears stick to the forests. With most of Denali's streams fed by glaciers, the fishing is poor and bears must rely on vegetation for 85% of their diet. As a result, most male grizzlies here range from only 300lb to 600lb, while their cousins on the salmon-rich coasts can easily top 1000lb.

There's no guarantee of seeing a grizzly, but most park bus drivers say they spot around five to eight per day along the road.

Moose

Anywhere between 2000 and 2500 moose roam the park, and they are almost always found in stands of spruce and willow shrubs (their favorite food). Backpackers should be wary when plowing blindly through areas of thick ground cover, especially in early

DENALI PLANNING GUIDE

Consider making reservations at least six months in advance for a park campsite during the height of summer, and at least three months ahead for accommodations outside the park. The park entrance fee is $10 per person, good for seven days. Vehicles are charged another $20.

When to Come

From May 15 to June 1, park services are just starting up and access to the backcountry is limited. Visitor numbers are low but shuttle buses only run as far as Toklat River. From June 1 to 8, access increases and the shuttle buses run as far as Eielson Visitor Center. After June 8, the park is in full swing till late August.

Shuttle buses stop running after the second Thursday after Labor Day in September. After a few days in which lottery-winning Alaska residents are allowed to take their private vehicles past Mile 14, Park Rd closes to all traffic until the following May.

While most area lodges close, Riley Creek Campground stays open in winter and camping is free, though the water and sewage facilities don't operate. If you have the equipment, you can use the unplowed Park Rd and the rest of the park for cross-country skiing, snowshoeing or dog sledding.

Road Lottery

Every summer the park holds a road lottery for Alaskan residents. The winners get the opportunity to drive their cars along the normally closed Park Rd as far as the weather allows over four days in early September. Most years there are about 1200 lucky winners. For more details see www.nps.gov/denali.

What to Bring

Bring all your own gear if you're camping, as supplies are limited. Basic groceries and dehydrated meals can be purchased; enough for a few days camping in the backcountry, for example.

The park tends to be cool, cloudy and drizzly most of the summer. Don't forget your rain gear.

Reservations

From December 1 you can reserve campsites and shuttle buses online through the **Denali National Park Reservation Service** (907-272-7275; www.reservedenali.com).

Note that sites in the Sanctuary River and Igloo Creek campgrounds can only be reserved in person at the WAC two days in advance, and backcountry permits one day in advance.

September, when the bulls clash over breeding rights to the cows.

Caribou

All the park's caribou belong to the Denali herd – one of 32 herds in Alaska – which presently numbers around 2000 animals. The best time to spot caribou in large groups is in late summer, when the animals begin to band in anticipation of the fall migration. They're often spotted earlier in summer in small bands on the hillsides. Look for unusual patches of white that just don't seem to belong there.

Wolves

Consider yourself lucky if you spot a wolf in the park. Denali is home to a fluctuating population, with approximately 70 wolves living in the 10 packs currently being monitored. 'In summer, wolf packs are less likely to travel in a large group because they center their activity around a den or rendezvous site, with one or more adults often remaining there with the pups,' says park wildlife biologist Tom Meier. Your best shot at sighting a wolf is along Park Rd, or near Igloo Creek Campground.

Other Species

In addition to moose, caribou, wolves and bears, Denali is home to 33 other species of mammal – from wolverines to mice – as well as 159 varieties of birds (including the golden eagle, tundra swan, rock ptarmigan, jaeger sand great horned owl), 10 types of fish and a lone amphibian, the wood frog.

Ranger-Led Activities

If you're hesitant about venturing into the wilds on your own, or merely looking to kill some time until your desired backcountry unit opens, Denali offers a daily slate of worthwhile free ranger-led hikes and presentations.

Sled-Dog Demonstrations DOG SLEDDING

(Map p270; Park Headquarters; ⊙10am, 2pm & 4pm) **FREE** Denali is the only US national park where rangers conduct winter patrols with dog teams. In summer the huskies serve a different purpose: amusing and educating the legions of tourists who sign up for the park's free daily tours of the sled-dog kennels,

SCALING THE MOUNTAIN

So, has gazing at lordly Mt McKinley from the seat of an aircraft infected you with summit fever?

If so, you're suffering from a century-old sickness. James Wickersham, the US district judge in Alaska, made the first documented attempt to scale Denali, reaching the 7500ft mark of the 20,237ft peak in 1903. His effort inspired a rash of ensuing bids, including Dr Frederick Cook's 1906 effort (which he falsely claimed was a success) and the 1910 Sourdough Expedition, where four Fairbanks miners, carrying only hot chocolate, doughnuts and a 14ft spruce pole, topped out on the North Peak only to realize it was 850ft lower than the true, more southerly summit.

Success finally came in 1913 when Hudson Stuck, Henry Karstens, Robert Tatum and Walter Harper reached the top on June 7. From there they saw the spruce pole on the North Peak to verify the claims of the Sourdough Expedition.

The most important date for many climbers, however, is 1951. That year, Bradford Washburn arrived and pioneered the West Buttress route, by far the preferred avenue to the top. Not long after, Talkeetna's two most famous characters – Ray 'the Pirate' Genet and Don Sheldon – began to have an impact on the climbing world. Genet was an Alaskan mountaineer who made a record 25 climbs up Mt McKinley, while Sheldon was a legendary glacier pilot. The two worked closely in guiding climbers to the top and, more importantly, rescuing those who failed. Sadly, the town lost both in quick succession, with Sheldon dying of cancer in 1975 and Genet freezing to death on Mt Everest four years later.

Nowadays, Denali's storied mountaineering history adds considerably to the mythic business of scaling the peak. Between 1200 and 1300 climbers attempt it each year, spending an average of three weeks on the slopes. About 90% use the West Buttress route, which involves flying in a ski plane from Talkeetna to the 7200ft Kahiltna Glacier and from there climbing for the South Peak, passing a medical/rescue camp maintained by mountaineering clubs and the NPS at 14,220ft.

In a good season (April through July), when storms are not constantly sweeping across the range, more than 50% will be successful. In a bad year that rate falls below 40%, and several climbers may die. Particularly grim was the annus horribilis of 1991, when 11 lives were lost.

The most solemn way to appreciate the effect of the mountain is to visit the cemetery in Talkeetna, a restful spot set among tall trees on 2nd St, just off Talkeetna Spur Rd near the airport. Don Sheldon's grave is the most prominent, with the epitaph 'He wagered with the wind and won.' The Mt McKinley Climber's Memorial includes a stone for Ray Genet, despite the fact that his body was never removed from the slopes of Mt Everest. The most touching sight, however, is a memorial with the names and ages of all the climbers who've died on Mt McKinley and neighboring peaks.

If you're a seasoned alpinist you can mount an expedition yourself, or be among the 25% of Mt McKinley climbers who are part of guided ascents. If you're looking for a local guiding company, try **Alaska Mountaineering School** (☎907-733-1016; www.climbalaska.org), which charges $7000 to lead you up the mountain. Another acclaimed company with a high success rate is Seattle-based **Alpine Ascents** (www.alpineascents.com). Trips start at $7300 excluding meals, lodging and flights to Alaska. Book at least a year in advance.

People without high-altitude credentials would be better off opting for a mountaineering and glacier-travel course. Alaska Mountaineering School has packages from $425 for a two-day glacier-travel seminar at Matanuska Glacier.

Denali National Park Entrance Area

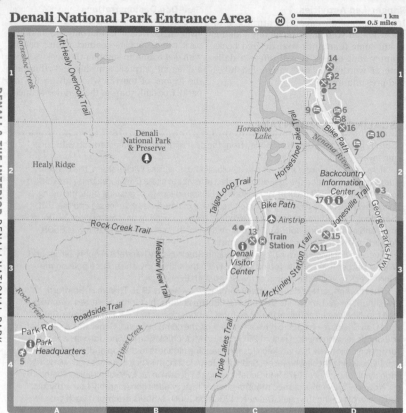

and dog demonstrations. The 40-minute show takes place at park headquarters; free buses head there from the visitor center, departing 40 minutes before each starting time.

Campground Programs　　GUIDED TOUR
(⊙7:30pm) At the Riley Creek, Savage River, Teklanika and Wonder Lake Campgrounds, rangers present 45-minute talks on Denali's wildlife and natural history, or whatever topic they want to expound upon. You're welcome to show up even if you're not camping.

Entrance-Area Hikes　　WALKING TOUR
To join a ranger on an easy, guided stroll (ranging from 30 minutes to 2½ hours) along the park's entrance-area trails, check out the schedule at the visitor center.

Discovery Hikes　　HIKING
Moderate-to-strenuous, three-to-five-hour hikes departing from Park Rd. The location

varies from day to day; you can find the schedule at the visitor center. Sign up there one or two days in advance and then go to the WAC to reserve a shuttle ticket. Shuttles leave at 8am.

Note that hiking is off trail, so be sure to have sturdy footwear and to pack rain gear, food and water.

Day Hiking
Even for those who have neither the desire nor the equipment for an overnight trek, hiking is still the best way to enjoy the park and to see the land and its wildlife. You can hike virtually anywhere that hasn't been closed to prevent an impact on wildlife.

For a day hike (which doesn't require a permit), try one of the options below or go it alone – just ride the shuttle bus and get off at any valley, riverbed or ridge that grabs your fancy. Check in at the BIC for suggestions.

Denali National Park Entrance Area

DENALI & THE INTERIOR DENALI NATIONAL PARK

Park Entrance Area
HIKING

A few short, well-maintained trails web the park entrance area.

The **Horseshoe Lake Trail**, accessed at Mile 1.2 of Park Rd, by the railroad crossing, is a leisurely 1.5-mile walk through the woods to the lake overlook, followed by a steep trail to the water's edge and beaver dam at the end. The **Taiga Loop Trail**, also commencing from the railroad tracks, turns west from the Horseshoe Lake Trail and leads to both Mt Healy Overlook Trail and Rock Creek Trail.

The moderate, 2.3-mile **Rock Creek Trail** leads west to the park headquarters and dog kennels. It's far easier hiking this trail downhill from the headquarters end, where the trail begins just before Park Rd. From here it crosses Rock Creek but doesn't stay with the stream. Instead, it climbs a gentle slope of mixed aspen and spruce forest, breaks out along a ridge with scenic views of Mt Healy and George Parks Hwy and then begins a rapid descent to its end at the Taiga Loop Trail.

The **Roadside Trail** parallels Park Rd and takes you 1.5 miles from the visitor center to park headquarters. The 1.6-mile **McKinley Station Trail** takes you from the visitor center to the WAC and also connects with the **Jonesville Trail** to Canyon.

Triple Lakes Trail
HIKING

When it opened in 2011, this 8.6-mile trail (six to eight hours) quickly gained a reputation as the entrance area's best day hike. The terrain and vegetation are more varied than on other trails, and there's a palpable feeling that you've truly entered the wilds.

From the McKinley Station Trail the path begins after a bridge crossing of Hines Creek. The trail is flat at first and the forest cover unusually lush. In about a mile you begin to climb switchbacks until eventually reaching a ridgetop affording yodel-inspiring views of the Alaska Range and the valleys formed by Hines Creek and the Nenana River.

After a long run along the ridgeline, the path begins to descend, first to the Triple Lakes and then to George Parks Hwy. After crossing the highway bridge it's a short walk to McKinley Village Lodge, where you can catch a shuttle ($5) back to the visitor center.

Mt Healy Overlook Trail
HIKING

The combination workout and rewarding views over the Nenana valley, Healy Ridge and other ridgelines makes this another highly popular day hike in the entrance area. The trail veers off the Taiga Loop Trail and makes a steep climb up Mt Healy, ascending 1700ft in 2.5 miles.

While you begin in a forest of spruce, alder and aspen, higher up you enter alpine tundra – a world of moss, lichen, wildflowers and incredible views. Keep an eye out for the large hoary marmots (a northern cousin of the groundhog), and the pika, a small relative of the rabbit. Plan on three to four hours for the return hike.

From the overlook (3425ft), hardy hikers can climb another mile to the high point of Healy Ridge (4217ft), or another 2 miles to the summit of Mt Healy (5714ft).

Savage River Loop Trail · HIKING

You can get to this trailhead by car (Mile 14), but you're better off taking the free Savage River Shuttle Bus as the small parking lot often fills up. The 2-mile loop is wheelchair accessible for the first half-mile and runs north from Park Rd on either side of the river.

People looking for a longer hike can continue past the bridge that marks the 'official' turnaround point along an informal trail paralleling the river's west bank.

Savage Alpine Trail · HIKING

New in 2013, this 4-mile trail begins at Savage River (Mile 15), ascends 1200ft to a windy alpine ridge with fabulous views and descends to the new Mountain Vista day-use area (Mile 13), where you can catch a park shuttle.

Backpacking

The park is divided into 87 backcountry units, and for 41 of these only a regulated number of backpackers (usually four to six) are allowed in at a time. You may spend a maximum of seven nights in any one unit, and a maximum of 30 consecutive nights in the backcountry. For more information download *A Denali Backpacking Guide* from the national park's website (www.nps.gov/dena).

Permits are needed to camp overnight and you can obtain these at the Backcountry Information Center (p280), where you'll also find wall maps with the unit outlines and a quota board indicating the number of vacancies in each. Permits are issued only a day in advance, and the most popular units fill up fast. It pays to be flexible: decide which areas you're aiming for, and be prepared to take any zone that's open. If you're picky, you might have to wait several days.

After you've decided where to go, the next step is to watch the required backcountry orientation video, followed by a brief safety talk that covers, among other things, proper use of the bear-resistant food containers (BRFCs) you'll receive free of charge with your permit. The containers are bulky, but they work – they've reduced bear encounters dramatically since 1986. It's also worth noting that you're required to pack out dirty toilet paper (you bury your waste), so be sure to carry at least a dozen ziplock bags. Finally, after receiving your permit, buy the topographic maps ($8) for your unit and then head over to the WAC to purchase a ticket on a camper bus ($34.50) to get you to the starting point of your hike.

For an overview of the different units in the park, check out the park's website for the brilliant Backcountry Camping and Hiking Guide, which includes unit-by-unit descriptions, including access points, possible hiking corridors, dangers and, maybe best of all, pictures from the area.

A MOUNTAIN BY ANY OTHER NAME

The Athabascans called it Denali or the 'Great One.' Their brethren to the south in the Susitna Valley called it Doleika, the 'Big Mountain.' The Aleuts meanwhile referred to it as Traleika. The first European to spot the peak, George Vancouver, didn't bother to call it anything, while Ferdinand von Wrangell, a prominent Russian administrator in the 19th century, wrote 'Tenada' on his maps. So why do we largely know North America's highest peak by the name McKinley?

During the gold-rush days, the mountain underwent yet another name change, this time to Densmore's Mountain in honor of a local prospector. But soon afterwards it was dubbed Mt McKinley, after William McKinley, an Ohioan who would soon become president of the United States. And that name seems to have stuck, at least officially.

But the name 'Denali' slowly began creeping back into people's minds, and finally made the maps in 1980 when the park was redesignated as Denali National Park & Preserve and the Alaskan Geographic Board officially renamed the mountain Denali. Despite these statewide changes, US map-makers still refer to Denali as McKinley. While it serves as an easy way to differentiate between park and mountain, it's mainly one stalwart congressman from Ohio, Ralph Regula, who keeps the name from changing. Every time Denali – we mean, um, McKinley – comes up for a name change, the congressman blocks it. But the blocking won't go on for long. Across the USA – and the world for that matter – many colonial and European names are being replaced by their original, aboriginal equivalents. Given that William McKinley never visited Alaska, it seems likely the mountain will one day return to the name it had for centuries, before there was such a place as Ohio, or even the USA.

LOCAL KNOWLEDGE

TRAIL-LESS HIKING

In most national parks in North America, hikers are constantly reminded to stay on marked trails in order to prevent soil erosion, deter damage to flora and fauna, and minimize the risk of getting lost. But Alaska – being Alaska – operates a little differently. Since most national parks in the state don't have an extensive network of marked trails, visitors are actively encouraged to get off the beaten track and explore the backcountry on their own.

Hiking without a signposted trail can be an intimidating experience to the average city dweller, especially if you're sharing the domain with bears, moose and various other unseen fauna (not to mention mosquitoes). The key to successful backcountry travel is being able to use a compass and read a topographic map. Riverbeds are easy to follow and make excellent avenues for the backpacker. Formed by glaciers during the last ice age, the river valleys never fill, though individual braids can get dangerously high and fast and must be forded with caution. Ridges are also good routes to use if the weather isn't foul.

If you've never veered off the beaten path, consider launching your trail-less hiking career in Denali National Park. Denali's 92-mile-long Park Rd provides an excellent transport link into the depths of the park with regular hop on, hop-off shuttle buses plying the route. Additionally, thanks to its high latitude, most of the park is above the treeline, allowing hikers to enjoy broad vistas across obstacle-free tundra. Not only does this mean Park Rd will be rarely out of sight (even when it's 5 miles away), it also prevents any surprise encounters with wildlife.

The treeline in Denali is at 2700ft. Above this you'll usually find tussock or moist tundra – humps of watery grass that make for sloppy hiking. Climb above 3400ft, however, and you'll be in alpine or dry tundra, making the going a lot easier. Note that cross-country hikers shouldn't walk in a line; rather, rangers recommend that you fan out to avoid creating trails.

Regardless of where you're headed, remember that 5 miles is a full-day trip for the average backpacker in Denali's backcountry.

A good compromise in Denali for those unsure of entering the backcountry on their own is to take a ranger-led Discovery Hike (ie hiking without a trail but *with* a guide); see p270.

Cycling

No special permit is needed to cycle on Park Rd, but cycling off road is prohibited. Camper buses and some shuttle buses will carry bicycles, but only two at a time and only if you have a reservation. Many cyclists ride the bus in and cycle back out, carrying their gear and staying at campsites they've reserved along the way. It's also possible to take an early morning bus in, ride for several hours and catch a bus back the same day. The highest point on the road is Highway Pass (3980ft). The entrance area is at 1585ft.

Denali Outdoor Center   BICYCLE RENTAL
(Map p270; www.denalioutdoorcenter.com; Mile 238.9, George Parks Hwy; bike per hr/day $8/40) You can rent bicycles at this Canyon fixture – minimum two-hour rental. Rates include a helmet, water bottle, tools and lock.

Tours

Some travelers confuse 'shuttle buses' and 'tour buses.' The former are purely for getting around the park. The latter ply the same routes, but with drivers who give narrated tours. If you're lucky and have a congenial driver on a park shuttle, you can get good lowdown on what's what without paying the extra cost of a tour.

The following narrated tours all include a packed lunch. See www.nps.gov/dena for more and www.reservedenali.com to make reservations.

Natural History Tour   GUIDED TOUR
(adult/child $69.50/34.75) Get your fill of all things Denali on this four- to five-hour trip out to Primrose Ridge (Mile 17).

Tundra Wilderness Tour   GUIDED TOUR
(adult/child $118.50/59.25) This seven- to eight-hour tour to Toklat River (Mile 53) focuses on wildlife viewing.

Kantishna Experience   GUIDED TOUR
(adult/child $165/82.50) The longest tour (12 hours) goes to the end of the road at the old mining area of Kantishna (Mile 92).

ATVs

Denali ATV Adventures   ADVENTURE SPORTS
(Map p270; ☎907-683-4288; www.denaliatv.com; Mile 238.6, George Parks Hwy) Offers two- and four-hour butt-busting rides ($105 to $185).

Note that you're not allowed to make this kind of cacophony in the national park. Instead, the trips skirt the park's fringes. The Stampede Trail is particularly popular.

Flightseeing

Most flightseeing tours around Denali leave from Talkeetna, but some companies also operate out of the park area.

Era Helicopters   SCENIC FLIGHTS
(Map p270; ☑ 907-683-2574; www.eraflightseeing.com; Mile 238, George Parks Hwy) Will take you up on a 35-minute Denali tour ($350) or a 50-minute flight that includes a glacier landing ($490). Heli-hiking trips are also available. The helipad is on the northern side of the Nenana River Bridge, at the southern end of Canyon.

Kantishna Air Taxi   SCENIC FLIGHTS
(☑ 907-683-1223; www.katair.com) Based at Skyline Lodge, and flies out of Kantishna, the park entrance and Healy. Hour-long flightseeing excursions around Mt McKinley are $250 per person from Kantishna.

River Rafting

Thanks to Denali tourists, the Nenana River is the most popular white-water-rafting area in Alaska. The river's main white-water stretch begins near the park entrance and ends 10 miles north, near Healy. It's rated class III and IV, and involves standing waves, rapids and holes with names such as 'Coffee Grinder' in sheer-sided canyons. South of the park entrance the river is much milder, but to many it's just as interesting as it veers away from both the highway and the railroad, increasing your chances of sighting wildlife.

Rafting companies offer similar guided trips on both stretches in which either the guide does all the work or you help paddle. Advanced reservations (no deposit) are accepted, and all trips include dry suits and shuttle pickups. The canyon and the easier 'wilderness' paddles go for about $89, and last around three hours.

Denali Outdoor Center   RAFTING
(Map p270; ☑ 907-683-1925; www.denalioutdoorcenter.com; Mile 238.9, George Parks Hwy) Considered one of the finest rafting outfits, with good equipment, a safety-first philosophy and friendly guides. Also offers half-day excursions and inflatable kayak tours from $127.

Denali Raft Adventures   RAFTING
(Map p270; ☑ 907-683-2234; denaliraft.com; Mile 238.6, George Parks Hwy) You can wave at trains as you saunter down the Nenana River between Canyon and Healy on class I to IV rapids with this outfit. Its office is in Canyon.

Courses

Murie Science & Learning Center OUTDOORS
(Map p270; www.murieslc.org; Mile 1.5, Park Rd; ☺ 9:30am-5pm; ⓘ) Representing eight of Alaska's arctic and subarctic parks, the center is *the* place to come for information on research taking place within the park and around the state. During the summer there are presentations and half-day 'Denaliology' courses, as well as multiday field seminars (coordinated with Alaska Geographic), teacher training and youth camps.

Denali Education Center   ADVENTURE
(☑ 907-683-2597; www.denali.org; Mile 231, George Parks Hwy; ⓘ) Offers day and extended educational/backpacking programs, including a number specifically designed for seniors and youths.

🛏 Sleeping

You definitely want something reserved in midsummer – even if it's just a campsite – before you show up. Note the Denali Borough charges a 7% accommodations tax on top of listed prices (except for campsites).

🛏 Within the Park

Kantishna excepted, lodgings are not available inside park boundaries, so if you want overnight shelter within the park you'll need a tent or RV.

Wonder Lake Campground   CAMPGROUND $
(Mile 85, Park Rd; tent sites $16) This is the jewel of Denali campgrounds, thanks to its eye-popping views of Mt McKinley. The facility has 28 sites for tents only, but does offer flush toilets and piped-in water. If you're lucky enough to reserve a site, book it for three nights and then pray that the mountain appears during one of the days you're there.

Also, pack plenty of insect repellent and maybe even a head net – the bugs are vicious in midsummer.

Riley Creek Campground   CAMPGROUND $
(Map p270; Mile 0.2, Park Rd; tent sites $14, campsites $22-28) At the park's main entrance, and within earshot of George Parks Hwy, this is Denali's largest and most developed campground. It's open year-round and has 146

sites for tents and RVs, piped-in water, flush toilets and evening interpretive programs. Walk-ins have their own section in C lot.

The location is convenient for access to Riley Creek Mercantile (p278; with wi-fi), the WAC, visitor center and many hikes.

Savage River Campground CAMPGROUND $
(Mile 13, Park Rd; campsites $22-28) Despite its name, this is a mile short of the actual river and close to the new Mountain Vista rest area. It's one of only two campgrounds with a view of Mt McKinley. The 33 sites can accommodate both RVs and tents, with such amenities as flush toilets, piped-in water and evening presentations.

Teklanika River Campground CAMPGROUND $
(Mile 29, Park Rd; campsites $16) There are 53 sites, flush toilets, piped-in water and evening programs at this campground, popular with tenters, RVers and the occasional wolf or two. You can drive to the campground but you must stay a minimum of three days if you do, and you can't use your vehicle until you're ready to return to the park entrance.

Sanctuary River Campground CAMPGROUND $
(Mile 23, Park Rd; tent sites $9) The next campground down Park Rd from Savage River, nicely set on the banks of a large glacial river. The seven sites can't be reserved in advance, however, and there's no piped-in water. The area is great for day hiking, though.

Head south to trek along the river or climb Mt Wright or Primrose Ridge to the north for an opportunity to photograph Dall sheep.

Igloo Creek Campground CAMPGROUND $
(Mile 34, Park Rd; tent sites $9) This small, waterless, seven-site camping area marks the beginning of true bear country. The day hiking around here is excellent, especially the numerous ridges around Igloo Mountain and Cathedral that provide routes into alpine areas.

🛏 Kantishna

The Park Rd ends at this privately owned island of land, an old gold-mining enclave that was outside the park's original boundary but was enveloped by additions in 1980. Kantishna provides the ultimate lodging location. Many options include meals and round-trip transportation from the park entrance.

★**Camp Denali** LODGE $$$
(907-683-2290; www.campdenali.com; cabins per person without bath per minimum 3-night stay $1690) Verging on legendary, Camp Denali has been the gold standard among Kantishna lodges for the last half-century. Widely spread across a ridgeline, the camp's simple, comfortable cabins elegantly complement the backcountry experience while minimizing impact on the natural world.

Think of it as luxury camping, with gourmet meals, guided hikes, free bicycle and canoe rentals, killer views of the mountain, and staff so devoted to Denali that you'll come away feeling like the beneficiary of a precious gift. If you can't handle the outhouses or the seven-minute walk to the bathroom, book the nearby, affiliated North Face Lodge (907-683-2290) with en-suite rooms for the same price.

Denali Backcountry Lodge LODGE $$$
(907-376-1992, 877-233-6254; www.denalilodge. com; s/d incl meals $593/978) The last lodge on the road, this is a great-looking place on the banks of Moose Creek with comfortable modern cabins and common areas. Transport, meals and guided activities are included.

Skyline Lodge LODGE $$$
(907-683-1223; www.katair.com; d without bath $275) This four-room, solar-powered lodge serves as Kantishna Air Taxi's base of operations. Guests have use of a common area, dining room, bath and shower block, and decks overlooking the Kantishna valley. Add $60 per person for meals.

Kantishna Roadhouse LODGE $$$
(800-942-7420; www.kantishnaroadhouse.com; d incl meals $990) Owned by park concessionaire Doyon, Kantishna Roadhouse has clean modern cabins, a beautiful dining room, bar and guided activities. Room rates include round-trip transport from the park entrance and various guided activities. Note there is a two-day minimum stay.

🛏 Canyon

Canyon is as close as the Denali area comes to a 'village.' In essence, it's a convenient, if not particularly attractive, service center consisting of a thin strip of wooden shops, accommodations, gas stations and stores clustered either side of the George Parks Hwy, roughly a mile north of the park entrance area (a walking path links the two).

The western side of the road is dominated by two cruise-line-owned hotels, including the Denali Princess Wilderness Lodge. The eastern side harbors a skinny line of shops, restaurants and outdoor-adventure specialists.

Crow's Nest   264

CABIN $$

(Map p270; 907-683-2723, 888-917-8130; www.denalicrowsnest.com; Mile 238.5, George Parks Hwy; cabins $179-199;) Rustic but proud might describe the feel of the recently refurbished Nest rooms, arranged in terraced rows that afford better and better views the higher you go. Beds are fluffy and comfortable and cabins have pleasant terraces and en-suite bathrooms. The lodge runs a free shuttle bus into the park (5am to 10pm). The on-site Overlook Restaurant was being refurbished at last visit.

Denali Park Salmon Bake Restaurant & Cabins   79 → no bath

CABIN $$

(Map p270; 907-683-7283; www.thebakerocks.com; Mile 238.5, George Parks Hwy; cabins without/with bath $69/149;) These standard cabins come with TVs, heaters and baths and are on the dingy side of clean. The economy rooms have shared bath and a shingle exterior with a white tarpaulin roof cover, giving the place a bit of a work-camp atmosphere. Notwithstanding, Salmon Bake is a big player in Canyon, running a popular bar, restaurant and shuttle bus.

Denali Princess Wilderness Lodge

HOTEL $$$

(Map p270; 907-683-2282; www.princesslodges.com; Mile 238.5, George Parks Hwy; r from $269;) The high-roofed, perennially busy reception hall at this giant 'lodge' carries the slightly antiseptic essence of a cruise ship, which is fitting as 80% of its guests are cruisers bused up from the coast. The splayed grounds constitute a medium-sized resort overlooking the choppy Nenana River and exhibit multiple restaurants, shops, hot tubs and accommodations blocks.

It's all very comprehensive, but oddly lacking in soul, for want of a better word.

Grande Denali Lodge

HOTEL $$$

(Map p270; 907-683-5100; www.denalialaska.com; r $271;) The pro here is the location, perched like an eagle's nest over the George Parks Hwy and high above the cacophony of Canyon. The con is the price, which doesn't really match the plain, unimaginative rooms. Solution: linger in the lodge's comfy communal areas and admire the stupendous view.

The affiliated **Denali Bluffs Hotel** (Map p270; r $204;) is further down the hillside.

McKinley Village

Six miles south of the park entrance, McKinley Village (Mile 229–231) sits at a cozy bend of the Nenana River. Though small, the area is far less commercialized than Canyon and is served by a courtesy bus ($5, 6am to 10pm) running between Denali Park Village, Canyon, the visitor center and the WAC. If you need to withdraw money, Denali Park Village has an ATM in the lobby.

Denali Grizzly Bear Resort   229 + tax

CABIN $

(907-683-2696; www.denaligrizzlybear.com; Mile 231.1, George Parks Hwy; campsites $25, tent cabins from $33, cabins $69-269;) The 'Grizzly' spans pretty much every price range and configuration, from wooded campsites by the Nenana River, to platform tent cabins, to 23 well-spaced cabins in various styles. Some cabins are modern and come with private bath, river views and kitchen, while others have tons of Alaskan character (including one log cabin that was dismantled and brought in from Fairbanks).

There's also a 72-room hotel with river-facing rooms and cabin-like interiors. Communal amenities include hot showers and laundry facilities.

Denali Park Village $199   but (view?)

LODGE $$$

(800-276-7234; www.denaliparkvillage.com; Mile 231, George Parks Hwy; r $209-289;) The former McKinely Village Lodge underwent a rebranding in 2014, but the log-cabin-style complex is still a fine place to enjoy a deckside drink overlooking the Nenana River. Rooms sport a liberal use of wood, but overall it's a generic-looking place with online deals making it much more attractive at times.

The lodge runs a courtesy shuttle to the Denali Visitor Center, WAC and Canyon. It's free for guests and $5 for everyone else.

Carlo Creek

Located 12 miles south of the park entrance (Mile 224), this is one of the best places to stay near Denali, especially for independent travelers looking for a chilled-out experience that includes a gorgeous mountain backdrop. Most of the businesses here are family run, with some now seeing the second or third generations taking over.

There's good hiking nearby (stop in at the youth hostel to get the lowdown on area tramps) and the Denali Mountain Morning Hostel, Perch Restaurant and Cabins and Panorama Pizza Pub all offer shuttle service to the park. It's definitely nice to have wheels, though, if you decide to stay here.

Denali Mountain Morning Hostel ✔ HOSTEL $
(☎907-683-7503; www.hostelalaska.com; Mile 224.1, George Parks Hwy; dm & tents $32, cabins $75-160; ☎) Perched beside the gurgling Carlo Creek, this is the area's only true hostel. Only open during summer, the hostel features a hotchpotch of tent-cabins, log cabins and platform tents. There's a fire pit, and visitors can cook meals and swap tales in the 'octagon' – the hostel's common area.

Laundry facilities are available and the hostel offers free shuttle service to/from the WAC four times a day.

Carlo Creek Lodge ✔ CABIN $$
(☎907-683-2576; www.denaliparklodging.com; cabins without bath $84-90, with bath $120-145; @☎) The 32-acre grounds are treed, the views are grand and the hand-hewn log cabins are filled with genuine old-Alaskan charm. Now in the hands of the grandson of the original homesteaders who settled this scenic little plot by the creek, the lodge has a fresh feel but still a healthy respect for tradition.

Communal amenities include a laundry room, spiffy shower block, barbecue and cooking areas.

McKinley Creekside Cabins ✔ CABIN $$
(☎907-683-2277; www.mckinleycabins.com; cabins $139-199, cafe breakfast $10-12; ☺cafe 6am-10pm; ☎) This is a friendly, well-run place with the most modern cabins in Carlo Creek. Given that the grounds aren't well treed, it's best to get a creekside cabin so you can enjoy the warble of the water and the wide-open views from your porch. The popular cafe at the front of the premises serves some tasty home fare, including breakfasts.

Perch Restaurant & Cabins ✔ CABIN $$
(☎907-683-2523; www.denaliperchresort.com; cabins without/with bath incl breakfast buffet $89/129; ☎) The best cabins here sit creekside, in particular the stylish A-frame No 3. Shared-bath cabins look to be on slightly too-friendly (close) terms with each other. Note that Perch runs a free shuttle bus to/from the park.

🏕 Healy

Healy (Mile 249.5), a pleasant decentralized community about 12 miles north of the park entrance, has a range of lodging options, but you'll need your own vehicle if you plan to stay here.

★EarthSong Lodge ✔ CABIN $$
(☎907-683-2863; www.earthsonglodge.com; Mile 4, Stampede Rd; cabins $165-225; ☎) North of Healy, off Mile 251, George Parks Hwy, this spotlessly clean lodge is pretty much on its own in green fields above the treeline. The private-bath cabins have an appealing at-home styling, with decorative touches such as sprays of wildflowers and hand-carved ornaments.

Breakfast and dinner are available in the adjacent Henry's Coffeehouse and there are sled-dog demos, a nightly slide show and dog-sled and cross-country-skiing tours in winter. The lodge is just a short climb away from stunning views of Mt McKinley, and just in case you wanted to know more about that mountain, proprietor Jon Nierenberg, a former Denali ranger, quite literally wrote the book on hiking in the park's backcountry.

Denali Dome Home B&B ✔ B&B $$
(☎907-683-1239, 800-983-1239; www.denalidomehome.com; Mile 0.5, Healy Spur Rd; r with breakfast $190; ☎) This is not a yurt but a huge, intriguing geodesic house on a 5-acre lot, offering one of the best B&B experiences in Alaska. There are seven modern rooms (with partial antique furnishings), an open common area with fireplace, and a small business area.

The owners are absolute oracles of wisdom when it comes to Denali, and do a bang-up job with breakfast. They also offer car rental.

Denali Park Hotel ✔ MOTEL $$
(☎907-683-1800; www.denaliparkhotel.com; Mile 247, George Parks Hwy; r $129-139; ☎) 'Moose in the grounds!' is a regular cry at this hotel that's actually more like a motel in terms of facilities and appearance. The communal areas are a different matter, encased inside a couple of old Alaska Railroad carriages and impossible to miss from the main road.

🍴 Eating & Drinking

Groceries are limited and expensive in the Denali area, so stock up in Fairbanks, Anchorage or Wasilla. Inside the park itself there are no restaurants, except Morino Grill. Luckily, the neighboring towns are not far apart, so there's a good variety of eating and drinking options to choose from.

Many of the area's restaurants double as bars and feature live music, open mikes, karaoke nights and the like during the week. Check out the Denali Salmon Bake, Prospectors Pizzeria & Ale House and Panorama Pizza Pub.

✗ Within the Park

Riley Creek Mercantile   DELI $
(Map p270; Mile 0.2, Park Rd; ⊘7am-11pm; 🐾) Next to the Riley Creek Campground, the mercantile has a decent selection of groceries, as well as fresh coffee, deli sandwiches and wraps. There's also a small selection of camping supplies, such as gas, head nets and trail mix.

Wilderness Access Center   CAFE $
(Map p270; Mile 0.5, Park Rd; ⊘5am-7pm; 🐾) With a limited array of backpacker-oriented foods, sandwiches and coffee.

Morino Grill   BURGERS $$
(Map p270; Mile 1.5, Park Rd; mains $8-11; ⊘11am-6pm; 🐾) This cafeteria-style establishment is the only eatery within the park. It has burgers, paninis and veggie chili, as well as seafood chowder and reindeer stew. There's a cafe and to-go section at the front, but the sandwiches are pricier than at the Mercantile.

✗ Canyon

★ Black Bear Coffee House   CAFE $
(Map p270; 📞907-683-1656; Mile 238.5, George Parks Hwy; sandwiches $10; 🐾) Serving coffee worthy of a hip Seattle-based barista, along with jolly decent coconut cake and megastrong wi-fi, this place is a knee-weakening apparition to people who've been living off camping food for the last few weeks.

Sled Dog Groceries & Liquors SUPERMARKET $
(Map p270; 📞907-683-7467; www.sleddogliquor. com; Mile 238.4, George Parks Hwy; snacks $3-5; ⊘7am-2am) An excellent combo of groceries, beer growlers and insomniac-friendly opening hours makes this the best store in Canyon.

★ Prospectors Pizzeria & Ale House
                                        PIZZERIA $$
(Map p270; 📞907-683-7437; http://prospectorspizza.com; Mile 238.9, George Parks Hwy; pizza $16-28, sandwiches $12-14; ⊘11am-11pm, bar to 1am) Perennially busy and with good reason! Set in

the Old Northern Lights Theatre building, this cavernous alehouse-cum–pizza parlor has quickly become one of the most popular eating establishments in the park area. In addition to a menu with two-dozen oven-baked pizza choices, there are some 50 beers available on tap from almost all of Alaska's small breweries.

Denali Salmon Bake   AMERICAN $$
(Map p270; 📞907-683-7283; www.thebakerocks. com; Mile 238.5, George Parks Hwy; burgers $16, mains $19-29; ⊘7am-11pm) The better-on-the-inside 'Bake' offers some quirky starters, such as Yak-a-dilla (locally raised yak quesadilla) and a well-regarded halibut and chips. The bar is open 24/7 and there's a free 24-hour shuttle. Popular and *very* casual.

✗ McKinley Village

★ 229 Parks   ORGANIC $$$
(📞907-683-2567; www.229parks.com; Mile 229, George Parks Hwy; dinner $24-34; ⊘8-11am & 5-10pm Tue-Sun; 🐾) 🌿 South of McKinley Village, this stylish timber-frame hideaway is quintessentially modern Alaskan: locally owned, organic and fervently committed to both the community and environment. Everything is made on-site, including the bread and butter, and the menu changes daily, though it usually features local game dishes and a veritable cornucopia of vegetarian options.

And don't worry if you can't finish every mouthful: scraps go to feed local sled dogs. Reservations definitely recommended.

✗ Carlo Creek

Perch Restaurant & Cabins   AMERICAN $$
(📞907-683-2523; www.denaliperchresort.com; breakfast $8-9, dinner mains $14-26; ⊘6-11am & 5-10pm) It's called the Perch for a reason, as the restaurant sits high on a moraine above Carlo Creek, with an almost-eye-level view of the surrounding peaks. It's just a quick jaunt from the highway, however, and on a sunny day a meal or drink on the deck should be mandatory. Perch serves great steaks and salmon dishes, and has a decent wine and Alaskan beer selection. There's a free shuttle to and from the park.

Panorama Pizza Pub   PIZZERIA $$
(📞907-683-2623; www.panoramapizzapub.com; Mile 224, George Parks Hwy; 12in pizzas $16-18; ⊘5-10pm, bar until 1am) This eatery was once the family's gift shop but now offers good

beer, burgers and pizza pies, with midsummer salads coming from a Healy-based organic grower. Later at night the place becomes more 'pub' than 'pizzeria' with locals, travelers and seasonal workers congregating for live music, open mike and pub quizzes.

Panorama shares a free shuttle with Perch Restaurant so you can get here even if you aren't staying in Carlo Creek.

✖ Healy

Miner's Market & Deli DELI **$**
(Mile 248.4, George Parks Hwy; ⊗24hr, deli 6am-3pm) A surprisingly good selection of groceries (including fresh produce) can be purchased at this market attached to a gas station. The deli even sells breakfast, sandwiches and Prospectors Pizzeria slices.

Rose's Café DINER **$$**
(☑907-683-7673; Mile 249.5, George Parks Hwy; mains $10-20; ⊗7am-8pm; 🐾) This classic breakfast, burger and pie joint is your best bet in town. The covered outdoor seating area out the back and authentic diner-style counter seating adds to its *Nighthawks*-meets-*Easy Rider* appeal.

★49th State Brewing Company BREWERY
(www.49statebrewing.com; Mile 248.4, George Parks Hwy; ⊗3pm-late) You can have the *best* evening out in Denali at this multifarious place which is 1) a brewpub brewing its own fine ales; 2) a wonderful flame-grilled restaurant; 3) a live-music venue and 4) a dedicated purveyor of dozens of whiskeys. A celebratory atmosphere is generated at the communal tables both inside and out, where fun games shorten the wait for your food.

Also out front is the famous Magic Bus from the Sean Penn film *Into the Wild*. The actual bus used by Chris McCandless is 28 miles along the nearby Stampede Trail (see below). Brewery tours with free tastings take place on Fridays at 4pm.

DENALI & THE INTERIOR DENALI NATIONAL PARK

THE STAMPEDE TRAIL & THE MAGIC BUS

The Stampede Trail was an overgrown, semi-abandoned mining road in April 1992 when an idealistic 24-year-old wanderer called Chris McCandless made camp in an abandoned bus west of Healy, equipped with little more than a rifle, 10lb of rice and a copy of Louis L'Amour's *Education of a Wandering Man* in his bag. His quest: to attempt to survive on his own in the unforgiving Alaskan wilderness.

McCandless' death several months later, in August 1992, was famously chronicled in the book *Into the Wild* by Jon Krakauer in 1996. But it was Sean Penn's cinematic rendering of the book in 2007 that brought the story to international attention and turned the Stampede Trail and the so-called 'Magic Bus' into a pilgrimage site for a stream of romantic young backpackers.

The deluge of hikers has led to problems. Thanks to two dangerous river crossings along the Stampede Trail's muddy if relatively flat route, some of the more amateurish hikers have found they've bitten off more than they can chew. As a result, search-and-rescue teams are called out five or six times a year to aid stranded or disorientated travelers and, in 2010, a Swiss woman tragically drowned while trying to cross the Teklanika River.

Today the Magic Bus – a 1946 International Harvester (number 142) abandoned by road builders in 1961 – continues to sit incongruously amid the taiga-tundra in an increasingly deteriorating state. A plaque in memory of McCandless adorns the faded interior, which is filled with graffiti scribbled by travelers from around the world inspired by his story. Many of them stay the night inside.

If you're hiking to the bus, it's approximately 28 miles from the start of the Stampede Trail, which begins 2 miles north of Healy (the first 8 miles are accessible in a vehicle). Go prepared, preferably in a group, and take extreme precautions when crossing the Savage and Teklanika Rivers (and if they're flowing high, don't cross them at all). Bears are common in the area and the mosquitoes are savage. Alternatively, you can take an ATV tour along the trail in summer, or head out in winter on a dog-sledding trip from EarthSong Lodge (p277).

A replica of bus 142 sits outside the 49th State Brewery Company in Healy.

DENALI & THE INTERIOR DENALI NATIONAL PARK

☆ Entertainment

Charles Sheldon Center CULTURAL CENTER
(www.denali.org; events $25; ⊙ 8pm mid-May–mid-Sep) At the back of the Denali Park Village in McKinley Village, this community center holds local talks and speeches, art shows and theatrical and musical performances, all designed to 'inspire personal connections to Denali.'

Shopping

You can get all sorts of nonessentials in Canyon's gift shops from moose-crossing stickers to Sarah Palin penknives.

Denali Bookstore BOOKS
(Map p270; Mile 1.5, Park Rd; ⊙9am-7pm) Across from the Denali Visitor Center. It has field guides, topographic maps, coffee-table books and Alaskan literature.

Denali Mountain Works OUTDOOR EQUIPMENT
(Map p270; Mile 239, George Parks Hwy; ⊙ 9am-9pm) This jam-packed Canyon store sells camping gear, clothing and pretty much anything you'd need for a few days in the backcountry. It also rents out tents, stoves and other outdoor gear, and has dehydrated meals.

ℹ️ Information

MEDICAL SERVICES

Canyon Clinic (☎907-683-4433; Mile 238.8, George Parks Hwy; ⊙9am-6pm) Only open during summer months but on call 24 hours.
Healy Clinic (☎907-683-2211; Healy Spur Rd) In the Tri-Valley Community Center, 13 miles north of the park and a half-mile east of George Parks Hwy.

MONEY

There are ATMs in most of Canyon's big hotels. The closest full-service bank is in Healy.

TELEPHONE

You can get cell-phone reception up to Mile 5 on Park Rd.

TOURIST INFORMATION

Backcountry Information Center (BIC; Map p270; ☎907-683-9510; Mile 0.5, Park Rd; ⊙9am-6pm) If you want to overnight in Denali's backcountry, you'll need to come to the BIC, just across the parking lot from the WAC.
Denali Visitor Center (Map p270; ☎907-683-2294; www.nps.gov/dena; Mile 1.5, Park Rd; ⊙ 8am-6pm) The place to come for an executive summary of Denali National Park, with quality displays on the area's natural and human history. Every half-hour in the theater,

the beautifully photographed, unnarrated film *Heartbeats of Denali* provides a peek at the park's wildlife and scenery.

You can also pick up a selection of park literature here, including the NPS' indispensable *Alpenglow* booklet, which functions as a user's manual to Denali.

Wilderness Access Center (WAC; Map p270; ☎907-683-9274; Mile 0.5, Park Rd; ⊙5am-7pm) There's a general-purpose info desk, cafe, snack and gear shop, but the WAC's main function is as the park's transport hub and campground-reservation center. Pay your park-entrance fee and bus tickets here (except interagency, handicapped and senior passes, which are purchased at the visitor center).

ℹ️ Getting There & Away

Located on George Parks Hwy, about four hours north of Anchorage and two hours south of Fairbanks, Denali is easy to access without your own vehicle.

BUS

Both northbound and southbound bus services are available from Denali National Park. **Alaska Bus Guy** (☎907-720-6541; www.alaskabusguy.com) departs Denali at 1pm for Anchorage ($74, 4½ hours) and will stop anywhere along the George Parks Hwy. Northbound buses depart Anchorage at 7am. **Alaska/Yukon Trails** (☎800-770-7275; www.alaskashuttle.com) offers an almost-identical schedule to Anchorage, but also forges north to Fairbanks ($55, three hours) via Healy and Nenana at 1:15pm. **Park Connection** (☎800-266-8625; www.alaskacoach.com) runs two buses a day from major Canyon hotels to Anchorage ($80/90, 7am/2pm) and one a day to Seward ($155, 7am). From Anchorage, buses leave at 7am and 3pm for Denali.

TRAIN

The most enjoyable way to arrive or depart from the park is aboard the **Alaska Railroad** (☎907-265-2494; www.alaskarailroad.com), with its viewing-dome cars that provide sweeping views of Mt McKinley and the Susitna and Nenana valleys along the way. All trains arrive at the depot beside the visitor center, only staying long enough for passengers to board. The northbound *Denali Star* departs from Denali at 4pm and reaches Fairbanks at 8pm. The southbound train departs Denali at 12:30pm and gets into Anchorage at 8pm. The one-way fare to/from Anchorage starts at $124; to/from Fairbanks is $53.

ℹ️ Getting Around

You'll find the area between Canyon and McKinley Village well served by public transport. North or south of there you may need your own car, though Denali Mountain Morning Hostel (p277) in

Carlo Creek now provides limited transport to the WAC, as does Panorama Pizza Pub (p278).

From Canyon, it's a not-unpleasant 2-mile walk to the park entrance area.

Within the park itself is a good system of free and paid shuttle buses.

WITHIN THE PARK

Shuttle buses are big, clunky, school-bus-style affairs aimed at wildlife watchers and day hikers, with the occasional bus also carrying bicycles. The drivers are concessionaire employees, not NPS naturalists, but most provide unofficial natural-history information en route. Day hikers don't need a backcountry permit and can get off anywhere (and multiple times) along Park Rd. After hiking, flag down the next bus that comes along and produce your bus-ticket stub. Due to space considerations, you might have to wait a bus or two during peak season. The bus to Wonder Lake heads into the park as early as 5:45am, but the usual ones to Toklat or Eielson start running around 7am. The last return bus (from Eielson) leaves around 6:30pm; check carefully when the last bus from your destination returns. Also note the exact schedule changes every year. It's wise to reserve a seat as far in advance as possible. The cost varies, and there are three-for-two passes, allowing three days of travel for the price of two. Sample fares include Savage River (Mile 14, free), Toklat River (Mile 53, $27), Eielson Visitor Center (Mile 66, $34.50), Wonder Lake (Mile 85, $47.25) and Kantishna ($51.50).

Camper buses ferry overnight campers, backpackers and cyclists, offering ample space to stow gear. To take these buses you must have a campsite or backcountry unit reserved along Park Rd, or be toting a bicycle. If you don't have a campground booking, you can't ride *in* on the camper bus, but you can probably hitch a ride *back* on one. The buses cost $31.50 to anywhere along the road. As with shuttle buses, it's good to reserve as far ahead as possible.

The free **Riley Creek Loop Bus** makes a circuit through the park entrance area, picking up at the visitor center every half-hour and stopping at the Murie Science & Learning Center, Horseshoe Lake trailhead, WAC, park headquarters and Riley Creek Campground. The park also has a free **Dog Sled Demo Bus**, which departs the visitor center for the park headquarters 40 minutes before each show.

OUTSIDE THE PARK

The useful **Salmon Bake Shuttle** runs from the WAC/visitor center to Healy via Canyon's hotels. It's particularly handy for those wishing to enjoy an evening microbrew at 49th State Brewing Company (p279). Tickets are $3 one way or $5 for a day pass. Buses run 5:30am to 3am.

Many other restaurants and lodges run their own shuttle buses, which means you can get about reasonably well without your own vehicle. Some charge $5 while others are free if you're staying or eating (or if the driver can't be bothered charging you). Some have regular pickups, while others will come for any potential customer at any time. Check the listings in Sleeping and Eating & Drinking for shuttles to your destination and also inquire at the WAC.

If you need a taxi, try **Caribou Cab** (📞907-683-5000) based in Healy.

GEORGE PARKS HIGHWAY

This ribbon of highway, drizzled ever so lovingly over vast stretches of wilderness, offers one of Alaska's top road journeys. From a beginning at the junction with Glenn Hwy (35 miles north of Anchorage) the Parks Hwy runs 327 miles to Fairbanks, Alaska's third-largest city. Along the way it's a veritable Denali Alley, with a state park, national park and highway named after the Great One. And while there's no doubt about everyone's final destination, the rest is no mere sideshow. There are views that won't be outdone later, a half-dozen local favorite hikes and paddles, and one spunky former boomtown that's now most everyone's idea of a good time.

Mileposts along the highway indicate distances from Anchorage.

Talkeetna

POP 876

A railway hub and proverbial base camp for the Alaskan climbing fraternity, Talkeetna sits in the savage shadow of Mt McKinley, whose bulk towers over the surrounding taiga like a sugar-frosted Kilimanjaro. Talkeetna is also a town with a healthy sense of its own ludicrousness. Its mayor since 1997 has been a 17-year-old cat – repeat: *a cat* – called Stubbs. The stealthy feline leader, who once rubbed shoulders with Sarah Palin (former mayor of the neighboring town of Wasilla), presides over a settlement that sits firmly on the tourist circuit thanks to its spectacular setting and well-preserved frontier history. Almost all of the attractive log and clapboard buildings that line Talkeetna's Main St date from between 1916 and 1940.

Talkeetna has acted as a staging post for alpinists embarking on Denali expeditions ever since people have been climbing it, and it's not hard to see why. On the 30% of days when the mountain is visible, it provides an alluring backdrop, with the town's attractive wooden buildings nestled in the foreground.

Talkeetna isn't a large place and can be easily reached on a day trip from Anchorage. Arriving by train is a good option. It's a gentle half-mile stroll from the station to Talkeetna's main drag. If you have more time to spare, Talkeetna is good for fishing, river-float trips and expensive flightseeing tours of Denali that offer options to land briefly on glaciers. Book ahead.

Talkeetna is reached by turning at Mile 98.7 on George Parks Hwy onto Talkeetna Spur Rd. This 14-mile paved road ends at the junction with Main St.

◉ Sights & Activities

Fairview Inn   HISTORIC BUILDING

(Main St; ◷ noon-late) Though not an official museum, the Fairview Inn might as well be. Founded in 1923 to serve as the overnight stop between Seward and Fairbanks on the newly constructed Alaska Railroad, the inn is listed on the National Register of Historic Places.

Its old plank-floored saloon is classic Alaska: its walls are covered with racks of antlers, various furry critters and lots of local memorabilia. One corner holds Talkeetna's only slot machine; another is devoted to President Warren G Harding. When the railroad was finished in 1923, Harding arrived in Alaska and rode the rails to the Nenana River, where he hammered in the golden spike. Talkeetna locals swear (with grins on their faces) that he stopped at the Fairview Inn on the way home, was poisoned and wound up dying in San Francisco less than a week later. Ever since, the Fairview has remained a fine place to be poisoned.

Talkeetna Historical
Society Museum   MUSEUM

(☑ 907-733-2487; admission $3; ◷ 10am-6pm) A block south of Main St, look for this small complex of restored buildings that includes the town's 1936 schoolhouse, a fully furnished trapper's cabin and a train depot. There are exhibits devoted to bush pilots and trapping and mining artifacts, but the real highlight is the talks given by park rangers about Mt McKinley using a fantastic scale model of the mountain.

Pick up the museum's *Historic Walking Tour* brochure if you want to head out and explore more old buildings around town.

Mountaineering
Ranger Station   RANGER STATION

(☑ 907-733-2231; cnr 1st & B Sts; ◷ 8am-5:30pm) Whether you're intrigued or boggled by high-altitude alpinism, this ranger station provides an excellent window into that rarefied world. In addition to coordinating the numerous Mt McKinley expeditions during spring and summer, the station functions as a visitor center, with maps, books, photos and video presentations about the Alaska Range. Ranger-led activities begin daily at 11:30am and 1pm.

Hurricane Turn Train   TRAIN

Sometimes called the 'Local' or the 'Bud Car,' this flagstop train (one of the last still running in America) provides a local rural service from Thursday through Sunday (and some major holidays) in summer. Departure from Talkeetna is at 12:45pm for the trip north to Hurricane Gulch, where the train turns around and heads back the same day.

This 'milk run' takes you within view of Mt McKinley and into some remote areas, and because the train goes slower and is less noisy than the *Denali Star*, your chances of spotting wildlife are greater. You also have a better opportunity to mingle with local residents. The round-trip adult fare for the 5½-hour (100-mile) journey is $75.

Hiking & Cycling

One of the easiest but most scenic walks in the area begins at the end of Main St, on the sandy banks of the Talkeetna River. There are pinch-yourself views of Mt McKinley across the waterway on a clear day.

Just south of town, a cycling/walking route parallels Talkeetna Spur Rd almost 14 miles back to Glenn Parks Hwy. At Mile 12 (2 miles south of town), the road begins to climb and, behind you, McKinley suddenly fills up half the sky.

Just a little further is the turn for Comsat Rd, which quickly leads to the Talkeetna Lakes Park Day-Use Area, offering short hikes around X and Y Lakes.

From the lakes you can either retrace your route back to town or continue up Comsat Rd and take the first left at Christiansen Lake Rd. In a short while, you'll pass Christiansen Lake (where you can swim) and then reach a dead end with a lookout over the river flats and, if you're lucky, Mc-Kinley in the distance.

The trail past the stop sign leads to Beaver Rd, which eventually runs into F St. You can follow this road back to Talkeetna Spur Rd just south of town. Pick up a copy of *Talkeetna Town & Trail Map* for a rough map of this and other routes.

⚐ Tours

Flightseeing

When in Talkeetna, it's pretty much mandatory to go flightseeing around Mt McKinley, both because it's an intrinsically exhilarating experience and because flights are actually cheaper from here than from within Denali National Park. There are four local operations, all well established and all similar with regards to safety, professionalism and price. Plan on spending anywhere from around $200 to $400 per person for a flight.

K2 Aviation   SCENIC FLIGHTS
(☑907-733-2291; www.flyk2.com; 14052 E 2nd St; 1hr trip from $205; ⊙7am-9pm) Aside from standard flightseeing tours, this company teams up with a Denali National Park concessionaire to offer fly-in multiday hiking trips.

Talkeetna Air Taxi   SCENIC FLIGHTS
(☑907-733-2218; www.talkeetnaair.com; 14212 E 2nd St; per person from $205; ⊙10am-6pm) Offers four different trips year-round to see Denali from every conceivable angle, starting with the one-hour South Face tour. It's an extra $85 to land on a glacier.

Fishing

Fishing around Talkeetna is amazing, with runs of every species of Pacific salmon plus grayling, rainbow trout and Dolly Varden.

Phantom Salmon Charters   FISHING
(☑907-733-2328; www.phantomsalmoncharters. com; 22228 Talkeetna Spur Rd; ⊙7am-7pm) Arranges fishing charters. Pop into its office for details.

Nature & River Tours

Denali Zipline Tours   ZIP LINE
(☑907-733-3988; www.denaliziplinetours.com; Main St; $149) This zipline strung up in Talkeetna's forest canopy opened in the summer of 2012. It has nine lines and three high-flying suspension bridges, meaning you can stay up in the trees for three hours. It's the most northerly zipline in North America.

Mahay's Jet Boat Adventures   BOAT
(☑907-733-2223; www.mahaysjetboat.com; adult/child $70/53) This brisk jet-boat tour on the Susitna River covers 130 miles and ventures into white water in Devil's Canyon. For some it offers a good overview of trapper and native history. Others claim it's more a 'trap' of the tourist variety.

Talkeetna River Guides   RAFTING
(☑907-733-2677; www.talkeetnariverguides.com; Main St) To get out onto Talkeetna's many nearby waterways, Talkeetna River Guides will put you in a raft for a placid two-hour float on the Talkeetna River ($79) or a four-hour float on the Chulitna River through Denali State Park ($129).

Alaska Nature Guides   WALKING
(☑907-733-1237; www.alaskanatureguides.com; from $59) Offers nature walking tours around Denali State Park and Talkeetna.

🛏 Sleeping

The Matanuska-Susitna Borough slaps a 5% accommodations tax on top of the following prices.

Talkeetna Camper Park   CAMPGROUND $
(☑907-733-2693; www.talkeetnacamper.com; Talkeetna Spur Rd; RV sites $32-38; ⊙Apr-Oct) An RV-only camper park near the railway station (and the railway tracks!), but close to town. Showers are $4.

Fairview Inn   HISTORIC HOTEL $
(☑907-733-2423; Main St; r without bath $55) Above the bar, the tiny but brightly painted flophouse rooms are first come, first served.

River Park Campground   CAMPGROUND $
(tent sites $10) This informal place (with self check-in) at the end of Main St is a bit scruffy, but close to the river and the action. No RVs.

Talkeetna Roadhouse   HISTORIC HOTEL $
(☑907-733-1351; www.talkeetnaroadhouse.com; Main St; dm/d/tr $21/68/99, 4-person cabins $131; ☎) The real Alaskan deal, this roadhouse dates from 1917 and maintains seven small private rooms, a bunkroom and a couple of rustic cabins out back. In keeping with the old-time setting, it's shared bath all the way, though the antique-strewn sitting room does offer free wi-fi. In early summer expect to see scores of climbers coming in and out the doors.

★ **Denali Fireside Cabins & Suites** CABIN $$
(☑907-733-2600; www.denalifireside.com; Talkeetna Spur Rd; ste/cabin $169/189; ☜) Upscale, centrally located (for town) and embellished with only-in-Alaska decor, this place is a jolly good deal for the price, and far more intimate than the large lodges beloved by cruise passengers. The separate cabins look sparkling new and are equipped with fireplaces, decks and kitchenettes.

Meandering Moose Lodge LODGE $$
(☑907-733-1000; www.meandering-moose-lodging.com; 14677 E Cabin Spike Ave; cabins with breakfast $85-165, B&B r with breakfast $80-145; ☜) Sitting a couple of miles northeast from the center of town, this collection of cabins nicely balances rustic charm and creature comforts. Private log cabins can hold up to 10 people (there's lots of extra space in funky hideaway lofts) and feature full kitchens and bathrooms (except the lowest-priced ones, which share).

The B&B cabin features modern rooms, a shared living space and kitchen and an interior design that wouldn't be out of place in a high-end suburb.

There's a shuttle service from Talkeetna and its train station.

Talkeetna Alaskan Lodge LODGE $$$
(☑907-733-9500; www.talkeetnalodge.com; Mile 12.5, Talkeetna Spur Rd; r $285-415) This high-end Alaska Native Corporation–owned lodge has a hillside setting that could hardly offer more perfect views of the Alaska Range. Rooms are spacious and quietly stylish, and cruise-ship and noncruise-ship guests are housed in different buildings. This is a place to enjoy good service and fine surroundings, but in an atmosphere as relaxed as a roadside diner.

The lodge can arrange almost any activity you care for in Talkeetna, from flightseeing to dog-sled tours. Check the website for frequent room deals.

✖ Eating

You won't go hungry for food or choice in Talkeetna, and just to make it easy, almost everything is crowded onto a few blocks off Main St.

★ **Talkeetna Roadhouse** BREAKFAST $
(☑907-733-1351; Main St; breakfast $9-14, dishes $5-7; ☺breakfast, lunch & dinner; ☜) This venerable, colorful establishment has the best breakfast in town. Half-orders are adequate,

full orders are mountain-sized. The restaurant also doubles as a bakery, cooking up giant cinnamon rolls in the morning, and lasagne, pasties and salads during the day. The long table seating is great for meeting other travelers.

Mountain High Pizza Pie PIZZERIA $
(☑907-733-1234; www.mhpp.biz; Main St; pizza slices from $3.50, sandwiches $5.50-10.50; ☺11am-10pm; ☜🖥) Casual and quirky (with Buddhist-inspired tie-dye hangings and knotted wood sculptures adorning the walls), this pizzeria-cum-diner delivers the melted-cheese goods. The outdoor-seating area seems a bit of an afterthought, but it's popular with those looking to down some Alaskan microbrews with their grub.

Nagley's Store SELF-CATERING $
(Main St; ☺7am-10pm) In a historic building across from the park at the start of Main St. Groceries are pricey, but there are daily lunchtime fresh burritos, coffee, soup and salads. A well-stocked beer and spirit shop is attached.

Wildflower Café SANDWICHES $$
(☑907-733-2694; Main St; sandwiches $16, mains $29-35; ☺11am-9pm) Yummy burgers, grilled salmon sandwiches, large wholesome mains and a deck facing Main St are just a few reasons this place is constantly abuzz with diners. There's also a good salad-menu selection if you need to fill up on greens.

West Rib Pub & Grill BURGERS $$
(☑907-733-3663; www.westribpub.info; Main St; burgers & sandwiches $9.95-15.95; ☺noon-2am) Located at the back of Nagley's Store, this is a really terrific place to soak in Talkeetna's chilled-out live-and-let-live vibe, rubbing shoulders with visitors and locals alike. It's got burgers, salmon and halibut, plenty of craft brews and, if it's sunny, outdoor seating.

Foraker Restaurant SEAFOOD $$$
(☑907-733-9500; Mile 12.5, Talkeetna Spur Rd; mains $20-39; ☺6:30-11am & 5-9pm) With a jaw-dropping view of McKinley and the Alaska Range from the elevated deck, it's well worth taking the shuttle or walking out to this Talkeetna Alaksan Lodge restaurant for a meal. The fine dining puts the emphasis on fresh fish, and the 'Inside Passage Seafood Cioppino' plate serves as the menu's 'greatest hits', containing salmon, shrimp, cod, crab and mussels.

Drinking

Pretty much every joint in town will serve you a beer, and most of them have fine outdoor perches for people watching. The Fairbanks Inn also has a beer garden out back in summer.

Denali Brewing Company BREWERY
(www.denalibrewingcompany.com; Main St; ⊙ 11am 8pm) Beer from this popular local microbrewery has already found its way right across the state. Fortunately it's also available in Talkeetna. For $2 you can sample a 5oz taster, or if you splash out $35 you can purchase a 2.25-gallon party pig. There's an outdoor garden facing Main St, where you can relax and enjoy whatever tipple you choose.

☆ Entertainment

There's live music or some kind of performance at least a few nights a week at the Fairview Inn, the **Twister Creek Restaurant** (www.denalibrewingcompany.com; Main St; ⊙ 9am-10pm) beside the Denali Brewing Company, and at Talkeetna Roadhouse.

The **Denali Arts Council** (www.denaliartscouncil.org; D St) based in the Sheldon Community Arts Hangar across from the museum, runs theatrical performances and an arts program throughout the summer. It also sponsors a family-friendly live outdoor music show in the Village Park (corner of Main St and Talkeetna Spur Rd) on Friday evenings.

Shopping

Not surprisingly, Talkeetna has a range of gift shops, selling all manner of kitsch and collectibles.

Artisans Open Air Market ARTS & CRAFTS
(⊙ 10am-6:30pm Fri-Mon) Located outside the Sheldon Community Arts Hangar, this weekend arts fare offers a smorgasbord of local and native crafts, clothing, storybooks, jewelry and more.

❶ Information

There are fickle ATMs in Nagley's and Twister Creek Restaurant. Almost all eating and drinking establishments have free wi-fi.

Talkeetna-Denali Visitor Center (⊙ 9am-7pm) is 14 miles from town at the junction of the George Parks Hwy. You'll pass it if you drive into Talkeetna.

❶ Getting There & Away

Check the notice board outside the post office (behind Sheldon Community Arts Hangar) for information on shared rides.

BUS

Alaska Bus Guy (☑ 907-720-6541; www.alaskabusguy.com) runs vans to Anchorage ($74), leaving at 4pm, and to Denali National Park ($74) at 9:30pm. **Alaska/Yukon Trails** (☑ 907-479-2277; www.alaskashuttle.com) has buses departing from Talkeetna Roadhouse daily at 10:15am heading for Denali Park ($65, three hours) and continuing on to Fairbanks ($92, 6½ hours). They also leave at 4:15pm for Anchorage ($59, 2½ hours). **Denali Overland Transportation** (☑ 907-733-2384; www.denalioverland.com; Denali Dry Goods Store, Main St) runs shuttles to and from Anchorage and less often to and from Denali ($95 per person, based on four-person minimum). The schedule is very loose.

TRAIN

From mid-May to mid-September, the **Alaska Railroad** (☑ 907-265-2494; www.akrr.com) *Denali Star* train stops daily in Talkeetna on its run between Anchorage ($76) and Fairbanks ($105). Talkeetna to Denali costs $76.

❶ Getting Around

The **Sunshine Transit** (☑ 907-354-3885) shuttle runs from town out to the George Parks Hwy, making stops anywhere riders request. Buses run about every 30 minutes from 7:15am to 4:45pm. You can catch the bus at the Roadhouse, and also find the full schedule there.

Talkeetna Taxi (☑ 907-355-8294, www.talkeetnataxi.com) offers service within town and also charters during the climbing season.

Denali State Park

At 325,240 acres, Denali State Park is the fourth-largest state park in Alaska and is roughly half the size of Rhode Island. The park covers the transition zone between the coastal region and the spine of the Alaska Range, and among the dense forests you can look forward to distant shots of towering peaks, including Mt McKinley and the glaciers on its southern slopes. Some say that on a clear day this panorama is the most spectacular mountain view in North America.

The park is largely undeveloped but does offer a handful of turnouts, trails, rental cabins and campgrounds that can be reached from George Parks Hwy, which runs through

1. Dall sheep, Denali National Park (p263) 2. Mt McKinley (p265)
3. Park Road (p265) 4. Root Glacier (p325), Wrangell-St Elias
National Park

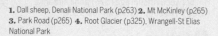

CHRISTIAN KOBER / GETTY IMAGES ©

Denali & the Interior Highlights

Visitors often come to the Interior for Mt McKinley, but they stay for the rest. There are few places in Alaska where the wildlife is so commonly spotted, where pure wilderness is so easily accessed, or where so many legendary highways criss-cross, offering unique adventure after adventure to the willing.

Wilderness Park

There's more untracked wilderness and wildlife at Wrangell-St Elias National Park than at Denali National Park, and only a fraction of the visitors. A junction of several mountain ranges, the park is an adventure playground with world-class glacier trekking, backcountry hiking and paddling.

Legendary Wildlife

Having a close encounter with Alaska's wildlife is on the bucket list of every visitor. Whether it's a grizzly bear or moose, a Dall sheep or one of hundreds of bird species you're wanting to see, this region won't disappoint.

Rough Riding

It's a bouncy ride along the dirt of the 135-mile Denali Hwy – a marvelous landscape of glaciers, braided river valleys, chain lakes and panoramas of the Alaska Range – but that just means you'll be sharing the road with fewer vehicles.

The Great One

The tallest mountain in North America, Mt McKinley sets the stage for one of the world's toughest climbs and most stunning alpine landscapes. Take in views of the mountain from stops along the Park Road or splash out on a bush-plane flight around the summit.

the park. In general, though, you need to be better prepared for any hiking and backpacking adventures than at the same-named national park to the north. But this may be the state park's blessing, for it means it lacks the crowds and there are no long waits or tight regulations. At the height of summer, experienced backpackers may want to consider this park as a hassle-free and cheaper alternative.

The entrance to the park is at Mile 132.2 of George Parks Hwy.

◎ Sights

Alaska Veterans' Memorial   MONUMENT
(Mile 147.5, George Parks Hwy) A poignant war memorial to Alaskan veterans who've served in all military branches (army, navy and air force), located in a wild but peaceful setting near Byers Lake. It was constructed in 1983. The Denali State Park Visitor Center is nearby.

🏃 Activities

The excellent hiking trails and alpine routes crossing the park are popular with locals. Keep in mind that in the backcountry, open fires are allowed only on the gravel bars of major rivers. Pack a stove if you plan to camp overnight.

The Chulitna River runs through the park. Floats can be arranged in Talkeetna.

Byers Lake Loop Trail   HIKING
(Mile 147, George Parks Hwy) If you only have a few hours, but want to get away from it all, head out on this easy 4.8-mile hike around the lake. The path begins at Byers Lake Campground, passes six hike-in campsites on the other side and then returns to the original campground after a bridge crossing.

If you want to go for a paddle across the lake, you can rent canoes or kayaks at the Byers Lake Campground through Southside River Guides (☑ 907-733-7238; per hr/day $15/45).

Kesugi Ridge Traverse   HIKING
For a moderate to difficult three- to four-day (24.7-mile) hike above the treeline with superb views of McKinley and the Alaska Range, try this popular hike connecting the Little Coal Creek Trail with the Byers Lake Loop Trail. You can begin from either end but most hikers start at the Little Coal Creek trailhead as the switchback ascent to the ridgeline is easier.

Troublesome Creek Trail   HIKING
This fickle route begins at a posted trailhead in the parking area at Mile 137.6 of George Parks Hwy and ascends alongside the creek until it reaches the treeline. From here you enter an open territory of alpine lakes and big country views, where the route is marked only by rock cairns as it heads north to Byers Lake or along Kesugi Ridge to Little Coal Creek (36 miles). For more see p72.

The trail experiences regular washouts and is also often awash with bears, hence its 'troublesome' moniker.

🛏 Sleeping

McKinley View Lodge   HOTEL $
(☑ 907-733-1555; www.mckinleyviewlodge.com; Mile 134.5, George Parks Hwy; r $75-100; ⊙ cafe 8am-8pm) Charming's the word at this highway stop older than the highway itself. The place was first homesteaded in 1962 and is now run by Jean Carey Richardson, a children's author and daughter of the original owner. Come here for quaint economical rooms, decent cafe grub and a fork-dropping McKinley view.

Byers Lake Campground   CAMPGROUND $
(Mile 147, George Parks Hwy; campsites $10, cabins $60) In addition to its 73 sites, this campground offers walk-in sites along the loop trail around the lake, and state park's Byers Lake cabins 1, 2 and 3. You can drive to cabin 1, cabin 2 is a half-mile hike from there, while cabin 3 is a further 70yd beyond that. Cabins can be reserved in advance online at the Alaska Division of Parks (☑ 907-745-3975; www.alaskastateparks.org).

Denali Viewpoint North
Campground   CAMPGROUND $
(Mile 162.7, George Parks Hwy; campsites $10) This handy outpost in the north of the park (closer to the national park) has 20 sites around a parking lot and a few walk-in sites in a level glade up a slope.

★ Mt McKinley Princess
Wilderness Lodge   HOTEL $$
(☑ 907-733-2900; www.princesslodges.com; Mile 133, George Parks Hwy; r from $125; @ 🔊) More isolated, spread out and economical than other Princess lodges, the McKinley retains a laid-back rustic atmosphere that's not a million miles from a national park lodge. The view of the iconic mountain (should it reveal itself) from the main building's deck is probably worth the room rate alone.

Throw in hot tubs, a small cardio room and wooded grounds with four short trails and you'll quickly forget the cruise crowds.

ℹ️ Information

Denali State Park Visitors Center (http://dnr.alaska.gov/parks/units/denali1.htm; Mile 147, George Parks Hwy; ⊙8am-5pm Thu-Sun) At the Alaska Veterans' Memorial, just north of Byers Lake Campground. Volunteer staff are usually well informed about the area, and maps and brochures are available for sale.

Cantwell & Broad Pass

The northern boundary of Denali State Park is at Mile 168.5, George Parks Hwy. Situated at Mile 203.6, Broad Pass (2300ft) is a dividing line: rivers to the south drain into Cook Inlet, while waters to the north flow to the Yukon River. The area is at the treeline and worth a stop for some hiking. The mountain valley, surrounded by tall white peaks, is unquestionably one of the most beautiful spots along George Parks Hwy or the Alaska Railroad – both use the low gap to cross the Alaska Range.

North from the pass, George Parks Hwy descends 6 miles to Cantwell (population 211), at the Denali Hwy junction. At the junction you'll find gas and convenience stores. The 'town' itself is 2 miles west, on the extension of the Denali Hwy. If you need to stay, there are a few places around, including Cantwell RV Park (☑907-768-2210; cantwellrvpark.worldpress.com; campsites/RV/cabin $16/30.50/65; 🛜), which has showers and laundry. The RV park is half a mile west of the George Parks Hwy, on the road into town.

Nenana

POP 341

The only significant town encountered between Denali National Park and Fairbanks is Nenana (nee-*na*-nuh, like 'banana'), which lies at the confluence of the Nenana and Tanana (*tan*-uh-naw, not like 'banana') Rivers. Though the big industry here is barging freight downstream, for visitors and northerners alike the community is most famous for the Nenana Ice Classic, an eminently Alaskan game of chance in which prognosticators attempt to profit by guessing when the ice will break up on the Nenana River.

Historically, Nenana (Mile 305, George Parks Hwy) was little more than a roadhouse until it was chosen as the base for building the northern portion of the Alaska Railroad in 1916. The construction camp quickly became a boomtown that made history on July 15, 1923, when President Warren G Harding arrived to hammer in the golden spike on the northern side of the Tanana. The sickly Harding, the first president ever to visit Alaska, missed the spike the first two times, or so the story goes, but finally drove it in to complete the railroad.

Most shops and businesses can be found off A St, which runs four blocks from the very helpful Nenana Visitor Center (☑907-832-5435; www.nenana.org; ⊙8am-6pm), at the entrance to town, to the train station beside the river.

◉ Sights

Nenana Train Station   HISTORIC BUILDING
In preparation for the president's arrival the following year, the Nenana train station was built in 1922 at the north end of A St. Extensively restored in 1988, it's now on the National Register of Historic Places. The building includes the jumbled Alaska Railroad Museum (⊙9:30am-6pm), which displays railroad memorabilia and local artifacts ranging from ice tongs to animal traps. East of the station, a monument commemorates Harding's visit.

St Mark's Episcopal Church   CHURCH
(cnr Front & Market Sts) Within eyeshot of the train station, this handsome church dates from 1905. The interior has a few lovely handcrafted features, including an altar with traditional Athabascan beadwork.

Alfred Starr Nenana Cultural Center   CULTURAL CENTER
(⊙9am-6pm) This riverfront center informs visitors about local culture and history.

Taku Chief   MONUMENT
The *Taku Chief* river tug once pushed barges along the Tanana River and now spruces up the grounds outside the visitor center.

🛏️ Sleeping & Eating

Rough Woods Inn & Café   INN $$
(☑907-832-5299; www.roughwoodsinn.biz; 623 A St; r $95-140; 🛜) Between the visitor center and train station, this inn is more noted for food, especially breakfasts ($6 to $10), though some of the rooms have kitchenettes that may be of use to travelers.

DENALI HIGHWAY

Still appearing ominously as a dotted line on maps, this 135-mile road was opened in 1957 as the only route to the national park. It became a secondary route after George Parks Hwy was completed in 1972, and now from mid-May to October sees a light but steady flow of hikers, hunters, mountain bikers, anglers and birdwatchers. A highway in only the titular sense, Denali is basically a gravel road from Cantwell, just south of Denali National Park on George Parks Hwy, to Paxson on Richardson Hwy.

Most of the highway is at or near the treeline, running along the foothills of the Alaska Range and through glacial valleys where you can see stretches of alpine tundra, enormous glaciers and braided rivers. All that scenery is a blessing, because the road itself, though perfectly passable in a standard auto, is slow going. Expect to average just 35mph, taking six hours from end to end.

There are no established communities along the way, but the roadhouses provide food, beds and sometimes gas. Most of the development is at the Paxson end. If you're driving, fill up with gas at Paxson or Cantwell.

Cantwell to Tangle Lakes

Within 3 miles of the Cantwell turnoff, the pavement ends, rough gravel takes over and the road ascends into the sort of big-sky territory that will dominate it for the duration.

There are stellar views of Mt McKinley starting at Mile 124. At Mile 85, climb a small hill for a spellbinding panorama of the Alaska Range, including Mt Debora and Mt Hess. From a lookout at Mile 37, you'll have no trouble identifying the MacLaren Glacier to the north. This is also where the highway peaks out at 4068ft.

◉ Sights & Activities

Eskers OUTDOORS
The Denali area abounds in fascinating geological features, from majestic glaciers to the easy-to-overlook thin ridges of silt, sand and gravel known as eskers. These deposits, once contained by glacier walls, remain as elongated mounds after the ice melts and around Mile 59 the highway actually runs on top of one.

Crazy Dog Kennels DOG SLEDDING
(☑907-388-6039; www.denalihighwaytours.com; kennel tour $15) ✎ On the MacLaren River's far side is the summer operation of two-time Yukon Quest champ John Schandelmeier and his wife, Zoya DeNure, an Iditarod finisher. Impassioned about their pups, they run the only dog yard in Alaska that rescues unwanted sled dogs and turns them into racers. In August and September, overnight trips are available on a husky-pulled wheeled cart for $350 per person (two person minimum).

Denali Jeep Excursion DRIVING TOUR
(☑907-683-5337; www.denalijeep.com; Mile 238.6, George Parks Hwy; adult/child $169/99) These jeep tours offer the opportunity to experience the highway for those without their own car. The five-hour trips go roughly halfway along the road from Cantwell. Jeeps travel in convoy with a guide and are equipped with CBs to aid communication. You can either handle the driving yourself, or travel as a passenger.

Hiking

Several potential hiking trails – none signposted – branch off the highway in the dozen or so miles after Gracious House Lodge, a roadhouse at Mile 82. Use topographical maps and ask at lodges for clear directions and the latest on conditions.

Paddling

At Mile 118, pull in to begin a float down the silt-choked **Nenana River** if you have your own kayak or raft. The river can be paddled in class I to II conditions from here to George Parks Hwy, 18 river miles distant. Novices should pull out at that point, as after the highway it gets way hairier.

🛏 Sleeping & Eating

There are two official campgrounds on the Denali Hwy, but between Cantwell and Tangle Lakes there are scores of pullouts that are ideal for informal camping.

Brushkana Creek Campground CAMPGROUND $
(Mile 104.3, Denali Hwy; campsites $12) If you can't find your own little hideaway tent spot off the highway, this campground offers 22 not-very-private sites, a picnic shelter, drinking water and a meat rack for the hunters who invade the area in late summer and fall.

MacLaren River Lodge LODGE $$
(☑907-822-5444; www.maclarenlodge.com; Mile 42, Denali Hwy; dm/r with shared bath $25/60, cabins $150; 🐾) The lodge sits on the edge of the

MacLaren River and features a bar and restaurant open for breakfast, lunch and dinner. The dorm is set inside Whitney's Cabin, the oldest cabin on the Denali Hwy, while the rooms are remodeled Atco units.

Tangle Lakes to Paxson

After several miles of lonely road, the Denali Hwy suddenly gets busier and better maintained as it descends into the Tangle Lakes Archeological District, a protected area containing over 500 archaeological sites, but also a magnet for birders, anglers and paddlers. Pavement begins around Mile 21. Most of the lakes – as many as 40 in springtime – can be seen from the Wrangell Mountain Viewpoint at Mile 13.

Activities

Paddling

If you just want to paddle around pretty Round Tangle Lake for a few hours, you can rent a canoe (per hour/day $5/35) from Tangle River Inn (p292).

Delta River Canoe Route CANOEING
This 35-mile paddle starts at Tangle Lakes Campground and ends a few hundred yards from Mile 212.5 of the Richardson Hwy. After crossing Round Tangle Lake, the route continues to Lower Tangle Lake, where you must make a portage around a waterfall.

Below the falls is a set of class III rapids that you must either line for 2 miles or paddle if you're an experienced hand. Be warned, though, that every year canoeists damage their boats beyond repair on these rapids and have to hike 15 miles back to the Denali Hwy. After the rapids, the remainder of the route is a much milder trip, though there are still class II sections.

For a more thorough overview and map, download the *Delta National Wild and Scenic River* brochure from the BLM website (www.blm.gov/ak/st/en/prog/nlcs/delta_nwsr.html).

Upper Tangle Lakes Canoe Route CANOEING
Though an easier and shorter paddle than the Delta River Route, this one does require four portages (unmarked but easy to work out in the low-bush tundra). The route starts at the Delta Wayside at Mile 21.7 of the Denali Hwy, and then passes through Upper Tangle Lake before ending at Dickey Lake,

9 miles to the south. There is a 1.2-mile portage into Dickey Lake.

From here, experienced paddlers can continue by following Dickey Lake's outlet to the southeast into the Middle Fork of the Gulkana River. For the first 3 miles the river is shallow and mild, but then it plunges into a steep canyon where canoeists have to contend with class III and IV rapids. Most canoeists choose to line their boats, though some make a portage. Allow seven days for the 76-mile trip from Tangle Lakes to Sourdough Creek Campground on the Gulkana River off the Richardson Hwy.

All paddlers trying this route must have topo maps. The useful BLM brochure *Gulkana National Wild River Floater's Guide* can be downloaded at www.blm.gov/ak/st/en/prog/nlcs/gulkana_nwr.html.

Hiking

There are eight designated hikes within the so-called Tangle Lakes Archeological District, which lies between mileposts 16 and 37. You can pick up more details at www.blm.gov/ak/st/en/fo/gdo/tangle_lakes_archeological.html.

Osar Lake Trail HIKING
(Mile 37) On the southern side of the highway, this easy 8-mile trail leads to Osar Lake and wide views of the MacLaren River valley. In August and September you'll be sharing the path with hunters.

MacLaren Summit Trail HIKING
(Mile 37) Starting across the road from the Osar Lake Trail, this 3-mile, mostly dry route runs north across the tundra to MacLaren Summit.

Landmark Gap Trail HIKING
(Mile 24.6) This 3-mile trail leads north to Landmark Gap Lake, at an elevation of 3217ft. You can't see the lake from the highway, but you can spot the noticeable gap between the Amphitheater Mountains.

Glacier Lake Trail HIKING
(Mile 30) A new and drier route to Glacier Gap Lake has replaced an older, boggier one. It's approximately 2 miles long.

Swede Lake Trail HIKING
(Mile 16.2) From a trailhead on the southern side of the highway, this path (mostly used by motorized vehicles and mountain bikers) runs south about 10 miles to the Middle Fork of the Gulkana River. From here there's access to the Alphabet Hills and Dickey Lake.

🛌 Sleeping

Tangle Lakes Campground　　CAMPGROUND $
(Mile 21.5, Denali Hwy; campsites $12) On the shores of Round Tangle Lake, this 45-site campground charges $6 for walk-ins. Walk the short Tangle Ridge Hiking Trail for first-rate views of the Tangle Lakes and Alaska Range.

★ Denali Highway Cabins　　CABIN $$
(☑ 907-822-5972; www.denalihwy.com; Denali Hwy; cabins with breakfast $160-200; 🛜) A couple of hundred feet up the Denali Hwy, this place is pure Alaskan gold. It's got pedigree (it's the oldest running lodge on the highway), authority (it's run by naturalist Dr Audubon Bakewell, co-author of the *Birding in Alaska* guide) and fine accommodations.

The modern log cabins, each with a private balcony, sit along the Gulkana River, and feature real flush toilets, among other civilized comforts. There are also surprisingly cozy prefab tents ($150, shared bath) and a communal 'great room' with books, grand piano and painting easel. You can rent kayaks ($40 to $50) and bicycles ($35 to $45) and take part in highly regarded birding and river tours.

Tangle River Inn　　LODGE $$
(☑ 907-822-3970; www.tangleriverinn.com; Mile 20, Denali Hwy; r without/with bath $82/107.50, cabins $157.50; 🛜) Though it may appear at first like a truck stop, this is in fact a well-run lodge with a good range of sleeping options. There are private cabins, family rooms and a bunkhouse (groups only) spread across the gravel hilltop. The restaurant serves tasty home-style meals with tranquil views of Sugarloaf Mountain and the Tangle Lakes thrown in for free.

The lodge is popular with anglers but come June, birdwatchers flock from all corners of the world to set their binoculars on Arctic warblers, wheateaters and golden plovers, among many other winged worthies.

FAIRBANKS

POP 32,204

The only thing that constitutes a 'city' in interior Alaska, Fairbanks often feels more like a crossroads than a conventional metropolis. But at the nexus of some truly epic routes – north to the Arctic, east to Canada and south to Denali – the mix of people in this once-rough-and-ready gold-rush town is rarely boring. Stay long enough and you'll meet the cross-continental cyclist who's pedaled up from Tierra del Fuego, the disorientated cruisers bused in from Seward, the Arctic-bound adventurers stocking up on supplies in Fred Meyer, and the bush pilots heading out to Kobuk, Chalkyitsik or some other chilly Arctic landing strip.

Fairbanks isn't particularly pretty – its 'downtown' is soporific and, in the rest of the city, the local businesses lie clustered around dull strung-out strip malls. However, there are saving graces. The modern university campus gives the city a young and forward-thinking demographic, while caught in the right light on a long summer's evening, the Chena River is a pleasant place to float or have a picnic (or both). If you come during the frigid winter, Fairbanks is the start or end point of the Yukon Quest 1000-mile dog-sled race and ground zero for viewing the aurora borealis.

History

The city was founded in 1901, as a result of a journey ET Barnette undertook up the Tanana River on the SS *Lavelle Young*. Barnette was hauling supplies to the Tanacross goldfields but a detour up the shallow Chena River stranded him at what is now the corner of 1st Ave and Cushman St. Barnette could have been just another failed trading-post merchant in the Great White North, but local miners convinced him to set up shop. The following year the Italian prospector Felix Pedro (who had incidentally been one of Barnette's first customers) struck gold 12 miles north.

A large boomtown sprang to life amid the hordes of miners stampeding into the area, and by 1908 more than 18,000 people resided in the Fairbanks Mining District. In the ensuing decade, other gold rushes largely drained the population, but ironically the city's gold-mining industry was to outlast any other in the state.

While WWII and the construction of the Alcan and military bases produced the next boom in the city's economy, nothing affected Fairbanks quite like the Trans-Alaska Pipeline. From 1973 to 1977, when construction of the pipeline was at its height, the town was bursting at its seams as the principal gateway to the North Slope.

The aftermath of the pipeline construction was just as extreme. The city's population shrank and unemployment crept toward 25%.

By the late 1990s, however, the city was on the rebound – thanks to tourism and, once again, gold. Just north of town is the Fort Knox Gold Mine – Alaska's largest. In 2010 Fort Knox produced 349,729oz of gold and employed more than 400 workers.

◉ Sights

★ **University of Alaska Museum of the North** MUSEUM
(Map p294; ☎907-474-7505; www.uaf.edu/museum; 907 Yukon Dr; admission $12; ☑9am-7pm) In an architecturally abstract igloo-and-aurora-inspired edifice sits one of Alaska's finest museums, with artifact-rich exhibits on the geology, history, culture and trivia of each region of the state. You are greeted by an 8ft 9in, 1250lb stuffed bear and then sign-posted around sensibly laid-out exhibits that include woolly mammoth tusks, Alaska Native kayaks and Blue Babe, a 36,000-year-old bison found preserved in the permafrost by Fairbanks-area miners.

The museum theater runs three films several times daily (admission $5); *Dynamic Aurora* is a multimedia look at the northern lights; *Winter* talks about, you guessed it, winter; and *You are Here* discusses the museum itself. Upstairs, the **Rose Berry Alaska Art Gallery** covers 2000 years of northern works, ranging from ancient ivory carvings to wood masks and contemporary photographs.

Fountainhead Antique Auto Museum MUSEUM
(Map p294; www.fountainheadmuseum.com; 212 Wedgewood Dr; admission $10; ☑11am-9pm Sun-Thu, to 6pm Fri & Sat) For a state with so few highways, this is a surprisingly comprehensive collection of 70 working antique vehicles, highlighting both the evolution of the automobile from the late 19th century as well as motor-vehicle history in Alaska. To get here, head east down College Rd and turn left on Margaret Ave. Then follow the signs into the Wedgewood Resort.

Creamer's Field Migratory Waterfowl Refuge NATURE RESERVE
(Map p294) Birds have been migrating through this idyllic little stretch of farmland for millennia, and when the local dairy finally shut its doors, the community rallied to preserve the land. More than 100 species can now be seen in summer, including thousands of sandhill cranes during August.

The **Farmhouse Visitor Center** (Map p294; ☑9:30am-5pm) has a handbook to help you get the most out of the short trails through the nearby boreal forest and wetlands (bring bug spray). Volunteers also lead one-hour nature walks at 7pm Monday through Friday.

Large Animal Research Station WILDLIFE RESERVE
(☎907-474-5724; www.uaf.edu/lars; guided walks $10; ☑10am, noon & 2pm) If you can't make a trip to the Arctic for a little wildlife observation, consider visiting this research station that tends herds of musk oxen, reindeer and caribou. The station studies the animals' unique adaptations to a sub-Arctic climate, and viewing areas outside the fenced pastures allow a free look at the herds any time. To see the facility itself, you must partake in a 45-minute guided walk.

To reach the station, head north from the university campus on Farmers Loop Rd, bear left onto Ballaine Rd and then turn left again on Yankovich Rd. The center is 1.2 miles up on the right.

Pioneer Park HISTORIC SITE
(Map p294; ☎907-459-1087; Airport Way; ☑stores & museums noon-8pm, park 24hr; 🚗) Like many cities with little surviving history, Fairbanks attempts to recreate the 'old' days in a historical theme park. Suffice to say, it doesn't always work. The most prominent sight in rather dowdy 44-acre Pioneer Park is the **SS Nenana**, a hulking stern-wheeler that once

---

INVESTIGATING CLIMATE CHANGE

Alaska in general, and Fairbanks in particular, is sometimes referred to as 'ground zero' for climate change, a region in which melting permafrost is threatening to damage roads, airstrips and – potentially – the Alaska oil pipeline. The renowned **International Arctic Research Center** (IARC; Map p294; www.iarc.uaf.edu), based in Fairbanks on the University of Alaska campus, has taken upon itself to become a leading authority on these warming effects. Its work includes investigating the impacts of climate change, assessing how much of it is human-made, and looking at ways in which the international community can prepare and adapt for the future.

Fairbanks

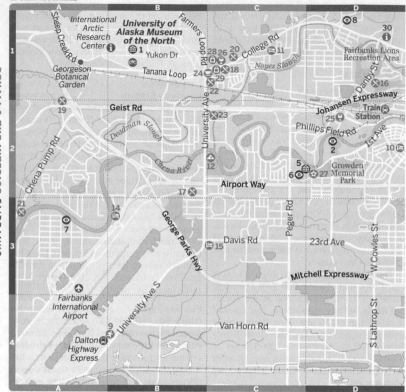

plied the Yukon River. However, many of the old cabins in Gold Rush Town are relocated historic buildings.

Fleeting distractions can be found in the Pioneer Museum (Map p294; ☎907-456-8579; ⊙11am-8pm May-Sep) FREE. More interesting is the Pioneer Air Transportation Museum (admission $3), chock-full of aviation history. A miniature train, the Crooked Creek & Whiskey Island Railroad, gives rides ($2) around the park for a global overview.

To get to Pioneer Park, take the MACS Blue or Red Line bus.

◉ Downtown Fairbanks

Morris Thompson
Cultural & Visitors Center   CULTURAL CENTER
(Map p298; www.morristhompsoncenter.org; 101 Dunkel St; ⊙8am-9pm) There are a few contenders for 'best visitor center in Alaska' but this one, an ingenious mix of museum,

info point and cultural center, has to be in the top two or three. Inside are exhibits on Alaskan history and native culture, as well as daily movies and cultural performances. Outside, on the grounds, don't miss the historic cabin and funky moose-antler arch.

The on-site Tanana Chiefs Conference Cultural Programs are designed to share native culture with the wider world, and also ensure it survives to the next generation. There are one-hour cultural performances ($10; 1pm, 3pm and 6:30pm), live craft-making demonstrations (1pm to 6pm Monday to Friday) and the opportunity to make your own crafts under the guidance of native artists.

Fairbanks Community & Dog
Mushing Museum   MUSEUM
(Map p298; 410 Cushman St; ⊙10am-7pm Mon-Fri, 11am-3pm Sun) FREE A small but packed museum that traces the city's history through old photos, newspaper clippings and his-

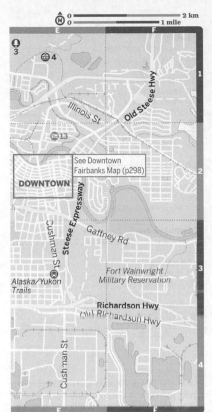

torical artifacts from daily life. One room focuses exclusively on sled-dog history and culture.

🏃 Activities

Fairbanks has plenty to keep outdoor enthusiasts enthusiastic. Much of the best trekking and paddling, however, is well out of town. In winter the rivers freeze up, making ideal ski-touring trails.

Cycling

Fairbanks has a network of cycle routes in and around the city, and cycling is a decent way to get around if you don't have a car. One of the more popular and scenic rides (about 17 miles long) is to head north on Illinois St from downtown, and then loop around on College Rd and Farmers Loop Rd/University Ave. Pick up a free *Bikeways* map at the Morris Thompson Cultural and Visitors Center.

**Alaska Outdoor
Rentals & Guides**   BICYCLE RENTAL
(Map p294; www.2paddle1.com; Pioneer Park; per 3hr/day $19/27; ⏲11am-7pm) Located on the river behind Pioneer Park, this small hut rents out mountain bikes.

Paddling

On long summer days (and nights), floating or canoeing down the Chena River is a quintessential Fairbanks activity. For extended backcountry expeditions, head to the visitor center for suggestions.

Several local places rent out boats and run shuttles to put-ins and take-outs: Alaska Outdoor Rentals & Guides will set you up with a canoe for $41 per day and, for another $24, pick you up downstream at the Pump House Restaurant. You'd be a party pooper if you didn't stop off at various riverside pubs along the way in what locals call the Great Fairbanks Pub Paddle.

Chena & Tanana Rivers   CANOEING
Those looking for an overnight – or even longer – paddle should try a float down the Chena River from Chena Hot Springs Rd, east of Fairbanks, or a pleasant two-day trip down the Tanana River. The popular 60-mile Tanana trip usually begins from the end of Chena Pump Rd and finishes in the town of Nenana, from where you can return with your canoe to Fairbanks on the Alaska Railroad.

Gold Panning

If you've been bitten by the gold bug, Fairbanks is an ideal area to try your hand at panning. Get handouts and up-to-date information at the Alaska Public Lands Information Center in the visitor center. Popular places include the Discovery Claim on Pedro Creek off the Steese Hwy (across from the Felix Pedro Monument), and several other locations further up the Steese Hwy.

Recreational gold panning can be done as part of the Gold Dredge No 8 (p296) tour.

👉 Tours

Northern Alaska Tour Co   SCENIC FLIGHTS
(907-474-8600; www.northernalaska.com) The Arctic Circle may be an imaginary line, but it's become one of Fairbanks' biggest draws, with small air-charter companies doing booming business flying travelers on sightseeing excursions across it. This company's tours fly to Coldfoot and return by bus along the Dalton Hwy for $369 to $419.

Fairbanks

Gold Dredge No 8   CULTURAL TOUR
(www.golddredgeno8.com; 1755 Old Steese Hwy N; admission incl lunch $14.95) The arrival of the Alaska Railroad in 1923 prompted major mining companies to bring their money and their three-story-high mechanized dredges to the region. The behemoths worked nonstop, making mincemeat of the terrain. The most famous of these, Gold Dredge No 8, a five-deck, 250ft dredge, ran from 1928 to 1959 and recovered 7.5 million ounces of gold.

Now listed as a national historic site, this is probably the most-viewed dredge in the state. Despite the official address, it's off the Old Steese Hwy at Mile 10, Goldstream Rd.

Note that individual travelers must join a scheduled tour to enter, which includes an opportunity to do some recreational gold panning.

Alaska Tails of the Trail   DOG SLEDDING
(☑ 907-455-6469; www.maryshields.com; adult/child $35/25; ☺ tours 10am & 7:30pm) Well-known musher and writer Mary Shields (the first woman to complete the Iditarod) offers an intimate two-hour glimpse into the life of a dog team and the Alaskans who raise and love them. You're asked to call first to confirm space and then make an online reservation.

The kennels are just north of the Large Animal Research Station (p293) on the UAF campus. Transportation is available for $20, round trip.

Riverboat Discovery   BOAT TOUR
(Map p294; ☑ 907-479-6673; www.riverboatdiscovery.com; 1975 Discovery Dr, Mile 4.5, Airport Way; adult/child $59.95/35.95; ☺ 9am & 2pm) This 3½-hour tour navigates the Chena River on a historic stern-wheeler, stopping at a replica of an Athabascan village as well as the riverfront home and kennels of the late Susan Butcher, four-time winner of the Iditarod. The boat leaves from **Steamboat Landing** (Map p294), a replica of a historic trading post, complete with a restaurant and massive touristy gift shop.

✻ Festivals & Events

Summer Solstice Celebrations   CULTURAL
(www.downtownfairbanks.com) Festivities take place around June 21, when the sun shines for almost 23 hours, and include foot races, arts-and-crafts booths and the Midnight Sun Festival and Midnight Sun Baseball Game.

Golden Days CULTURAL

Fairbanks' largest summer happening, staged in the third week of July, commemorates the city's golden past, with beer, sourdough pancakes and events ranging from rubber-ducky races to horse-and-rider shootouts.

World Eskimo-Indian Olympics CULTURAL

(www.weio.org; Carlson Center, 2010 2nd Ave) Held on the second-last weekend in July at the **Carlson Center** (Map p294), this four-day event attracts indigenous people from across the Far North, who display their athletic prowess in contests such as the Alaska High Kick and test their pain thresholds in games such as the Knuckle Hop. There's also dancing, cultural performances and plenty of traditional regalia.

🛏 Sleeping

Fairbanks has more than 100 B&Bs, many of which are in the downtown area; visit the visitor center for brochures. Fairbanks has an 8% bed tax.

Ah, Rose Marie B&B B&B $

(Map p298; ☏ 907-456-2040; www.ahrosemarie. com; 302 Cowles St; s/d $65/90; 🛜) This long-running and well-regarded B&B is split into two units: an original 80-year-old Dutch-built cottage with its charming heritage atmosphere, and a next door annex with a stylish modern interior. A super-friendly father-and-son team run the units, and while the son is a font of information on outdoor activities (he's cycled the Dalton Hwy in winter), the father prides himself (among other things) on his breakfasts.

Sven's Basecamp Hostel HOSTEL, CAMPGROUND $

(Map p294; ☏ 907-456-7836; www.svenshostel. com; 3505 Davis Rd; tent site $7, tipi/cabin $22/60; 🛜) Sven, from Switzerland, welcomes all kinds of travelers and vagabonds to this fine, multifarious hostel. This is where you'll meet some of Alaska's most intrepid explorers and hear the best travel tales. Accommodations are in cabins, tipis or your own tent. Showers are coin-operated and there's table football, books, a movie room and kitchen. Sven also rents bikes and canoes ($35 a day).

Billie's Backpackers Hostel HOSTEL $

(Map p294; ☏ 907-479-2034; www.alaskahostel. com; 2895 Mack Blvd; tent site $20, dm $30; @🛜) An easy-breezy international scene make this place regularly full in summer. Billie's has typical hostel amenities such as showers, laundry and kitchen, but it also offers nice touches such as a mosquito-netted communal tent for campers and free use of bicycles.

The hostel is off the MACS Red Line and not far from the university. From College Rd turn right on Westwood Ave and walk one block south.

THE NORTHERN LIGHTS

Fairbanks' best attraction is also its furthest-flung: the aurora borealis, better known as the northern lights, which take place 50 to 200 miles above Earth. As solar winds flow across the upper atmosphere, they hit gas molecules, which light up much like the high vacuum electrical discharge of a neon sign. The result is a solar-powered light show of ghostly, undulating colors streaming across the sky. In the dead of winter, the aurora can be visible for hours. Other evenings 'the event,' as many call it, lasts less than 10 minutes, with the aurora often spinning into a giant green ball and then fading. Milky-green and white are the most common colors of the lights; red is rare. In 1958 the sky was so 'bloody' with brilliant red auroras that fire trucks rushed to the hills surrounding Fairbanks, expecting to find massive forest fires.

This polar phenomenon has been seen as far south as Mexico, but Fairbanks is the undisputed aurora capital. Somebody in northern Minnesota might witness fewer than 20 'events' a year, and in Anchorage around 150, but in Fairbanks you can see the lights an average of 240 nights a year. North of Fairbanks, the number begins to decrease, and at the North Pole the lights are visible for fewer than 100 nights a year.

Regrettably, from May to mid-August there's too much daylight in Alaska to see an 'event,' but generally in late summer the aurora begins to appear in the Interior and can be enjoyed if you're willing to be awake at 2am. By mid-September the lights are dazzling and people are already asking, 'Did you see the lights last night?'

The best viewing is in Fairbanks' outlying hills, away from city lights, or at the University of Alaska Fairbanks.

Downtown Fairbanks

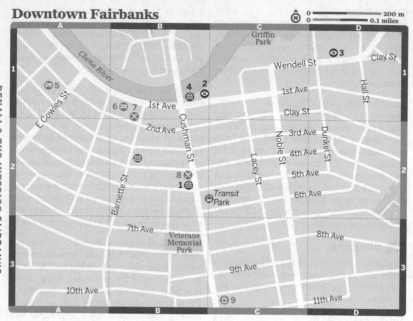

Downtown Fairbanks

◎ Sights
1 Fairbanks Community & Dog
  Mushing Museum B2
2 Golden Heart Plaza............................ B1
3 Morris Thompson Cultural &
  Visitors Center D1
4 Yukon Quest Headquarters................. B1

⊟ Sleeping
5 Ah, Rose Marie B&B A1
6 Bridgewater Hotel................................ B1

✕ Eating
7 Gambardella's Pasta Bella.................. B1
8 McCafferty's Coffee House B2

🏠 Shopping
9 Alaska House Art Gallery C3

ⓘ Information
Alaska Public Lands
  Information Center................... (see 3)

**Chena River State
Recreation Area**   CAMPGROUND $
(Map p294; walk-in/drive-up sites $10/17, RV sites
$28; ��) This lushly wooded campground
has 61 sites, tables, toilets, fireplaces, water

and a boat launch. It's served by the MACS
Red, Yellow and Blue lines.

Bridgewater Hotel   HOTEL $$
(Map p298; ☑907-456-3642; www.fountainhead-
hotels.com; 723 1st Ave; r $130; ℗@�) Your
best affordable option in what passes for
downtown in Fairbanks, the Bridgewater is
on the Chena River and abuts a pretty river-
side walking path. Rooms, while unlikely to
blow your mind, will keep you comfotable
and there's a decent buffet breakfast and a
handy free 'around town' shuttle. It's part of
a small family-run chain of four local hotels.

Minnie Street B&B Inn   B&B $$
(Map p294; ☑907-456-1802; www.minniestreet-
bandb.com; 345 Minnie St; r without/with bath
$139/169, ste $219-239; �) North of downtown, this spacious B&B literally occupies
a square block of turf. Near matching-sized
breakfasts are served by the friendly owners, as well as bountiful advice on what to
do around Fairbanks. Four suites come with
their own full kitchens and bathrooms, and
for the ultimate in privacy and space you
can rent an entire house for six ($219). All
guests have access to an outside deck and
barbecue.

Alaska Heritage House B&B
B&B $$

(Map p294; ☑907-456-4100; www.alaskaheritagehouse.com; 410 Cowles St; r $130-220; ☞) Probably the fanciest B&B in town, Heritage House was built in 1916 by Arthur Williams as a way to lure his future wife up to the Great White North to marry him. The home is on the National Historic Register, and each room has its own flair.

Pike's Waterfront Lodge
LODGE $$$

(Map p294; ☑907-456-4500; www.pikeslodge.com; 1850 Hoselton Rd; r from $235, cabins $279; ☻☞) This upscale lodge has an enviable position on the green banks of the Chena River. Room decor tilts toward the matronly, but there's also a row of spiffy log cabins with their own grass lawn.

Service is quick and friendly, local artwork adorns the public spaces, and amenities include a steam room, sauna, exercise facilities and the popular Pike's Landing (Map p294; mains $25-33), with its Alaskan-sized deck facing the river.

In 2003, the Iditarod dog-sled race finished here due to lack of snow further south. The event is memorialized in a pleasant iris garden.

✗ Eating

✗ Downtown

The downtown area has a handful of restaurants in close proximity, representing a range of ethnic cuisines, including Thai, Greek and Italian.

McCafferty's Coffee House
CAFE $

(Map p298; 408 Cushman St; ☺7am-8pm Mon-Thu, to 11pm Fri, 9am-11pm Sat, 9am-5pm Sun; ☞) Espresso emporium with good daily soups and baked goods. Striking up a conversation with the person on the next table is almost obligatory. There's a recording studio upstairs and live music adds atmosphere on Friday and Saturday nights.

Gambardella's Pasta Bella
ITALIAN $$

(Map p298; ☑907-457-4992; www.gambardellas.com; 706 2nd Ave; mains $17-28; ☺11am-10pm) In a city founded by an Italian, one would expect a decent *ristorante* and though Gambardella's can't compete with the chefs in Bologna or Catania, it's a welcome sight in Fairbanks – and very popular. Italophiles should find the pasta al dente and the homemade bread pleasantly aromatic.

✗ University Area

Lemongrass
THAI $

(Map p294; ☑907-456-2200; 388 Old Chena Pump Rd; mains $9-11; ☺11am-4pm & 5-10pm) Ignore the out-of-the-way, strip-mall setting, which is ugly even by Fairbanks' standards. Lemongrass does the best Thai food north of Anchorage.

Pita Place
FALAFEL $

(Map p294; www.pitasite.com; 3300 College Rd; half/full pita $4.75/8; ☺11am-6pm Wed-Sat; ☑) A humble food stand with a couple of pews indoors and picnic tables outside. The pitas are filled with falafel and made entirely from scratch.

Hot Licks
ICE CREAM $

(Map p294; www.hotlicks.net; 3453 College Rd; cones $3.50, sundaes $5-7; ☺noon-10pm) On warm days, the line for the homemade ice cream is insane. Find out why with a double-scoop cone of the fresh daily specials.

Sam's Sourdough Café
DINER $$

(Map p294; ☑907-479-0523; University Ave, at Cameron St; mains $11.95; ☺6am-11pm) Considered by many to be the town's best diner, this place serves up sourdough pancakes all day long, as well as burgers and the usual diner suspects. It's not fancy, but that's the point.

Wolf Run Restaurant
AMERICAN, FUSION $$$

(Map p294; ☑907-458-0636; 3360 Wolf Run; mains $24-38; ☺11am-9pm Tue-Thu & Sun, to 10pm Fri & Sat) Set in an old timber house that has recently been spruced up, Wolf Run has long been known for its generous, super-sweet dessert plates, but lately has also excelled at gourmet food with a strong Middle Eastern influence. Of note are the mezze plates, including a fine hummus dish, plus treats such as salmon on a cider plank.

There's an outside patio should the weather cooperate.

✗ Airport Way & Around

Cookie Jar
BREAKFAST $

(Map p294; ☑907-479-8319; www.cookiejarfairbanks.com; 1006 Cadillac Ct; breakfast $8-10; ☺6:30am-8pm Mon-Thu, to 9pm Fri & Sat, 8am-4pm Sun; ☞☝) Though bizarrely situated behind a pair of car dealerships off Danby St, Cookie Jar lives up to its name as one of Fairbanks' top spots to indulge a sweet tooth. It's also a great little breakfast and lunch shop with filling specials and an endless cup of coffee. Kids' menu available.

Fred Meyer SUPERMARKET $
(Map p294; ☑907-474-1400; cnr Old Airport Rd & Airport Way; ⊗7am-11pm) An airplane-hangar-sized store with every grocery imaginable, plus bulk foods, an extensive salad bar and all sorts of ready-to-eat fare. Excellent if you're stocking up for the Dalton Hwy.

Pump House Restaurant STEAKHOUSE $$$
(Map p294; ☑907-479-8452; www.pumphouse.com; Mile 1.3, Chena Pump Rd; dinner $18-36; ⊗lunch & dinner) Located 4 miles from downtown, this national historic site was once a pump house during the gold-mining era. It's loaded with character and collectibles, but the food is undistinguished and the dining area takes itself a bit too seriously. Fortunately the guests don't, which still makes this a great place to turn dinner into an evening overlooking the Chena River.

The MACS Yellow Line goes by here.

Alaska Salmon Bake SALMON BAKES $$$
(Map p294; ☑907-452-7274; www.akvisit.com; adult/child $33/13; ⊗5-9pm; ⊛) Hungry souls should take in the touristy, tasty, tongue-in-cheek salmon bake at Pioneer Park, which serves all-you-can-eat grilled salmon, halibut, cod, prime rib and countless sides. A $6 shuttle bus is available from major hotels.

✗ Around Fairbanks

Some of the most recommended places to eat in town are actually just outside town. The following are in Fox, reached by heading north on Steese Hwy and turning onto the Old Steese Hwy. The brewery is practically right at the intersection of the two highways, while Turtle Club is a mile further down.

Silver Gulch Brewery BURGERS $$
(☑907-452-2739; Mile 11, Old Steese Hwy; mains $15-34; ⊗4-10pm Mon-Fri, 11am-10pm Sat & Sun) This cavernous, slightly overdone brewpub (the northernmost microbrewery in the US) makes jolly good beer, but plenty of people come just for the pub grub. There are free brewery tours at 3pm on Wednesday and Friday.

Turtle Club RIBS $$
(☑907-457-3883; www.alaskanturtle.com; Mile 10, Old Steese Hwy; dinner $23-37; ⊗6-10pm Mon-Sat, 5-9pm Sun) Not a club but more of a roadhouse reputed for its prime ribs. Reservations are recommended.

☕ Drinking & Nightlife

★Hoodoo Brewing Co BREWERY
(Map p294; ☑907-459-2337; www.hoodoobrew.com; 1951 Fox Ave; ⊗3-8pm Tue-Fri, 11am-8pm Sat) A new Pacific Northwest–style brewery with an on-site tasting room that's kitted out in modern, minimalist decor. Get the four-beer sampler, which includes a stout, IPA and some pale blonde beers with interesting Germanic flavors. There's a refined non-pub-like atmosphere inside, especially on Saturday afternoon when it runs free brewery tours (4pm).

Pump House Saloon PUB
(Map p294; Mile 1.3, Chena Pump Rd) Enjoys the riverfront ambience of the Pump House Restaurant, but with a bar menu that won't break the bank.

College Coffeehouse CAFE
(Map p294; ☑907-374-0468; 3677 College Rd; ⊗7am-11pm Mon-Fri, 8am-11pm Sat & Sun; ☎) In the Campus Corner Mall, this is one of the best spots in Fairbanks to pick up on the student vibe. Frequent live music.

Marlin BAR
(Map p294; 3412 College Rd) A subterranean dive hosting Fairbanks' edgiest musical acts most nights of the week.

☆ Entertainment

As Alaska's third-biggest city, Fairbanks always has something on the go. For the low-down on live music, movies and such, check the listings in 'Latitude 65,' printed each Friday in the *Fairbanks Daily News-Miner*.

Palace Theatre & Saloon THEATER
(Map p294; ☑907-452-7274; www.akvisit.com; adult/child $18/9; ⊗show 8:15pm) Pioneer Park comes alive at night in this historical theater with honky-tonk piano, cancan dancers and other acts in the 'Golden Heart Revue.'

Blue Loon LIVE MUSIC
(www.theblueloon.com; Mile 352.5, George Parks Hwy) One of the Fairbanks area's most popular nightspots, the Loon features live bands and DJs, dancing, food and lots of good beer. A couple of times a summer it may even pull in an older big-name act such as the Violent Femmes or the Bare Naked Ladies. To get here, head out of town a few miles on George Parks Hwy.

🛍 Shopping

Alaska House Art Gallery   ARTS & CRAFTS
(Map p298; www.thealaskahouse.com; 1003 Cushman St; ⊘11am-7pm Mon-Sat) In a log building at the southern end of downtown, the gallery specializes in indigenous and native-themed creations. Artists can often be found on the premises demonstrating their talents or telling stories.

Gulliver's Books   BOOKS
(Map p294; www.gullivers-books.com; 3525 College Rd; ⊘9am-9pm Mon-Fri, to 8pm Sat, 11am-6pm Sun; 🛜) Next to Campus Corner Mall, this is by far the best bookstore in town, selling new and used books and plenty of Alaskan titles.

Beaver Sports   SPORTS
(Map p294; www.beaversports.com; 3480 College Rd; ⊘10am-8pm Mon-Fri, to 7pm Sat, 11am-5pm Sun) Sells mountain bikes and mountains of every species of wilderness equipment. There's also a handy message board for exchanging info with fellow adventurers or securing used gear.

ℹ Information

Wi-fi is common around town and there are free computers at the visitor center.
Alaska Public Lands Information Center (Map p298; www.alaskacenters.gov/fairbanks.cfm; ⊘8am-6pm) Encased in the Morris Thompson Cultural and Visitors Center, this is the place to head if you're planning on visiting any state or national parks and reserves in the region. Pick up one of its detailed tree brochures on the Steese, Elliot, Taylor or Denali Hwys.
Fairbanks Memorial Hospital (☑907-452-8181; 1650 W Cowles St) Emergency care; south of Airport Way.

Key Bank of Alaska (100 Cushman St) Has an ATM. Most strip-mall areas also have a bank and ATM.

ℹ Getting There & Away

AIR
Alaska Airlines (☑800-252-7522; www.alaskaair.com) flies direct to Anchorage (where there are connections to the rest of Alaska, the Lower 48 and overseas) for around $250 round trip. There are also handy direct flights to Seattle ($390) with Delta Airlines. **Air North** (☑800-661-0407; www.flyairnorth.com) flies to Dawson City. For travel into the Bush, try Ravn Alaska (p417), **Warbelow's Air Ventures** (☑907-474-0518; www.warbelows.com) or **Wright Air Service** (☑907-474-0502; www.wrightair.net).

BUS
Alaska Bus Guy (☑907-720-6541; www.alaskabusguy.com) departs Fairbanks at 7am for Denali National Park ($70, three hours) and Anchorage ($145, 10½ hours), and will make stops anywhere along George Parks Hwy. Interior Alaska Bus Line (p419) leaves at 9.30am from the downtown Transit Park on Sunday, Wednesday and Friday for Delta Junction ($60, two hours) and Tok ($95, 5½ hours), where you can transfer to a bus for Glennallen and Anchorage. At Whitehorse you can catch the company's bus to Skagway. Alaska/Yukon Trails (p417) leavess daily around 9am from various points in Fairbanks (including the hostels) and travels down the George Parks Hwy to Denali ($55, three hours), Talkeetna ($92, seven hours) and Anchorage ($99, 10 hours). The company also has a 7am service to Dawson City ($265, nine hours), and Whitehorse via the Taylor Hwy.

CAR & MOTORCYCLE
If you're driving to Fairbanks from Canada, you'll likely be coming up the Alcan. It's a good 12 hours from Whitehorse to Fairbanks, with little

---

THE YUKON QUEST: ALASKA'S 'TOUGH' DOG RACE

Like a handful of other Alaskan towns, Fairbanks bills itself as the dog-mushing capital of the world. The town's claim to fame is the Yukon Quest, which takes place each February and covers 1023 miles between here and Whitehorse along many of the early trails used by trappers, miners and the postal service. Though less famous than the Iditarod, mushers will attest that the Quest is tougher. One female musher described it to us as being like childbirth – unbelievably painful at the time but worth it afterwards.

Over the race's course, teams climb four mountains more than 3000ft high and run along hundreds of miles of the frozen Yukon River. While the Iditarod has 25 rest stops, the Quest has only six. The Yukon Quest has its new headquarters (Map p298; cnr 1st Ave & Cushman St; ⊘10am-6pm Mon-Fri, 11am-4pm Sat & Sun) in the old Log Cabin Visitor Center. There's a small exhibit on the grueling race and a gift shop where proceeds go toward the race organization. Mushers are usually on hand with dogs from 11am to 4pm to talk and answer questions.

en route, save for Tok and a few other highway service communities. From Anchorage, it's six hours to Fairbanks up George Parks Hwy.

TRAIN

Alaska Railroad (☑ 907-458-6025; www. alaskarailroad.com) leaves Fairbanks daily at 8:15am from mid-May to mid-September. The train gets to Denali National Park ($53) at noon and Anchorage ($179) at 8pm. The **station** (☉ 6:30am-3pm) is at the southern end of Danby St. MACS (p302) Red Line buses run to and from the station.

❶ Getting Around

TO/FROM THE AIRPORT

Super-modern and well laid out, **Fairbanks International Airport** (Map p294; www.dot.state. ak.us/faiiap) is at the west end of Airport Way, 4 miles from town. MACS Yellow Line buses swing by seven times a day Monday to Friday (three times on Saturday) between 7:30am and 7:15pm, charging $1.50 and taking you past some Airport Way motels en route to the Transit Park. Most of the main hotels along Airport Way and in downtown have airport shuttles. Free phones are available in the baggage claim.

CAR

All the national rental agencies (Avis, National, Budget, Payless, Hertz) have counters at the airport. However, to drive on the unpaved roads around Fairbanks, including the Dalton Hwy, you'll need to contact **Dalton Highway Auto Rentals** (Map p294; ☑ 907-474-3530; www. arctic-outfitters.com; 3820 University Ave, east ramp of Fairbanks International Airport). Expect to pay $200 to $250 a day (mileage may be extra, depending on how many days you rent) when everything is added up. Note that rental taxes are very high (18%) and so are gas prices. You must be at least 30 years of age.

PUBLIC TRANSPORTATION

MACS (Metropolitan Area Commuter Service; www.co.fairbanks.ak.us/transportation) runs buses roughly hourly from around 6:15am to 8:15pm Monday to Friday. There's a more-limited service on Saturday and none on Sunday. The **Transit Park** (Map p298; cnr Cushman St & 5th Ave) is the system's central hub. The Blue and Red lines run in loops linking the university district and downtown. The Green route heads to North Pole; the Yellow to the airport. The fare on all routes is $1.50, or you can purchase an unlimited day pass for $3. Schedules are posted on bus stops and also online.

TAXI

Cabs charge around $3 per mile, with a $1 flag fall. Try **Alaska Cab** (☑ 907-455-7777) or **Yellow Cab** (☑ 907-455-5555).

AROUND FAIRBANKS

There are a number of day trips and longer adventures to be had in the outlying areas. Along the Steese and Elliot Hwys you'll find plenty of good hiking and paddling.

Chena Hot Springs Road

This fireweed-lined, forest-flanked corridor parallels the languid Chena River 56 miles to the Chena Hot Springs Resort, the closest hot springs to Fairbanks and also the most developed. The road is paved and in good condition. From Mile 26 to Mile 51 it passes through **Chena River State Recreation Area**, a 397-sq-mile preserve encompassing the valley and nearby alpine areas. Some of the Fairbanks area's best hiking, canoeing and fishing can be found here, usually just steps from the road.

◉ Sights & Activities

Trail maps are sometimes available at the start of hiking trails, but it's best to drop by the Morris Thompson Cultural and Visitors Center (p294) in Fairbanks beforehand as it's always stocked.

Ice Museum   MUSEUM
(admission $15) Most of this museum's ice art is the work of Steve Brice, one of the world's premier ice sculptors. There are tours every two hours from 11am to 7pm to see the life-size jousting knights, chandeliers and a bar where martinis are served in ice glasses. Just remember the ice loo is only for show. It's next to Chena Hot Springs Resort.

Chena River   CANOEING
With no white water and comparatively few other hazards, the peaceful Chena River offers a variety of day and multi-day canoeing possibilities, with access points all along Chena Hot Springs Rd.

Granite Tors Trail Loop   HIKING
The 15-mile Granite Tors Trail Loop (which is accessed from the Tors Trail State Campground, at Mile 39.5) ascends into an alpine area with unusual tors (isolated pinnacles of granite rising out of the tundra). The first set is 6 miles from the trailhead, but the best group lies 2 miles further along the trail.

This eight- to 10-hour trek gains 2700ft in elevation. There's a free-use shelter midway.

Angel Rocks Trail HIKING

A moderate two- to three-hour, 3.5-mile loop trail that leads to Angel Rocks, large granite outcroppings near the north boundary of the recreation area. The elevation gain is a modest 900ft.

The trail is also the first leg of the **Angel Rocks–Chena Hot Springs Traverse**, a more difficult, 8.3-mile trek that ends at the Chena Hot Springs Resort. Roughly halfway along the traverse is a free-use shelter.

The posted trailhead for Angel Rocks is just south of a rest area at Mile 49. The lower trailhead for the Chena Dome Trail is practically across the road.

Chena Dome Trail HIKING

The upper trailhead for the most popular hike in the area, Chena Dome Trail, is at Mile 50.5. The trail follows the ridge for almost 30 miles in a loop around the Angel Creek drainage area. The first 3 miles to the treeline make an excellent day hike.

Chena Hot Springs SPRING

The burbling Chena Hot Springs were discovered by gold miners in 1905 and quickly became the area's premier soaking spot. At the heart of a 40-sq-mile geothermal area, the springs produce a steady stream of water that, at 156°F (69°C), must be cooled before you can even think about bathing in it.

You can only enjoy the waters at this 'resort,' which has aging indoor facilities (with chlorinated waters) and a large outdoor, boulder-ringed pool with pure hot-spring water for adults only.

Other activities at the resort include mountain biking, hiking, horseback riding and fishing the local streams for grayling.

Tours

Geothermal Renewable Energy Tours ENVIRONMENTAL TOURS

(⊙2pm & 4pm) ✐ **FREE** The US's biggest oil state also hides a potentially rich source of geothermal energy, as these tours at the hot springs resort will demonstrate. The Chena plant was inaugurated in 2006 and these interesting tours will enlighten you on the ins and outs of the valuable renewable resource.

Sleeping & Eating

There are a number of sleeping options in the area, including three popular state-run campgrounds and eight public-use cabins ($35 to $60). Three of the cabins are on the road, while the rest are accessible via short but often very wet hikes. The cabins vary in size, sleeping between four and nine people, and can be reserved via the **Alaska Division of Parks and Outdoor Recreation** (☑907-451-2695; www.alaskastateparks.org).

Rosehip State Campground CAMPGROUND $

(Mile 27, Chena Hot Springs Rd; campsites $10) The largest of the area's three campgrounds, Rosehip has a nature trail and 36 treed, well-spaced sites, some right on the riverbank.

Chena Hot Springs Resort RESORT $$$

(☑907-451-8104; www.chenahotsprings.com; Mile 56.6, Chena Hot Springs Rd; campsites $20, r $199-249, yurts with outhouse $65, restaurant mains $20-35) ✐ This come-as-you-are complex is at its best in winter when snow covers the ground and the aurora lights up the sky. Otherwise the rooms are a bit overpriced in summer, especially the older wing, which is getting a little tatty. The resort's **restaurant** whips up

Chena Hot Springs Road

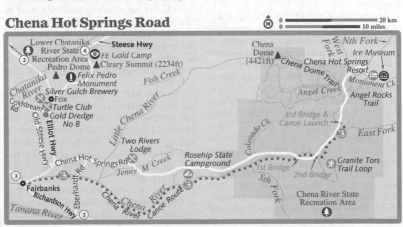

decent meals, and the adjacent bar doesn't quite overpower you with Yukon Quest memorabilia.

Two Rivers Lodge PUB $$$
(Mile 16, Chena Hot Springs Rd; mains $24-36; ⊙5-10pm Tue-Fri, 3-10pm Sat & Sun) Steak, seafood and poultry are the focus at this rustic lodge, complete with hunting trophies, but good roadhouse meals (burgers, ribs, sandwiches) are found in the lounge.

❶ Getting There & Away

Chena Hot Springs Resort runs a shuttle service from Fairbanks ($125 round trip, two-person minimum), but you'd be better off renting a car. Hitchhiking is not the grand effort it is on the Elliot Hwy, because of the heavy summer usage of the recreation area.

Steese Highway

The scenic but severely lonely Steese Hwy follows an old miners' trail 162 miles from Fairbanks to the Athabascan village of Circle on the Yukon River. This hilly and winding road is paved for the first 53 miles, and then has a good gravel base to the mining settlement of Central. In the final 30 miles it narrows and becomes considerably rougher and more twisty. While an interesting drive, the route's main attraction – Circle Hot Springs – has been closed for several years.

It may be worth a short drive up the highway to see the **Felix Pedro Monument** (Mile 16.6, Steese Hwy), which commemorates the miner whose gold strike gave birth to Fairbanks. The stream across the highway – now known as Pedro Creek – is where it all happened.

Beyond this is the **FE Gold Camp** (Mile 27.9), a national historic site. The camp was built in 1925 for the dredging that went on from 1927 to 1957 and removed an estimated $70 million in gold (at yesterday's prices).

A few miles beyond, the landscape opens up, revealing expansive vistas as well as evidence of forest-fire activity. There are several state campgrounds, including **Cripple Creek BLM Campground** (Mile 60, Steese Hwy; campsites $6), which is the uppermost access point to the Chatanika River canoe route.

Access points for the **Pinnell Mountain Trail** are at Mile 85.6 and Mile 107.3. The first trailhead is **Twelvemile Summit**, which offers remarkable alpine views and

is often snowy well into June. Even if you have no desire to undertake the three-day trek, the first 2 miles is an easy climb past unusual rock formations.

The **Birch Creek Canoe Route** begins at Mile 94, where a short road leads down to a canoe launch on the creek. The wilderness trip is a seven- to 10-day, 110-mile paddle to the exit point, at Mile 140.5 or 147.2 of the highway. The overall rating of the river is class II, but there are some class III and possibly class IV rapids that require lining your canoe.

Eagle Summit (3624ft), at Mile 107, has a parking area for the second trailhead of the Pinnell Mountain Trail. A climb of less than a mile leads to the mountaintop, the highest point along the Steese Hwy and a place where the midnight sun can be observed skimming the horizon around the summer solstice. On a clear day, summiting here can feel like ascending to heaven. The peak is also near a caribou migration route.

Twenty miles later, the highway passes through **Central** (Mile 127.5), a former supply stop on the trail from Circle City, and finally to **Circle** itself (Mile 162), once a bustling town of 1200 people, with theaters, dance halls and 28 saloons. Circle, on the Yukon River, grew up during the Klondike Gold Rush (1897–98) and was erroneously named by original settlers who thought it sat on the Arctic Circle (which actually lies 50 miles to the north).

Elliot Highway

From the crossroad with the Steese Hwy at Fox, just north of Fairbanks, the Elliot Hwy extends 154 miles north and then west to Manley Hot Springs, a small settlement near the Tanana River. Along the way are a number of free campgrounds as well as public-use cabins (per cabin $25) that need to be reserved through the BLM (☎907-474-2251) in Fairbanks.

The first half of the highway is paved, the rest is gravel, and there's no gas and few services until you reach the end. The diversions along the way are comparatively few, but the leisurely, scenic drive, coupled with the disarming charms of Manley Hot Springs, makes it a worthwhile one- or two-day road trip.

At Mile 11 is the **Lower Chatanika River State Recreation Area**, a 400-acre unmaintained park offering fishing, boating

und content

At Mile 28, look for the Wickersham Dome trailhead parking lot and an information box. From here, trails lead to two public-use cabins. Lee's Cabin is a 7-mile hike in and overlooks the White Mountains. Borealis-Le Fevre Cabin is a 20-mile hike over the White Mountains Summit Trail.

At Mile 49.5, you'll enter (probably without realizing it) the 'settlement' of Joy (population 30), named for Joy Griffin, an original homesteader. Stop at the tumble-down wooden shop/cafe known variously as Wildwood General Store, or Arctic Circle Trading Post, which sells Arctic-themed souvenirs, coffee and rather nice muffins. Stock up as there aren't many more places like this further north.

Ten miles before the junction with the Dalton Hwy, at Mile 62, a 500yd spur road on the right leads to the public-use Fred Blixt Cabin.

Livengood (lye-ven-good), 2 miles east of the highway at Mile 71, has no services and is little more than a maintenance station with a scattering of log shanties. Here, the Elliot Hwy swings west and in 2 miles, at the junction of the Dalton Hwy, the pavement ends and the road becomes a rutted, rocky lane. Traffic evaporates and until Manley Hot Springs you may not see another vehicle.

The rustic, privately managed Tolovana Hot Springs (907-455-8708, www.tolovanahotsprings.com; 2-/4-/6-person cabins $60/120/150) can be accessed on a taxing 11 mile overland hike south from Mile 93. Facilities consist of outdoor wood tubs bubbling with 125°F (51°C) to 145°F (62°C) water, outhouses, a drinking-water barrel and three cabins that must be reserved in advance. The trailhead isn't signposted, so contact the managers for directions.

At Mile 110, a paved side road runs 11 miles to the small Athabascan village of Minto (population 180), which isn't known for welcoming strangers.

Beyond Minto, the Elliot Hwy briefly becomes winding and hilly, and then suddenly, at Mile 120, there's chip-sealing for the next 17 miles. Hutlinana Creek is reached at Mile 129, and a quarter-mile east of the bridge (on the right) is the start of an 8-mile creekside trail to Hutlinana Warm Springs, an undeveloped thermal area with a rock-wall pool. The springs are visited mainly in winter; in summer, the buggy bushwhack seems uninviting.

WORTH A TRIP

NORTH POLE, ALASKA

Well, it *seemed* like a good idea: back in the 1940s, a development corporation bought up a sleepy homestead southeast of Fairbanks and, in a bid to attract toy manufacturers, named it North Pole. Though the Fortune 500 companies never came knocking, a steady stream of smirking tourists and their starry-eyed kids have been wandering through ever since.

Today this community of 2200 souls, 12 miles south of Fairbanks, would be a forgettable clutch of churches and fast-food franchises if it weren't for its name and year-round devotion to the Yuletide. Streetlights are decorated with candy-cane stripes, local businesses work Santa into their name no matter how, and streets bear such festive monikers as Mistletoe Lane. At the North Pole Post Office (325 S Santa Claus Lane), hundreds of thousands of letters arrive annually, simply addressed to 'Santa Claus, North Pole, Alaska.'

The town's biggest attraction is Santa Claus House (www.santaclaushouse.com; 101 St Nicholas Dr, off Richardson Hwy; 8am-8pm), between the North Pole exits. The sprawling barn-like store holds endless aisles of Christmas ornaments and toys, a live Santa to listen to your Christmas wishes, a giant statue of Santa and the 'North Pole' – a candy-striped post.

From the bridge it's another 23 miles southwest to Manley Hot Springs.

Manley Hot Springs

POP 72

The town of Manley Hot Springs (http://fairbanks-alaska.com/manley-hot-springs.htm) may be one of the loveliest discoveries you'll make around the Fairbanks area. At the end of a long, lonely road, this well-kept town is full of friendly people, tidy log homes and luxuriant gardens. Located between Hot Springs Slough and the Tanana River, the community was first homesteaded in 1902 by JF Karshner, just as the US Army Signal Corps arrived to put in a telegraph station. A few years later, as the place boomed with miners from the nearby Eureka and Tofty districts, Frank Manley arrived and built a four-story hotel. Most of the miners are gone now, but Manley's name – and the spirit of an earlier era – remains. In modern times the town has been a hotbed of high-level dog mushing: Charlie Boulding, Joe Redington Jr and four-time Iditarod champ Susan Butcher have all lived here.

🏃 Activities

Hot Springs
SPRING
(☑907-672-3231; admission per hr $5; ⊙24hr) Just before crossing the slough, you pass the town's namesake hot springs, privately owned by famously hospitable Chuck and Gladys Dart. Bathing takes place inside a huge, thermal-heated greenhouse that brings to mind a veritable Babylonian garden of grapes, Asian pears and hibiscus flowers.

Deep in this jungle are three spring-fed concrete tubs, each burbling at different temperatures. Pay your money (which gives you sole access to the springs for an hour), hose yourself down and soak away in this deliriously un-Alaskan setting. Heed the signs to not pick the fruit, but do call ahead to reserve a time slot.

Manley Boat Charters
BOAT TOUR
(☑907-672-3271; boat rental per hr $75) Across the slough and 3 miles beyond the village is the broad Tanana River, just upstream from its confluence with the Yukon. Frank Gurtler of Manley Boat Charters can take you fishing or just show you the sights along the waterway.

Iditarod Kennels
DOG SLEDDING
(☑907-672-3412; www.joeredington.com; tours adult/child $25/15) Run by famed dogsled racer Joe Redington Jr, these 1½-hour kennel tours delve into the history of dog mushing and racing, as well as Manley itself and the ways and means of rural living. Reservations are preferred to drop-ins.

🛏 Sleeping & Eating

Public Campground
CAMPGROUND $
(campsites $5) The slough-facing campground is just past the bridge. Pay at the roadhouse. Showers are available for $5.

Manley Roadhouse
HISTORIC HOTEL $$
(☑907-672-3161; www.manleyroadhouse.com; r without/with bath $70/120; ⊙restaurant 8am-8pm) Facing the slough, this antique-strewn, century-old establishment has clean, un-complicated rooms and is the social center of town. The bar boasts an impressive array of liquor and beer choices, while the **restaurant** (mains $17-25) offers home-style cooking on communal tables in the adjacent sitting room.

Manley Trading Post
SELF-CATERING $
(⊙10am-5pm) For groceries, expensive gas, liquor and postal services.

ℹ Getting There & Away
With so little traffic on Elliot Hwy, hitching is ill-advised – though if someone *does* come along, they'll likely take pity on you. You can rent a vehicle in Fairbanks, however, or contact **Warbelow's Air Ventures** (☑907-474-0518; www.warbelows.com), which has flights to Manley Hot Springs for $170 (round trip) on Monday, Wednesday and Friday.

THE ALCAN/ALASKA HIGHWAY
One of the most impressive engineering feats of the 20th century, the Alcan stretches 1390 miles from Dawson Creek, British Columbia, to Delta Junction, Alaska. A drive up (or down) the Alaska Hwy is one of those once-in-a-lifetime road trips that many folks dream of and very few actually accomplish.

The highway was famously punched through the wilderness in a mere eight months in 1942, as part of a WWII effort to protect Alaska from expansionist Japan. Commonly known as the Alcan, short for 'Alaska–Canada Military Hwy,' it remains the only year-round overland route that links the 49th state to the Lower 48.

Approximately 300 of its miles, paved and well maintained, are within Alaska, between Fairbanks and the Yukon Territory border. The 98-mile stretch from Delta Junction to Fairbanks is 'technically' the Richardson Hwy, but most figure this to be the final leg of the Alcan and we, too, treat it as such.

Fairbanks to Delta Junction
From Fairbanks, Richardson Hwy runs 98 relatively unscenic miles to Delta Junction, with little of interest save a few campsites and recreation areas, and some neat well-tended Ukrainian farms. From Delta

Junction, the Richardson continues to the south via Glennallen to Valdez, while the Alcan branches off and passes through Tok en route to Canada.

Chena Lakes Recreation Area (Mile 346.7, Richardson Hwy; campsites $10-17, RV sites $25) was the last phase of an Army Corps of Engineers flood-control project prompted by the Chena River's flooding of Fairbanks in 1967.

Two separate parks make up the area, offering nature paths, paved trails and swimming, plus canoe, sailboat and paddleboat rentals. Three campground loops provide access to about 80 sites. Note that the entrance to the recreation area is 2 miles off the Richardson Hwy. Follow the signs after you exit.

Salcha River State Recreation Site (Mile 323.3, Richardson Hwy; campsites $10) offers access to the Salcha and Tanana Rivers for fishing and boating ($10 boat launch). It has a basic camping area on a gravel bar, plus the reservable **Salcha River Public-Use Cabin** (☑907-451-2705; www.dnr.state.ak.us/parks/cabins; per night $35) right by the boat dock. To reach the state recreation site, turn in at the Salcha Marine boat dealership.

Harding Lake State Recreation Area (Mile 321.5, Richardson Hwy; campsites $10, day-use parking $10, boat launch $10) is 43 miles from Fairbanks and 1.5 miles northeast of the Alcan. The 90-site wooded campground features more amenities than most in the area, with a ranger office, picnic shelters, horseshoes, volleyball, swimming, canoeing and fishing (char and pike) in the natural lake. Five group walk-in sites are on the water.

Not far from the sprawl of Delta Junction is the turnoff at Mile 293.7 for **Tenderfoot Pottery** (www.tenderfootpottery.com; pieces $25-65; ⊙9am-9pm), a small studio run by a local ceramicist.

Delta Junction

POP 949

For most visitors, Delta Junction is notable for a technicality: it proclaims itself the end of the Alcan, as the famous highway joins Richardson Hwy here to complete the route to Fairbanks. The town began as a construction camp and picked up its name as it lies at the junction between the two highways. Most travelers use the town as a fuel and grocery stop, with a quick visit to the historic Sullivan Roadhouse, and Rika's Roadhouse and Landing. The big **Deltana Fair** (www.deltanafair.com), with giant vegetables,

livestock shows, parades and live music, is on the last weekend of July.

◉ Sights

Big Delta State Historical Park　　PARK
(☑907-895-4201;　http://dnr.alaska.gov/parks/units/deltajct/bigdelta.htm; Mile 274.5, Richardson Hwy; ⊙8am-8pm) **FREE** A few miles north of town is the area's best attraction. The 10-acre historical park on the Tanana River preserves **Rika's Roadhouse and Landing**, an important crossroads for travelers, miners and soldiers on the Fairbanks–Valdez Trail from 1909 to 1947. You can easily spend a couple of hours here wandering the pretty grounds and exploring buildings stocked with displays of turn-of-the-century farming and roadhouse life.

Sullivan Roadhouse　　HISTORIC BUILDING
(⊙9am-6pm) **FREE** Across the parking lot from the visitor center, this classic log structure (on the National Register of Historic Places) was built in 1906 to serve travelers along the Fairbanks–Valdez Trail. In 1997 the cabin was moved, log by log, from Fort Greely to its present location and now serves as a museum with a collection of exhibits dedicated to travel in Alaska in the early 1900s – the roadhouse era.

⊨ Sleeping & Eating

Delta Junction is blessed with scads of nearby campgrounds and no bed tax. Eating options in town are limited.

Big Delta State Historical Park　　CAMPGROUND $
(☑907-895-4201; www.rikas.com; Mile 274.5, Richardson Hwy; campsites $5; ⊙8am-8pm) Just off the parking lot is a small wooded campground. Within the park, look for the à la carte **Packhouse Pavilion Restaurant** (sandwiches $7.50; ⊙9am-5pm), which sells tasty sandwiches and baked goods.

Clearwater State Recreation Site　　CAMPGROUND $
(campsites $10) With 16 wooded and well-spaced sites, most overlooking the peaceful Clearwater Creek, this is a lovely little spot to spend a night. The site is 13 miles northeast of town. To get there, first follow Richardson Hwy and then turn right on Jack Warren Rd, 2.4 miles north of the visitor center. Head 10.5 miles east and look for signs to the campground. Clearwater Creek has good grayling fishing and some paddling options.

Quartz Lake State Recreation Area

CAMPGROUND $

(Mile 277.8, Richardson Hwy; campsites $10) Covering 600 acres north of town (3 miles from the Richardson Hwy), this area has two camping areas: one by Lost Lake and another closer to the entrance. Both are accessible by road, and there is additional primitive camping at Bluff Point, accessible by a 3-mile trail starting near the lake. Also starting near the lake is a rugged 1.7-mile trail (one way) to Bert Mountain (1820ft).

The public-use **cabins** (http://dnr.alaska.gov/parks/cabins; per night $35) are another option.

Garden B&B

B&B $$

(☑ 907-895-4633; www.alaskagardenbandb.com; 3103 Tanana Loop Extension; r without/with bath $89/109, cabin $129; ☎) ✐ Located on what is possibly the neatest-looking farm you'll ever see, the Garden B&B grows its own vegetables (many of which find their way onto your breakfast plate) and tends its own flower garden. The rooms are instantly inviting – the cabins have kitchenettes – and the hosts are lovely.

Kelly's Alaska Country Inn

MOTEL $$

(☑ 907-895-4667; www.kellysalaskacountryinn. com; 1616 Richardson Hwy; s/d $129/139; ☎) Two blocks north of the visitor center, Kelly's has spacious, clean rooms, some with kitchenettes.

IGA Food Cache

SUPERMARKET $

(Mile 266, Richardson Hwy; ⊙6:30am-10pm Mon-Sat, 8am-9pm Sun) A half-mile north of the visitor center, this grocery store features a bakery, deli and espresso cart and also sells homemade soup and other ready-to-eat items to go.

Buffalo Center Drive-In

BURGERS $$

(☑ 907-895-4055; Mile 265.5, Richardson Hwy; burgers $12; ⊙9am-10pm May-Sep) Novel Alaskan drive-in where they'll bring heaped burger baskets out to your car, or you can enjoy them on an adjacent patio. The patties and relishes are high quality and they also serve ice cream. Cash only.

❶ Information

Delta Junction Visitor Center (www.delta-chamber.org; Mile 1422, Alaska Hwy; ⊙8am-8pm) More a gift shop than a visitor center, this place is usually jammed with RVers clamoring to purchase 'End-of-the-Alaska-Highway' certificates ($1).

❶ Getting There & Away

Interior Alaska Bus Line (p419) stops in Delta Junction on Monday, Wednesday and Friday on its run between Fairbanks ($45) and Tok. From Tok you can continue to Glennallen and Anchorage. Alaska/Yukon Trails pass through on their way to/from Fairbanks and Dawson City (Sunday, Tuesday and Friday), or Whitehorse (Monday, Wednesday and Saturday).

Tok

POP 1258

If you've just stumbled carsick out of your bruised Buick after several hundred miles on the Alcan, Glenn or Taylor Hwys, Tok (pronounced *Toke*) might – briefly – seem like heaven on Earth. But after you've spent a night at one of its cheap motels, exhausted its oversized visitor center and given a cursory glance to the crapshoot of kitschy gift shops and eating joints, there's little reason to linger.

The town was born in 1942 as a construction camp for the highway, and was called Tokyo Camp until anti-Japanese sentiment caused locals to shorten it to Tok. From here, the rest of the state beckons: the Alcan heads 206 miles northwest to Fairbanks; the Tok Cutoff and Glenn Hwy reaches 328 miles southwest to Anchorage; and the Taylor Hwy curls back 161 miles to Eagle.

⏟ Sleeping

There is no bed tax in Tok. Hurray!

Main Street Motel

MOTEL $

(☑ 907-883-6246; www.mainstreetmotelalaska. com; Mile 1312.7, Alcan Hwy; r from $85; ᴘ☎) Ask Alcan truckers to name the best accommodations in Tok and they'll probably surprise you with this boring-looking motel box that seems like a four-out-of-10 from the outside, but scores 10 out of 10 on most internal barometers, including friendliness, cleanliness and – important if you're on the Alcan – its welcoming 24-hour reception.

Tok River State Recreation Site

CAMPGROUND $

(Mile 1309, Alaska Hwy; campsites $15) On the Tok River's east bank, 4.5 miles east of Tok, this pleasant 27-site campground has a boat launch and picnic shelter.

Moon Lake State Recreation Site
CAMPGROUND **$**

(Mile 1331.5, Alaska Hwy; campsites $15) Fourteen sites sit next to placid Moon Lake, 17 miles west of Tok.

Mooseberry Inn
B&B **$$**

(☑ 907-883-5496; www.amooseberryinn.com; Mile 1316, Alaska Hwy; r $109-169; 🛜) Just 2.5 miles west of Tok, this B&B has cute and comfy rooms, private balconies and big breakfasts in a homey family atmosphere, making it one of the best options outside of town. The friendly owner speaks German. To get here, head south of the Alcan at Mile 1316 on Scooby Rd, then take a quick right on Maes Way.

✖ Eating & Drinking

Beaver Fever Cafe
CAFE **$**

(☑ 907-883-5658; Mile 1314, Alaska Hwy; snacks $4-12; ⊙ 7am-2pm Mon-Fri) You quickly learn never to judge a book by its cover in Alaska, and nowhere is this cliché more true than in this little log cabin with its amateurish hand-painted sign, where you can procure possibly the best coffee on the Alcan (Seattle's Caffe d'Arte, no less, if you're a coffee snob) backed up by burritos, sandwiches and baked goods.

Fast Eddy's
DINER **$$**

(☑ 907-883-4411; Mile 1313.3, Alaska Hwy; burgers $8-12, pizzas $14-22; ⊙ 6am-11pm; 🛜🚗) Perhaps the most famous eatery on the Alcan, Eddy's delivers decent diner food with surprisingly less attitude than you might think. And such large portions!

❶ Information

Tok Mainstreet Visitors Center (⊙ 8am-7pm Mon-Sat, from 9am Sun) Tok's main 'sight' is its visitor center, but it's a good one with ultra-friendly staff and info on pretty much everywhere and everything within a 500-mile radius.

❶ Getting There & Away

BUS

Interior Alaska Bus Line (☑ 800-770-6652; www.alaskadirectbusline.com) passes through Tok on Sunday, Wednesday and Friday, stopping at the village of Texaco. From there, buses head northwest to Fairbanks ($95, four hours) and southwest to Anchorage ($130, eight hours). **Alaska/Yukon Trails** (☑ 800-770-7275; www.alaskashuttle.com) runs vans on Sunday, Tuesday and Friday from Fairbanks to Dawson City and will stop in Tok only if it

already has at least two people starting from Fairbanks. The fare from Tok is $125.

HITCHHIKING
Check the message board at the Tok Mainstreet Visitors Center if you're trying to hitch a ride through Canada. Note that the Canadian customs post has developed a tough reputation and hitchhikers, especially Americans, may be turned back for having insufficient funds.

Tok to Canada
The journey from Tok to the Canadian border comprises 92 miles of the paved but often frost-heaved Alcan as it weaves through low-slung mountains and vast wetlands. Thirteen miles east of Tok sits Tetlin Junction, where Taylor Hwy branches off toward Eagle, with connections via the Top of the World Hwy to Dawson City.

Shortly after the junction you'll reach the 932,000-acre **Tetlin National Wildlife Refuge** (http://tetlin.fws.gov), which skirts the highway's south side all the way to the border. Waterlogged by countless lakes, marshes, streams and rivers, the refuge is a home or migratory pit stop for 180 species of bird. The best viewing is typically from April to early June, when swans, geese, ducks, sandhill cranes and raptors are on their way through.

Two USFWS campgrounds are available just off the highway, and backcountry camping is permitted throughout the refuge. **Lakeview Campground** (Mile 1256.7, Alaska Hwy; campsites free) features 11 sites on a hillside overlooking beautiful Yager Lake, from where you can see the St Elias Range to the south on a nice day. **Deadman Lake Campground** (Mile 1249.3, Alaska Hwy; campsites free) has 15 sites, a boat ramp and a short nature trail. Presentations by rangers are held weekdays at 7pm.

The **Tetlin National Wildlife Refuge Visitor Center** (Mile 1229, Alaska Hwy; ⊙ 8am-4:30pm), a sod-covered log cabin with a huge viewing deck, overlooks the Scotty and Desper Creek drainage areas. The Mentasta and Nutsotin Mountains loom in the distance. The cabin is packed with interpretive displays on wildlife, mountains and Athabascan craftwork; beading demonstrations take place regularly.

Ten miles on, you'll reach the Canadian border. The spot is marked by an observation deck and plaque. Another 18 miles beyond is the Canadian customs post, just outside Beaver Creek.

TAYLOR HIGHWAY

The Taylor Hwy runs 161 miles north from Tetlin Junction (13 miles east of Tok) through the lovable tourist trap of Chicken to the sleepy, historic community of Eagle on the Yukon River. Wildfires in 2004 and 2005 scarred many sections of the scenic drive, including around Mt Fairplay, Polly Summit and American Summit. But the large swaths of burnt spruce forest create an interesting 'Seussical' landscape, scenic in its own way. The route was once infamously rough, but these days the only white-knuckle stretch is the last 65 miles from Jack Wade Junction to Eagle. The highway closes in winter (generally from October to May), when you can still get to Eagle by plane, snow machine or dog sled.

The highway takes paddlers to both the Fortymile River and the Yukon-Charley Rivers National Preserve, and also offers much hiking. Many of the trailheads are unmarked, so it's necessary to have good topographic maps. Many trails are off-road-vehicle tracks that hunters use heavily in late summer and fall.

By Alaskan standards summer traffic is light to moderate until Jack Wade Junction, where the majority of vehicles continue east to Dawson City, Yukon, via the Top of the World Hwy. Hitchhikers aiming for Eagle from the junction will need patience. Leave Tok or Dawson with a full tank of gasoline, as roadside services are limited.

The first section of the Taylor, from Tetlin Junction (Mile 0) to just shy of Chicken, is now paved. Within 9 miles of Tetlin Junction you'll begin to climb Mt Fairplay (5541ft). At Mile 35 a lookout near the summit is marked by an interpretive sign describing the history of Taylor Hwy. From here you should have superb views of Mt Fairplay and the valleys and forks of Fortymile River to the north. The surrounding alpine area offers good hiking for those wanting to stretch their legs.

The first state campground is the 25-site **West Fork Campground** (Mile 49, Taylor Hwy; campsites $10), but there are informal camping spots all along the road. Travelers packing gold pans can try their luck in West Fork River, which is also the first access point for a canoe trip down Fortymile River.

Chicken

POP 7

After crossing a bridge over Fortymile River's Mosquito Fork at Mile 64.4, Taylor Hwy enters dusty Chicken, once a thriving mining center and now more of a punchline than an actual community. The town's name allegedly originated at a meeting of resident miners in the late 1800s. As the story goes, the men voted to dub their new tent-city 'Ptarmigan,' since that chicken-like bird (now the Alaskan state bird) was rampant in the area. Trouble is, no-one could spell it. The town's name has been Chicken ever since. Lest you forget, a colossal horror-flick-inspired **mascot** sits high above town on a knoll near Pedro Dredge.

TOP OF THE WORLD HIGHWAY TO DAWSON CITY

Northeast of Chicken, at Jack Wade Junction (Mile 95.7, Taylor Hwy), the Taylor Hwy meets the Top of the World Hwy, gateway to Dawson City. This grail of the Klondike Gold Rush is now one of the Far North's most intriguing, fun-drunk towns. It's also just 79 miles away, with a stop at the international border. Be forewarned, though: Canadian customs is open only from 8am to 6pm Alaska time (call the Tok Visitor Center on ☑907-883-5775 to confirm). Arrive too late and you'll be camping in the parking lot until morning. Also remember that these days even US citizens will be required to show a passport.

Beyond the border, the highway – mainly paved now, but with lots of gravel patches under repair – lives up to its name, twisting along high-country ridgetops with flabbergasting views and all sorts of hiking options. There's significant wildfire damage around this area, but you'll still get some lovely panoramas. After 66 miles of this you wind your way down to the Yukon River, where a car ferry conveys you across to Dawson City.

If you're without wheels, you can ride along the Top of the World Hwy with **Alaska/Yukon Trails** (☑800-770-7275; www.alaskashuttle.com), which has buses that travel from Fairbanks to Dawson City ($265 one way, minimum two passengers) on Sunday, Tuesday and Friday. For more on Dawson City, consult Lonely Planet's *British Columbia*, which covers the Yukon Territory.

In retrospect, the naming was a savvy move. Nowadays, folks flock here for 'Go peckers!' coffee mugs, 'I got laid in Chicken' caps and pictures of themselves in front of the Chicken Poop outhouses. In the third weekend of June, check out the increasingly popular **Chickenstock Music Concert** (see its Facebook page for details).

Sights & Activities

Chicken's work-camp appearance is no act and an old pile of rusting pipes is as likely to be labeled a tourist attraction as some pun on chickens.

Mining History & Gold Panning

Dominating the town's skyline (after Monster Chicken, of course) is the **Pedro Gold Dredge**, which worked creeks in the area from 1959 to 1967. Chicken Gold Camp runs tours ($8).

The camp also offers **gold panning** (four hours $10) near the dredge, and more advanced recreational mining down the road at a working claim where you can sluice your way to riches (per day $25 to $60). It's not unheard of for visitors to come away with an ounce of gold after a day's work.

Just north of Chicken is **Chicken Creek Bridge**, built on tailing piles from the mining era. The creek, and most other tributaries of the Fortymile River, is covered from end to end by active mining claims.

Kayaking

The nearby **Fortymile River** is a popular recreational kayak route. Chicken Gold Camp rents out kayaks (half-day $35). Shuttle services are also available for $45. The bridge over South Fork (Mile 75.3) marks the most popular access point for the Fortymile River.

Sleeping & Eating

There's no bed tax in Chicken.

Chicken Gold Camp   CABIN, CAMPGROUND $
(www.chickengold.com; campsites/RV sites $14/28, s/d cabin $90/125; ⊙cafe 7:30am-7:30pm; 🛜) On a spur road to the right as you enter Chicken, this camp offers Chicken's toniest setting with workaday cabins and a gravel camping area. It's a friendly, family-run place, however, and the **cafe** (sandwiches $11) in the Chicken Creek Outpost is a good hang-out.

Goldpanner   CABIN, CAMPGROUND $
(www.townofchicken.com; Mile 66.8, Taylor Hwy; campsites $16.20, RV sites $26-40, 2-/4-person cabins $99/119; ⊙8am-10pm; 🛜) Just before Chicken Creek is another gravel lot featuring cabins, rooms, a gift shop and the only flush toilets in Chicken. Goldpanner also offers 'hostel' rooms, though these are really just bare singles and doubles ($75/85).

Chicken Creek Cafe, Saloon & Mercantile Emporium   DINER $
(www.chickenalaska.com; breakfast & dinner $7-15; ⊙7:30am-7pm) Profiting the most from chicken kitsch seems to be this row of clapboard buildings across from Chicken Gold Camp. The gift shop is extensive, the saloon has hats from every corner of the world, and the cafe, unsurprisingly, features lots of chicken on the menu, plus that wilderness staple – cinnamon buns.

Getting There & Away

If you haven't got a car, the Alaska/Yukon Trails bus stops at the Chicken Creek Cafe on its way between Fairbanks and Dawson City on Sunday, Tuesday and Friday.

Fortymile River

Historic Fortymile River, designated as Fortymile National Wild River, offers an excellent escape into scenic wilderness for paddlers experienced in lining their canoes around rapids. It's also a step back into Alaska's gold-rush era; the river passes abandoned communities, including Franklin, Steele Creek and Fortymile, as well as some present-day mining operations. The best place to start paddling is at the **South Fork Bridge Wayside** (Mile 75, Taylor Hwy), as the access points south of here on Taylor Hwy are often a little too shallow for an enjoyable trip.

Many canoeists paddle the 40 miles from South Fork Bridge to the **Fortymile Bridge Wayside** (Mile 112, Taylor Hwy). This two- to three-day trip involves three sets of class III rapids. For a greater adventure, continue paddling the Fortymile into the Yukon River; from here, head north to Eagle at the end of the Taylor Hwy. This trip is 140 miles, takes seven to 10 days and requires lining your canoe past several sets of rapids in Fortymile River.

See the 'Fortymile Wild and Scenic River' pages on the BLM (www.blm.gov/ak) website for route planning, maps and more.

Eagle Canoe Rentals, in Eagle, is the closest place to get an expedition-worthy canoe or raft.

Eagle

POP 88

From Jack Wade Junction, the Taylor Hwy continues north 58 miles on one of the worst (though highly scenic) stretches of highway in Alaska to Eagle. This quaint hamlet of log cabins and clapboard houses is one of the better-preserved boomtowns of the Alaskan mining era. The original settlement, today called Eagle Village, was established by the Athabascans long before Francois Mercier arrived in the early 1880s and built a trading post in the area. A permanent community of miners took up residence in 1898, and in 1900 President Theodore Roosevelt issued a charter that made Eagle the first incorporated city of the Interior.

The gold strikes of the early 1900s, most notably at Fairbanks, began drawing residents away from Eagle. At one point, it's said, the population of Eagle dipped to nine residents, seven of whom served on the city council. When the Taylor Hwy was completed in the 1950s, however, the town's population increased to its present level.

In 2009 floods wiped out most of Front St and badly damaged the village's historic core. As a result, the passenger tour boat from Dawson City no longer docks here. Still in operation are the Eagle Campground (☑ 907-883-5121; campsites $10; north of Fort Egbert, and Falcon Inn B&B (☑ 907-547-2254; 220 Front St; s/d $125/145; ☎), a beautiful log building with rooms with either private or shared baths and a deck overlooking the Yukon River.

◉ Sights & Activities

Historic Buildings

Residents say Eagle has the state's largest 'museum system,' boasting five restored turn-of-the-20th-century buildings. If you're spending a day here, the best way to see the buildings and learn the town's history is to take the Eagle Historical Society's (www.eagleak.org; tour $7; ☺ 9am) two-hour town walking tour. In addition to Eagle City Hall and the Log Church, the tour takes you into the restored Fort Egbert, originally built in 1899 by the US Army as part of its effort

to maintain law and order in the Alaskan Interior.

Paddling

During its heyday, Eagle was an important riverboat landing for traffic moving up and down the Yukon. Today it's a departure point for the many paddlers who float along the river through the Yukon-Charley Rivers National Preserve. The 165-mile trip extends from Eagle to Circle, at the end of the Steese Hwy northeast of Fairbanks. Most paddlers take six to 10 days, though some require as few as three.

It's not a difficult paddle, but it must be planned carefully. Kayakers and canoeists should come prepared for insects, but can usually camp either in public-use cabins or on open beaches and river bars, where winds keep the bugs at bay. They also need to be prepared for extremes in weather; freezing nights can be followed by daytime temperatures of 90°F (32°C).

Eagle Canoe Rentals (☑ 907-547-2203; www.eaglecanoerentals.com) rents canoes for the trip to Circle ($285). It can also arrange transportation. The Yukon-Charley Rivers National Preserve Visitor Center (www.nps.gov/yuch; ☺ 8am-5pm) in Eagle is also worth contacting. The center is off 1st St, near the river and airstrip.

❶ Getting There & Around

There are no buses to Eagle. If driving, check at the Tok Mainstreet Visitors Center for the latest road conditions. **Everts Air Alaska** (☑ 907-450-2300; www.evertsair.com) flies to Eagle from Fairbanks ($170, 9am Monday to Friday).

TOK CUTOFF & GLENN HIGHWAY

The quickest path from the Alcan to Anchorage, the paved Tok Cutoff and Glenn Hwy offers some of the best hiking, boating and gawk-worthy scenery in the state. The rugged 328-mile route is graced by both the Wrangell and Chugach Mountains. Glennallen and Palmer are significant-sized communities along the way.

Tok Cutoff

Narrow and forest-flanked, the Tok Cutoff runs 125 miles from Tok to Gakona Junction. There it meets the Richardson Hwy, which heads 14 miles south to Glennallen, the eastern terminus of the Glenn Hwy. There are glorious views of towering Mt Sanford and the Wrangell Mountains on a clear day.

The first of only two public campgrounds on Tok Cutoff pops up at Mile 109.5 as you drive south from Tok. **Eagle Trail State Recreation Site** (campsites $15), near Clearwater Creek, has 35 sites, drinking water and toilets. The historic Old Slana Cutoff Hwy, which at one time extended from Tok to Valdez, now provides a leisurely 20-minute **nature walk** in the vicinity of the campground. Look for the posted trailhead near the covered picnic shelters.

Another 45 miles southwest along the highway, just north of the Nabesna Rd junction, is the 240-acre **Porcupine Creek State Recreation Site** (Mile 64.2, Tok Cutoff; campsites $15), offering 12 wooded sites in a scenic spot along the creek. A mile north along the highway you'll find a historical marker and the first views of Mt Sanford (16,237ft), a dormant volcano.

Officially, the Tok Cutoff ends at Gakona Junction, where it merges with the Richardson Hwy. Nearby is **Gakona Lodge** (907-822-3482; www.gakonalodge.com; Mile 2, Tok Cutoff; r with shared bath $95, cabins with bath $120-150, tipi $35;), a lovely log roadhouse dating from 1905 and listed on the National Register of Historic Places. Even if you aren't staying the night, the friendly owners will let you snoop around. Rooms are small, in keeping with the old-time atmosphere, and the warped floorboards in the hallways are a source of both amusement and pride. In addition to accommodations, the roadhouse has a **dining room** (mains $8 to $15, open 5:30pm to 9:30pm), **Trapper's Den Tavern** (a former US Army Corp of Engineers supply room) and, according to some, a resident ghost. Fishing tours are offered on the Klutina and Gulkana Rivers, which offer some of Alaska's best salmon fishing.

From Gakona Junction, follow the Richardson Hwy 14 miles south to the Glenn Hwy junction.

Glenn Highway

Among Alaska's most jaw-dropping drives, the Glenn runs 189 miles from the Richardson Hwy at Glennallen through the Chugach Range to Anchorage, merging with the George Parks Hwy just after Palmer. Appropriately, most of this corridor has been declared a National Scenic Byway. Along the route, outdoor opportunities abound: there's great alpine hiking around Eureka Summit, easy access to the humbling Matanuska Glacier, and some of the state's best white water in the nearby Matanuska River. Note there is a 5% bed tax in this area.

Glennallen
POP 554

Glennallen (the name is a combo of two early explorers: Edwin Glenn and Henry Allen) is a small, strung-out community that sits at the confluence of two of Alaska's most important highways: the Glenn and the Richardson. Turnoffs for the Denali and Edgerton Hwys are also close by. Yet this geographic importance has done little to enliven Glennallen's appeal, which is limited to a gas station, a visitor center and a smattering of so-so eating and sleeping services. If you overnight here, admire the views of the icy Wrangell Mountains, top up your gas tank and use the ATM, before heading off somewhere more interesting.

Within town, the **Copper River Valley Visitor Center** (9am-7pm), at the exact junction of the highways, is useful if you need a stack of brochures. West of here, you'll find the region's only full-service bank, a **Wells Fargo** (Mile 187.5, Glenn Hwy), which has an ATM.

Sleeping & Eating

Antler's Rest B&B   B&B $
(907-822-4007; www.antlersrest.com; 3rd St; r $95) A lovely, pristine and very private B&B tucked away behind Glennallen's busy crossroads. Expect large rooms, a relaxing lounge and formidable breakfasts. It's about a mile north of Omni Park's Place.

Northern Nights Campground   CAMPGROUND $
(907-822-3199; www.northernnightscampground.com; Mile 188.7, Glenn Hwy; campsites/RV sites $25/40; 8am-8pm;) Sites don't have much privacy but this is a clean, well-run, centrally located campground. There are also showers, laundry, strong free wi-fi and complimentary coffee in the morning.

Caribou Hotel   MOTEL $$
(907-822-3302; www.caribouhotel.com; Mile 187, Glenn Hwy; r from $150;) In a town with little competition, or panache, the Caribou often gets a bad rap. But if you think of it as a staging post rather than a romantic getaway, the

dated rooms and utilitarian motel decor will be a little easier to swallow. Granted, it's a tad overpriced.

Omni Park's Place SUPERMARKET $
(Mile 187, Glenn Hwy; ⊙ 7am-10pm Mon-Fri, 8am-9pm Sat, 9am-9pm Sun) Has a large, well-stocked grocery selection and a deli.

Tok Thai THAI $$
(cnr Glenn & Richardson Hwys; dishes $10) Bangkok street food is the last thing you expect to see at a dusty road junction in freezing cold, or sweltering mosquito-ridden (depending on the season), Alaska. Thus, all hail Tok Thai's well-worn purple food truck. Judging by its pad thai noodles – a good barometer for any Thai restaurant – the food's jolly good, and cheap.

All 23 listed menu items go for $10.

ℹ Getting There & Around

For hitchhikers, Glennallen is notorious as a place for getting stuck when trying to thumb a ride north up the Alcan. Luckily, buses are available. Interior Alaska Bus Line (p419) passes through town every Monday, Wednesday and Friday en route between Anchorage ($75, five hours) and Tok ($65, three hours), where you can connect to Fairbanks. Book ahead.

Soaring Eagle Transit (p419) connects to Anchorage ($50) and Valdez ($40) on Tuesday, Thursday and Saturday. It also has a local shuttle linking Glennallen with Copper Center and Gulkana ($3).

Kennicott Shuttle (p419) vans run to and from McCarthy in Wrangell-St Elias National Park daily in summer (round-trip same day/different day $109/149, four hours, 7am). You'll need to make a reservation.

Tolsona Creek to Matanuska Glacier

West of Glennallen, the Glenn Hwy slowly ascends through woodland into wide-open high country, affording drop-dead-gorgeous views of the Chugach and Talkeetna Mountains, and limitless hiking opportunities. If you're driving, anticipate plenty of stops to get out and coo over the scenery.

From Little Nelchina River at around the Mile 140 mark, the Glenn Hwy begins to ascend and Gunsight Mountain comes into view (you have to look hard to see the origin of its name). From Eureka Summit (Mile 129.3), the highway's highest point (3222ft), you can see both Gunsight Mountain and the Chugach Mountains to the

south. The Nelchina Glacier spills down in the middle here and the Talkeetna Mountains strut to the northwest. The open view extends to the west, where the highway drops into the valley that separates the two mountain chains.

From here the Glenn Hwy begins to descend, and the surrounding scenery fires the imagination as the Talkeetna Mountains loom in the distance and you pass the sphinx-like rock formation known as the Lion's Head (Mile 114). A half-mile further, the highway reaches the first viewpoint of Matanuska Glacier. To the north is Sheep Mountain, aptly named as you can often spot Dall sheep on its slopes.

🏃 Activities

Chickaloon-Knik Nelchina Trail System HIKING
Once a gold miner's route used before the Glenn Hwy was built, today this network of dirt roads and rough trails extends to Palmer and beyond, and is popular with backpackers and off-road vehicles alike. The system is not maintained regularly and hikers attempting any part of it should have extensive outdoor experience and the appropriate topographic maps.

The main access point is at Mile 118.5 in a large parking lot off the highway. There are five main hikes, ranging from two to three hours (8.5 miles) for the trail to Knob Lake, to three to four days (32 miles) for the Belanger Pass & Syncline Mountain Trail. The latter can also be mountain biked in one long day.

The trailhead rest area is also a popular vantage point for birdwatchers. With a bit of patience you might be able to get the fixed spotting scopes to reveal a variety of raptors resting in the trees in the wide valley below. In particular, be on the lookout for the hawk owl, which is visible during the day.

Sheep Mountain Lodge Trails HIKING
The lodge (Mile 113.5) maintains a network of easy-to-follow trails in the overlooking hills. The paths are open to all, and outstanding views and the chance to see Dall sheep are among the highlights. Nonguests can park in the lodge's gravel lot or at the nearby airstrip.

Mae West Lake Trail HIKING
A pullout at Mile 169.3 marks the start of this mile-long trail to a long, narrow lake fed by Little Woods Creek.

Lost Cabin Lake Trail   HIKING
This trail winds 2 miles to the lake and is a berry picker's delight from late summer to early fall. Look for the trailhead at a pullout on the southern side of the Glenn Hwy at Mile 165.8.

Tours

If you want to get into, over or onto the mountains, contact Blue Ice Aviation (907-354-6040; www.blueiceaviation.com; Mile 115, Glenn Hwy), which runs standard flight-seeing and backpacking tours and more extreme custom trips such as glacier cycling!

Sleeping & Eating

Lake Louise State Recreation Area   CAMPGROUND $
(campsites $15) At Mile 160, a 19-mile spur road runs north to this scenic recreation site popular among Alaskans keen on swimming, boating and angling for grayling and trout. There are 52 campsites in two campgrounds, and a few lodges and numerous private cabins around the lake as well.

Tolsona Wilderness Campground   CAMPGROUND $
(907-822-3865; www.tolsona.com; Mile 173, Glenn Hwy; campsites $25, RV sites $35-40;) The first campground west of Glennallen, this private facility has more than 80 sites bordering Tolsona Creek. In addition to coin-operated showers, there are laundry facilities, and wi-fi in the main office.

Sheep Mountain Lodge   LODGE $$
(907-745-5121; www.sheepmountain.com; Mile 113.5, Glenn Hwy; r with shared bath $99, cabins $169-199;) Among the finest and most scenically situated lodges along the highway, Sheep Mountain features a cafe, bar, sauna (free for cabin guests), comfortable log cabins and a bunkhouse dorm with free showers. The lodge also maintains a lovely network of easy trails in the surrounding hills. The restaurant (mains $23-28) serves the area's best meals.

Tundra Rose Guest Cottages   CABIN $$
(907-745-5865; www.tundrarosebnb.com; Mile 109.5, Glenn Hwy; 2-/4-person cottages $148/158) In a glacier-view setting that's as pretty as the name implies, this family-run place has a more cozy and personal atmosphere than Sheep Mountain Lodge. The owners also run the Grand View Cafe (Mile 109.75, Glenn Hwy; sandwiches $8-11; 8am-9pm;) just down the road.

Eureka Lodge   DINER $$
(907-822-3808; www.eurekalodge.com; Mile 128, Glenn Hwy; mains $10-18; 7am-8pm Wed-Mon) A typical roadside Alaska diner where taxidermic animals stand guard over truck drivers tucking into home cooking. The lodge is at a high point on the Glenn Hwy, meaning the weather can go through four different seasons by the time you finish your cheeseburger. Grab a massive muffin and the cheapest coffee in Alaska (25¢) for the road.

It also rents rooms ($115 to $125) if you're too knackered to press onto Glennallen.

Matanuska Glacier to Palmer

One of Alaska's most accessible ice tongues, Matanuska Glacier nearly licks the Glenn Hwy as it stretches 27 miles from its source in the Chugach Mountains. Beyond the glacier, almost 12 miles past Sutton, is the junction with the Fishhook-Willow Rd, which provides access to Independence Mine State Historical Park. The highway then descends into the agricultural center of Palmer.

From Palmer, the Glenn Hwy merges with the George Parks Hwy and continues south to Anchorage, 43 miles away.

Sights & Activities

Matanuska Glacier   GLACIER
Some 18,000 years ago this glacier covered the entire area where the city of Palmer sits today. It must have appeared a supernatural force back then, whereas these days it's *merely* a grand spectacle and open geological classroom.

Entry to Matanuska is via Glacier Park Resort (Mile 102), which charges $20 to follow its private road to a parking lot at the terminal moraine. From there, a self-guided trail will take you a couple of hundred yards onto the gravel-laced ice, carved and braided with translucent blue streams and pitted with deep ponds.

To go further, duck into the office of MICA Guides (907-351-7587; www.micaguides.com; Mile 102.5, Glenn Hwy), where you'll be outfitted with a helmet, crampons and trekking poles, and led on a 1½-hour glacier tour ($45), a three-hour trek ($69) or a six-hour ice-climbing excursion ($129).

There's also a 500yd-long zipline ($49).

Alpine Historical Park　　HISTORIC BUILDING
(Mile 61, Glenn Hwy; ⊙ 9am-6pm) FREE A picnic
or photo-op stop, the park preserves several
buildings, including the Chickaloon Bunkhouse and the original Sutton post office,
which now houses a museum.

Purinton Creek Trail　　HIKING
The trail starts at Mile 91 (look for the sign-
post) and continues 12 miles to the foot of
Boulder Creek. Most of the final 7 miles run
along the river's gravel bars. The accompanying Chugach Mountains scenery is excellent, and you'll find good camping spots
along Boulder Creek.

☞ Tours

Nova　　RAFTING
(☑ 800-746-5753; www.novalaska.com; Mile 76.5,
Glenn Hwy, Chickaloon; ⊛) Almost across the
highway from the King Mountain State Recreation Site sits the headquarters of one of
Alaska's pioneering rafting companies. Nova
offers daily floats on the Matanuska River.
Wilder half-day trips feature class IV rapids
around Lion's Head ($95 to $99 per person).

From early June to mid-July there's also
the extremely popular evening Lion's Head
run, departing at 7pm and including a riverside cookout. Nova can also guide you on
glacier hikes (from $70) and extended river
trips on the Matanuska, Talkeetna, Copper,
Chickaloon and Tana Rivers for anywhere
from $475 to $2900.

⌷ Sleeping

**Matanuska Glacier
State Recreation Site**　　CAMPGROUND $
(Mile 101, Glenn Hwy; campsites $15) Just steps
from outrageous glacier vistas in the rest-
area parking lot sits this campground with
12 tree-shrouded sites. At the far edge of the
lot is the mile-long interpretative Edge Nature Trail.

**King Mountain
State Recreation Site**　　CAMPGROUND $
(Mile 76, Glenn Hwy; campsites $15) This 22-site
campground on the banks of the Matanuska
River has excellent views of King Mountain
to the southeast.

RICHARDSON HIGHWAY

This is about as postcard perfect as you can
get without leaving the cozy confines of your
vehicle. Sprinkles of wildflowers shimmer in
the wind along the roadside, while off in the
distance the sheltering shoulders of the Alaska and Chugach Mountains stand guard. To
the south, you get access to the vast wilderness of Wrangell-St Elias National Park, and
every step of the way there are chances to
hike, cycle (many cyclists go ahead and do
the entire route) and stop for photos.

Alaska's first highway, the Richardson runs
266 miles from Fairbanks to Valdez. However,
the 98-mile stretch between Fairbanks and
Delta Junction is popularly considered part
of the Alcan, and our coverage of the Richardson thus begins at Delta Junction, where the
Alcan branches away to the east.

The Richardson was originally scouted in
1919 by US Army Captain WR Abercrombie,
who was looking for a way to link the gold
town of Eagle with the warm-water port of
Valdez. At first it was a telegraph line and
footpath, but it quickly turned into a wagon
trail following the turn-of-the-20th-century
gold strikes at Fairbanks.

Along the way it passes waterfalls, glaciers, five major rivers and the Trans-Alaska
Pipeline, which parallels the road most of
the way.

Delta Junction to Glennallen

Richardson Hwy runs 151 relatively untraf-
ficked miles from Delta Junction to Glennallen. The route has plenty of curves, hills
and frost heaves, but is otherwise in fine
condition.

Donnelly Creek & Around

After departing Delta Junction's 'Triangle,'
where the Alcan merges with Richardson
Hwy at Mile 266, the highway soon passes
Fort Greely (Mile 261) and, a few minutes later, the Alaska Pipeline's Pump Station No 9.

A turnoff at Mile 243.5 offers one of the
best views you'll get of the pipeline, as it
plunges beneath the highway. Interpretive
signage provides an overview of the pipeline's history and engineering, including
a fascinating explanation of how 'thermal
siphons' protect the permafrost by sucking
heat from areas where the pipeline is buried.
There are also spectacular panoramas to the
southwest of three of the highest peaks in
the Alaska Range. From south to west, you
can see Mt Deborah (12,339ft), Hess Mountain (11,940ft) and Mt Hayes (13,832ft).

Another interesting turnoff, at Mile 241.3, overlooks the calving grounds of the Delta buffalo herd to the west. In 1928, 23 bison were relocated here from Montana for the pleasure of sportsmen and today they number more than 400. The animals have established a migratory pattern that includes summering and calving along the Delta River. If you have binoculars you may be able to spot dozens of the beasts.

The first public campground between Delta Junction and Glennallen is just after Mile 238, where a short loop road leads west to **Donnelly Creek State Recreation Site** (campsites $10), which has 12 sites. This is a great place to camp, as it's seldom crowded and is extremely scenic, with good views of the towering Alaska Range. Occasionally the Delta bison herd can be seen from the campground.

At Mile 225.4 you'll find a viewpoint with picnic tables and a historical marker pointing out what little ice remains of **Black Rapids Glacier** to the west. Once known as the 'Galloping Glacier,' this ice river advanced 3 miles in the winter of 1936 to almost engulf the highway.

From here, the highway ascends into alpine country and the scenery turns gonzo, with the road snaking under sweeping, scree-sided peaks. At Mile 200.5, a gravel spur leads 2 miles west to **Fielding Lake State Recreation Site** (campsites free), where a willow-riddled 17-site campground sits in a lovely area above the treeline at 2973ft.

In another 3 miles the highway crests its highest point, **Isabel Pass** (3000ft). The pass is marked by a sign dedicated to Captain Wilds Richardson, after whom the highway is named. From this point you can view Gulkana Glacier to the northeast and the Isabel Pass pipeline camp below it.

For much of the next 12 miles the highway parallels the frothing headwaters of the Gulkana River as it pours toward Paxson.

Paxson & Around

At Mile 185.5 of the Richardson Hwy, the junction with the Denali Hwy, you'll find the small service center of Paxson (population 43).

Ten miles south on the Richardson Hwy, a gravel spur leads 1.5 miles west to **Paxson Lake BLM Campground** (Mile 175.5, Richardson Hwy; campsites $6-12). With 50 sites around the lakeshore, this is the highway's best public campsite.

Over the next 20 miles, the highway descends from the Alaska Range, presenting sweeping views of the Wrangell Mountains to the southeast and the Chugach Mountains to the southwest.

At Mile 147.5, the BLM's 42-site **Sourdough Creek Campground** (campsites $6-12) provides canoeists and rafters another access to the popular Gulkana River. Located in scrubby forestland that bugs seem to love, the campground has a boat launch, a fishing deck and trails leading to a river observation shelter.

Once you reach Gulkana River Bridge, you are 3 miles south of Gakona Junction, where Tok Cutoff heads northeast to Tok, and 11 miles north of Glennallen, where the Richardson Hwy intersects with the Glenn Hwy.

🏃 Activities

Paxson to Sourdough Float   CANOEING
(www.blm.gov/ak) Experienced paddlers can travel the main branch of the Gulkana River, which roughly parallels the Richardson Hwy from Paxson Lake BLM Campground to Sourdough Creek Campground. This is a 45-mile, three- to four-day journey involving several challenging rapids, including the class IV **Canyon Rapids**.

Although there's a short portage around these rapids, rough class III waters follow. If you're interested in the route, the BLM offers the super-informative 17-page *Gulkana River Users Guide for Paxson to Sourdough Float* for download from its website.

Sourdough to Gulkana Bridge Float   CANOEING
From Sourdough Creek Campground, you can take a placid, 35-mile river float to the highway bridge at Gulkana (Mile 126.8), making for a pleasant one- or two-day paddle.

All the land from Sourdough Creek Campground south belongs to the Ahtna Native Corporation, which charges boaters to camp. The exceptions – three single-acre sites – are signposted along the riverbanks and have short trails leading back to the highway.

Raft rentals and shuttle services for many of the area's rivers, including the Gulkana, can be arranged through **River Wrangellers** (☏907-822-3967; www.riverwrangellers.com).

Copper Center

The diminutive, typically Alaskan settlement of Copper Center, 14 miles south of Glennallen, sits just off the Richardson Hwy beside the iconic, fast-flowing Copper River.

The 'town' first took root in 1898 as a way station on the disastrous Valdez Glacier trail to the Klondike goldfields. For the 4000 or so would-be prospectors who made it over the Valdez Glacier, utilizing the so-called 'All-American route,' this was about as far as they got. Exhaustion and a calamitous scurvy outbreak at Copper Center prevented them from getting much further.

Once the prospectors had passed on (or away), Copper Center settled down to become just another gnarled Alaskan settlement on the frontier. These days it supports a small riverside community of 328 people and is notable for its rafting and fishing opportunities. Tragically the community's most historic building, the wood-paneled Copper Center Hotel, burnt down in 2012 and is in the process of being rebuilt. The business is temporarily bivouacked in an adjacent cabin.

◉ Sights & Actvities

George Ashby Museum MUSEUM
(Mile 101, Old Richardson Hwy; admission by donation; ☉ 10am-5pm Mon-Sat, from 11am Sun) A tiny museum set in two old log cabins that explains the remarkable fate of the 'stampeders' who attempted to reach Klondike via the cursed Valdez Glacier trail in 1898. It's eye-opening reading.

Klutina Salmon Charters FISHING
(☑907-822-3991; www.klutinasalmoncharters.com; Mile 101, Old Richardson Hwy) Sitting at the confluence of of two legendary fishing rivers (Klutina and Copper), this professional outfit offers all kinds of fishing trips. It also runs a riverside campground (tent/RV sites $20/29).

🛏 Sleeping & Eating

Copper River Princess Wilderness Lodge HOTEL $$
(☑800-426-0500; www.princesslodges.com; 1 Brenwick Craig Rd; r from $179; @🛜) More intimate than the other Princess lodges, this secluded retreat just off the Richardson Hwy, 14 miles south of Glennallen, is frequented primarily by groups of cruise-line vacationers, but can still offer a comfortable indulgence for DIYers on their way in or out of Wrangell-St Elias National Park.

There are two restaurants, country-lodge furnishings and a handy daily shuttle ($5) to the Copper Center community and national park visitor center.

Old Town Copper Center Inn & Restaurant AMERICAN $$
(☑907-822-3245; www.oldtowncoppercenter.com; Mile 101, Old Richardson Hwy; breakfast $10-12; ☉ 7am-8pm; 🛜) Guns are welcome, but keep them in your holster, explains a sign in the temporarily relocated Copper Center Lodge. What might read as facetious anywhere else is par for the course in rural Alaska. But, fear not, the cozy restaurant is friendly to out of towners and the breakfasts and apple cinnamon buns are a treat. It also rents rooms (double $149).

❶ Getting There & Around

Soaring Eagle Transit (p419) buses pass through Copper Center on Tuesday, Thursday and Saturday heading to Valdez ($40), Anchorage ($50) and Glennallen ($3).

Glennallen to Valdez

One of Alaska's most spectacular drives, the 115 miles of the Richardson Hwy between Glennallen and Valdez lead through a paradise of snowy summits, panoramic passes and stunning gorges.

Nine miles south of Glennallen is a turnoff to the Wrangell-St Elias National Park Visitor Center. Just south of the visitor center, at Mile 106, Old Richardson Hwy loops off the main highway, offering access to Copper Center. Old Richardson Hwy rejoins the Richardson at Mile 100.2.

You'll reach a lookout over **Willow Lake** at Mile 87.6. The lake can be stunning on a clear day, with the water reflecting the Wrangell Mountains, a 100-mile chain that includes 11 peaks over 10,000ft. The two most prominent peaks visible from the lookout are Mt Drum, 28 miles to the northeast, and Mt Wrangell (14,163ft), Alaska's largest active volcano, to the east. Some days you can see a plume of steam rising from its crater.

Squirrel Creek State Campground (Mile 79.6, Richardson Hwy; campsites $15) is a scenic 25-site camping area on the banks of the creek. You can fish for grayling and rainbow trout here.

Fourteen miles further along, you'll reach what used to be the Little Tonsina River State Recreation Site. Though it's closed, a path leads down to the water, where anglers can fish for Dolly Varden most of the summer.

At Mile 28.6 the turnoff to Worthington Glacier State Recreation Site leads you to the glacier's face via a short access road. The recreation area includes outhouses, picnic tables and a large, covered viewing area. The mile-long, unmaintained Worthington Glacier Ridge Trail begins at the parking lot and follows the crest of the moraine. It's a scenic hike and follows the edge of the glacier, but exercise caution: never hike on the glacier itself due to its unstable crevasses.

As the highway ascends toward Thompson Pass (Mile 26; 2678ft) it climbs above the treeline, and the weather can be windy and foul. On the other side, several scenic turnoffs with short trails descending the ridgelines allow lucky early summer visitors to ooh and aah at a riot of wildflowers.

Blueberry Lake State Recreation Site (Mile 23, Richardson Hwy; tent & RV sites $14) offers 15 sites and several covered picnic shelters in a beautiful alpine setting surrounded by lofty peaks. There's good fishing for rainbow trout in the nearby lakes.

At Mile 14.8 you'll reach the northern end of narrow Keystone Canyon. Tucked away in a little bend is an abandoned hand-drilled tunnel that residents of Valdez began but never finished when they were competing with Cordova for the railroad to the Kennecott copper mines. A historical marker at the entrance briefly describes how nine companies fought to develop the short route from the coast to the mines, leading to the 'shootout in Keystone Canyon.'

For the next 2 miles you'll pass through the dark-walled canyon and, like everyone else, make a stop at two high, full-throated waterfalls: Bridal Veil Falls and, half a mile further, Horsetail Falls.

Leaving the canyon at Mile 12.8, the road begins a long, gradual descent into Valdez.

WRANGELL-ST ELIAS NATIONAL PARK

Imagine an area the size of Switzerland. Now strip away its road network, eradicate its towns and cities and take away all but 40 of its eight million people. The result would be something approximating Wrangell-St Elias National Park. Comprising 53,000 sq miles of brawny ice-encrusted mountains, Wrangell-St Elias is the second-largest national park in the world after Northeast Greenland, meaning there's plenty of room for its 45,000-or-so annual visitors to get lost – very, very lost. The park's vital statistics are mind-boggling. If Wrangell-St Elias were a country it would be larger than 70 of the world's independent nations. Its biggest glacier covers an area larger than the US state of Rhode Island. Plenty of its mountain peaks have never been climbed. And that's even before you've started counting the bears, beavers, porcupines and moose.

Yet perhaps the strangest thing about the park is how comparatively few people visit it. For every eight tourists who track north to Denali, only one intrepid traveler tackles the little-known wilderness of Wrangell. Why? Good question. Granted, most of the park is desolate and doesn't have the infrastructure or satellite towns of Denali, though it does support one small settlement, McCarthy (seven hours by road from Anchorage), along with some improbable copper-mining history preserved for posterity by the NPS in nearby Kennecott.

So, how do you tackle such an immense place? Ninety-five per cent of visitors enter the park via the tiny, off-the-grid settlements of McCarthy and Kennecott, accessible by bush plane or a single unpaved road that branches off the Richardson Hwy near Copper Center. Between them, these hamlets have several eating establishments, a store and a hardy year-round population of around 40 people who practice subsistence hunting and grow their own vegetables. Popular activities in the area include glacier hiking, ice climbing and historical tours of Kennecott's mine buildings.

Unlike Denali, you don't need a backcountry permit for overnight hikes, but you are encouraged to leave an itinerary at any of the ranger stations, where you can also get advice and pick up a bear canister for your trip. There's a refundable deposit required for the canister.

You can also drop by the visitor center in Kennecott for maps and ideas for both day and overnight hikes. There are literally two full folders of options. Popular overnight hikes include Donoho Peak, Erie Lake and McCarthy Creek.

OFF THE BEATEN TRACK

NABESNA ROAD

For connoisseurs of roads less traveled, Alaska offers few lonelier motorways than the Nabesna Rd, jutting 42 miles south from the Tok Cutoff into the northern reaches of Wrangell-St Elias National Park.

Turning onto the Nabesna Rd, you'll find yourself in a place the signs call Slana (population 124). Somewhere back through the trees there's an Alaska Natives settlement on the northern banks of the Slana River, where fish wheels still scoop salmon during the summer run. Also in the area are more recent settlers: in the early 1980s this was one of the last places in the USA to be opened to homesteading.

Before continuing, stop in at the NPS **Slana Ranger Station** (☑907-822-7401; Mile 0.5, Nabesna Rd; ☺8am-5pm Apr-Sep), where you can get info about road conditions and hikes, purchase USGS maps, peruse displays and collect the free *The K'elt'aeni*, the official guide to Wrangell-St Elias National Park, which has a *Nabesna Road Guide* section.

In the 4 miles between the ranger station and the park entrance you'll pass a handful of accommodations. Offbeat and friendly is **Huck Hobbit's Homestead** (☑907-822-3196; campsites/cabins per person $5/30) 🐾, a wind-and-solar-powered, 87-acre wilderness retreat. Cabins are rustic, but include a cooking area and shower block. Stay an extra day here if you can. The scenery is beautiful and you can rent canoes for a half-day float down the gentle Slana River ($60 per canoe, including shuttle).

Upon entering the park proper, the Nabesna Rd turns to gravel. It's manageable in a 2WD vehicle for the first 29 miles, but after that several streams flow over it, making it impassable in high water (check at the ranger station for the latest on road conditions). At mile 28.2, **Kendesnii Campground** (☑907-822-5234; campsites free) is the only official NPS campground in Wrangell-St Elias National Park. It's new, remote and has 10 sites and vault toilets. Maintenance ends at Mile 42, though a rough track continues 4 miles to the private Nabesna Gold Mine, a national historic site.

For a comparatively easy hike, try the 3-mile **Caribou Creek Trail** (Mile 19.2, Nabesna Rd), which ascends 800ft from the road to a dilapidated cabin with unbeatable views of the surrounding peaks. A tougher walk is the 2.5-mile **Skookum Volcano Trail** (Mile 36.2, Nabesna Rd), which climbs 1800ft through a deeply eroded volcanic system, ending at a high alpine pass frequented by Dall sheep.

☞ Tours

Some of the best outfitters and guides in the state operate in Wrangell-St Elias.

St Elias Alpine Guides ADVENTURE TOUR
(☑888-933-5427; www.steliasguides.com; Motherlode Powerhouse, McCarthy) One of the best guiding companies in the state, operating in one of the finest wildernesses on the planet. Need we say more. It leads great Kennecott Mill Town tours ($25), half-day hikes on Root Glacier ($75), ice climbing ($130), or a whole stash of truly adventurous stuff, including first ascents of unclimbed mountain summits.

Based in McCarthy with another office in Kennecott.

Kennicott Wilderness Guides ADVENTURE TOUR
(☑907-554-4444; www.kennicottguides.com; Main St, Kennecott) The other local guiding firm, also extremely experienced, offering small-group ice climbing and glacier excursions from $75, and a wide variety of multi-day hiking trips.

Copper Oar ADVENTURE TOUR
(☑800-523-4453; www.copperoar.com; Motherlode Powerhouse, McCarthy) Offers a popular full-day float along the Kennicott, Nizina and Chitina Rivers, with a return to McCarthy by bush plane. The high point is going through the vertical-walled Nizina Canyon. This trip costs $290 per person (two-person minimum). The company also offers multi-day paddles, glacier and alpine hikes. It's affiliated with St Elias Alpine Guides.

Wrangell Mountain Air SCENIC FLIGHTS
(☑907-554-4411; www.wrangellmountainair.com; Main St, McCarthy) Has a fantastic reputation and can do a backcountry drop or a wide range of scenic flights from $110 (35 minutes) to $255 (1½ hours) per person (two-person minimum).

McCarthy Road

Edgerton Hwy and McCarthy Rd combine to form a 92-mile route into the heart of Wrangell-St Elias National Park. The 32-mile Edgerton Hwy, fully paved, begins at Mile 82.6 of the Richardson Hwy. If you want to camp before reaching the park, the best bet is lovely **Liberty Falls State Recreation Site** (Mile 24, Edgerton Hwy; campsites $10), where the eponymous cascade sends its waters rushing past several tent platforms.

The end of Edgerton Hwy is 10 miles beyond, at little Chitina. McCarthy Rd then begins, auspiciously enough, after you pass through a single-lane notch blasted through a granite outcrop. The dirt route is a rump shaker, but even a regular car can make it if you go slow (35mph maximum) and stay in the center to avoid running over old rail spikes (contact Ma Johnson's Hotel in McCarthy about car-rental companies that will let you take their vehicles on the road; see p323). The road was substantially upgraded in 2012.

From here for 60 miles eastward you trace the abandoned Copper River and Northwest Railroad bed that was used to transport copper from the mines to Cordova. The first few miles offer spectacular views of the Chugach Mountains, the east-west range that separates the Chitina Valley lowlands from the Gulf of Alaska. Peaks average 7000ft to 8000ft. Below is the mighty Copper River, one of the world's great waterways for king and red salmon.

At Mile 14.5 the access road to the trailheads for the **Dixie Pass, Nugget** and Kotsina Trails begin across from the Strelna airstrip.

Just a couple of miles further up, at Mile 17, the one-lane, 525ft-long **Kuskulana River Bridge** spans a steep-sided gorge and is a vertigo-inducing 238ft above the riverbed. Built in 1910, the historic railway span has long been known as 'the biggest thrill on the road to McCarthy.'

Another 43 miles along, the road ends at the **Kennicott River**. To get into McCarthy or Kennecott, cross the river on the narrow footbridge. On the other side, a **shuttle** (☎907-554-4411; one way $5; ◷9am-8:30pm) can take you to McCarthy (half a mile) or Kennecott (4.5 miles), or you can walk or cycle the distance. There's parking for private vehicles by the bridge for $10 a day.

Chitina

POP 126

Chitina is the last taste of civilization before McCarthy, a riverside hamlet on the frontier where rustic house lots are littered with antediluvian vehicles and the road signs are used for target practice by locals with guns (count the bullet holes). Notwithstanding, the scenery is pretty, there's good hiking and wildlife-viewing opportunities and Chitina is one of the few places you can easily watch **fish wheels** at work. The wheels, which look much like a paddle wheel with baskets, sit just off the banks and turn with the river's current. When a fish is caught in a basket, it's lifted up and then deposited into a trough. A slow day might see no salmon caught, while a great day could see a dozen.

To see the fish wheels, head out to the airport and follow the side road down toward the runway. Keep left and shortly you'll be within view of the Copper River and the wheels. To watch **dip netters** – fishing with a large net attached to a pole either from the shore or a small boat – in action, head down O'Brien Creek Rd, which is just past Gilpatrick's Hotel Chitina. There are some fantastic views along the way of the Copper River Valley.

Chitina has a grocery store, a laundry with showers, ranger station, and restaurant and saloon in **Gilpatrick's Hotel Chitina** (☑907-823-2244; www.hotelchitina.com; Mile 33, Edgerton Hwy; r $165, mains $15-18). You can camp for free along the road to O'Brien Creek or at the lakes outside town. The best place to stay in town is **Chitina Guest Cabins** (☑907-823-2266; www.pawandfeathers. com; Mile 32.2, Edgerton Hwy; dm $75, cabins with breakfast $175) in a bit of forested land just off the highway, though only kids aged 12 and up can stay here. Although the well-made and comfortably furnished cabins have no showers or toilets, the outhouses are spotless (and dare we say even stylish?) and a shower block was in the works at the time of writing. Bicycles and canoes are available free to cabin guests, while hostel guests have access to a kitchen and outdoor eating area under a giant mosquito net.

McCarthy

Some tap Hollywood to get their Wild West kicks, but the savvy roll into McCarthy where, after sharing a couple of beers in the Golden Saloon with grizzly locals sporting Klondike-era beards, you have to blink to check you haven't been transported back to 1914. McCarthy took root in the early 1900s to serve as a rambunctious escape hatch for bored miners bivouacked at the 'dry' mining town of Kennecott 5 miles up the road and for a couple of decades it served its debauch purpose.

When the Kennecott mines went the way of the dodo in 1938, McCarthy clung on – but only just. These days, a year-round population of 25-or-so hardy souls get around on ATVs rather than horses and have swapped their cowboy hats for baseball caps, though the place still has the feel of a genuine frontier town bereft of the national-park orderliness of nearby Kennecott. Come here for freedom, adventure, high-spirited Saturday nights and a warts-'n'-all taste of life off the grid.

◉ Sights

McCarthy-Kennecott Historical Museum   MUSEUM
(◔2-7pm) This old railroad depot is worth a quick visit to view the historical photographs, mining artifacts and model of McCarthy in its heyday. The road splits at the museum, with one lane bending back 500ft to downtown (such as it is) McCarthy, and the other continuing toward Kennecott, 4.5 miles up the road.

Wrangell Mountain Center   CULTURAL CENTER
(☑907-554-4464; www.wrangells.org; 🖈) At the end of downtown McCarthy, check out this environmental NGO/community center with summer field courses for university students, arts and science programs for children, writing workshops and interpretative walks. The center sits in the Old Hardware Store and is always open.

☞ Tours

McCarthy Then & Now   WALKING
(tours $10) These historical walking tours of McCarthy usually kick off in the mornings from Main St. Check at Ma Johnson's Hotel for when the next one is running.

🛏 Sleeping

There are camping and lodging options on either side of the Kennicott River. There's also good camping at the foot of the Root Glacier. It's important to camp away from the road and be bear savvy, as many habituated bears have been reported in the area.

Wi-fi is available throughout town on the Copper River network ($8.95 per day).

Lancaster's Hotel   HOTEL $
(☑907-554-4402; www.mccarthylodge.com; Main St; d/tr/q without bath $99/149/179) Run by the same guys as Ma Johnson's Hotel, the Lancaster is an even lower 'frills' option for those who want to soak in the Main St vibe but are on a tighter budget. There's no kitchen, but a reading room is available and you can store your bags when you head out into the wilds.

Glacier View Campground   CAMPGROUND $
(☑907-554-4490; www.glacierviewcampground. com; campsites $24, cabins without bath $95; ◔restaurant 10am-10pm) A half-mile back from the river at the road's end, this very friendly place has stony sites with just enough scrub and space to maintain your privacy, hot showers ($10) and mountain

bikes for hire (full day $25). The on-site restaurant enjoys a good local reputation for its burgers ($15), and is blessed with views of Root Glacier from the deck.

★ **Ma Johnson's Hotel**   HISTORIC HOTEL $$
(☑907-554-5402; www.mccarthylodge.com; Main St; s/d/tr without bath $129/169/179) Copper-boom-era hotel that has yet to make it into the second half of the 20th century – let alone the first half of the 21st. The old-fashionedness is intentional and strangely refreshing. Small rooms don't have electrical sockets (charge your phone in the lobby), bathrooms are shared and every floorboard creaks.

But it's comfortable and atmospheric, and you can't beat sitting on the front deck imagining you've got a walk-on role in a remake of *Butch Cassidy and the Sundance Kid.*

Kennicott River Lodge & Hostel   CABINS, HOSTEL $$
(☑907-554-4441; www.kennicottriverlodge.com; dm $40, cabins without bath from $115) A short walk back from the road's end is this handsome two-story log lodge with private and dorm cabins. Amenities include a great communal kitchen and common room, a bright outhouse and a Finnish sauna. Views look over to the fantastical Root Glacier in the distance.

Currant Ridge Cabins   CABIN $$
(☑907-554-4124; www.currantridgecabins.com; Mile 56.7, McCarthy Rd; cabins $195) ✱ On a mountainside not far from the 'end of the road,' these well-designed log cabins feature bathrooms (including bathtubs), full kitchens and large decks for taking in the outrageous mountain views. During the summer season, all power is provided by photovoltaic panels.

✖ Eating & Drinking

McCarthy (and nearby Kennecott, too) offers some great food, not just for where you are, but for anywhere.

Roadside Potatohead   TEX-MEX $
(breakfast $8-11, burritos $10; ⊙7am-5pm) Fantastic food shack where the signature burritos are a meal in a tortilla stuffed with curly fries, eggs, cheese and jalapeños. It also serves the best (and possibly only) lattes for 100 miles. Decor is Potatohead toys and dusty Lonely Planets. The menu is written on old pieces of cardboard.

McCarthy Center   GROCERIES $
(Main St; ⊙10am-6pm) Small shop that makes a big effort to procure the healthy hiking essentials – including decent fruit and camping food – and a few treats such as ice cream.

Golden Saloon   BREAKFAST $$
(Main St; mains $11-15; ⊙8am-10pm) Connected to McCarthy Lodge, this is the area's only true bar, with pool, frequent live music and an always-intriguing cast of drinkers and beards. Food-wise, there's breakfast in the morning and a casual bar menu from 5pm to 10pm.

McCarthy Lodge   INTERNATIONAL $$$
(☑907-554-4402; www.mccarthylodge.com; Main St; meals $40; ⊙6-11pm) ✱ One of the more pleasant absurdities of McCarthy is the way you can enjoy expertly prepared gourmet food in what, superficially, looks like Tombstone circa 1881. Although it may be 200 miles from the nearest supermarket, the Lodge kitchen has been setting a spell over the taste buds of visitors for years and gaining rave reviews from food and wine experts.

Most evenings there's a set four-course meal (per person $40 with wine), including artistically laid-out local salmon, duck and greenhouse veggies plucked yards from your table.

🛍 Shopping

Wild Alpine   OUTDOOR EQUIPMENT
(☑907-529-9624; ⊙7:30am-7:30pm May-Sep) This guiding company has a decent little store that sells some useful backcountry gear, including bear spray and camp food. It also rents bikes (half/full day $20/40) and crampons.

ℹ Getting There & Around

AIR

Copper Valley Air (☑907-822-4200; www.coppervalleyairservice.com) has twice-weekly flights from Anchorage or McCarthy via Gulkana from $275 one way. **Wrangell Mountain Air** (☑907-554-4411; www.wrangellmountainair.com) offers daily scheduled flights between McCarthy and Chitina ($129 one way). Both use the tiny gravel McCarthy Airport.

BICYCLE

You can rent mountain bikes at Wild Alpine. This is an excellent way of getting between McCarthy and Kennecott (4.5 miles).

BUS

The **Kennicott Shuttle** (☑ 907-822-5292; www. kennicottshuttle.com) leaves Glennallen daily at 7am for McCarthy (round trip same/different day $109/149) and departs at 4:30pm for the return trip. It's about four hours each way, with a few scenic stops and some driver commentary thrown in. Reservations are essential.

Kennecott

Between 1911 and 1938, Kennecott was the serious 'dry' working town to free-living, hard-drinking McCarthy. These days it harbors the more interesting sights and activities, due to its mining history and proximity to hiking trails and glaciers.

◎ Sights & Activities

Kennecott Visitor Center   MUSEUM
(⊘ 9am-5:30pm) The center, which sits in the town's former post office, is done out like a general store. The cans of dusty baked beans are just for show, but you can buy bear spray and outdoor books. Information and a short film on the copper boom cost nothing. There are also five 15-minute ranger-led walks around town daily that begin here.

Kennecott Glacier   GLACIER
'Oh no, they destroyed this valley!' If you're like 99% of visitors, that's exactly what you'll think as you reach Kennecott and look across the valley at a rolling landscape of dirt and rubble. But no, that isn't a dump of mine tailings from the copper-boom days, but the Kennicott Glacier moraine. The ice is buried underneath.

The glacier is thinning terribly and has dropped 175ft in height over the past eight decades. As one interpretation sign notes, in the 1930s some locals didn't even realize they lived in a valley, so high was the ice field.

Kennecott Mill Town   HISTORIC SITE
Pretty much all of Kennecott comprises the mill town and there are dozens of old wood and log buildings that have been restored, stabilized or purposely left in a state of decrepitude. You're welcome to wander around the outside of the buildings at will, or you can join daily tours.

One of the most interesting ruins is the 14-story **Concentration Mill & Leaching Plant** (tour $25), which used to process the copper ore through a multistage process. You can only enter the mill on a two-hour tour led by St Elias Alpine Guides (p320), but this is highly recommended both for the stunning views from the top floors and the chance to get up close and personal with the hulking machinery. There are three tours daily.

KENNECOTT'S COPPER BOOM

In 1900 miners 'Tarantula Jack' Smith and Clarence Warner reconnoitered Kennicott Glacier's east side until they arrived at a creek and found traces of copper. They named the creek Bonanza, and was it ever – the entire mountainside turned out to hold some of the richest copper deposits ever uncovered.

Eventually, a group of investors bought the existing stakes and formed the Kennecott Copper Corporation, named when a clerical worker misspelled Kennicott (which is why, nowadays, the town is spelled with an 'e' while the river, glacier and other natural features get an 'i'). First the syndicate built its railroad: 196 miles of track through the wilderness, including the leg that's now McCarthy Rd and Cordova's famous Million Dollar Bridge. The line cost $23 million before it even reached the mines in 1911.

From 1911 until 1938 the mines operated around the clock and reported a net profit of more than $100 million. By 1938 most of the rich ore had been exhausted, and in November that year the mine was closed permanently. With the exception of a steam turbine and two large diesel engines, everything was left behind, and Kennecott became a perfectly preserved slice of US mining history.

Unfortunately, when the railroad bed was converted to a road in 1974, Kennecott also became the country's biggest help-yourself hardware store. Locals were taking windows, doors and wiring, while tourists were picking the town clean of tools, railroad spikes and anything else they could haul away as souvenirs.

In 1998 the NPS purchased the mill, power plant and many of the buildings from private owners as the first step to restoring them. At the time of writing, the old mill town was undergoing extensive renovations.

Hiking & Backpacking

There are a few excellent hikes around town and a backcountry bonanza if you're able to fly by bush plane deeper into the national park.

Root Glacier Trail   HIKING

Beginning at the far edge of town past the Concentration Mill, the Root Glacier Trail is an easy 4- or 8-mile round-trip route out to the sparkling white-and-blue ice. Signposts mark the route and the path itself is clear and well used as far as the primitive Jumbo Creek campsites.

From here you can head left to the glacier or continue straight another 2 miles along a rougher track. At the end, the Erie Mine Bunkhouse will be visible on the slopes above you. Check at the visitor center for the latest on the conditions on the climb. Most of this trail can also be ridden on a mountain bike.

Bonanza Mine Trail   HIKING

Another excellent hike from Kennecott follows this alpine trail – a round trip of almost 9 miles. Begin on the Root Glacier Trail and turn off to the right at the clearly marked junction. This is a steep uphill walk with 3800ft of elevation gain. Once above the treeline, the view of the confluence of the Root and Kennicott Glaciers is stunning.

Expect three to five hours for this hike up if the weather is good and half that time to return. Water is available at the top, but carry at least a quart (1L) if the day is hot. Snow lingers higher up until early June.

🛏 Sleeping

Kennicott Glacier Lodge   HOTEL $$

(☑907-258-2350; www.kennicottlodge.com; Main St; s/d from $165/175; 🛜) Some of Kennecott's historic mining buildings have been restored, including this grande dame, which hits the jackpot with a mix of modern comforts and old-school charm (bathrooms are shared). The Glacier Lodge is a little more touristy than McCarthy's Ma Johnson's (p323).

Rooms are cozy (those at the front have stupendous glacier views) and the hotel offers nice little extras, such as lending out bear spray.

🍴 Eating & Drinking

Kennicott Glacier Lodge   AMERICAN $$

(☑907 258 2350; www.kennicottlodge.com; lunch $9-13, dinner $33-36) You'll need a reservation for the lodge's well-regarded family-style dinners, which are set three-course meals. There's only one seating: at 7pm.

Tailor Made Pizza   PIZZA $$

(slice $6, pizzas $16-32; ⊙11:30am-6pm) Delicious, filling slices and whole pizzas are served straight from this antediluvian Anchorage bus transformed into a food cart. It's just off the main road on a glacier-view flat.

Kodiak, Katmai & Southwest Alaska

Best Cheap Things To Do

➡ Izembek National Wildlife Refuge (p345)

➡ Cycling around Kodiak (p333)

➡ Aleutian WWII National Historic Area (p346)

➡ Audubon Society hike (p331)

Best Places to See Brown Bears

➡ Brooks Falls (p339)

➡ Kodiak National Wildlife Refuge (p331)

➡ Izembek National Wildlife Refuge (p345)

➡ Aniakchak National Monument (p337)

Why Go?

The elongated Alaska Peninsula marks the extreme western extension of the North American continent. Tapering out into the Bering Sea like a curled crocodile's tail, it's a jumble of treeless emerald hills, precipitous cliffs and conical snow-capped peaks heavy with reminders of an erstwhile Russian culture and a still surviving Aleut one.

In the east sit Kodiak Island and Katmai National Park, where you can indulge in what are, arguably, the best salmon fishing and brown-bear viewing opportunities on the planet.

Equally special are the surreal landscapes of the lower peninsula and the nebulous Aleutian islands that lie beyond. The MV *Tustumena,* an economical ferry, weaves its way twice monthly between Kodiak and Dutch Harbor, stopping at half a dozen pin-prick sized, off-the-grid communities along the way. Replete with breaching whales, smoking volcanoes and poignant WWII sites, this could well be the best water-based excursion in the state.

When to Go

Kodiak

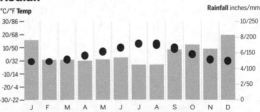

Jun Decent bear viewing and salmon fishing but with fewer crowds at the hot spots.

Jul Salmon are running, bears are fishing and humans are hoping to glimpse them both.

May–Sep The MV *Tustumena* ferry runs to the Lower Alaska Peninsula and Aleutian Islands.

History

Of all the state's regions, Southwest Alaska has had the most turbulent history, marked by massacres, violent eruptions and WWII bombings.

When Stepan Glotov and his Russian fur-trading party landed at present-day Dutch Harbor in 1759, there were more than 30,000 Aleuts living on Unalaska and Amaknak Islands. After the Aleuts destroyed four ships and killed 175 fur hunters in 1763, the Russians returned and began a systematic elimination of Aleuts, massacring or enslaving them. It's estimated that by 1830 only 200 to 400 Aleuts were living on Unalaska.

The Russians first landed on Kodiak Island in 1763 and returned 20 years later when Siberian fur trader Grigorii Shelikof established a settlement at Three Saints Bay. Shelikof's attempts to 'subdue' the indigenous people resulted in another bloodbath where more than 1000 Alutiiqs were massacred, or drowned during their efforts to escape.

The czar recalled Shelikof and in 1791 sent Aleksandr Baranov to manage the Russian-American Company. After an earthquake nearly destroyed the settlement at Three Saints Bay, Baranov moved his operations to more stable ground at present-day Kodiak. It became a bustling port and was the capital of Russian America until 1804, when Baranov moved again, this time to Sitka.

Some violence in Southwest Alaska was caused by nature. In 1912 Mt Katmai on the nearby Alaska Peninsula erupted, blotting out the sun for three days and blanketing Kodiak with 18in of ash. Kodiak's 400 residents escaped to sea on a ship, but soon returned to find buildings collapsed, ash drifts several feet high and spawning salmon choking in ash-filled streams.

The town was a struggling fishing port until WWII, when it became the major staging area for operations in the North Pacific. At one point Kodiak's population topped 25,000, with a submarine base at Women's Bay, an army outpost at Buskin River and gun emplacements protecting Fort Abercrombie.

Kodiak was spared from attack during WWII, but the Japanese bombed Unalaska only six months after bombing Pearl Harbor, and then invaded Attu and Kiska Islands. More hardship followed: the Good Friday Earthquake of 1964 leveled downtown Kodiak and wiped out its fishing fleet; the king-crab fishery crashed in the early 1980s; and the *Exxon Valdez* oil spill soiled the coastline at the end of that decade. But this region rebounded after each disaster, and today Unalaska and Kodiak are among the top three fishing ports in the country.

Getting There & Away

Alaska Airlines (800-252-7522; www.alaskaair.com) and **PenAir** (800-448-4226; www.penair.com) service the region and one or the other provides daily flights to Kodiak, King Salmon, Unalaska, Dillingham and Bethel. Ravn Alaska (p417) also flies to Kodiak from a number of destinations throughout Alaska, including Anchorage.

The most affordable way to reach the region is via the **Alaska Marine Highway ferry** (800-642-0066; www.ferryalaska.com), which has stops at Kodiak, Unalaska and a handful of small communities in between.

KODIAK ISLAND

Kodiak is the island of plenty. Consider its famous brown bears, the largest ursine creatures in the world. Thanks to an unblemished ecosystem and an unlimited diet of rich salmon that spawn in its lakes and rivers, adult male bears can weigh up to 1400lb.

Part of the wider Kodiak archipelago and the second largest island in the US after Hawaii's Big Island, Kodiak acts as a kind of ecological halfway house between the forested Alaskan panhandle and the treeless Aleutian Islands. Its velvety green mountains and sheltered ice-free bays were the site of the earliest Russian settlement in Alaska and are still home to one of the US's most important fishing fleets.

Largely off the big cruise-ship circuit, the island's main attraction – beyond the obvious lure of its bears – is its quiet Alaskan authenticity. Only a small northeastern section of Kodiak is populated. The rest is roadless wilderness protected in the Kodiak National Wildlife Refuge.

Elsewhere, Kodiak harbors one of the largest coast-guard stations in the US, hides smatterings of abandoned WWII defenses and retains some genuine Russian colonial heritage. On a (rare) sunny day it's a sublime place to be.

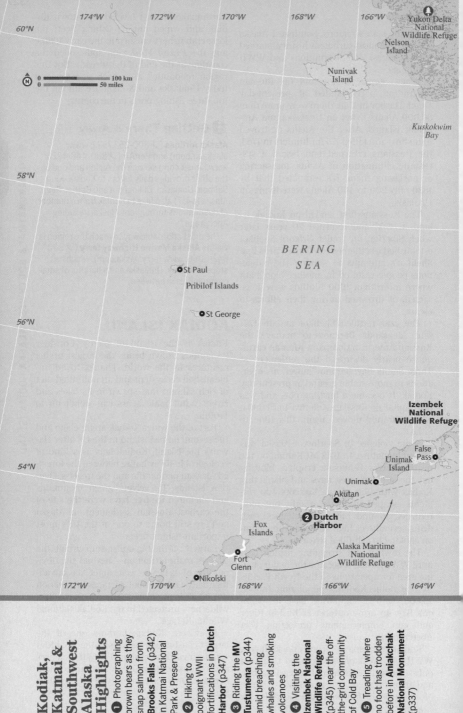

Kodiak, Katmai & Southwest Alaska Highlights

1 Photographing brown bears as they snap salmon from **Brooks Falls** (p342) in Katmai National Park & Preserve

2 Hiking to poignant WWII fortifications in **Dutch Harbor** (p347)

3 Riding the **MV Tustumena** (p344) amid breaching whales and smoking volcanoes

4 Visiting the **Izembek National Wildlife Refuge** (p345) near the off-the-grid community of Cold Bay

5 Treading where no foot has trodden before in **Aniakchak National Monument** (p337)

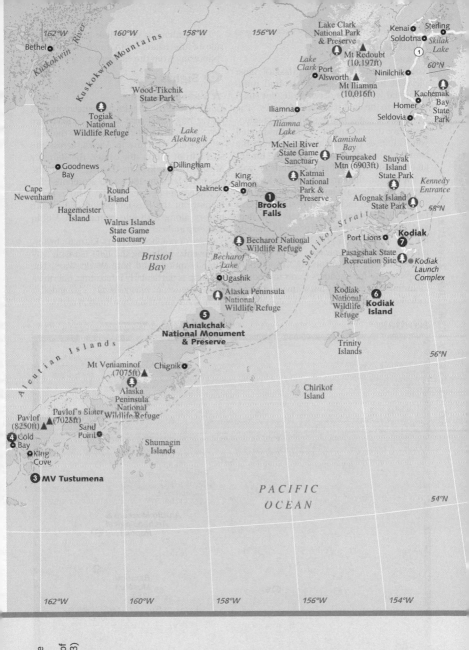

162°W 160°W 158°W 156°W

Bethel

Kuskokwim River

Kuskokwim Mountains

Lake Clark
National Park
& Preserve

Kenai
Soldotna
Sterling
*Skilak
Lake*

Mt Redoubt
(10,197ft)

60°N

*Lake
Clark* Port
Alsworth
Mt Iliamna
(10,016ft)

Ninilchik

Togiak
National
Wildlife Refuge

Wood-Tikchik
State Park

*Lake
Aleknagik*

Iliamna

Homer
Seldovia

Kachemak
Bay
State
Park

*Tliamna
Lake*

McNeil River
State Game
Sanctuary

*Kamishak
Bay*

Fourpeaked
Mtn (6903ft)

Shuyak
Island
State Park

*Kennedy
Entrance*

Goodnews
Bay

Dillingham

Naknek
King
Salmon

Katmai
National
Park &
Preserve

Afognak Island
State Park

58°N

Cape
Newenham

Round
Island

❶
**Brooks
Falls**

Shelikof Strait

Hagemeister
Island

Walrus Islands
State Game
Sanctuary

Becharof National
Wildlife Refuge

Port Lions

Kodiak

❼

*Bristol
Bay*

*Becharof
Lake*

Pasagshak State
Recreation Site

● *Kodiak
Launch
Complex*

Ugashik

Alaska Peninsula
National
Wildlife Refuge

Kodiak
National
Wildlife
Refuge

❻
**Kodiak
Island**

❺
**Aniakchak
National Monument
& Preserve**

Trinity
Islands

56°N

Aleutian Islands

Mt Veniaminof
(7075ft)

Chignik

Alaska
Peninsula
National
Wildlife Refuge

*Chirikof
Island*

Pavlof
(8250ft)
Pavlof's Sister
(7028ft)

Sand
Point

*Shumagin
Islands*

❹ Cold
Bay

King
Cove

❸ **MV Tustumena**

*PACIFIC
OCEAN*

54°N

162°W 160°W 158°W 156°W 154°W

Kodiak

POP 6457

Kodiak is one of outback Alaska's most pleasant towns; big enough to find uninterrupted wi-fi and a decent latte, but small enough to be laid-back and friendly. The locals are a congenial bunch who passionately love their town and aren't afraid to tell you. Glimpses of onion domes through the standard shopping mall architecture hint at an erstwhile Russian heritage, while crowds of trawlers in the harbor testify to Kodiak's mantle as Alaska's largest fishing center with 650 boats, including the state's largest trawl, longline and crab vessels. The fleet and the 12 shore-based processors include the *Star of Kodiak,* a WWII vessel converted into a fish plant downtown.

Despite its hardworking reputation, there's plenty for outsiders to do in Kodiak, including two excellent museums and a historical park.

The settlement of Kodiak is on the east side of the island, with three main roads splintering from the city center.

◉ Sights

★ Baranov Museum MUSEUM

(☑907-486-5920; www.baranovmuseum.org; 101 Marine Way; adult/child $5/free; ⊙10am-4pm Mon-Sat, to 3pm winter) Housed in the oldest Russian structure in Alaska, across the street from the visitor center, the Baranov Museum fills Erskine House, which the Russians built in 1808 as a storehouse for precious sea-otter pelts. Today it holds many items from the Russian period of Kodiak's history, along with fine examples of Alutiiq basketry and carvings.

A set of notebooks covers Katmai's historical events, including the 1964 tsunami, volcanic eruptions and both World Wars. The gift shop is particularly interesting, offering a wide selection of *matreshkas* (nesting dolls), brass samovars and other Russian crafts.

Kodiak

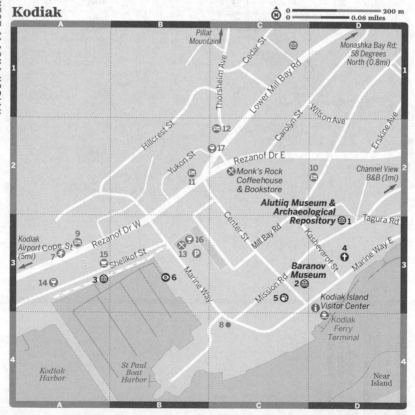

Holy Resurrection Cathedral   CHURCH
(📞907-486-5532; 385 Kashevarof St) Near the Alutiiq Museum on Mission Rd, Holy Resurrection Church serves the oldest Russian Orthodox parish in the New World, established in 1794. The present church, marked by its beautiful blue onion domes, was built in 1945 and is the third one to occupy this site. There are no specific opening times. Try the door handle.

Kodiak National Wildlife Refuge Visitor Center   WILDLIFE RESERVE
(📞907-487-2626; 402 Center St; ⏱9am-5pm; 🚸) This excellent visitor center focuses on the Kodiak brown bear, the most famous resident of the refuge, with an exhibit room that's especially well suited for children, a short film on the bears and a bookstore. A variety of kids' programs are offered, with the schedule posted on the front door. Interested in seeing a big bruin? Stop by here first.

Kodiak

★**Alutiiq Museum & Archaeological Repository**   MUSEUM
(📞907-486-7004; www.alutiiqmuseum.org; 215 Mission Rd; adult/child $7/free; ⏱10am-4pm Tue-Fri, noon-4pm Sat) The Alutiiqs (not to be confused with the Aleuts) are the subject of this brilliant Alaska Native museum. They were the original inhabitants of the Kodiak archipelago and many of them remain members of the Russian Orthodox Church. Like most native groups their population was decimated during the 19th century, thus the museum guards some precious native heritage.

There's information on the Alutiiq language (now being taught again in local schools), exhibits on masked dancing and details of some 1000-year-old petroglyphs found in the archipelago.

St Paul Boat Harbor   HARBOR
The pulse of this city can be found in its two boat harbors. St Paul Boat Harbor is downtown and the larger of the two. Begin with the **Harbor Walkway** (Shelikof St), where a series of interesting interpretive displays line the boardwalk above the docks. Then descend to the rows of vessels, where you can talk to the crews or even look for a job.

Fort Abercrombie State Historical Park   PARK
This military fort, 4.5 miles northeast of Kodiak, off Monashka Bay Rd, was built by the US Army during WWII for a Japanese invasion that never came. In the end, Kodiak's lousy weather kept the Japanese bombers away from the island. The fort is now a 186-acre state historical park, sitting majestically on the cliffs above scenic Monashka Bay.

Between its pair of 8in guns is Ready Ammunition Bunker, which stored 400 rounds of ammunition during the war. Today it contains the small **Kodiak Military History Museum** (📞907-486-7015; adult/child $3/free; ⏱1-4pm Fri-Mon).

Just as interesting as the gun emplacements are the tidal pools found along the park's rocky shorelines, where an afternoon can be spent searching for sea creatures.

🏃 Activities

Hiking
The Kodiak area has dozens of hiking trails, but few are maintained and trailheads are not always marked. Windfall can make following the track difficult, or even totally conceal it. Still, hiking trails are the best avenues to the natural beauty of Kodiak Island.

KODIAK, KATMAI & SOUTHWEST ALASKA KODIAK

The best source of hiking information is the Alaska Division of Parks (p335) or the excellent *Kodiak Audubon's Hiking & Birding Guide,* a large waterproof topographical map with notes on the trails and birds, sold at various places around town, including the Kodiak National Wildlife Refuge Visitor Center (p331) for $12.

For transportation and company on the trail, the local **Audubon Society** offers group hikes almost every Saturday and Sunday from May to October, meeting at 9:30am at the ferry terminal. You can get a list of the hikes and the contact person from the Kodiak Island Visitor Center (p335) or the Kodiak National Wildlife Refuge Visitor Center.

Pillar Mountain   MOUNTAIN

The de rigueur hike for anyone with a couple of hours to spare, Pillar Mountain is the 1270ft summit that overlooks Kodiak town, with its sentinel wind turbines on top. If you want to get a glimpse of the island's velvety greenness and enjoy a bird's-eye view of the town, this provides instant gratification.

Pick up the bumpy dirt road to the top by walking or driving north up Thorsheim Ave and turning left on Maple Ave, which runs into Pillar Mountain Rd. You'll end up where the giant wind turbines slice through the fog. It's 2 miles one-way.

Barometer Mountain   HIKING

At 2452ft it might not sound tall, but climbing Barometer is a tough grunt that shouldn't be taken lightly. With loose stones and a couple of steep sections near the top you'd better have good balance and strong knees, especially on the way down.

The 4-mile out-and-back trail – easily visible from the road – starts just past the airport runway as you head south on Chiniak

Rd where there's a pullover and small sign. The path bends through trees at the start, then branches uphill through high bushes, and ultimately follows a steep open ridge. The views from the summit are as staggering as your gait. Take plenty of water.

Termination Point   HIKING

This 5-mile loop starts at the end of Monashka Bay Rd and branches into several trails near Termination Point, a spectacular peninsula that juts out into Narrow Strait. Most hiking is done in a lush Sitka spruce forest. If you're nervous about your navigational skills, simply hike the coastal half of the loop and then backtrack.

North Sister Mountain   HIKING

Starting 150ft up a creek bed a mile before the end of Monashka Bay Rd, this trail (find it on the left side of the creek bed) first leads up steeply through dense brush, but then levels off on alpine tundra. The summit of North Sister (2100ft) is the first peak seen (to your left), about a mile from the trailhead. The other two Sisters are also accessible from here.

Pyramid Mountain   HIKING

Two trails, both of which start on Anton Larsen Bay Rd, lead to the top of Pyramid Mountain (2401ft). Avoid the easternmost trail, accessed from the golf course, which is brush-choked and hard going. Instead, continue west to Anton Larsen Pass, where the other trail begins in the parking area on the right. It's a steep but easy-to-follow 2-mile climb to the top.

Anton Larsen Pass   HIKING

This 5-mile loop is a scenic ridge walk and a far easier alpine hike than Barometer Mountain. The trail begins just north of the gravel

---

KODIAK FOR CHILDREN

If the kids are tagging along in Kodiak, cross the Zharoff Memorial Bridge to Near Island, where you'll find several attractions well suited to families. Best of all, they're free.

Kodiak Fisheries Research Center (☎907-481-1800; www.kodiakak.us; Trident Way; ⊗8am-4:30pm Mon-Fri; ⊕) Opened in 1998 to house the fisheries research being conducted by various agencies, the center has an interesting lobby that includes displays, touch tanks, a large **aquarium** and a 19ft Cuvier's beaked whale skeleton.

North End Park (Trident Way; ⊕) Reached as soon as you cross the bridge, the small park is laced with forested trails that converge at a stairway to the shoreline. At low tide you can search the tidepools here for starfish, sea anemones and other marine life.

St Herman Harbor (Dog Bay Rd; ⊕) Kodiak's 'other' harbor is on Near Island (cross the bridge from downtown) and is a great place to look for sea lions and eagles.

parking lot, at the pass on the left side of Anton Larsen Bay Rd. A well-defined trail leads you through meadows; at a fork, the trail heads right to cross a bridge and climbs to a broad alpine ridge. Once on top, use the rolling ridge to skirt a distinctive, glacial valley before descending back to the fork in the trail.

Cycling

On a clear, sunny day, cycling on Kodiak's 75 miles of paved, relatively quiet roads is heaven. Traffic is only thick around the town and thins out dramatically south of the airport. A spin down to Bell's Flats (10 miles south of town) for lunch in Java Flats (p334) cafe is a must. And why stop there? The mainly unpaved, 12-mile Anton Larsen Bay Rd is popular with mountain bikers and crosses a mountain pass to the island's west side, where you'll find quiet coves and shorelines to explore. With long daylight hours a ride down to Pasagshak Bay 46 miles to the south of Kodiak town is not out of the question.

58 Degrees North   BICYCLE RENTAL
(☑907-486-6249; 1231 Mill Bay Rd; per 24hr $30; ⊙11am-6pm Mon-Sat) A friendly outdoor shop that rents out mountain bikes. If you are planning to do a lot of bike exploration, purchase the *Kodiak Island Mountain Bike Guide*.

Paddling

With its many bays and protected inlets, scenic coastline and offshore rookeries, Kodiak is a kayaker's dream. Unfortunately, there is nowhere in Kodiak to rent a kayak.

Alaska Wilderness Adventures   KAYAKING
(☑907-487-2397; www.kodiakswildside.com; full-day tours $145-160) Specializes in whale watching and photography tours, along with seeing other marine wildlife such as sea otters and puffins, from kayaks. Destinations depend on where the wildlife is.

🖝 Tours

Several companies provide either a city tour of Kodiak or a day-long scenery-viewing tour that includes Baranov Museum, Pillar Mountain and Fort Abercrombie State Historical Park. But Kodiak is one place where you should skip the ground tour and hit the water.

Galley Gourmet   BOAT
(☑907-486-5079; www.galleygourmet.biz; 1223 Kouskov St; dinner cruise $150) Along with

whale-watching and harbor cruises, Marty and Marion Owen offer a delightful dinner cruise onboard their 42ft yacht. Marty navigates the boat while Marion whips up meals – such as salmon Kiev with king-crab sauce or apricots and marinated halibut wrapped in bacon – and serves them on white table linen with views of coastal scenery and wildlife.

Kodiak Adventures Unlimited   TOURS
(☑907-486-8766; www.kodiakadventuresunlimited.com; 105 Marine Way; ⊙8am-5pm Mon-Fri, to 3pm Sat & Sun) A clearinghouse of sorts for private tours and charters, the very friendly Kodiak Adventures Unlimited can book you bear-viewing tours as well as halibut and guided river fishing excursions. The office overlooks St Paul Harbor.

Fish n Chip Charters   FISHING
(☑907-487-2267; www.fishingkodiak.net; 301 Cope St; day trip $350) These guys can sort you out with what is – let's face it – the quintessential Kodiak experience: fishing. Captain Dave has a newly refurbished boat and decades of experience. Equipment is provided and you can get your catch processed afterward.

Helios Sea Tours   BOAT
(☑907-486-5310; www.kodiakrivercamps.com; 5hr tours $160-290) Offers three-, five- and seven-hour bird- and whale-watching tours on a small 27ft vessel. Also stops at some WWII sites.

🎊 Festivals & Events

Kodiak Crab Festival   CULTURAL
(www.kodiak.org) The town's best event, it was first held in 1958 to celebrate the end of crabbing season. Today the week-long event in late May features parades, a blessing of the fleet, foot and kayak races, fishing-skills contests (such as a survival-suit race) and a lot of cooked king crab.

Bear Country Music Festival   MUSIC
Features country, bluegrass and Alaskan music in mid-July.

🛏 Sleeping

Lodging is expensive in Kodiak and there's an 11% sales and bed tax on top of all tariffs. The most current list of B&Bs is on the website of the visitor center (www.kodiak.org).

Russian Heritage Inn   HOTEL $
(☑907-486-5657; www.russianheritageinn.com; 119 Yukon St; r $95-105; 🅿🛜) You pick this motel for location and price. All rooms have

microwaves, coffeemakers and small refrigerators. There's not much that's Russian about it apart from the name.

Fort Abercrombie State Historical Park
CAMPGROUND $

(www.dnr.alaska.gov/parks/units/kodiak/ftaber.htm; Mile 4, E Rezanof Dr; tent & RV sites $10) Four-and-a-half miles northeast of Kodiak, this park has 13 wooded sites in a delightfully mossy forest. A few are walk-in, and feel very secluded. Trails meander around the bluffs, beach and small lake, and it's a great place to wander.

Buskin River State Recreation Site
CAMPGROUND $

(Mile 4.5, W Rezanof Dr; campsites $10) Four miles southwest of the city, this 168-acre park includes a 15-site rustic campground, the closest to the city, along with a self-guided nature trail and good salmon fishing in the Buskin River.

★ Channel View B&B
B&B $$

(☎907-486-2470; www.kodiakchannelview.com; 1010 Steller Way; r/ste $125/135; 🐾) Run by a couple of world travelers, history buffs and art collectors, Channel View offers a a range of subtle delights: historic Kodiak photos, fossils collected from the island and arranged in a rainy rock garden, and original artwork from travels abroad. Room options include a single or queen, a studio apartment or a one-bedroom apartment.

There are views of the channel below through fir trees and from a spacious deck. Host Mary is a fifth-generation islander, and serves full gourmet breakfasts.

Mrs Potts Bed & Breakfast
B&B $$

(☎907-539-1414; www.mrspottsbnb.com; 223 Mill Bay Rd; r $119-129; 🐾) Mrs Potts is actually Beth Davis; the Potts moniker came about due to her penchant for teapots (count them, there are more than 50). Running this new B&B handily located in a cute house near the harbor is her other passion and it shows. Enjoy glorious breakfasts; clean, cozy rooms; and wonderful Kodiak hospitality.

Best Western Kodiak Inn
HOTEL $$

(☎907-486-5712, 888-563-4254; www.kodiakinn.com; 236 W Rezanof Dr; r $175-195; 🐾) Kodiak's largest and most upscale motel is downtown and has 81 rooms along with a fine restaurant, outdoor hot tub and airport-shuttle service. Suites run to $259 and are quite large.

Shelikof Lodge
HOTEL $$

(☎907-486-4141; www.shelikoflodgealaska.com; 211 Thorsheim Ave; r $130; 🐾) Nicest rooms downtown for what you pay, plus a good restaurant and a lounge. A bonus is the airport shuttle service, which is rare in Kodiak.

✗ Eating

★ Java Flats
CAFE $

(Bell's Flats; breakfast $6-9, lunch $10-12; ⊙6am-3pm Tue-Fri, 7am-3pm Sat & Sun; 🐾) Saying you have the best baking within a 100-mile radius doesn't always mean much in Alaska where 100 miles is often the distance to the nearest gas station, but, take it on trust, the homemade cookies at Java are to visiting homo sapiens what salmon is to Kodiak's oversized bears – delicious! It also serves mean soups, sandwiches and salads.

Java is located at Bell's Flats 10 miles south of Kodiak town, but is well worth the journey – even if you're cycling.

Mill Bay Coffee & Pastries
CAFE $

(www.millbaycoffee.com; 3833 E Rezanof Dr; breakfast $5-7, lunch $10-14; ⊙8am-6pm Mon-Sat; 🐾) Possibly the last place in the world you expect to find a French bakery, yet here it is. In a nondescript strip mall on the outskirts of Kodiak, Mill's French owners knock out buttery croissants and light fluffy sponges that wouldn't look out of place on the Champs-Élysées.

Monk's Rock Coffeehouse & Bookstore
CAFE $

(202 W Rezanof Dr; sandwiches $6-8; ⊙10am-6pm Mon-Fri) Part cafe, part library of Russian Orthodox books and icons, Monk's is an out-of-the-ordinary eating place thanks to its on-site bookshop that might have stepped straight out of Vladivostok. Sofas are comfortable, staff are friendly and the soups are recommended, especially the borscht.

Safeway
SUPERMARKET $

(2685 Mill Bay Rd; sandwiches $6-8; ⊙6am-midnight) If you're stocking up with food for a long ferry ride, look no further.

Old Powerhouse
JAPANESE $$

(☎907-481-1088; 516 Marine Way; lunch special $8-10, dinner $15-22; ⊙11:30am-2pm & 5-9pm Tue-Thu, 11:30am-2pm & 5-10pm Fri & Sat, 5-9pm Sun) The best fish in Kodiak are in this historic power plant, which has been beautifully renovated into a Japanese seafood restaurant. The waterfront location places you on an outdoor deck, or in a solarium, watching fishing boats glide right past, while feasting on almost all-local sushi and seafood or excellent *udon, soba* and *yakisoba* noodles.

Aquamarine Cafe & Sweets   AMERICAN $$
(☑907-486-2999; 508 W Marine Way; lunch $10, dinner $15-25) It's not often that Kodiak gets a new restaurant, so much interest greeted the opening of this rather hip spot in late 2014. The trendy decor pays a nod to Kodiak's seafaring culture while the food puts quality over quantity with tasty meat and fish dishes served with sides of rice and homemade buns. Cool but casual.

🍸 Drinking & Nightlife

Clustered around the city waterfront and small-boat harbor are a handful of bars that cater to Kodiak's fishing industry. If you visit these at night you'll find them interesting places, overflowing with skippers, deckhands and cannery workers drinking hard and talking lively.

★ Kodiak Island Brewing Co   MICROBREWERY
(☑907-486-2537; www.kodiakbrewery.com; 117 Lower Mill Bay Rd; ◔noon-7pm) For proof that craft-brewing has reached the frontier, call into Kodiak's only microbrewery. It operates a taproom rather than a pub, meaning you can bring your own food as you sample their latest ales, including the signature Liquid Sunshine. Tours of the small brewing operation are available on request.

Henry's Great Alaskan   PUB
(512 Marine Way; ◔11:30am-10pm Mon-Thu, to 10:30pm Fri & Sat, noon-9:30pm Sun) Henry's bills itself as a restaurant but is really more of a bar. Located on the mall in front of the small-boat harbor, it's hopping with fishermen and their friends. It's not as dark or claustrophobic as other venues and has a decent pub menu.

Harborside Coffee & Goods   CAFE
(216 Shelikof St; ◔6:30am-7pm Mon-Sat, 8am-7pm Sun; 🛜) The best cuppa in town can be procured at this fount of fishing-boat gossip right on the harborside. A strong double shot goes down well while surfing the equally strong wi-fi.

B'n'B Bar   BAR
(326 Shelikof St; ◔9am-late) Across from the harbor, B'n'B claims to be Alaska's oldest bar, having served its first beer in 1899. It's a fisher's bar with a giant king crab on the wall, as well as the most level pool table in a town that feels an earthquake now and then.

Rendezvous   BAR
(11653 Chiniak Hwy; ◔11:30am-late) This bar and restaurant is a 15-minute drive out of town past the coast-guard base, but its atmosphere is worth the gas (even at $5 a gallon). It hosts the best live music in Kodiak, with singers taking to the stage several times a month.

ℹ️ Information

Alaska Division of Parks (☑907-486-6339; 1400 Abercrombie Dr; ◔8am-4:30pm Mon-Fri, varies Sat & Sun) Maintains an office at Fort Abercrombie State Historical Park (p331), 4.5 miles northeast of the city off Monashka Bay Rd, and is the place for information on trails, campgrounds and recreational cabins.

Kodiak Island Ambulatory Care Clinic (☑907-486-6188; Suite 102, 1202 Center St; ◔8am-6pm Mon-Fri, 9am-3pm Sat) For emergency and walk-in medical care.

Post Office (419 Lower Mill Bay Rd) The main post office is just northeast of the library.

Kodiak Island Visitor Center (☑907-486-4782, 800-789-4782; www.kodiak.org; 100 Marine Way; ◔8am-5pm Mon-Fri) Next to the ferry terminal, with brochures and maps of the city. Hours tend to vary during summer.

Wells Fargo (☑907-486-3126; 202 Marine Way) Has an ATM and a king-crab display in its lobby.

ℹ️ Getting There & Away

Both **Alaska Airlines** (☑907-487-4363, 800-252-7522; www.alaskaair.com) and its contract carrier Ravn Alaska (p417) fly to Kodiak daily. Fares are approximately one-way/return $250/500. The airport is 5 miles south of Kodiak on Chiniak Rd. Other than the offerings from a few motels, there is no shuttle service into town. **A&B Taxi** (☑907-486-4343) charges $20 for the ride.

Between May and September Alaska Marine Highway's MV *Tustumena* stops at **Kodiak Ferry Terminal** (☑907-486-3800; www.alaskaferry.org; 100 Marine Way) several times a week, coming from Homer (one-way $74, 9½ hours). Twice a month the 'trusty *Tusty*' continues west to Unalaska and Dutch Harbor ($293 one-way from Kodiak). Several times a month the MV *Kennicott* sails to Kodiak from Homer and Whittier (one-way $91, 10 hours). The office in the ferry terminal, next to the Visitor Center, prints out tickets. Arrive at least two hours before sailing.

ⓘ Getting Around

There's no public transport in Kodiak. You can procure car rental at the airport. **Budget Rent-A-Car** (☑ 907-487-2220; airport terminal), among others, has a desk, but it isn't cheap. Bank on around $75 to $90 a day. Other options are to call a taxi, walk, or – if you're heading outside town – rent a bicycle from 58 Degrees North (p333).

Around Kodiak

More than 100 miles of paved and gravel roads head from the city into the wilderness that surrounds Kodiak. Some are rough tracks, manageable only by 4WD, but others can be driven or hitched along to reach isolated stretches of beach, which make great fishing spots and superb coastal landscapes. These scenic areas are the true attractions of Kodiak Island.

South of Kodiak, Chiniak Rd winds for 48 miles to Cape Greville, following the edge of three splendid bays. The road provides access to some of Alaska's best coastal scenery and there are plenty of opportunities to view sea lions and puffins offshore, especially at Cape Chiniak near the road's southern end.

Just past Mile 30 of Chiniak Rd is the junction with Pasagshak Bay Rd, which continues another 16.5 miles due south. Along its way it passes **Pasagshak River State Recreation Site** (Mile 8.7, Pasagshak River Rd; tent/RV sites $10/28), which has 12 campsites near a beautiful stretch of rugged coastline, 45 miles from town. This small riverside campground is famous for its silver- and king-salmon fishing and for a river that reverses its flow four times a day with the tides.

At the end of the road is **Fossil Beach**, where you'll find not only the namesake fossils emerging from the cliffs, but also a few surfers braving the cold to catch the perfect wave.

Kodiak National Wildlife Refuge

This 2812-sq-mile preserve, which covers the southern two-thirds of Kodiak Island, all of Ban and Uganik Islands, and a small section of Afognak Island, is the chief stronghold of the Alaska brown bear. An estimated 3500 bears reside in the refuge and the surrounding area, which is known worldwide for brown-bear hunting and to a lesser degree for salmon and steelhead fishing. Birdlife is plentiful: more than 200 species have been recorded, and there are 600 breeding pairs of eagles that nest within the refuge. Flowing out of the steep fjords and deep glacial valleys and into the sea are 117 salmon-bearing streams that account for 65% of the total commercial salmon harvest in Kodiak.

The refuge's diverse habitat ranges from rugged mountains and alpine meadows to wetlands, spruce forest and grassland. No roads enter the refuge, and no maintained trails lie within it. Access into the park is by charter plane or boat out of Kodiak, and most of the refuge lies at least 25 air miles away.

Like most wilderness areas in Alaska, an extensive trip into the refuge is something that requires advance planning and some money. Begin before you arrive in Alaska by contacting the **Kodiak National Wildlife Refuge Headquarters** (☑ 907-487-2600; http://kodiak.fws.gov; 1390 Buskin River Rd, Kodiak).

If you're looking for somewhere to sleep, the Kodiak office of the US Fish & Wildlife Service (USFWS) administers nine cabins in the refuge, none accessible by road. The closest to Kodiak are **Uganik Lake Cabin** and **Veikoda Bay Cabin**. Go to www.reserveusa.com to book them ($45 per night each). Contact the **refuge visitor center** (☑ 907-487-2626; http://kodiak.fws.gov; 402 Center St; ◉ 9am-5pm) for more information.

🐾 Activities

Mid-July to mid-September is the best time to see bears, and the most common way to do it is with a bear-sighting flight. The average tour is a four-hour trip that includes two hours on the ground photographing bears, and costs $450 to $550 per person.

Kodiak Treks   BEAR WATCHING
(☑ 907-487-2122; www.kodiaktreks.com; tours per person $375) 🌿 Offers low-impact, small-group bear-watching trips from its remote lodge on an island in Uyak Bay. Noted bear biologist Harry Dodge leads guests from the lodge, by boat and boot, to various viewing spots to view up to two dozen bears. Costs cover lodging, meals and equipment but not your charter flight to Uyak Bay.

Kingfisher Aviation   BEAR WATCHING
(☑ 907-486-5155, 866-486-5155; www.kingfisheraviation.com) Four-hour bear-viewing excursions take place in either Kodiak or Katmai on the mainland depending on the season. You are transported on four-passenger float planes.

Afognak Island State Park

Afognak Island lies just north of Kodiak Island in the archipelago. Some 75,000 acres of Afognak are protected in the pristine Afognak Island State Park, which has two public-use cabins: Laura Lake Cabin and Pillar Lake Cabin. The cabin at Pillar Lake is a short walk from a beautiful mile-long beach. Both cabins are accessed by floatplane, cost $35 a night, and are reserved through Alaska Division of Parks (☑907-486-6339; www.alaskastateparks.org). You can check the cabin availability and make reservations online six months in advance.

Shuyak Island State Park

The northernmost island in the Kodiak Archipelago, remote and undeveloped Shuyak is 54 air miles north of Kodiak. It's only 12 miles long and 11 miles wide, but almost all the island's 47,000 acres are taken up by Shuyak Island State Park, featuring forests of virgin Sitka spruce and a rugged shoreline dotted with secluded beaches. Otters, sea lions and Dall porpoises inhabit offshore waters, while black-tailed deer and a modest population of the famous Kodiak brown bear roam the interior.

Kayakers enjoy superb paddling in the numerous sheltered inlets, coves and channels; the area boasts more protected waterways than anywhere else in the archipelago. Most of the kayaking takes place in and around Big Bay, the heart of the state park. From the bay you can paddle and portage to four public cabins and other protected bays.

The park's four cabins are on Big Bay, Neketa Bay and Carry Inlet. The cabins ($75 per night) are cedar structures with bunks for eight, woodstoves, propane lights and cooking stoves but no running water. Shuyak Island cabins are also reserved through Alaska Division of Parks (p335) and can be reserved six months in advance online.

ALASKA PENINSULA

The Alaska Range doesn't suddenly stop at Mt McKinley. It keeps marching southwest to merge with the Aleutian Range and form the vertebrae of the Alaska Peninsula, Alaska's rugged arm that reaches out for the Aleutian Islands. This volcanic peninsula stretches some 550 miles from Cook Inlet to the tip at Isanotski Strait. It includes Alaska's largest lakes – Lake Clark, Iliamna Lake and Becharof Lake – and some of the state's most active volcanoes, with Mt Redoubt and Mt

---

OFF THE BEATEN TRACK

ANIAKCHAK – A BLANK SPOT ON THE MAP

More people orbit the earth annually than set foot in Aniakchak National Monument (www.nps.gov/ania), the least visited segment of the US National Park Service's 400 protected areas. Here the annual visitor count routinely struggles to break a 'score.' High travel costs, volatile weather, 1000lb bears (lots of 'em), and a curious lack of knowledge about the area's Garden of Eden landscapes deter the bulk of would-be adventurers. What they're missing defies written description. Imagine a kind of psychedelic cross between Crater Lake and the Ngornongoro Crater with a bit of the Colorado River thrown in for good measure. Aniakchak's centerpiece is a 6-mile-wide caldera (a massive crater formed when a volcano collapses inward) that sits in the middle of the narrow Alaska Peninsula. The caldera has a dramatic effect on the local weather causing clouds to billow over the edges of the crater rim in what have been christened 'cloud Niagaras.'

Though known to Alaskan natives for centuries, Aniakchak lay pretty much undiscovered until 1931 when it was explored by a Jesuit priest named Bernard Hubbard, who wrote about it enthusiastically in publications such as the New York Times. These days it sees a tiny trickle of intrepid visitors. Most fly to Port Heiden and trek up and over the crater rim carrying folding microkayaks, before descending to Surprise Lake, the remains of a much bigger lake that once sat in the crater. After a portage around a set of dangerous rapids called The Gates, at a cleft in the crater rim, basic kayaking skills are required to cruise down the class II rapids of the Aniakchak River toward the Pacific Ocean where an old cannery cabin and a prearranged floatplane pickup awaits. By all accounts, it's the trip of a lifetime and one not many get the opportunity to make. For more information contact the Katmai National Park Headquarters (p338) in King Salmon.

Iliamna topping more than 10,000ft in height. Wildlife abounds, communities do not.

The peninsula's most popular attraction, Katmai National Park and Preserve, has turned King Salmon into the main access point. Two other preserves – McNeil River State Game Area and Lake Clark National Park and Preserve – also attract travelers, while the Alaska Marine Highway stops at four small communities along the peninsula on its way to the Aleutians.

King Salmon

POP 426

King Salmon is the kind of place where you arrive just after breakfast and are on first-name terms with half the town by dinner-time. Almost all the people who fly in are bound for nearby Katmai National Park – the 'town' acts as both staging post and official nexus (the park HQ and visitor center are both near the airport). The oversized airport runway is testament to the erstwhile presence of the US Air Force, which was stationed here until the 1990s. These days, you're more likely to bump into hunters and fishers than pilots. They even hunt brown bears in King Salmon, where they are abundant and regarded as pests by some locals.

Tourists bound for Katmai's Brooks Camp on floatplanes rarely linger here more than a few hours. However, if you get stuck overnight, King Salmon is a friendly enough place with two restaurants, two basic places to stay, and a river lined with floatplanes and boat docks.

There's a 10% room tax.

Sleeping & Eating

Antlers Inn   INN $$

(☑907-246-8525, 888-735-8525; www.antlersin nak.com; r/ste $195/250; 🐾) Antlers beckons you into the unfussy laid-back confines of the Antlers Inn, a friendly, family-run inn with shared bathrooms. Suites have kitchenettes and private baths, but – in typical 'Bush' style – are overpriced. The airport and what passes for downtown are within salmon-hooking distance.

Eddie's Fireplace Inn   AMERICAN $$

(☑907-246-3435; Airport Rd; breakfast $11-14, dinner $20-32; ⊙8am-9pm; 🐾) Pure outback Alaska with a grizzly yarn-spinning clientele, friendly wait staff and a straightforward no-nonsense menu that never strays too far from burgers and fried fish. Dig in

like a local and you'll soon forgive them the crumby plastic tablecloths and all-pervading essence of cigarette smoke.

King Ko Inn   AMERICAN $$

(☑907-246-3377; www.kingko.com; 100 Airport Rd; mains $16-25; ⊙11am-9pm; 🐾) Positively posh compared to Eddie's, Ko's can rustle up such exotic delicacies as French-onion soup and Italian fettuccine alongside the usual Alaskan suspects. Film posters of Alaska-themed movies adorn the walls. It also rents expensive cabins ($195 to $215).

❶ Information

Katmai National Park Headquarters (☑907-246-3305; ⊙8am-4:30pm Mon-Fri) Recently relocated to the old US Air Force base, the park HQ is run by enthusiastic and knowledgeable rangers. Don't miss the fabulous film about the hard-to-reach Aniakchak National Monument.

King Salmon Visitor Center (☑907-246-4250; ⊙8am-5pm) Adjacent to the airport with topographical models, books, gifts and informed staff.

❶ Getting There & Away

Alaska Airlines (☑800-252-7522; www. alaskaair.com) and Penair (p327) fly up to eight times daily between Anchorage and King Salmon during summer (around $600 round-trip).

Katmai National Park & Preserve

'Expensive, but worth it' are perhaps the four most common words used to describe marvelous Katmai.

A national monument since 1918 and a national park since 1980, Katmai National Park & Preserve (☑907-246-3305; www.nps. gov/katm; King Salmon) is famous for its salmon-trapping brown bears, epic sportfishing potential and unusual volcanic landscapes. A visit to Katmai, unconnected to the main Alaskan road network and covering an area the size of Wales, is for most people a once-in-a-lifetime experience involving meticulous preplanning and a big wad of cash. Nearly all park visitors fly in from Anchorage to the pinprick settlement of King Salmon before transferring to a floatplane to access the main tourist area of Brooks Camp. Here they will stand spine-tinglingly close to 1000lb brown bears utilizing their formidable ursine power to paw giant salmon out of the river (better still, some bears catch the fish clean in their chops). Brooks Camp, 35 miles east of King Salmon, is the most heavily visited section of the park and is equipped with a rustic lodge plus a couple of short trails. The park headquarters and visitor center is located in King Salmon.

Brooks Camps' bear season is relatively short, but more adventurous visitors can charter floatplanes and guides to take them out to other bear viewing areas on the coast between June and October. Although without roads and prone to inclement weather, the coast is speckled with some surprisingly comfortable overnight accommodation at several fly-in backcountry lodges. Beware. None of these places are cheap and all need to be booked in advance. Visit www.katmailand.com for details.

In keeping with other Alaskan wilderness parks, Katmai's infrastructure is basic with only one road connecting Brooks Camp to the park's other main lure, the intriguing **Valley of a Thousand Smokes**. The peculiar landscape of this trippy valley is the result of a 1912 double volcano. It covered the area in a rain of ash and opened up countless smoke vents, which jetted hot steam skyward. The post-apocalyptic spectacle served as Katmai's original raison d'être and led to the area being declared a national monument in 1918. These days, the notably less smoky valley plays second fiddle to Katmai's bear-viewing, but can still be visited on a daily bus ride from Brooks Camp.

Katmai supports a healthy population of 2200 brown bears. Many of the bears arrive with instinctual punctuality at **Brooks Falls** on July 1 for the annual salmon spawning, which lasts until the end of the month. The bears return in September for a second showing to feed on the dead salmon carcasses. Brooks Camp receives about 10,000 visitors in a typical summer season so the viewing platforms can get busy. The platforms offer close-ups of the bears standing astride the falls with their mouths agape and paws at the ready. The rest of the park's visitors fan out over Katmai's 6400-sq-miles using chartered floatplanes. Fishing trips are popular and rainbow trout are plentiful in the park's large lakes. Despite Katmai's dense bear population (two bears per sq mile in places) only two serious human-bear incidents have been recorded in 100 years – a testament to fine park management.

LAKE CLARK NATIONAL PARK & PRESERVE

Only 100 miles southwest of Anchorage, Lake Clark National Park and Preserve features spectacular scenery that is a composite of Alaska: an awesome array of tundra-covered hills, mountains, glaciers, coastline, the largest lakes in the state and two active volcanoes. The centerpiece of the park is spectacular Lake Clark, a 42-mile-long turquoise body of water ringed by mountains. But the park is also where the Alaska Range merges into the Aleutian Range to form the Chigmit Mountains, and is home to two volcanoes: Mt Iliamna and Mt Redoubt. Despite its overwhelming scenery and close proximity to Alaska's largest city, less than 5000 visitors a year make it to this 5625-sq-mile preserve.

Hiking is phenomenal, but Lake Clark is best suited to the experienced backpacker. For any pretrip planning, contact the **NPS Park Headquarters** (☑907-644-3626; www.nps.gov/lacl; 240 West 5th Ave, Ste 236, Anchorage; ☺8am-5pm Mon-Fri). Port Alsworth, the main entry point for the park, has a **ranger station** (☑907-781-2117; ☺8am-5pm Mon-Fri, 9am-6pm Sat & Sun) with displays and videos on the park. There you'll find information on both the 50-mile historic **Telaquana Trail** and **Twin Lakes**, where dry tundra slopes provide easy travel to ridges and great views.

Float trips down any of the three designated wild rivers (the Chilikadrotna, Tlikakila and Mulchatna) are spectacular and exciting, with waterways rated from Class III to Class IV. The best way to handle a boat rental is through **Alaska Raft & Kayak** (☑907-561-7238, 800-606-5950; www.alaskaraftandkayak.com; 401 W Tudor Rd, Anchorage; ☺10am-6pm Mon-Sat), which rents out inflatable sea kayaks and canoes (per day $75) and 14ft to 16ft rafts (per day $100) in Anchorage. The shop will also deliver the boat to Lake Clark Air in Anchorage for your flight into the national park and pick it up when you return.

To reach the park, you will need to arrange with an Anchorage charter pilot for drop-off at the start of your adventure; consider **Lake Clark Air** (☑907-781-2208, 888-440-2281; www.lakeclarkair.com), which flies daily to Port Alsworth for a round-trip fare of $450.

ENRIQUE R. AGUIRRE AVES / GETTY IMAGES ©

1. Hallo Bay
Stunning views on the Katmai coast.

2. Red Fox
Wild-watching is popular at Katmai National Park & Preserve (p338).

3. Bay of Islands
Paddling (p342) is excellent in Katmai.

4. Brown Bear
Katmai has a strong population of brown bears (p339).

History

In June 1912 Novarupta Volcano erupted violently and, with the preceding earthquakes, rocked the area now known as Katmai National Park and Preserve. The wilderness was turned into a dynamic landscape of smoking valleys, ash-covered mountains and small holes and cracks fuming with steam and gas. Only one other eruption in documented historic times – on the Greek island of Santorini in 1500 BC – displaced more ash and pumice.

If the eruption had happened in New York City, people living in Chicago would have heard the explosion; the force of the eruption was 10 times greater than the 1980 eruption of Mt St Helens, in the state of Washington. For two days, people in Kodiak could not see a lantern held at arm's length, and the pumice, which reached half the world, lowered the average temperature in the northern hemisphere that year by 2°F. In history books, 1912 is remembered as the year without a summer, but the most amazing aspect of this eruption, the most dramatic natural event in the 20th century, was that no one was killed. Katmai is that remote.

In 1916 the National Geographic Society sent Robert Grigg to explore the locality. Standing at Katmai Pass, the explorer saw for the first time the valley floor with its thousands of steam vents. He named it the Valley of 10,000 Smokes, and the name stuck.

🏃 Activities

Bear Watching

Brooks Camp has three established bear-watching areas. From the lodge, a dirt road leads to a floating bridge over the river and the first observation deck – a large platform dubbed 'Fort Stevens' by rangers, for the Alaskan senator who secured the funding for it. From here you can see the bears feeding in the mouth of the river or swimming in the bay.

Continue on the road to the Valley of 10,000 Smokes, and in half a mile a marked trail winds to Brooks Falls. Two more viewing platforms lie along this half-mile trail. The first sits above some riffles that occasionally draw sows trying to keep their cubs away from aggressive males at the falls.

The last deck at the falls is the prime viewing area, where you can photograph the salmon making spectacular leaps or a big brownie at the top of the cascade waiting with open jaws to catch a fish. At the peak of the salmon run, there might be eight to 12 bears here, two or three of them atop the falls themselves. The observation deck holds 40 people, and in early to mid-July it will be crammed with photographers, forcing rangers to rotate people on and off.

Hiking

Hiking and backpacking are the best ways to see the park's unusual backcountry. Like Denali National Park in Alaska's Interior, Katmai has few formal trails; backpackers follow river bars, lake shores, gravel ridges and other natural routes. Many hiking trips begin with a ride on the park bus along the dirt road to Three Forks Overlook, in the Valley of 10,000 Smokes. The bus will also drop off and pick up hikers and backpackers along the road – or you can walk its full 23-mile length.

The only developed trail from Brooks Camp is a half-day trek to the top of **Dumpling Mountain** (2520ft). The trail leaves the ranger station and heads north past the campground, climbing 1.5 miles to a scenic overlook. It then continues another 2 miles to the mountain's summit, where there are superb views of the surrounding lakes.

Paddling

The area has some excellent paddling, including the Savonoski Loop (p342), a five- to seven-day adventure. Other popular trips include a 30-mile paddle from Brooks Camp to the Bay of Islands and a 10-mile paddle to Margot Creek, which has good fishing and lots of bears.

Kayaks are the overwhelming choice for most paddlers due to high winds blowing across big lakes, and possible rough water. Accomplished paddlers should have no problem, but the conditions can sometimes get dicey for novices.

Lifetime Adventures KAYAKING
(☏907-746-4644,800-952-8624; www.lifetimeadventures.net; single/double folding kayaks $55/65 per day, folding bikes $30) Located in King Salmon or Anchorage, Lifetime Adventures rents out folding kayaks and folding mountain bikes.

👉 Tours

Independent Tours

The only road in Katmai is 23 miles long. It's a scenic traverse of the park that leads from the lodge, past wildlife-inhabited meadows and river valleys, and ends at **Three Forks Overlook**, which has a sweeping view of the

Valley of 10,000 Smokes. Katmailand runs the lodge at Brooks Camp. It has a daily round-trip by bus to Three Forks Overlook, leaving at 9am, with three hours at the cabin, and returning at 4:30pm.

Each bus carries a ranger who talks during the bus trip and leads a short hike from the cabin into the valley below. Views from the cabin include almost 12 miles of barren, moonlike valley where the lava once oozed down, with snowcapped peaks beyond. It's an amazing sight.

The fare is a steep $88 per person (with a packed lunch $96). Sign up for the tour at the Katmailand office across from the lodge as soon as you arrive at Brooks Camp. The bus is filled most of the summer, and you often can't get a seat without making a reservation a day or two in advance.

Brooks Lodge also offers an hour-long flightseeing tour around the park for $165 per person (two people minimum).

Package Tours

Because of the logistics of getting there and the need to plan and reserve so much in advance, many visitors arrive in Katmai as part of a one-call-does-it-all package tour. A shockingly large number are part of a one-day visit, spending large sums of money for what is basically an hour or two of bear watching.

★**Hallo Bay Bear Camp**   BEAR WATCHING
(☎907-235-2237, 888-535-2237; www.hallobay.com) This ecofriendly camp is on the outside coast of Katmai National Park and is designed exclusively for bear watching. The cabins are simple but comfortable, and the camp can handle only 12 guests at a time. In such an intimate setting, the bear watching can be surreal at times. Packages include lodging, meals and guides, and begin at $950 per person for one night.

Katmailand   BEAR WATCHING
(☎907-243-5448, 800-544-0551; www.katmailand.com) The concessionaire of Brooks Lodge offers packages that are geared for either anglers or bear watchers. Its one-day tour to see the bears of Brooks Falls is $669 per person from Anchorage. A three-night angler's package, including all transportation, lodging and meals, costs $1740 per person based on double-occupancy.

Lifetime Adventures   CAMPING
(☎907-746-4644, 800-952-8624; www.lifetimeadventures.net) If you have the time, this out-fit offers a seven-day camping adventure that includes hiking in the Valley of 10,000 Smokes and kayaking near Margot River. The cost is $2300 per person and includes the flight from Anchorage, charters into the park, all equipment and guides.

🛏 Sleeping & Eating

If you plan to stay at Brooks Camp, either at the lodge or in the campground, you must make a reservation. Walk-ins are not accepted. If you don't have a reservation, you're limited to staying in King Salmon and visiting the park on day trips.

Campground   CAMPGROUND $
(☎518-885-3639, reservations 877-444-6777; www.recreation.gov; tent sites $12) Each year, reservations for the campground are accepted from the first Monday in January. It might be easier to win the lottery than to get a reservation for July bear watching; often the sites are completely booked before the end of the first week of January. There's a seven-night maximum stay in July.

The campground holds a maximum of 60 people and reservations are made by person. If you don't provide the names of everyone in your party when you make your reservation, space will be held for just one person. The campground, for obvious reasons, is surrounded by an electrical fence.

Brooks Lodge   LODGE $$$
(Katmailand; ☎907-243-5448, 800-544-0551; www.katmailand.com; d per person incl flight 1/2/3 nights $1006/1351/1696) The lodge has 16 basic but comfortable rustic rooms. Each room has two bunk beds and a private bath (with shower); rooms are spread over a main lodge and six individual cabins. Accommodation is booked as part of a package tour that includes transportation from Anchorage. Bears often stalk the grounds.

A store at Brooks Camp sells limited supplies of freeze-dried food, white gas (for camp stoves), fishing equipment, flies, and other essentials...such as beer. You can also sign up for all-you-can-eat meals at Brooks Lodge without renting a cabin (renters pay too): for adults, breakfasts are $15, lunches $20 and dinners $35. Also in the lodge is a lounge with a huge stone fireplace, soft chairs and bar service in the evening (including cocktails). Campers can take hot showers ($8).

❶ Getting There & Away

Most visitors to Katmai fly into King Salmon on **Alaska Airlines** (☎800-252-7522; www.alaskaair.com) for between $600 and $650 round-trip. Once you're in King Salmon, a number of air-taxi companies offer the 20-minute floatplane flight out to Brooks Camp. **Katmai Air** (☎907-243-5448, 800-544-0551; www.katmailand.com/air-services), the Katmailand-affiliated company, charges $196 per round trip.

The Lower Peninsula

Most visitors to the little fishing villages on the western peninsula arrive on the Alaska Marine Highway's MV *Tustumena,* which sails from Kodiak to Unalaska and Dutch Harbor. The ferry usually stops for an hour or two: long enough to get out and walk from one end of the village to the other, and for most people, that's ample. If you decide to stay over at any village, you'll be able to find food and shelter, and then return to Anchorage through **PenAir** (☎800-448-4226; www.penair.com). A one-way flight from the peninsula communities to Anchorage ranges from $475 to $525.

Chignik

The first notable settlement west of Kodiak is isolated Chignik, which harbors a couple of fish canneries and a seasonal population that fluctuates between 100 and 200 people. The MV *Tustumena* stops at Chignik on most, but not all, of its runs. Check ahead.

Sand Point

On the northwest coast of Popof Island, Sand Point is the largest commercial fishing base in the Aleutians with a population of 992 split approximately 50-50 between Aleut and non-Native. It was founded in 1898 by a San Francisco fishing company as a trading post and cod-fishing station, but also bears traces of Aleut, Scandinavian and Russian heritage. The town's **St Nicholas Chapel**, a Russian Orthodox church, was built in 1933 and is now on the National Register of Historical Places. The *Tustumena* ferry only stops for an hour in Sand Point, meaning you'll have to be a very fast runner to make it the half-mile to the **Sand Point Tavern** (⊙3pm-2am Sun-Thu, to 3am Fri & Sat) for a beer and a game of pool.

THE TRUSTY TUSTY

The easiest way to see 'Bush Alaska' without flying is to hop onto the Alaska Marine Highway ferry on its route to the eastern end of the Aleutian Islands between May and September. The MV *Tustumena,* a 290ft vessel that holds 220 passengers, is one of only two ferries in the Alaska Marine Highway fleet rated as an oceangoing ship; hence its nickname, the 'Trusty *Tusty*.' It is also one of the oldest vessels in the fleet, serving with valor since 1964.

Riding the *Tusty* is truly one of the best bargains in public transportation. The scenery and wildlife are spectacular. You'll pass the perfect cones of several volcanoes, the treeless but lush green mountains of the Aleutians, and distinctive rock formations and cliffs. Whales, sea lions, otters and porpoises are commonly sighted, and birdlife abounds (more than 250 species).

Viewing wildlife and scenery depends, however, on the weather. It can be an extremely rough trip at times, deserving its title 'the cruise through the cradle of the storms.' The smoothest runs are from June to August, while in the fall 40ft waves and 80-knot winds are the norm. That's the reason for the barf bags near the cabins and travel-sickness medication in the vending machines. The tiny bar – three stools, two tables – is called the Pitch and Roll Cocktail Lounge.

Cabins are available (doubles cost $311 each way) and are a worthwhile expense, but book at least three months in advance. Otherwise you can pitch a tent on deck (bring duct tape) or pitch your sleeping bag in the solarium. The *Tusty* has power outlets but no wi-fi or decent cell-phone coverage. The restaurant serves breakfast, lunch and dinner at set times and the food isn't bad. There is also a coffee machine and a vending machine. To save mone,y stock up with your own snacks.

The ferry's stops can vary slightly, but the most common route is (east to west): Homer, Kodiak, Chignik, Sand Point, King Cove, Cold Bay, False Pass, Akutan and Dutch Harbor.

King Cove

At the Alaska Peninsula's western end, near the entrance to Cold Bay, is King Cove, founded in 1911, when a salmon cannery was built. Today, with a population of 756, it is a commercial fishing base and home to Peter Pan Seafoods, whose salmon cannery is the largest operation under one roof in Alaska.

Cold Bay

Cold, treeless and very sparsely populated, Cold Bay is one of the more interesting stops on the *Tustumena* ferry route, primarily because the boat pulls in for a three-hour stopover, long enough to step ashore and get a taste of this desolate land and its off-the-grid community. If you put your name down for the wildlife-tour lottery on the *Tustumena* (and get lucky) you'll enjoy a free guided tour of nearby Izembek National Wildlife Refuge (www.fws.gov/refuge/Izembek) and possibly see a brown bear

The tiny trickle of visitors are of the hunting and fishing persuasion. Bears, waterfowl and ptarmigan are hunted, and salmon is abundant. In summer, the silence is broken when the *Tustumena* pulls in and takes passengers off to the wildlife refuge via the visitor center (☑907-532-2445). The refuge's main viewing point is an interpretive lookout at Grant Point overlooking the Bering Sea.

Cold Bay owes its existence to WWII. In 1942 a massive airstrip was built to deter a possible Japanese invasion. The airstrip remains – the fifth largest in the state – though these days it handles flights to Anchorage plus the odd emergency jumbo landing. Huge brown bears have been known to patrol the airport perimeter fence.

Surprisingly, there are two accommodation options: the Bearfoot Inn (☑907-532-2327; www.bearfootinnalaska.com; Cold Bay; r $75-90), which doubles as a bar and grocery, and the Cold Bay Lodge (☑907-532-2767; www.cblodge.weebly.com; s/d $130/260). It's conceivable to stay for two days in Cold Bay if you're on the MV *Tustumena*, although this means you'll miss out on Dutch Harbor.

ALEUTIAN ISLANDS

Where the Alaska Peninsula ends, the Aleutian Islands begin: a jagged 1100-mile arc that stretches across the north Pacific to within 500 miles of Russia's Kamchatka Peninsula. This is a barren, windswept and violent place, as 27 of the 46 most active volcanoes in the US form islands here.

For most visitors, the Aleutians are limited to three stops aboard the Alaska Marine Highway's MV *Tustumena*.

False Pass

This small but picturesque fishing village (population 46) on the tip of Unimak Island looks across a narrow passage at the Alaska Peninsula. False Pass sits in the shadow of the snowy Roundtop Volcano. There's a basic store at the end of the jetty and (usually) some locals selling jewelry. The *Tustumena* ferry docks for two hours.

Akutan

This community of around 1000 on Akutan Island was founded as a fur-trading post in 1878, but today supports a stalwart group of fish-processing workers and some Aleuts. Its Russian Orthodox Alexander Nevsky Chapel dates from 1918. The *Tustumena* ferry reaches here at 5:30am to pick up a few fishers. Most other passengers stay in their bunks/sleeping bags.

Unalaska & Dutch Harbor

POP 3580

On the road from the ferry terminal to Unalaska and Dutch Harbor, two things catch your eye: concrete pillboxes and crab pots. In a nutshell, that's the story of these twin towns on Unalaska and Amaknak Islands: the pillboxes are a reminder of the islands' violent WWII past, while the crab pots acknowledge the important role of commercial fishing in the towns' future.

Located at the confluence of the Pacific Ocean and the Bering Sea, one of the world's richest fisheries, Dutch Harbor is the only natural deepwater port in the Aleutians. More than 400 vessels call here each year from as many as 14 countries. From this industrialized port of canneries and fish-processing plants, the newly rebuilt Bridge to the Other Side arches over to the residential community of Unalaska.

The area, and Dutch Harbor in particular, shot into the limelight in 2007, when Discovery Channel's *Deadliest Catch* (now in its 10th season) emerged as a popular TV reality show. Each week viewers tune in to watch crab boats and their crews battle four-story-high waves, icy temperatures and paralyzing fatigue, to fill their holds with a gold mine of king crab, before heading back to Dutch Harbor.

Ironically, since the dramatic crash of the king-crab fishery in 1982, it has been pollock, an unglamorous bottom fish, that has been the backbone of Unalaska and Dutch Harbor's economy. Pollock accounts for more than 80% of all seafood processed, and is the reason the towns have been the country's number-one commercial fishing port for the past 20 years. In 2006 Dutch Harbor set a record when 911 million pounds of seafood, at an export value of $165 million, crossed its docks.

During the 1970s Unalaska and Dutch Harbor were Alaska's version of the Wild West, with drinks, money and profanity flowing freely at every bar in town. With the crash of the king crab, the towns became more community-oriented, and with the recent drop of the pollock fishery, residents

are now trying to survive another downturn in the boom-and-bust cycle of fishing.

Unfortunately, short-time visitors returning on the ferry don't have an opportunity to soak in the color and unique character of these towns. To stay longer, you need to splurge on an expensive airline ticket. Those who do discover that a few days in Unalaska and Dutch Harbor can be a refreshing cure from an overdose of RVs, cruise ships and tour buses.

◉ Sights

★ Aleutian WWII National Historic Area   HISTORIC SITE

In 1996 Congress created this 134-acre national historic area to commemorate the bloody events of WWII that took place on the Aleutian Islands.

To learn about the 'Forgotten War,' begin at the **Aleutian WWII Visitor Center** (☑907-581-9944; 2716 Airport Beach Rd; adult/child $4/free; ◷1-6pm Wed-Sat), near the airport, in

Unalaska & Dutch Harbor

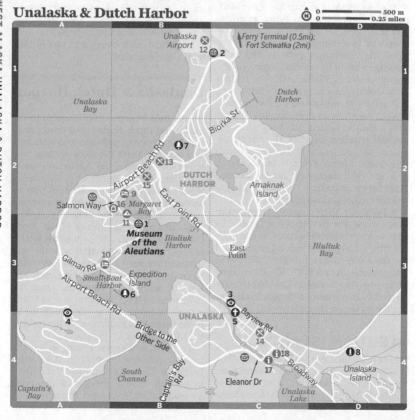

the original air-control tower built in 1942. Downstairs, exhibits relive the Aleutian campaign, including the bombing of Dutch Harbor by the Japanese. Upstairs is the re-created air-control tower, and in a theater you can watch documentaries about the war.

Most of the park preserves **Fort Schwatka**, on Mt Ballyhoo, the highest coastal battery ever constructed in the US. Looming nearly 1000ft above the storm-tossed waters of the Bering Sea, the Army fort encompassed more than 100 concrete observation posts, command stations and other structures built to withstand earthquakes and 100mph winds. The gun mounts here are still among the best preserved in the country, and include tunnels and bunkers that allowed gunners to cart ammunition from one side of the mountain to the other.

The 1634ft mountain of military artifacts is behind the airport and can be reached on foot or by vehicle via Ulakta Rd, picked up half a mile north of the ferry terminal, along Ballyhoo Rd. If you are on foot, it will take you an hour to climb the gravel road to the top, but the views of Unalaska Island on the way up, and on top, are excellent. Pick up the free *Fort Schwatka Self-Guided Tour* brochure at the visitor center.

★**Museum of the Aleutians**　　　　MUSEUM
(☑907-581-5150; www.aleutians.org; 314 Salmon Way; adult/child $7/3; ⊙11am-5pm Tue-Sat, noon-5pm Sun) This small but impressive museum is one of the best native cultural centers in Alaska. It relives the Aleutian story from prehistory through the Russian America period

to WWII and the present. Exhibits are broken into sections on Russian colonization, the WWII evacuation of the Aleuts, the modern fishing industry and – most interesting – displays of the tools, boats and grass baskets that allowed these clever and creative people to live in such a harsh environment.

Church of the Holy Ascension　　　CHURCH
(Broadway) Unalaska is dominated by the Church of the Holy Ascension, the oldest Russian-built church still standing in Alaska. It was built in 1825 and then enlarged in 1894, when its floor plan was changed to a *pekov* (the shape of a crucifix). Overlooking the bay, the church with its onion domes is the town's most haunting symbol. It contains almost 700 pieces of art, ranging from Russian Orthodox icons and books to the largest collection of 19th-century paintings in Alaska.

The best time to view the interior of the church is after services, 6:30pm on Saturday and 11am Sunday.

Outside the church is a small graveyard, where the largest grave marker belongs to Baron Nicholas Zass. Born in 1825 in Archangel, Russia, he eventually became bishop of the Aleutian Islands, and all of Alaska, before his death in 1882. Next door to the graveyard is the **Bishop's House**.

Bunker Hill　　　　HISTORIC SITE
Part of the national historic area, this coastal battery was known to the military as Hill 400, and was fortified with 155mm guns, ammunition magazines, water tanks, 22 Quonset huts and a concrete command post at the

KODIAK, KATMAI & SOUTHWEST ALASKA UNALASKA & DUTCH HARBOR

Unalaska & Dutch Harbor

top. You can easily hike to the peak of Bunker Hill along a gravel road picked up just after crossing the bridge to Amaknak Island.

USS Northwestern Memorial   MONUMENT

In a disheveled hillside graveyard along the bay is the USS *Northwest* memorial named for a 19th-century freight ship turned floating WWII bunkhouse that was destroyed by Japanese bombs in 1942. To get there, follow Bayview Rd to the southeast end of town.

In 1992, for the 50th anniversary of the event, the propeller was salvaged by divers and is now part of the memorial. US and Alaskan flags fly gallantly in the (usually) strong winds.

Sitka Spruce Park   PARK

(Biorka Dr) This national historical landmark within Dutch Harbor is where the Russians planted Sitka spruce in 1805. It's the oldest recorded afforestation project in North America. Three of the gnarly spruce are said to be the originals. The park also features interpretive displays and a short trail to an edge-of-the-cliff overlook.

Expedition Park   PARK

(off Gilman Rd) Bald eagles are as common as crows in and around Unalaska and Dutch Harbor. There are so many birds that locals view them as scavengers, which they are by nature, rather than the majestic symbol of the USA. One of the best places to photograph them up close and in a somewhat natural setting is Expedition Park, at the end of Bobby Storrs Boat Harbor.

🏃 Activities

Hiking

Because of the treeless environment, hiking is easy here. And don't worry about bears – there aren't any. Before hiking anywhere, even Mt Ballyhoo or Bunker Hill, you must obtain a permit (per person $6 daily, $15 weekly) from the **Ounalashka Corporation** (📞 907-581-1276; www.ounalashka.com; 400 Salmon Way; ⊙ 8am-5pm Mon-Fri). Also call Unalaska's **Parks, Culture & Recreation Department** (PCR; 📞 907-581-1297; 37 S 5th St; ⊙ 6am-10pm Mon-Fri, 8am-10pm Sat, noon-7pm Sun), which organizes hikes in summer for locals and visitors.

Uniktali Bay   HIKING

There are few developed trails, but an enjoyable day can be spent hiking to Uniktali Bay, a round-trip of 8 to 10 miles.

From Captain's Bay Rd, turn east on a gravel road just before Westward Cannery. Follow the road for a mile to its end; a foot trail continues along a stream. In 2 miles, the trail runs out, and you'll reach a lake in a pass between two 2000ft peaks. Continue southeast to pick up a second stream, which empties into Uniktali Bay. The bay is undeveloped, and a great place to look for glass floats washed ashore from Japanese fishing nets.

Ugadaga Bay Trail   HIKING

On the southeast side of Unalaska, this pleasant hike is 2.2 miles one-way along an ancient portage route. More recently, the US military ran communications lines from Unalaska all the way to Seattle, and you'll see remnants of it in eroded spots. Seal hunters were using the portage as late as the 1960s.

Paddling

The many protected harbors, bays and islets of Unalaska Island make for ideal sea-kayaking conditions. The scenery is stunning and the wildlife plentiful. It is possible to encounter Steller's sea lions, sea otters and harbor porpoises.

Aleutian Adventure Sports   ADVENTURE SPORTS

(📞 907-581-4489;   www.aleutianadventure.com) Has kayak rentals for $69 and $89 per day for single and double kayaks respectively, as well as an introductory kayak class for $75. It also offers guided trips.

👉 Tours

If you're planning to return with the ferry, a van tour is the best way to see a lot in your short stay. Book in advance if you can.

Extra Mile Tours   GUIDED TOUR

(📞 907-581-1859;   www.unalaskadutchharbortour. com; 2/4hr tour $50/90) Operator Bobbie Lekanoff is very knowledgeable in indigenous and WWII history, and knows every single flower and bird.

🛏 Sleeping

On top of prices listed there's an 8% hotel tax.

Ounalashka Corporation   CAMPGROUND $

(📞 907-581-1276; www.ounalashka.com; 400 Salmon Way; permits daily/weekly per person $6/15) This native corporation owns most of the land out of town and allows camping if you obtain a permit.

Grand Aleutian Hotel   HOTEL $$

(📞 907-581-3844, 866-581-3844; www.grandaleutian.com; 498 Salmon Way; r $164-184, ste $254;

☎) Updated rooms with memory-foam mattresses appeal to TV crews and travelers on a loose budget. The grand views from every window help make up for the slightly utilitarian – if new and clean – digs. Aside from the rougher Harbor View Inn it's your only option. Book ahead!

Harbor View Inn MOTEL $$

(☑907-581-3844; 88 Salmon Way; s/d $99/110) Affiliated with the Grand Aleutian Hotel, this basic 30-room inn is between a shipyard and a fish-processing plant. The smell of cigarette smoke competes with the pong of fish, and the bar downstairs is noisy. Grin and bear it – it's the only budget option in town.

Eating

There are 10 places to eat in Unalaska and Dutch Harbor, two in supermarkets, five affiliated to the Grand Aleutian Hotel and one at the airport. The only two truly indie places are Amelia's and Dutch Harbor Fast Food.

Dutch Harbor Fast Food ASIAN $

(☑907-581-5966; 3rd St & Broadway Ave; mains $10-12; ⊙11am-10pm Mon-Sat, to 6pm Sun) Don't let the name fool you: this is a sit-down place serving great Asian staples such as chow mein, fried rice and pho. The pad thai comes in a pile the size of your face and is highly recommended.

KODIAK, KATMAI & SOUTHWEST ALASKA UNALASKA & DUTCH HARBOR

THE FORGOTTEN WAR

The image of the world's most powerful nation reeling under the occupation of a belligerent foreign power probably sounds like the plot of a Hollywood disaster movie involving aliens. Yet, this seemingly unthinkable scenario actually took place (minus the aliens) in 1942, when the Imperial Japanese Army invaded the islands of Attu and Kiska in the US territory of Alaska. The Japanese occupied the two tiny islands on the westernmost tip of Alaska's Aleutian archipelago for an uncomfortable 13 months in a little remembered chapter of WWII dubbed the Aleutian Campaign or the 'Forgotten War'. It cost more than 3000 lives.

Views vary about the Japanese military's motives. Their Aleutians Islands campaign began when they bombed Dutch Harbor on Unalaska Island on June 3 and 4, 1942 to soften up US defenses for a largely uncontested seaborne invasion of Attu and Kiska two days later. Some claim it was to deflect US attention away from the ongoing Battle of the Midway; others reason that it was primarily a defensive measure designed to protect Japan's northern coastline.

At the time, undefended Attu, which lies more than 1000 miles west of the Alaskan mainland, supported a small population of 54 native Aleutians, all of whom were captured and promptly shipped off to prison camps in Japan. Located 200 miles to the southeast, Kiska was uninhabited, save for 10 American military personnel working at a remote navy weather station. Faced with a well-armed contingent of 1250 Japanese invaders, the US weather monitors didn't stand a chance. Nine of the soldiers were quickly captured and taken prisoner. The 10th, Petty Officer William C House, employing a superhuman level of bravery and tenacity, managed to hold out for nearly two months in the island's bleak, rain-lashed interior, living in caves and feeding on worms and grass. He finally emerged, emaciated and on the verge of starvation, 50 days later. Despite being taken prisoner, House survived the war and served with distinction in the US Navy until 1966.

As the tide in the war began to turn in America's favor in 1943, plans to retake Attu and Kiska were secretly hatched. Attu was ultimately taken back by a 15,000-strong US invasion force in May 1943 after two weeks of heavy hand-to-hand fighting with Japanese troops bent on gyokusai (honorable suicide). Of Attu's 2500 occupying Japanese soldiers, only 29 were taken alive.

Kiska was a different proposition. A wary force of 35,000 US and Canadian soldiers landed on the island on August 15, but were met with no resistance. The Japanese army, realizing the uselessness of another costly rearguard action, had secretly evacuated the island two weeks previously. Jumpy and hampered by fog, it took the American-Canadian force eight days to fully ascertain that the island was empty. In the interim, 300 soldiers died from cold, disease and 'friendly fire'.

Attu and Kiska remain uninhabited today with no regular flights or boat connections. For war memorabilia you will find more accessible memorials in Dutch Harbor's Aleutian WWII National Historic Area (p347) and Kodiak's Fort Abercrombie State Historical Park (p331).

Safeway
SUPERMARKET $

(2029 Airport Beach Rd; sandwiches $6-8; ⊘ 7am-11pm) As is often the case in the more remote parts of Alaska, the local Safeway is a passable place to grab a coffee and sandwich.

Amelia's
MEXICAN $$

(☑ 907-581-2800; Airport Beach Rd; breakfast $7-13, dinner $14-29; ⊘ 7am-10pm) This Dutch Harbor restaurant does a little of everything, from breakfast and burgers to seafood and pasta, but the majority of its menu is Mexican, including almost a dozen types of burritos. Amazingly, none of them is stuffed with crab or halibut.

Harbor View Bar & Grill
PIZZA $$

(☑907-581-7246; 88 Salmon Way; pizza $16-30; ⊘11:30am-1am Mon-Thu, 11:30am-2am Fri & Sat, noon-10pm Sun) At the eponymous inn, this place has pizza, salads, pasta and burgers. Attached is **Harbor Sushi** (⊘5-10:30pm Mon-Sat, to 9:30pm Sun), the best sushi in a town that knows its seafood. The rocking bar is the best place to meet a proud extra from the early seasons of *Deadliest Catch* (the reason for its local nickname, the 'Unisleaze').

Airport Restaurant
ASIAN $$

(breakfast & lunch $9-14, dinner $15-27; ⊘9am-11pm) A godsend of a restaurant located at an airport notorious for bad weather. Better than the usual franchise food, it does American staples along with some excellent Vietnamese dishes: try the Airport Surf – a *banh mi* (Vietnamese sandwich) in disguise. The bar is open late.

Chart Room
SEAFOOD $$$

(☑907-581-7120; 498 Salmon Way; mains $22-40; ⊘6-11pm Mon-Sat, 10am-2pm, 6-9:30pm Sun) The swankiest restaurant in Dutch Harbor and, by definition, the Aleutian Islands, the Chart Room has more meat than seafood on its menu. It's best known for its weekend buffet brunch spread ($25), which includes king-crab legs, made-to-order omelets and chocolate-dipped strawberries. Otherwise try the local halibut, salmon, shrimp and king crab, and great sushi.

Drinking

Cape Cheerful Lounge
BAR

(498 Salmon Way; ⊘3pm-midnight Mon-Sat, noon-10pm Sun) The Grand Aleutian Hotel bar is more refined than the Harbor View and when the sun is out drinkers move to an outdoor deck. The good pub-grub menu includes sliders and barbecued meals ($12 to $18).

Shopping

Alaska Ship Supply
SOUVENIRS

(☑907-581-1284; www.alaskashipsupply.com; 487 Salmon Way; ⊘7am-10pm) Like a remote outpost of Costco with a few unique extras. The *Deadliest Catch* hoodies make a good 'only in Dutch Harbor' souvenir. If you're not after fishing-trawler fashion, stock up on groceries or drop by the espresso cafe.

ⓘ Information

Iliuliuk Family & Health Clinic (☑907-581-1202; 34 LaVelle Ct; ⊘walk-in 8:30am-6pm Mon-Fri, to 1pm Sat) Just off Airport Beach Rd near Unalaska City Hall; has a walk-in and 24-hour emergency service.

Key Bank of Alaska (☑907-581-1233; 100 Salmon Way) Across from the Grand Aleutian Hotel in Dutch Harbor; has a 24-hour ATM.

Post Office Unalaska (82 Airport Beach Rd); Dutch Harbor (Airport Beach Rd) The Dutch Harbor post office is near the Grand Aleutian Hotel.

Unalaska/Port of Dutch Harbor Convention & Visitors Bureau (☑907-581-2612, 877-581-2612; www.unalaska.info; cnr 5th & Broadway, Unalaska; ⊘8am-5pm Mon-Fri, 10am-3pm Sat) Located in the Burma Street Russian Church, originally a military chapel built during WWII. Also opens when the ferry is in.

ⓘ Getting There & Around

The MV *Tustumena* from Homer ($351) and Kodiak ($293) calls at Dutch Harbor twice monthly between May and September. The **ferry terminal** is approximately 3 miles north of Unalaska off Ballyhoo Rd. It stops in town for eight hours before returning east.

The only other way to get out of town is by air. It's serviced by **PenAir** (☑800-448-4226; www.penair.com) but you book the ticket through **Alaska Airlines** (☑800-252-7522; www.alaskaair.com). There are three to four flights daily and a one-way ticket is $500 to $600. Beware: Dutch Harbor's notoriously fickle weather can delay flights, hence PenAir's local nickname 'When Air?' The airport is on Amaknak Island.

A cab to downtown Unalaska costs $10 to $12 from the airport, or $14 to $16 from the ferry. There are cabs all over Unalaska and Dutch Harbor, including **Aleutian Taxi** (☑907-581-1866). There's a long list in the airport terminal.

To get out and see the island by car, look no further than **North Port Car Rental** (☑907-581-3880), which is located at the airport and has vehicles from around $75 a day. A mountain bike is another way to get around as the extensive, lightly used dirt roads left over from the WWII buildup make for great riding. You can hire a mountain bike from Aleutian Adventure Sports (p348) for $40/120 per day/week.

The Bush

Best Protected Wilderness Areas

➜ Gates of the Arctic National Park & Preserve (p364)

➜ Arctic National Wildlife Refuge (p360)

➜ Kobuk Valley National Park (p364)

➜ Bering Land Bridge National Preserve (p358)

Best Places for Birdwatching

➜ Nome (p353)

➜ St Lawrence Island (p369)

➜ Bering Land Bridge National Preserve (p358)

➜ Barrow (p368)

Why Go?

In a state where unbounded wilderness is the norm, the Bush is like the frontier on the frontier. Towns and townly comforts are few, roads are fewer, and most of the region is accessible only by flying, floating or walking in. Yes, it takes effort to reach the ends of the earth, but the rewards are equal to the task.

In western Alaska, you can head out on extended hikes or wilderness paddles, swagger through Nome's gold-rush saloons or fly into isolated Native villages to meet the people who thrive year-round in this formidable landscape. In Arctic Alaska, explore the mythical vastness of preserves like Gates of the Arctic National Park and the Arctic National Wildlife Refuge. Here the mandate is 'self-discovery,' which may be as much about teaching us our physical limits as about our puny insignificance in the grand scale of nature.

When to Go

Nome

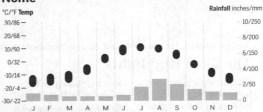

Mar The Iditarod, the world's most famous dogsled race, concludes in Nome.

Jun Barrow Iñupiat celebrate the Nalukataq Festival after the spring's whale harvest.

Jun–Aug Enjoy 24-hour sunlight above the Arctic Circle.

History

The history of the Bush is largely the history of Alaska Natives. By their own accounts, they've been here since the beginning. Archaeologists say it's not been as long as that: perhaps 6000 years for the ancestors of today's Athabascans, and about 3000 years for the Iñupiat, Yupiks and Aleuts. Either way, they've displayed remarkable ingenuity and endurance, thriving as fishers, hunters and gatherers in an environment few else could even survive in.

Europeans arrived in Alaska in the 1800s, with traders and missionaries setting up shop in numerous communities along the western coast. Whalers entered the Bering Sea around the middle of the century, and soon expanded into the Arctic Ocean. By 1912 they had virtually decimated the bowhead whale population.

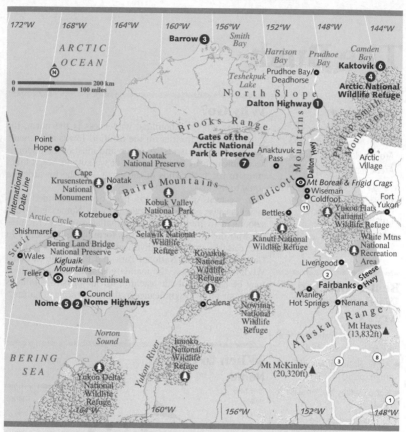

The Bush Highlights

❶ Traveling up the famed **Dalton Highway** (p360), aka the Haul Rd, to the edge of the world

❷ Exploring the **Nome highways** (p358) for stunning Arctic scenery and endless hiking and camping opportunities

❸ Watching the midnight sun in **Barrow** (p368) in June and staying for the Nalukataq Festival

❹ Following caribou herds on a backcountry excursion inside the **Arctic National Wildlife Refuge** (p360)

❺ Exploring gold-rush history on the beaches, streets and bleak tundra of **Nome** (p353)

❻ Watching polar bears outside the tiny Arctic village of **Kaktovik** (p360)

❼ Entering the almost virgin **Gates of the Arctic National Park & Preserve** (p364) and making your own path across this unblemished wilderness

The most climactic event in the Bush, however, was the gold rush at Nome, triggered in 1898 (just two years after the discovery of gold in the Klondike) by the 'Three Lucky Swedes.' The stampede drew as many as 20,000 fortune chasers across to the Seward Peninsula, giving the region, ever so briefly, the most populous town in Alaska. Even today Nome remains the only significant non-Native community in the Bush.

Throughout the 20th century, progress in transportation, communications and social services transformed the remote region. 'Bush planes' made the area relatively accessible, and towns like Barrow, Kotzebue, Nome and Bethel became commercial hubs, in turn bringing services to the smaller villages in their orbit. Political and legal battles resulted in more schools and better health care, while the 1971 *Alaska Native Claims Settlement Act* turned villages into corporations and villagers into shareholders. Today, anywhere you go in the Bush you'll find residents engaged in a fine balancing act – coping with the challenges of the 21st century, while at the same time struggling to keep alive the values, practices and links to the land that they've passed down through countless generations and maintained for millennia.

ⓘ Getting There & Around

The Bush is, almost by definition, road-less. You can drive (or get a shuttle bus) up the Dalton Hwy to Deadhorse, and around Nome on an insular road network reaching out to a few surrounding destinations, but everywhere else it's fly-in only.

Alaska Airlines and Ravn Alaska are the main carriers, with Nome, Kotzebue and Barrow the main hubs. Regional airlines fly to smaller villages and provide air-taxi services into the wilderness.

WESTERN ALASKA

Western Alaska is home to Iñupiat, intrepid prospectors and some of the state's least-seen landscapes. Too far north (and too close to the Arctic Ocean and Bering Sea) for trees, the terrain is instead carpeted with coral-like tundra grasses and flowers, and patrolled by herds of caribou and musk ox. Highlights of the area include regional hubs like Nome and Kotzebue, and the vast tracts of little-explored wilderness in the Noatak and Bering Land Bridge National Preserves.

Nome
POP 3505

Warning: Your first sight of Nome could be decidedly underwhelming. Huddled on the ice-encrusted shores of the Bering Strait and inhabiting one of the wildest and most westerly parts of mainland America, this hard-bitten grid of unkempt houses and unpaved road,s backed by snow-speckled expanses of bleak tundra, isn't quite the boomtown it was in 1900.

Nome owes its existence to three 'lucky' Swedes who scooped up the first nuggets of a bonanza of easily extractable gold at Anvil Creek in 1898, hot on the heels of Klondike.

Thanks to fires, storms and the corrosive effects of the Bering Strait weather, few of Nome's gold-rush-era buildings remain, though a detectable Wild West spirit still haunts the town's downbeat bars and gritty streets, where rattling trucks kick up mini-tornadoes of choking dust.

Amazingly, gold can still be mined in Nome and the town continues to attract the odd recreational prospector as it once attracted Wyatt Earp. Otherwise most of the 8000 or so annual visitors are what you might call untypical vacationers. Some come for esoteric but rewarding birdwatching opportunities, while the bulk fly in to witness the final lap of the epic Iditarod dogsled race that wraps up here in March.

Whatever your reason for visiting, you can kill a surreal day or two hiking across the unforgiving tundra, or warming up in several well-worn bars where locals compare gun calibers, and mullets have never gone out of fashion.

Disconnected from the main Alaskan road grid, Nome has three insular roads, all of which dead-end in the icy tundra just below the Arctic Circle. Anchorage lies 537 crow-flying miles to the southeast, while Siberian Russia bristles a mere 160 miles across the Bering Strait. You can almost taste the vodka.

◉ Sights

Drop by the Nome Visitor Center for information on the various gold-rush-era buildings still standing in the downtown area. And, while wandering about, be on the lookout for dredge buckets. During Nome's golden heyday there were more than 100 dredges in use, each employing hundreds of buckets to scoop up gravel and dirt. Today

Nome

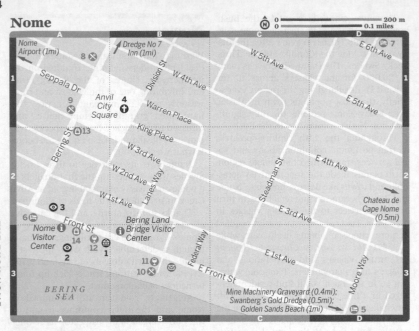

Nome

⊙ Sights
1 Carrie McLain Museum.........................A3
2 Donald Perkins Memorial Plaza..........A3
3 Iditarod Finish-Line Arch.....................A2
4 St Joseph Church.................................B1

🛏 Sleeping
5 Aurora Inn...D3
6 Nome Nugget Inn..................................A2
7 Nome Recreation Center......................D1

⊗ Eating
8 Airport Pizza...A1
9 Pingo Bakery...A1
10 Polar Café...B3

🍸 Drinking & Nightlife
11 Board of Trade Saloon.........................B3
12 Breaker's Bar..A3

🛍 Shopping
13 Chukotka Alaska...................................A2
14 Maruskiya's of Nome............................A3

you'll see the buckets all over town, many used as giant flowerpots.

Golden Sands Beach   BEACH
Sand zero, so to speak, of Nome's famed gold rush, this beach is still open to recreational mining and all summer long you can watch

miners set up work camps along the shore. Some will pan or open a sluice box right on the beach, while the more serious rig a sluice and dredging equipment onto a small pontoon boat and anchor it 100yd offshore.

From this Rube Goldberg machine–like contraption they will spend up to four hours underwater in wet suits (pumped with hot air from the engine), essentially vacuuming the ocean floor. Miners are generally friendly, and occasionally you can even coax one to show you their gold dust and nuggets. If you catch the fever, practically every gift shop and hardware store in town sells black-plastic gold pans. As you're panning, think about the visitor who, while simply beachcombing in 1984, found, at the eastern end of the seawall, a 3.5in nugget that weighed 1.29oz, and remember that gold's now worth well over $1300 per ounce.

The beach stretches a mile east of town along Front St. At the height of summer, a few local children may be seen playing in the 45°F (7°C) water, and on Memorial Day (in May), more than 100 masochistic residents plunge into the ice-choked waters for the annual **Polar Bear Swim**.

Across from the beach, just past the Tesoro Gas Station, sits a **Mine Machinery Graveyard**. With no roads connecting

Nome to the rest of the world, once a piece of equipment makes the barge-ride here, it stays until it turns to dust.

Swanberg's Gold Dredge LANDMARK
One mile east of the town, and fronting the beach, is this poignantly abandoned gold dredge that was in operation until the 1950s. A boardwalk with various interpretative signs traverses the tundra to allow a close-up look. In the evening herds of musk ox can sometimes be seen in the nearby fields.

Carrie McLain Museum MUSEUM
(223 Front St; ⊙1-5pm Tue-Sat) **FREE** It's amazing how much information you can stuff into a very small space. Bivouacked in the basement of the Kegoayah Kozga Public Library, Nome's small museum does a commendable job of showcasing the surprisingly interesting history of this isolated town. There are some Native culture displays, but the focus is on the gold rush and Nome's history in the early 20th century.

Among racks of mining equipment, historical documents and photo albums, you can see the preserved body of Fritz the sled dog, one of the leaders of the famed 1925 race to deliver diphtheria serum to Nome (the inspiration for the annual Iditarod dogsled race).

St Joseph Church CHURCH
(Anvil City Sq) Built in 1901, when there were 20,000 people living in Nome, this church and its spire was located on Front St and used as a beacon for seamen. By the 1920s, after the population of the city had plummeted to less than 900, the Jesuits abandoned the structure. It was used for storage by a mining company until 1996, when the city purchased and moved it to Anvil City Sq.

In the grassy square fronting the church, look for statues of the Three Lucky Swedes, dredge buckets and the 'world's largest gold pan.'

Iditarod Finish-Line Arch LANDMARK
This imposing structure, a distinctly bent pine tree with burls, is raised over Front St every March in anticipation of the mushers and their dogsled teams ending the 1049-mile race here.

Donald Perkins Memorial Plaza PLAZA
Next to the Nome Visitor Center is this plaza, containing a collection of old mining detritus.

🏃 Activities
If you're well prepared and the weather holds, the backcountry surrounding Nome can be **hiking** heaven. Though there are no marked trails in the region, the area's three highways offer perfect access into the tundra and mountains. What's more, the lack of trees and big, rolling topography make route-finding fairly simple: just pick a point and go for it. For those who'd like a little more direction, a multipage list of suggested day hikes is available from the Nome Visitor Center.

Also providing great info on local trekking is the Bering Land Bridge Visitor Center. Every second Saturday during the summer the center leads very popular and free **guided day hikes** as well as **birding tours** in May and June. Contact the center for exact times and dates.

Anvil Mountain HIKE
The climb up 1062ft Anvil Mountain is the closest hike to Nome and the only one that can be easily pulled off without a car. To start, follow Bering St out of town to where it changes to the Teller Hwy. About 2.5 miles down the Teller Hwy turn right on the Dexter Bypass and look for an obvious dirt road, about half a mile in, climbing up the hillside.

It's about a half mile to the summit, through wonderful wildflower patches. At the top you'll find the giant parabolic antennae of the Cold War–era **White Alice Communications System**, plus great views of town and the ocean, as well as the odd passing musk ox.

☞ Tours
The visitor center can hook you up with operators for fishing, hunting and dogsled rides, as well as snowcat and snowmobile tours in season.

Bering Air SCENIC FLIGHTS
(📱443-5464; www.beringair.com; tours per person $250) Offers 90-minute helicopter tours of the area (two person minimum).

Nome Discovery Tours TOUR
(📱443-2814; tours $65-185) Nome's most intimate, highly recommended tours are run by Richard Beneville, an old song-and-dance man who decided to hang up his tap shoes to live out in the Alaska wilds. He offers everything from two-hour tundra exploration drives to full-day excursions to Teller, during which you'll drop in on an Iñupiat family, or to Council, with fishing along the way.

THE BUSH NOME

Akau Alaska Gold & Resort TOUR
(☎866-431-8541; www.akaugold.com; Old Glacier Creek Rd) This 'resort' offers gold panning, sluicing and metal-detecting trips (from $150) and tours of old gold-rush-era ruins and machinery. It can throw in accommodations and meal packages if you wish to stay in the lodge and cabins; these are 7 miles outside Nome on Old Glacier Creek Rd, which branches off the Nome–Teller Rd. You get to keep any gold nuggets you might unearth.

Wilderness Birding Adventures BIRDWATCHING
(☎694-7442; www.wildernessbirding.com) This well-regarded Alaskan-run company offers small group birding trips around Nome in June and November. A highlight is a search for the beach-nesting McKay's bunting, which breeds in the Bering Strait. Check the website for dates and pricing.

🛏 Sleeping

You can camp like a gold-rush miner for free on Golden Sands Beach, but do so a bit down the beach as the street sweepers dump debris here daily. Showers ($5) are available at the **Nome Recreation Center** (208 E 6th Ave; ⊙5:30am-10pm Mon-Fri). Further from town it's unofficially permissible to camp just about anywhere: simply hike away from the road corridor, avoid private property and active mining claims, and clean up after yourself. About 40 miles north of town, there is also the lovely, free Salmon Lake Campground (p359), run by the Bureau of Land Management (BLM).

Nome tacks on 11% bed and sales taxes to its accommodations prices. Book rooms well in advance in summer and up to a year before Iditarod.

THE BUSH NOME

NOME: KLONDIKE'S SEQUEL

Type the words 'Alaska' and 'gold rush' into an internet search engine and your first result will probably contain the word 'Klondike.' There's just one small problem: Klondike is in the Yukon Territory in Canada. Its erroneous listing as an Alaskan gold rush came about because of the key role Alaska played as a supply center and point of embarkation for thousands of American 'stampeders' heading north in 1897.

The first true Alaskan gold rush ignited near present-day Nome in 1898 when three Swedish prospectors (the 'Three Lucky Swedes,' as they became known), blown off course in a small boat, discovered gold deposits in a river called Anvil Creek near Cape Nome. Coming so soon after the mania in the Yukon and giving fresh wind to many of the disgruntled and semi-destitute stampeders, Nome acted as Klondike's frenzied sequel, a kind of *Godfather Part II* with an equally colorful cast of despicable characters.

Nome's rise was meteoric. By 1899 when gold was discovered on Nome's beaches, Klondike's stampeders were leaving Dawson City in their droves to descend on the region. The nascent city, which hadn't even existed two years previously, briefly morphed into the largest in Alaska with over 20,000 hardy souls squeezed into makeshift wooden buildings or saggy canvas tents on the beach. Rather like Klondike, Nome attracted an abnormally high number of unsavory characters, including US lawman and veteran of the Gunfight at the OK Corral, Wyatt Earp, who set up and ran the profitable Dexter Saloon in town, a bar that allegedly doubled as a brothel.

The beauty of Nome's gold was that it was easily extractable. As much of it lay deposited on the beach, you didn't need heavy-duty dredging equipment to retrieve it, although dredges were often used. With seasonal sea access via steamship, the region was easier to reach than Klondike and thus attracted its fair share of chancers, no-hopers and blatant criminals. Within months of the strike, the fledgling settlement, in contrast to the relatively law-abiding Dawson City (well-policed by the Canadian Mounties), was filled with debauchery. Hold-ups, gambling, prostitution, fist-fights, drunkenness and robbery became endemic.

'Drunken gamblers groveled in the dust; women, shameless scarlet women of exceedingly grotesque character but universally décolleté, reveled as recklessly as their tipsy companions,' wrote prudish new arrival Sara Fell in 1900.

The frenzy of Nome had died by about 1905 and the town quickly reinvented itself as a small but stable settlement, known since 1972 as the end-point for the Iditarod dogsled race. It wasn't Alaska's last gold rush. Fairbanks hit the jackpot in 1902 but it never reached the heights of Nome and its brief flirtation with notoriety.

★ **Dredge No 7 Inn**   B&B $$
(☑ 304-1270; www.dredge7inn.com; 1700 Teller Hwy; ste incl breakfast $145-155; 🖥) A cozy apparition in the unashamedly basic confines of Nome, Dredge No 7 is a modern inn that strikes a nice balance between rustic charm and some fine Martha Stewart–inspired flourishes. Thirteen bright private suites share a spacious kitchen and common areas decked out with leather sofas and fireplace, and breakfast items are left in your room.

The inn is about a mile north of town on a large lot with open views across the tundra from the back deck. It also has a new annex, the **Sluicebox** (☑ 304-1270; 608 East D St; ste $155), in town.

Solomon Bed & Breakfast   B&B $$
(☑ 443-2403; www.solomonbnb.com; s/d with breakfast $150/160; 🖥) ✔ Is Nome not remote enough for you? Then head 34 miles down Kougarok Rd to this guesthouse run by the Village of Solomon, a federally recognized Native tribe. Inside a converted historic schoolhouse (built in 1939) you'll find four guest rooms, each with private bath and patio overlooking the tundra. Meals are available at an extra cost, and canoes and kayaks by request. The Last Train to Nowhere (p359) is just down the road and there's good fishing nearby. Airport pickups offered.

Chateau de Cape Nome   B&B $$
(☑ 443-2083; cussy@nome.net; 1105 E 4th Ave; r from $115) Overlooking the tundra and the Bering Sea on the far eastern edge of town is another excellent inn run by a descendant of gold-rush-era pioneers. Owner 'Cussy' Kauer and her homestay are troves of local history, and the B&B is just a short walk from Golden Sands Beach. Try to get a room with a view.

Nome Nugget Inn   HOTEL $$
(☑ 443-4189; www.nomenuggetinnhotel.com; 315 Front St; r $110-120; 🖥) In the thick of what passes for downtown, the slightly disheveled Nugget has 45 smallish rooms, about half with ocean views. The clapboard front and memorabilia-laden lobby promise much, but the rooms are compact and characterless – think cheap motel. The best part of the interior is the old saloon with views of the Bering Sea, now an exclusive sitting room for guests.

Coffee is available in the lobby.

Aurora Inn   HOTEL $$
(☑ 443-3838; www.aurorainnome.com; 302 Front St; d $175; 🖥) Nome's most hotel-like accommodations are at the far edge of town, and just a short walk to Golden Sands Beach. The neat and tidy Aurora offers generic-style comfort in simple no-surprises rooms, some with full kitchenettes.

✖ Eating

There are almost a dozen places to eat in Nome, mostly sit-down restaurants offering that odd Arctic mix of pizza, Chinese and American-style grub.

Opening hours are sometimes casual, with businesses displaying cryptic signs like 'open most days about 9am or 10am, occasionally as early as 7am; some days we aren't here at all.' You have been warned.

★ **Pingo Bakery**   BAKERY, CAFE $
(☑ 387-0654; 308 Bering St; breakfast $10; ⊙ 11:30am-3pm & 5:30-8pm Wed-Fri, 7:30am-3pm & 5:30-8pm Sat, 7:30am-5pm Sun) For Pingo shout 'bingo!', especially if you arrive on a day when this precious three-table cafe is open. Best way to find out? Follow your nose. You'll catch the heady aroma of freshly baked cinnamon buns long before you see the flashing neon sign. Snack-seekers grab the croissants, cookies and big buns. Larger appetites tackle the roasted halibut pizza.

Airport Pizza   PIZZA, AMERICAN $$
(☑ 443-7992; 406 Bering St; pizzas $15-34; ⊙ 7am-11pm; 🖥🍴) The inaptly named Airport Pizza is not at the airport and sells far more than just pizza. No matter. Nome's most popular restaurant (vociferously recommended by locals) is where you'll bump into practically everyone you met on the plane from Anchorage the previous day. Thick pizzas headline the menu but it also does good steaks, burgers, desserts and draft beers. Reliable wi-fi too.

Polar Café   AMERICAN $$
(☑ 443-5191; 204 Front St; mains $19-28; ⊙ 6am-10pm; 🖥) This popular waterfront eatery serves straightforward food that hits the spot – at least in Nome. As a bonus it has open views of the Bering Sea, friendly service and a $10 salad bar.

🍺 Drinking

Even by Alaskan standards, drinking in Nome is legendary. There are more saloons here than in the rest of Bush Alaska combined, which unfortunately means drunks wandering the streets, sometimes from morning till night. Most bars are clustered around Front St and can be classified as 'dives.'

Breaker's Bar BAR
(243 Front St; ⊙10am-midnight) Dive in with the beards and the baseball caps and listen to Nomers discuss gun preferences and tussles with local grizzly bears. The decor's retro without even realizing it and the floor smells like 1973. Pool shooters play 'winner stays on' out back.

Board of Trade Saloon BAR
(212 Front St; ⊙10am-2am) Dating back to the callow years of the gold rush, this saloon claims to be the oldest on the Bering Sea and was (is?) certainly the most notorious. Call it behind the times, but it still had its Halloween decorations up at last visit – in May!

Shopping

Chukotka Alaska ARTS & CRAFTS
(309 Bering St; ⊙11am-11pm) Sells indigenous crafts and has a good book collection. The friendly owner will talk your ear off if you give him the chance.

Maruskiya's of Nome ACCESSORIES, CRAFT
(Front St; ⊙9am-5pm Mon-Sat) *The* place to go for your 'There's No Place Like Nome' T-shirt.

Information

Bering Land Bridge Visitor Center (www.nps.gov/bela; 179 Front St; ⊙8am-5pm Mon-Fri, 9am-3pm Sat) In the Sitnasuak Native Corporation building, this National Park Service (NPS) center represents the Bering Land Bridge National Preserve near Nome, a fly-in-only park good for birdwatching, hunting and hot springs. Inside are displays on mammoths, early Alaska Native culture and reindeer herding, plus info on the preserve.

Nome Visitor Center (443-6624; www.visitnomealaska.com; 301 Front St; ⊙8am-7pm Mon-Fri, 10am-6pm Sat & Sun) Make this your first stop in Nome: the extremely helpful staff will load you up with brochures, advice and coffee.

Wells Fargo (109a Front St) In the historic Miner's and Merchant's Bank building (dating from 1904); has a 24-hour ATM.

Getting There & Around

Nome is well served by **Alaska Airlines** (800-252-7522; www.alaskaair.com), which offers at least two daily flights to Anchorage for $500 to $600 round-trip (book well in advance). Most flights take roughly 90 minutes, but some through Kotzebue can take literally half a day with waits and transfers. Check ahead.

Nome's tiny airport is a little more than a mile from town. It's an easy walk or catch a cab for $6 per person. Try **Mr Kab** (443-6000).

If renting a vehicle, book well ahead of time. **Stampede Rent-A-Car** (443-3838; 302 Front St; vehicles per day $100-160) is at the Aurora Inn and offers SUVs, vans and pickups. Dredge No 7 Inn also rents out trucks for $100 a day. Both offer unlimited miles. When budgeting for a rental, keep in mind that gas in Nome is expensive and your vehicle likely won't get good mileage.

Hitchhiking is possible and locals are really good about picking people up. But you must be patient – and willing to sit in the back of an open pickup on very dusty roads. Hitchhiking is never completely safe anywhere, and travelers who decide to hitch should be aware that they are taking a potentially serious risk.

Around Nome

Radiating east, north and northwest from Nome are its finest features: three gravel roads, each offering passage into a land of sweeping tundra, crystal-clear rivers and rugged mountains. Along the way you'll find some of the best chances in Alaska to see waterfowl, caribou, bears and musk oxen. But be prepared: there's no gas and few other services along Nome's highways; instead, you'll encounter road-shrouding dust, rocks and narrow elevated sections of road that can easily dump you into a marsh. Going slow is key. Take twice as long as you would on pavement.

Nome–Council Road

This 73-mile route, which heads northeast to the old mining village of Council, is perhaps the best excursion if you have time for only one of Nome's roads. For the first 30 miles it hugs the glimmering Bering Sea coastline and passes a motley, but very photogenic, array of shacks, cabins, tepees and Quonset huts used by Nome residents as summer cottages and fishing and hunting camps. Natives have hunted and fished in this area for millennia, and the many depressions dotting the landscape are the sites of former camps.

On sunny days, the miles of beaches outside Nome beckon – but note how far inland autumn storms have tossed driftwood. At Mile 22 the road passes Safety Roadhouse, a dollar-bill-bedecked dive of a watering hole, and then crosses the birders' wonderland of Safety Sound, which once formed the eastern edge of the Bering Land Bridge. Ten miles further along is Bonanza Crossing, on the far side of which is the Last Train to Nowhere, a series of abandoned locomotives. Just to the north is the ghost town of Solomon, which

THE LAST TRAIN TO NOWHERE

In all of Bush Alaska, it's almost certainly the most-photographed landmark: a set of steam locomotives, utterly out of place and out of time, moldering on the Arctic tundra off the Nome–Council Rd, hundreds of miles from the nearest functioning railway. Dubbed the 'Last Train to Nowhere,' the three engines first plied the elevated lines of New York City in the 1880s, until Manhattan switched from steam to electric-driven trains. In 1903 the upstart Council City & Solomon River Railroad purchased the locomotives and transported them north, hoping to profit by servicing inland mines from the coast. Though the company surveyed some 50 miles of potential track, only half of that was built. By 1907 the operation went belly-up. Six years later a powerful storm sealed the Last Train's fate by destroying the Solomon River railroad bridge and stranding the engines on the tundra forever. Truly, it was the end of the line.

was originally established in 1900 and once boasted a population of 1000 people and seven saloons. The town was destroyed by a storm in 1913, relocated to higher ground and then further decimated by the 1918 flu epidemic. These days there's a B&B open in summer in the former schoolhouse.

Near Mile 40 you pass the first of two **gold dredges** within a couple of miles of each other. By 1912 almost 40 dredges worked the Seward Peninsula, and many are still visible from the Nome road system. The two on this road are in the best shape and are the most picturesque. Nome–Council Rd begins climbing after the second dredge and reaches **Stookum Pass** at Mile 53. There's a parking area at the pass, so you can pull off and admire the views or take a hike on the nearby ridges.

The road ends at Mile 73 at **Council**. Actually, the road ends at the banks of the Niukluk River, and Council is on the other side. Most of the houses here are weekend getaways for people living in Nome, and there are currently no year-round residents. Locals drive across the river – with the water often reaching their running boards. Tourists with rental vehicles should stay put. There are no services or shops in Council, but the Niukluk is an excellent place to fish for grayling.

Kougarok Road

Also known as Nome-Taylor Rd, Kougarok Rd leads 86 miles north from Nome through the heart of the Kigluaik Mountains. Along the way are a few artifacts from the gold-rush days, and the best mountain scenery and hiking in the area. You can access the highway two ways: from its juncture off Nome–Council Rd just east of town, or via the Dexter Bypass, which spurs off Nome–Teller Rd a few miles northeast of Nome.

The Kigluaiks spring up almost immediately, flanking the road until around Mile 40, where the free, BLM-operated **Salmon Lake Campground** (Mile 40, Kougarok Rd) is beautifully situated at the northern end of the large Salmon Lake. The facility features nine willow-girdled sites with tables, fire rings and an outhouse. The outlet for the Pilgrim River, where you can watch sockeye salmon spawn in August, is close.

Just before Mile 54 is Pilgrim River Rd, a rocky lane that heads northwest. The road climbs a pass where there's great ridge walking, then descends into a valley dotted with small tundra lakes. Less than 8 miles from Kougarok Rd, Pilgrim River Rd ends at the gate of **Pilgrim Hot Springs**. A roadhouse and saloon were located here during the gold rush, but they burnt down in 1908. Later there was an orphanage for children who lost their parents in the 1918 influenza epidemic. If you want to enter the hot spring area, first check in at the Nome Visitor Center as you'll need to fill out a form.

Kougarok Rd crosses Pilgrim River at Mile 60, the Kuzitrin River at Mile 68 and the Kougarok Bridge at Mile 86. This is one of the best areas to look for herds of musk oxen. At all three bridges you can fish for grayling, Dolly Varden trout and salmon, among other species.

Beyond the Kougarok Bridge the road becomes a rough track impassable to cars. The extremely determined, however, can shoulder a pack and continue overland for a very challenging, boggy, unmarked 30-plus miles to **Serpentine Hot Springs**, inside the **Bering Land Bridge National Preserve**. A free, first-come, first-served bunkhouse-style cabin here sleeps 15 to 20, and there's a bathhouse for slipping into the 140°F to 170°F (60°C to 76.5°C) waters. Almost no-one hikes

THE BUSH AROUND NOME

both ways; consider chartering a plane in or out. Check at the Bering Land Bridge Visitor Center for flight operators and also to pick up its informative brochure on the springs.

Nome–Teller Road

This road leads 73 miles (a one-way drive of at least two hours) to Teller, a year-round, subsistence Iñupiat village of 256 people. The landscape en route is vast and undulating, with steep climbs across spectacular rolling tundra. Hiking opportunities are numerous, as are chances to view musk oxen and a portion of the reindeer herd communally owned by families in Teller. The huge Alaska Gold Company dredge, which operated until the mid-1990s, lies just north of Nome on the Nome–Teller Rd.

Teller lies at the westernmost end of the westernmost road in North America. This wind-wracked community overlooks the slate waters of the Bering Sea and stretches along a tapering gravel spit near the mouth of Grantley Harbor. Roald Amundsen, one of the greatest figures in polar exploration, returned to earth here after his legendary 70-hour airship flight over the North Pole on May 14, 1926. In 1985 Teller again made the

headlines when Libby Riddles, then a Teller resident, became the first woman to win the Iditarod dogsled race.

With rising sea levels and melting permafrost, there are plans to move Teller, but the move, if it happens, will take several years.

ARCTIC ALASKA

Perhaps the least-visited portion of the state, Alaska's Arctic region is tough and expensive to reach. But for those with a penchant for moon-like dystopian towns, you might have just hit the jackpot. Of course, there's also plenty of outdoor stuff to do: paddling the numerous rivers, backpacking in little-visited national parks and preserves or driving the precarious and prodigious Dalton Hwy. Arctic Alaska has no cities, but 'hubs' like Bettles, Barrow and Coldfoot will get you started.

Dalton Highway

One of only two roads to cross the Arctic Circle in North America and reaching a latitude of 70° north, 2° higher than Canada's Dempster Hwy, the Dalton is a truly epic drive. Also known as Haul Rd, the punishing truck

---

WORTH A TRIP

ARCTIC NATIONAL WILDLIFE REFUGE

Seldom has so much furor involved a place so few have ever been. The Arctic National Wildlife Refuge (ANWR; www.fws.gov/refuge/arctic) is a 19.6-million-acre wilderness in Alaska's northeast corner, straddling the eastern Brooks Range from the treeless Arctic Coast to the taiga of the Porcupine River Valley. For years the refuge has been at the core of a white-hot debate over whether to drill beneath its coastal plain, which is thought to contain billions of barrels of crude oil and natural gas.

Beyond the bragging rights of visiting one of the most remote regions of the world, ANWR attracts with its boundless wilderness and surprisingly diverse wildlife. This 'Serengeti of the north' is home to dozens of land mammals, including grizzlies, musk ox, Dall sheep and the second largest herd of caribou in North America. Over 20 rivers cut through the region, several suitable for multiday paddles, as well as the four highest peaks in the Brooks Range. For adventurers, photographers and lovers of all things untamed and untrammeled, there are few more appealing destinations.

Visiting ANWR (an-wahr) is easier said than done. There are no visitor facilities, and even reaching the refuge can be tricky. There's only one place it can be accessed by car: just north of Atigun Pass on the Dalton Hwy, where the road and the refuge briefly touch.

To get deep into ANWR, you will need to fly. For a list of charter companies, consult the refuge's website. Wilderness Alaska (☑ 345-3567; www.wildernessalaska.com; 1-week trips $3400-5000) offers over 20 different ANWR trips from rafting to following the caribou herds.

One of the gateways to the refuge is Kaktovik, an Iñupiat village on the northern shore of Barter Island in the Beaufort Sea, 160 miles east of Deadhorse. Kaktovik is the place to see polar bears in the wild, especially in September when they feed close to the town. For more information (and accommodations), contact the village's Waldo Arms Hotel (☑ 640-6513; www.waldoarms.com).

route cuts 414 miles from Alaska's Interior to the North Slope, paralleling the Trans-Alaska Pipeline to its source at the Prudhoe Bay Oil Field. Along the way you can contemplate boreal forest, the Gothic majesty of the Brooks Range and the chilling flatness of the Arctic tundra.

Fueled by crude-oil fever, the Dalton was built in a whirlwind five months in 1974. For the ensuing two decades, however, it was effectively a private driveway for the gas companies, until a bitter battle in the state legislature opened all but the last 8 miles to the Arctic Ocean (accessible now by private tours out of Deadhorse).

Though the Dalton is slowly being tamed (there are intermittent paved sections as far as Coldfoot these days) and thousands of ordinary tourists drive it every summer, it's still not an easy road. In summer the 28ft-wide corridor is a dusty minefield of potholes and frost heaves, its embankments littered with blown tires. Paint scratches and window chips are inevitable, which is why most car-rental companies don't allow their vehicles here. There are few services – telephones, tire repair, fuel, restaurants – and none for the final 225 miles from Wiseman to Deadhorse.

The road is open year-round, but only tackle it between late May and early September, when there's virtually endless light and little snow and ice. Drive with headlights on, carry two spares, extra water and fuel, and always slow down and swing wide for oncoming trucks. Expect a 40mph average and two hard days to reach Deadhorse.

☞ Tours

Tour prices are comparable to the cost of renting (and fueling) your own vehicle and so offer a reasonable alternative to those not keen on tackling the challenges of the Dalton on their own.

Northern Alaska Tour Company TOUR
(📞474-8600; www.northernalaska.com) Offers all sorts of packages, including a three-day tour ($1089 per person, based on double occupancy) that involves a drive up or down the Dalton (with a flight going the other way).

Trans Arctic Circle Treks TOUR
(📞479-5451; www.transarctictreks.com) Tours to the Arctic Circle from Fairbanks start at $189 per person by vehicle, and $439 per person if you fly.

❶ Information

For more info on the highway, visit the Alaska Public Lands Information Center in the Morris Thompson Cultural & Visitors Center (p294) in Fairbanks for a copy of the *Dalton Highway Visitor Guide*. It covers history, safety, services, accommodations, points of interest and wildlife, and also includes mileage charts and maps.

Also check out the website of the **BLM Central Yukon Field Office** (www.blm.gov/ak/st/en/prog/recreation/dalton_hwy.html), the agency that maintains the highway's campgrounds, rest areas and visitor center.

❶ Getting There & Around

Amazing, but true: you can catch a bus to the Arctic Ocean. The vans of **Dalton Highway Express** (Map p294; 📞474-3555; www.daltonhighwayexpress.com; 3820 University Ave S) head north twice a week between Fairbanks and Prudhoe Bay from early June to late August, but only if they have bookings. Vans stop overnight at Deadhorse and give you time to take an early morning oil-field tour before returning the next day. As it's a 16-hour journey one-way, you may wish to fly back. Warning: spending more than a day in Deadhorse can invoke serious cabin fever. The one-way fare to the Arctic Circle is $84, Coldfoot $106, Wiseman $125 and Deadhorse $250.

Trucks and SUVs can be rented in Fairbanks.

Mile 0 to 175

Mile 0 of the Dalton is at the junction with the Elliot Hwy, 84 miles from Fairbanks. Immediately, the Haul Rd announces itself: the pavement ends and loose gravel and blind curves begin. A road sign informs you that the speed limit is 50mph – for the next 416 miles!

This first section of highway carries you through scraggy boreal (taiga) forest. At Mile 56 the highway crosses the 2290ft-long, wooden-decked Yukon River Bridge – the only place where the legendary waterway is spanned in Alaska. On the far bank is the tiny BLM-run Yukon Crossing Visitor Contact Station (www.blm.gov/ak/st/en/prog/recreation/dalton_hwy.html; ⊙9am-6pm Jun-Aug), small on exhibits, but big on friendly advice.

On the opposite side of the highway is the Yukon River Camp (📞474-3557; www.yukonrivercamp.com; r with shared bath $199), a utilitarian truck stop with work-camp-style rooms, showers, costly gas, a gift shop and a restaurant (⊙9am-9pm).

The road then clambers back out of the river valley, across burned-over patches of forest (the remains of Interior-wide fires in 2004 and 2005), and into an alpine area with

THE ALASKA PIPELINE

Love it or loathe it, if you're driving Alaska's Richardson or Dalton Hwys, the Trans-Alaska Pipeline will be your traveling companion. The steely tube, 4ft wide and 800 miles long, parallels the highways from Prudhoe Bay on the Arctic Ocean down to Valdez, Alaska's northernmost ice-free port. En route, it spans 500-odd waterways and three mountain ranges, transporting about 600,000 barrels of crude oil per day – 12% of US domestic production – to tankers waiting in Prince William Sound. Back in its heyday, the pipeline was carrying around 2 million barrels per day. With dwindling reserves, however, they've cut down the flow and expect to continue to reduce it unless new sources, such as those in the Arctic National Wildlife Refuge, are opened up for drilling.

Before construction began in 1974, the debate over the pipeline was among America's hardest-fought conservation battles. Boosters viewed the project as a grand act of Alaskan pioneering, and opponents called it an affront to all that's wild and wonderful about the 49th state. After the pipeline's completion – three years and $8 billion later – the late University of Alaska president William R Wood likened it to 'a silken thread, half-hidden across the palace carpet.' Many have had less kind words for it, especially in light of the numerous spills that have occurred over the years.

For about 380 of its miles, the Trans-Alaska Pipeline – like most pipelines – runs underground. Elsewhere it can't, because the 110°F to 55.6°F (43.3°C to 13°C) oil it carries would melt the permafrost. It's in those places – particularly where it crosses the highway – that you'll get your best look at the line. Especially good views can be had at Mile 243.5 of the Richardson Hwy south of Delta Junction, on the Dalton Hwy at the Yukon River crossing, and at the spur road to Wiseman. Just north of Fairbanks you can walk right up to the pipeline, stand under it, and even move in for a kiss if you are so inclined (as some are).

Be forewarned, however: elsewhere it's a bad move to get too close to the pipeline. After September 11, 2001, officials identified the pipe as Alaska's number one terrorist target, ramping up security and for a while even operating a checkpoint on the Dalton Hwy. Their fears weren't entirely unfounded: in 1999, Canadian Alfred Reumayr was arrested for plotting to blow up the pipeline (apparently to make big profits on oil futures). In 2001, a drunken hunter also shot it with a .338-caliber rifle and 285,000 gallons spewed out. Officials say the pipeline has been shot – with no spillage caused – dozens of other times.

the 40ft-high granite tor of Finger Mountain beckoning to the east. You pass the imaginary line of the Arctic Circle at Mile 115, and for good 24/7 views of the sun, continue to Gobblers Knob, a hilltop lookout at Mile 132. From Gobblers Knob northward, the pyramids of the Brooks Range begin to dominate the scene. In the next 50 miles you'll cross several grayling-rich streams, including Prospect Creek, which, in January 1971, experienced America's lowest-ever temperature: -80°F (-62°C).

Coldfoot

At Mile 175, in a mountain-rimmed hollow, you'll arrive in Coldfoot. Originally Slate Creek, it was renamed when the first settlers, a group of greenhorn miners, got 'cold feet' at the thought of spending the 1898 winter in the district and headed south. Coldfoot was a ghost town by 1912, but nowadays there is an airstrip, post office and trooper detachment. There's also Coldfoot Camp (☑474-3500;

www.coldfootcamp.com; r $198; ☺24hr), a truck stop with the last gas until Deadhorse, spartan rooms and a restaurant with passable diner-style fare. Frozen Foot Saloon is Alaska's northernmost bar if you care for a tipple.

A world apart is the Arctic Interagency Visitor Center (☑678-5209; CentralYukon@ blm.gov; ☺11am-10pm Jun-Aug), on the opposite side of the highway. This impressive $5-million structure opened in 2004 and features museum-quality displays about the Arctic and its denizens. As the visitor center employees will tell you, the area's best lodging is down the highway 5 miles at Marion Creek Campground (Mile 180, Dalton Hwy; tent & RV sites $8). This 27-site campground almost always has space and is in an open spruce forest with stunning views of the Brooks Range.

You can hire charter flights to Gates of the Arctic National Park & Preserve and the Arctic National Wildlife Refuge with Coldfoot-based Coyote Air Service (☑678-5995; www.flycoyote.com).

Wiseman

POP 18

Those seeking a bed – or wanting an antidote to Coldfoot's culture of the quick-and-dirty – should push on to Wiseman, a century-old log-cabin village accessible via a short dirt spur road at Mile 189. The only authentic town on the Dalton, Wiseman occupies an enviable spot, overhung by peaks and fronting the Middle Fork of the Koyukuk River. Its heyday was 1910, when it replaced the original Coldfoot as a hub for area gold miners.

The **Wiseman Historical Museum** (474-3500), near the entrance to town, is only open to tour bus groups, but individual travelers might try to see if Wiseman's wise man, Jack Reakoff, is around. This engaging, urbane trapper will discourse at length about local history and wildlife. Many buildings from the gold-rush era still stand, including those of **Arctic Getaway Alaska Cabin Rentals** (678-4456; www.arcticgetaway.com; cabins incl breakfast $110-240), which offers a sunny two-person cabin and antique-laden four-person cabins. All come with breakfast and have kitchenettes available for making other meals. At **Boreal Lodge** (678-4556; www.boreallodge.com; s/d without bath $80/100, cabin $150) next door, the rooms are cheaper but more institutional. There's a full kitchen for guests.

Mile 190 to 414

North from Wiseman the Dalton skirts the eastern edge of Gates of the Arctic National Park. Dall sheep are often visible on the mountain slopes, and by Mile 194 the first views appear of the massive wall of **Sukakpak Mountain** (4459ft) looming dead ahead. At Mile 235 you kiss the woods goodbye: the famed **Last Spruce** (now dead) stands near a turnout on the highway's east side.

Atigun Pass (Mile 242), at an elevation of 4739ft, is the highest highway pass in Alaska and marks the Continental Divide. The view from the top – with the Philip Smith Mountains to the east and the Endicotts to the west – will steal your breath away.

Once you reach the turnoff for the Galbraith Lake Campground at Mile 275, the Brooks Range is largely behind you. From here on it's all rolling tundra. Hiking and camping options are limitless, wildflowers and berries grow in profusion, and wildlife is rather easy to spot, not least because from May 10 to August 2 the sun never sets.

At the beginning and end of summer, watch for migrating waterbirds thronging roadside ponds, and caribou – members of the 31,000-head Central Arctic herd – grazing nearby. Also, keep an eye out for weird polar phenomena such as pingos – protuberant hills with a frozen center – and ice-wedge polygons, which shape the tundra into bizarre geometric patterns.

THE BUSH DALTON HIGHWAY

LOCAL KNOWLEDGE

CYCLING THE HAUL ROAD

Every summer a few dozen hardy souls tackle this epic route under their own power. It's not a place to learn the ins and outs of long-distance cycling, but for the prepared and experienced it can be a trip of a lifetime.

Most riders catch the shuttle van to Deadhorse and ride back to Fairbanks, as it can be difficult to coordinate with the van's return schedule (twice a week but only if there are customers going both ways). Count on eight to 12 days to complete the route, with long days in the saddle and primitive camping at night. Water is available in streams but make sure to treat it first.

Changing weather systems can blow in quickly so be prepared for snow, icy rains and also hot temperatures (sometimes in the same day). Road conditions can also deteriorate fast. As Welshman Rob Hickman told us after he completed the route in June 2011 as part of a Pan-American Hwy ride to Tierra del Fuego, after rains, 'a decent gravel road could turn to a ready-mix slurry.' Other sections he described as like riding on 'ball bearings.'

But truck drivers were surprisingly good about giving riders like him a bit of space, and it was seldom more than 30 minutes between vehicles. With everyone aware of the dangers and hardships of the Dalton, it was never a problem to flag drivers down for backup when a bear had gotten too close, or even for a drink of water on a long stretch.

And if that makes Haul Rd sound a little too tame, you can always try the ride in winter, pulling your supplies behind you on a sleigh. It's been done.

Deadhorse

Deadhorse is a sprawling industrial dystopia that supports the huge Prudhoe Bay Oil Field at the north end of Dalton Hwy. Its statistics make grim reading: 54 days of consecutive darkness in winter, a permanent population of less than 50, bitter winds even in July, and an architectural style best described as Stalinist Siberian meets *Mad Max 2*. No right-minded traveler would come here if it wasn't the end point of a truly epic journey – the Dalton Hwy. That said, a night in the military-camp-like confines of the Prudhoe Bay Hotel, with its industrial carpets and nail-biting, calendar-checking oil workers, at the conclusion of an exhausting road trip is an experience you probably won't forget.

🏃 Activities

Having come this far, most travelers venture to dip their toe in the Arctic Ocean on a brief organized excursion.

Arctic Ocean Shuttle   BUS TOUR
(☑474-3565; www.arcticoceanshuttle.com; tours per person $59; ⊘tours 8:30am & 3:30pm) You must book these 1½-hour tours at least 24 hours in advance online or through your tour/bus company. Remember that the body of water you see at Deadhorse is Lake Colleen *not* the Arctic Ocean. The only way to see the real thing is on this tour. The tour starts early, but you can book it through the Dalton Highway Express to ensure you connect with your 8am return bus heading south to Fairbanks.

🛏 Sleeping & Eating

All Deadhorse accommodations follow the same booking policy: unless you're an oil worker and have reserved through a company, you can only book up to two weeks in advance. But book you should.

As there are no restaurants in Deadhorse, each hotel runs its own cafeteria where you can eat as much as you like (included in the room price). It's good chow too.

Prudhoe Bay Hotel   HOTEL $$
(☑659-2449; www.prudhoebayhotel.com; dm with shared bath $125, r with private bath $160; � 🛜) 'Take your boots off at the door!' proclaims the sign. The Prudhoe Bay is that kind of hotel. Long corridors with industrial carpets are full of weather-beaten oil workers wandering around in their hole-y socks. But, after the long haul up the Dalton Hwy, it's – weirdly – just what you need: a truly Alaskan experi-

ence. Rooms are surprisingly cozy (with TVs), but the best deal is the cafeteria. Grab as much food as you can stuff in your rucksack – it's all included. Nonguests can also eat here (breakfast/lunch/dinner $12/15/20).

Deadhorse Camp   HOTEL $$
(☑474-3565; Dalton Hwy, Mile 413.6; d with shared bath $199; 🛜) A more downbeat version of the Prudhoe Bay Hotel that's less conveniently situated on the edge of 'town.' Bathrooms are shared.

Aurora Hotel   HOTEL $$$
(☑670-0600; Colleen Lake Dr; s/d $160/270; 🛜) The Aurora is newer and much larger than the Prudhoe Bay Hotel and comes with some handy extras. The fitness room will save you jogging around outside with the grizzly and polar bears. It overlooks Colleen Lake but is almost a mile from the airport.

🛈 Getting There & Away

The only road connection is via the Dalton Hwy. Dalton Highway Express heads south at 8am on Sunday and Wednesday (June to August). The 16-hour journey to Fairbanks costs $250.

From **Deadhorse Airport** (☑659-2553) there are daily flights to Anchorage ($450 one way) plus connections to Barrow ($250 one way). The ultra-friendly airport is opposite the Prudhoe Bay Hotel.

Gates of the Arctic National Park & Preserve

Standing in the middle of the Gates of the Arctic National Park & Preserve (www.nps.gov/gaar), 8 million acres of uninhabited mountains and tundra located between the Dalton Hwy and the Bering Strait, you could quite conceivably be living in the year 2014 BC, so raw is the surrounding landscape. Unchanged in four millennia, the park is part of a contiguous wilderness that stretches for over 27,000 sq miles – the equivalent of nearly two Switzerlands – harboring no roads, no cell-phone coverage and a population of precisely zero. To the southwest lies desolate Kobuk Valley National Park (www.nps.gov/kova), known for its arctic sand dunes and migrating caribou, while, adjoining it to the west, Noatak National Preserve (www.nps.gov/noat) is comprised of a giant untouched river basin covered in tundra.

Not surprisingly, you don't come to these parks to stroll along interpretive boardwalks looking for the nearest hot-dog concession, or even follow something as rudimentary as a trail (there aren't any). Tackled alone, this is a land for burly and brave travelers with advanced outdoor experience, plenty of time on their hands and – ahem – a flexible budget (read: it's costly). If you're less intrepid, fear not. You can sign up with one of a handful of agencies and go on a guided backcountry or flightseeing tour.

Gates of the Arctic is the most accessible of the three parks as it starts just 5 miles west of the Dalton Hwy, meaning you can technically hike in, although charter flights out of Coldfoot and Bettles are more common. Noatak and Kobuk Valley are both reached via charters out of the small settlement of Kotzebue.

Within the parks are dozens of rivers to run, miles of valleys and tundra slopes to hike and, of course, the 'gates' themselves: Mt Boreal and Frigid Crags, which flank the north fork of the Koyukuk River. In 1929 Robert Marshall found an unobstructed path northward to the Arctic through these landmark peaks and his name for the passage has stuck ever since.

The parks contain no visitor facilities, campgrounds or trails, and the NPS is intent upon maintaining its virgin quality. Unguided trekkers, paddlers and climbers entering the park should check in at one of the ranger stations for a backcountry orientation.

Bettles (population 12) is the main gateway to Gates of the Arctic, offering meals, lodging and air transport into the backcountry. Other visitors fly in from Coldfoot on the Dalton Hwy, or hike in directly from Wiseman, just north of Coldfoot. To the north, the remote Alaska Native village of Anaktuvuk Pass is another access point if traveling by foot, though you'll need to fly here first. Contact the Anaktuvuk Ranger Station for more information on visiting the park from here.

◉ Sights & Activities

Hiking
Most backpackers enter the park by way of charter air-taxis, which can land on lakes, rivers or river bars. Once on the ground they often follow the long, open valleys for extended treks or work their way to higher elevations where open tundra provides good hiking terrain.

While this appears to make planning an impossibly vague task, the landscape limits the areas that aircraft can land or pick you up, as well as where you can hike. Park staff suggest consulting flight and guide companies, as well as topographic maps, for possible routes and then running it by them to make sure the area is not overused. If it is, they can suggest alternatives.

The only treks that don't require chartering a plane are those beginning from the Dalton Hwy (near Wiseman), or from the village of Anaktuvuk Pass. For hikes from the highway, which lead into several different areas along the eastern border of the park, stop at the Arctic Interagency Visitor Center in Coldfoot for advice and assistance in trip planning. Several well-known routes in this area are showing too much wear and even beginning to affect the livelihood of subsistence hunters.

Hiking into the park from Anaktuvuk Pass is surprisingly one of the more economical options, as you only need to pay for a regular scheduled flight to the village from Fairbanks. From the airstrip it's just a few miles' hike into the northern edge of the park. You can camp for free by the airstrip if needed, but elsewhere get permission until you enter the park.

Paddling
Floatable rivers in the park include the John, Alatna, Noatak, Kobuk, Koyukuk and Tinayguk. The waterways range in difficulty from Class I to III, and you should consult the park or guide companies about possible routes.

Canoes can be rented in Bettles at the Bettles Lodge (p365) for around $270 per week.

☞ Tours

Arctic Wild   ADVENTURE SPORTS
(☑ 479-8203; www.arcticwild.com) Arrange a fantastic eight-day guided backpacking trip in Gates of the Arctic National Park for $3900 per person, or a 10-day canoeing/hiking trip on the Noatak River from $4900 per person. Trips run in August.

Brooks Range Aviation   SCENIC FLIGHTS
(☑ 692-5444; http://brooksrange.com) These guys run four- to five-hour flightseeing tours of Gates of the Arctic and Kobuk Valley National Parks with a brief landing in each. You'll need to overnight in Bettles.

🛏 Sleeping

Bettles Lodge   LODGE
(☑ 692-5111; www.bettleslodge.com) A 1952 vintage six-room lodge (now a National Historic Site) providing accommodations in the tiny settlement of Bettles. There's a common area with books and games, and decent

THE BUSH GATES OF THE ARCTIC NATIONAL PARK & PRESERVE

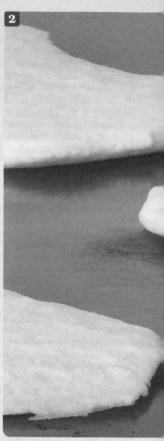

JOSEF FRIEDHUBER / GETTY IMAGES ©

SCOTT DICKERSON / DESIGN PICS / GETTY IMAGES ©

3

1. Brooks Range
Skiing in Arctic Alaska (p360).

2. Northern Alaska
Polar bears climbing out of the icy Arctic waters.

3. Off the beaten track
Camping in Gates of the Arctic National Park & Preserve (p364).

4. Native Alaskans
Iñupiat family in northwestern Alaska.

meals are provided. Even better, the lodge organizes multiple trips and tours in Gates of the Arctic National Park. It's not posh but it's peaceful. Phone for packages and rates.

ℹ Information

For more information, check out the park's website. If the 'Plan Your Visit' section doesn't answer all your questions, contact the park directly.

Anaktuvuk Ranger Station (☎ 661-3520; www.nps.gov/gaar) Can help you plan your trip from Anaktuvuk.

Arctic Interagency Visitor Center (☎ 678-5209; CentralYukon@blm.gov; ⊙ 11am-10pm Jun-Aug) In Coldfoot; has info for those accessing the park from the Dalton Hwy.

Bettles Ranger Station & Visitor Center (☎ 692-5495; www.nps.gov/gaar; ⊙ 8am-5pm daily Jun-Sep, 1-5pm Mon-Fri winter) In a log building less than a quarter mile from the airstrip.

ℹ Getting There & Away

Wright Air Service (☎ 474-0502; www.wrightairservice.com) flies daily from Fairbanks to Bettles ($340 round-trip) and Anaktuvuk Pass ($380 round-trip). **Bettles Air Service** (☎ 692-5111; www.bettlesair.com) also covers these routes.

From Bettles it's necessary to charter an air-taxi to your destination within the park. Most areas can be reached in under two hours. Check with Brooks Range Aviation (p365) or Bettles Air Service for air charters.

From Coldfoot on the Dalton Hwy you can hire a charter flight with Coyote Air Service (p362).

Barrow

POP 4346

Barrow is the northernmost settlement in the USA, and the largest Iñupiat community in Alaska. Originally called Ukpeagvik, which means 'place to hunt snowy owls,' the town is situated 330 miles above the Arctic Circle. It's a flat, bleak, fogbound and strangely evocative place locked in almost perpetual winter. It's also a town of surprising contradictions.

On one hand, Barrow's wealth is famous: due to the spoils of North Slope petroleum it boasts facilities, such as its Iñupiat Heritage Center, that are unusual in a town this size. On the flip side, it's an Arctic slum packed with ramshackle structures wallowing in frozen mud.

It's also at once ancient and modern. Iñupiat have dwelled here for at least two millennia and still run the place: Barrow, as the seat of the North Slope Borough (a countylike government covering an area larger than Nebraska), is the administrative and commercial hub of Alaska's Far North. Yet locals have retained much of their traditional culture, best symbolized by the spring whale harvests and seen during the Nalukataq Festival staged in June to celebrate successful hunts.

Barrow's appeal is as much the Iñupiat culture, served up by some of Alaska's warmest citizens, as its novel latitude. The midnight sun doesn't set here for 82 days, from May to early August.

Barrow lies along the northeasterly trending shore of the icebound Chukchi Sea, and is divided into two sections. Directly north of the airport is Barrow proper: it's home to most of the hotels and restaurants and interlaced with a warren of gravel streets, including Stevenson St, which runs along the water. Heading east along the shore takes you past Isatquaq, or Middle Lagoon, and then into Browerville. This is a more residential area but it's also where the heritage center, post office and grocery store are located. It's about 2 miles from one end of town to the other, making it easy enough for people to walk if the weather cooperates for long enough.

◉ Sights & Activities

The main thing to do at the 'top of the world' is bundle up, stand on the shore of the Arctic Ocean, dip something of yourself in the water and gaze toward the North Pole.

Iñupiat Heritage Center   CULTURAL CENTER (www.nps.gov/inup; Ahkovak St; admission $10; ⊙ 8:30am-5pm Mon-Fri, 1-4pm Sat & Sun) This 24,000-sq-ft facility houses a museum, a gift shop and a large multipurpose room where short traditional dancing-and-drumming performances take place each afternoon ($20). Local craftspeople often assemble in the lobby to sell masks, whalebone carvings and fur garments and are happy to talk about craft and technique. In the center's galleries, displays include everything from poster-sized, black-and-white portraits of local elders to a 35ft-long replica of a bowhead skeleton to a detailed (and artifact-rich) breakdown of traditional whaling culture and hunting practices.

Point Barrow   LANDMARK Follow the shore 12 miles northeast of the city and you'll come to Point Barrow, a narrow spit of land that's the northernmost extremity of the US (though not, as locals sometimes claim, North America). In the winter and spring this is where polar bears den; in the summer it's the featured stop of organized tours. You can also take a taxi out there ($50 round-trip), but you'll have to walk the last section in.

Barrow Arctic Science Consortium   LECTURE
(www.arcticscience.wordpress.com; Beach Rd; ⊙lectures 1:30pm Sat) Hosts free scientific lectures most Saturdays. It's located at the Ilisagvik College, about 3 miles east of town on Beach Rd. See the website for lecture details.

Hiking
You can stroll the gravel roads, or gray-sand beaches, that parallel the sea to view *umiaks* (traditional kayaks), giant jawbones of bowhead whales, fish-drying racks and the jumbled Arctic pack ice that even in July spans the horizon.

On the waterfront opposite Apayauk St at the southwest end of town (turn left as you exit the airport) is Ukpiagvik, the site of an ancient Iñupiat village marked by the remains of semi-subterranean sod huts. From that site, continue southwest out of town and when the road splits go left toward Freshwater Lake. After about 3 miles you'll come to a row of satellite dishes that face directly out and not up. It's an odd sight, making for an interesting photo, and drives home just how far north you are.

Birding & Wildlife-Watching
Not many people would describe Barrow as 'paradise,' except, perhaps, for birders. At least 185 avian species make a stop here during the summer months. Most serious twitchers are on organized tours, but anyone with binoculars will find a few hours out of town a rewarding experience. In the absence of trees, birds nest on the ground and are easy to spot. Snowy owls are common.

If you want to see a polar bear, it's best to take a tour. But don't get your hopes up too high: they're tough to spot, especially in the summer months.

 Tours

Tundra Tours   TOUR
(☑852-3900; www.tundratoursinc.com; tours per person $150) Tundra Tours is run out of the Top of the World Hotel and its five-hour May-to-September day-trips are one of the better ways to piece together Barrow's essential sights. The trip includes a tundra walk to Iñupiat sod huts, a visit to Barrow Point and a look around the Iñupiat Heritage Center.

OFF THE BEATEN TRACK

ST LAWRENCE ISLAND
Way out in the Bering Sea only 40 miles from mainland Russia and 125 miles southwest of Nome, St Lawrence Island isn't the kind of place you pop into on your way to somewhere else. Inhabited primarily by Alaskan and Siberian Yupik, it provides a good opportunity to watch birds and sea mammals. There are basic hotels in its two main settlements Gambell and Savoonga, and a new road system allows for easier access to birding areas. Ravn Alaska (p417) flies to Gambell from Nome daily for around $500 round-trip, but birders are probably better off hitching onto an organized trip with Wilderness Birding Adventures (p356). Trips are run to coincide with the spring and fall migrations (ie early June and early September).

Wilderness Birding Adventures   BIRDWATCHING
(☑694-7442; www.wildernessbirding.com) Runs small-group birding tours to the Arctic region, including Barrow.

⚘ Festivals & Events

Nalukataq Festival   CULTURAL
The Nalukataq Festival is held in late June, when the spring whaling hunt has been completed. Depending on how successful the whaling captains have been, the festival lasts anywhere from a few days to longer than a week. It's a rare cultural experience and one of the best reasons to visit Barrow.

One Iñupiat tradition calls for whaling crews to share their bounty with the village, and during the festival you'll see families carrying off platters and plastic bags full of raw whale meat. Dishes served include *muktuk*, the pink blubbery part of the whale, which is boiled, pickled or even eaten raw with hot mustard or soy sauce.

The main event of the festival is the blanket toss, in which locals use a sealskin tarp to toss people into the air – the effect is much like bouncing on a trampoline. For the jumper, the object is to reach the highest heights (this supposedly replicates ancient efforts to spot game in the distance) and inevitably there are a number of sprains and fractures.

THE BUSH BARROW

🛏 Sleeping

Camping is not advised around Barrow due to extreme weather and the potential for up-close encounters with curious, carnivorous polar bears. Given Barrow's compact size, it's possible to catch a morning flight in and a late evening flight out and still see just about everything you're likely to see. Alternatively, you can tack it onto a trip to Prudhoe Bay.

Book well in advance if you do plan to spend the night, and note that there's a 5% bed tax.

King Eider Inn   INN **$$**
(☑ 852-4700; www.kingeider.net; 1752 Ahkovak St; s/d $185/194; 🖤) With a snug log-cabin feel, wood-post beds and an inviting fireplace in the lobby, the Eider is a pleasant antidote to the dystopia outside. It's almost directly across from the airport exit.

Barrow Airport Inn   HOTEL **$$**
(☑ 852-2525; airportinn@barrow.com; 1815 Momegana St; r incl breakfast $125; 🖤) A few minutes' walk from the airport, the 15 rooms here are simply furnished but do the trick for a night's stay. Some have kitchenettes, but these are usually booked far in advance by research teams.

⭐ **Top of the World Hotel**   HOTEL **$$$**
(☑ 852-3900; www.tundratoursinc.com; 3060 Eben Hopson St; s/d $273/293; @🖤) Recently rebuilt a quarter of a mile to the east in the Browerville neighborhood, the Top of the World still lives up to its name (it's the northernmost hotel in North America), but after the move it's also surprisingly plush, with large airy communal spaces, topical arctic mosaics, boutique-style rooms and the best restaurant in Barrow – by far.

The catch? Like most things in Barrow, it's mega-expensive.

🍴 Eating

Barrow has a handful of places to eat, though none of them look much like restaurants from the outside. Pizza, Japanese, Chinese, Mexican and Korean can all be procured. However, Barrow is a 'damp' town (one that permits the possession of alcohol but bans the sale of it), so don't expect to be throwing back lagers with your chimichangas or kimchi.

Niggivikut Restaurant   AMERICAN **$$**
(☑ 852-3900; 3860 Eben Hopson St; mains $15-33; ⊙ 6am-10pm Mon-Sat, 8am-10pm Sun) You can get pancakes pretty much anywhere in the US, but only in the Niggivikut can you enjoy them while gazing wistfully at the iceberg-choked Arctic Ocean. This new restaurant in the Top of the World Hotel has booths in front of large Arctic-facing windows, a no-surprises American menu and keen-to-please staff.

Sam & Lee's Chinese Restaurant   CHINESE **$$**
(☑ 852-5556; cnr Nachik & Kiogak Sts; breakfast mains $12-15, lunch & dinner mains $18; ⊙ 6am-2am) Ostensibly a Chinese restaurant, this joint has good American-style breakfasts and all-you-can-eat lunch buffets on weekdays ($14). In addition to the food, the bright diner atmosphere and lively staff make this a popular local hangout.

Arctic Pizza   INTERNATIONAL, PIZZA **$$**
(☑ 852-4222; 125 Apayauq St; mains $19-24; ⊙ 11:30am-11:30pm) Pizza's just half of it. This Arctic Ocean–abutting restaurant's multifarious menu also includes pasta, Chinese food, burgers, salads, soup, sandwiches and nachos. The decor – that of an unkempt diner – promises little, but the food, spurred on by the vicious winds outside, warms you up nicely.

AC Store   SUPERMARKET **$$**
(cnr Stuaqpak & Agvik Sts; ⊙ 7am-10pm Mon-Sat, 9am-9pm Sun) Over in Browerville, across from the Iñupiat Heritage Center, this supermarket has quick eats and groceries at diet-inducing prices. Many visitors come by just to take pictures of the $10-plus gallons of milk.

ℹ Information

You can pick up a map and information guide at the airport and most restaurants and hotels. The airport has strong and free wi-fi, as do hotels.
Post Office (cnr Eben Hopson & Tahak Sts) To send your postcards from the top of the world.
Wells Fargo (cnr Agvik & Kiogak Sts) Has a 24-hour ATM.

ℹ Getting There & Around

While you can get to Barrow in the winter by ice road, it's best to fly. Wiley Post–Will Rogers Memorial Airport is served by Alaska Airlines (p358) and Ravn Alaska (p417) with daily flights to Fairbanks ($550 round-trip), Anchorage ($750 round-trip) and Deadhorse ($250 one way).

The airport is an easy stroll from all three hotels, and most other points of interest can also be reached by walking. However, cabs are available for a flat fee of $5. Try **Arctic Cab** (☑ 852-2227).

Understand
Alaska

Alaska Today

Alaska's economic, political and social chatter tends to follow hot-button national trends. Like the rest of the US, Alaskans grapple with resource management, environmental responsibility, same-sex marriage, the legalization of marijuana, systemic poverty, recovery from the Great Recession, and a number of related social issues that mirror those in the Lower 48. But being so big, so isolated and so independent, Alaska's discourse often diverges from that of the mainstream at its very roots.

Media

Alaska Dispatch News (www.adn.com) Alaska's largest newspaper just went through a name/brand change.
Alaska Magazine (www.alaskamagazine.com) Highlights outdoor and cultural wonders.
Alaska Public Radio Network (www.alaskapublic.org) Has 26 community stations.

Reality TV

The Deadliest Catch (Discovery Network) Crab fishing in the Bering Sea.
Gold Rush (Discovery Network) Hapless miners destroy the permafrost in search of fortune.
Ultimate Survival Alaska (National Geographic) Survival in the woods.

Books

Ordinary Wolves (Seth Kantner) A tale about a boy growing up white in Bush Alaska, and his struggles to be accepted into the Native culture.
Coming Into The Country (John McPhee) Powerful journalistic storytelling captures the offbeat and eccentric essence of Alaska's wild men and women.
Alaska A History (Claus Naske and Herman Slotnick) The definitive tome on The Great Land's cultural, geographic and political history.

Social Outlooks

The world looks a lot different from a subsistence village in the Bush than from a drive-up espresso shop in an Anchorage mini-mall.

Alcoholism, suicide, violence and drug abuse are very high in rural Alaskan communities. The rate of rape in Alaska is nearly three times the national average, and child sexual assault is six times higher. Social issues affect an especially large portion of Alaskan Native communities, which make up 14.7% of the population. And while high wages (even for blue-collar jobs) help Alaskans meet the even higher cost of living, around 12 per cent of households are still considered food insecure.

On a social equality front, Alaska was the first US state to ban same-sex marriage. In 2014 the law was being challenged in Federal Court. That same year, the state recognized 20 Alaska Native languages as official languages in an effort to honor native heritage and preserve linguistic traditions.

Economy

Since the early 1980s, Alaska's economy has been fueled by oil. Nearly 85% of the state's general fund revenue comes from taxes on oil and gas production, and residents receive an annual dividend check from the Alaska Permanent Fund of around $5000 for a family of four. Thanks to oil, residents do not pay state taxes on income, sales or inheritance, though you will often find local city and bed taxes.

But the problem with such a narrow economy based largely on mineral extraction is that the minerals run out. Alaskan oil production has been in decline for the past two decades from its peak of 2 million barrels a day in 1988 to just around 500,000 today. In 2014 both Shell and Conoco-Phillips suspended plans to drill in the Chukchi and Beaufort Seas, citing federal regulations and permitting standards. In response, the Alaska legislature is pushing hard to get a gas pipeline built from the North Slope oilfields to markets in the Lower 48 and to create a pro-oil environment that taxes profits less heavily than before. The controversy over drilling in the Arctic Refuge is ongoing with no end in sight.

Alaska's other major industries similarly rely on the state's natural resources. Logging and mining play a large part in the state's economic portfolio, and commercial fishing, rebuilt on expanding markets for wild salmon, brings in around $5.8 billion annually.

But Alaska's beauty is arguably the state's greatest natural resource. With 1.7 million visitors in the summer months alone, tourism is growing, and it's now the second-largest employer in the state.

Politics

Alaskan politics push heavily toward conservative and libertarian values. The state has voted for Republican candidates in all but one presidential election. The Alaskan Independence Party is a strong statewide libertarian-inspired group that works toward abolishing taxes and making Alaska an independent country.

With Sarah Palin fading into the distance (or moving from politics to punditry) her successor, Governor Sean Parnell, also a Republican, is working to create a pro-business economy to attract further investment in North Slope oil exploration. Palin tax policies that placed more oil money in Alaska state coffers helped create a $17 billion rainy day fund for the state (not to mention the $48 billion permanent fund), but they were rolled back during the Parnell administration. Along with tax credits for big oil, Palin worked to attract more investment in exploration. In recent years, Parnell has run deficits against this surplus to capitalize underfunded retirement systems for public employees, using $2 billion in savings in 2014 and predicting another $1.1 budget deficit for 2015.

In 2008 Democrat Mark Begich defeated long-time Republican Senator Ted Stevens. A few days later Stevens was indicted on corruption charges, but the case was ultimately thrown out due to prosecutorial misconduct. Begich's seat was up for grabs in the November 2014 US election, bringing in tons of Super PAC money to the state as Republicans and Dems battled for control of the senate.

The state currently has legalized medicinal marijuana, and a November 2014 ballot measure to legalize the growth, sale and consumption of marijuana for recreational use (like in Colorado and Oregon) appears likely to win.

Environmental Issues

Environmentalists appear to be winning the battle for hearts and minds, but pro-mining, pro-oil and pro-logging legislation and projects are still in the works.

In 2014 the EPA effectively blocked the creation of the controversial Pebble Mine Project, announcing a

POPULATION: **735,132**

AREA: **586,400 SQ MILES**

HIGHEST POINT: **MT MCKINLEY (20,237FT)**

GDP: **$44.5 BILLION**

NUMBER OF DAYS WITHOUT THE SUN IN BARROW: **84**

if Alaska were 100 people

67 would be Caucasian
15 would be Alaska Native
6 would be Hispanic
3 would be African American
5 would be Asian
2 would be Pacific Island Origin
2 would be other

USA in land area
(% of land area)

Alaska — 16
California — 4
Rhode Island — 0.03
Texas — 7
New York — 1

population per sq mile

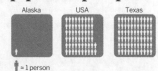

Alaska   USA   Texas

≈ 1 person

Films

Grizzly Man Werner Herzog's darkly incisive documentary follows Timothy Treadwell's life (and death) among grizzlies.
Alone in the Wilderness Dick Proenneke builds a cabin in the woods in this Walden-esque 1960 homemade documentary.
Into the Wild Visually stunning adaptation of Jon Krakauer's book.

Dos & Don'ts

Don't overdress Alaska is extremely casual.
Do dress warm Layers are your best bet.
Do let someone know When you head into the backcountry.
Do bring $500 extra For the excursion to the middle of nowhere.

Myths

Everyone lives in igloos Though many go without modern plumbing, no one in Alaska lives in an igloo.
Everyone drives sled dogs to work In Bush Alaska, driving a snow machine is far more common than a dog team.
There's snow year-round Even up in Barrow the snow disappears for the summer; it sticks around on the higher mountains, though.
There are penguins in Alaska Penguins are found only in the southern hemisphere.

Fun Facts

3 million lakes in Alaska.
100,000 glaciers are found here.
6640 miles of coastline.

large set of restrictions that would make the project too costly to implement. Located in the southwest near Bristol Bay, this would have been one of the biggest opencast mines in the world – a mile deep and about the size of Manhattan. The mining project was opposed by native communities and the area's salmon fisheries.

In other states protests are staged to save a wetland or a woodlot or a park; in Alaska the battleground is an entire ecosystem. At almost 20 million acres, the Arctic National Wildlife Refuge (ANWR) is the size of South Carolina, encompassing 18 major rivers and the greatest variety of plant and animal life – including 36 species of land mammals – of any conservation area in the circumpolar north. The North Slope is also home to 36 trillion cubic feet of natural gas, making it one of the world's largest proven reserves. The fight to 'drill, baby, drill' is still raging, but, with stiffer federal regulations and continued pushback, several oil companies have slowed or halted their Arctic exploration operations in Alaska.

Plans to build one of the US' largest hydroelectric dam projects in years were approved by federal regulators in 2013. The Susitna-Watana Dam would create a 735ft dam in the wilderness between Anchorage and Fairbanks, costing upward of $5 billion. The project is moving forward, but it has triggered backlash from environmentalists, who cite potential damage to the delicate salmon spawning grounds nearby. A Federal Appeals Court Decision ruling that allows logging and road-building in Tongass National Forest is another hot-button issue for environmentalists.

Alaskans are acutely aware of the issues, both local and global, that they face. Few question global warming in Alaska because the proof is evident. Receding glaciers, grasshoppers appearing in the Mat-Su Valley and Native villages slipping into the sea quickly end any debate about climate change in the Far North.

Alaska is known for its abundance of wildlife, yet this, too, is disappearing. In 2008 the polar bear was listed as a threatened species by the US Department of the Interior. The number of Cook Inlet beluga whales has also decreased so dramatically in recent years that they are being considered for listing under the Endangered Species Act, and the king salmon run was so weak up the Kenai and Yukon Rivers in 2014 that even residents with subsistence rights were restricted from filling their quotas.

History

The Aleuts called it Alaxsxaq – where the sea breaks its back. The Russians christened it Bolshaya Zemlya or the Great Land. Today, it's simply known as Alaska. The history of this vast subcontinent – the largest of the US's 50 states – is unique to the Americas and has all the trappings of an epic tale.

There are massive migrations, cultural annihilation, deeds of sale, gold rushes, wartime strategics, oil booms and reparations. The modern political, economic and cultural histories are largely cut from the exploitation of the vast natural resources of this great frontier, while the spirit of adventure – from the first bold souls who came here to early fur trappers and modern-day independent thinkers – permeates the ethos of a land that continues to reinvent itself well into the 21st century.

The complete skeleton of a thalattosaur, a marine reptile that lived 200 million years ago, was found in Southeast Alaska, near Kake, in 2011.

Early Alaskans

Many parts of Alaska's early history are still under debate; at the heart of this is how North America was first populated. Some say the first Alaskans migrated from Asia to America between 15,000 and 30,000 years ago, during an ice age that lowered the sea level and created a 900-mile land bridge linking Siberia and Alaska. The nomadic groups who crossed the bridge were not bent on exploration but on following the animal herds that provided them with food and clothing. Others posit that there was more continued contact between the Old and New Worlds, with continual migrations and commerce by boat.

The first major migration, which came across the land bridge from Asia, was by the Tlingits and the Haidas, who settled throughout the Southeast and British Columbia, and the Athabascans, a nomadic tribe that settled in the Interior. The other two major groups were the Iñupiat, who settled the north coast of Alaska and Canada (where they are known as Inuit), and the Yupik, who settled Southwest Alaska. The smallest group of Alaska Natives to arrive was the Aleuts of the Aleutian Islands. The Iñupiat, Yupik and Aleuts are believed to have migrated 3000 years ago and were well established by the time the Europeans arrived.

TIMELINE	28,000–13,000 BC	2000–1500 BC	AD 1741
	The first Alaskans arrive, migrating across a 900-mile land bridge from Asia to North America – or perhaps by boat. They settle throughout the state and establish unique civilizations.	Permanent settlements in high Arctic areas start to form, first in Siberia, then spreading across Alaska and Canada and into Greenland.	Danish explorer Vitus Bering, employed by Peter the Great of Russia, becomes the first European to set foot on Alaska. His lieutenant returns to Europe with pelts that trigger a rush across the Aleutian chain.

The matrilineal Tlingit and Haida cultures were quite advanced. The tribes had permanent settlements and a class system that included chiefs, nobles, commoners and slaves – though upward (and downward) mobility were still possible. These tribes were noted for their excellent wood carving, especially carved poles, called totems, which can still be seen in Ketchikan, Sitka and many other places in the Southeast. The Tlingits were spread across the Southeast in large numbers and occasionally went as far south as Seattle in their huge dugout canoes. Both groups had few problems gathering food, as fish and game were plentiful in the Southeast.

Many tribes of the Pacific Northwest, including the Tlingit and Haida, celebrated 'potlatches.' These unique gatherings were in many ways designed to redistribute goods. Nobles would host the feasts, give gifts, free (or sometimes kill) slaves, and occasionally throw large copper shield-like objects into the ocean as a sign of their wealth. The practice was suppressed by Western interests (and even made illegal for a time) but remains today in some forms. Recent evidence indicates that Athabascan tribes also celebrated a version of the potlatch, possibly indicating a continual exchange of ideas and technologies between the numerous tribes.

Life was not so easy for the Aleuts, Iñupiat and Yupik. With much colder winters and cooler summers, these people had to develop a highly effective sea-hunting culture to sustain life in the harsh regions of Alaska. This was especially true for the Iñupiat, who could not have survived the winters without their skilled ice-hunting techniques. In spring, armed only with jade-tipped harpoons, the Iñupiat, in skin-covered kayaks called *bidarkas* and *umiaks*, stalked and killed 60-ton bowhead whales. Though motorized boats replaced the kayaks and modern harpoons the jade-tipped spears, the whaling tradition lives on in places such as Barrow.

Age of Exploration

There are over 2700 identified archaeological sites in Alaska. With extremely difficult field conditions, only a few of them have been thoroughly investigated. The limited evidence indicates these date back just 12,000 years – less than other parts of the Americas.

Due to the cold and stormy North Pacific, Alaska was one of the last places in the world to be mapped by Europeans.

Spanish Admiral Bartholomé de Fonte is credited by many with making the first European trip into Alaskan waters in 1640, but the first written record of the area was made by Vitus Bering, a Danish navigator sailing for the Russian tsar. In 1728 Bering's explorations demonstrated that America and Asia were two separate continents. Thirteen years later, Bering became the first European to set foot in Alaska, near Cordova. Bering and many of his crew died from scurvy during that journey, but his lieutenant returned to Europe with fur pelts and tales of fabulous seal and otter colonies, and Alaska's first boom was under way. The Aleutian Islands were quickly overtaken, with settlements at Unalaska and Kodiak Island. Chaos followed, as bands of Russian hunters robbed and

1778	1784	1784	1804
British explorer Captain James Cook looks for the Northwest Passage, but is eventually turned back by 12ft ice walls. British and American fur traders rush north, competing with Russian interests.	Russian Grigorii Shelikhov establishes the first permanent European settlement at Kodiak Island. Eight years later he is granted a monopoly on furs as head of the Russian-American Company.	With the introduction of European diseases, thousands of Alaska Natives perish.	With four warships, Aleksandr Baranov defeats the Tlingit at Sitka and then establishes New Archangel (Sitka's former name) as the new capital of the Russian-American Company.

NATIVE STRUGGLES

While Alaska lacks the great wars between indigenous peoples and settlers that occurred in other parts of the United States, the settlement by Russian fur traders, whalers and other outside forces had a lasting impact on Alaska's Native tribes. Before European contact, there were an estimated 80,000 people living in Alaska – a figure the state would not reach again until WWII.

Diseases introduced by Europeans were the biggest killers, but there were also limited violent clashes, especially between Russian fur traders and the Aleut. Slavery and the introduction of alcohol were other primary factors in the reduction of Alaska Native populations; some estimates indicate that during the Russian-American period the Aleut lost 80% of its tribe, and the Chugach, Tlingit, Haida and Dena'ina each lost 50%. The whalers that arrived at Iñupiat villages in the mid-19th century were similarly destructive, introducing alcohol, which devastated the lifestyles of entire villages. When the 50th anniversary of the Alaska Hwy was celebrated in 1992, many Alaska Natives and Canadians called the event a 'commemoration' not a 'celebration,' due to the destructive forces that the link to Canada and the rest of the USA brought.

murdered each other for furs, while the Aleuts, living near the hunting grounds, were almost annihilated through massacres, disease and forced labor. By the 1790s Russia had organized the Russian-American Company to regulate the fur trade and ease the violent competition.

The British arrived when Captain James Cook began searching the area for the Northwest Passage. On his third and final voyage, Cook sailed north from Vancouver Island to Southcentral Alaska in 1778, anchoring at what is now Cook Inlet before continuing on to the Aleutian Islands, Bering Sea and Arctic Ocean. The French sent Jean-François de Galaup, comte de La Pérouse, who in 1786 made it as far as Lituya Bay, now part of Glacier Bay National Park. The wicked tides within the long, narrow bay caught the exploration party off guard, killing 21 sailors and discouraging the French from colonizing the area.

The last shot of the Civil War was fired in the Bering Sea by the CSS *Shenandoah* on June 22, 1865, 74 days after the Battle of Appomattox.

Having depleted the fur colonies in the Aleutians, Aleksandr Baranov, who headed the Russian-American Company, moved his territorial capital from Kodiak to Sitka, where he built a stunning city, dubbed 'an American Paris in Alaska.' But Russian control of Alaska remained limited, and at the height of their residency, only 800 full-time Russian inhabitants lived here.

Seward's Folly

By the 1860s the Russians found themselves badly overextended: their involvement in Napoleon's European wars, a declining fur industry and the long lines of shipping between Sitka and the heartland of Russia

1857	1867	1878	1880
Coal mining begins at Coal Harbor and a new chapter in mineral extraction starts.	Secretary of State William H Seward negotiates the US purchase of Alaska from Russia for $7.2 million. It takes six months for Congress to approve the treaty.	Ten years after a salmon saltery is opened in Klawock on Prince of Wales Island, a San Francisco company builds the first salmon cannery in Alaska.	Led by Tlingit Chief Kowee, Richard Harris and Joe Juneau discover gold in Silver Bow Basin. The next year miners change their tent city's name from Harrisburg to Juneau.

were draining their national treasury. The country made several overtures to the USA to purchase Alaska, but it wasn't until 1867 that Secretary of State William H Seward signed a treaty to purchase the state for $7.2 million – less than 2¢ an acre.

By then the US public was in an uproar over the purchase of 'Seward's Ice Box' or 'Walrussia,' and on the Senate floor, the battle to ratify the treaty lasted six months. On October 18, 1867, the formal transfer of Alaska to the Americans took place in Sitka. In post Civil War America, Alaska remained a lawless, unorganized territory for the next 20 years.

This great land, remote and inaccessible to all but a few hardy settlers, stayed a dark, frozen mystery to most people, but eventually its riches were uncovered. First it was through whaling, then the phenomenal salmon runs, with the first canneries built in 1878 on Prince of Wales Island.

The Alaskan Gold Rush

What truly brought Alaska to the world's attention was gold. The promise of quick riches and frontier adventures was the most effective lure Alaska has ever had and, to some degree, still has today. Gold was discovered in the Gastineau Channel in the 1880s, and the towns of Juneau and Douglas sprang up overnight. In 1896, one of the world's most colorful gold rushes took place in the Klondike region of Canada's Yukon Territory, just across the border.

Often called 'the last grand adventure,' the Klondike Gold Rush occurred when the country and much of the world was suffering a severe recession. When the banner headline of the *Seattle Post-Intelligencer* bellowed 'GOLD! GOLD! GOLD! GOLD!' on July 17, 1897, thousands of people quit their jobs and sold their homes to finance a trip to the newly created boomtown of Skagway. From this tent city almost 30,000 prospectors tackled the steep Chilkoot Trail to Lake Bennett, where they built crude rafts to float the rest of the way to the goldfields. Nearly as many people returned home along the same route, broke and disillusioned.

The number of miners who made fortunes was small, but the tales and legends that emerged were endless. The Klondike stampede, though it only lasted from 1896 to the early 1900s, was Alaska's most colorful era and earned the state the reputation of being the country's last frontier.

Within three years of the Klondike stampede Alaska's population doubled to 63,592, including more than 30,000 non-Native people. Nome, another gold boomtown, was the largest city in the territory, with 12,000 residents, while gold prompted the capital to be moved from Sitka to Juneau. Politically, this was also the beginning of true

To enter Canada on the Chilkoot Trail, miners were required to carry a year's supply of food, including 400lb of flour and 200lb of bacon.

1882	1884	1896	1898
A US Navy cutter shells Angoon in retaliation for an uprising and then sends a landing party to loot and burn what remained of the Native village.	Local governing begins. Alaska is named the District of Alaska, the first step toward statehood.	Oil is discovered in Cook Inlet, but there is no major extraction from Alaska for another seven decades.	Klondike Gold Rush turns Skagway into Alaska's largest city, with a population of 10,000. Canadian Mounties describe the lawless town as 'little better than a hell on earth.'

Alaskan 'state building' – railroads were built, governing bodies were created, support industries were established, and a non-voting Alaskan delegate was sent to Congress in 1906. Nevertheless, it was still largely a transient state, with men outnumbering women five to one, and few people building their lifelong homes here.

World War II

In June 1942, only six months after their attack on Pearl Harbor, the Japanese opened their Aleutian Islands campaign by bombing Dutch Harbor for two days and then taking Attu and Kiska Islands. Other than Guam, it was the only foreign invasion of US soil during WWII and is often dubbed 'the Forgotten War' because most Americans are unaware of what happened in Alaska. The battle to retake Attu Island was a bloody one. After 19 days and landing more than 15,000 troops, US forces recaptured the plot of barren land, but only after suffering 3929 casualties, including 549 deaths. Of the more than 2300 Japanese on Attu, fewer than 30 surrendered, with many taking their own lives.

The Alcan & Statehood

Following the Japanese attack on the Aleutian Islands in 1942, Congress panicked and rushed to protect the rest of Alaska. Large army and airforce bases were set up at Anchorage, Fairbanks, Sitka and Whittier, and thousands of military personnel were stationed in Alaska. But it was the famous Alcan (also known as the Alaska Hwy) that was the single most important project of the military expansion. The road was built by the

BUILDING THE ALCAN

A land link between Alaska and the rest of the USA was envisioned as early as 1930, but it took WWII to turn the nation's attention north to embark on one of the greatest engineering feats of the 20th century: constructing a 1390-mile road through remote wilderness.

Deemed a military necessity and authorized by President Franklin Roosevelt only two months after the attack on Pearl Harbor, the Alcan was designed to be an overland route far enough inland to be out of range of airplanes transported on Japanese aircraft carriers. The exact route followed old winter roads, trap lines and pack trails, and by March 9, 1942, construction had begun. Within three months, more than 10,000 troops, most of them from the US Army Corps of Engineers, were in the Canadian wilderness. They endured temperatures of -30°F (-34.4°C) in April, snowfalls in June and swarms of mosquitoes and gnats for most of the summer.

When a final link was completed near Kluane Lake in late October, the Alcan was open, having been built in only eight months and 12 days.

1900	1913	1915	1923
The capital is moved from Sitka to Juneau, but as yet there are no roads to the capital.	Walter Harper, an Alaska Native, becomes the first person to summit Mt McKinley. He is joined by Harry Karstens, who later becomes the first superintendent of Denali National Park.	Anchorage is founded when Ship Creek is chosen as a survey camp to build the Alaska Railroad and after a year is a tent city of 2000.	President Warren G Harding comes to Alaska to celebrate the completion of the Alaska Railroad. The first president to visit Alaska dies within two weeks of his trip.

UNCLE TED

Ted Stevens was already a decorated WWII pilot and Harvard Law School graduate when in 1953, after accepting a position in Fairbanks, he moved to Alaska with his wife by driving the Alaska Hwy in the dead of winter. A mere six months later, Stevens was appointed the US Attorney for Fairbanks and was eventually elected as a state representative. In 1968 Stevens was appointed US senator for Alaska and held that position until 2009, never receiving less than 66% of the vote after his first election in 1970.

Such longevity allowed Stevens to break Strom Thurmond's record as the longest-serving Republican senator in 2007, with 38 years and three months of continual service. For the majority of Alaskans, Stevens had always been their senator – the reason many dubbed him 'senator for life.'

The senator was duly noted for his ability to bring home the 'pork': in 2008 the Feds returned $295 per Alaskan citizen in local projects (other states average only $34 per person). In 2005 Stevens was ridiculed by the national media when, in a speech from the Senate floor, he angrily opposed diverting the Bridge to Nowhere funds to help New Orleans recover from Hurricane Katrina. Congress dropped the specific allocation for the bridge, but Alaska still received the money and simply spent it elsewhere.

Stevens' legendary Senate tenure came to an end in 2009. The previous year, a jury found him guilty of federal corruption – failing to report tens of thousands of dollars in gifts and services he had received from friends – and convicted him of seven felony charges. Stevens vowed to appeal the decision, but in November Alaskans had had enough and narrowly voted him out of office in his bid for an eighth term. The indictment was dismissed after a federal probe found evidence of prosecutorial misconduct.

In 2010 Stevens was killed in a not-unusual Alaskan accident: a small-plane crash (outside Dillingham in Southwest Alaska).

military, but Alaska's residents benefited, as the Alcan helped them access and make use of Alaska's natural resources.

In 1916 Alaska's territorial legislature submitted its first statehood bill. The effort was first quashed by the Seattle-based canned-salmon industry, which wanted to prevent local control of Alaska's resources; then the stock market crash of 1929 and WWII kept Congress occupied with more-demanding issues. But the growth that came with the Alcan, and to a lesser degree the new military bases, pushed Alaska firmly into the American culture and renewed its drive for statehood. When the US Senate passed the Alaska statehood bill on June 30, 1958, Alaska had made it into the Union and was officially proclaimed the country's 49th state by President Dwight Eisenhower the following January.

Alaska entered the 1960s full of promise, but then disaster struck: the most powerful earthquake ever recorded in North America (registering

1935	1942	1959	1964
The first of 200 Depression-era families from Minnesota, Wisconsin and Michigan arrive in the Matanuska Valley to begin farming as part of Franklin Roosevelt's New Deal experiment and Palmer is established.	Japan bombs Dutch Harbor for two days during WWII and then invades the remote Aleutian Islands of Attu and Kiska. Americans build the Alcan (Alaska Hwy).	Alaska officially becomes the 49th state when President Dwight Eisenhower signs the statehood declaration on January 3. The state's population swells.	North America's worst earthquake, 9.2 on the Richter scale, takes place on Good Friday, devastating Anchorage and Southcentral Alaska, with 131 people losing their lives.

9.2 on the Richter scale) hit Southcentral Alaska on Good Friday morning in 1964. More than 100 lives were lost, and damage was estimated at $500 million. In Anchorage, office buildings sank 10ft into the ground, and houses slid more than 1200ft off a bluff into Knik Arm. A tidal wave virtually obliterated the community of Valdez. In Kodiak and Seward, 32ft of the coastline slipped into the Gulf of Alaska, and Cordova lost its entire harbor as the sea rose 16ft.

The Alaskan Black-Gold Rush

The devastating 1964 earthquake left the newborn state in a shambles, but a more pleasant gift from nature soon rushed Alaska to recovery and beyond. In 1968 Atlantic Richfield discovered massive oil deposits underneath Prudhoe Bay in the Arctic Ocean. The value of the oil doubled after the Arab oil embargo of 1973. However, it couldn't be tapped until there was a pipeline to transport it to the warm-water port of Valdez. And the pipeline couldn't be built until the US Congress, which still administered most of the land, settled the intense controversy among industry, environmentalists and Alaska Natives over historical claims to the land.

The *Alaska Native Claims Settlement Act* of 1971 was an unprecedented piece of legislation that opened the way for a consortium of oil companies to undertake the construction of the 789-mile pipeline. The act allocated $962.5 million and 99 million acres (including mineral rights) to Alaska Natives. Half of the money went directly to the Native villages, while the other half funded the creation of 12 Native corporations. There are now 13 Native corporations in Alaska; they manage land, invest in diverse endeavors and provide dividends to Native peoples.

The Trans-Alaska Pipeline took three years to build, cost more than $8 billion – in 1977 dollars – and, at the time, was the most expensive private construction project ever undertaken.

The oil began to flow on June 20, 1977, and for a decade oil gave Alaska an economic base that was the envy of every other state, accounting for as much as 80% of state government revenue. With oil proceeds, the state created the Alaska Permanent Fund – which grew from just $700,000 to over $44 billion today. Full-time residents still receive annual dividend checks.

In the explosive growth period of the mid-1980s, Alaskans enjoyed the highest per-capita income in the country. The state's budget was in the billions. Legislators in Juneau transformed Anchorage into a stunning city, with sports arenas, libraries and performing-arts centers, and provided virtually every bush town with a million-dollar school. From 1980 to 1986 this state of only half a million residents generated revenue of $26 billion.

From Pump Station No 1 to Valdez, the Trans-Alaska Pipeline crosses three mountain ranges, 34 major rivers and 500 streams.

HISTORY THE ALASKAN BLACK-GOLD RUSH

1968	1971	1973	1980
Oil and natural gas are discovered at Prudhoe Bay on the North Slope. The next year the state of Alaska stages a $900 million North Slope oil-lease sale.	President Richard Nixon signs the *Alaska Native Claims Settlement Act* to pave the way for the Trans-Alaska Pipeline. Alaska Natives give up claims in return for nearly $1 billion and 44 million acres.	The first Iditarod Trail Sled Dog Race is held on an old dog-team mail route blazed in 1910. The winner covers the 1049-mile race between Wasilla and Nome in 20 days.	President Jimmy Carter signs the *Alaska National Interests Lands Conservation Act* (ANILCA), preserving 79.54 million acres of wilderness and creating or enlarging 15 national parks.

Disaster at Valdez

For most Alaskans, the abundant oil made it hard to see beyond the gleam of the oil dollar. Reality hit hard in 1989, when the *Exxon Valdez*, a 987ft Exxon oil supertanker, rammed Bligh Reef a few hours out of the port of Valdez. The ship spilled almost 11 million gallons of North Slope crude oil into the bountiful waters of Prince William Sound. Alaskans and the rest of the country watched in horror as the oil spill quickly became too large to contain, spreading 600 miles from the grounding site. State residents were shocked as oil began to appear elsewhere, from the glacier-carved cliffs of Kenai Fjords to the bird rookeries of Katmai National Park. The spill eventually contaminated 1567 miles of shoreline and killed an estimated 100,000 to 250,000 birds and 2800 sea otters, also decimating fish populations. The fisheries are just now recovering from the spill, as are animal populations, though you can still find oil just below the sand on many beaches.

Today the oil, like other resources exploited in the past, is simply running out. That pot of gold called Prudhoe Bay began its decline in 1988 and now produces less than half of its 1987 peak of two million barrels a day. The end of the Cold War and the subsequent downsizing of the US military in the early 1990s was more bad economic news for Alaska. Alaskan state revenues, once the envy of every other state governor in the country, went tumbling along with the declining oil royalties. With more than 80% of its state budget derived from oil revenue, Alaska was awash in red ink from the early 1990s until 2004, managing a balanced budget only twice.

Out of the Channel: the Exxon Valdez Oil Spill in Prince William Sound (1999), by John Keeble, is an in-depth account of Exxon's response and cover-up, which the author contends did more damage than the original spill.

The Alaskan Way of Life

Cut off from the rest of the United States, this great northern oasis has been attracting renegades, free thinkers, roughneck profiteers and nature lovers from the very beginning. Alaska is about independence, rugged individualism and taking care of business. It's a state of transient workers, rugged frontiersmen and women, and down-home sensibilities, and a place that attracts the eccentric in all of us. And that's what makes the Alaskan way of life so fascinating.

Regional Identity

Most of Alaska may be rural, road-less areas collectively known as the Bush, but most Alaskans are urban. Almost 60% of the residents live in the three largest cities: Anchorage, Fairbanks and Juneau.

The vast majority of households in rural Alaska participate in subsistence living. Studies show that 86% use game and 95% use fish. There are also Alaskans who gather and hunt the majority of their food and live in small villages that can only be reached by boat, plane or, in the winter, snowmobile. But the majority live in urban neighborhoods, work a nine-to-five job and shop at the supermarket.

And most Alaskans are newcomers. Only 30% of the state's population was born in Alaska; the rest moved there – including all but one of its eight elected governors. Such a transient population creates a melting pot of ideas, philosophies and priorities. What they usually have in common is an interest in the great outdoors: they were lured here to either exploit it or enjoy it, and many residents do a little of both.

Thus debates in Alaska usually center on access to land, resources, and, in particular, the wilderness. There are some liberal bastions of environmentalism, Juneau and Homer being the best known, but over the years Alaskans have moved to the right, voting for Republican presidents, fighting tax increases and becoming one of the first states to pass a constitutional amendment banning same-sex marriages.

Travelers come to visit and marvel at the grand scenery. But Alaskans are here to stay, so they need to make a living in their chosen home, a land where there is little industry or farming. They regard trees, oil and fish as an opportunity to do that.

According to a marketing research firm, Anchorage has three coffee shops per 10,000 residents, beating out even Seattle, and making it, per capita, the country's mocha mecca.

Lifestyle

In Anchorage, residents can shop at enclosed malls, spend an afternoon at one of 162 parks, go in-line skating along paved bike paths, or get in their car and drive to another town. By contrast, in Nunapitchuk, 400 miles west of Anchorage on the swampy tundra of the Yukon–Kuskokwim Delta, the population is 517, there are no roads to or within town, homes and buildings are connected by a network of boardwalks, and there is just one store and a health clinic.

Rural or urban, Alaskans tend to be individualistic, following few outside trends and, instead, adhering to what their harsh environment dictates. Mother Nature and those -30°F (-34.4°C) winter days are responsible for the Alaskan dress code, even in Anchorage's finest restaurants. Alaskans also like to take care of things on their own, and many seek out spartan and tough living conditions. In the Bush, most homes feature a big pile of old airplane parts, broken-down cars and construction materials in the front yard – you never know when a hard-to-find part may come in handy.

American visitors may find that most of the locals they meet in towns and cities have lifestyles similar to their own. They work, they love their weekends, they live in a variety of homes big and small, and they participate in double-coupon days at supermarkets. Even in remote villages there are satellite TV dishes and internet access to the rest of the world.

But Alaska also has social ills, exacerbated in a large measure by the environment. The isolation of small towns and the darkness of winter have contributed to Alaska being one of the top 10 states for binge and heavy drinking, and sixth overall for the amount of alcohol sold per capita. Since the 1980s, Alaska has seen some of the highest per capita use of controlled drugs in the country, and its suicide rate is twice the national average. Alcohol abuse and suicide rates are higher for Alaska Natives than other populations.

To survive this climate and to avoid such demons, you have to possess a passion for the land and an individualistic approach to a lifestyle that few, other than Alaskans, would choose.

Sports

Women won the 1049-mile Iditarod Trail Sled Dog Race five out of six years from 1985 to 1990, and finished second the one year they didn't win it.

The state sport of Alaska, officially adopted in 1972, is dog mushing, and the biggest spectator event is the Iditarod. But there are other spectator sports in Alaska that you don't have to bundle up to watch, including baseball. The **Alaska Baseball League** (www.alaskabaseballleague. org) features six semipro teams of good college players eyeing the major leagues. Teams include Fairbanks' **Alaska Goldpanners** (www.goldpan ners.com) and the **Anchorage Bucs** (www.anchoragebucs.com). Major leaguers who have played in Alaska include sluggers Barry Bonds and Mark McGwire.

The state's most unusual sporting event is the **World Eskimo-Indian Olympics** (www.weio.org) in July, when several hundred athletes converge on Fairbanks. For four days Alaska Natives compete in greased-pole walking, seal skinning, blanket tosses and other events that display the skills traditionally needed for survival in a harsh environment.

Alaska in the Popular Imagination

Alaska has a role in the collective imagination as a mysterious, often frozen, dramatically scenic land. Not surprisingly, the state's portrayal in popular media often reflects this idea.

Literature

Two of the best-known writers identified with Alaska were not native to the land nor did they spend much time there, but Jack London and Robert Service turned their Alaskan adventures into literary careers.

The first print run of Jack London's *Call of the Wild* – 10,000 books – sold out in 24 hours. London, an American, departed for the Klondike Gold Rush in 1897, hoping to get rich panning gold. Instead he produced 50 books of fiction and nonfiction in just 17 years, and became the country's highest-paid writer of the day.

Service, a Canadian bank teller, was transferred to Dawson City in 1902 and then wrote his first book of verse, *The Spell of the Yukon*. The work was an immediate success and contained his best-known ballads,

'The Shooting of Dan McGrew' and 'The Cremation of Sam McGee.' Both portray the hardship and violence of life during the gold rush.

Alaska's contemporary luminaries of literature are no less elegant in capturing the spirit of the Far North. Kotzebue author Seth Kantner followed his critically acclaimed first novel, *Ordinary Wolves,* with the equally intriguing *Shopping for Porcupine,* a series of short stories about growing up in the Alaska wilderness. One of the best Alaska Native novels is *Two Old Women* by Velma Wallis, an Athabascan born in Fort Yukon. This moving tale covers the saga of two elderly women abandoned by their migrating tribe during a harsh winter.

Other Alaskans who have captured the soul of the Far North include Nick Jans, whose *The Last Light Breaking* is considered a classic on life among the Iñupiat, and Sherry Simpson, who chronicles living in Fairbanks in the series of wonderful stories, *The Way Winter Comes.* For entertaining fiction using Alaska's commercial fishing as a stage, there's Bill

THE IDITAROD – LOVE IT OR LEAVE IT?

The Iditarod is one of the most iconic races in the world, and mushing is one of Alaska's most beloved pastimes. Supporters of the sport say sled dogs are born and bred to run, and if you've ever been tethered to a team flying across the frozen tundra, you'd probably agree. But a growing number of opponents say races like the Iditarod are cruel. Numerous reports of underfed, beaten and culled sled dogs at operations in Canada, Colorado and Alaska beg the question: should you support a race that has seen the death of 140-plus dogs since 1973? Should you even take a tourist trip on a dog sled?

History of the Race

In 1948 Joe Redington Sr arrived in Alaska with just $18 in his pocket, and used $13 of it to cover a filing fee for a 101-acre homestead in Knik. By accident – some say fate – Redington's homestead was located only a few hundred feet from the historic Iditarod Trail, an old dogsled mail route from Seward to Nome. Redington was fascinated by the Iditarod Trail and the famous 'serum run' that saved the town of Nome from diphtheria in 1925, when mushers used the trail to relay medical supplies across Alaska.

Worried that snowmobiles might replace sled dogs, Redington proposed an Anchorage–Nome race along the historic trail, and then staged the first 1049-mile Iditarod in 1973. Alaska's 'Last Great Race,' the world's longest sled-dog event, was born. The Iditarod is held in early March, when the temperatures are in the low teens and snow coverage is good.

Pros & Cons

People for the Ethical Treatment of Animals (PETA) is absolutely opposed to dog sledding, while other groups like the Sled Dog Action Coalition and US Humane Society support recreational mushing as long as cruel practices (like beating dogs) do not occur. One issue is that winning times are dropping – from 20 days in 1973 to around 10 today – putting greater stress on the dogs, who suffer from ulcers, bruised and lacerated paws, and damaged lungs. On the Iditarod, about one or two dogs die each year (20 died in 2005), and around a third end up dropping out of the race. There's also the questionable practice of culling, where hundreds of substandard dogs are either given away or euthanized by their owners to ensure faster pedigrees. Race supporters cite new standards put in place to ensure the safety of dogs, including veterinarian checkups, mandatory breaks and drug tests.

Top Resources

Sled Dog Action Coalition (www.helpsleddogs.org)

PETA (www.peta.org)

Iditarod (www.iditarod.com)

McCloskey, whose three novels have characters ranging from the greenhorn fisherman to the hard-nosed cannery manager, with the plotline leaping from one to the next. His first, *Highliners,* is still his best.

Small cabins and long winter nights filled with sinister thoughts have also given rise to Alaska's share of mystery writers. Dean of the Alaskan whodunit is *New York Times* best seller Dana Stabenow, whose ex-DA investigator Kate Shugak has appeared in around 20 novels, some of which are free as e-books. Sue Henry is equally prolific with musher-turned-crime-solver Jessie Arnold in novels such as *Murder on the Iditarod Trail* and *Cold Company.*

Alaska is also popular ground for nonfiction. Jon Krakauer's *Into the Wild* explores the lost journeyer Chris McCandless and mankind's desire to seek isolation and connection with the earth. John McPhee's 1991 classic *Coming into the Country* explores the explosive personalities of Alaska's fringe.

Cinema, TV & Music

The War Journal of Lila Ann Smith (2007), by Irving Warner, is a moving historical novel, based on the invasion of Attu by the Japanese in WWII, and the Aleuts who became prisoners of war.

Hollywood and Alaska occasionally mix, especially in Hyder. This tiny, isolated town (population 83) has been the setting for numerous films, most recently *Insomnia* (2002), in which Al Pacino plays a cop sent to a small Alaskan town to investigate a killer played by Robin Williams. There's also *Bear Island* (1978), loaded with stars, and *Ice Man* (1984), about scientists who find a frozen prehistoric man and bring him back to life. The 2007 movie *Into the Wild* featured many Alaska locations, including Anchorage, Healy, Denali National Park, Cantwell and the Copper River.

Recent Hollywood tax breaks have led to more films being shot in the 49th state: in 2010 Drew Barrymore and John Krasinski were on location filming *Everybody Loves Whales,* and more films are being lined up.

Alaska has also been the backdrop for TV, including the Emmy Award–winning series *Northern Exposure,* but reality TV is where it's hit the mother lode. The Discovery channel has basically staked its lineup on Alaska; there are new shows, like *Alaskan Bush People,* and the ever popular crab-fight-fest, *Deadliest Catch.* Everywhere in between you have spin-offs about gold mining, ice-trucking, survival and logging.

Alaskan composer John Luther Adams won a Pulitzer Prize for Music in 2014 for his *Become Ocean* composition, which is inspired by the waterways and rhythms of Alaska. Singer-songwriter Jewel was raised in Homer and got her start playing local bars with her father.

Alaska Natives

Alaska Natives play an integral part in the Great Land's modern-day politics, culture and commerce. While their cultural imprint stretches back 10,000 years, present-day traditions and practices are evolving, dying off and transforming as the tide of Western influences sweeps through the state. Economically and politically, much of the work of the tribes happens on a village level, while the 13 Native corporations established by the *Alaska Native Claims Settlement Act* manage vast land and financial assets.

The People

Before 1940, Alaska Natives were in the majority. They now represent just 16% of the population. With 36,000 Alaska Natives, Anchorage is sometimes called the state's 'largest Native village.' Tribes once inhabited separate regions: the Aleuts and Alutiiqs lived from Prince William Sound to the Aleutian Islands; the Iñupiat, Yupik and Cupik occupied

Above Totem mural, Juneau (p116)

Alaska's northern and western coasts; the Athabascan populated the Interior; and the Tlingit, Haida, Eyak and Tsimshian lived along the southeast coasts. Urban migration has blurred lines.

Two-thirds of Alaska Natives live in villages within their ancestral lands. Though outwardly modern, the heart of village life is still the practice of subsistence hunting, fishing and gathering – around 50% of village diets still come from subsistence food gathering. Though critical to rural economies, the customs and traditions associated with subsistence are also the basis of Native culture. Subsistence activities are cooperative, helping maintain community bonds, preserve traditional festivities and oral histories, facilitate a spiritual connection to the land, and provide inspiration and material for artists.

Language

Alaska has at least 20 distinct Native languages. Native language use varies: the last Eyak speaker died in 2008, Haida has only a handful of speakers remaining, but Yupik is still spoken by about half the population. Even so, few children are currently learning any Native language as their mother tongue, though there is a mounting interest to ensure Native-language preservation and instruction.

Many of the Native tribes have specialized vocabularies. For instance, modern linguists say the Iñupiat have about 70 terms for ice and the Yupik language has 50 words for snow.

Arts & Crafts

Alaska Natives produce much of the state's most creative work. Not content to rest on tradition, contemporary indigenous artists push boundaries and reinterpret old forms.

Traditionally, Native artisans gathered their materials in the fall and began work in December, when cold weather forced them to remain inside. Materials varied according to what the local environment or trade routes could supply, and included wood, ivory, bone, antler, birch bark and grasses.

Production of Native crafts for a Western market began in the 18th century with Iñupiat ivory carvers and, later, Aleut basket weavers, adapting traditional forms for collectors. Today, the sale of Native art comprises a large slice of the economy in many Bush communities.

Carving

Ivory carving is practically synonymous with the Iñupiat, though they will also use wood, bone and antler. In addition to sculptures depicting hunting scenes or wild animals, scrimshaw (known as 'engraved ivory') is also produced. These incredibly detailed etchings often present a vignette of daily life on a whale bone or walrus tusk.

Yupik carvings tend to have more intricate surface detailing, and feature stylized designs. Red clay paint is sometimes used for coloring.

Natives of the Southeast, such as the Haida and Tlingit, have a lively woodcarving tradition that's heavy on abstractions based on clan sym-

---

Top Places to See Native Art

University of Alaska Museum of the North (p293)

Alaska Native Medical Center (p161)

Iñupiat Heritage Center (p368)

Totem Heritage Center (p82)

Sitka National Historical Park (p109)

Alaska Native Heritage Center (p160)

Ilanka Cultural Center (p205)

Alutiiq Museum & Archaeological Repository (p331)

REINDEER GAMES

At the turn of the 20th century, numerous Sami people, from northern Scandinavia and Russia, were brought to Alaska to teach reindeer husbandry to the Iñupiat. Domesticated reindeer are not native to these lands, though their wild cousins, the caribou, are. Franklin D Roosevelt's Reindeer Act prohibited the ownership of reindeer herds by non-Natives in Alaska. Today reindeer play an important role in Native economies – and the sausage meat tastes great!

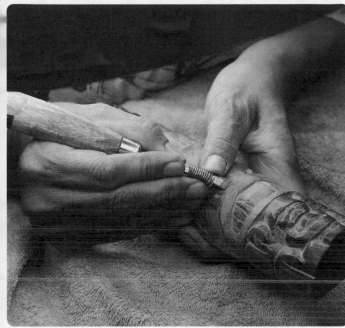

Woodcarving, Sitka (p107)

bols. Their totem poles are known worldwide but they are also masters at wood masks and bentwood boxes.

Purchasing ivory and bone crafts made from at-risk species is a personal decision for visitors to Alaska. Across the globe, it's a frowned-upon practice, particularly where ivory poaching poses serious risks to wildlife populations. In Alaska, it's a bit different. Alaska Natives are permitted to hunt endangered species – and most experts say that Alaska Native harvests have no impact on populations of species like whales. They also use every part of the animal, rely on the meat for their subsistence lifestyle and make a little extra spending money by creating some amazing crafts from bone and ivory.

Dolls & Masks

All Native groups share a love of dolls, and traditionally used them in ceremonies, as fertility symbols, for play and for teaching young girls about motherhood. Modern doll-making is said to have begun in the 1940s in Kotzebue with the work of Ethel Washington, and continues today as one of the most vibrant Native art forms. Dolls can look realistic or be deliberate caricatures, such as the Chevak area 'ugly-faced' dolls with their wrinkled leather faces and humorous expressions.

Masks were traditionally used by Yupik and Iñupiat peoples for midwinter hunting festivals. Today you can find wonderful examples carved in wood and sewn from caribou.

Baskets

Perhaps no single form represents indigenous art better than basketry. Decorative patterns are geometric or reflect the region's animals, insects or plants. Athabascans weave baskets from alder, willow roots and birch bark; the Tlingit use cedar bark and spruce root; Yupik often decorate

Tlingit ceremony, Anchorage (p158)

their baskets with sea-lion whiskers and feathers, and a few dye them with seal guts. Iñupiat are famous for using whale baleen, but this is in fact a 20th-century invention.

The Aleuts are perhaps the most renowned basket weavers. Using rye grass, which is tough but pliable, artists create tiny, intricately woven pieces that are highly valued.

Embroidery & Clothing

Athabascan women traditionally decorated clothing with dyed quills, but after Europeans introduced beads and embroidery techniques they quickly became masters of this decorative art. Their long, hanging baby belts are often purchased as wall hangings.

Both Haida and Yupik are renowned for *mukluks* (knee-high boots) and decorative parkas.

Challenges

There are 229 federally recognized tribes in Alaska, but no reservation system. In 1971 Alaska Natives renounced claims to aboriginal lands in return for 44 million acres of land, $962.5 million and 100 shares per person in regional, urban and village corporations. While the settlement was a cause of pride, it has done little for employment and household income.

There are many other social challenges. Few issues are as serious as alcohol abuse, which has led to a high rate of fetal alcohol syndrome, domestic violence, crime and suicides. Since 1980 the state has allowed local control of alcohol and 120 villages now have some form of prohibition. Needless to say, you shouldn't introduce alcohol to Native dry villages. Other challenges include recruiting sufficient teachers, police officers and medical professionals to the Bush, and improving the diet of Native people.

Alaskan Landscapes

It's one thing to be told Mt McKinley is the tallest mountain in North America; it's another to see it crowning the sky in Denali National Park. It's a mountain so tall, so massive and so overwhelming, it has visitors stumbling off the park buses. As a state, Alaska is the same, a place so huge, so wild and so unpopulated, it's incomprehensible to most people until they arrive.

The Land

Dramatic mountain ranges arch across the landmass of Alaska. The Pacific Mountain System, which includes the Alaska, Aleutian and St Elias Ranges, as well as the Chugach and Kenai Mountains, sweeps along the south before dipping into the sea southwest of Kodiak Island. Further north looms the imposing and little-visited Brooks Range, skirting the Arctic Circle.

In between the Alaska and Brooks Ranges is Interior Alaska, an immense plateau rippled by foothills, low mountains and magnificent rivers, among them the third longest in the USA, the mighty Yukon River, which runs for 2300 miles. North of the Brooks Range is the North Slope, a coastal plain of scrubby tundra that gently descends to the Arctic Ocean.

The Alaska Volcano Observatory website (www. avo.alaska.edu) has webcams and a 'volcano alert' map so you can see what's shaking and where.

In geological terms Alaska is relatively young and still very active. The state represents the northern boundary of the chain of Pacific Ocean volcanoes known as the 'Ring of Fire' and is the most seismically active region of North America. In fact, Alaska claims 52% of the earthquakes that occur in the country and averages more than 13 each day. Most are mild shakes, but some are deadly. Three of the six largest earthquakes in the world – and seven of the 10 largest in the USA – have occurred in Alaska.

Most of the state's volcanoes lie in a 1550-mile arc from the Alaska Peninsula to the tip of the Aleutian Islands. This area contains more than 65 volcanoes, 46 of which have been active in the last 200 years. Even in the past four decades Alaska has averaged more than two eruptions per year. If you spend any time in this state, or read about its history, you will quickly recognize that belching volcanoes and trembling earthquakes (as much as glaciers and towering peaks) are defining characteristics of the last frontier.

Southeast Alaska

Southeast Alaska is a 500-mile coastal strip extending from north of Prince Rupert right across to the Gulf of Alaska. In between are the hundreds of islands of the Alexander Archipelago, and a narrow strip of coast, separated from Canada's mainland by the glacier-filled Coast Mountains. Winding through the middle of the region is the Inside Passage waterway; a lifeline for isolated communities, as the rugged terrain prohibits road-building. High annual rainfall and mild temperatures have turned the Southeast into rainforest, broken up by majestic mountain ranges, glaciers and fjords.

Prince William Sound & Kenai Peninsula

Like the Southeast, much of this region (also known as Southcentral Alaska) is a jumble of rugged mountains, glaciers, steep fjords and lush forests. This mix of terrain makes Kenai Peninsula a superb recreational area for backpacking, fishing and boating, while Prince William Sound, home of Columbia Glacier, is a mecca for kayakers and other adventurers.

Geographically, the Kenai Peninsula is a grab-bag. The Chugach Range receives the most attention, but in fact mountains only cover around two-thirds of the peninsula. On the east side of the peninsula is glorious Kenai Fjords National Park, encompassing tidewater glaciers that pour down from one of the continent's largest ice fields, as well as the steep-sided fjords those glaciers have carved. Abutting the park in places, and taking in much of the most southerly part of the Kenai Peninsula, is Kachemak Bay State Park, a wondrous land of mountains, forests and fjords.

Covering much of the interior of the peninsula, the Kenai National Wildlife Refuge offers excellent canoeing and hiking routes, plus some of the world's best salmon fishing. On the west side, the land flattens out into a marshy, lake-pocked region excellent for canoeing and trout fishing.

Prince William Sound is completely enveloped by the vast Chugach National Forest, the second-largest national forest in the US.

Southwest Alaska

Stretching 1500 miles from Kodiak Island to the international date line, the Southwest is spread out over four areas: the Kodiak Archipelago including Kodiak Island, the Alaska Peninsula, the Aleutian Islands and Bristol Bay. For the most part it is an island-studded region with stormy weather and violent volcanoes. This is the northern rim of the Ring of Fire, and along the Alaska Peninsula and the Aleutian Islands is the greatest concentration of volcanoes in North America.

Southwest Alaska is home to some of the state's largest and most intriguing national parks and refuges. Katmai National Park & Preserve, on the Alaska Peninsula, and Kodiak National Wildlife Refuge are renowned for bear watching. Lake Clark National Park & Preserve, across Cook Inlet from Anchorage, is a wilderness playground for rafters, anglers and hikers.

Roadside Geology of Alaska (1988), by Cathy Connor and Daniel O'Haire, explores the geology you see from the road, covering everything from earthquakes to why there's gold on the beaches of Nome – not dull reading by any means.

ALASKA'S GLACIERS

Alaska is one of the few places in the world where active glaciation occurs on a grand scale. There are an estimated 100,000 glaciers in Alaska, covering 28,000 sq miles, or 3% of the state, and containing three-quarters of all Alaska's fresh water. The effects of glaciation, both from current and ice age glaciers, are visible everywhere and include wide U-shaped valleys, kettle ponds, fjords and heavily silted rivers.

Glaciers are formed when the snowfall exceeds the rate of melting and the solid cap of ice that forms begins to flow like a frozen river. The rate of flow, or retreat, can be anything but 'glacial,' and sometimes reaches tens of yards per day. While most of Alaska's glaciers are in rapid retreat, roughly 2% of them are advancing – actually growing in size.

Glaciers are impressive-looking formations, and because ice absorbs all the colors of the spectrum except blue, they often give off a distinct blue tinge. The more overcast the day, the bluer glacial ice appears. The exceptions are glaciers that are covered with layers of rock and silt (the glacier's moraine) and appear more like mounds of dirt. For example, the Kennicott Glacier in Wrangell-St Elias National Park is often mistaken for a vast dump of old mine tailings.

The largest glacier in Alaska is the Malaspina, which sits at the southern base of Mt St Elias and blankets 850 sq miles.

One of the most spectacular sights is watching – and hearing – tidewater glaciers 'calve' icebergs (the act of releasing small to massive chunks of glacier). Tidewater glaciers extend from a land base into the sea (or a lake) and calve icebergs in massive explosions of water. Active tidewater glaciers can be viewed from tour boats in Glacier Bay National Park, Kenai Fjords National Park and Prince William Sound, which has the largest collection in Alaska.

Most of the Aleutian Islands and part of the Alaska Peninsula form the huge Alaska Maritime National Wildlife Refuge, headquartered in Homer. The refuge encompasses 3.5 million acres and more than 2500 islands, and is home to 80% of the 50 million seabirds that nest in Alaska.

Denali & the Interior

With the Alaska Range to the north, the Wrangell and Chugach Mountains to the south and the Talkeetna Mountains cutting through the middle, the Interior has a rugged appearance matching that of either Southeast or Southcentral Alaska.

Mountains are everywhere. The formidable Alaska Range creates a jagged spine through the interior's midsection, while the smaller ranges – the Chugach, Talkeetna and Wrangell to the south and the White Mountains to the north – sit on the flanks. From each of these mountain ranges run major river systems. Spruce and birch predominate in the lowland valleys with their tidy lakes. Higher up on the broad tundra meadows, spectacular wildflowers show their colors during summer months. Wildfire also plays its role here, wiping out vast swaths of forest nearly every summer.

The big name here, of course, is Denali National Park, blessed with the continent's mightiest mountain and abundant wildlife. Wrangell-St Elias National Park, located in the region's southeast corner, is the largest national park in the US and a treasure house of glaciers and untouched wilderness. Up in the Interior's northeast is Yukon-Charley Rivers National Preserve, located at the nexus of two of the state's legendary waterways.

The Bush

This is the largest slice of Alaska and includes the Brooks Range, Arctic Alaska and western Alaska on the Bering Sea. The remote, hard-to-reach Bush is separated from the rest of the state by mountains, rivers and vast roadless distances.

The mighty Brooks Range slices this region in two. To the north, a vast plain of tundra sweeps down to the frozen wasteland of the Arctic Ocean. In the western reaches, near towns such as Nome and Kotzebue, you'll find more tundra, as well as a flat landscape of lakes and slow-moving rivers closer to the Bering Sea, and rolling coastal hills and larger mountains heading toward the interior.

The Bush has several national parks and preserves. Gates of the Arctic National Park & Preserve spans the spires of the Brooks Range and offers spectacular hiking and paddling. Near Kotzebue is Kobuk Valley National Park, known for the Great Kobuk Sand Dunes and the oft-paddled Kobuk River, with the mountain-ringed Noatak National Preserve just to the north.

Major Vegetation Zones of Alaska

With its vast territory extending from the frigid Arctic Ocean to the temperate Gulf of Alaska, and encompassing mountain ranges, river valleys, sweeping plains, island chains and a range of climatic conditions, Alaska harbors a diversity of ecosystems. Most of the state, however, can be categorized into three large zones: tundra, taiga and temperate forest.

Tundra

Tundra comes from the Finnish word for barren or treeless land. Of course, tundra isn't completely barren but often a bewitching landscape of grasses, herbs, mosses, lichens and, during the short summer, wildflowers. Nevertheless, tundra soil is generally poor, the diversity of plants

Want to see if Mt McKinley is clouded over before you visit? Check out Denali National Park's webcam for the latest conditions (www.nps.gov/dena/photos-multimedia/webcams.htm).

ALASKAN LANDSCAPES MAJOR VEGETATION ZONES OF ALASKA

is low and the growing season extremely short: sometimes plants have as little as one-and-a-half months a year to sprout.

Lowland tundra extends along the coastal regions of the Arctic, and the deltas of western Alaska around Nome. What's referred to as upland tundra covers the land at higher elevations above the treeline throughout the Alaska Range, as well as across the Brooks Range and all along the Aleutians.

The Great Kobuk Sand Dunes comprise a 25-sq-mile swath of sand, 40 miles above the Arctic Circle. Remnants of ancient glaciers, some dunes rise 100ft high.

Taiga

Taiga, also called boreal forest, runs from Interior Alaska through Canada and down past the Great Lakes. Taiga forests are low and damp, often broken up with lakes and bogs. The most common species of trees are white spruce, black spruce, birch and aspen. Trees tend to be short and scraggly, and grow in thickets.

Most of Interior Alaska (at lower elevations) is covered in taiga. It's great moose habitat, so keep your eyes peeled in such areas.

Between the taiga and tundra is a transitional area in which species from either zone may be found. On the ride up the Dalton Hwy, a famous 'Last Spruce' is a curious testament to the fact that while transitions rarely have exact boundaries, they do have to end somewhere.

Coastal Temperate Forest

Alaska's temperate forests are found, no surprise, in southeastern Alaska, along the Gulf of Alaska, as well as the eastern edge of the Kenai Peninsula. They form part of the system of coastal rainforests that runs north from the Pacific Northwest and are dominated by Sitka spruce and other softwoods. Precipitation is high in this region and the winters mild; as a result trees can grow to be giants over 229ft tall. It's no surprise that Alaska Natives from this region are masters at woodcarving, and created the splendid totem pole culture that is now famous around the world.

CLIMATE CHANGE & ALASKA

Alaska's temperatures are rising, causing permafrost to melt, coastlines to erode, forests to die (or push north into new territory), and Arctic sea ice and glaciers to melt at alarming rates (90% of Southeast glaciers are retreating rapidly). Some scientists now predict the Arctic Ocean will be entirely ice-free in summer by 2040, or even sooner. Meanwhile, Portage Glacier can no longer be viewed from its visitor center, and Mendenhall Glacier is expected to retreat totally onto land and cease being a tidewater glacier within five years.

Northern Alaska is ground zero when it comes to global warming, and with the vast majority of the land sitting on permafrost – and aboriginal traditions and whole ecosystems inextricably tied to the frozen earth and sea – the very balance of nature has been thrown into disaccord. At Shishmaref, a barrier island village on the Seward Peninsula, residents have watched with horror as homes have literally slipped into the Bering Sea due to the loss of protective sea ice that buffers them against storms. And Shishmaref is just one of 160 rural communities the US Army Corps of Engineers has identified as being threatened by erosion. Relocation plans have already begun for several of these.

Paradoxically, in Juneau sea levels are dropping as billions of tons of ice have melted away, literally springing the land to new heights. In some areas the land is rising 3in a year, the highest rate in North America. As a result, water tables are dropping, wetlands are drying up and property lines are having to be redrawn.

Beyond the disaster for humans, the changes to the Alaskan landscape and climate will have dramatic effects on the highly adapted organisms that call this place home. In Juneau, the rising land has already caused channels that once facilitated salmon runs to silt up and grass over. In the far north, melting summer sea ice is expected to put such pressure on the polar bear that in 2008 the animal was listed as a 'threatened' species.

Mt McKinley reflected in a tundra pond in Denali National Park (p263)

Climate

Oceans surround 75% of Alaska, the terrain is mountainous and the sun shines at a low angle. All this gives the state an extremely variable climate, and daily weather that is infamous for its unpredictability.

For visitors, the most spectacular part of Alaska's climate is its long days. At Point Barrow, Alaska's northernmost point, the sun doesn't set for two-and-a-half months from May to August. In other Alaskan regions, the longest day is on June 21 (the summer solstice), when the sun sets for only two hours in Fairbanks and for five hours in the Southeast. Even after sunset in late June, however, there is still no real darkness, just a long twilight.

Southeast Alaska

The Southeast has a temperate maritime climate; like Seattle, but wetter. Juneau averages 57in of precipitation (rain or snow) annually, and Ketchikan gets 154in, most of which is rain as winter temperatures are mild.

Prince William Sound & Kenai Peninsula

Precipitation is the norm in Prince William Sound. In summer, Valdez is the driest of the towns; Whittier is by far the wettest. In all communities, average July daytime temperatures are barely above 60°F (15.5°C). So no matter what your travel plans are, pack your fleece and some bombproof wet-weather gear.

Weather-wise, the Kenai Peninsula is a compromise: drier than Prince William Sound, warmer than the Bush, wetter and cooler (in summer) than the Interior. Especially on the coast, extremes of heat and cold are unusual. Seward's normal daily high in July is 62°F (16.5°C). Rainfall is quite high on the eastern coasts of the peninsula around Seward and

> The heaviest recorded annual snowfall in Alaska was 974.5in at Thompson Pass, north of Valdez, in the winter of 1952–53.

Kenai Fjords National Park; moderate in the south near Homer and Seldovia; and somewhat less frequent on the west coast and inland around Soldotna and Cooper Landing.

Anchorage

Shielded from the dark fury of Southcentral Alaska's worst weather by the Kenai Mountains, the Anchorage Bowl receives only 14in of rain annually and enjoys a relatively mild climate: January averages 13°F (-10.5°C) and July about 58°F (14.5°C). Technically a sub-Arctic desert, Anchorage does have more than its fair share of overcast days, however, especially in early and late summer.

Southwest Alaska

With little to protect it from the high winds and storms that sweep across the North Pacific, the Southwest is home to the very worst weather in Alaska. Kodiak is greatly affected by the turbulent Gulf of Alaska and receives 80in of rain per year, along with regular blankets of pea-soup fog and occasional blustery winds. On the northern edge of the Pacific, Unalaska and the Alaskan Peninsula receive less rain (annual precipitation ranges from 60in to 70in), but are renowned for unpredictable and stormy bouts of weather. Southwest summer temperatures range from 45°F to 65°F (7°C to 18°C). For the clearest weather, try visiting in early summer or fall.

Denali & the Interior

In this region of mountains and spacious valleys, the climate varies greatly and the weather can change on a dime. In January temperatures can sink to -60°F (-51°C) for days at a time, while in July they often soar to above 90°F (32°C). The norm for the summer is long days with temperatures of 60°F to 70°F (15.5°C to 21°C). However, it is common for Denali National Park to experience at least one dump of snowfall in the lowlands between June and August.

Here, more than anywhere else in the state, it's important to have warm clothes while still being able to strip down to a T-shirt and hiking shorts. Most of the area's 10in to 15in of annual precipitation comes in the form of summer showers, with cloudy conditions common, especially north of Mt McKinley. In Denali National Park, Mt McKinley tends to be hidden by clouds more often than not.

In the Interior and up around Fairbanks, precipitation is light, but temperatures can fluctuate by more than 100°F during the year. Fort Yukon holds the record for the state's highest temperature, at 100°F (37.8°C) in June 1915, yet it once recorded a temperature of -78°F (-61°C) in winter. Fairbanks has the odd summer's day that hits 90°F (32°C) and always has nights during winter that drop below -60°F.

Wrangell-St Elias, Kluane and Glacier Bay National Parks and Tatshenshini-Alsek Provincial Park collectively form one of the largest World Heritage sites at 24.34 million acres.

The Bush

Due to its geographical diversity, the Bush is a land of many climates. In inland areas, winter holds sway from mid-September to early May, with ceaseless weeks of clear skies, negligible humidity and temperatures colder than anywhere else in America. Alaska's all-time low, -80°F (-62°C), was recorded at Prospect Creek Camp, just off the Dalton Hwy. Closer to the ocean winter lingers even longer than inland, but it is incrementally less chilly.

During the brief summer, visitors to the Bush should be prepared for anything. Barrow and Prudhoe Bay may demand a parka: July highs there often don't hit 40°F (4.5°C). Along the Dalton Hwy and around Nome, the weather is famously variable. Intense heat (stoked by the unsetting sun) can be as much a concern as cold.

MAJOR PARKS OF ALASKA

PARK	FEATURES	ACTIVITIES
Admiralty Island National Monument	wilderness island, chain of lakes, brown bears, marine wildlife	bear watching, kayaking, canoeing, cabin rentals
Chena River State Recreation Area	Chena River, alpine areas, granite tors, campgrounds, cabin rentals	backpacking, canoeing, hiking
Chugach State Park	Chugach Mountains, alpine trails, Eklutna Lake	backpacking, mountain biking, paddling, hiking, campgrounds
Denali National Park	Mt McKinley, brown bears, caribou, Wonder Lake, campground	wildlife viewing, backpacking, hiking, park bus tours
Denali State Park	alpine scenery, trails, views of Mt McKinley, campgrounds	backpacking, hiking, camping
Gates of the Arctic National Park & Preserve	Brooks Range, Noatak River, treeless tundra, caribou	rafting, canoeing, backpacking, fishing
Glacier Bay National Park & Preserve	tidewater glaciers, whales, Fairweather Mountains	kayaking, camping, whale-watching, lodge, boat cruises
Independence Mine State Historical Park	Talkeetna Mountains, alpine scenery, gold mine ruins, visitor center	mine tours, hiking
Kachemak Bay State Park	glaciers, protected coves, alpine areas, cabin rentals	kayaking, backpacking, boat cruises
Katmai National Park & Preserve	Valley of 10,000 Smokes, volcanoes, brown bears, lodge	fishing, bear watching, backpacking, kayaking
Kenai Fjords National Park	tidewater glaciers, whales, marine wildlife, steep fjords, cabin rental	boat cruises, kayaking, hiking
Kenai National Wildlife Refuge	chain of lakes, Russian River, moose, campgrounds	fishing, canoeing, wildlife watching, hiking
Kodiak National Wildlife Refuge	giant bears, rich salmon runs, wilderness lodges, cabin rentals	bear watching, flightseeing, cabin rentals
Misty Fjords National Monument	steep fjords, 3000ft sea cliffs, lush rainforest	boat cruises, kayaking, cabin rentals, flightseeing
Tracy Arm-Fords Terror Wilderness Area	glaciers, steep fjords, a parade of icebergs, marine wildlife	boat cruises, kayaking, wildlife watching
Wrangell-St Elias National Park	mountainous terrain, Kennecott mine ruins, glaciers	backpacking, flightseeing, rafting, biking, mine tours

National, State & Regional Parks

One of the main attractions of Alaska is public land, where you can play and roam freely over an area of 384,000 sq miles, more than twice the size of California. The agency in charge of the most territory is the **Bureau of Land Management** (BLM; www.blm.gov/ak; 133,594 sq miles), followed by the **US Fish & Wildlife Service** (USFWS; www.fws.gov; 120,312 sq miles) and the **National Park Service** (www.nps.gov; 84,375 sq miles).

Alaska's national parks are the crown jewels as far as most travelers are concerned, and attract more than two million visitors a year. The most popular units are Klondike Gold Rush National Historical Park, which draws 860,000 visitors a year, and Denali National Park, home of Mt McKinley, which sees around half that number. Other busy units are Glacier Bay National Park, a highlight of every cruise-ship itinerary in the Southeast, and Kenai Fjords National Park in Seward.

Salmon fishing, Bristol Bay

Alaska State Parks (www.alaskastateparks.org) oversees 119 units that are not nearly as renowned as most national parks, and thus far less crowded at trailheads and in campgrounds. The largest is the 1.6-million-acre Wood-Tikchik State Park, a roadless wilderness north of Dillingham. The most popular is Chugach State Park, the 495,000-acre unit that is Anchorage's after-work playground.

Both the BLM and the USFWS oversee many refuges and preserves that are remote, hard to reach and not set up with visitor facilities such as campgrounds and trails. The major exception is the Kenai National Wildlife Refuge, an easy drive from Anchorage, and a popular weekend destination for locals and tourists alike.

For more pre-trip information, contact the **Alaska Public Lands Information Centers** (www.alaskacenters.gov).

In 2012, only 19 people visited Southwest's vast and volcanic Aniakchak National Monument & Preserve.

Environmental Issues

With its vast tracts of pristine land and beloved status as America's last wild frontier, Alaska's environmental issues are, more often than not, national debates. These days the focus of those debates (and a fair amount of action) centers on the effects of global warming and resource management, especially the push for mining and drilling in reserve lands.

Land

The proposed Pebble Mine development in Bristol Bay has been one of the most contentious environmental issues of the past decade. The stakes are huge for all sides. Pebble is potentially the second-largest ore deposit of its type in the world, with copper and gold deposits estimated to be worth a staggering $500 billion. But the minerals would be extracted from near the headwaters of Bristol Bay and require a 2-mile-wide open pit that could pollute streams that support the world's largest run of wild salmon. That has an unlikely alliance of environmentalists, commercial fishers and Alaska Natives up in arms. Their voices might be making a difference: in 2013 one of the two major investors, Anglo American, backed out.

Oil exploration in the Arctic National Wildlife Refuge (ANWR) is another unresolved issue, despite a political battle that has raged in the Lower 48 since the earliest days of former president Ronald Reagan. The refuge is often labeled by environmentalists as America's Serengeti, an unspoiled wilderness inhabited by 45 species of mammals, including grizzly bears, polar bears and wolves. Millions of migratory birds use the refuge to nest, and every spring the country's second-largest caribou herd, 150,000 strong, gives birth to 40,000 calves there.

Though estimates of the amount of recoverable oil have dropped considerably in the past few years, industry is still eager to jump in, and politicians continue to argue that ANWR can help the country achieve energy independence.

Fisheries

The problems of resource exploitation are not restricted to oil, gas and minerals. After the king crab fishery collapsed in 1982, the commercial fishing industry was rebuilt on pollack, whose mild flavor made it the choice for imitation crab, and fish sandwiches served at fast-food restaurants. Pollack has been called 'the world's largest fishery,' but since 2006, when a record 730 million pounds were processed at Dutch Harbor, the fishery has been slipping backwards. Fishing quotas have been reduced these past few years, however, and the stock may make a comeback if all goes well.

But pollack is not alone. At least four times since 1997 the salmon runs of Bristol Bay and Kuskokwim River have been declared economic disasters; in recent years the river has been closed at different times to sport, commercial or subsistence fishing. In 2014, it was closed to all three. The reason for the fishery's collapse remains a mystery, though theories about climate change and its many effects as well as overfishing have the most traction.

Rural Issues

Waste management is a hot issue in Alaska's rural communities, many of which are unconnected to the rest of the state by convenient transportation routes. Though burning garbage is still a common way of reducing trash, as is dumping, more and more communities have begun to build recycling centers, practice composting and haul back to Anchorage whatever they can. A free program called Flying Cans now takes bundled aluminum cans from rural communities to recycling plants in Anchorage via scheduled cargo flights. Energy-saving education programs are also making their way across the state, as are greenhouses. The latter are expected to have a positive impact on both nutrition and the amount of fuel used to supply rural villages with fresh produce.

For more information on environmental issues, contact these conservation organizations:

Alaska Sierra Club (www.alaska.sierraclub.org)
No Dirty Gold (www.nodirtygold.org) A campaign opposing abusive gold mining around the world, including the proposed Pebble Mine.
Southeast Alaska Conservation Council (www.seacc.org)
Wilderness Society (www.wilderness.org)

Village Voices (www.ruralcap. com) is an informative quarterly magazine focusing on the issues facing rural Alaska Natives, including the high costs of energy, homelessness, the legacy of Head Start and poor nutrition.

Alaskan Wildlife

Alaska's vast landscape and waters allow the space for wild creatures to roam, and wildlife watching is a major draw for visitors to the state. Spotting wildlife can be as dramatic as a flight over feeding grizzlies or as simple as a walk to see moose in an Anchorage park.

Land Mammals

Alaska boasts one of the earth's great concentrations of wildlife, and some species that are threatened or endangered elsewhere – brown bears, for example – thrive in the 49th state.

Above Polar bears

Bears

There are three species of bear in Alaska: brown, black and polar. Of these, you're most likely to see brown bears, as they have the greatest range.

Brown and grizzly bears are now listed as the same species *(Ursus arctos)* but there are differences. Browns live along the coast, where abundant salmon runs help them reach weights exceeding 800lb, or 1500lb in the case of the famed Kodiak. Grizzlies are browns found inland and subsist largely on grass. Normally a male weighs from 500lb to 700lb, and females half that. The most common way to identify any brown bear is by the prominent shoulder hump, easily seen behind the neck when the animal is on all fours.

Alaska has an estimated 32,000 brown bears, or more than 98% of the US population. In July and August you can see the bears fishing alongside rivers. In early fall they move into tundra regions and open meadows to feed on berries.

Though black bears *(Ursus americanus)*, which may also be colored brown or cinnamon, are the USA's most widely distributed bruin, their range is limited in Alaska. They live in most forested areas of the state, but not north of the Brooks Range, on the Seward Peninsula, or on many large islands, such as Kodiak and Admiralty. The average male black weighs from 180lb to 250lb.

Polar bears *(Ursus maritimus)* dwell only in the far north and their adaptation to a life on sea ice has given them a white, water-repellent coat, dense underfur, specialized teeth for a carnivorous diet (primarily seals), and hair that almost completely covers the bottom of their feet. A male polar bear weighs between 600lb and 1200lb. Plan on stopping at the zoo in Anchorage, or taking a lengthy side trip to Barrow or Kaktovik, if you want to see one.

Moose

Moose are long-legged in the extreme, but short-bodied despite sporting huge racks of antlers. They're the world's largest members of the deer family, and the Alaskan species is the largest of all. A newborn weighs 35lb and can grow to more than 300lb in five months; cows weigh 800lb to 1200lb; and bulls 1000lb to more than 1600lb, with antlers up to 70in wide.

The moose population ranges from an estimated 120,000 to 160,000, and historically the animal has been the most important game species in Alaska. Some 20,000 are officially hunted each year.

Caribou

Although more than a million caribou live in Alaska across 32 herds, they are relatively difficult to view as they inhabit the Interior north up to the Arctic Sea. This is a shame as the migration of the Western Arctic herd, the largest in North America with almost 500,000 animals, is one of the great wildlife events left on earth. The herd uses the North Slope for its calving area, and in late August many of the animals cross the Noatak River and journey southward.

Caribou range in weight from 150lb to more than 400lb. The animals are crucial to the Iñupiat and other Alaska Natives, who hunt more than 30,000 a year to support their subsistence lifestyle.

The best place to see caribou is Denali National Park.

Wolves

While gray wolves are struggling throughout most of the USA, in Alaska their numbers are strong despite predator control programs. In total, about 7000 wolves live in Alaska, spread throughout almost every region of the state. Adult males average 85lb to 115lb, and their pelts can be gray, black, off-white, brown or yellow, with some tinges approaching red. Wolves travel, hunt, feed and operate in the social unit of a pack. In

MICHAEL DEYOUNG / DESIGN PICS / GETTY IMAGES ©

Lynx

the Southeast their principal food is deer, in the Interior it's moose and in Arctic Alaska it's caribou.

Mountain Goats & Dall Sheep

Often confused with Dall sheep, mountain goats have longer hair, short black horns and deep chests. They range throughout the Southeast, fanning out north and west into the coastal mountains of Cook Inlet, as well as the Chugach and Wrangell Mountains. Good locations to see them include Glacier Bay and Wrangell-St Elias National Park.

Dall sheep are more numerous and widespread, numbering close to 80,000, and live in the Alaska, Wrangell, Chugach and Kenai mountain ranges. They are often seen at Windy Corner, on the Seward Hwy and in Denali National Park. Another good spot is on the Harding Ice Field trail in Seward.

The best time to catch rams in a horn-clashing battle for social dominance is right before the mating period, which begins in November.

TOP PLACES TO SEE...

Brown Bears Katmai National Park & Preserve (p338), Anan Creek Wildlife Observatory (p95)

Moose Kenai National Wildlife Refuge (p240), Denali National Park (p263)

Seals Tracy Arm, Prince William Sound

Humpback Whales Glacier Bay National Park & Preserve, Sitka

Puffins St Lazaria Island National Wildlife Refuge, Gull Island

Caribou

Lynx
This intriguing-looking feline has unusually large paws to help it move swiftly over snowpack as it hunts snowshoe hare, its primary food source. Lynx inhabit most forested areas of Alaska, but your chances of seeing one depends on the hare population, which fluctuates over an eight- to 11-year cycle.

Beavers & River Otters
Around lakes and rivers you stand a good chance of seeing river otters and beavers or, at the very least, beaver lodges and dams. Both animals live throughout the state, with the exception of the North Slope. Otters range from 15lb to 35lb, while beavers weigh between 40lb and 70lb, although 100lb beavers have been recorded in Alaska.

Fish & Marine Mammals
Whales
The three most common whales seen in coastal waters are the 50ft-long humpback, the smaller bowhead whale and the gray whale. The humpback is the most frequently seen on cruise ships and ferries, as they often lift their flukes (tails) out of the water to begin a dive, or blow every few seconds when resting. Biologists estimate 1000 humpbacks migrate to the Southeast and more than 100 head to Prince William Sound each year.

Tour boats head out of almost every Southeast Alaska port loaded with whale-watching passengers. You can also join such trips in Kenai Fjords National Park and in Kodiak.

At the **Sitka WhaleFest** (http://sitkawhalefest.org) in early November, visitors and locals gather to listen to world-renowned biologists talk about whales, and then hop on boats to go look for them.

Dolphins & Porpoises

Dolphins and harbor porpoises are commonly seen in Alaskan waters, even from the decks of public ferries. Occasionally, passengers will also spot a pod of orcas (killer whales), and sometimes belugas, both large members of the dolphin family. Orcas, which can be more than 20ft long, are easily identified by their high black-and-white dorsal fins.

The white-colored beluga ranges in length from 11ft to 16ft and weighs more than 3000lb. There are two populations of belugas in Alaska: the endangered Cook Inlet area population, and the Bering Sea area population. In the spring and fall, roughly May and September, pods of the Cook Inlet belugas feed in Turnagain Arm, right outside Anchorage. Lines of cars pull to the side of the Seward Hwy to watch these mammals surface; the best pullout is aptly named Beluga Point. The 74,500 belugas that live off Alaskan shores travel in herds of 10 to several hundred.

Salmon

Five kinds of wild salmon can be found in Alaska: sockeye (also referred to as red salmon), king (or chinook), pink (or humpie), coho (or silver) and chum. For sheer wonders of nature it's hard to beat a run of thousands of salmon swimming upstream to spawn. From late July to mid-September, many coastal streams are so choked with the fish that at times individuals have to wait their turn to swim through narrow gaps of shallow water.

In the heart of Anchorage, Ship Creek supports runs of king, coho and pink. From a viewing platform you can watch the fish spawning upriver and also the locals trying to catch one for dinner. In downtown Ketchikan, you can watch salmon in Ketchikan Creek.

Seals & Sea Lions

The most commonly seen marine mammal, seals are often found basking in the sun on ice floes. Six species exist in Alaska, but most visitors will encounter the harbor seal, whose range includes the Southeast, Prince William Sound and the entire Gulf of Alaska. The average male weighs 200lb, reached by a diet of herring, flounder, salmon, squid and small crabs.

The ringed and bearded seals inhabit the northern Bering, Chukchi and Beaufort Seas, where sea ice forms during winter.

Steller sea lions, the largest member of the 'eared seals' family, range from Japan to California, but are divided from the Gulf of Alaska into two stocks: the endangered Western stock and the threatened Eastern stock. Females can weigh close to 800lb, while males can reach 2500lb. A day trip in Kenai Fjords National Park will take you to sea lion haul-outs, where you can view a crowd of them resting on rocks.

Walruses

Like the seal, the Pacific walrus is a pinniped (fin-footed animal) but this much larger creature is less commonly spotted. Walruses summer in the far northern Chukchi Sea and though they may number over 200,000, most visitors are likely only to encounter the tusks of these creatures in the carving of a Native artist.

Above Tufted puffins
Right Harbor seals

Bald eagles

Birds

Alaska's vast open spaces and diversity of habitat make it unusually rich in birdlife. Over 445 species have been identified statewide.

Bald Eagles

While elsewhere in America the bald eagle (a magnificent bird with a wingspan of over 8ft) is on the endangered species list, in Alaska it's commonly sighted in the Southeast, Prince William Sound and Dutch Harbor in the Aleutian Islands.

Ptarmigan

The state bird is a cousin of the prairie grouse. Three species can be found throughout Alaska in high, treeless country.

Seabirds & Waterfowl

Alaskan seabirds include the crowd-pleasing horned and tufted puffins, six species of auklet and three species of albatross (which boast a wingspan of up to 7ft). The optimum way to see these is on a wildlife cruise to coastal breeding islands such as St Lazaria Island, home to 1500 pairs of breeding tufted puffins.

An amazing variety of waterfowl migrate to Alaska each summer, including trumpeter swans, Canada geese, eider, the colorful harlequin duck and five species of loon.

Tundra Species

Tundra birds such as wheateaters, Smith's longspurs, Arctic warblers, bluethroats and snowy owls are big draws for amateur twitchers. Prime viewing areas include Nome, Barrow, and the Dalton and Denali Hwys.

Survival Guide

Directory A–Z

Accommodations

Alaska offers typical US accommodations, along with many atypical options such as mountain cabins or luxury lodges in the middle of the wilderness. We have recommendations for all types and budgets. The price range for a double per night is as follows:

$ less than $100

$$ $100 to $200

$$$ more than $200

Advance bookings are wise as the Alaskan tourist season is short, and rooms fill quickly in such places as Juneau, Skagway and Denali National Park. You will receive better accommodation rates during the shoulder seasons of April through May and September through October.

Rates listed are for high season: June through August. Listed rates do not include local taxes. In most towns you will be hit with a local sales tax *and* a bed tax, with the combination ranging from 5% to 12% for cities such as Anchorage and Juneau.

The most affordable accommodations are hostels, campsites (bring your tent!) and campground cabins. Motels, both individually owned and national chains, are well scattered in cities and most towns. Even small rural hamlets will have a motel. The larger centers will also have a number of B&Bs, which will range from basic rooms to plush accommodations, housing the peak-of-summer tourists.

As to be expected, Alaska is the land of wilderness lodges. Many of these are geared toward anglers and remote fishing opportunities, must be booked well in advance, and require floatplane transport to reach. Tribal companies and the cruise ship industry (for the land portions of their tours) are also responsible for a growing number of luxury hotels popping up across the state.

B&Bs

For travelers who want nothing to do with a tent, B&Bs can be an acceptable compromise between sleeping on the ground and sleeping in high-priced lodges. Some B&Bs are bargains, and most are cheaper than major hotels, but plan on spending $75 to $130 per night for a double room.

Many visitor centers have sections devoted to the B&Bs in their area, and courtesy booking phones. You can contact B&B reservation services to book rooms before your trip.

Alaska Private Lodgings (☎907-235-2148; www.alaskabandb.com) Statewide.

Anchorage Alaska Bed & Breakfast Association (☎907-272-5909, 888-584-5147; www.anchorage-bnb.com)

Bed and Breakfast Association of Alaska (www.alaskabba.com) Statewide.

Fairbanks Association of Bed & Breakfasts (www.fabb.biz)

Camping & Caravan Parks

Camping is king in Alaska and with a tent you'll always have cheap accommodations in the Far North. There are state, federal and private campgrounds from Ketchikan to Fairbanks. Nightly fees range from free to $15 for rustic public campgrounds and from $30 to $55 to park your RV in a deluxe private campground with full hookup and heated restrooms with showers. Many towns that cater to tourists operate a municipal campground. For commercial campgrounds there's the **Alaska Camp-**

ground Owner's Association (☎866-339-9082; www.alaskacampgrounds.net).

Hostels

Thanks to an influx of backpackers and foreign travelers each summer, the number of hostels offering budget accommodations in Alaska increases annually. There are now more than 40, and there's even one in tiny McCarthy.

Alaska's hostels offer budget bunkrooms and kitchen facilities for nightly fees that range from $10 to $35. Most are around $25 a night. The best statewide hostel organization is the **Alaska Hostel Association** (www.alaskahostelassociation.org).

Hotels & Motels

Hotels and motels are often the most expensive lodgings you can book, and they tend to be full during summer. Without being part of a tour or having advance reservations, you may have trouble finding a bed available in some towns.

Resorts

Resorts – upscale hotels that have rooms, restaurants, pools and on-site activities – are not as common in Alaska as elsewhere in the USA, but are increasing due to the patronage of large companies, such as Princess Tours.

Customs Regulations

For a complete list of US customs regulations, visit the official portal for **US Customs & Border Protection** (www.cbp.gov). Click on 'Travel' and then 'Know Before You Go' for the basics.

Travelers are allowed to bring personal goods (including camping and hiking equipment) into the USA and Canada free of duty, along with food for two days and up to 100 cigars, 200 cigarettes and 1L of liquor or wine.

There are no forms to fill out if you are a foreign visitor bringing a vehicle into Alaska, whether it is a bicycle, motorcycle or car, nor are there forms for hunting rifles or fishing gear. Hunting rifles (handguns and automatic weapons are prohibited) must be registered in your own country, and you should bring proof of registration. There is no limit to the amount of money you can bring into Alaska, but anything over $10,000 must be registered with customs officials.

Keep in mind that endangered species laws prohibit transporting products made of bone, skin, fur, ivory etc through Canada without a permit. Importing and exporting such items into the USA is also prohibited. If you have any doubt about a gift or item you want to purchase, call the **US Fish & Wildlife Service** (USFWS; ☎800-767-6198; www.fws.gov) in Anchorage or check the website.

Hunters and anglers who want to ship home their salmon, halibut or rack of caribou can do so easily. Most outfitters and guides will make the arrangements for you, including properly packaging the game. In the case of fish, most towns have a storage company that will hold your salmon or halibut in a freezer until you are ready to leave Alaska. When frozen, seafood can usually make the trip to any city in the Lower 48 without thawing.

Discount Cards

Most museums, parks and major attractions will offer reduced rates to seniors and students, but most accommodations, restaurants and small tour companies will not.

➡ Best seniors card for US travelers to carry is issued by the **American Association of Retired Persons** (AARP; ☎888-687-2277; www.aarp.org).

➡ For students, an **International Student**

Identity Card (www.isic.org) will often result in discounts for attractions in cities and major towns.

➡ There are no Hostelling International chapters in Alaska so the HI card is of little use in the Far North.

Electricity

120V/60Hz

120V/60Hz

Embassies & Consulates

International travelers needing to locate the US embassy in their home country should visit the **US Department of State** (http://usembassy.state.gov), which has links to all of them. There are no embassies in Alaska, but there are a handful of foreign consulates in Anchorage to assist overseas travelers with unusual problems.

Canadian Consulate (✆907-264-6734; Ste 220, 310 K St)

Danish Consulate (✆907-276-1221; Suite 610, 425 G St)

French Consulate (✆907-561-3280; Ste 106, 1675 C St)

German Consulate (✆907-274-6537; Ste 650, 425 G St)

Japanese Consulate (✆907-562-8424; Ste 1300, 3601 C St)

Norwegian Consulate (✆907-375-5565; Suite 200, 310 K St)

UK Consulate (✆907-786-4848; UAA, 3211 Providence Dr)

Food

Many travelers are surprised that food prices in a Fairbanks or Anchorage supermarket are not that much higher than what they're paying at home. Then they visit their first restaurant and a glance at the menu sends them into a two-day fast. Alaskan restaurants are more expensive than most other places in the country because of the short tourist season and the high labor costs for waiters and chefs.

Restaurant prices in this book are usually for a main dish at dinner and do not include drinks, appetizers, dessert or tips. Restaurants can be divided into budget, midrange and top end:

$ less than $12
$$ midrange, $12 to $27
$$$ top end, more than $27

The mainstay of Alaskan restaurants, particularly in small towns, is the main-street cafe. It opens early in the morning serving eggs, bacon, pancakes and oatmeal, and continues with hamburgers, fries and grilled sandwiches for lunch. There is almost always halibut and salmon on the dinner menu. Most small towns also have a hamburger hut – a small shack or trailer with picnic tables outside – serving burgers, hot dogs, wraps or fried fish.

While places catering to vegans are rare throughout Alaska, you will find at least one health food store in most midsize towns and cities, as well as a number of restaurants advertising 'vegetarian options.' Alternatively, search out Chinese and other Asian restaurants for the best selection of meatless dishes. Also keep in mind that Carrs, Safeway and other large supermarkets often have well-stocked salad bars, self-serve affairs at $6 per pound.

BEARS IN ALASKA

Too often travelers decide to skip a wilderness trip because they hear too many bear stories. Your own equipment and outdoor experience should determine whether you take a trek into the woods, not the possibility of meeting a bear on the trail. The **Alaska Department of Fish & Game** (www.adfg.state.ak.us) emphasizes that the probability of being injured by a bear is one-fiftieth the chance of being injured in a car accident on any Alaskan highway.

The best way to avoid bears is to follow a few commonsense rules. Bears charge only when they feel trapped, when a hiker comes between a sow and her cubs, or when enticed by food. Sing or clap when traveling through thick bush, and don't camp near bear food sources or in the middle of an obvious bear path. Stay away from thick berry patches, streams choked with salmon, or beaches littered with bear droppings.

Set up the spot where you will cook and eat at least 30yd to 50yd away from your tent. In coastal areas, many backpackers eat in the tidal zone, knowing that when the high tide comes in, all evidence of food will be washed away.

At night try to place your food sacks 10ft or more off the ground by hanging them in a tree. Or consider investing in a lightweight bear-resistant container. A bear usually finds a food bag using its great sense of smell. Avoid odorous foods, such as bacon or sardines, in areas with high concentrations of bears, and don't take food, cosmetics or deodorant into the tent at night.

Gay & Lesbian Travelers

The gay community in Alaska is far smaller and much less open than in major US cities, and Alaskans in general are not as tolerant of diversity. In 1998 Alaska passed a constitutional amendment banning same-sex marriages. However attitudes are slowly changing. A 2014 poll found 47% of Alaskan voters in favor of same-sex marriage.

In Anchorage, the only city in Alaska of any real size, you have **Identity Inc** (✆907-929-4528; www.identityinc.org), which has a gay and lesbian helpline, a handful of openly gay clubs and bars, and a weeklong **PrideFest** (http://alaskapride.org) in mid-June. The **Southeast Alaska Gay & Lesbian Alliance** (www.seagla.org) is based in Juneau and offers links and travel lists geared to gay visitors. The list is short, however, because most towns do not have an openly active gay community. In rural Alaska, same-sex couples should exercise discretion.

Health

There is a high level of hygiene found in Alaska, so most common infectious diseases will not be a significant concern for travelers. Superb medical care and rapid evacuation to major hospitals are both available.

➡ The cost of health care in the USA and Alaska is extremely high. It's essential to purchase travel health insurance if your regular policy doesn't cover you when you're abroad.

➡ No special vaccines are required or recommended for travel to Alaska

➡ In recent years, paralytic shellfish poisoning (PSP) from eating mussels and clams has become a problem in Alaska. For a list of beaches safe to clam, check with the **Alaska Division of Environmental Health** (www.dec.alaska.gov/eh).

➡ Tap water in Alaska is safe to drink, but you should purify surface water taken from lakes and streams that is to be used for cooking and drinking. The simplest ways to purify water is to boil it thoroughly or use a high-quality filter.

➡ The most dangerous health threat outdoors is hypothermia. Dress in layers topped with a well-made, waterproof outer layer and always pack wool mittens and a hat.

➡ Due to Alaska's long summer days, sunburn and windburn are a primary concern for anyone trekking or paddling. Use a good sunscreen on exposed skin, even on cloudy days, and a hat and sunglasses for additional protection.

➡ Alaska is notorious for its biting insects, including mosquitoes, black flies, no-see-ums and deer flies. Wear long-sleeved shirts, pants that can be tucked into socks and a snug cap. Use a high-potency insect repellent and head nets in areas where there are excessive insects.

Insurance

A travel insurance policy to cover theft, loss and medical problems is a smart investment. Coverage depends on your insurance and type of ticket, but should cover delays by striking employees or company actions, or a cancellation of a trip. Such coverage may seem expensive but it's nowhere near the price of a trip to Alaska or the cost of a medical emergency in the USA.

Some policies offer lower and higher medical-expense options; the higher ones are chiefly for countries such as the USA, which have extremely high medical costs. There is a wide variety of medical and emergency repatriation policies and it's important to talk to your healthcare provider for recommendations.

Worldwide travel insurance is available through the **Lonely Planet** (www.lonelyplanet.com/travel_services) website. You can buy, extend and claim online any time – even if you're already on the road.

Access America (☑800-284-8300; www.accessamerica.com)

Insuremytrip.com (☑800-487-4722; www.insuremytrip.com)

Travel Guard (☑800-826-4919; www.travelguard.com)

Internet Access

It's easy to surf the net, make online reservations or retrieve email in Alaska. Most towns, even the smallest ones, have internet access at libraries, hotels and internet cafes. Access ranges from free at the library to $5 to $10 an hour at internet cafes. If you are hauling around a laptop, wi-fi is common in Alaska at bookstores, motels, coffee shops, airport terminals and even bars. The internet icon (@) shows when accommodations or other businesses have an internet terminal, and a wi-fi icon (☞) for anywhere that has wireless internet access. If you're not from the US, remember you will need an AC adapter and a plug adapter for US sockets.

Legal Matters

Despite the history of marijuana in Alaska – it was once legal for personal use – possession of small amounts is now a misdemeanor punishable by up to 90 days in jail and a $2000 fine. The use of other drugs is also against the law and results in severe penalties, especially for cocaine, which is heavily abused in Alaska.

The minimum drinking age in Alaska is 21 and a government-issued photo ID (passport or driver's license) will be needed if a bartender questions your age. Alcohol abuse is also a problem in Alaska, and it's a serious offense if you are caught driving under the influence of alcohol (DUI). The blood alcohol limit in Alaska is 0.08% and the penalty for DUI is a three-month driver's license revocation. You may also be given a fine and jail time.

If you are stopped by the police for any reason while driving, remember there is no system of paying on-the-spot fines and bribery is not something that works in Alaska. For traffic violations, the officer will explain your options to you and many violations can often be handled through the mail with a credit card.

The legal age of consent in Alaska is 16 and travelers should note that they can be prosecuted under the law of their home country regarding age of consent, even when abroad.

Maps

Unlike many places in the world, Alaska has no shortage of accurate maps. There are detailed US Geological Survey (USGS) topographical maps to almost every corner of the state, even though most of it is still wilderness, while every visitor center has free city and road maps that are more than adequate to get from one town to the next. See **Google Maps** (http://maps.google.com) for free downloadable maps and driving directions.

For trekking in the backcountry and in wilderness areas, the USGS topographical maps are worth the $6-per-quad cost. The maps come in a variety of scales, but hikers prefer the smallest scale of 1:63,360, with each inch equal to a mile. Canoeists and other river runners can get away with the 1:250,000 map.

You can order maps in advance directly from **USGS** (☑888-275-8747; www.usgs.gov) or you can view and order custom topo maps from cartography websites such as **Mytopo** (☑877-587-9004; www.mytopo.com). GPS units and accompanying mapping software that includes Alaska are available from **Garmin** (www.garmin.com) and **DeLorme** (www.delorme.com).

Money

Prices quoted are in US dollars unless otherwise stated. US coins come in denominations of 1¢ (penny), 5¢ (nickel), 10¢ (dime), 25¢ (quarter) and the seldom seen 50¢ (half-dollar). Quarters are the most commonly used coins in vending machines and parking meters, so it's handy to have a stash of them. Notes, commonly called bills, come in $1, $2, $5, $10, $20, $50 and $100 denominations. Keep in mind that the Canadian system is also dollars and cents but is a separate currency.

ATMs

In Alaska ATMs are everywhere: banks, gas stations, supermarkets, airports and even some visitor centers. At most ATMs you can use a credit card (Visa, MasterCard etc), a debit card or an ATM card that is linked to the Plus or Cirrus ATM networks. There is generally a fee ($1 to $3) for withdrawing cash from an ATM, but the exchange rate on transactions is usually as good as, if not better than, what you'll get anywhere else.

Cash

Hard cash still works. It may not be the safest way to carry funds, but nobody will hassle you when you purchase something with US dollars. Most businesses along the Alcan in Canada will also take US dollars.

Credit Cards

Like in the rest of the USA, Alaskan merchants are ready and willing to accept just about all major credit cards. Visa and MasterCard are the most widely accepted cards, but American Express and Discovery are also widely used.

Places that accept Visa and MasterCard are also likely to accept debit cards. If you are an overseas visitor, check with your bank at home to confirm that your debit card will be accepted in the USA.

Moneychangers

Banks are the best place to exchange foreign currencies as the exchange counters at the airports typically have poorer rates. **Wells Fargo** (☑800-956-4442; www.wellsfargo.com), the nation's sixth-largest bank, is the dominant player in Alaska with more than 400 branches, eight in Anchorage alone. Wells Fargo can meet the needs of most visitors, including changing currency and offering 24-hour ATMs.

Tipping

Tipping in Alaska, like in the rest of the USA, is expected. The going rate for restaurants, hotels and taxis is about 15%. It is also common for visitors to tip guides, including on bus tours. If you forget, don't worry: they'll remind you.

Bars If you order food at the table and your meal is brought to you, tipping is the same as at a restaurant: 15%. If you are simply having a drink or appetizer at the bar, it's 10%.

Restaurants From 15% for cafes and chain eateries to 20% for upscale restaurants.

Taxis Tip 15%.

Tour guides Tip 10% for a bus tour guide, $15% to 20% for wilderness guides leading you on a glacier trek or white-water rafting trip.

Traveler's Checks

Although slowly becoming obsolete thanks to ATMs, the other way to carry your funds is the time-honored method of traveler's checks. The popular brands of US traveler's checks are American Express and Visa, but keep in mind that most banks won't cash them unless you have an account with them, and that stores or motels will only denominations of $100 or less.

Opening Hours

Banks Open 9am to 4pm or 5pm Monday to Friday; 9am to 1pm Saturday (main branches).

Bars & Clubs In cities, bars open until 2am or later, especially at weekends. Clubs stay open to 2am or beyond.

Museums & Sights Large museums and sights usually open virtually every day of the year. Smaller places open daily in the summer, open weekends only or can be completely closed in low season.

Post Offices Open 9am to 5pm Monday to Friday; noon to 3pm Saturday (main branches open longer).

Restaurants & Cafes Breakfast at cafes and coffee shops is served from 7am or earlier. Some restaurants open only for lunch (about noon to 3pm) or dinner (about 4pm to 10pm, or later in cities). Asian restaurants often have split hours: 11am to 2pm and 4pm.

Shops Open 10am to 8pm/6pm (larger/smaller stores) Monday to Friday; 9am to 5pm Saturday; 10am to 5pm Sunday (larger stores).

Post

The **US Postal Service** (☎800-275-8777; www.usps. com) is one of the world's busiest and most reliable, but even it needs another day or two to get letters and postcards to and from Alaska. With an abundance of internet cafes and the availability of internet at libraries and hostels and hotels, think email for quick notes to friends and family. For packages, especially heavy ones, it's faster to use private carriers in Alaska such as **United Parcel Service** (☎800-742-5877; www.ups.com) or **Federal Express** (☎800-463-3339; www.fedex.com).

Public Holidays

Public holidays for Alaskan residents may involve state and federal offices being closed, bus services curtailed, and shop and store hours reduced.

New Year's Day January 1

Martin Luther King Day Third Monday in January

Presidents' Day Third Monday in February

Seward's Day Last Monday in March

Easter Sunday Late March or early April

Memorial Day Last Monday in May

Independence Day (Fourth of July) July 4

Labor Day First Monday in September

Columbus Day Second Monday in October

Alaska Day October 18

Veterans' Day November 11

Thanksgiving Day Fourth Thursday in November

Christmas Day December 25

Telephone

Cell Phones

Cell phones work in Alaska and Alaskans love them as much as anywhere else in the USA. When calling home or locally in cities and towns, reception is excellent, but overall, in a state this large, cell phone coverage can be unpredictable and sporadic at times. The culprits in most cases are mountains.

Most travelers still find their cell phones to be very useful. Before you head

---

PRACTICALITIES

➜ Alaska has more than 30 daily, weekly and trade newspapers, with the *Anchorage Daily News* being the largest and the closest thing to a statewide newspaper.

➜ The largest cities have local TV stations, and radio stations are found all over Alaska.

➜ NTSC is the standard video system (not compatible with PAL or SECAM).

➜ Voltage in Alaska is 120V – the same as everywhere else in the USA.

➜ There is no national sales tax in the USA and no state sales tax in Alaska, but towns have a city sales tax plus a bed tax.

➜ Almost every town in Alaska has a laundromat, the place to go to clean your clothes ($3 per load) or take a shower ($3 to $5).

➜ US distances are in feet, yards and miles. Dry weights are in ounces (oz), pounds (lb) and tons, and liquids are in pints, quarts and gallons (4 quarts).

➜ The US gallon is about 20% less than the imperial gallon.

➜ There is no statewide smoking ban in Alaska but a growing number of cities, including Anchorage, Juneau, Nome, Palmer, Skagway and Unalaska have a city ban on smoking in bars, restaurants and clubs.

north, however, check your cell phone provider's roaming agreements and blackout areas. It may be possible for international travelers to purchase a prepaid SIM card that can be used in their mobile phones for local calls and voicemail. You can also purchase inexpensive cell phones from AT&T for $10 along with prepaid cards for calls at 10¢ a minute or $2 a day.

Phone Codes

Telephone area codes are simple in Alaska: the entire state shares ✆907, except Hyder, which uses ✆250. Phone numbers that begin with ✆800, ✆877 and ✆866 are toll-free numbers and there is no charge for using one to call a hotel or tour operator. If you're calling from abroad, the country code for the USA is ✆1.

Phonecards

The best way to make international calls is to first purchase a phonecard. There's a wide range of phonecards sold in amounts of $5, $10 and $20, available at airports, convenience stores and internet cafes. Most towns and villages in Alaska have public pay phones that you can use to call home if you have a phonecard or credit card.

Time

With the exception of several Aleutian Island communities and Hyder, a small community on the Alaska–British Columbia border, the entire state shares the same time zone, Alaska Time, which is one hour earlier than Pacific Standard Time – the zone in which Seattle, Washington, falls. When it is noon in Anchorage, it is 4pm in New York, 9pm in London and 7am the following day in Melbourne, Australia. Although there is a movement to abolish it, Alaska still has Daylight Saving Time when, like most

of the country, the state sets clocks back one hour in November and forward one hour in March.

Tourist Information

The first place to contact when planning your adventure is the **Alaska Travel Industry Association** (www.travelalaska.com), the state's tourism marketing arm. From the ATIA you can request a copy of the *Alaska Vacation Planner,* an annually updated magazine; a state highway map; and schedules for the Alaska Marine Highway ferry service.

Almost every city, town and village has a tourist contact center, whether it is a visitor center, a chamber of commerce or a hut near the ferry dock. These places are good sources of free maps, information on local accommodations and directions to the nearest campground or hiking trail.

Most trips to Alaska pass through one of the state's three largest cities. All have large visitor centers that will send out city guides in advance.

Anchorage Convention & Visitors Bureau (✆907-276-4118; www.anchorage.net)

Fairbanks Convention & Visitors Bureau (✆907-456-5774, 800-327-5774; www.explorefairbanks.com)

Juneau Convention & Visitors Bureau (✆907-586-1737, 800-587-2201; www.traveljuneau.com)

Travelers with Disabilities

Thanks to the American Disabilities Act, many state and federal parks have installed wheelchair-accessible sites and restrooms in their campgrounds. You can call the **Alaska Public Lands Information Center** (✆907-271-2599; www.alaskacenters.

gov) to receive a map and campground guide to such facilities. The Alaska Marine Highway ferries, the Alaska Railroad and many bus services and cruise ships are also equipped with wheelchair lifts and ramps to make their facilities easier to access. Chain motels and large hotels in cities and towns often have rooms set up for disabled guests, while some wilderness guiding companies are experienced in handling wheelchair-bound clients on rafting and kayaking expeditions.

Access Alaska (✆907-248-4777; www.accessalaska.org) Includes statewide tourist information on accessible services and sites.

Access-Able Travel Source (www.access-able.com) A national organization with an excellent website featuring travel information and links.

Challenge Alaska (✆907-344-7399; www.challengealaska.org) A nonprofit organization dedicated to providing recreation opportunities for those with disabilities.

Flying Wheels Travel (✆877-451-5006; www.flying-wheelstravel.com) A full-service travel agency specializing in disabled travel.

Society for Accessible Travel & Hospitality (✆212-447-7284; www.sath.org) Lobbies for better facilities and publishes *Open World* magazine.

Visas

Since September 11, the US has continually fine-tuned its national security guidelines and entry requirements. Double-check current visa and passport regulations before arriving in the USA, and apply for visas early to avoid delays. Overseas travelers may need one visa, possibly two. For citizens of many countries a US visa is required, and if you're taking the Alcan or the Alaska

DIRECTORY A–Z VOLUNTEERING

Marine Highway ferry from Prince Rupert in British Columbia, you may also need a Canadian visa. The Alcan begins in Canada, requiring travelers to pass from the USA into Canada and back into the USA again.

Canadians entering the USA must have proof of Canadian citizenship, such as a passport; visitors from countries in the Visa Waiver Program may not need a visa. Visitors from all other countries need to have a US visa and a valid passport. On the website of the **US State Department** (www.travel. state.gov) there is a 'Temporary Visitors to the US' page with tips on how and where to apply for a visa and what to do if you're denied one.

Note that overseas travelers should be aware of the process to reenter the USA. Sometimes visitors get stuck in Canada due to their single-entry visa into the USA, used up when passing through the Lower 48. Canadian immigration officers often caution people whom they feel might have difficulty returning to the USA. More information about visa and other requirements for entering Canada is available on the website of the **Canada Border Services Agency** (www.cbsa-asfc.gc.ca).

Visa Application

Apart from Canadians and those entering under the Visa Waiver Program, foreign visitors need to obtain a visa from a US consulate or embassy. Most applicants must now schedule a personal interview, to which you need to bring all your documentation and proof of fee payment. Wait times for interviews vary, but afterward, barring problems, visa issuance takes from a few days to a few weeks. If concerned about a delay, check the US State Department website, which provides a list of wait times calculated by country.

Your passport must be valid for at least six months

longer than your intended stay in the USA. You'll need a recent photo (2in by 2in) and you must pay a $100 processing fee, plus, in a few cases, an additional visa issuance fee (check the State Department website for details). In addition to the main nonimmigration visa application form (DS-156), all men aged 16 to 45 must complete an additional form (DS-157) that details their travel plans.

Visa applicants are required to show documentation of financial stability, a round-trip or onward ticket and 'binding obligations' that will ensure their return home, such as family ties, a home or a job.

Visa Waiver Program

The Visa Waiver Program (VWP) lets citizens of some countries enter the USA for tourism purposes for up to 90 days without having a US visa. Currently there are 36 participating countries in the VWP, including Austria, Australia, Belgium, Denmark, Finland, France, Germany, Iceland, Ireland, Italy, Japan, the Netherlands, New Zealand, Norway, Spain, Sweden, Switzerland and the UK.

Under the program you must have a round trip or onward ticket that is nonrefundable in the USA, a machine-readable passport (with two lines of letters, numbers and <<< along the bottom of the information page) and be able to show evidence of financial solvency.

As of 2009, citizens of VWP countries must register online prior to their trip with the **Electronic System for Travel Authorization** (ESTA; http://esta.cbp.dhs.gov), an automated system used to determine the eligibility of visitors traveling to the US.

Volunteering

For many travelers the only way to enjoy Alaska is to volunteer. You won't get paid,

but you're often given room, board and work in a spectacular setting. Most volunteer roles are with federal or state agencies and range from trail crew workers and campground hosts to volunteering at the **Arctic Interagency Visitor Center** (☑678-5209; CentralYukon@blm.gov; ⏰11am-10pm Jun-Aug) in Coldfoot and collecting botanical inventories.

Alaska State Parks (☑907-269-8708; www. alaskastateparks.org)

Bureau of Land Management (BLM; ☑907-271-5960; www.ak.blm.gov)

Chugach National Forest (☑907-743-9500; www.fs.fed. us/r10/chugach)

Student Conservation Association (☑907 543 1700; www.thesca.org)

Tongass National Forest (☑907-225-3101; www.fs.fed. us/r10/tongass)

Women Travelers

While most violent crime rates are lower here than elsewhere in the USA, women should be careful at night in unfamiliar neighborhoods in cities like Anchorage and Fairbanks or when hitching alone. Use common sense; don't be afraid to say no to lifts. If camping alone, have pepper spray and know how to use it.

Alaska Women's Network (www.alaskawomensnetwork. org) Has listings of women-owned B&Bs and travel agencies across the state.

Anchorage Planned Parenthood Clinic (☑907-563-7419; 4001 Lake Otis Pkwy) Offers contraceptives, medical advice and services.

Women's Flyfishing (www. womensflyfishing.net) Alaska's premier outfitter for women-only fly-fishing trips and a great web resource for women arriving in Alaska with a fly rod.

Transportation

GETTING THERE & AWAY

Whether you're from the US or overseas, traveling to Alaska is like traveling to a foreign country. By sea it takes almost a week on the Alaska Marine Highway ferry to reach Whittier in Prince William Sound from the Lower 48. By land a motorist in the Midwest needs 10 days to drive straight to Fairbanks.

If you're coming from the US mainland, the quickest, and least expensive, way to reach Alaska is to fly nonstop from a number of cities. If you're coming from Asia or Europe, it's almost impossible to fly directly to Alaska as few international airlines maintain a direct service to Anchorage. Most international travelers come through the gateway cities of Seattle, Los Angeles, Minneapolis and Vancouver.

Entering the Country

Since the September 11 terrorist attacks, air travel in the USA has permanently changed and you can now expect vigilant baggage screening procedures and personal searches. In short, you're going to have to take your shoes off. Non-US citizens should be prepared for an exhaustive questioning process at immigration.

Crossing the border into Alaska from Canada used to be a relaxed process – US citizens often passed across with just a driver's license. Now this process has also become more complicated, and all travelers should have a passport and expect more substantial questioning and possible vehicle searches.

Passport

If you are traveling to Alaska from overseas, you need a passport. If you are a US resident passing through Canada, you will need a passport to re-enter the USA. Make sure your passport does not expire during the trip, and if you are entering the USA through the Visa Waiver Program (VWP) you *must* have a machine-readable passport. If you are traveling with children, it's best to bring a photocopy of their birth certificates. If one parent is traveling with children alone, they will likely be asked for a letter of agreement from the other parent.

Air

Airports & Airlines

The vast majority of visitors to Alaska, and almost all international services, fly into **Ted Stevens Anchorage International Airport** (ANC; Map p158; www.dot.state.ak.us/anc; ☎). International flights arrive at the north terminal; domestic flights arrive at the south terminal and a complimentary shuttle service runs between the two every

---

CLIMATE CHANGE & TRAVEL

Every form of transport that relies on carbon-based fuel generates CO_2, the main cause of human-induced climate change. Modern travel is dependent on airplanes, which might use less fuel per kilometer per person than most cars but travel much greater distances. The altitude at which aircraft emit gases (including CO_2) and particles also contributes to their climate change impact. Many websites offer 'carbon calculators' that allow people to estimate the carbon emissions generated by their journey and, for those who wish to do so, to offset the impact of the greenhouse gases emitted with contributions to portfolios of climate-friendly initiatives throughout the world. Lonely Planet offsets the carbon footprint of all staff and author travel.

15 minutes. You'll find bus services, taxis and car-rental companies at both terminals. The airport has the usual services, including baggage storage, ATMs, currency exchange, free wi-fi, and courtesy phones to various Anchorage hotels.

Alaska Airlines (AS; ☎800-426-0333; www.alaskaair.com)

American Airlines (AA; ☎800-443-7300; www.aa.com)

Condor Airlines (DE; ☎800-524-6975; www.condor.de)

Delta Air Lines (DL; ☎800-221-1212; www.delta.com)

Frontier Airlines (2F; ☎800-432-1359; www.frontier airlines.com)

JetBlue (☎800-538-2583; www.jetblue.com)

PenAir (☎800-448-4226; www.penair.com) Aleutian Islands, Alaska Peninsula and Bristol Bay.

Ravn Alaska (☎800-866-8394; www.flyravn.com)

Sun Country Airlines (SY; ☎800-359-6786; www.sun country.com)

US Airways (US; ☎800-428-4322; www.usairways.com)

Tickets

Due to its lack of direct and international flights, Anchorage, and thus Alaska, is not the most competitive place for airfares. Begin any ticket search by first checking travel websites and then compare the prices against the websites of airlines that service Alaska, particularly Alaska Airlines, as it often has internet specials offered nowhere else. For a good overview of online ticket agencies and lists of travel agents worldwide, visit **Airinfo**(www.airinfo.aero).

Seattle serves as the major hub for flights into Alaska. Alaska Airlines owns the lion's share of the market, with 20 flights per day to Anchorage as well as direct flights to Ketchikan, Juneau and Fairbanks.

You can also book a non-stop flight to Anchorage from a number of other US cities. Delta flies in from Minneapolis, Atlanta and Salt Lake City. American Airlines arrives in Anchorage from Dallas; US Airways from Phoenix; JetBlue from Long Beach; Frontier from Denver. Alaska Airlines, naturally, flies nonstop from numerous cities including Los Angeles, Denver, Chicago and Portland.

Condor has direct seasonal flights to Frankfurt in Germany from both Anchorage and Fairbanks.

Land

What began as the Alaska-Canada Military Hwy is today the Alcan (the Alaska Hwy). This amazing 1390-mile road starts at Dawson Creek in British Columbia, ends at Delta Junction and in between winds through the vast wilderness of northwest Canada and Alaska. For those with the time, the Alcan is a unique journey north. There are several ways of traveling the Alcan: bus, car or a combination of Alaska Marine Highway ferry and bus.

Bus

A combination of buses will take you from Seattle via the Alcan to Alaska, but service is limited and the ride is very long. From Seattle, **Greyhound Canada** (☎800-661-8747; www.greyhound.ca) goes to Whitehorse, a 60-hour-plus ride. A one-way ticket is around $200 if you purchase in advance online. From Whitehorse, **Alaska/Yukon Trails** (Map p294; ☎800-770-7275; www.alaskashuttle. com) leaves Sunday, Tuesday and Friday for Fairbanks for $400.

Car & Motorcycle

Without a doubt, driving your own car to Alaska allows you the most freedom. You can leave when you want, stop where you feel like it and plan your itinerary as you go

along. It's not cheap driving to Alaska, and that's not even considering the wear and tear from the thousands of miles you'll put on your vehicle.

The Alcan is now entirely paved and, although sections of jarring potholes, frost heaves (the rippling effect of the pavement caused by freezing and thawing) and loose gravel still exist, the infamous rough conditions of 30 years ago no longer prevail. Food, gas and lodging can be found almost every 30 to 50 miles along the highway, with 100 miles being the longest stretch between fuel stops.

On the Canadian side, you'll find kilometer posts (as opposed to the mileposts found in Alaska), which are placed every 5km after the zero point in Dawson Creek. Most Alcan veterans say 300 miles a day is a good pace – one that will allow for plenty of stops to see the scenery or wildlife.

Along the way, **Tourism Yukon** (☎800-661-0494; www.travelyukon.com) operates a number of visitor centers stocked with brochures and maps.

Hitchhiking

Hitchhiking is probably more common in Alaska than it is in the rest of the USA, and even more so on rural dirt roads such as the McCarthy Rd and the Denali Hwy than it is on the major paved routes. Hitchhiking is never entirely safe in any country and we don't recommend it. That said, if you're properly prepared and have sufficient time, thumbing your way along the Alcan can be an easy way to see the country while meeting local people and saving money.

The Alcan seems to inspire the pioneer spirit in travelers who drive along it. Drivers are good about picking up hitchhikers, much better than those across the Lower 48; the only problem is that there aren't really enough of them.

Any part of the Alcan can be slow, but some sections are notoriously bad. The worst is probably Haines Junction, the crossroads in the Yukon where southbound hitchhikers often get stranded trying to thumb a ride to Haines in Southeast Alaska.

If you'd rather not hitchhike the entire Alcan, take the Alaska Marine Highway ferry from Bellingham, WA, to Haines, stick your thumb out and start hitchhiking from there; you'll cut the journey in half but still travel along the highway's most spectacular parts.

Sea

As an alternative to the Alcan, you can travel the Southeast's Inside Passage. From that maze of a waterway, the **Alaska Marine Highway** (AMHS; ☑800-642-0066; www.dot.state.ak.us/amhs) and cruise ships then cut across the Gulf of Alaska to towns in Prince William Sound.

Tours

Package tours can often be the most affordable way to see a large chunk of Alaska, if your needs include the better hotels in each town and a full breakfast every morning. But they move quickly, leaving little time for an all-day hike or other activities.

Companies offering Alaska packages:

Alaska Heritage Tours (☑877-777-2805, 877-777-2805; www.alaskaheritagetours.com)

Alaska Wildland Adventures (☑800-334-8730; www.alaskawildland.com)

Gray Line (☑800-478-6388; www.graylineofalaska.com)

Green Tortoise Alternative Travel (☑800-867-8647, 415-956-7500; www.greentortoise.com)

GETTING AROUND

Air

As a general rule, if there are regularly scheduled flights to your destination, they will be far cheaper than charter flights on the small airplanes known in Alaska as 'bush planes.' This is especially true for **Alaska Airlines** (☑800-252-7522; www.alaskaair.com). Other airlines:

➡ **PenAir** (☑800-448-4226; www.penair.com) Aleutian Islands, Alaska Peninsula and Bristol Bay.

➡ **Ravn Alaska** (www.flyravn.com) Fairbanks, Nome, Barrow, Deadhorse, Valdez and Kodiak.

➡ **Wings of Alaska** (☑907-789-0790; www.wingsofalaska.com) Southeast Alaska.

Bush Planes

With 75% of the state inaccessible by road, small, single-engine planes known as 'bush planes' are the backbone of intrastate transport. They carry residents and supplies to desolate areas of the Bush, take anglers to some of the best fishing spots in the country and drop off backpackers in the middle of untouched wilderness.

In the larger cities of Anchorage, Fairbanks, Juneau and Ketchikan, it pays to compare prices before chartering a plane. In most small towns and villages, you'll be lucky if there's a choice.

Bush aircraft include floatplanes, which land and take off on water, and beach-landers with oversized tires that can use rough gravel shorelines as air strips. Fares vary with the type of plane, its size, the number of passengers and the amount of flying time. On average, chartering a Cessna 185 that can carry three passengers and a limited amount of gear will cost up to $400 for an hour of flying time. A Cessna 206,

a slightly larger plane that will hold four passengers, costs up to $400 to $450, while a Beaver, capable of hauling five passengers with gear, costs on average $500 to $550 an hour. When chartering a plane to drop you off in the wilderness, you must pay for both the air time to your drop-off point and for the return to the departure point.

Double-check all pickup times and places when flying to a wilderness area. Bush pilots fly over the pickup point and if you're not there, they usually return to base, call the authorities and still charge you for the flight. Always schedule extra days around a charter flight. It's not uncommon to be 'socked in' by weather for a day or two until a plane can fly in. Don't panic: they know you're there.

Bicycle

For those who want to bike it, Alaska offers a variety of cycling adventures on paved roads under the Arctic sun that allows you to peddle until midnight if you want. A bicycle can be carried on Alaska Marine Highway ferries for an additional fee and is a great way to explore small towns without renting a car.

Most road cyclists avoid gravel, but cycling the Alcan (an increasingly popular trip) does involve riding over some gravel breaks in the paved asphalt. Mountain bikers, on the other hand, are in heaven on gravel roads such as Denali Hwy in the Interior.

Anchorage's **Arctic Bicycle Club** (☑907-566-0177; www.arcticbike.org) is Alaska's largest bicycle club and sponsors a wide variety of road-bike and mountain-bike tours during the summer. Its website includes a list of Alaska cycle shops.

If you arrive in Alaska without a bicycle, some towns have rentals; expect to pay $30 to $50 a day. You can take your bicycle on the airlines for an excess luggage fee of $50 per flight or ship it in advance to **Chain Reaction Cycles** (☏907-336-0383; www.chainreactioncycles.us) in Anchorage, which will assemble your bicycle and hold it until you arrive.

Boat

The **Alaska Marine Highway** (AMHS; ☏800-642-0066; www.dot.state.ak.us/amhs) calls at 35 ports across 3500 miles of coastline from Bellingham, WA, to Dutch Harbor in the Aleutians. There are nine regular vessels serving four main regions: the Southeast (Ketchikan up to Skagway), the Cross-Gulf Route (Juneau to Whittier), Southcentral Alaska (Prince William Sound, the Kenai Peninsula and Kodiak), and the Southwest (the Alaska Peninsula and the Aleutian Islands).

The Southeast is also served by the **Inter-Island Ferry Authority** (☏866-308-4848; www.interislandferry.com), which connects Ketchikan with Prince of Wales Island, and **Haines-Skagway Fast Ferry** (☏888-766-2103; www.hainesskagwayfastferry.com; one way adult/child $36/18) servicing Skagway and Haines.

Bus

Shuttle buses (usually 12-seater vans) cover most of Alaska's main highways in the summer, though they don't always run daily. Check individual websites for schedules and prices and book in advance.

Alaska Park Connection (☏800-266-8625; www.alaskacoach.com) Seward to Denali National Park via Anchorage and Talkeetna; May to September.

Alaska/Yukon Trails (Map p294; ☏800-770-7275; www.alaskashuttle.com) Runs from

Fairbanks to Anchorage via Denali National Park on the George Parks Hwy. Also covers Fairbanks to Dawson City via Tok on the Taylor/Top of the World Hwys; and Fairbanks to Whitehorse on the Richardson/Alcan Hwys.

Dalton Highway Express (☏907-474-3555; www.daltonhighwayexpress.com) Plies the Dalton Highway between Fairbanks and Prudhoe Bay, June to August.

Homer Stage Line (Map p246; ☏907-868-3914; www.stagelineinhomer.com) Runs from Homer to Anchorage, and between Homer and Seward.

Interior Alaska Bus Line (☏800-770-6652; www.alaskadirectbusline.com) Runs shuttles from Anchorage to Fairbanks via Glennallen and Tok on Glenn and Richardson Hwys.

Kennicott Shuttle (☏907-822-5292; www.kennicottshuttle.com) Runs a summer shuttle between Glennallen and McCarthy in Wrangell-St Elias National Park.

Seward Bus Line (☏907-563-0800, 888-420-7788; www.sewardbuslines.net) Seward to Anchorage and Whittier.

Soaring Eagle Transit (☏907-822-4545; www.soaringeagletransit.com) Runs from Anchorage to Glennallen and onto Valdez.

Yukon-Alaska Tourist Tours (☏866-626-7383, Whitehorse 867-668-5944; www.yukonalaskatouristtours.com) Daily bus service from Skagway to Whitehorse.

Car & Motorcycle

Not a lot of roads reach a lot of Alaska but what pavement there is leads to some seriously spectacular scenery. That's the best reason to tour the state in a car or motorcycle, whether you arrive with yours or rent one. With personal wheels you can stop and go at will and sneak away from the RVers and tour buses.

Automobile Associations

AAA (☏800-332-6119; www.aaa.com), the most widespread automobile association in the USA, has one office in Alaska, **Anchorage Service Center** (☏907-344-4310), which offers the usual including maps, discounts and emergency road service.

Fuel & Spare Parts

Gas is widely available on all the main highways and tourist routes in Alaska. In Anchorage and Fairbanks the cost of gas will only be $0.10 to $0.15 per gallon higher than in the rest of the country. Along the Alcan, in Bush communities such as Nome, and at that single gas station on a remote road, they will be shockingly high.

Along heavily traveled roads, most towns will have a car mechanic, though you might have to wait a day for a part to come up from Anchorage. In some small towns, you might be out of luck. For anybody driving to and around Alaska, a full-size spare tire and replacement belts are a must.

Insurance

Liability insurance – which covers damage you may cause to another vehicle in the event of an accident – is required when driving in Alaska but not always offered by rental agencies because most Americans are already covered by their regular car insurance. This is particularly true with many of the discount rental places. Major car agencies offer Collision Damage Waiver (CDW) to cover damage to the rental car in case of an accident. This can up the rental fee by $15 a day or more and many have deductibles as high as $1000. It's better, and far cheaper, to arrive with rental car insurance obtained through your insurance company, as a member of AAA, or as a perk of many credit cards, including American Express.

TRANSPORTATION CAR & MOTORCYCLE

Rental & Purchase

For two or more people, car rental is an affordable way to travel, far less expensive than taking a bus or a train. At most rental agencies, you'll need a valid driver's license, a major credit card and you'll also need to be at least 21 years old (sometimes 25). It is almost always cheaper to rent in town rather than at the airport because of extra taxes levied on airport rentals.

Read any rental contract carefully, especially when it comes to driving on gravel or dirt roads. Many agencies, particularly those in the Fairbanks area, will not allow their compacts on dirt roads. If you violate the contract and have an accident, insurance will not cover repairs. Also be conscious of the per-mile rate of a rental. Add up the mileage you aim to cover and then choose between the 100 free miles per day or the more expensive unlimited mileage plan.

Affordable car-rental places, are always heavily booked during the summer. Try to reserve vehicles at least a month in advance.

MOTORHOME

RVers flock to the land of the midnight sun in astounding numbers. This is the reason why more than a dozen companies, almost all of them based in Anchorage, will rent you a motorhome. Renting a recreational vehicle is so popular you have to reserve them four to five months in advance.

ABC Motorhomes (☎800-421-7456; www.abcmotorhome.com)

Clippership Motorhome Rentals (☎800-421-3456; www.clippershiprv.com)

Great Alaskan Holidays (☎907-248-7777, 888-225-2752; www.greatalaskanholidays.com)

Alaska Railroad

Road Conditions & Hazards

For road conditions, closures and other travel advisories for the Alaska highway system, even while you're driving, contact the state's **Alaska511** (☑511, outside Alaska 866-282-7577; http://511.alaska.gov).

Local Transportation

In cities and most mid-size towns there will be taxi service, and at almost every Alaska Marine Highway port there'll be van service into town. There is also limited local bus service in some cities, with the most extensive systems in Anchorage, Fairbanks, Juneau and Ketchikan.

Capital Transit (☑907-789-6901; www.juneau.org/capital-transit) Juneau and Douglas.

Ketchikan Bus (☑907-225-8726; www.borough.ketchikan.ak.us/145/Transit)

Metropolitan Area Commuter System (MACS; ☑907-459-1011; www.co.fairbanks.ak.us/transportation) Fairbanks and North Pole.

People Mover (☑907-343-6544, Rideline 343-6543; www.muni.org/departments/transit/peoplemover) Anchorage.

Train

Alaska Railroad

It took eight years to build it, but today the Alaska Railroad stretches 470 miles from Seward to Fairbanks, through spectacular scenery. You'll save more money traveling by bus down the George Parks Hwy, but few travelers regret booking the Alaska Railroad and viewing pristine wilderness from its comfortable cars.

SERVICES

The Alaska Railroad operates a year-round service between Fairbanks and Anchorage, as well as summer services (from late May to mid-September) from Anchorage to Whittier and from Anchorage to Seward.

The most popular run is the 336-mile trip from Anchorage to Fairbanks, stopping at Denali National Park. Northbound, at Mile 279 the train passes within 46 miles of Mt McKinley, a stunning sight from the viewing domes on a clear day. It then slows down to cross the 918ft bridge over Hurricane Gulch.

The ride between Anchorage and Seward may be one of the most spectacular train trips in the world. From Anchorage, the 114-mile trip begins by skirting the 60-mile-long Turnagain Arm on Cook Inlet and then swings south, climbs over mountain passes, spans deep river gorges and comes within half a mile of three glaciers.

The Anchorage–Whittier service, which includes a stop in Girdwood and passes through two long tunnels, turns Whittier into a fun day trip. So does riding Alaska Railroad's *Hurricane Turn*, one of America's last flag-stop trains, which departs from Talkeetna.

RESERVATIONS

You can reserve a seat and purchase tickets, even online, through **Alaska Railroad** (☑800-544-0552; www.akrr.com); highly recommended for the Anchorage–Denali service in July and early August.

White Pass & Yukon Route

Built during the height of the Klondike Gold Rush, it's still possible to travel the White Pass & Yukon Railroad from Skagway to Carcross in the Yukon and complete the journey to Whitehorse by bus.

Reservations are highly recommended any time during the summer. Contact **White Pass & Yukon Route** (☑800-343-7373; www.whitepassrailroad.com) for information.

Glossary

Alcan or **Alaska Hwy** – the main overland route into Alaska. Although the highway is almost entirely paved now, completing a journey along this legendary road is still a special accomplishment. The Alcan begins at the Mile 0 milepost in Dawson Creek (northeastern British Columbia, Canada), heads northwest through Whitehorse, the capital of the Yukon Territory (Canada), and officially ends at Delta Junction (Mile 1390), 101 miles southeast of Fairbanks.

AMS – acute mountain sickness; occurs at high altitudes and can be fatal

ANWR – Arctic National Wildlife Refuge; the 1.5-million-acre wilderness area that oil-company officials and Alaskans have been pushing hard to open up for oil and gas drilling

ATV – all-terrain vehicle

aurora borealis or **northern lights** – the mystical snakes of light that weave across the sky from the northern horizon. It's a spectacular show on clear nights and can occur at almost any time of the year. The lights are the result of gas particles colliding with solar electrons and are best viewed from the Interior, away from city lights, between late summer and winter.

bidarka – a skin-covered sea kayak used by the Aleuts

BLM – Bureau of Land Management; the federal agency that maintains much of the wilderness around and north of Fairbanks, including cabins and campgrounds

blue cloud – what Southeasterners call a break in the clouds

breakup – when the ice on rivers suddenly begins to melt, breaks up and flows downstream; many residents also use this term to describe spring in Alaska, when the rain begins, the snow melts and everything turns to mud and slush

bunny boots – large, over-sized and usually white plastic boots used extensively in subzero weather to prevent the feet from freezing

Bush, the – any area in the state that is not connected by road to Anchorage or is not part of the Alaska Marine Highway

cabin fever – a winter condition in which Alaskans go stir-crazy in their one-room cabins because of too little sunlight and too much time spent indoors

cache – a small hut or storage room built high off the ground to keep supplies and spare food away from roaming bears and wolves; the term, however, has found its way on to the neon signs of everything from liquor stores to pizza parlors in the cities

calve – (of an ice mass) to separate or break so a part of the ice becomes detached

capital move – the political issue that raged in the early 1980s, concerning moving the state capital from Juneau closer to Anchorage; although residents rejected funding the move north in a 1982 state election, the issue continues to divide Alaska

cheechako – tenderfoot, greenhorn or somebody trying to survive their first year in Alaska

chum – not your mate or good buddy, but a nickname for dog salmon

clear-cut – an area where loggers have cut every tree

d-2 – the lands issue of the late 1970s, which pitted environmentalists against developers over the federal government's preservation of 156,250 sq miles of Alaskan wilderness as wildlife reserves, forests and national parks

dividend days – the period in October when residents receive their Permanent Fund checks and Alaska goes on a spending spree

Eskimo ice cream – an Iñupiat food made of whipped animal fat, berries, seal oil and sometimes shredded caribou meat

fish wheel – a wooden trap powered by a river's current

that scoops salmon or other large fish out of a river into a holding tank

freeze-up – the point in November or December when most rivers and lakes ice over, signaling to Alaskans that their long winter has started in earnest

humpie – a nickname for the humpback or pink salmon, the mainstay of the fishing industry in the Southeast

ice worm – a small, thin black worm that thrives in glacial ice and was made famous by a Robert Service poem

Iditarod – the 1049-mile sled-dog race run every March from Anchorage to Nome. The winner usually completes the course in less than 14 days and takes home $50,000

Lower 48 – an Alaskan term for continental USA

moose nuggets – hard, smooth droppings; some enterprising resident in Homer has capitalized on them by baking, varnishing and trimming them with evergreen leaves to sell during Christmas as Moostletoe

mukluks – lightweight boots of sealskin trimmed with fur, made by the Iñupiat

muktuk – whale skin and blubber; also known as *maktak*, it is a delicacy among Iñupiat and is eaten in a variety of ways, including raw, pickled and boiled

muskeg – the bogs in Alaska, where layers of matted plant life float on top of stagnant water; these are bad areas in which to hike

North Slope – the gentle plain that extends from the Brooks Range north to the Arctic Ocean

no-see-um – nickname for the tiny gnats found throughout much of the

Alaskan wilderness, especially in the Interior and parts of the Brooks Range

NPS – National Park Service; administers 82,656 sq miles in Alaska and its 15 national parks include such popular units as Denali, Glacier Bay, Kenai Fjords and Klondike Gold Rush National Historical Park

Outside – to residents, any place that isn't Alaska

Outsider – to residents, anyone who isn't an Alaskan

permafrost – permanently frozen subsoil that covers two-thirds of the state but is disappearing due to global warming

petroglyphs – ancient rock carvings

portage – an area of land between waterways over which paddlers carry their boats

potlatch – a traditional gathering of indigenous people held to commemorate any memorable occasion

qiviut – the wool of the musk ox, often woven into garments

RVers – those folks who opt to travel in a motorhome

scat – animal droppings; however, the term is usually used to describe bear droppings. If the scat is dark brown or bluish and somewhat square in shape, a bear has passed by; if it is steaming, the bear is eating blueberries around the next bend.

scrimshaw – hand-carved ivory from walrus tusks or whale bones.

sourdough – any old-timer in the state who, it is said, is 'sour on the country but without enough dough to get out;' newer residents believe the term applies to anybody who has survived an Alaskan winter; the term also applies

to a 'yeasty' mixture used to make bread or pancakes

Southeast sneakers – the tall, reddish-brown rubber boots that Southeast residents wear when it rains, and often when it doesn't; also known as 'Ketchikan tennis shoes,' 'Sitka slippers' and 'Petersburg pumps' among other names

squaw candy – salmon that has been dried or smoked into jerky

stinkhead – an Iñupiat 'treat' made by burying a salmon head in the sand; leave the head to ferment for up to 10 days then dig it up, wash off the sand and enjoy

taku wind – Juneau's sudden gusts of wind, which may exceed 100mph in the spring and fall; often the winds cause horizontal rain, which, as the name indicates, comes straight at you instead of falling on you; in Anchorage and throughout the Interior, these sudden rushes of air over or through mountain gaps are called 'williwaws'

tundra – vast, treeless plains

UA University of Alaska

ulu – a fan-shaped knife that Alaska Natives traditionally use to chop and scrape meat; now used by gift shops to lure tourists

umiaks – leather boats made by the Iñupiat people

USFS – US Forest Service; oversees the Tongass and Chugach National Forests, and the 190 cabins, hiking trails, kayak routes and campgrounds within them

USFWS – US Fish & Wildlife Service; administers 16 federal wildlife refuges in Alaska, more than 120,312 sq miles

USGS – US Geological Society; makes topographic maps, including those covering almost every corner of Alaska

Behind the Scenes

SEND US YOUR FEEDBACK

We love to hear from travelers – your comments keep us on our toes and help make our books better. Our well-traveled team reads every word on what you loved or loathed about this book. Although we cannot reply individually to postal submissions, we always guarantee that your feedback goes straight to the appropriate authors, in time for the next edition. Each person who sends us information is thanked in the next edition – the most useful submissions are rewarded with a selection of digital PDF chapters.

Visit **lonelyplanet.com/contact** to submit your updates and suggestions or to ask for help. Our award-winning website also features inspirational travel stories, news and discussions.

Note: We may edit, reproduce and incorporate your comments in Lonely Planet products such as guidebooks, websites and digital products, so let us know if you don't want your comments reproduced or your name acknowledged. For a copy of our privacy policy visit lonelyplanet.com/privacy.

OUR READERS

Many thanks to the travelers who used the last edition and wrote to us with helpful hints, useful advice and interesting anecdotes:

Anthony & Maureen Benedict, Anne Berger, Robert Claassen, Naldi Dalia, Laura Fortey, Aaron Hurd, Christina Kloss, Alex Konik, Marietta Lieb, Deidre Mahoney, Monse Murcia, Isabel Heim Vadis

AUTHOR THANKS

Brendan Sainsbury

Thanks to all the untold bus drivers, tourist info volunteers, burger-flippers, bush pilots and backcountry guides who helped me during my research. Special thanks to my wife, Liz, and eight-year-old son, Kieran, for their company on the road.

Greg Benchwick

Alaskans are remarkably generous people. I want to especially thank my great friends Kris and Jess Klain for their hospitality and rip-roaring adventures. Perry and Lois of Sound Paddler helped me review kayak information around Prince William Sound. My beautiful guide Ilene kept us afloat on our paddle to Columbia Glacier, and Stephanie in Seldovia is a chart-topping rock star. Huge props to my co-writers and my intrepid editors. My love for Alaska came from my Dad, Paul, and my friend for life, Julian.

Catherine Bodry

Researching guidebooks feels like a lonely endeavour until you begin adding up all the people who helped you along the way: Buckwheat in Skagway, Leslie in Haines, Darren on Prince of Wales, Jeanie in Wrangell, and Alexandra – this time in Juneau! – for restaurant recs. The LP A-Team: Alex, Sarah, Brendan, Greg, Alison Lyall and everyone working support. My peeps in Anchorage, and Alaska itself: so addicting and wonderful and my favorite place to call home.

ACKNOWLEDGEMENTS

Climate map data adapted from Peel MC, Finlayson BL & McMahon TA (2007) 'Updated World Map of the Köppen-Geiger Climate Classification', Hydrology and Earth System Sciences, 11, 1633-44.
Cover photograph: Canoeing in Chugach National Forest, Michael DeYoung/Alamy.

THIS BOOK

This 11th edition of Lonely Planet's *Alaska* guidebook was researched and written by Brendan Sainsbury, Greg Benchwick and Catherine Bodry. The previous edition was written by Jim DuFresne, Catherine Bodry and Robert Kelly. This guidebook was produced by the following:

Commissioning Editor
Sarah Reid

Destination Editor
Alexander Howard

Product Editors Kate James, Martine Power

Senior Cartographer
Alison Lyall

Senior Layout Designer
Katherine Marsh

Assisting Editors Andrew Bain, Michelle Bennett, Justin Flynn, Victoria Harrison, Kate Kiely, Kellie Langdon, Anne Mulvaney, Erin Richards, Jeanette Wall, Simon Williamson

Assisting Cartographer
Hunor Csutoros

Cover Researcher
Naomi Parker

Thanks to Sasha Baskett, Andi Jones, Claire Naylor, Karyn Noble, Angela Tinson, Tony Wheeler

Index

Airbnb:
cartwell, 73, nobath

Go North:
    178 economy

NOTES

Map Legend

Sights
- Beach
- Bird Sanctuary
- Buddhist
- Castle/Palace
- Christian
- Confucian
- Hindu
- Islamic
- Jain
- Jewish
- Monument
- Museum/Gallery/Historic Building
- Ruin
- Shinto
- Sikh
- Taoist
- Winery/Vineyard
- Zoo/Wildlife Sanctuary
- Other Sight

Activities, Courses & Tours
- Bodysurfing
- Diving
- Canoeing/Kayaking
- Course/Tour
- Sento Hot Baths/Onsen
- Skiing
- Snorkeling
- Surfing
- Swimming/Pool
- Walking
- Windsurfing
- Other Activity

Sleeping
- Sleeping
- Camping

Eating
- Eating

Drinking & Nightlife
- Drinking & Nightlife
- Cafe

Entertainment
- Entertainment

Shopping
- Shopping

Information
- Bank
- Embassy/Consulate
- Hospital/Medical
- Internet
- Police
- Post Office
- Telephone
- Toilet
- Tourist Information
- Other Information

Geographic
- Beach
- Hut/Shelter
- Lighthouse
- Lookout
- Mountain/Volcano
- Oasis
- Park
- Pass
- Picnic Area
- Waterfall

Population
- Capital (National)
- Capital (State/Province)
- City/Large Town
- Town/Village

Transport
- Airport
- BART station
- Border crossing
- Boston T station
- Bus
- Cable car/Funicular
- Cycling
- Ferry
- Metro/Muni station
- Monorail
- Parking
- Petrol station
- Subway/SkyTrain station
- Taxi
- Train station/Railway
- Tram
- Underground station
- Other Transport

Note: Not all symbols displayed above appear on the maps in this book

Routes
- Tollway
- Freeway
- Primary
- Secondary
- Tertiary
- Lane
- Unsealed road
- Road under construction
- Plaza/Mall
- Steps
- Tunnel
- Pedestrian overpass
- Walking Tour
- Walking Tour detour
- Path/Walking Trail

Boundaries
- International
- State/Province
- Disputed
- Regional/Suburb
- Marine Park
- Cliff
- Wall

Hydrography
- River, Creek
- Intermittent River
- Canal
- Water
- Dry/Salt/Intermittent Lake
- Reef

Areas
- Airport/Runway
- Beach/Desert
- Cemetery (Christian)
- Cemetery (Other)
- Glacier
- Mudflat
- Park/Forest
- Sight (Building)
- Sportsground
- Swamp/Mangrove

OUR STORY

A beat-up old car, a few dollars in the pocket and a sense of adventure. In 1972 that's all Tony and Maureen Wheeler needed for the trip of a lifetime – across Europe and Asia overland to Australia. It took several months, and at the end – broke but inspired – they sat at their kitchen table writing and stapling together their first travel guide, *Across Asia on the Cheap*. Within a week they'd sold 1500 copies. Lonely Planet was born.

Today, Lonely Planet has offices in Franklin, London, Melbourne, Oakland, Beijing and Delhi, with more than 600 staff and writers. We share Tony's belief that 'a great guidebook should do three things: inform, educate and amuse'.

OUR WRITERS

Brendan Sainsbury

Coordinating Author; Denali & the Interior; Kodiak, Katmai & the Southwest; The Bush An expat Brit from Hampshire, England, now living near Vancouver, Canada, Brendan has long relished the thrill of masochistic endurance events in remote wilderness areas and thus jumped at the chance to cover Alaska for Lonely Planet. He particularly relished getting his hands numb in Nome, re-reading Jack London, and bussing it along the Top of the World Highway from Chicken to the Yukon. When not scribbling research notes for Lonely Planet in countries such as Cuba, Peru, Spain and Canada, Brendan likes refining his cross-country skiing technique, strumming old Clash songs on the guitar, and experiencing the pain and occasional pleasures of following Southampton Football Club.

Read more about Brendan at:
lonelyplanet.com/members/brendansainsbury

Greg Benchwick

Kenai Peninsula, Prince William Sound Greg Benchwick first came to Alaska in college when he spent a summer working in the canneries, tramping in the parking lots of the Kenai Peninsula and exploring the underbelly of Alaska's subcultures. He later returned as a Lonely Planet writer. For this edition, he visited Prince William Sound for the first time, including a bluewater paddle to Columbia Glacier to shoot video for the website. He also hiked the Russian Lakes Trail with friends and shot his first gun! Greg lives in Colorado with his 100-pound Anatolian shepherd and 30-pound daughter. Follow him on twitter @greentravels. Greg also wrote the Cruising in Alaska, Outdoor Activities & Adventures, Alaska Today, History, The Alaskan Way of Life, Alaska Natives and Alaska's Best Hikes & Paddles chapters.

Read more about Greg at:
lonelyplanet.com/members/gbenchwick

Catherine Bodry

Juneau & the Southeast, Anchorage & Around Catherine is a travel writer who covers Alaska, Asia and as many other places as she can. For Lonely Planet, she's contributed to guidebooks to Thailand and Canada as well as Alaska, and to LonelyPlanet.com, BBC Travel, Trail Runner Magazine, Korean Air's Morning-Calm and more. In love with motion, she spends any time not traveling daydreaming about traveling. She's a trail runner in love with mountains, curry and second-class bus rides in foreign countries. Find out more about her at www.catherinebodry.com. Catherine also wrote the Alaskan Landscapes and Alaskan Wildlife chapters.

Read more about Catherine at:
lonelyplanet.com/members/catherinebodry

Published by Lonely Planet Publications Pty Ltd
ABN 36 005 607 983
11th edition – April 2015
ISBN 978 1 74220 602 8
© Lonely Planet 2015 Photographs © as indicated 2015
10 9 8 7 6 5 4 3
Printed in China